The Politics of Tradition

PUBLISHED FOR

THE CENTER OF INTERNATIONAL STUDIES

PRINCETON UNIVERSITY

A list of other Center publications appears
at the back of this book

The Politics of Tradition
Continuity and Change in
Northern Nigeria
1946-1966

C. S. WHITAKER, JR.

PRINCETON, NEW JERSEY
PRINCETON UNIVERSITY PRESS
1970

L.C. Card: 68-56323

SBN: 691-03079-0

NOTE: Popularly known as "the Northern knot"
and much favored in that area of Nigeria as an
embroidery, the figure on the jacket and cover
of this book was adopted in 1959 upon attainment
of regional self-government as an official insignia
of the later Government of the Northern Region
of the Federal Republic of Nigeria. To the author
and others, it has also seemed highly appropriate
as a symbol for the interwoven threads of varying
cultural, social, and political influences which profoundly characterized that regime.

This book has been composed in Linotype Caledonia

Printed in the United States of America
by Princeton University Press, Princeton, New Jersey

For my mother, Edith McColes Whitaker

Contents

Acknowledgments

IN THE COURSE of the 10 years between now and when I first arrived in London to begin study of the Hausa language and read background materials on Northern Nigeria in English libraries, I have incurred a considerable number of debts of warm gratitude. To former colleagues Professors M. G. Smith and R. L. Sklar special thanks are due for unflagging expert assistance and moral encouragement. Professor Kenneth Robinson, formerly Director of the Institute of Commonwealth Studies (now Vice-Chancellor, University of Hong Kong), opened valuable doors and graciously put at my disposal his knowledge of and facilities for study of African politics. I have also enjoyed insightful scholarly comment and helpful criticism from many others at various stages of the work. They include Professors Harry Eckstein, James S. Coleman, Charles Nixon, Julian H. Franklin, Rupert Emerson, Dwaine Marvick, H. H. Smythe, David G. Smith, Nikki Keddie, Mr. Dennis Austin and Mr. Anthony M. Kirk-Greene. And I have benefited much from the critical intelligences of U.C.L.A. graduate students, some of whom also served as devoted research assistants: notably Gerald J. and Tammara Bender, Mrs. Pauline Halpern Baker, Mrs. Deborah Smith, and Mr. Ralph Young. Drs. A. N. Allot and Frederick Parsons, then of the School of Oriental and African Studies, University of London, did their best to impart their great Hausa proficiency to a novice.

In Nigeria itself my work could not have been done nor I personally sustained without the help, support, and hospitality I encountered generally; but I hope I may be forgiven for recording particular appreciation to the following: Alhaji Adamu Husseini; M. Adamu Ciroma; Alhaji Ali Akilu; Mr. D. J. Pott; Mr. John Smith; Alhaji Aminu Kano; Mr. James Laurence; Mr. J. P. P. Gibbs; Alhaji Maitama Sule; Mr. Michael Strong; A. Alhaji MacIver; M. Alwan Nair; Alhaji Muhammadu; *Magajin Gari* of Kazaure; Miss Christine Nuttall; Mr. Sunday Dankaro; Mr. E. D. O. Iloanya; Mr. Chief Rotimi Williams, Q.C.; M. I. Ade Yusuf; Dr. Abubakar Imam; Alhaji Ibrahim Imam; Mr. N. A. B. Kotoye; Mr. S. T. Oreidin; Mr. M. J. Dent; M. Mustapha Dambatta; the late Alhaji Isa Suleiman Wali; Mr. J. G. Davies; Mr. J. S. Tarka; M. Garba Abuja; M. Hassan Naibi; Mr. Boyd L. Hornor; and again Mr. Anthony M. Kirk-Greene.

In addition to the Center of International Studies, Princeton University, which has sponsored the publication of this book and much of its preparation, other institutions which have contributed their resources to make my research and writing possible are: The African Studies Center, U.C.L.A.; The Social Science Research Council of New York; and the Institute of Commonwealth Studies, University of London.

Finally I wish to acknowledge the conscientious and professional efforts of Mr. Roy Grisham of Princeton University Press, who served as editor for this volume, and Mr. S. H. C. Tatham who prepared the index.

All of these parties are of course absolved of any responsibility for the use to which I have put their help in the form of this book.

C. S. Whitaker, Jr.

London September 1969

The Politics of Tradition

The Theoretical Context and Setting

Social science literature dealing with phenomena of social, economic, and political change, has in recent years been dominated by the concept of modernization. The fundamental contention underlying this book is that for these purposes this concept is an inadequate tool of analysis, at least in terms of universal applicability. I happen to have arrived at this conclusion through research into one people's response to certain forms of modern representational institutions, an experience covering 20 years. Any fundamental conclusion (even if essentially negative) based on a single case is obviously itself open to legitimate critical scrutiny, and there is no attempt here to evade responsibility for it. It should be pointed out, however, that this particular contention is in line with the thinking of a growing number of social scientists who have recently been concerned with similar phenomena. This thinking has stemmed from both empirical examination and conceptual reflection.

In purely conceptual terms, the principal objection to the prevailing notion of modernization is that it unsoundly rests on a strictly a priori assumption that for all societies there is only one direction of significant change, culminating in the essentials of modern Western society. This conceptual attachment to a unilinear model of change has on reflection seemed to critics to be partly rooted in a naive faith in general social evolution or the inevitability of "progress" and partly in implicit cultural and ideological bias which arbitrarily (even if unconsciously) places the societies that one is most familiar with or admiring of at the top of a descending scale of human virtue. A closely related objection is that the concept entails a dichotomization of significant social qualities which are not necessarily mutually exclusive and thence the attribution of each of the two sets of qualities thus derived to imaginary classes of societies, called "modern" and "traditional" respectively. The essence of the empirically based objections is that the work of many scholars dealing with a wide range of cultural and geographical contexts suggests that the image of any apparently "premodern" society implicit in this approach is often false or significantly distorted; and/or that the acquisition of ostensibly "modern" qualities is possible under a considerable diversity of cultural conditions.[1] These views are consistent with the

---

[1] I plan to edit a collection of articles reflecting these views based on selected studies done in Africa, the Near and Far East, and Latin America.

analysis to be presented here; but rather than rest my theoretical argument on an acceptance of this general attack, it seems appropriate to consider the issues in the terms to which this study first led me.[2]

The tendency inherent in the idea of modernization to formulate a contrast between traditional and modern societies, based on supposedly mutually exclusive social qualities, derives, as others have observed, from the work of such sociology greats as Maine, Morgan, Weber, Tonnies, and Durkheim. These scholars have all advanced parallel concepts of a dichotomous relationship of principles of behavior which they believe underlie Western history—status and contract, *societas* and *civitas*, traditional and rational authority, *Gesellschaft* and *Gemeinschaft*, mechanical and organic solidarity, respectively. Thanks largely to their enormous influence, "modern" is a term that has become shorthand for the sum of economic, social, and political attitudes, institutions, and patterns of behavior historically associated with the Western experience of industrialization. Conversely, "traditional society" is tantamount to a reference to the balance of all other attitudes, institutions, and patterns of behavior. These terminological distinctions therefore reflect a fundamental proposition that might be stated as follows: the essential difference between societies identified as traditional and modern is not simply a matter of temporal sequence; rather it is that members of the one group consistently act and think differently from members of the other in a variety of basic contexts of social action.

Thus the notion of modernization has involved the conceptualization of mutually exclusive classes of societies in terms of certain analytical categories, logical constructs, or what Weber called "ideal types"—all these being terms for logically alternative principles of action which the behavior of people in modern and traditional societies respectively suggests to the mind of an observer. Thus Weber and others all characteristically insist that the "ideal types" or principles of action they formulated, like all analytical categories or heuristic devices or logical constructs, are not the same thing as the reality itself—i.e. the actual behavior of the people concerned. These principles of action supposedly do not, in other words, purport to describe or predict what, in fact, a given people do or will do. Rather, they constitute abstractions which the mind derives from observing beha-

[2] This book is a revised and updated version of my doctoral dissertation, "The Politics of Tradition: A Study of Continuity and Change in Northern Nigeria, 1946-60", Princeton University, 1964.

vior in an effort to understand its implications. The difference between a categorical statement about reality and a heuristic device may be illustrated as follows: "the earth is round" is a categorical statement about reality (it implies that the earth is in fact round); thinking or conceiving of the earth *as if* it were round is a heuristic device (it does not imply that the earth is in fact round). In "thinking the earth round", one expects only that so doing will help one to discover the actual shape of the earth (i.e. that it is elliptical), and perhaps other related properties of the earth as well. Similarly, in the case of the Weberian "ideal types", the expectation is that thinking of differences in the behavior of whole societies in terms of logically alternative principles of behavior (norms) will help one better to analyze and understand the actual behavior of those societies. Again, the types involved do not in principle commit one to any particular view of how a given people will, in fact, behave in particular circumstances.

Interestingly Weber himself first warned about the danger of supposedly heuristic devices becoming, by sleight of mind, as it were, descriptive or predictive assertions. He wrote: "The logical classification of analytical concepts on the one hand and the empirical arrangements of the events thus conceptualized appear to be so bound up together that there is an almost irresistible temptation to do violence to reality in order to prove the real validity of the construct".[3] The most cursory examination of the statements of certain contemporary scholars indicates that this elusive borderline usually has indeed not been observed.[4] The philosopher of science, Carl G.

[3] *The Methodology of the Social Sciences* (Glencoe, Ill., 1949), pp. 102-103, quoted in Reinhart Bendix, "Tradition and Modernity Reconsidered", *Comparative Studies in Society and History*, Vol. ix, No. 3 (April 1967), 314.

[4] The following quotations represent no more than a small sample of what is a pervasive tendency in a literature too vast to be exhausted here. These examples were selected because they are more explicit.

> All of the present relatively nonmodernized societies will change in the direction of greater modernization. They will change in that direction regardless of whether their members wish it or whether the members of some other society or societies wish to force change upon them. . . .
> The various sources of explosive subversion of the structures of relatively nonmodernized societies will be explored throughout this work in summary below. . . . I have tried to give here sufficient reasons why members of relatively nonmodernized societies cannot expect to avoid these problems. Once the contacts are made, attempts will be made to use some structures of the relatively modernized societies. Once those attempts are made, the existing structures will begin to disintegrate, some explosively. The structures of the relatively modernized societies do constitute for the first time in social history, a sort of general social solvent for all other social types. Marion J. Levy,

Hempel, some years ago impressively demonstrated in terms less tenative than Weber's apprehension, that in truth such distinctions are

---

Modernization and The Structure of Societies; A Setting for International Affairs, 2 vols., Princeton, 1966, pp. 31, 128.

Movement from one sub-type (of society) to another appears to be reversible, but shifts from one model to another are one-directional, namely from Agrarian toward Industrial settings. Thus "underdeveloped" countries confront an inescapable challenge; they must industrialize or face extinction. The more "civilized" a society, the more unavoidable is the quandary. There is no way to "turn the clock back" and those who have tried have been rudely blasted out of their hermitages by shells and bombs. Only the most "primitive" peoples in inaccessible regions can hope to perpetuate their traditional ways, but even here the power of industrial technology has brought great changes.

Toynbee asserts that elements in his spectrum are interdependent, despite their seeming autonomy, so that a borrower finds he cannot limit his borrowing to one element, but must go on to borrow more: "one thing follows another". This tends to confirm our hypothesis about the functional interdependence of institutions in our models, and the tension or disequilibrium in transitional settings where dysfunctional elements have been introduced from external sources. . . . It is only after they have borrowed the innovations that they discover they have opened their doors to a modern "Trojan horse". Fred W. Riggs, "Agraria and Industria", in W. J. Siffen, ed., *Toward the Comparative Study of Public Administration* (Bloomington, Ind., 1957) p. 100; and *Administration in Developing Countries: The Theory of Prismatic Society* (Boston, 1964), p. 47.

The process of political development in neo-traditional oligarchies quite clearly revolves around the replacing of traditional bonds of social organization and allegiance with new bonds which are more functionally distinct and which can better represent the interests common to a developing country. . . .

The basic issue (in "transitional oligarchies") is the adaptation of institutions of Western origin to local conditions. Moreover, they present a common picture of social tension. . . . Beneath the Westernized leadership, parochial and sectional loyalties remain extremely strong. As a result, they tend to be inherently unstable societies in which the uneven process of change and disruption is dominant. . . . Max F. Milikan and Donald K. M. Blackmer, eds., *The Emerging Nations* (Boston, 1961), pp. 81, 82-83.

The politics of historic empires, of tribe and ethnic community, or of colony must give way to the politics necessary to produce an effective nation-state which can operate successfully in a system of other nation-states. . . .

Although to a limited extent the political sphere may be autonomous from the rest of society, for sustained political development to take place it can only be within the context of a multidimensional process of social change in which no segment or dimension of the society can long lag behind. Lucian W. Pye, "The Concept of Political Development", *Annals of the American Academy of Political and Social Science* (March 1965), pp. 7, 11.

It may be stated, then, as a second general hypothesis for purposes of this study, that the institutionalization of these two kinds of authority—that based upon personal loyalty and solidarity between superior and subordinate and that based upon the impersonal, disinterested conception of bureaucratic "office"—within the same society again results in instability and strain, and that integration within the political system of such a society can come only through one of these types of authority giving way to the other. Lloyd A. Fallers, *Bantu Bureaucracy* (Cambridge, Eng., n.d.), pp. 19-20.

typically just plain spurious.[5] In effect, Hempel argues that such analytical constructs as are typical of Weber and his intellectual heirs represent an attempt to win for their observations the status of scientific respectability without burdening them with meeting the demands of systematic proof. The ideal type is often no more, in other words, than an ordinary hypothesis in heuristic clothing. To appreciate how basic this objection is to my book, one need only ask why proponents of the kind of constructs in question should favor them over any other. Typically, the answer given is that the choice depends upon "the extent to which they draw attention to significant phenomena and relationships".[6] The logical corollary to that idea is that there can also be bad constructs which obscure significant phenomena and relationships. Clearly, without having recourse to relevant data there can be no objective way to decide between alternative constructs, or indeed, no cogent reason to use any. To do so, however, is to place the constructs concerned on the same footing as any tentative hypothesis; to refuse to do so is to be committed to views without foundation.

The theoretical argument of this book, then, is that data concerning the experience of political change in the period dealt with fail to confirm many of the hypotheses or pseudo-hypotheses that have been deliberately or otherwise derived from the conceptualization of change as "modernization". In other words, the contention is that uncritical acceptance and use of the constructs associated with the idea of modernization would have obscured significant phenomena and relationships. These ramifications of the material to be presented here may better be appreciated if we first delve a little further into the implications of the idea of modernization in more general terms.

It is important to note that the scholars in question are typically very aware that human behavior certainly does not always conform to either traditional or modern models of behavior—hence one reason for the usual caveat that a pattern of behavior or institution (i.e. formalized principles of action, norms, or rules) never exists in "pure" form in any society. Thus the modernization proposition is strictly speaking not "think of modern and traditional societies as if their members conformed to certain norms", but rather, "think of these

[5] American Philosophical Association (Eastern Division), *Science, Language and Human Rights; Symposium: Problems of Concept and Theory Formulation in the Social Sciences* (Philadelphia, 1952), pp. 71-134.

[6] Fred W. Riggs, "Agraria and Industria—Toward a Typology of Comparative Administration", in William J. Siffen, ed., *Toward the Comparative Study of Public Administration* (Bloomington, Ind., 1957), p. 28.

societies as if their members *tended* to conform to them". The crucial distinction, then, is a matter of the *relative emphasis* which different societies place on alternative attitudes, values and principles of action. It must also be said of this kind of caveat, however, that seldom if ever is operational content given to the notion of relative contrasts. Presumably it could mean that "most people" in a society act according to one or the other set of principles, or that all people do so "in most instances" or that there are differences of qualitative emphasis, i.e. the principles are pursued more *intently* in some sense.

Next, it should be noted that the models of traditional and modern societies consist not merely of one or two isolated alternative principles, but of two whole sets of such principles. Furthermore, all the principles belonging to one set are mutually consistent and supportive of each other, and mutually antagonistic or exclusive with respect to all the principles in the other set. The various pair-sets of qualities (Parsons calls them "pattern variables"[7]) which this mode of analysis has generally yielded are by now familiar to students of socio-political change; only some of the most important ones need be noted and briefly interpreted here for illustrative purposes:

Context of action	Tendency of traditional society	Tendency of modern society
orientation toward established socio-political institutions, rules, arrangements	prescription	innovation
criteria of role recruitment and allocation	ascription	achievement
criteria of distribution of rewards	privilege and status	performance, skill, contribution to objective goals
quality of official relationships	diffuse functions, personal loyalty	specific functions, impersonal loyalty
sanctions of authority	divine, sacred	secular
criteria of membership and participation	particularistic	universalistic

Prescription/innovation: In traditional societies people generally approve of and (given the opportunity) act to foster conformity to the ways and rules (including social and political norms) established in the past; whereas, in modern societies, people generally approve of and (given the opportunity) act to foster such changes (including

[7] Talcott Parsons, *Structure and Process in Modern Societies* (Glencoe, Ill., 1960); see also his *The Social System* (Glencoe, Ill., 1951), and, with Edward A. Shils (eds.), *Toward a General Theory of Action* (Cambridge, Mass., 1951).

changes in social and political norms) as facilitate improvement in the "objective conditions of life" (supply, cost and quality of goods, services, conveniences, etc.).

Ascription/achievement: In determining who shall hold various positions, jobs, or offices, traditional societies pay greater attention to "who a person is" (e.g. the family he was born into); whereas modern societies usually insist more on evidence of "what a person can do" (scholastic examinations, quality and quantity of output, etc.). The divergent criteria of distribution of rewards and prestige follow to a large extent from the ascription/achievement emphasis, since different amounts of reward and prestige attach to various roles.

Diffuseness/specificity: Official relationships in traditional societies are normally such that the duties or functions which a subordinate may be called on to render at the request of a superior are not fixed and, in fact, frequently extend beyond those related to the subordinate's office, as such; whereas in modern societies, the range of duties and functions which officeholders are required to perform are defined and circumscribed either by formal contractual undertakings or conventional understandings.

Sacred/secular: The obligation to obey authority in traditional societies is normally reinforced by, if not inseparable from, belief in some sort of religious or supernatural ordination (at least) of the person exercising supreme authority; whereas in modern societies authority and the obligation to obey it ultimately derive from mundane claims and acknowledgements only.

Particularistic/universalistic: Criteria of membership, judgment, and participation predominate in traditional and modern societies respectively. The principle of universalism requires that the eligibility, worth, and treatment of persons in regard to a social role or institution should not be determined by considerations that are irrelevant to the stated functions of that role or institution. Particularistic criteria consist of considerations that are irrelevant in this sense (e.g. no green-eyed children may attend school). Clearly, the universalistic/particularistic distinction must be regarded as an example par excellence of a difference in degree only as between modern and traditional societies.

Several important observations follow. The first is that the supposedly heuristic "ideal types" thus extrapolated consist of logical or normative antinomies; they are cast in the form of either/or relationships. In regard to each context of action, the operative principle

9

is a contradiction of another principle, and the sum total of these contradictions constitute the "ideal difference", as it were, between modern and traditional classes of societies. A second observation is that the contradictory or mutually exclusive relationship of the contrasting qualities is not altered by qualifying their incidence. In other words, caveats about relative emphasis or disclaimers regarding "pure" cases are not inconsistent with the assumption of mutual exclusivity, nor can those who employ these models reasonably deny this. Thus, to give one example, it cannot be that a society at one and the same time "usually" gives precedence to considerations of birth and also "usually" to considerations of performance. "Most people" in a given society cannot simultaneously insist on universalistic and particularistic bases of social membership and participation. In sum, so long as the claim is that there is a necessary divergence of qualities, then these conflicting qualities cannot both be maximized in the same context; to this extent, relative no less than absolute differences necessarily imply mutual exclusivity of these types or classes of society.

A third important observation involves the conception of the *process* of change to which these formulations necessarily involve. I have elsewhere called this conception "eurhythmic".[8] The idea is, the constituent elements in any process of change are always mutually supportive and consistent, both with respect to various spheres of society (economy, polity, cult, etc.) and to various aspects of any action within a given sphere (normative, psychological, institutional, etc.). In other words, once any significant new element is introduced into a society, a host of changes follow which are all in keeping with the character and impact of the initial innovation. The connection between the assumption that processes of change are always eurhythmic and the conceptualization of the substance of change, in terms of mutually exclusive social qualities, seems clear enough. If innovation inevitably produces a kind of chain reaction of mutually reinforcing consequences, then all preexisting antithetical qualities will necessarily be driven out or displaced. Points of functional reinforcement or viable combination between fundamental elements of modern and traditional societies, respectively, are not possible if such a process is set in motion. If the traditional society which accepts one major feature of a modern society must accept virtually all of them, than any significant change in that direction must

[8] C. S. Whitaker, Jr., "A Dysrhythmic Process of Political Change", *World Politics*, Vol. 19, No. 2 (January 1967), pp. 190-217.

eventually involve a complete shift from one type of society to the other.

The supposed movement of societies between the "ideal types" of social behavior denoted by the concept of modernization brings me to a final set of general observations about such movement. It was suggested above that the conceptual precepts of Weber and others were principally derived from a retrospective analysis of historic changes in Western societies, notably in Weber's case, a movement from a "patrimonial" to a "rational" bureaucracy. Now if the situation of change is not one of a consummated historical movement, but one in which some contemporary "traditional" society is currently in the process of being exposed to certain "modern" influences, the proposition about modernization subtly changes accordingly. This subtle conceptual reformulation is from "think of the difference between the past and present state of certain societies as a conflict of certain principles of action" to "think of (traditional society) as being presented with an ultimate and unavoidable choice between mutually incompatible attitudes, institutions, and principles of action". It is interesting to note in this connection that the very term characteristically applied by scholars in the Weberian tradition to such situations—"transitional"—is indicative of the notion that societies subjected to important "modern" stimuli are on the way from one state of affairs to another predefined end. The basic alternatives of such people are either virtually total displacement of their indigenous order or virtually complete rejection of "modernity". Furthermore, such people are by this formulation necessarily doomed to an intermediate fate of severe strain, conflict, psychic stress, and instability.

One difference between the context of Weber's discussion of Western experiences *over time* and that of what might be called (in place of transitional) *confrontation* societies, is that characteristically, in the latter, "modern" innovations exist side by side with traditional arrangements *in time*. Thus to conceive of the confrontation situation simply as an unavoidable choice between incompatible arrangements, is to prejudge the response, to rule out possibilities that are at least conceivable but which would present not one or two but several possible outcomes. Among the possibilities that come to mind are: (1) in certain contexts of action a conflict of existing and novel arrangements might not arise either because (a) a given element of modernity might in fact coincide with a traditional preconception, (b) a given element of a "modern" society might be normatively neutral for the "traditional" society, (c) the modern element might prove to be

11

positively instrumental, functional, or reinforcing in relation to a given "traditional" pattern; (2) insofar as conflicts of norms do arise, the response of the "traditional" society might be to leave them unresolved, i.e. to persist in states of uncertainty or inconsistency.

What I am suggesting, in other words, is that the modernization conception prematurely precludes or fails to leave room for circumstances or contingencies that could mitigate potential clashes based on conflicting norms, man's capacity to persist in double-mindedness or to work at cross purposes, and what might be called creative adaptations to change, action that succeeds in utilizing or manipulating new or alien elements to serve established ends and values (and vice-versa).

Once the possibility of such exigencies is entertained, it becomes reasonable to imagine that confrontation societies face a far greater range of alternatives than just two, for example:

(1) total rejection of modernity and total retainment of tradition
(2) total acceptance of modernity and total displacement of tradition
(3) partial acceptance of modernity and partial retainment of tradition
(4) partial rejection of modernity and total retainment of tradition
(5) partial displacement of tradition and total acceptance of modernity
(6) total retainment of tradition and total acceptance of modernity

(it will be noticed that the last permutation listed here closely corresponds to a notion, perhaps encountered most frequently a propos of African countries, that a happy synthesis or fusion of all that is best in both modern and traditional systems is possible. What precisely is meant by this notion is unclear. However, insofar as opposing norms do form *any* part of a confrontation situation—and nothing I have said above is to be taken to imply that conflicts of norms may *not* be a real aspect of a confrontation situation—synthesis or fusion, in the sense of change that involves the simultaneous and full realization of both the norms or values of "modernity" and those of the traditional society, is necessarily precluded. Interestingly, however, precisely some such notion of synthesis or fusion served to rationalize the deliberate retainment of important elements of the traditional emirate system of government in Northern Nigeria—at the same time that it served to promote modifications of both traditional and modern institutions. For this reason, the notion of synthesis must be reckoned with in the body of this book).

As a model of socio-political change, the applicability of Western experience to the situation of confrontation societies may have another very serious drawback. The West's development of the socio-political forms associated with the term "modernity" took place as a graduated series of responses to a sequence of economic developments summed up in the term "industrialization". But the essence of the situation of confrontation societies is that they experience these same socio-political forms torn from their original economic context. Modernity, to the extent the confrontation society experiences it, preceded industrialization, and it may well be that many of the socio-political forms resulting from industrialization will not have the same impact when the socio-political forms do not involve the same economic concomitants. The likelihood of important discrepancies is perhaps further enhanced by the fact that leaders and policy-makers in the confrontation societies are acutely conscious of some of the implications of the Western experience and are in a position to innovate selectively.

People seldom seem able or willing to change established ways of behaving as rapidly as their societies can absorb new institutional forms. Particularly in highly stratified societies, a well-entrenched elite may profit indefinitely from a tendency of people to adhere to old political expectations and attitudes of social deference. That the confrontation society typically does not spontaneously generate and design its new political forms to fit internal political exigencies, but often grafts onto the society forms initially designed to cope with problems and conditions which may not be those of the confrontation society, seems bound to complicate and proliferate the possibilities in the outcome of various formal innovations. At the very least, a natural possibility in the confrontation situation is that alien political forms may be accepted without a corresponding commitment to the values originally associated with them.

Finally, political continuity may not always derive simply from atavisms of indigenous popular behavior or environmental conditions unfavorable to the internalization of new institutional arrangements. It may also be fostered by the very situation of active coexistence of indigenous and alien arrangements. In this kind of political world, people may not be so much divided in their responses as dualistic and ambivalent. Virtually at every turn in this situation, modern and traditional conceptions, roles, and functions can interact dynamically; this interaction itself can be a profound force for continuity, or for change in a number of previously novel directions. Tertiary forms, i.e. neither pristinely traditional nor unequivocally modern, may emerge.

To reiterate, "confrontation society" is a term I have employed to help conceptualize situations in which aspects of institutions of different historical origins actually coexist and interact. It emphatically does not constitute a reappearance in a new guise of the polar concepts and evolutionary assumptions of the older scholarly tradition just discussed. On the contrary, it represents a rejection of them in favor of a perspective which remains open to the possibility that institutions of radically different origin, form, and function may be difficult or impossible to accommodate mutually in some important respects but not in others. It is precisely on the point of this possibility that, I am tentatively suggesting here, the old scholarly tradition can be misleading.

This point is also essential for appreciating the manner in which the materials in this book are presented. For, to show the actual, as opposed to the formerly presumed relationship of certain phenomena I have been obliged, to borrow a classic phrase, "to speak with the vulgar", i.e. to pose issues in terms of tradition *versus* modernity, but only in order to demonstrate the difficulties with that formulation according to my own findings: that is, "while thinking with the learned"—about the course of political change in Northern Nigeria.

Furthermore, it is not suggested here that Northern Nigeria is typical even of confrontation societies. Indeed, in terms of political continuity, Northern Nigeria's experience seems conspicuous even among other African societies, which often appear to be paradigms of confrontation generally. Nor is it contended that the 20 years covered in this study is an adequate timespan on which to base general conclusions about lasting patterns of continuity and change. Yet a score of years is hardly a nonce, while a further fundamental difficulty with "modernization theory" has been not merely a failure to indicate a length of time in which the supposed either/or dynamic of change can be expected to operate, but indeed a tendency to deal in ultimate eventualities where Keynes' well-worn caveat against doing so was never more appropriate. If Northern Nigeria functioned for 20 years under "contradictory institutions" without succumbing to any fate envisioned by modernization theory, then it may well be that its experience can shed light on other cases, past, present, and future.

More general significance especially may be derived if in such cases one is able to identify some of the forces and factors that promoted a result other than that pointed to by modernization theory. I believe this is done for Northern Nigeria in this book. A more precise characterization of that result and of those forces and factors must be left to a concluding chapter, where we can reconsider these theoretical points against the background of a detailed account of actual events and developments of the period.

As IT EXISTED up to 1966, the northern region of Nigeria contained more than one-half the population of the Federation or Federal Republic of Nigeria, the most populous nation in Africa. Nigeria accounted for more than the combined populations of all other West African states. Alone, Northern Nigeria's population exceeded that of any other political unit on the African continent, save Nigeria itself and perhaps the United Arab Republic.[9] The territory of Northern Nigeria comprised nearly 300,000 square miles; it is 720 miles wide, from its border with Dahomey in the west to the Cameroon Republic in the east, and 410 miles long, from its northern neighbor, the Niger Republic, to the rest of Nigeria in the south (the eastern, western, and midwestern regions).[10] Northern Nigeria was divided into 13 provinces. The regional capital, centrally located at Kaduna, incorporated a city of some 150,000 people. Two major rivers, the Niger and the Benue, each running about 500 miles and connected to important tributaries, join within this region at the southerly town of Lokoja and flow southwards to the Niger Delta and the Bight of Benin. The latter, and the Gulf of Guinea, represented Northern Nigeria's only navigable access to the sea.

Roughly 70% of the population of Northern Nigeria and approxi-

[9] The Nigerian census conducted in 1952-53 recorded a total of 16,835,582 people in Northern Nigeria, out of a grand total for Nigeria of 31,168,000. The latest census conducted in 1963 placed Nigeria's total population at 55,620,268, with 29,758,875 people in the northern region. This surprising increase in population may be attributable to inaccuracy of the earlier census, an exceptionally high rate of population growth, manipulation of the censuses for political purposes, and most likely some of all these factors together. Many of the statistical breakdowns contained in the 1952-53 census were not made available in connection with the 1963 census. The most useful compilation, based on both censuses to date, is the *Northern Nigeria Statistical Yearbook, 1964* (Kaduna, 1965). Unless otherwise noted, figures cited in this study are taken from this publication.

[10] It will be noted throughout this book that "Northern Nigeria" is always capitalized, while "southern" in "southern Nigeria" is not. The reason is simply that formally no such unit as "southern Nigeria" existed in the period of this study. For the sake of convenience, however, the term is used when the eastern, western and midwestern regions are referred to collectively.

mately one-half its territory lay within kingdoms, mostly ancient in origin, which the British, who ruled over this land from 1900 to 1960, called emirates, after the Arabic word for a Muslim ruler (Amir). All but a very small and dwindling minority of the people of these emirates are Muslims or adherents of Islam, a religion which claimed 70% of the people of Northern Nigeria. The focus of this book is on the *internal* political experience of Northern Nigeria as it relates, primarily, to the affairs of the emirates between 1946 and 1966. External influences, including those of the southern part of the northern region (commonly referred to in this book and elsewhere as the "Middle Belt") and of southern Nigeria, are only discussed in this book insofar as they impinged on that experience. It is evident, however, that Northern Nigeria's population and size made it the dominant influence in Nigeria as a whole in this period and that by the same token, the nature of Northern Nigeria's influence was principally determined by what happened in the emirates. It follows that to say this study concerns the political and geographical heartland of Africa is no more than a slight exaggeration, and perhaps an important perspective.

The 13 provinces of Northern Nigeria were commonly grouped into two broad areas—the upper or far North, and the Middle Belt or riverain area—and sometimes into four—the Far North Provinces: Sokoto, Kano, Bornu, Bauchi (North); the Central provinces: Zaria, Niger (North), Bauchi (except the northern part); the Plateau and Cameroon Mountains provinces: Plateau, Sardauna; and the southern riverain provinces: Adamawa, Benue, Kabba, Ilorin. At least one emirate was to be found in each of the 13 provinces except Kabba, and most provinces contained several emirates. It was a sign of the dominance of the emirate as a political form in Northern Nigeria that the names of eight of the provinces were derived from that of the largest emirate respectively situated in them. Five provinces (Sokoto, Kano, Bornu, Katsina, and Ilorin) were composed exclusively of emirates, and in four others the great majority lived in emirates. Some large provinces were subdivided into divisions consisting of one or more emirates. In official administrative nomenclature, emirates (like all other types of local administrative units in the region) were styled Native Authorities (unlike most other areas of former British Africa where this originally colonial usage was dropped along with the attainment of independence). Thus, for example, Kano emirate was synonymous with the Kano Native Authority (N.A., giving rise to the Hausa neologism *en'e*). Native Administrations, in principle, referred to the total operations of the Native Authorities, but these two terms were conventionally used interchangeably, as they often are in this book.

"Most of Northern Nigeria is an open savannah land with scattered hills and thin woods, which northwards gradually changes to almost desert, yet remains within the range of the summer rains. Landscape and climate vary in the great undulating Central Plateau, with hills of granite and sandstone ranging from 2,000 to well over 5,000, and in the Cameroon Mountains along the eastern frontier. The southern riverain area is a lowland but with ranges of hills rising towards its western and southern boundaries, humid and partly covered with high rain forest."[11]

"Climate, and especially rainfall, varies in a north-south direction, and so to a lesser extent does temperature; but throughout the area there is a common agricultural cycle falling into two clearly marked seasons—a short rainy period from mid-May to September, and a long dry spell which begins with the harvest, October to December, and is followed by two cold months, finishing with the hot dry months of the harmattan, February to May. Vegetation is denser in the south, and the profitable savannah cash crops, such as cotton and groundnuts or tobacco, do not flourish there. Intensive farming is limited to the rainy season; and although some marsh cultivation is carried on in the rainless months, the dry season is traditionally the period of concentrated craft production, long-term trading expeditions, marriage celebrations, hunting, bush clearing for new farms, and formerly, slave raids and war."[12]

The total number of distinct ethno-linguistic groups indigenous to Northern Nigeria in precolonial times is unknown, but a conservative estimate is about 250. However, the 1952-53 census lists four northern groups numbering in the millions—Hausa, 5.5 million; Fulani, over three million; Kanuri, well over a million—who resided overwhelmingly in emirates. The nonemirate Tiv people were recorded as over three quarters of a million strong, but the latest census lists them at almost one and a half million.

[11] *Northern Nigeria Statistical Yearbook, 1964.*
[12] M. G. Smith, *Government in Zazzau, 1800-1950* (London, 1960), p. 1.

The earlier census records an average literacy rate for the region as a whole of under 7%. This figure took into account literacy in a corrupted form of Arabic script called *ajami* in Hausa. Considering only literacy in Roman letters (in which most newspapers, government publications, and memoranda, were written), the literacy rate was 2.5%. These calculations, however, include the nonemirate people, whose earlier historic exposure to Christian missionaries gave them a substantial lead in Western education. In the provinces composed exclusively of Muslim emirate peoples the literacy rate was much lower (Sokoto, 1.3%, Kano, 1.1, Bornu, 1.2, Katsina 2.0). Assuming a doubling or even tripling of the literacy rate among the emirate peoples between 1952 and 1966, one was still dealing with literacy rates low even for contemporary Africa. Similarly, while the number of children attending school in Northern Nigeria has officially doubled in these years, the percentages for the great emirates were still strikingly low (Sokoto, 3.2%, Bornu 4.1, Kano, 4.9).

By 1966 less than 10% of Northern Nigerians were living in towns of 20,000 or more (there were 12 such towns), although 9 of the 12 were in emirates. The average population density for the region is recorded in the 1952-53 census as 60 per square mile. Again, however, the population in the area of the emirates tended to be considerably more densely settled, with some emirates having very high rates indeed (e.g. Kano, 229 thousand and Katsina, 157 thousand).

Approximately 90% of the male working population of Northern Nigeria were engaged in nonindustrial pursuits. 80% were farmers; approximately 10% earned their livelihood in forestry and animal husbandry, fishing and hunting. Only a portion of the remainder represented skilled and semiskilled, salaried workers employed by governmental agencies and private manufacturing enterprises. The annual per capita cash income of Northern Nigeria in the period under study did not exceed 30 pounds, or 100 dollars, and very likely this figure is high in relation to the emirate peoples. The cash-earning resources of the region included groundnuts, cotton and tobacco, and among minerals, tin, columbite, and limestone. Primarily for domestic use, the north grew a wide variety of grains and cereals and bred all of Nigeria's cattle. Under the 1962-68 Nigerian Development Plan, the construction of a Niger dam promised to make Northern Nigeria the nation's source of hydroelectric power. Agriculture, however, earned 85% of the country's foreign exchange; Northern Nigeria's primary source of public revenue was in the form of a share of Nigeria's import and export taxes on foreign trade. The official currency was the Nigerian pound, exchangeable at par with British sterling.

In the period of this study, economic development was pursued with noteworthy vigor. A 1963 study, conducted under the auspices of the Northern Ministry of Trade and Industries with the cooperation of British Industrial firms, was able to boast the following advances: "Factories built in Northern Nigeria during the period 1960-63 produce a variety of products and the total investment in industrial development in this short time approximate £20,000,000, of which about £5,000,000 is from Northern Nigerian sources. . . . Within the Federal National income growth, Northern Nigeria has shown the most rapid growth. From 1950 to 1957 the national income of the North increased more than twice as fast as that of either of the other regions. Since 1957, Northern Nigeria has at least maintained her share of the Federal total so that by 1960 her national income had risen to a total of about £560 million, at 1960 prices—an increase of 68 per cent over the decade, compared with a 75 per cent increase in Federal national income."[13] However, these data did not obscure or seriously alter the reality of Northern Nigeria's relatively backward base of development in comparison with that of southern Nigeria, nor the low levels of conventional socioeconomic development indices even in absolute terms, as reflected in the statistics presented here. Indeed, consciousness of socioeconomic "backwardness" throughout the period of this study constituted a very significant element of the attitude of any politically aware Northerner.

The bulk of the emirates are known historically as the Hausa States. They were conquered mostly between 1804 and 1810 in a *jihad*, or Islamic holy war, led by members of another people, the Fulani. Today in all but two of these Hausa emirates, the core of the ruling class is Fulani and the masses of subjects are Hausa or *Habe*. *Habe* is a Fulani word meaning non-Fulani; Hausa, properly a linguistic and cultural designation, is also commonly applied to the *Habe* and Fulani collectively, for the Fulani rulers soon became assimilated to the culture and language of their subjects. (The *Habe* dynasties of Abuja and Daura emirates survived the *jihad* and remain in power today.) However, the British also applied the term emirate to states in which Fulani rule was established over kingdoms founded originally by the Nupe and by the Yoruba peoples, a few which the Fulani fabricated out of a conglomeration of ethnic and mostly pagan

[13] Northern Nigeria, Ministry of Trade and Industries, *The Industrial Potentialities of Northern Nigeria* (Kaduna, 1963), pp. 13, 16.

19

groups, the *Habe* states which survived the *jihad* (including the transplanted *Habe* enclave of Abuja), and other indigenous states never conquered by the Fulani, notably the huge kingdom of Bornu, near Lake Chad, where the Kanuri people are dominant, and Argungu, a remnant of a once mighty empire. British usage stemmed from the apparent facts that Islam was the state religion in all of these and that they all had generally become acculturated to a common type of government and administration. Accordingly, unless otherwise noted or qualified, observations made in this book about the emirates of Northern Nigeria are meant to apply to all of them.

The Hausa states did serve as the nucleus of this acculturative process, however, as the often related myth of their historical origin itself suggests. According to the legend, a traveler from Bagdad, one Bayajidda, who had previously spent some time in Bornu, arrived in the Hausa village of Daura where he found that a menacing snake, lodged in the village well, was preventing the people from drawing water. Bayajidda slew the snake; the queen of the village married him as a reward; and their children were three sets of twins who became the rulers of Kano and Rano, Katsina and Zaria (or Zazzau), and Gobir and Daura. These, together with Biram whose king was furnished by another son of Bayajidda by a Bornu princess, form the Hausa *Bakwai* or seven "true" Hausa states. Another seven states—the *banza bakwai*, or bastard seven—were according to the legend formed by seven sons born of Bayajidda and a concubine who had been his other reward for killing the snake. Students of this part of the world speculate that the legend not only expresses the cultural and linguistic unity of the Hausa, but indicates that an actual wave of Berber migration into the area, probably during the ninth or tenth centuries, helped to shape that culture.[14]

The Hausa culture of this era was very rich. The traditional agricultural pursuits of the people were combined with crafts that foreshadowed relatively advanced technology—such as iron-smelting, cloth-weaving and dyeing—and trade which included a vigorous trans-Saharan commerce that was to provide the vehicle for a slow but steady infiltration of religious and cultural influences from the Islamic

---

[14] H. R. Palmer, *Sudanese Memoirs* (Lagos, 1958); M. G. Smith, "The Beginning of Hausa Society: A.D. 1000-1500", in J. Vansina et al., eds., *The Historian in Tropical Africa* (London, 1964), pp. 339-54; S. J. Hogben and A.H.M. Kirk-Greene, *The Emirates of Northern Nigeria* (London, 1966), pp. 3-5, 145-48.

lands to the north and east.[15] The Hausa appear to have been primarily patrilinial in family organization, and in political organization ever more centralized, elaborate, and complex with the passage of time. The main initial impetus to political development was undoubtedly internecine war. Latterly Islam—in which, ideally, prescribed social and political forms, as well as faith, go hand in hand—was the most formative influence, though locally the religion was in fact modified through contact with preexisting religious beliefs and practices.[16]

By 1500 Hausa social and political institutions had assumed a distinctive and durable shape. These included a sharp division between the ruling and subject classes (*sarakuna* and *talakawa*); subdivision of *sarakuna* into royals and nobles, eunuchs, slaves, and free clients (whose differences in status corresponded to an elaborate system of state offices and titles); a system of administration based on territorial subunits, or fiefs, supervised by royal appointees who acted through agents (*jekadu*); systematic tribute or taxation, the state treasury; and presiding over this structure, the king (*sarki*, singular of *sarakuna*) and his council of advisors.

Internecine wars, competition for trade, wars and relations involving the great neighboring empires of the western Sudan (Mali, Songhai, and to the east of Hausaland, Kanem, and its derivative, Bornu), and slave-raiding in pursuit of military and economic advantage dictated the political preoccupations of the Hausa states from the 14th to the 19th centuries. The deepening penetration of Islam during this period was accompanied by, among other currents, the growth of a class of influential religious preachers (*Imams*) and scholars (*malams*). The Fulani people were and are mostly nomadic cattle-herders, but in this period an increasing number of them became sedentary among the Hausa. From among the settled Fulani (*Fulanin gida*, as distinct from the *bororoje* or "cow Fulani") emerged some of the most active and earnest malams and imams. One Fulani preacher and scholar, Shehu Usman dan Fodio, became especially prominent and influential in the state of Gobir about 1800. It was he who sounded the fateful cry of *jihad* against the *Habe* kings.

Commentaries on the *jihad* have advanced various underlying

---

[15] See E. W. Bovill, *Caravans of the Old Sahara* (London, 1933); a more recent but not identical edition is *The Trade of the Golden Moors* (London, 1955).

[16] See Joseph H. Greenberg, *The Influence of Islam on a Sudanese Religion*, American Ethnological Society, Monograph No. 10 (New York, 1946); and J. S. Trimingham, *A History of Islam in West Africa* (London, 1962).

motives for it, some of them ulterior. Perhaps the baldest version of the latter interpretation is contained in S. J. Hogben's first edition of *The Muhamaden Emirates of Northern Nigeria,* the gist of which is that the *jihad* represented a skillfully executed plot, masquerading under the guise of a movement for religious purification, to install Fulani in place of Habe monarchs.[17] A more recent work appears to offer the hypothesis that because the authority of the *Habe* kings rested on a syncrestic blend of Islamic and pre-Islamic precepts, any exhortation to Islamic orthodoxy was ipso facto subversive.[18] Neither of these interpretations do justice to the deep feeling of moral indignation—toward the pernicious standards of official conduct evidently prevalent at the time—which dan Fodio exhibits in his writings (few of which have been translated into English).[19] Shehu dan Fodio's de-

[17] "At the beginning of the nineteenth century conditions in the Western Sudan underwent a violent change in consequence of an event which is generally known as the Fulani Conquest and is qualified as a jihad. . . . Religion was often made a pretext for the acquisition of worldly power. It had as its confessed object the purification of the Muslim religion, and it was directed against the corrupt rulers of Hausaland who had been supposedly oppressing or ignoring the rights of the Muslim subjects.

"In reality, it was originally a national fight of the Fulani, both Muslim and pagan, against the forces of Yunfa, the King of Gobir, who had decreed their extermination. Only after the victory, when the pagan Fulani, who had borne more than their full share in order to achieve it, had retired to their flocks and herds, did the malams who had been the leaders, exploit the opportunity under the cloak of religion to oust the native rulers and put themselves into their places, with Usman dan Fodio at their head. Henceforth this movement was no longer confined to a particular race; yet from its very nature, it appealed more strongly to the fanatical and more highly strung element in the Fulani clans, and for this reason perhaps it has been called the Fulani Conquest. Furthermore, the Fulani, by reason of the greater powers of initiative given by their clan organization, were convenient instruments for the successful working of a coup".

[18] "It is true that over certain matters Islam, which had been long established in Hausaland, made many concessions to the indigenous religion of the Hausa. This was particularly marked in the institution of monarchy. Indeed, as far as the Habe monarchs were concerned, they practiced a calculated syncretism whereby their authority as Moslem monarchs was boosted by, and to a considerable extent depended on, their respect for Habe religious rites and social practices. Thus, the Fulani attack on their 'reversion to paganism' was an attack on the very authority by which they ruled. . . .

"It becomes clear in this light that the attacks of Usman dan Fodio struck at the very heart of Yunfa's power, and Yunfa's anti-Islamic measures were probably designed to prevent Usman the reformer, from gaining more adherents. The antagonism between the two was not really that between believer and infidel, even though the Fulani liked to depict Yunfa as an unbeliever, but between radical reformer and a conservative willing to compromise in pursuit of stable government". Michael Crowder, *The Story of Nigeria* (London: Faber and Faber, 1962), p. 81.

[19] See M. Hisket, "*Kitab-el-Farq*: A work on the *Habe* Kingdoms Attributed to 'Upman dan Fodico' ", *Bulletin of the School of Oriental and African Studies,* London, Vol. 23, Part 3 (1960). This is a short work which does, however, pro-

scriptions of the conditions of the time are confirmed by those of contemporary European travelers, other leader-publicists of the *jihad*, and the elderly living inhabitants of the surviving *Habe* states who have been interviewed by the anthropologist M. G. Smith.[20]

Upon completion of the *jihad*, dan Fodio retired in Sokoto (which he had made his headquarters in 1809), leaving the political consummation of his reforms to others. Men to whom dan Fodio had presented a green flag and whom he had directed to prosecute the *jihad* in various territories, including the *Habe* states, remained as rulers in those territories, founding dynasties from which with few exceptions the Fulani emirs have been drawn ever since. (Yakubu, the trusted pupil of dan Fodio who received authority to establish the present emirate of Bauchi, was not Fulani, but Gerewa, a people indigenous to the area, as have been all Emirs of Bauchi down to the present.) The seat of supreme authority in the empire, which together these territories constituted, remained in Sokoto after the death of dan Fodio in 1817. Before that, however, Shehu had divided the imperial administration between his son Bello and his brother Abdullahi. Abdullahi was charged with supervision of all the western territories (which included the *banza bakwai*); he resided in Gwandu while Bello supervised the other states from Sokoto. This division was administrative rather than political, which is seen in the fact that the descendants of Bello inherited Shehu's title of *Sarkin Musulmi* (Commander of the Faithful), the throne of Sokoto emirate, and the ultimate allegiance of the other states as a whole, while the descendants of Abdullahi could lay claim to the throne of Gwandu only (an arrangement never completely satisfactory to either Abdul-

---

vide an insight into both the nature of dan Fodio's objectives and the exploitive and oppressive tendencies of the society of his day which he denounced. A longer work, the *Bayan Wujab al Hijra Alal Ibad*, which reportedly "sets out the binding obligations of the jihad on Muslims and discusses 'pagan' and Muslim government in detail", has been paraphrased by M. G. Smith and discussed in "Historical and Cultural Conditions of Corruption Among the Hausa", *Comparative Studies in Society and History* Vol. 6, No. 2 (January 1964), pp. 164-94. According to Smith, the condemned Habe practices include use of elaborate titles, illegal appropriation of property, compulsory military service commutable for cash, the giving of gifts to one who conducts subjects before the ruler, bribery of judges and legal assessors, illegal taxes on merchants and travelers, confiscation of commoners' beasts which strayed among the ruler's, etc. See also Hajji Said, *History of Sokoto* (London, 1948); and E. J. Arnett, *The Rise of the Sokoto Fulani*, a paraphrased translation of a historical work by dan Fodio's son, Muhammed Bello, entitled *Infagal Maisuri* (London, 1910); another work by dan Fodio's brother, Abdullahi, is *Tazyin al Waraquat*, tr. Mervyn Hisket (Ibadan, 1963).

20 *Ibid.*

lahi or his successors). To dan Fodio's impassioned indictment in the name of Islamic ideals, of exploitation and oppression under *Habe* rule, Bello and Abdullahi added their own treatises in similar vein. All of them normally wrote in Arabic (occasionally some wrote a vernacular in Ajamic script). That in time virtually all of the condemned *Habe* practices found their way back into the system of government of the emirates (along with newly invented variations) is obviously no reflection on the standards they set. Rather it indicates that their less righteous successors were spared the inconvenience of having to answer for their conduct. The absence of restraining influences was due partly to the fact that ordinary subjects were unable to read Arabic (and that the rulers made no effort otherwise to disseminate the contents of the documents) and partly to the reality that learned Muslim devouts, like their Christian counterparts in an earlier era, lacked means of enforcement.

In an illuminating discussion, M. G. Smith has delineated some forces and conditions that encouraged progressive departure from the tenets and prescriptions associated with the *jihad* in the direction of forms and practices characteristic of *Habe* rule.[21] He notes that the new imperial regime was from the outset rendered vulnerable to such a development, partly by the participation in the *jihad* and its aftermath of opportunistic seekers after power and wealth for their own sake, combined with practical difficulties of exercising control over the vast area encompassed by the *jihad* (1,100 miles east to west, by 400 miles north to south) from Sokoto, situated almost at its westernmost extreme.

Another difficulty stemmed from the customary grouping of the Fulani into separate and rival clans and rival lineages within clans, a practice that was translated into the institutions of the state, including the monarchy. In other words, succession to the throne was not governed by any rule of primogeniture. In terms of royal authority, rivalry meant intrigue or fear of it, which in turn stimulated the Fulani emirs to seek unchallengeable positions of power. The impulse to autocracy (bordering at times on absolutism) that the condition of insecurity generated within the ruling circle of Fulani clearly did not reduce the social and political distance between the monarchy and its *Habe* subjects (although it did promote the elevation of selected *Habe* into positions of trust and delegated authority, as we shall see). Indeed, reapproximation of *Habe* norms of government

---

[21] *Ibid.*, pp. 175-76.

on the part of Fulani went hand in hand with redoubled insistence on the necessity and sanctity of the Fulani mission of conquest and domination. Fulani emirs asserted claims to superior religious authority at the same time that they induced loyalty to the throne in the form of the license given their subordinate officials to engage in imposition of mass levies, receipt of bribes and gifts (*gaisuwa*, literally "greetings"), exaction of arbitrary fines, and other practices proscribed by dan Fodio's deductions from the doctrines of Islam. Of course such license only enhanced the value of offices, which in turn excited deeper envy and more intense rivalry for their possession. Furthermore, sharing the proceeds of these practices with a superior was not merely a means for subordinates to demonstrate loyalty; for the superior it also represented an important source of financial remuneration, which reinforced his vested interest in allowing the practices.

External assaults on the Fulani regimes and Fulani fear of them also contributed to the vicious circle of insecurity, autocracy, and oppression. The military forces of displaced former *Habe* kings which had withdrawn to other areas and been replenished, like Katsina and Gobir *Habe* to the north at Maradi, and of states the Fulani never succeeded in conquering—Bornu and Kebbi (Argungu)—harassed the Fulani with hostile forays virtually throughout the balance of the 19th century. Slave-raiding and holding (not only of non-Muslims, as Islam enjoins), helped provide the military strength the Fulani needed to repulse these enemies, as well as providing a source of labor. Perhaps the last arc of the vicious circle was the reality that the established, familiar and tried machinery of *Habe* government offered the most effective and expeditious means of organizing resistance to external and internal threats alike. Many of the superficial innovations that resulted from the Fulani conquest were maintained (e.g. *alkalai*, or Muslim judges and priests within the capital towns); but by and large, "the proper forms of Muslim law and administration were reserved by the Fulani for themselves, other groups such as the Tuareg and the Arabs, and for privileged members of the subject population".[22]

Such was the situation prevailing on January 1, 1900, the day Northern Nigeria was officially declared a British Protectorate under High Commissioner Sir Frederick Lugard, following a period in which the authority of the British government in the area had been

[22] *Ibid.*, p. 181.

vested in a commercial enterprise, the Royal Niger Company.[23] Like dan Fodio, Lugard was partly inspired by a zeal to reform away what to his British mind were evil elements in the system of government in the emirates. Significantly, the evil elements to Lugard, and those dan Fodio and his lieutenants had denounced in the name of Islam, were largely identical, although there is no evidence that Lugard or his successors ever made much use of indigenous moral precedents. Perhaps part of the reason was that the British, like the masses of emirate subjects, never saw the relevant political documents. Instead, Lugard spoke of "natural" justice, a notion he himself had to define for the circumstances in which he found himself.

These circumstances involved practical problems which, just as much as the aims Lugard envisioned, had their parallel in the history of the *jihad*. Essentially the problems grew out of having to control a vast and populous area with inadequate facilities for travel and communication, to win recognition and respect for a new regime from an alien people (which meant the necessity of demonstrating effectiveness), to come to terms with the prejudices and hostility of still powerful antecedent rulers.[24] Nor were Lugard's difficulties alleviated by a British government that had only reluctantly endorsed the idea of a Protectorate and was unprepared or unwilling to commit substantial resources to the venture. Lugard had to start with a grant of £135,000 and the services of about a dozen British "political officers". Within three years Lugard with the help of African troops had achieved victory over the military forces of the resisting emirs. But British military victory no more solved the long-term problems of communication and control than had the Fulani conquest before it.

[23] The fullest account of this period is in J. E. Flint's excellent biography of the Royal Niger Company's chief, *Sir George Goldie and the Making of Nigeria* (London, 1960).

[24] In the first three years following the proclamation of the Protectorate, Fulani emirs showed defiance on several occasions. The Emir of Kontagora, a notorious slave-raider, answered Lugard's command to stop the practice with the epigram: "Can you stop a cat from mousing? I shall die with a slave in my mouth". The emirs of Nupe and Abuja offered resistance and sabotage; Yola was unbending; the Emir of Keffi's titled client, the *Magaji*, slew a British resident when he ordered cessation of slaving; and the famous reply of the Sultan of Sokoto, Attahiru, to Lugard's overtures for collaboration was, "From us to you. I do not consent that any one from you should ever dwell with us. I will never agree with you. I will have no dealings except as between Mussulmans and Unbelievers, War, as God Almighty has enjoined on us. There is no power of strength save in God on high. This with salutations". *The Occupation of Hausaland* (Arabic documents tr. ed. H. F. Blackwell) (Lagos: Government Printer, 1927), p. 14 and *passim*. Also see Margery Perham, *Native Administration in Nigeria* (London: Oxford University Press, 1937), p. 37.

Like the Fulani conquerors, Lugard perceived that a solution for his problems presented itself in the form of the already effectively functioning system of government, which by then offered such obvious additional advantages as religious justification for authority, a formal code of law (the Islamic *Shari'a*), specialized judicial institutions, a more centrally controlled apparatus of administration, the custom of taxation, and, above all, the people's habit of obeying state authority—cultivated and ingrained by the centuries-old tradition of monarchy and hardened by Fulani despotism.

It might be said that the essential difference between the British and Fulani regimes was that while Fulani rulers systematically abandoned and concealed the original ideals of their mission, the British response was to construct a system designed to satisfy expedience and idealism simultaneously. Lugard called this system indirect rule, or the system of native administration. Retaining for the conqueror's own use the political techniques, institutions, and influence of an ostensibly vanquished regime was an inspiration that obviously originated neither with Lugard nor in Northern Nigeria. But Northern Nigeria probably is the classic case of articulation of such an expedient into a creed for the political and moral transformation of subject people in the image of their alien masters. In time, the principles of Lugard's system were adopted as official doctrine in almost all the British colonial territories in Africa.

To introduce the flavor of indirect rule, which will be repeatedly manifested in the substance of this book, here is a typical recital by one of the creed's apostles, Major Burdon (one of Lugard's original cadre of "political officers", or Residents):

> Our aim is to rule through existing chiefs, to raise them in the administrative scale, to enlist them on our side in the work and progress of good government. We cannot do without them. To rule directly would require an army of British magistrates . . . which both the general unhealthiness of the country and the present poverty forbid. My hope is that we may make of these born rulers a high type of British official, working for the good of their subjects in accordance with the ideals of British Empire, but carrying on all that is best in the constitution they have evolved for themselves, the one understood by, and therefore best suited to the people.[25]

We shall turn in the next chapter to a fuller examination of the later political implications of the uncomfortable mixture of aspirations em-

---

[25] Quoted in Crowder, *Story of Nigeria*, pp. 193-94.

27

bodied in this and similar statements. For the moment, the important point to be noted is that the execution of indirect rule had left intact the essential institutions of traditional government in the emirates for the time when Northern Nigeria confronted a fundamentally new objective of colonial rule—namely, to introduce and develop democratically representative institutions of government in Nigeria, along with other African territories. This sudden turn of events was certainly never envisaged by Lugard at all, and only a few of the responsible British officials at the time had given any serious thought to how the new policy was to fit in with the system Lugard had initiated and they had nurtured. We shall see that those who *had* entertained such thoughts did not agree in their conclusions, and that in this state of official irresolution about the role and future of traditional institutions in the emirates, the new policy was set in motion. Nevertheless, a new policy was applied, the British carried out their withdrawal, and the major elements of emirate traditional institutions, to the surprise of many, survived these developments. How and why they survived, and what effect the survival had on government and politics in Northern Nigeria are questions I shall deal with in this book.

Britain's new policy was applied at three levels of Nigerian government—local, regional, and national. Nigeria had existed as a colonial *administrative* entity from the time the Protectorate of Northern Nigeria was combined with the Colony and Protectorate of Southern Nigeria in 1914. But in order for Nigeria to benefit as a unit from British policy after the war, all Nigerian *political* institutions had to be evolved from scratch. Thus between 1946 and 1960, the year of Nigerian independence, leaders drawn from the multifarious ethnic nationalities and communities that made up Nigeria engaged in a process of deliberating, negotiating, and operating a series of complicated constitutions in pursuit of a mutually acceptable framework for Nigerian nationhood.[26] The detailed story of those years and that

[26] The first postwar Nigerian constitution, the so-called Richards Constitution, after the colonial governor of Nigeria, Sir Arthur Richards, was introduced in 1946, but without benefit of prior consultation with Nigerian representatives. Nigerian resentment over this omission accelerated the replacement of the Richards Constitution with the "Macpherson Constitution" of 1951, whose sponsor was assured that its arrangements had at least the provisional backing of African representatives following a series of prior conferences at the provincial, regional, and national levels. The third was the Conference on the Review of the Nigerian Constitution held at Ibadan in 1950. Under the Richards Constitution, the Northern Provinces were for the first time accorded representation in the Legislative Council of Nigeria, while additional advisory councils were introduced in the regions—or in

process, of the forces in Nigeria which helped promote new colonial policy in the first place, and of the obstacles encountered then and seemingly overcome, has been admirably chronicled and analyzed by distinguished scholars of Nigeria[27] and therefore need not be recounted here. Certain aspects of the story will be referred to later, but only insofar as they have a bearing on the particular topics of this study. At this point, for purposes of background, it may be helpful to advance two general observations about postwar Nigerian nationalism and constitutional development. The first is that the most formidable obstacle to the achievement of 1960 was the profound cultural, religious, social, and political differences that existed and will likely exist for the foreseeable future between the emirates of Northern Nigeria and the rest of Nigeria.

In 1950-51 Northern and southern leaders clashed over the issue of the balance of representation in the Nigerian Legislative Council. The Northerners insisted on and finally won a 50 percent allocation of seats on the grounds that the size of the population of the Northern Region warranted it. Clearly they also regarded the recognition of this demand as indispensable to the realization of northern interests. In 1953 leaders of the Northern Peoples' Congress (NPC), a political party primarily identified with the dominant social, political, and religious institutions of Northern Nigeria (i.e. those found in the emirates) threatened to reject the whole proposition of common Nigerian political institutions unless further basic concessions were made by the two principal southern nationalist parties, the National Council of Nigeria and the Cameroons (later called the National Council of Nigerian Citizens, or NCNC) and the Action Group (AG).

---

the Northern Provinces, the Eastern Provinces and the Western Provinces, as these units were then officially called. Most African members of the Legislative Council were chosen by and from the members of the Regional Councils, who, in turn, were nominated by the governor. The Macpherson Constitution provided for elections to each of the regional councils, regional executive authority over a defined range of subjects, and African Ministers of Government. The fundamental departure of the 1954 Constitution was that certain powers were enumerated to the central government, leaving residual powers to the Regions (as they were now officially called)—which meant that Nigeria had moved from a unitary system of government to a genuinely federal system. (The constitution also contained a list of concurrent powers.) The Constitutional Conference held in London in 1953, at which delegates of all the important political parties in Nigeria were present, preceded this major change. Additional London conferences, at which various amendments to the 1954 Constitution were adopted, were convened in 1957, 1958, and finally in 1960, on the eve of independence.

[27] James S. Coleman, *Nigeria: Background to Nationalism* (Berkeley, 1958); Kalu Ezera, *Constitutional Developments in Nigeria* (London, 1960); Richard L. Sklar, *Nigerian Political Parties* (Princeton, 1963).

Each party's main support came from the two ethnic groups that dominated the two largest constituent regions of the federation remaining at the time, the Ibo people in the eastern region and the Yoruba people of the western region.

As is now well known and documented, both Ibo and Yoruba traditional societies were relatively "open" compared with the traditional society of the emirates. Another fundamental contrast was in the far greater degree to which the peoples of southern Nigeria, being closer to the sea (the historical avenue of modern Western contact with Nigeria), had been exposed to and had absorbed the typically coastal African experiences of Western education, the international market system, and Christian missionary activity. (Lugard initially barred Christian missions from the emirates, thus keeping his promise to the emirs not to interfere with the Islamic religion.) Ostensibly the occasion for the crisis of 1953 was disagreement over a timetable for Nigerian independence. The southern parties specifically endorsed 1956; the NPC was unwilling to commit itself, proposing instead the formula "as soon as practicable". But most observers would agree that the roots of the crisis were to be found in the profound socio-cultural contrasts between north and south.

The second important observation about terminal colonialism in Nigeria arises out of the fact that British concessions took the form of a federal constitution (the "Lyttleton Constitution" of 1954) in which the constituent regions of Nigeria retained jurisdiction over precisely those matters that most vitally affected the condition and future of the emirates as political entities. Thus Northern Nigeria exercised exclusive jurisdiction in local government and chieftaincy affairs, regulations governing elections to regional parliaments, the judiciary and legal institutions within the region, recruitment and regulation of separate regional public services (e.g. civil services), and education (up to and including the secondary-school level). These remained prominent features of Nigeria's "independence" constitution. In other words, the constitution of Nigeria placed the issue of the fate of Northern traditional institutions in the hands solely of the political leaders of Northern Nigeria. Federalism by itself did not assure the perpetuation of traditional emirate institutions in Northern Nigeria. But in light of most southern Nigerian leaders' natural distaste for all that the emirates politically represented, Nigerian federalism surely made continuity in the emirates possible.

In Nigeria *regional* self-government (i.e. surrender by the British to Africans of all powers within the purview of regional authority), preceded national independence. The timing was indicative of the acute sense of separate ethnic and regional identity that was to characterize relationships between the main components of the Federation throughout the two decades of its existence as discussed in this book. Both Eastern Nigeria and Western Nigeria became self-governing in 1957 (the Midwestern Region was carved out of the Western Region in 1960). Northern Nigeria's self-government came in 1959, on the deliberately symbolic date of March 15, the anniversary of the fall of the seat of the Fulani empire, Sokoto, to Lugard's troops.

The beginning point of this study of continuity and change is the end of the Second World War, a watershed marked politically in Nigeria by the introduction of national parliamentary political forms under the Richards Constitution of 1946. Up to that time, as I have said, the traditional political system of the emirates was only slightly modified by colonial rule, though often in certain respects important to its subsequent development. The traditional system continued, but in a new context and subject to external forces and considerations brought on by the superimposition of representational political forms. The empirical focus of this book is the mutual interplay of influences between those forms and that system. Because the traditional system coexisted with new institutions, my references to it are not confined to the preparliamentary era. Rather specific contrasts before and after 1945 must be noted in the relevant place. Otherwise it is possible and indeed necessary to speak of the traditional system in continuous terms extending up to January 1966, when parliamentary institutions were overthrown by a military coup d'état.

My central subject has naturally determined the method of its presentation—which is to reiterate and elaborate specific features of traditional and modern influences, including the impact of colonial administration, as they relate to the topic of continuity and change in each of nine substantive chapters which all deal with a different aspect of the interplay of these influences. The method has unavoidably involved a certain degree of repetition of facts and themes, but only insofar as it has seemed essential to clarity of analysis.

It will be seen that there are important variations among the emirates in terms of historical and demographic setting and even traditional political structure which had significant implications and consequences in the period of this study. The major features of traditional political organization shared by all the emirates amply justify their characterization as a "system", however. Thus although specific features will be encountered (again) separately and in closer detail in the various chapters, it will be helpful to briefly set forth at the outset the salient characteristics of the traditional system as a whole.

Emirship: Eligibility for this supreme office of the traditional state is limited, in the first instance, to members of hereditary dynasties. In practice, but not usually by formal rule, only a member of a royal dynasty who holds an office of state is selected as an emir. In the vast majority of cases the dynasty is Fulani, although there are important exceptions. [The Hausa word for emir is *sarki*, plural: *sarakuna*.]

Succession: Succession is not limited or regulated by any rule of primogeniture, which means that any descendant of the founder of the dynasty, however distant, is technically eligible to succeed to the throne. However, convention in some emirates limits the succession to sons, and in others to grandsons, of emirs. A son of an emir in Hausa is *dan sarki*, grandson: *jikan sarki*. The absence of any automatic order of succession promotes intense competition among members of royal families which always ensues upon the death of an incumbent emir. This competition is structured; it is waged between rival solidary groups composed of members of different lineages within the royal dynasty, or, in those few emirates having a multi-dynastic structure, between members of rival dynasties. Within lineages there may also be rivalry between individuals. The successor is chosen by a *Kingmakers Council* invariably composed of members of the ruling circle who by birth are themselves ineligible. Each emir rules in association with a council of state (*majalisar sarki*, literally "emir's council") over which he customarily enjoys the right of veto. Appointments to the important offices and traditional titles of state are made by the emir in association with his *majalisa*. Eligibility for the traditional titles (*sarautu*; sing., *sarauta*) customarily varies with the particular *saruauta* concerned. A principal distinction is drawn between hereditary and nonhereditary *sarautu*. Three major classes of hereditary offices and titles may be distinguished: those "belonging" to free noble families (in Hausaland proper they are usually Fulani) whose ancestors were leaders in the conquest of the state, those occupied by vassals—descendants of local chiefs who gave their allegiance to the new rulers, and those customarily awarded to descendants of slaves. It is important to note that customarily slaves frequently exercised enormous power, a circumstance which largely derived from the system of rival lineage and dynastic competition; being ineligible to succeed to the throne and totally dependent upon the emir's patronage, slaves were delegated powers and authority which in the hands of eligible persons would represent a potential threat to the reigning emir. The emir exercises his discretion in appointing to office individuals from within the hereditary families concerned.

Nonhereditarily reserved titles (titles "in the gift of the emir") are gained through three principal avenues of personal attachment to the emir—kinship, marriage, and clientage. *Clientage*, a relationship of personal loyalty, normally exists between superior and subordinate at all levels of the hierarchy of state offices and titles. *Sarautu*, "in the gift of the emir", like emirship itself, are subject to competition between rival solidary lineage and dynastic groups. In fact, access to these offices—and the influence, wealth, power, and prestige that go along with them—is a primary focus of political interest and action in the traditional state. On gaining the throne, an emir is expected to favor his lineage-mates and other supporters with such offices and titles; to do so he often must dismiss officeholders belonging to a rival solidary group. The prospect of gaining office is a primary motive for any follower's support and loyalty in relationship to a candidate for royal succession.

Kudin sarauta: literally "money for office and title", this is the Hausa term for the principal means by which individuals belonging to various classes of eligibles compete, i.e. through giving gifts in cash or kind to the person or persons having the authority to award the *sarauta*. A more euphemistic name for gifts in cash and kind that exchange hands between superiors and subordinates at all levels of the administrative hierarchy as expressions of loyalty, influence, and power (the value depending on the status of the giver and the receiver) is *gaisuwa* (literally "greetings").

The most important offices of state are councillorships (membership in the emir's council) and district headships (authority over the territorial subunits or districts of the kingdom). Special traditional titles usually attach to these offices—*Waziri, Galadima, Magajin Gari, Ciroma, Tafida, Madawaki, Sardauna*, etc. Technical departments of the state administration (health, agriculture, etc.) are of post-British origin, but the heads of the departments became important offices. Usually the general title of *Wakili* (literally "deputy" of the emir) is attached to these offices. Each properly traditional title such as *Madawaki* and *Galadima*, is an exclusive property of the holder in each emirate.

In most emirates "household titles" (traditional titles of persons performing domestic duties within the palace) are also found although in dwindling numbers. Large numbers of courtiers, or personal retainers (*fadawa*), form part of the royal entourage. *Fadawa* and other types of retainers surround noble families, and indeed, any holder or seeker of office and title (*Masu-neman sarauta*). Lesser retainers include *Yaran sarki* (literally "emir's boys"), and *jekadu* ("messengers"), after the British-instituted residential district headship in place of fief-holding. A final category of the court offices is made up of menial servants (*barori*, sing.: *bara*) having miscellaneous duties.

Holders of minor posts in the state bureaucracy (clerks and technical functionaries), are collectively referred to as *ma'aikitan sarki* (literally, "employees of the emir") or *ma'aikitan "en'e"* ("employees of the N.A. or Native Authority").

Those holding state titles and offices, and their kin, are collectively referred to as *sarakuna*, in other words, the ruling class. All others are commoners, or *talakawa*. In Hausaland the vast majority of *talakawa* are *Habe* (non-Fulani). Nomadic Fulani are all *talakawa*, but there are many sedentary Fulani who are also *talakawa* (i.e. unconnected in any way with the ruling class). By virtue of clientage and vassalage individual *Habe* may also be *sarakuna*, however. Last but by no means least important, lesser forms of clientage—between commoners and *sarakuna* (not to be confused with clientage within the class of *sarakuna*)—provide a channel for individual *talakawa* to secure protection and favors from individual *sarakuna*. Otherwise *talakawa* are by definition traditionally excluded from participation in the traditional system of government and politics.

Part One of this book deals with formulation of policy—why and how the officials involved fashioned a program of reform based on both traditional and modern conceptions of government. Part Two is concerned with the practical results of the policy in the emirates. Part Three treats the reciprocal influences of regional and emirate politics.

PART ONE

The Path of Reform

CHAPTER 1

Perspectives on Reform

IN THIS CHAPTER I seek to trace the assumptions, interests, and experiences that led Nigerian policy-makers after World War II to decide that, rather than adopt British local political forms outright, it would be better to try to modify traditional emirate institutions to fit the functions and objectives of modern democratic local government. Significantly this policy was couched in terms of a doctrine of "gradualism".

In one sense the term served well as a rationale for the deliberate perpetuation of the local traditional emirate system into the new era of British-type parliamentary political institutions at the regional level. Preference for gradual rather than abrupt or revolutionary change is of course commonly associated with a genuine, concomitant interest in the fruits of stability and with the obvious desirability of preserving those benefits of an existing system that are compatible with the objectives of change. So understood, the Northern policy could hope to command general respect. Perhaps just as commonly, however, the profession of such a policy may serve to cloak a reluctance to undergo change at all, or to do so in any fundamental respects. In this sense, the Northern version of gradualism was motivated by considerations of both principle and expediency. These mixed motivations were related to two peculiarities of official policy that are important to note at the outset of this discussion—the substance of the policy, and the identity of its proponents.

As propounded in Northern Nigeria, the doctrine of gradualism was inherently ambiguous, in that it obscured the crucial distinction between questions of an appropriate *pace* of change and the *degree* or *extent* of change to be sought. To conceive of the course of change as involving a slow progression away from one state of affairs toward another is one thing; to regard it as entailing fusion or synthesis of two originally separate sets of arrangements is quite another matter. The validity of the fusion or synthesis approach depended strictly on the question of whether salient features of the British and emirate systems of "local government", respectively, are in fact compatible, and to what extent. Only through a careful and detailed comparison of these features can the answer to that question be determined; in Chapter 3 I undertake to do just this, in an effort to assess the dimensions and implications of the policy of gradual change within the framework of traditional emirate institutions.

It will be apparent from the statements below, made in behalf of the policy, that the official policy of gradualism did implicitly accommodate the two different meanings without trying to come to grips with the objective validity of the second connotation. The failure was no doubt partly explainable in terms of psychological comfort and convenience, but it also clearly offered certain tactical advantages, which brings us to the second important initial observation—the identity of the policy-makers.

In postwar Northern Nigeria, at least three distinguishable groups among the policy-makers espoused the doctrine of gradualism: senior British officers posted in the North, key traditional authorities, and the new group of Western-educated government ministers and NPC politicians. But each group had its own slant on the subject of reform, stemming from disparate goals and interests. Yet the second and third groups overlapped considerably in both background and outlook, while there were also certain significant differences of view within each of the three groups. It may be incidentally noted here that the leaders of radical parties in the North, like militant nationalist leaders in southern Nigeria, held still other views about the future of local government in the emirates, but these views were closer to revolution than reform, and in any case the leaders were unable to achieve the power necessary to become policy-makers. Thus, to understand how these multifarious elements found a mutually congenial rationale in the form of the doctrine of gradualism, the views of each group must be closely examined.

BRITISH ATTITUDES

As is true elsewhere in formerly British Africa, the initial major impetus toward democratization of local government in Northern Nigeria came from the Colonial Office in London,[1] where officials were fairly sensitive to developments in the politically more restless parts

---

[1] The policy was laid down in the *Despatch of the Secretary of State for Colonies*, 1947, excerpted and reproduced in A.H.M. Kirk-Greene, ed., *The Principles of Native Administration in Nigeria: Selected Documents, 1900-1947* (London, 1965). Democratization of local government also formed the main topic of discussion at the Cambridge Summer School Conferences of 1947 and 1951. According to Kalu Ezera, the African Governors Conference, convened in London in November 1947, also concerned itself primarily with questions of African local government reform under the guidance of "policy papers prepared by Colonial Officer policy-planners". *Constitutional Developments in Nigeria* (Cambridge, Eng., 1960), pp. 82-86.

of Africa, including southern Nigeria. But as is well known, it was characteristic of British colonial practice to allow maximum scope for interpretation and implementation of policy to the officials of each colony affected. And although the role of the Colonial Office in this instance appears to have been more aggressive than usual, the policy enunciated was very broad, and a large measure of discretion in its detailed formulation and application was permitted the various territorial administrations, including that of Nigeria.[2] The Nigerian colonial administration, in turn, followed its usual custom of turning over a large share of responsibility to regional administrations. Thus the senior British officials of the Northern Provinces (as the Northern Region was then called) were bound, initially at least, to exercise a decisive influence on the course of change.

The reaction of British officials in the north to the proposition of democratic reforms in the emirates was strongly conditioned by the type of colonial policy they were pursuing long before the war. Indeed, the history of indirect rule helped shape the British attitude in at least three respects. First, the policy of indirect rule had embodied certain preconceptions regarding the *process* of reform or change —especially how change could and should be brought about in the Northern emirates. Thus, as might be expected, British officials, most of whom had spent their entire careers observing certain well-defined procedures in relation to the emirates, continued to apply them in their approach to the process of democratization, even though in *content* such reforms were novel. Second, indirect rule had rested on the assumption that the basic goals of traditional emirate government might be altered or supplemented without destroying traditional forms and institutions. The officials had always worked on the premise that to assure that this result was both necessary and desirable. They were to cling to these assumptions after the war, being partly encouraged by an indecisiveness on the part of the Colonial Office regarding the future position of the emirate Native Administrations under the new dispensation. Finally, the mere fact that the conceptions, assumptions, and premises of indirect rule had been operative in the past meant that the British officials in Northern Nigeria had

[2] Cf. L. Gray Cowan, *Local Government in West Africa* (New York, 1958), p. 64, where Professor Cowan states that "no effort was made to draw up a common form for these local government institutions for all of British Africa. Instead, it was left to the governments of each colony, under the general directives of the colonial offices, to work out the detailed reforms which would best fit the needs of the territory concerned".

already taken certain steps and shunned others in relation to the traditional political system, steps and omissions which now seemed to set limits on what could or should be done about democratization. At the very least, these realities influenced official estimates of the pace at which democratization should and could occur, but they probably also prejudiced their view of the proper extent of change.

THE special conditions that led Lugard to develop for Northern Nigeria the administrative technique or system known as indirect rule were noted in the introduction—severe restrictions in funds and personnel; the grip of indigenous monarchs whose authority rested on conquest backed up by effective occupation and the popularly accepted claim that they were indispensable guardians of religion; the emirs' command of an impressive apparatus of administration, including well-developed procedures of direct taxation and an institutionalized judiciary. All this made it prudent for Lugard to uphold indigenous authority as an instrument of British rule.

Yet the rationale of the British conquest was that British suzerainty would lead to the eradication of what the British regarded as evils of traditional government. British efforts, the officials believed, would gradually alter the system to conform with basic British standards of justice, public integrity, and popular welfare. This rationale, of course, implied that British control and supervision were essential, that British rule was necessary to instill virtues which the traditional system could not or would not otherwise assume. The rationale therefore rested on a profound contradiction.

The nub of the difficulty was that the British proposed to rely on the continuing efficacy of the very system they sought to transform. Ultimately British administration meant to impose its own standards, but immediately it had to support traditional norms and techniques of traditional government, for these imparted the required stability and popular compliance. In the beginning, Lugard's officers were up against the dilemma in the form of the problem of law and order. Without the physical resources necessary to assure the rudiments of effective administration, they were obliged to assess each proposed innovation in terms of its probable impact on the disciplined relation of subject to ruler, and to refrain from measures that might impair that discipline. In the very early years the British were deeply uncertain of being able to retain their hold should the emirs themselves undertake to mobilize resistance; the initial reception by the emirs hardly encouraged British officers to be sanguine about the longer range reaction to British rule. Thus due regard had to be paid to acquiring and maintaining the goodwill of the traditional rulers. British misgivings over basic physical security, as such, later subsided, but the awareness remained, that whatever the objective of administration success eventually required the acquiescence if not active cooperation of the peasants with their overlords, and that of both vis-à-vis the British Administration. The more a given British innovation was a departure from tradition, the more attention had to be paid to these realities of fundamental dependence. Thus a conflict between the twin goals of stability and progress lay at the heart of the colonial edifice, bedeviling nearly every major venture into reform, from the very first days of Lugard on.

A crucial proviso to Lugard's original dictum that traditional customs were to be respected, stated, "insofar as they are not repugnant to natural justice." Accordingly this yardstick was summarily brought to bear against traditional practices blatantly at odds with British ideals, such as slave-raiding and bartering and the punishment of certain offenses by physical torture of mutilation. But Lugard was bound to acknowledge that the peasants, if not the British, would be weighing the political strength of their emirs by traditional standards.[3]

Measures which evidently were compromises with British ideals inevitably resulted. Lugard's policy on slavery was a striking instance. Slavery as such was not abolished. A proclamation gave slaves the right to manumit themselves by petition to a court. But those who could be induced to continue the relationship with their masters were confirmed in their status. Lugard reasoned that since slavery had been the principal source of wealth among the ruling classes, to end it abruptly would undermine their position. Emirs were repeatedly assured that the British did not intend to "interfere with domestic slavery", while Lugard explained to the Colonial Office that his policy was necessary to mitigate "complete dislocation of social

[3] The classic application of the injunction against slave-raiding occurred in the notorious case of the Emir of Kontagora, Ibrahim, who made the infamous and much-quoted boast that like a cat fond of mousing, he would "die with a slave in his mouth". (See note 12, Intro.) Even in this case, however, Lugard went to some lengths to temporize. Ibrahim was deported, but later reinstated. A second relapse was also officially pardoned in time, though afterwards he was closely watched. How prevalent the use of theoretically prescribed punishments—such as amputation of the hand for the crime of theft and stoning to death for adultery —actually was, is a matter of controversy. In any case, Lugard explicitly outlawed the punishments. See Northern Nigeria, *Annual Reports, 1900-11* (London, pp. 71, 92.

conditions," but that the policy would permit the institution to expire gradually.[4] Lugard similarly defended his decision to maintain flogging as a penalty for specified offenses, on the grounds that customary usage had made it an especially effective device.[5] Corporal punishment was in fact retained throughout the colonial period, in spite of the efforts of high officials in postwar Britain to have it abolished.[6]

The fact that the system of traditional taxation was already institutionalized later permitted services and projects of a modern public welfare nature to be introduced, but it is interesting to note that Lugard originally recognized the institution primarily in order to allow traditional rulers to live up to their accustomed material standards. He was seeking, in fact, to compensate the emirs for the decline in their wealth and prestige which the British pacification had inevitably caused.[7] Thus the proportion of public revenue he originally allotted the emirs as "personal emolument" (in some cases as high as 40 percent of the total for an emirate) was emphatically more in keeping with prevailing Hausa notions of the proper level of remuneration for public office than with those current in Lugard's own society. In like manner, one of Lugard's successors, C. L. Temple, was

[4] *Ibid.*, p. 409. For a detailed discussion of Hausa slavery before and after the British conquest, see M. G. Smith, "Slavery and Emancipation in Two Societies (Zaria and Jamaica)", in *Social and Economic Studies*, Vol. 3, No. 4 (1954), pp. 239-90.

[5] *Ibid.*, pp. 133-34. Lugard argued that the traditional stipulation that the official must keep a shell or stone in his armpit while wielding the cane made the practice relatively humane.

[6] In 1946 Arthur Creech-Jones, the Secretary of State for the Colonies, sought to have the administration of corporal punishment confined to the Nigerian Supreme Court. In 1950 a successor, James Griffiths, wanted the provision abolished altogether. Neither was successful, for in each case the British administration in Nigeria had to take into account the views of influential emirs who held that abolition would seriously undermine their power.

[7] "The advent of the British and overthrow of the Fulani domination was heralded by the peasantry as an excuse for the repudiation of any obligation to pay taxes, even in a province so well organized as Kano—the very center of Fulani rule. The new Government prohibited internecine war and armed slave raids, and the Fulani were thus left powerless to enforce taxation. It was urgently necessary to take some action without delay. If the Fulani were to be maintained in their position as rulers, and the upper classes were not to be reduced to beggary and to become outcasts, it devolved upon the Government to assist them to levy the taxes they could no longer levy themselves . . . but it is important to recollect that it was not undertaken merely—or even primarily—for the sake of creating revenue, but resulted inevitably as a part of the task involved by the assumption of administrative control in the country, and was the necessary result of supporting the system of native rulers in the Protectorate, without whom it would be impossible to administer the country effectively. Since under the new regime, the native chiefs had lost the income they derived from slave-raiding and from taxes on traders, it became the more urgent to assure to them a regular income from the tribute of the peasantry". Northern Ngieria, *Annual Reports, 1900-11*, p. 218.

to justify his inauguration of a *beit-al-mal*, or "native treasury", possibly the most significant of all colonial innovations, on the grounds that "the only alternative to some such system . . . is a Civil List, and the eclipse for all practical purposes, of the Native Administrations as responsible rulers under the guidance of the Protectorate Administration".[8] Temple's apprehension was that as technical services and personnel expanded, emirs stood to lose their traditionally all-important power of appointment and promotion in favor of some type of "outside" agency, and also to forfeit the popular esteem which would inevitably be accorded the agents of popular benefits unless the emirs themselves attained control of some of the new dispensations. And indeed, the *beit-al-mal* did in time enable the Native Administrations to enjoy a substantial measure of fiscal independence in relation to the center, which gave concrete expression to a dualism of authority in the Northern governmental system.

Lugard himself held with the modern notion that economic reward should be dispensed in accordance with social utility, and he sought to make this a principle of Native Administration. Here again however, he had to face up to some unwelcome consequences of upholding tradition. An emir's conduct had to meet certain demands and expectations. While Lugard deplored what he regarded as a useless "palace clique" (idle princes, title-holders without office, eunuchs, palace slaves, and other members of the royal entourage), he nonetheless concluded that to cut them off precipitately might embitter the emirs—and what would be worse—spawn an entire class of influential malcontents.[9] Lugard was content to rely on the hope (a vain one on the whole, it would appear[10]) that the emirs themselves would in time come to regard nonofficial camp followers as an unwanted drain on steadily dwindling purses.

Other relevant instances might be adduced. Important policies which reflected constant temporizing included the severely restricted scope afforded Christian missions in the emirates by the administration, the special design of educational curricula and techniques of teaching, and the quality of justice and legal processes. But undoubtedly the most poignant of all the adjustments the British made was in the traditional relationship of ruler to subject. Its essentially despotic features had been revealed to Lugard and his officers in the course of investigating the incidence and techniques of taxation current at the time of their arrival. Their early reports and memoranda

---

[8] *Ibid.*, p. 778. [9] See *ibid.*, p. 796. [10] Cf. below, Chap. 6.

refer repeatedly to the prevalence of various extortionary practices, and more recent official interpretations of British objectives in Northern Nigeria have reiterated the indictment.[11] Immediate steps were taken to eradicate arbitrary exactions nakedly supported by force or the threat of it; in time the steps were largely successful. But subtler, less visible forms of corruption, such as embezzlement, bribery, and many variations emerged even as the British stamped out the old excesses. The ubiquity of corruption continued, as we shall see, to constitute the greatest drawback from a modern vantage point—the "sting in the tail", as the future Prime Minister of Nigeria was to call it, of Native Administration. In this context, Margery Perham's biography of Lugard describes how the dilemma of indirect rule tended to lower British standards with respect to the conduct of traditional officials: "The gap between the two standards, British and traditional, was narrowed partly by forcing the emirs to act according to British standards. But it was sometimes closed by the administrators themselves meeting the emirs half-way, by partially suspending their own ideals, by supporting at times a corrupt and selfish aristocracy and teaching themselves to regard as irremediable a measure of abuse. Some of the early Residents, while admitting the danger, urged upon the writer that direct rule being quite impracticable, some acceptance of abuse was inescapable if the whole structure of indigenous society were not to break down."[12]

An integral aspect of this see-little-evil approach was, as Smith observes, the rule that in the emirates British officers were always to be accompanied on their tours of outlying areas by a representative of the emir (*yaran sarki*), which of course made it impossible for complaints to be lodged without the emir finding out about it.[13]

Apart from their own estimates of the need for accommodation, the British were often responsive to an emir's assessments and claims. It would appear, for example, that Lugard was in this way persuaded to vest in certain emirs one of the most significant trappings of power they possess today—the authority to hand down the death penalty (subject to approval by the Governor) and in their capacity as judges, notwithstanding the anomaly (from a British or any modern

[11] See C. W. Cole (Senior District Officer), "Village and District Councils in the Northern Provinces of Nigeria", in *Journal of African Administration*, Vol. 3, No. 2 (April 1951); *Duties of the Administrative Officer in Northern Nigeria* (Kaduna, 1952).

[12] Perham, *Lugard: Years of Authority*, Vol. 2: p. 152.

[13] M. G. Smith, *Government in Zazzau* (Oxford, 1960), p. 215.

standpoint) that these emirs were allowed to exercise simultaneously both executive and judicial authority.[14] Many lesser concessions were routinely made by Residents in day-to-day administration.

The obligation to restrain themselves from consistently applying standards of good government taken for granted in British society must have frequently been distressing to officers who had imbibed the ideals of a colonial *mission civilisatrice*. Morally, however, the idea of indirect rule was not without its redeeming features; indeed, it provided an alternate ideal. It offered the justification of respect for African principles of social and political organization in an age when to denigrate "primitive" cultures (which all cultures of black peoples were then widely assumed to be) was a pervasive and unabashed Western impulse. From Lugard on, it was characteristic of the partisans and practitioners of British indirect rule to avow regard for African customs. Far from being mere sham, the ideal of tolerance no doubt helped to make the highly ambivalent role of the British administrative officers psychologically tenable. The ideal especially appealed to their romantic imagination. Was it not true, furthermore, that Hausa and British political traditions (monarchy, stratification, an established religion) had important features in common? Thus the ideal of tolerance represented a vindication of indirect rule which was reassuring and persuasive when all else seemed compromised. In particular, the British officers in Northern Nigeria scrupulously exercised this spirit with respect to Islam—and consequently, with respect to social and political forms and behavior which they were persuaded, rightly or wrongly, went along with that religion.

In this light, it is easy to understand how, with the added weight of Lugard's expository writings, indirect rule eventually assumed the dignity of a "philosophy" of colonial administration, despite its having been germinated in accidental circumstances and notwithstanding its obvious resemblance to the age-old devices of conquerors. But far from resolving the moral and logical contradictions, the ele-

[14] "I had much personal discussion with the Emir of Kano on the subject of the *Jakadas*, and other matters connected with taxation, which I have already reported. He asked that powers of inflicting a death sentence should be granted to his native court. These powers, which, of course, have always been exercised by the Emirs, I have withheld until the native judiciary should have proved itself sufficiently pure to exercise them. Sokoto and Kano have both done admirable judicial work, and I therefore concurred in the extension of his powers provided that he obtained (in accordance with the Native Courts Proclamation) the concurrence of the Resident before a death-sentence was carried into execution". Northern Nigeria, *Annual Reports, 1900-11*, Report for 1904, p. 244.

vation of indirect rule into a formal doctrine merely caused them to be reintroduced in the form of more subtle casuistries.

In indirect rule as a "philosophy", British officers were always furnished with two often mutually exclusive sets of criteria for evaluating administrative action. On the one hand, there were the norms of good government as conceived by their own society, which colonial government was seeking to instill. Accordingly the performance of the Native Administrations could be judged by the degree to which it approximated them. On the other hand, there was the original cast of traditional society; practices might also be justified according to their tendency to maintain its cohesion. Since virtually all the important matters of Native Administration that came to the attention of the British administration could be construed as falling under one or the other category of objectives, an acceptable construction could always be placed on almost anything that was done. The principles of the "philosophy" helped to sanction practically every specific course of action.

In practice, far from every act of Native Administration *was* countenanced. But the presence of ambivalent guideposts created some tortuous paths for British conduct. In their dealings with emirs, British officials had to be alternatively censorious and permissive, to applaud alike orthodoxy and innovation, to expose emirs favorably to alien values while confirming the essential preferability of traditional culture, to encourage Native Administrations to become responsible organs of government, but to insist on control remaining indefinitely in the hands of the colonial government, to allocate resources and rewards on the principle of functional rationality and yet uphold ancient privileges, to defend the surveillance over the Native Administrations on grounds of the welfare of the peasantry, but to discourage direct contact between commoners and British officers. Such dualistic aims begot dual structures: native courts (applying the Maliki school of Islamic law) and British courts (employing English common law and statutes); Nigeria Police (officered by Britons) and N.A. police; the town of traditional habitation (*birni*) and the towns of "stranger settlement" (*tundun wada, sabon gari*).[15] Withal, any suggestion that the system entailed dualistic elements was to be deprecated

[15] *Tudan wada* was for Northern Muslims who were not natives of the emirate involved; *sabon gari* was mostly for people of non-Northern origin whether Muslim or not, and non-Muslim Northerners. They were located in different parts of the outskirts of the *birni*. Both represent an attempt to contain as much as possible the potentially disruptive incursion of cosmopolitan influence.

(!), it being contended, in Lugard's words, that the system represented not "two sets of rulers—the British and the Native—working either separately or in cooperation, but a single Government in which the Native Chiefs have clearly-defined duties and an acknowledged status equally with the British Officials".[16] Not surprisingly, the whole system produced its British critics, including a prominent missionary who castigated it very sharply indeed.[17]

In later years Lugard himself deplored the unfortunate extent to which he felt his system had been carried in the direction of accommodating traditional patterns.[18] In so doing, he expressed the dilemma characteristic of his own system, for Lugard was inclined to attribute an apparent susceptibility to immobility of the whole operation to his successors' failure to comprehend its original purposes and requirements.[19] Evidently he had assumed that increasingly, with time and appropriate guidance, the conduct of Native Administration would more and more faithfully reflect the aims of its British patrons. He also assumed, however, that an indefinite number of extraneous standards and functions could be injected into an existing and integral political order without jeopardizing its coherence.

Ultimately the deepest source of the difficulties Lugard complained of was the stubborn fact of a limit beyond which traditional roles and institutions could not be redefined to suit these extraneous purposes and yet retain their identity, their credibility, and hence their influence. If the nexus of traditional political conceptions, convictions, relationships, and loyalties was to be relied on to furnish elements deemed indispensable to colonial government—such as social discipline—clearly some of the concrete interests, aims, and satisfactions which sustained that nexus had to be sanctioned. At crucial

[16] *Instructions to Political and other officers on subjects chiefly Political and Administrative* (1906), cited in Perham, *Lugard*, Vol. 2, p. 144.

[17] Walter R.S. Miller was a leader of the Church Missionary Society who spent over 40 years in Northern Nigeria. His frequently acid comments on Fulani rulers and British administrators (e.g., "For forty-one years in this country I was accustomed to hearing a futile, placid justification of everything being done administratively by men who felt it necessary to keep their end up".) are scattered among five publications: *Reflections of a Pioneer* (London, 1936); *Yesterday, Today, and Tomorrow in Northern Nigeria* (London, 1938); *Have We Failed in Nigeria?* (London, 1947); *Success in Nigeria? Assets and Possibilities* (London, 1948); *Walter Miller: An Autobiography, 1872-1952* (Zaria, 1952).

See also W. R. Crocker, *Nigeria: A Critique of British Colonial Administration* (London, 1936); Edmund E. Morel, *Nigeria: Its Peoples and Problems* (London, 1911); and D. W. Bittinger, *Educational Experiment in the Sudan* (Elgin, Ill., 1941).

[18] See Perham, *Lugard*, Vol. 1, pp. 480-88.

[19] *Ibid.*

points, therefore, Lugard's successors (from Temple to Cameron), like himself, were obliged to choose between emphasizing one or the other class of values, British or traditional.[20]

But the logical and moral embarrassments of indirect rule are not of direct concern here (although until recently the matter remained very inadequately explored in scholarly studies dealing with the subject).[21] It should be noted that British ambivalence undoubtedly quickened the disaffection with the colonial system of those "progressive" Northerners who later looked to the British administration for an unequivocal lead in realizing ideals practiced in Britain.[22] In the present context the main significance of normative ambivalence in indirect rule lies in the kind of strategy of reform and change it necessarily implied, and perhaps more importantly, in the possibilities it precluded.

[20] In a chapter of her earlier study, *Native Administration in Nigeria* (London, 1937), entitled "The Governorship of Sir Donald Cameron", Miss Perham is again instructive in this connection. Of all Lugard's successors up to that date, Cameron appears to have been the most concerned with innovations and improvements in Native Administration in the direction of modern criteria of government, most notably in his insistence that the British administration should only recognize traditional authorities "desired by the people". He did not, of course, introduce elections; popular acceptability was evidently to be determined through recognition and use of traditional procedures of selection—which in the case of the emirates were hardly such as to occasion in practice much of a departure from the status quo ante. According to Miss Perham, even Cameron, however, felt constrained to pass on to his Residents "warnings in the old tradition not to expect too much of chiefs, not to undermine their authority by direct action, nor to be too ready to recommend punishments and depositions" (p. 336). For Cameron's views and those of other British governors between his and Lugard's tenure, see the documents extracted in Kirk-Greene, *Principles of Native Administration in Nigeria, passim.* See also Mary Bull, "Indirect Rule in Northern Nigeria, 1906-1911", in Kenneth Robinson and Frederick Madden, eds., *Essays in Imperial Government* (Oxford, 1963).

[21] The more candid recent accounts are Perham's biography of Lugard, already cited, and the essay by Mary Bull's article cited in the note above, which is especially good on the "double standards" of indirect rule. Also an article by Ronald Cohen contains the following penetrating comment: "Initiative and Innovation were often approved officially, and privately condemned". See "The Analysis of Conflict in Hierarchical Systems: An example from Kanuri Political Organization", in *Anthropologica*, Vol. 4, No. 1 (1962), p. 99.

[22] In *Reflections of a Pioneer*, Walter Miller concluded that "after living among the Hausas for thirty years and getting into very close contact with members of almost every group and social status, I am convinced that there is a growing dislike of the present system, and that before long, British administrators will be faced with a powerful plea for direct British rule, leading to a more progressive and widely based rule of the people for the people. . . . Unless the present native administration can adapt itself to more modern ideas, I foresee a widespread revolt before long against obscurantism, tending towards more democratic institutions and a more representative administration". Quoted in the *Daily Comet*, Nigeria, November 25, 1950, p. 1.

Insofar as the paramount goal of administration was conceived to be the maintenance of external (British) control and the encouragement of internal change only to the degree consistent with the first consideration, the idea of indirect rule was serviceable, indeed, rational. This formulation of "ambivalence" could be translated positively as "flexibility". By the same token, the precepts of indirect rule could not function as a *political charter* or even sanction the spontaneous creation of one. That is, indirect rule could not furnish the masses of Africans subjected to Native Administration with a set of binding widely understood and agreed-upon political principles— which they clearly needed to have if they themselves were to undertake control of their rulers, or on their own to press for reform. The very existence of such a political charter or constitution would have meant the surrender of British initiative, a redefinition of the administrative goal as being subordinate to a political end. Thus it was not simply that the British administration inadvertently neglected to disseminate thoroughly and precisely its objectives in the realm of reform throughout Hausaland, but rather that the logic of controlled change ruled out such a step.

To preserve the framework of a stratified polity meant change had to begin at the top and spread downward. Had the British somehow been able to measure out ahead of action exactly how much reform was compatible with particular quantity of stability or continuity, or had the structure of power in Hausaland been less hierarchical, then the articulation of a program might have been possible. Such speculations are, of course, both fanciful and idle. As it was, indirect rule could not actively work to promote among the peasants that condition of predictability and clarity about the obligations and aims of Native Administration which effective political action on their own initiative would have presupposed. In this light, it becomes intelligible, too, why the term *abokin talakawa* (literally, "friend of the commoners") was sometimes applied with stinging pejorative connotation to the "overzealous" British administrative officer by traditional rulers and fellow officers alike.

Nor is it difficult to understand, in turn, how a scholarly analysis of the political dynamics of one emirate as it existed between 1900 and 1950 could reduce the major innovations of a modern character successfully imposed by the British to the following: the abolition of slavery as a legal institution, but not as a social status; the regrouping of scattered feudatory fiefs into united districts under resi-

dent chiefs or district heads; the reduction, consolidation, and simpli-
fication of taxation; the introduction of a system of public exchequer
or treasury; and the addition of modern technical departments and
services to the assortment of traditional administrative functions
and structures.[23] The ready absorption by the emirate system of these
essentially formal and procedural innovations contrasts markedly
with the fate of British objectives which had they been realized would
have constituted profound structural change—such as impersonal
performance criteria for allocating offices, redefined goals or aims of
administrative service, and a benevolent relationship between the
rulers and the ruled—all of which met with equivocal reception.[24]

THE TERMINAL PHASE OF BRITISH RULE

I POINTED OUT in my introduction on Nigerian constitutional development that Lugard's conception of the proper objectives of British
colonial rule did not include self-government or independence for
the African territories. But as colonial officials in Nigeria and London
began to reckon with that goal, they were led to reconsider the system
of Native Administration. What role, if any, were the Native Administrations to play in a democratically self-governing Nigeria?

Over the years the increasingly greater contrast between the insistence in the southern regions on representative institutions and the apparent quiescence of the Northern emirates had given the question
ever greater relevance. The crux of the complicated issues involved
was this: to grant institutions of popular representation at the Nigerian center seemed logically to entail granting the institutions, on
demand, in the realm of local government as well. But conversely,
to perpetuate traditional institutions in areas where they appeared to
be "popularly acceptable" suggested either that the brand of democracy introduced at the center would have to be diluted considerably (if there was to be a unitary form of government for Nigeria), or that separate courses of development in local government would have to be permitted (which implied regional autonomy). The fate of Native Administrations in the emirates and the
constitutional future of Nigeria were therefore inseparable questions;
any proposal for one necessarily embodied a policy for the other. A
complete picture of the various official policy projections must await
a full chronicle of the ending of British administration in Nigeria. But

[23] Smith, *Government in Zazzau*, esp. Chaps. 6 and 7.
[24] *Ibid.*

a good impression of the major contending theories current when the prospect of self-government began to be entertained seriously (roughly at the beginning of the Second World War) can be gleaned from various sources.[25]

One school of thought envisioned the emirates eventually constituting unto themselves a self-governing nation (some versions of this theory have conserved a permanent role for British authority). Its proponents were silent on the nature of the structure required to bind the emirates together, but they deprecated a parliamentary regime. Their primary concern was to minimize dislocation of traditional authority and institutions. Hailey indicates that the most enthusiastic members of this school were to be found among the British officers serving in Northern Nigeria.[26] Indeed, many of these officers had become, in the words of one British officer who recently wrote to me, "more Moslem than the Moslems".

The wartime Governor-General of Nigeria, Sir Bernard Bourdillon, while staunchly advocating the preservation of Nigeria as a political unit and its development under some form of representative government, rejected Lord Hailey's view that "the principles of indirect rule, if not incompatible with the ideal of self-government by representative institutions, are at all events so alien to it that native institutions must be materially modified if they are to fit into any scheme involving an elected parliament".[27] His own opinion was that only changes of form, not principle, would be necessary to reconcile the system of Native Administration with central parliamentary institutions. On this presumption, Nigerian ministers, no less than British

[25] Perham, *Native Administration in Nigeria*, Chap. 26; Lord Hailey, *Native Administration in the British African Territories* (London, 1951), Vol. 3, pp. 65-69, 95-98, Vol. 4, pp. 5-12, 23-28; Hailey, *An African Survey* (London, 1937); Bernard Bourdillon, "Nigeria's New Constitution", in *United Empire*, Vol. 37 (March-April 1946); James S. Coleman, *Nigeria: Background to Nationalism* (Berkeley, 1958), pp. 272-74; Ezera, *Constitutional Developments in Nigeria*, pp. 84-86. There are several other important sources which, though they had a wide circulation, were originally published for official use only and have never been officially released from confidential classification. They include Hailey's *Native Administration and Political Development in British Tropical Africa* (London, 1940); Bourdillon's *Memorandum on the Future Political Development of Nigeria* (Lagos, 1942); and Report, *Colonial Office Summer School on African Administration*, African No. 1,173 (London, 1947). See also the extracts from Bourdillon's *Minute on the Appointment of Revenues and Duties as between the Central Government and the Native Administrations*, excerpted and reproduced in Kirk-Greene, *Principles of Native Administration in Nigeria*, pp. 226-37.

[26] Hailey, *Native Administration in British African Territories*, Vol. 3, p. 67.

[27] Hailey, *An African Survey*, p. 1,640.

colonial administrators, would be able to govern through traditional institutions. In retrospect, one might say that Bourdillon was the better prophet, even if Hailey emerges as the more cogent student of politics!

But Bourdillon's optimistic view of the reconcilability of the two structures of government presupposed a relatively protracted period of political development prior to the grant of self-government—time in which to work out the details of a modus vivendi. Bourdillon was most anxious that the precise terms—i.e. exactly how much modification of tradition or what manner of parliaments would be suitable —should not be prejudged. In this he confirmed Hailey's penetrating caveat that, "It is implicit in the philosophy of indirect rule that the nature of the political forms which may ultimately be involved should not be prematurely defined".[28]

If British officials in the North were at one extreme of the spectrum regarding the degree of desirable continuity and change, and Bourdillon occupied a middle position, Hailey's opinions placed him closest to the other end. This meant that while the first school was willing to sacrifice both the unity of Nigeria and its democratic development to the coherence of the emirates and the perpetuation of their customary institutions, and Bourdillon looked forward to reconciling these desiderata, Hailey was ready if necessary to promote national unity and democracy at the expense of the other objectives. In his capacity as advisor to the Colonial Office on Native Administration, he recommended not granting a separate future for the emirates. Insisting that the desirability of the democratic development of Nigeria as a whole logically extended to the level of local government, he also urged that the democratization of the emirate system be accelerated.

In both respects the Colonial Office subsequently proclaimed policies in keeping with Hailey's advice. It is significant, however, that Hailey had not sought to *preclude* the harmony of interests that Bourdillon envisioned. While evidently less sanguine than the Nigerian Governor-General, he too endorsed a wait and see attitude about the future of Native Administrations. Thus the Colonial Office did not have to choose between the positions of Hailey and Bourdillon on the issue of eventual reconcilability. Its line of least resistance was to allow the natural course of events to determine the outcome, and in the meantime leave the way open for alternative solu-

[28] *Ibid.*, p. 23.

tions. In fact, the decision to develop responsible institutions of government at the *regional* level—a policy which initially represented a second line of defense of the first school—owed much to the consideration that it would permit the pace and extent of democratization to be adjusted to the distinctive conditions and culture obtaining in most of the Northern provinces.[29] It could be argued, further, that the entire course of Nigeria's postwar civilian constitutional development—the movement from the essentially unitary structure of 1946 to "strong" federation in 1951 to "weak" federation in 1954— was determined largely by the attempt to perfect a parliamentary system at the center while keeping ajar the door to survival of traditional forms in the emirates.

Specifically, regionalization meant that the affairs of Native Administration or local government remained the responsibility of the regional chief commissioners (and later that of regional lieutenant governors, who afterward were called governors). Fatefully, it also kept local government from later being included among the subjects for constitutional negotiation and bargaining between the African political leaders of the various regions, who after 1951 shared responsibility with the British for defining local government policy.[30] The effect of all this, in turn, was to enable the Colonial Office to maintain to the very last a position of noncommitment regarding the fate of Native Administrations in the North. Its attitude on Native Administration in the southern provinces, where internal pressures to

[29] Similarly, the decision to use the Native Authorities as the basis of representation under the Constitution of 1946 is also partly attributable to this concern. See *The Political and Constitutional Future of Nigeria, Sessional Paper No. 4 of 1945: Governor of Nigeria's Despatch to the Secretary of State for the Colonials dated the 6th of December 1944* (Lagos, 1945). In this document then Governor Sir Arthur Richards states his view that, "what are needed are bodies where the affairs of each group of provinces can be discussed . . . in this way a chain of representation would be created from the Legislative Council to the people through the regional councils and the Native Authorities, and it would be a type of representation which would be in accordance with custom, would fit in naturally with existing institutions, and would be readily intelligible to the people themselves. . . . The individualism and the craving to paddle their own canoes which distinguishes the people of the Eastern Provinces, finds no counterpart in the disciplined and conservative North, where respect and affection for the Chiefs is a very real factor".

[30] Ezera, *Constitutional Developments in Nigeria*, p. 114, draws attention to the significant contrasts between the 1950 General Conference on the Nigerian Constitution's failure to make recommendations on questions of local government, with the fact that a historically comparable body (the Coussey Committee in Ghana, with its unitary structure), did make recommendations in this field. The contrast underlines the intimate connection between constitutional development and that of local government in Nigeria.

democratize had begun to build up, was correspondingly more favorable to fundamental change, beginning at least as early as 1948.[31]

In thus honoring the inveterate British bias against proceeding in advance of events, the Colonial Office provided the opportunity for British officials charged with interpreting and implementing democratization in the emirates not only to be flexible about timing, but also to exercise a substantial measure of discretion. And in the absence of firm direction from above, the local British officials could always justify continuing to protect the N.A. system in the North at the expense of progress in democratizing on the unexceptionable ground that it might yet play a major role even in a self-governing Nigeria.

In fact, to judge by one official statement of its goals in Northern Nigeria, the colonial government in Nigeria was assuming as late as 1947 that the institutional heir apparent of British power in the North were the Native Authorities rather than a new parliamentary regime: "The policy of the system of Indirect Rule practices in the Northern Provinces is to organize and improve indigenous administrative institutions as to form an efficient administration based upon modern conceptions, *which will eventually be fitted to bear the entire responsibility for all administrative action in the area.* The immediate aims of the system are identical with the long term policy and their achievement—as for instance the closer identification of Native Authorities with the Government of Nigeria by means of the new Constitution—represents successive steps toward the ultimate goal".[32] Whether or to what extent this particular statement was in accord with the thinking of the Colonial Office is problematical. It should be kept in mind, however, that the system of Native Administration represented Britain's distinctive contribution to conceptions of Western colonial purposes in Africa, and that Northern Nigeria constituted the classic case of its successful execution and development. It would not be unreasonable to suppose that there may have been special sympathy even in London for a course which at least would not exclude the possibility of the system's survival in some recognizable form.

[31] See Cowan, *Local Government in West Africa*, pp. 66-67.

[32] Emphasis added. Answer of the Chief Secretary to the Nigerian Government to the question asked by The Second Member for the Northern Provinces (The Honorable Malam Abubakar Tafawa Balewa)—"What is the policy of the present Indirect Rule System in the Northern Provinces and what are its immediate aims?" *Legislative Council of Debates* (March 25, 1947), p. 251.

In any case, it may now be seen how, commissioned on the one hand to democratize and armed on the other with an implicit sanction for maintaining existing institutions, the British administration in the North was left approximately in its accustomed position: in the middle of a conflict between innovation and prescription, progress and stability, intervention and autonomy, tutelage and concession, continuity and change.

Democratization simply presented itself as the latest in a series of reforms which British officers had sought to introduce into the structure of emirate government. Thus, despite the fact that democratization was an unprecedented kind of undertaking, from the standpoints of both the traditional system of government and the colonial administration, the basic considerations and assumptions that had previously conditioned British policy regarding innovations, remained in effect. The result was a decision to "democratize within the framework of traditional institutions", to avoid any action that might undermine their prestige and influence, to proceed, in short, with the heretofore dubious task of trying to induce fundamental change within the bounds of the established political order.

But in the newer context, the old precepts were almost a complete negation of what was said to be the goal. On questions of change we saw previously that there were two basic assumptions of indirect rule: first, that it was the British administration's role to propose reforms; second, that appropriate implementation should originate at the top of the traditional administrative hierarchy. The emirs, together with other key officials, were therefore regarded not only as the principal objects of change but also as its primary agents. At the same pace, indirect rule more or less deliberately eschewed the exercise of initiative by the peasants. No provision had been made before for them to act independently of their rulers. The peasants' one opportunity for political participation had derived from the uncertain possibility of contracting into that necessarily subservient relationship —i.e. clientage—which the traditional structure of authority offered. All the emphasis had been placed by the British on the attempt to redefine, from a British perspective, the functions and conditions of high traditional office.[33] But to introduce genuinely democratic local

[33] In his Memorandum, "Principles of Native Administration and Their Application", Sir Donald Cameron perhaps best captures this feature of indirect rule when he states: "It will be the primary duty and object of the Administrative Officers to educate the Native Authorities in their duties as rulers of their people according to civilized standards; to convince them that oppression of the peoples

government would be to universalize the basis of political participation, to completely reorient the direction of authority and transfer the source of ultimate political accountability to the peasants. Clearly indirect rule had not prepared the peasants to exercise these opportunities. It had also precluded any chance for them to acquire the minimum technical competence in the management of public affairs—which democratic local control seemed also to imply—the more so if the local initiation and maintenance of public services and projects was to be emphasized.

Thus, if some British officers were less devoted than others to the philosophical esprit of indirect rule, they were all acutely aware that the assumptions of the past were unavoidably visited on the present, and the foreseeable future. Surveying the prospects of early and fully democratized local government, the British were alternatively, and sometimes simultaneously, appalled at the potential for violent revolutionary upheaval, at the danger of reversion to precolonial conditions, and at the possibility that the meaning and implications of reform might not be comprehended by the peasantry. Surmising that it would be some time before the peasants could be sufficiently educated so as to avert any or all of these catastrophes, the British saw no completely satisfactory course. But for them the most prudent path lay in continuing to concentrate on trying to modify the conduct and attributes of traditional officials, thereby avoiding at least the one immediate pitfall of a serious decline in the level of technical proficiency in government. But the same prudence pointed as well, of course, to a need to avert any tendency toward an assumption of local political power by the peasants.

Starting in 1952 African political leaders steadily shared more and more in the defining of government policies. By 1959 they had assumed virtually complete control of the regional government. The fact that the policy of gradualism crystallized between these years and was maintained afterward indicates that it somehow accorded with their wishes as well as those of the British. At the same time,

---

is not sound policy or to the eventual benefit of the rulers; to bring home to their intelligence, as far as may be possible [!], the evils attendant on a system which holds the lower classes in suppression, so destroying individual responsibility, ambition and development amongst them; and to inculcate the unspeakable benefit of justice, free from bribery and open to all. The end to be sought is, in brief, just government according to civilised standards and the moral and material wellbeing and the social progress of the people. Quoted in *Duties of the Administrative Officer in Northern Nigeria* (Kaduna, 1952), p. 5. Cameron's Memorandum is excerpted and reproduced in Kirk-Greene, *Principles of Native Administration in Nigeria*, pp. 193-225.

it is obvious that the perspectives of the two were not identical. In other parts of British Africa, notably southern Nigeria itself, African leaders during the same period were busy using their newly won power to begin or to hasten a dismantling of the Native Administration system. The triumph of gradualism within postwar Northern Nigerian official circles therefore cannot be explained without an understanding of its special appeal to the new African segment of the policy-makers.

THE NORTHERN "CONSERVATIVES"

ONE KEY to the situation was the fact that the majority of that leadership was not really "new". In fact, it consisted mostly of relatives, clients, and appointees of Native Authorities, as well as some emirs themselves. Emirs were given a prominent place in the new parliamentary regime under the constitution—which allotted them a coordinate House of Chiefs and seats in the Cabinet (and consequently on important government committees and councils)—and special provisions governing elections to the House of Assembly helped initially to give them great influence in that body.[34] It was predictable that most emirs would seek to resist democratization, since above all it was their position of power, privilege, and prestige at which this policy was, in principle, aimed. With few exceptions the emirs reacted strongly to Tafawa Balewa's proposal in 1950 that an "independent" commission of inquiry (i.e. one that would include non-officials) be appointed as a preliminary to promulgating basic reforms.[35]

There were some exceptions to this attitude, which indicates the presence within the ranks of the traditional rulers of an opposing minority perspective on reform generally. One emir, especially (Malam Yahaya, the late Emir of Gwandu), actively identified himself with the cause of reform, personally introducing or supporting some of the relevant proposals in the legislature. His unique career and role are sketched more fully elsewhere in this book. Here it need only be noted that the few emirs who shared to some extent the advanced ideas of M. Yahaya saw the challenge of reform in terms of "purifying" their traditional role, instead of seeking to promote structural

[34] See below, Chap. 9.

[35] It is reliably reported that one prominent emir, for example, denounced Balewa's proposal as being "designed to promote ill-feeling", and that another equally prominent emir similarly condemned it as "the speech of a disgruntled man and designed to stir up trouble".

reordering of the traditional state. The term "purify" is apt, for these few were primarily motivated by an ideal of Islamic government; they were reformers, but not democratizers, in that they adhered to a paternalistic conception of political authority.

After Balewa's speech in 1950, the emirs were obliged to acquiesce in some important reforms, including one instituted on the eve of self-government, which promised eventually to have far-reaching consequences—the introduction of a Western criminal code of law. Yet the fact that, during the same period, they strenuously objected to significant proposals, suggested that most emirs were far from welcoming measures that appeared immediately and directly to threaten their position.

Fortunately for the emirs, the views of the Northern Ministers and the vast majority of the regional Assembly did not radically conflict with their own. From the beginning of representative government in Nigeria the overwhelming majority of Northern elected representatives were high Native Administration officials or employees of a lower rank whose appointments and careers necessarily owed a good deal to the good graces of emirs who headed the Native Administrations. And by virtue of their position of influence (and those helpful electoral devices to which I have referred), emirs frequently were able to secure or help promote the election of favorite candidates. This situation emphasized the dependency of successful politicians on traditional authority and reinforced traditional relationships of mutual obligation and loyalty. It accounted to a large extent for the outward harmony that throughout 1952 to 1965 prevailed between the two Northern legislative branches in general, and for their large area of agreement on local government matters in particular.

Yet it would be misleading to leave the matter there, for in terms of family origins these Native Administration political figures were not completely homogeneous, nor were their views as a group always the same as those of the bulk of emirs. Along with conservative-minded promoters of reforms who were relatively sympathetic to "tradition", the elected politicians included some critics who were instinctively hostile to the system of Native Administration. Each of these factions had its own motives for fostering the atmosphere of coexistence.

Typically, the "sympathetic" reformer was a high-born, upper-echelon member of a local hereditary-bureaucratic hierarchy for whom traditional institutions held both intrinsic and instrumental attractions. But even his pride of tradition and his vested interest in it were counterbalanced to some extent by two other values to which he had become especially sensitive, African self-determination and material development.

Thanks either to education or direct contact with the outside world, or both, he was aware of the virtually universal quest for the benefits of modern technology. And he had come to believe, along with other African leaders, that to affirm the human worth and dignity of Africans to himself and in the eyes of the world, the African politician had to encourage a pursuit of those benefits for and by Africans. "By" Africans, of course, presupposed self-government; hence for all his disdain for revolutionary social changes accompanying nationalist movements in southern Nigeria and elsewhere, the Western-educated traditionalist was also in this sense a believer in self-determination. He became an enthusiast of modern services, projects, and schemes for economic development, and a firebrand on the issue of the right of Africans to participate fully in the new political and economic institutions and enterprises that modern technology was creating. The most cursory reading of the postwar parliamentary debates at Kaduna and Lagos confirms the strength of such feelings among the most vehement neo-defenders of "tradition". The record suggests that as individuals they had not been immune to the sensation of humiliation generally experienced under alien rule. Indeed, their repeated utterances about these matters makes the "militants" in the south, whom they castigated constantly in this period as "Uncle Tomism" or "stoogism" the Northern conservative politician's reluctance to force the pace of Nigerian nationalism, seem very wide of the mark.

The reluctance of the Northern politician stemmed rather from his wanting to realize those aspects of the nationalist program he believed in, while also wanting to avoid those—in the realm of implied Northern internal political structure—he deplored and rejected. In the process of attaining independence and development, he wanted to ensure that the roots of power and authority in the emirates would be disturbed as little as possible. His allegedly retrograde attitude toward setting an early date for Nigerian independence masked his desire for an interval of time in which he might awaken traditional rulers to the potential benefits and requirements of material "progress", on the one hand, and the need to organize the North politically against the prospect of southern domination and Northern revolutionary upheaval, on the other. But knowing that the emirs more than appreciated how much the colonial regime had strengthened their power, he correctly anticipated that it would be difficult to reassure them that self-government was for them too.

In a nutshell, the role of the conservative reformer consisted first of calculating the internal political concessions necessary to satisfy the British conditions for transferring power—which were optional and which were not—then communicating accordingly with that traditional hierarchy of which he was both a member and a beneficiary. In later days it similarly consisted of weighing and interpreting to the hierarchy pressures in connection with economic development— how to acquire the requisite talent, skills, and financial resources without sacrificing the essentials of the traditional political order. As mediators of change, the effectiveness of the conservative reformers derived largely from the confidence of other members of the hierarchy that such reformers could be relied on not to jeopardize common political interests gratuitously. In another context, the historical evolution of the Northern Peoples' Congress, this mutual confidence constituted a political asset which at a crucial juncture enabled the "conservatives" to gain the upper hand. In the context of policies for local government, it placed them in a position to help guide, moderate, and ultimately limit reform under a banner of gradualism.

THE NORTHERN "CRITICS"

I HAVE SUGGESTED that within the ranks of the Native Administration employees elected as representatives there were also persons who, in contrast to the ones just described, were critical antagonists of the traditional system. The more severe "critic" shared the conservative reformer's exposure to Western education and his quickened sensitivity to new economic values, but lacked his parallel commitment to political tradition per se. Typically his own foothold in the traditional hierarchy was marginal and tenuous, enjoyed more by dint of special training and technical skill than through close blood or strong clientage relationships with his superiors. The paradigm of the type was the trained clerk, elementary schoolteacher, or technical specialist (forestry *malam*, drug dispenser, accountant) who was by birth a commoner or at least not a member of the royalty or prominent nobility. His experience imbued him with respect for the bureaucratic or "meritocratic" criteria of worth that had lifted him from obscurity. At the same time, he was almost totally dependent on the

Native Administration system, because until recently it had offered virtually the only accessible outlet for his talents (the recruitment policies of the Government Service had for a long time precluded employment there as an alternative; those of the expatriate firms had been only slightly more encouraging). Thus he was highly prone to feelings of frustration and resentment about the pervasive climate of personalism, fixed status, inherited prerogatives, and special treatment, the undervaluing of skill and qualifications—in short, from his point of view—the arbitrariness constantly encountered in the operations of the Native Administration.

In the early days of the postwar political and constitutional ferment, some of these N.A. employees ventured criticisms and concocted proposals which, though they were couched in a form designed to be palatable both to the Native Authorities and their conservative-reformer sympathizers, nonetheless implied a break with fundamental features of traditional government. Such proposals implied their authors' sympathy for modern, secular, and democratic standards of local government.[36]

In the Northern Assembly the critics were always in the minority. But a review of Assembly debates between 1952 and 1954 showed that approximately 20 of the 84 elected members at one time or another made statements or speeches of this character. Since no official opposition party candidates were elected before 1956, such utterances came wholly from within the ranks of the Northern Peoples' Congress. By 1956, however, the number of outspoken critics had declined; furthermore, they were to be found only on the opposition side of the House. Yet, with one exception, the early critics had not switched party affiliations; the exception was Malam Ibrahim Imam, a former secretary general of the NPC and probably the most

---

[36] A prime example was the article published by Yusuff Maitama Sule (then an elementary schoolteacher employed by the Kano Native Authority, later Federal Minister of Power and Chief Whip of the NPC in the Federal Government). In the *Daily Comet* for June 1, 1950, he argued that ". . . the system of election was followed by the ancient followers of Islam whose government we should try to copy as it agrees entirely with the principles of democracy. It is religiously hereditary and we failed to inherit it because of imperialism. The ordinary man—the *"talaka"* whose views and opinions should be respected and listened to, and who should have a say in the government of his own country if at all we are being governed democratically—has been neglected. . . . Having got an elected council in the centre and another in the ward, Northerners should next look for an elected Emir. The Emir should be amenable to those he rules. . . . If an Emir is really elected by his people he will be more respected by them and, I believe, he will respect them more as his loyal subjects". See profile of M. Maitama Sule in Appendix A, No. 26.

persistently and trenchantly critical Northern legislator of all.[37] Thus, for some reason, a number of the Native Administration NPC-elected members in effect withdrew during this period from an active or overtly critical stance—without, it is apparent, having imposed their demands.

Some of the reasons were obvious. The NPC had risen to power in the regional government; the critics formed only a minority of the parliamentary party; and a formal opposition had emerged. In these circumstances, the normal imperatives of party discipline would naturally overwhelm the critics within the legislature. But this does not wholly account for the failure of the critic to press his case within the party and in channels outside the legislature (e.g. the press) as he had done before. Some of the individuals concerned whom I interviewed offered explanations suggesting that as a group they consciously abated their activities during this period. By their own account they did not undergo a change of heart ideologically; rather, they appear to have been preoccupied with certain interrelated considerations involving the course of political development in the wider contexts of the Northern Region and Nigeria as a whole, which, taken together, usually dissuaded them from advocating rapid democratization in the emirates. These may be characterized as (1) the specter of domination of the North by southern political leadership, (2) the challenge of mass enfranchisement, and (3) the "backwardness" of the peasantry. These are factors that will be encountered again in connection with an analysis of the internal development of the NPC —which in fact parallels the advent and recession of the critics' drive for democratic reform of local government. But these points require initial comment here.

The antagonist and the protagonist of Native Administration shared an acute anxiety over the possibility that southern politicians would be elevated to positions of power over the North. This attitude stemmed partly from a past history of bad relationships between Northerners and southerners in the North, and partly from anxiety about the southerners' greater preparedness for participating in modern political activities. Nationalism in the southern regions of Nigeria represented the culmination of internal forces that had built up over a long period of time. Thus James S. Coleman's analysis of the roots of Nigerian nationalism in that area casts back almost half a century,

---

[37] See profile of A. Ibrahim Iman in Appendix A, No. 106.

pointing to such incipient revolutionary developments as the gradual burgeoning of a cash economy and export trade, the growth of an extensive system of communications and transport, the penetration by Christian missionaries and the concomitant development of Western schools and curricula—in short, to a sustained exposure to Western ways and institutions. In contrast, these currents had touched the Northern emirates only to a limited extent, while the colonial system's manipulation of the traditional order had deliberately inhibited acculturation. Hence the fear on the part of the Northern politician that greater sophistication and experience vis-à-vis the appropriate structures and techniques would give the southern politician a decisive advantage in strictly modern competitive political action.

Past animosity toward southern Nigerians was a product of their special position in the North, in combination with the cultural gulf existing between the two peoples, in language, religion, social relations and customs, and perhaps most fatefully of all, in traditional orientations toward political authority.[38] There had been just enough commercial activity in the North to attract colonies of southerners who operated either as private entrepreneurs or as agents of expatriate firms which naturally preferred them to Northerners because of educational qualification and experience. It had similarly been the habit of the colonial administration in the North to recruit southerners for secondary clerical posts and the like. The southerner's superior skill, together with the legal authority and powers he sometimes enjoyed by virtue of official duties, inevitably exposed him to temptations of abuse and arrogance toward the illiterate Northern peasant.

In 1959 thoughtful southerners acknowledged in retrospect that on the whole these temptations were withstood no better than in comparable historical circumstances—wherever an elite harbors notions of cultural superiority to a people over whom it wields politically unaccountable power and whose ignorance or reticence may inhibit recourse to available legal processes. The Kano riot of 1953, in which members of the southern and Northern communities clashed in some

[38] On the highly decentralized and egalitarian tendencies of the Ibo system of government see Simon Ottenberg, "Ibo Receptivity to Change", in William R. Bascom and Melville J. Herskovits, eds., Continuity and Change in African Cultures (Chicago, 1959). On the limited monarchy of the Yoruba people see Peter C. Lloyd, "The Traditional Political System of the Yoruba", in Southwestern Journal of Anthropology, Vol. 10 (Winter 1954), pp. 366-84; for an interesting comparison of Ibo, Yoruba, and Hausa psychological orientations see Robert A. Levine, Dreams and Deeds: Achievement Motivation in Nigeria (Chicago, 1966).

nasty incidents,[39] first unearthed the legacy of bitterness which had accumulated through an undeniably invidious relationship. Years later, the full magnitude of the feelings involved were revealed.[40]

It can easily be seen how the other two problems followed. The prospect of enfranchisement of the peasantry, who composed the overwhelming portion of the electorate, triggered an anxiety that Northerners would fall prey to the "rapacious and shrewd" southerners, that the political power the peasantry now ostensibly enjoyed might work to extend the southerners' grasp and elude the claims of the Northern elite. There were also indications—in the form of the rise of NEPU (the Northern, later Nigerian, Elements' Progressive Union), a radical Northern party—of the possibility of a successful "populist" movement which might equally deny those claims. Thus Malam Abubakar Tafawa Balewa, the future Prime Minister of Nigeria, who in this initial reform period epitomized the perspective of "severe critic" of the traditional system, repeatedly warned against the dangers of "unscrupulous politicians" and generally lamented the "unpreparedness", parochialism, and naïveté of the electorate.[41] Critics' fears were aggravated by the awareness that they lacked the backing of an organized mass political movement and the party machinery through which to arouse and secure the allegiance and support of the peasantry. Yet the constitutional changes that

[39] According to a report published under the authority of the Northern Regional government, atrocities included several instances of burning, mutilation, and castration of both Northerners and southerners. Fatalities totalled 15 Northerners and 21 southerners. 241 persons were wounded. *Report on the Kano Disturbances, 16th, 17th, 18th, and 19th May 1953* (Kaduna, 1953), esp. pp. 16, 21.

[40] In terms of the scale of violence, the Kano riots of 1953 paled to insignificance in comparison to the mass murders of Ibos in Northern Nigeria in May and September-October 1966, following the rise of Nigeria's first military government, under Maj. Gen. Johnson T. U. Aguyi-Ironsi, an Ibo. One knowledgeable and responsible observer privately stated to me in Kaduna in January 1967 that a conservative estimate of the total number of Ibos killed was 10,000, approximately 3,000 in May and the remainder in September and October (after a second Nigerian military government, under an officer of Northern "Middle-Belt" origin, Lt. Col. Yakubu Gowon, had overthrown the Ironsi regime). Hundreds of thousands of Ibos fled the North leaving the region literally void of any Ibo settlers by January 1967. For a perceptive interpretation of these events, especially from the viewpoint of the Northern Ibo community, see the article by the *London Observer* reporter Colin Legum, "The Tragedy of Nigeria", reproduced in *Africa Report,* Vol. 2, No. 8 (November 1966), pp. 23-24.

[41] See *Proceedings of the General Conference on Review of the Constitution,* January 1950 (Lagos, 1950), p. 68; *Nigeria Legislative Council Debates,* March 16, 1949, pp. 47, 474; March 30, 1949, pp. 723-24; August 21, 1948, p. 193; March 24, 1947, 1949, pp. 723-24; August 21, 1948, p. 193; March 24, 1947, p. 212; Northern Nigeria, *House of Assembly Debates,* January 21, 1947, pp. 17-18; Minutes, Northern Peoples' Congress Emergency Convention, 1953, mimeog., p. 1.

placed a premium on these assets proceeded apace. The net effect of the mounting pressures and uncertainties was to instill deep misgivings even in the critics about the necessity and desirability of complete and immediate democratic change; in expressing concern over the "backwardness" of the peasantry the critics were both summing up and justifying this attitude.

But their attitude stemmed from another source as well, and here we come to a matter that is perhaps especially significant for understanding the peculiar political position of the educated commoner in Northern Nigeria and thus the special magnetism the policy of gradualism exerted on him.

It has become a commonplace to observe in the developing areas the existence of a wide gap between the background, experience, values, and political outlook of the educated leadership, on the one hand, and the masses of citizens on the other. But in this respect, the position of the educated Hausa commoner is particularly unenviable. He is confronted with the stubborn fact of having to acquire the prestige and influence that is requisite to political leadership in a society which, as M. G. Smith has made clear, actually *disvalues* status mobility, evincing instead "a general preference for social continuity and for stability in the status order".[42] Thus the principle of recognition on the basis of objective merit, performance, and function—which had led to his disaffection with the Native Administration system in the first place—he knew was not widely shared by the very element, the peasants, in whom was to be vested the power to select political leaders. His credentials were often consciously rejected by them. In this sense, he was a politician without a "constituency", which was the older colonial conundrum turned inside out; the British typically worried that the peasants could not properly be represented by the educated few. It is interesting to note that the dilemma of the "critic" was foreshadowed by an informal official British appraisal of the Northern political situation in 1950 which contained the following observation:

> . . . little doubt arises that when some members of the "progressive" element claim a greater opportunity for the people to play a more active part in their Local Government affairs, they are staking a claim for themselves and their fellows. It is conceivable that the democratization of Local Government and the introduction of

[42] Smith, "The Hausa System of Social Status", *Africa*, Vol. 39, No. 3 (July 1959), p. 248 *passim*.

something in the nature of popular representation might not lead immediately to a greater participation in Local Government affairs by the "progressive" element. By extending the system of selection to afford an opportunity to the rural populations of a greater voice in choosing their representatives, it is by no means certain that preferences would not be given to the traditional representatives of the people, rather than to the class which is seeking entry into this sphere. The peasantry, which is genuinely still acutely "birth conscious", might well prefer blue-blooded mediocrity to the higher qualified parvenu.[43]

The fully prophetic quality of that last sentence is confirmed in other chapters (Five and Eight) which deal with the composition of representative institutions at local and regional government levels, respectively. But the particular relevance of this situation to the discussion at hand lies in the paradoxical fact that eventually it occurred to the critic that the solution to each of his various predicaments was to forge an alliance with traditional authority.

The struggle against a possible spread of southern influence to the North indicated a strategy of emphasizing the solidarity of traditional communities. The theme was to become a hallmark of the NPC, which used it effectively to discredit the claims of southern and Northern radical parties alike. "We felt", explained one critic, "that it would be politically self-defeating to try and take on the southerners, the British, and the emirs all at one time". In effect, the critic accepted a priority that would enable Northern political leadership to use the last foe against the others. In the early days of postwar constitutional negotiations, especially, emirs proved to be effective symbols, rallying points for interests of the North, including those shared by the otherwise hostile critics.

Perhaps the touchstone of this development was the assumption by the Sultan of Sokoto of the chairmanship of a public fund drive for purposes of defending the Northern point of view at a crucial juncture in those negotiations (the Emir of Katsina served as treasurer). The issue concerned primarily the distribution of seats in the Legislative Council between the Northern and southern provinces, the Northern leaders insisting that the population of the former entitled it to a 50-percent share. When it appeared that the southern leaders would not agree to that, the fund (called the *Kudin Taimakon*

[43] Document in possession of the author.

Arewa—literally "money to help the North") was launched with a view to carrying the Northern case directly to the Colonial Office if necessary.[44] Within the short space of five months the impressive sum of £23,000 was amassed.[45]

Furthermore, we shall see in a later chapter how the Native Administrations, in effect, provided the base for politically mobilizing the new organizational electorate. Similarly the answer to the social-status dilemma of the typical critic was eventually seen to be what amounted to a process of reciprocal recognition on the part of traditional and modern leadership. Briefly put, the idea was, if the Native Authorities were to welcome the educated elements to their ranks, the popular standing of the latter would in time be enhanced through being associated with the superior prestige and authority of traditional rulers. Acceptance of a prolonged tenure for those traditional rulers was of course implicit in the bargain.

Finally, with respect to the value of self-determination, many Northern Nigerians and British officials in the early stages of "nationalism" regarded increasing the power and responsibility of the Native Authorities as an earnest of the promise of independence from colonial rule. That the British should do so was a corollary to their hope that the Native Administrations would somehow turn out to be compatible with the new governmental forms being introduced in Kaduna and Lagos. As long as this hope was kept alive, it followed not only that the Native Authorities should be preserved, but that positive steps should be taken to improve their potential as responsible institutions of government, such as granting them an increased measure of autonomy. That Africans sometimes bolstered the British in this reasoning is revealed in the sentiments expressed by some of them at local advisory conferences that were convened to discuss the future of local government—conferences which, though they included educated commoners, tended to be heavily weighted on the side of traditional representation. Thus the Resident's report to the Northern Chief Commissioner on the 1950 Kano Provincial Conference observed that: "A very interesting feature of the Conference was the evident desire, on both sides that the powers of the Native Authorities and Native Authority Courts vis-à-vis Government should be increased rather than diminished. There is undoubtedly a very strong feeling among the general public in favor of local autonomy, in con-

---

[44] See *Daily Comet*, May 31, 1950, p. 1.
[45] Sardauna of Sokoto, in Northern Nigeria, *House of Assembly Debates*, December 6, 1950, p. 89.

formity with the principles of Islam, in all the Native Authorities of the Province, and it is improbable that any revision of local government which ignores the tradition and religion of the people will find favour in their eyes".[46]

A handbook for British officers published in 1952 captured the spirit of this rationalization in observing: "as the Native Authorities gain greater confidence and experience, the administrative officer finds himself more and more in the position of an advisor, rather than instructor".[47] It is doubly understandable that many nonofficial Africans increasingly felt that for British officers seemingly to dictate as they pleased on every facet of Native Administration was inconsistent with the idea of African emancipation. Thus the traditional ruling class was not alone in calling for a loosening of restrictions. Some of the bitterest critics of the conduct of Native Administration also became the most indignant objectors to allowing British officers to retain the power of intervention.[48] Of course the eventual Africanization of the Administrative Service offered an antidote to this irritant. But as long as British personnel occupied important posts, it was perhaps inevitable that the issue of African self-determination would be confounded in Northern Nigeria with that of the relationship of the Native Administrations to the center.

Assuming that the Native Administrations were indeed to be put on a popular and secular conciliar footing, relaxing central control was perfectly consistent with the desire to develop an effective system of democratic local government in the emirates. But in the absence of an early and decisive move in the direction of democratization, the net result of this new liberality was to enhance the capacity of traditional powers to resist fundamental change. Hence, the policy of granting Native Administrations greater autonomy reinforced that of gradualism, and vice-versa.

Similarly the desire to obtain foreign aid and investment capital for economic development added to the long-standing concern for political stability and thus stimulated a new appreciation of the contribution traditional political organization might make to this end. During the period in which plans of reform in local government were

[46] Document in possession of the author.
[47] *Duties of the Administrative Officer in Northern Nigeria* (Kaduna, 1952), p. 9.
[48] See, for example, the remarks of T. Ayilla Yogh and Patrick D. Fom, Northern Nigeria, *House of Assembly Debates*. Debate on the 1954 Native Authority Law, third session, 12th to 23rd February 1954, pp. 223-307.

being formulated, British officials were repeatedly drawing attention to an intimate connection between a government's proficiency in maintaining political stability and its prospects for receiving outside financial assistance. Such was the much enunciated theme of Sir Bryan Sharwood-Smith, Governor of Northern Nigeria from 1952 to 1957. In apparent allusion to the activities of radical Northern parties, he observed in one speech to the Northern House of Chiefs, that "I have referred in previous addresses and speeches to the necessity for stability. I make no apology for returning to this subject again. There can be no progress of any form whatsoever, political, social or economic, where there is confusion and lack of public confidence as to the future in the mind of the ordinary citizen. We must set our face, therefore, against those who seek to disrupt while claiming to reform".[49] In the aftermath of the 1953 Kano riots he again reiterated the point perhaps even more explicitly:

> For every modern state, stability is the one essential. Therefore, I ask you to remember your heritage and tradition of self-control so that you may ensure that in this Region stability persists, for without stability there can be no public confidence, no freedom of movement and no freedom of speech.
>
> Where there is no stability and where law and order are not rigorously maintained, trade, which is the life-blood of a people, cannot flourish, neither will the capital without which vast new undertakings cannot be contemplated, be forthcoming.
>
> Where there are potentialities combined with stability, capital flows in and trade flourishes.[50]

It is unlikely that the implications of such remarks were lost on Northern Nigeria political leaders, not least the critics. At least one Northern minister, formerly a member of a radical political party, would appear to have carried this line of thinking even further in arguing to me in 1959 that the habit of social discipline imparted by the traditional order represented "a natural economic advantage". It was clear that what he had in mind was something akin to what Marx called "primitive accumulation" and some African contemporaries have termed "human investment"—namely, the generation of economic development through the intensive use of "voluntary" cheap labor. The presence of a "natural" or traditional social leaven like

[49] February 25, 1952, *House of Chiefs Debates*, p. 3.
[50] Text reproduced in *Nigerian Citizen*, May 5, 1953, pp. 6-7.

hierarchy rendered less necessary recourse to "artificial" inducements such as charismatic appeals, or the use of various overt techniques of coercion or manipulation through new political structures. From this, it followed that economic development required less change in existing political structures than one might otherwise desire. The minister seemed very earnest in this, and it may well be that other former critics' views were altered through reflection on the elusive requirements of "development".

Some Echoes of Harmony

THE DEGREE to which any one of the considerations discussed above contributed to making gradualism the keynote of policy is probably unknowable, but in any case the proportions are less important than what they all added up to—and that was a profound unwillingness to push democratization to an early conclusion on the part of nearly everyone in a position to shape policy. Frequently the considerations I have identified above were reflected in attempts to enunciate and interpret the official position on local government reform—before, during, and after the rise of African leadership to power at the center. The following paragraphs are therefore presented as a partial selection of revealing statements in this regard during the seminal years of reform, beginning with Sir Arthur Richard's (then Governor of Nigeria) classic rendition of an old theme of indirect rule in 1946, the inaugural year of Nigeria's first modern constitution, in a speech to the Northern Residents' and Chiefs' Conference: "You have fine traditions and I want you to preserve them. You want progress, but progress which will be based on your own way of life, progress which will build on the foundations of your fathers, not the false progress which would destroy the social organization you know, whose roots are deep in your history, and leave you and your people without faith and without hope. A respect for authority and an appreciation of orderly advance are the best foundations of your future".[51]

In 1950 someone signing himself "Dan Sakkwato" (literally "a son of Sokoto", the emirate or the province) wrote a letter to the newspaper *Daily Comet* asking why N.A. officials shouldn't be held accountable to popular representatives. In an open letter the government public relations officer replied:

[51] *Summary of Proceedings* (Kaduna, 1946), p. 15.

"Dan Sakkwato" wishes to know who represents the peasants when the N.A. Estimates are being framed, and the reply is that the peasants are represented by their traditional rulers, the Native Authorities and representatives who are already in possession of the views of District and Village Heads and other Officials who are in a position to know the wishes of the people.

"Dan Sakkwato" claims to be a typical Northerner but if he is in fact the author of this article, he has no right to make such a claim in that he is both literate and obviously highly interested in political affairs.

The vast majority of the Northerners have neither of these attributes although there is indeed a slowly awakening interest in administrative affairs which is being fostered by Native Authorities and Administrative Officers in many ways, particularly by the inauguration of village councils on which councils more and more administrative and financial responsibility is ever being devolved.

When the time comes that "Dan Sakkwato" is indeed typical of peasants there will be no delay in evolving a system by which the peasant is given more direct representation than it is at present practicable to grant him.[52]

The following year in the same newspaper the position was amplified in a verbatim report on an Assembly debate: "Government was well aware that modernization and improvements in the local government system were needed, so indeed were the Native Authorities themselves, but was equally certain that these improvements could best be brought about, not by destroying the present traditional system, but by building a more democratic structure upon the firm foundation evolved by the people of the Region themselves in the past".[53] In rejecting two years later the proposal that Native Authority Councils should be popularly chosen, the Sardauna of Sokoto, the African Minister of Local Government who was to become the first premier of the Northern Region stated further: "The Regional Government has no intention of embarking on any hasty and ill-considered measures which could impair the authority or reduce the efficiency of the great Councils of the larger Emirates in particular, on whose wisdom and competence the well-being of millions of people depend".[54] It was noteworthy that on the same occasion he also

[52] "The North and Its Finance—A Reply", *Daily Comet*, May 19, 1950, p. 2.
[53] *Ibid.*, December 12, 1951, pp. 1, 4.
[54] Northern Nigeria, *House of Assembly Debates*, February 19, 1954, p. 224.

argued: "We in the North have not had to attempt . . . to set up an alien type of local government borrowed from another country as is the case in the other Regions. No, Mr. President, Sir, we have our own form of Local Government and this flexible bill, the N.A. Law of 1954, will enable us to develop and modify it so that, within the framework of our traditional system, we shall have an efficient and democratic form of Local Government which will compare favorably with that of any country".[55] By 1958 the government was sufficiently confident of its policy of gradualism to tell the independent Minorities Commission, appointed by the Colonial Office, to investigate "fears of minorities" in Nigeria in connection with constitutional development, that: "The Northern Regional Government has no major proposals for reorganization of its local government system up to the level of Native Authority. Its proposals are rather to stimulate development and growth following the principles that have been applied over the past half century, namely, where practicable to build on the indigenous institutions and to encourage development along democratic lines so that it is level with or just in advance of public need and demand while being within the competence and financial strength of the unit concerned".[56]

As the last statement implied, the policy was capable of receiving positive as well as negative emphasis. Indeed, the Northern Governor's speech from the throne the year following had suggested that within its confines some significant further changes might be in the offing. "A balance must be struck", he observed, ". . . between innovation and undue conservatism. It is my Government's policy that all local councils should progress steadily without overly rapid changes that lead to unbalance, but sufficiently fast to meet the genuine needs and wishes of the people for participation in local affairs".[57] But the year did not see any fundamental innovations,[58] and

[55] The *Sardauna's* sentiments were echoed by the (British) Civil Secretary in the parallel debate in the House of Chiefs. "The Regional Government does not believe", the latter confirmed, "that success in Local Government can best be achieved by sweeping away all of the old and well-tried system and imposing something new from outside. It believes in building on the traditional system in the North, adapting it to meet the changes required by modern times", March 3, 1954.

[56] *Memorandum to the Minorities Commission from the Government of the Northern Region* (London, 1958), Appendix W.

[57] *Speech by His Excellency, Sir Gawain Westray Bell, to the Northern House of Assembly, February 16, 1959*, p. 9.

[58] The Governor was referring to the government's intention "to introduce formal representative provincial councils". But as he noted, these were to be advisory bodies. See Chap. 2.

in 1960 the Minister for Local Government, Alhaji Maikano Dutse, made it clear once again that motions such as that tabled by M. Anga Soba, a NEPU member of the Assembly, proposing, "That all the present Native Authority Councils in this Region should be dissolved and replaced by elected members", were still well beyond acceptable limits. In his remarks, the Minister argued in a familiar vein that:

> The evidence of good local government is to be found in its ability to retain the confidence of the people and its ability to maintain law and order, providing those essential services which the people need and desire. Experience in this Region has conclusively shown that Native Authorities composed largely of selected [sic] members do not *necessarily*, and I repeat *necessarily*, provide the good government which the people have the right to enjoy. . . .

> There is no need to be discouraged by one or two failures, provided that the lessons from such failures are learned. One of the main lessons is that the full elective principle must be introduced gradually. As with human beings so with local authorities [sic] it is usually fatal to throw a baby into deep waters and expect it not to drown. . . .

> To teach this lesson the Government places great importance upon the development of District and Urban Councils as training grounds in democratic principle for the responsible leaders of the public. Here, in miniature, and without doing irreparable harm by mistakes, these leaders can learn the very difficult art of the government of their fellow citizens. . . .

> The motion proposed by the Honorable Member from Zaria North is highly unrealistic, impracticable, and irresponsible.[59]

All these official expressions of policy serve to remind us too, however, that for all their caution and distaste for undiluted and accelerated democratization, the policy-makers were for various reasons committed to making relevant changes in that direction. In 1963, for example, it was decided that all Native Authority Councils should have at least some elected members, and by the end of 1965 all did.[60] A few of the lesser emirate N.A.s even had an elected majority.

The essence of the response of gradualism was therefore neither

[59] Northern Nigeria, *House of Assembly Debates*, April 26, 1960, Cols. 516-23.
[60] *Northern Nigeria Local Government Yearbook: 1966*, prepared by the Department of Local Government, Institute of Administration, Ahmadu Bello University, Zaria.

simple "reaction" nor paralysis, but a continuing ambivalence between a commitment to change and a desire to uphold existing arrangements. Hence innovations in the field of local government *were* made in the postwar period. But having discovered some of the deeper springs of official policy, we are now better able to appreciate and understand the nature of the reforms that were in fact devised—and why, for the most part, they constituted a resolution of the ambivalence in favor of continuity.

CHAPTER 2

Devising the Framework

IN THE preceding chapter I indicated that the doctrine of gradualism was adopted by a heterogeneous group of policy-makers whose disparate purposes the doctrine suited alike. The shape of the reforms they devised as a consequence is the subject of this chapter.

Gradualism meant that with care and time the basic institutions of traditional government in the emirates could be made to accommodate the essential objectives, norms, and practices of modern democratic local government without sacrificing their integrity or identity as traditional institutions. Stated this way, the new doctrine's affinity to the earlier philosophy of indirect rule is readily apparent. Hence it might be expected that the attempt to devise a program of reform on the basis of this doctrine would encounter much the same kind of difficulties as previously attended colonial rule in Northern Nigeria. We shall see in this chapter that such in fact was the case.

Like that of indirect rule, the logic of the doctrine of gradualism in the field of local government clearly had to stand or fall on the question of whether the requisite innovations were ultimately compatible with irreducible elements of the traditional system. But since the utility of the doctrine did not necessarily depend on its having a strictly logical cogency (in fact, its greatest political usefulness was precisely in its imprecision), the gradualists themselves felt no compulsion to come to grips with such considerations. Those who propounded the doctrine characteristically were "loath"— one government official told me in 1959—"to speculate on such abstract issues". As the policy-makers defined their task, it was to get on with the business of devising such concrete measures of reform as would be consistent with the dual aims of change and continuity.

Thus in the period 1947-59 the Northern government promulgated a series of reforms that reflect the conceptions of gradualism. Miss Lucy Mair, the English scholar of traditional and colonial governments in Africa, has insisted that the central question to be asked of any attempt to introduce modern democratic local government within the framework of traditional institutions is, "how far an authority based on tradition can be an instrument of change".[1] The

[1] Mair, "Representative Local Government as a Problem in Social Change", in *Journal of African Administration*, Vol. 8, No. 1 (January 1958).

question unavoidably arises in relation to reforms that were introduced into the emirates: did they represent a means of fusing traditional and modern democratic local government? To arrive at any
conclusions, we will clearly need to answer a series of related questions. What exactly was meant by modern democratic local government in Northern Nigeria and how do specific characteristics of traditional emirate government compare with the end in view? How, if
at all, did the reformers seek to resolve any points of discrepancy
and how successful were their efforts? Were there any fundamental,
irresolvable incompatibilities? Or to state the central issue in another
way, did the reformers' adherence to the objective of retaining traditional institutions necessarily limit the extent to which they could
pursue modernization and democratization in local government?

This chapter deals with these questions, in part by analyzing the
historic evolution of the program of reform in local governments as it
unfolded after the war. I leave aside, for the moment, the related
question of how the program adopted worked out in practice, which
is the subject of the chapters in Part Three.

The discussion will first juxtapose the objectives of the program of
reform as a whole with the relevant features of the traditional system,
and then give a roughly chronological account of significant postwar
changes in the field of local government, in terms of their implications for the various values and interests in question. My main conclusion in this chapter is that because traditional emirates and modern democratic local government enjoy only limited elements of com-
patibility, and the reformers were primarily committed to continuity,
only such measures of reform as fell considerably short of an effective
program of modernization and democratization were acceptable to
those in power.

POINTS OF CONFLICT

A COMMON way of formulating problems of political change in non-
Western ex-colonial countries is to envision the ultimate objective in
terms of the "model" furnished by the relevant institutions of the
former "metropole". Thus David Apter calls the problem of change
in the former British Gold Coast that of "institutional transfer". But we
have seen that the whole proposition of reform in the emirates
rested rather on the expectation that, with limited modifications only,
traditional institutions would prove adequate to serve the same essential purposes as are associated with the British system (and pre-

sumably other comparable systems). Hence the institution-building approach was officially disclaimed. To draw up an inventory of the relevant English institutions with an eye to seeing how closely the program of reform resembled it, as such, is therefore inappropriate here.

Though a distinction between "change in accordance with the English model" and "modification in conformity with its purposes" may smack of hair-splitting, such a distinction had a practical import in Northern Nigeria. For it sanctioned formal departures from that model and also disarmed in advance any appraisals or criticisms based solely on the appearance of unorthodoxy. In other words, it legitimized what might be called a process of selective borrowing, whereby features of the British system, which ostensibly fit in with the maintenance of the traditional system, might conveniently be adopted, but those which did not, might be justifiably rejected.

For the policy-makers to have published a detailed statement of aims would hardly have been in keeping with that unwillingness to be bound to any predetermined course of action or set timetable which underlay the gradualist rationale. No obstacle to analysis would arise were there universally accepted functions and purposes of modern democratic local government, but, of course, there are none. By way of an authoritative definition of goals we have only such very general statements as that of the 1947 Secretary of State for the Colonies' Despatch, which says that the objective is "an efficient and democratic system of local government" (the word "representative" was later substituted in official nomenclature for "democratic"), without explaining what that state of affairs specifically consists of. The student of the period must therefore discover in some way the specific aims of a "democratic" reform of local government in the emirates.

A reasonable approach seemed to be to review literature on English local government,[2] extracting those items generally indicated as

[2] Herman Finer, *English Local Government* (London, 1933); W. A. Robson, *The Development of Local Government* (London, 1931); J. H. Warren, *The English Local Government System* (London, 1949); C. H. Wilson, *Essays on Local Government* (Oxford, 1948). In addition, studies that deal with the adaptation of aspects of the English system to areas in Africa which were found to be particularly suggestive for purposes of the present study, were especially Fred G. Burke, *Local Government and Politics in Uganda* (Syracuse, 1964); L. Gray Cowan, *Local Government in West Africa* (New York, 1958); Lloyd A. Fallers, *Bantu Bureaucracy* (London, 1957); Audrey I. Richards, ed., *East African Chiefs* (London, 1960); Ronald E. Wraight, *Local Government*, rev. ed. (London, 1956). Parts of Cowan's and Wraith's books deal with Northern Nigeria; otherwise these works examine comparable cases, i.e. where British indirect rule was the colonial

forming the principal functions and purposes of this system, and then to determine through interviews whether, or which of, these items actually also formed part of the Northern Nigerian policy-makers' understanding of a "modern democratic system of local government". The result is a summary list of aims which, I think, represents a fair statement of what the policy-makers claimed to be trying to achieve through reform in the emirates (though they would not necessarily choose to express themselves in the same language). As might be expected, if for no other reason than that the policy-makers were most familiar with them, British experience and practices in fact were the principal source of reference. Various policy-makers would no doubt also differ among themselves as to the relative importance to be attached to particular items; therefore, the order in which they are listed below does not necessarily reflect any order of priority. Distinctions are drawn in the list between (a) general functions and (b) structural principles (according to which local government ought properly to be conducted), although it is obvious that these two categories are closely interrelated:

(a) general functions

(1) provision of services (water supply, sanitation and health services, etc.)
(2) popular political participation
(3) provision of a convenient channel for expression of interests and grievances
(4) political education, leading to enhanced capacity for effective participation in higher levels of democratic government

(b) structural principles

(5) impartial dispensation and administration of services (as between segments of the community)
(6) impersonal recruitment, evaluation, deployment, etc. of technical or administrative staff (i.e. on the basis of objective standards of qualification and performance)
(7) conciliar processes of decision-making (decisions taken by majority vote of a group of community representatives)

---

policy and the traditional system was a centralized state. In both respects, however, there were significant differences. Consequently, the set of problems involved are not identical, although many points of similarity will be noted by those familiar with those studies.

(8) visibility or accessibility (important decisions normally taken in meetings open to the public at large)

(9) voluntary participation (elected councillors serve without remuneration)

(10) accountability or responsibility (policies and actions of councillors subject to control by the community—assured by means, at the very minimum, of its right periodically to elect the councillors by majority vote)

It may be pointed out that partially corroborative evidence for claiming that this does represent a fair extrapolation can be found in portions of the standard outline of a lecture once given by officials of the Northern government at its *Institute of Administration* to local Native Authority officials being trained to operate a system of local government:

What are the Reasons for Having "Local Government"? The main reasons are:

(a) Flexibility for variations in local conditions (religion and customs)

(b) Local knowledge

(c) Wider representation and participation (democracy)

(d) Confidence of peasants in those they know

(e) Cheaper than central services

(f) Local laws (rules and orders)

(g) Training in "government"

(h) Local desires are made more articulate[3]

The nature of the traditional political system of an emirate is at odds in many respects with these functions and purposes, which will already be obvious to the reader from many observations I have made. It will be useful, however, to note specific points of conflict in relation to the above summary list of functions and principles. But at the outset, one very fundamental discrepancy should be noted that is not immediately apparent from a more detailed comparison of specific features.

This concerns the emirates' original identity as quasi-sovereign states and related to the reality that the state as a form of political organization possesses certain distinctive characteristics which would seem to be wholly alien to local government in the usual sense. These crucial differences lie in the scope of authority, the basis of legitimacy,

---

[3] Institute of Administration, *Lecture Notes* (Series 1959), L. G. (59)79, p. 4.

and the range of functions involved, respectively. Thus Gabriel Almond has suggested that it is fundamental to the nature of the state that its authority is "ultimate, comprehensive, and legitimate".[4] These terms do apply to the authority embodied in the traditional Hausa-Fulani kingdoms, with the one possible qualification presented by their (now distant) relationship of ultimate allegiance to Sokoto. Such terms characterize the accepted authority of an emir in relation to the masses of his subjects. For these subjects traditionally there was no recognized source of appeal beyond that authority, and indeed, no specified limitations at all concerning the political objectives an emir might pursue or sanction. Legitimacy derived de facto from effective conquest and de jure from the binding force of religious obligation. By definition and in reality, the emirate's authority normally constituted the last resort of all political action.

None of these attributes is associated with the authority of any unit of local government, as local government is known in Britain. British units of local government typically came into being in response to certain specific problems and definite needs of local communities, a development that was stimulated by the circumstance that existing higher authorities either would not so respond or could not, it was felt, do so as effectively. The scope of such local government is anything but "comprehensive" and there is nothing "ultimate" about its claim on the community's loyalty. On the contrary, modern British local government characteristically operates on what Fred G. Burke rightly designates as the principle of ultra vires, according to which any exercise of its powers, except in connection with the performance of the specific functions legally permitted or allocated to it by the central political authority, is illegal. Whereas the legal and political efficacy of the traditional state or emirate inheres in its claim to be superior virtually to any other possible source of authority, that of any British-type unit of local government normally resides merely in its being authorized to carry out certain well-delimited duties or functions by a superior authority which has acknowledged or decided for some reason that for it to do so (and to do so in a particular way) is desirable.

In the case of the Hausa-Fulani kingdoms, it is true that these characteristic attributes of the state had been qualified further by

[4] Gabriel A. Almond, "Comparative Political Systems", in *The Journal of Politics*, Vol. 18 (August 1956), pp. 392-93, cited by Roy C. Macridis, "Interest Groups in Comparative Analysis" (same journal), Vol. 23 (February 1961), p. 30.

their subordination to the colonial power, which assigned or allowed them to exercise powers as it saw fit. Yet the colonial relationship did not actually result in the emirates being reduced, so far as their internal political constitution was concerned, to a position comparable to that of local government units in relation to a modern central government. The reason for this was simply that the colonial power used them *as states*, that is, it fully exploited the state-like quality of their authority—a point Miss Mair observes apropos of British colonial practice generally: " . . . the native authorities were not treated as local authorities in current sense of the word—that is bodies responsible for providing a defined range of public services and endowed with such legislative and executive powers as are essential for this purpose—but as miniature states, in which all the functions of the state were exercised subject to the supervision and control of the superior authority".[5] To this statement might be added the comment that in the emirates the colonial power had deliberately and with great success encouraged the population under the jurisdiction of Native Authorities to regard the latter precisely with the full awe and deference belonging to a sovereign executive.

Attention has been drawn to this theoretical nuance because it takes on highly practical significance in the context of the basic assumption that a system of modern local government could successfully be constructed in the emirates on the institutional foundations of traditional government. Indeed, it helps us to see why if for no other reason fundamental difficulties would inevitably arise over any attempt to do so. Inherent in the ultra vires concept as it applies to local government is the idea that the potential intervention of some central authority assures that local institutions will function strictly within their sphere of competence and in accordance with certain principles. Clearly such external restraints on local institutions are sheer anathema to the lofty pretensions of the authority of a state, and hence potentially subversive of the traditional authority of an emirate. It might be argued that both the suzerain of Sokoto in pre-European times and afterwards the colonial power formally occupied a position similar to that of the regional government in relation to individual emirates, but there was nonetheless a crucial departure involved in the latter relationship. The difference was that the regional government enjoyed its powers of intervention in relation to matters expressly set forth in a legal document, hence the respective respon-

[5] Mair, "Representative Local Government", p. 14.

sibilities of the local and central authorities were not determined in the essentially ad hoc fashion which formerly obtained. The theoretical restrictions operating on the Native Authorities, in other words, were more precisely defined, more fixed, and thus also more liable to strict observance.

The ever-present problem for the policy-makers, given its policy of preserving traditional authority, was the danger that actually enforcing such controls and restraints as were provided for in law might in effect undermine the *mystique* of state authority on which the emirate system rested.

Admittedly the importance popularly attached to any institution of modern local government may be diminished through overindulgence in control from above, whether or not the unit in question was originally a state in the sense indicated here. Apprehension about this is a common feature of center-locality relationships within modern Western democracies whose local units are of no such derivation. Implicit in the remarks of policy-makers in Northern Nigeria, however, was that their fears on this score had a more profound source and extended much further than is ordinarily the case. In the last analysis, their anxiety stemmed from the realization that one of the bona fides of traditional authority in the emirates was its claim to finality. To detract from that claim through open intervention was to run the risk that the peasant "subjects" of that authority might eventually see no reason to obey it. The more government intervened the more hastened might be the day when it would have to either supplant traditional institutions with a more effective (but "artificial") local system or employ "direct" or central authority—which were precisely the alternatives the policy-makers sought at all costs to avoid. One can therefore well understand why these policy-makers, like the colonial regime before them, always seemed to regard maintaining the appearance, even more than the substance, of local autonomy as a sine qua non of reform. To cite one expression of official policy which reflected this ticklish consideration: "Local authorities have responsibility for the maintenance of law and order. Their traditional character ensures for them the support of the vast majority of the people, which enables them effectively to carry out their many duties. Should their authority be substantially reduced by the assumption by the Regional Government of overly close control, that stability would inevitably decline to a dangerous degree".[6]

[6] *Recent Trends and Possible Future Developments in the Field of Local Gov-*

More specific difficulties emerged in trying to associate traditional institutions with the functions of modern democratic local government, which can be partly traced to the original identity of the emirates as states in the sense indicated. The theme occurs from time to time throughout the chapters of this book that are concerned with local government. But having pointed up the general problem, further connections will simply be noted in passing. I now turn to a discussion of points of conflict in relation to the above summary list of the functions and purposes ostensibly underlying the reform of local government in the emirates:

1. *Provision of services*

Providing local services is perhaps the most obvious objective of a system of local government and indeed most students regard that as its special raison d'etre. In any event, in other contexts this normally constitutes the focus of activity and consumes the bulk of time and energy of those concerned with the institution. One scholar has pointed out that, "although the democratic ideology is frequently called upon as a justification for the maintenance of local government in the West, the justification came after local governments evolved to solve specific local problems".[7]

In this sense, the path of evolution of local government in Northern Nigeria was not peculiar, in that local institutions there had assumed the function of administering services long before anyone suggested the goal of democratization. Otherwise any historical parallel breaks down in the face of the reality that this function was added as an afterthought to preexisting objects of government and that it was introduced structurally from above at the behest of an alien colonial regime. But the false analogy was not without influence. It is easy to see how, from the superficial fact that traditional institu-

ernment in the Northern Region of Nigeria, published by authority (Kaduna, 1952), p. 2. It will have occurred to the reader that the issue I have been discussing derives particular relevance from the fact that the nature of the traditional state was autocratic. While the issue is doubtless more acute by virtue of that fact, I would point out that it is clear from the context in which Gabriel Almond and others have attributed the above-mentioned distinctive characteristics to the authority of the state (as against other types of political organization) that they are meant to apply with equal validity to modern democratic states. If they do so apply, the issue would have arisen to some extent even if the traditional emirates had been more constitutional or democratic in character; hence, my deliberate emphasis on the "state" feature of traditional authority as one particular problem that confronted the attempt to reconcile traditional and modern government in Northern Nigeria.

[7] Burke, *Local Government and Politics in Uganda*, p. 314.

tions had already absorbed new technical functions without evident injury to their integrity, it might be inferred that they were capable of assuming any of the broader objectives of a system of modern democratic local government as well. In any event, something like this assumption must have underlain the hopes of sincere proponents of gradualism, and even of scholarly observers who at one time discerned a steady evolutionary development of the emirates toward a modern democratic local government system.[8]

The first of these formerly helpful conditions under colonial rule was that Native Administration services were always executed with the advice and guidance of British personnel in the employ of the government, persons who enjoyed technical qualification and training far beyond that of any of the locally recruited employees of the Native Authorities. The hard if often obscured truth about indirect rule, as it operated in practice, was that in many instances the "Native Authority services" had been such in name only, a situation candidly remarked on by Mr. R. S. Hudson, a Colonial Office official, as late as 1958 in his report: "It would be entirely wrong to imagine that all of these complicated services are in fact being run by the native authorities by which they are 'owned'. Many of them, and this applies to the more modern type of service, have to be partly and sometimes entirely managed by trained Regional staff".[9]

A second painful truth was pointed up by M. G. Smith's study of Zaria emirate under colonial rule; in relation to the broader perspectives of a modern and democratic conduct of local government, its implications are even more sobering than the first. A key to the original successful accommodation of new technical departments within the traditional bureaucracy was that they had been assimilated to traditional concepts and interests. Those same concepts and interests were at odds not only with the norms of colonial government, they were equally, if not more so, with any standards of modern and democratic local government. An excerpt from Smith's *Government in Zazzau* makes the point here:

[8] For example, Cowan, *Local Government in West Africa*, pp. 34, 73, 83.
[9] Provincial Authorities: *Report by the Commissioner* (Kaduna, n.d.), p. 6, para. 17. In the same report, Mr. Hudson warned: "The growth of the native authorities, accompanied by the wishful thinking of many of their supporters, is giving birth to the idea that the Native Authorities can do anything; that they should become more and more independent of the centre. This most dangerous idea has been fostered partly by the lack of knowledge of how the modern part of the native authorities' services work".

In their internal organization each of these new departments tended to repeat the [traditional] system of territorial administration, and most of these departments distributed most of their staff among the territorial districts. These new departmental heads also exercised considerable power to appoint their supporters to the new offices . . . the king . . . was careful to allocate departmental headships to his loyal kinsmen and strong supporters. . . . At the same time the king was concerned to protect his departmental heads from dismissal or punishment on charges of maladministration supported by the British. The departmental heads in turn sought to protect their loyal subordinates, kinsmen and clients, and to increase their own political standing and chances of promotion.

Thus the traditional objectives and practices of political and administrative action penetrated the new departments from the moment of their establishment. In consequence, the technical standards and intentions of the British Administration which introduced these departments have been substantially frustrated. . . .

The establishment and progressive expansion of these technical departments more than made up for the number of offices which had been put in abeyance by territorial reorganization in the initial years of British rule. . . . Such a sudden increase in the number of official employments multiplied the chances of successful political clientage, and thereby increased the participation of aristocratic Fulani whose traditional tenure of certain titles had been interrupted by the elimination of fiefs.[10]

One point requires further attention. Relations between the official of the Native Administration and the subjects of the emir are as poorly defined and regulated as are relations between these officials and the emir himself. This is especially true with regard to the new technical staff. The subject population (*talakawa*) are often ignorant of the powers and duties of the new officials. And since the duties and powers are subject to technical considerations and goals, they are also frequently subject to redefinition and change, so that information about the rights, functions, and authority of officials has to be kept up to date by continuous inquiry. The commoners' ignorance of the matters is coupled with their incapacity to take effective action against officials of any department who act ultra vires; in short, *talakawa* are largely defenseless against N.A. officials.[11]

[10] Smith, *Government in Zazzau*, pp. 231-33.
[11] *Ibid.*, p. 275.

Yet, given the prominent part which providing services admittedly plays in modern democratic local government and the demonstrated receptiveness of the traditional system to that function, this aspect of assumption that the two systems might be fused was perhaps not unreasonable so much as it was either innocent or disingenuous. The same may be said about such surface features of the traditional systems as territorial boundaries and subdivisions, administrative apparatus and staff, organized methods of gathering revenue, the ancillary judicial system, a council for discussing political affairs—all of which helped make the false contention of adaptability seem plausible. If, furthermore, one juxtaposes all the other functions or objectives outlined above with the dynamic features of traditional government (as modified by the impact of colonial rule), the points of incompatibility would seem to be glaring and fundamental.

2. Political participation

For all intents and purposes, the vast majority of the people in an emirate were precluded by the rules of the traditional system from effectively participating in the political process. In the absence of any form of institution of popular representation, the exercise of political power had remained the exclusive preserve of those who held political title and office (*masu-sarauta*). Access to that station was gained by such restrictive criteria as (Fulani) ethnicity, kinship (with royalty or nobility), hereditary vassalage, marriage (with royalty or nobility), and clientage (personal allegiance to persons themselves enjoying one or more of these preceding advantages). Even taking into account that *talakawa* (commoners) were occasionally newly elevated to the class of *masu-sarauta* by virtue of clientage, and after due weight is given the indirect, largely informal political influence wielded by the nonaristocratic class of *Malama* (religious teachers, learned men) and *Imams* (clerics), it remains true that only an insignificant portion of the numerically preponderant *talakawa* at any given time ever attained a politically relevant role, that is, one that had some bearing on the formation of public action and decisions.

3. Grievance articulation

The limited opportunities open to individuals to contract lesser clientage relationships, for example, a *talaka*, or nonofficial, with a minor office-holder, or *mai-sarauta*, did offer some chance for the former to secure protection against oppression (*zalunci*) at the hands of the latter's supporters and subordinates. Thus, while there is evidently some functional similarity between the traditional institution of clientage and the techniques and channels of *interest and grievance articulation* as they exist in a modern democratic system, the similarity is strictly limited. That is, the traditional device tended to be ineffectual in relation to superiors of the client's patron (every patron except the emir necessarily having one or more superiors), and its function was mostly defensive; indeed, to assert his interests and grievances effectively, the *talaka* had not so much to "articulate" as to counterplot, principally by means of gifts to his patron. Hence it was the *talaka*'s ability to pay that established the limits of his clientage opportunities.

4. *Political education for democratic participation*

Concerning political education for democracy at a higher level, the *talaka*'s traditional experience can hardly be viewed as anything else than negative, or irrelevant, especially in view of the lack of any opportunity for independently organized group political activity.

5. and 6. *Impartiality and impersonality*

Impartiality in dispensing and administering services ran afoul of the traditional notion that insofar as was possible and expedient, the amenities and resources at the disposal of a political office-holder should be used to reward the loyal members and supporters of his own lineage at the expense of its opponents. Indeed, the very motive of competition between lineages and dynasties for titles and offices, the rewards and weapons of traditional political power, was necessarily predicated on the acceptance of this assumption. Furthermore, as the above excerpt from Smith's study of Zaria suggests, a main attraction of political power was the pervasive assumption that its object, to put the matter bluntly, was to exact amenities and services from the community, not to dispense them. Characteristically the expectations of the ruled in this respect were not at variance with those of rulers.

As for the principle of *impersonality*, in matters touching technical or administrative staff, it follows from what I have already said that traditional administrative relationships were necessarily characterized by the very opposite quality. The recruitment, promotion, and even deployment of administrative personnel were above all a matter of loyalty to that higher person whose prerogative it was to make appointments to and thus influence tenure of office and/or title. Ultimately this meant an emir, but the exercise of such prerogatives was also "farmed out" to an emir's subordinates, such as department heads or territorial subchiefs, who in turn exercised them in relation to more minor offices under their administrative jurisdiction. Hence, personalism was not a pathological condition; rather it was the normal bond of union connecting a vast and complex network of hierarchical relationships of which the emir was the center and ultimate source.

It would therefore be accurate to say that no member of the traditional bureaucracy, not even those employed in the modern technical departments introduced by the British, could count on performance in the formal functions of his office to determine his fortunes. At the same time, a usual objective in each step of an administrative career was to advance to an office and maybe a title having higher prestige and remuneration.[12] But offices that were superior in these terms usually lay outside the technical functionary's line of work and might not call for the exercise of related skills. Consequently, personal ambition commonly extended beyond relevant occupational spheres. A "successful" career within the traditional bureaucracy was thus often marked by movement across quite diverse vocational lines.[13] For example, despite a chronic shortage of Northern school teachers, that profession had lost an undetermined number through their promotion to a higher *sarauta* (office and title) in some other branch of an N.A. Ironically, both British officers and reform-minded Northerners frequently complained about this in 1959.

[12] This is less true of those who held territorial office partially via familial or hereditary rights. Hereditary subchiefs or district heads (as against purely appointive chieftains) even today regard their office as the ne plus ultra in prestige. In pre-European days, moreover, eligibility for office was more strictly delimited in terms of rank-orders than is the case at present, various categories of persons (e.g. sons of chiefs, royal slaves, free clients) having been eligible to compete only for those offices and titles assigned to their particular status groups as a whole. Otherwise, it is important to note that in contrast to the society's traditional negative attitude toward intergenerational movement between classes and between various lower class occupations, nobility *within* rank-orders, and in more recent times within the ruling bureaucracy as a whole, was positively valued, indeed actively sought.

[13] The case of Alhaji Abubakar, *Dokajin Kano*, is perhaps extreme but illustrative. He began as a teacher in the Kano Middle School, which he eventually became headmaster of. Subsequently he was promoted to the post of Assistant Treasurer of the Native Authority and afterwards to that of Chief Scribe (General clerk). He is currently the District Head of the Gabasawa District of Kano (*Dokaji* being his traditional title). (*Who's Who in the Northern Region Legislature* [Kaduna, 1957], p. 67.) Alhaji Abubakar is a member of the noble Fulani family of Kano called Bornawa, his father having held the office and title of *Waziri*. He is a member of the Emir's Council as well as of the Northern House of Assembly and also sits on the Medical Advisory and Leprosy Boards of the Northern Region.

It is also noteworthy that the administrative organization of each emirate or Native Authority traditionally provided for only a limited number of offices and titles, and that exclusive possession was stipulated—the rule being that each office and title was unique and consecutive (there are several Northerners who hold the title *Magajin Gari*, for example, but at any one time there is only one *Magajin Gari* of Sokoto emirate). Consequently, in order to favor a kinsman or client with an appointment or promotion, it was usually necessary (barring the death of an incumbent) to dispossess someone else (preferably, if not invariably, someone identified with a rival lineage group). Hence personalism and favoritism had negative as well as possibly positive implications for all concerned, for these principles not only determined the opportunities available to office-seekers, they also rendered the successful ones insecure in their position. None (save the emir) enjoyed the assurance of permanency in office during good health and behavior. On the contrary, the traditional administrative system was a "spoils system" par excellence. A change at any echelon of the administrative hierarchy might, and usually did, occasion changes below.

Furthermore, even within solitary lineage groups it was prudent for an office-holder to make repeated demonstrations of his loyalty to the benefactor and protector above him, customarily by presentation of gifts from time to time—or sometimes that equally valued negotiable, information. Implicit in such practices was that the obligations of administrative office did not cease with execution of the duties of the office, but arbitrarily extended to satisfaction of informal and unpredictable demands.

In all these respects, the gulf separating accepted traditional administrative conduct and relationships from the conditions which presumptively prevail in a modern system of local government was all but absolute.

7. Conciliar process of decision-making

Despite superficial similarities of form, modern expectations in this context ran counter to traditional norms and practices. The power position of the emirs in relation to the councils with which they are traditionally associated is a complicated and controversial matter which must be discussed in more detail in a later chapter (Seven). Here the analysis need only be summarized. A conciliar political institution functioned in premodern times; however, it differed from the modern type of local government council in that the emirs, with the possible exceptions of Sokoto and Kano before 1819, could legitimately impose their will against the objections of their councillors, who lacked any constitutional authority to act on their own. In effect, a councillor's writ of responsibility extended only to the privilege of giving advice. In assigning each emir the status at law of "sole Native Authority" the colonial government had sought to confirm what they then thought was the established situation. Hence, despite later suggestions that to insist on conciliar decision-making was merely to reinstate the traditional constitution, a conciliar structure conforming to each would actually be antagonistic; a contradiction in terms.

8. *Visibility*

The related issue of the comparative *visibility of the decision-making process* in the two systems is even more readily disposed of. While modern local government council meetings are normally open to public inspection, those of the emir's *majalisa* (council) are invariably conducted in secret. Since the eternal struggle between hostile dynastic or lineage interests formed the substance of much of the *majalisa*'s deliberations, not only secrecy, but intrigue and conspiracy characterized its atmosphere. In the heydey of indirect rule, the British Resident, or another senior officer, customarily attended in the emir's palace a formal weekly session sometimes held at the Residency, while upon his departure more traditional business continued to be transacted in informal meetings which daily convened in the emir's palace.

9. *The principle of voluntary service*

The traditional notion was that political office should yield wealth as well as rank and prestige; in fact, these were the irreducible motives inspiring the quest for *sarauta*. Membership in the emir's council was synonymous with possession of a *sarauta*; a *sarauta* devoid of economic compensation is understandably regarded by the Hausa as less than useless. For to obtain and retain a *sarauta* customarily entails making substantial outlays to the person who bestows it, an investment which the *mai-sarauta* figures to more than recoup through exercise of various economically rewarding prerogatives of office. From this it follows that if offices and titles "no longer have economic rewards attached to them, they should either cease to be a source of competition or degenerate into *wasa* (play), to which no disciplinary force or importance attached. This is precisely what occurs [in Zaria emirate, about 1950]."[14]

10. *Popular accountability*

That a principle or mechanism of popular accountability could have no place in the traditional scheme of government follows as a matter of course from what has already been said, especially in regard to points 2, 3, 7, and 8.

One further contrasting aspect of modern local government objectives and emirate traditional institutions may be noted and disposed of here. An important assumption compared to more centralized institutions underlying British and other Western polities is that local governments offer certain practical advantages in the way of economy and efficiency. Economies are assumed to result from the superior ability of local institutions to make use of local talent at less cost, to take appropriate account of special community conditions and problems, and to tap local wealth for public purposes. Local government is expected to minimize administrative overhead and maximize exploitation of local resources. The assumption is reflected in the official outline lecture regarding the objects of local government in Northern Nigeria reproduced above.

No empirical means of assessing systematically the relative economy and efficiency of N.A. services against the hypothetical alternative of regional government management of the same services was available. A point that should be made here, however, is that efficiency and economy in local public services appear clearly to have been a secondary consideration in the thinking of the original architects of Native Administration. Lugard's efforts to approximate the living standards and social styles of traditional office-holders is one indication. The heavy dependence of the Native Administration services on the technical expertise and supervision of government personnel, as remarked by Hudson in 1957, was a product of the colonial regime, and is again indicative of the problems on this score.

Other aspects of colonial administration reflect the point, too, but the general reality seems sufficiently clear: that far from passing the test of comparative advantage in economy and efficiency in administering services, it was the performance of the Native Administrations

---

[14] M. G. Smith, *The Economy of Hausa Communites in Zaria* (London: H.M. Stationery Office, 1955), p. 98.

in terms of promoting the political security of the central or colonial authority that primarily mattered to its promotors.

These points of contrast and conflict have been considered in order to make apparent the profound difficulties inherent, so far as the emirates were concerned, in trying to simultaneously change and preserve in the same contexts. Thus, any program seeking to transform an emirate into a system of modern democratic local government would have had to deal with the following critical items: (1) the relationship between the central government and the Native Authorities; (2) the composition of the Native Authority councils; (3) the method of selecting the councillors; (4) the relationship of emirs to councillors; (5) the recruitment, regulation, and condition of service of N.A. employees, with special reference to the problem of nepotism and favoritism; (6) the relationship between local officials and the public, with special reference to the phenomenon of bribery and corruption.

These are in fact the six leading issues around which the whole dilemma of postwar reform of local government in the emirates revolved. With this background and agenda in mind, it will perhaps now be easier to understand the significance and outcome of specific efforts to reform these traditional systems in the period under study.

As LEGAL entities, the Native Authorities were begun in 1933 with the passage of a Native Authority Ordinance which was later superseded by the Ordinance of 1943. Neither law took cognizance of emirs' councils, which existed in every emirate, nor did they envisage conciliar organs at any other level of Native Administration. Under these Ordinances, the terms of the emir and the "Native Authority" were synonymous, as the adjective "sole" prefixed to the latter made abundantly clear. 1947 marked the beginning of a new era, in that the Secretary of State for the Colonies' Despatch of that year explicitly stated for the first time the British government's intention to fashion systems of modern democratic local government. The following year Sir John Macpherson arrived in Nigeria as its new governor and made a much-quoted declaration of intent to "devote my special interest to the problems of local government". But the whole idea had been in the air since Hailey's 1940 report to the Colonial Office. Thus, by the time the despatch appeared, the British administration in Northern Nigeria had already given some thought to how the new line of policy might be squared with the existing commitment to the perpetuity of Native Authority; it had even taken a few halting steps toward that end.

The Northern Provinces Residents' Conference of 1945 hit on the idea of making the village and the district the initial foci of local government development, fostering at that level of Native Administration the semblance of representative conciliar organs which democratization obviously implied. From such councils, the conference asserted, similar "Central Councils might in due course emerge".[15] The proposal was evidently a fair-haired child of gradualism. Its attraction lay in the fact that it allowed the new principle of popular representation to be introduced into the old system without immediately disturbing existing relationships of power and authority— which emanated, of course, from the emir and the bureaucracy he controlled at the center. In rudimentary form, such councils were in some emirates traditional at least at the village level, where village heads had long been accustomed to consulting village elders and notables. At the district level, such councils were traditionally unknown, districts having evolved out of what had been feudal possessions awarded by the emir. At both levels the more broadly representative kind of conciliar institution envisaged by the Residents' Conference represented an innovation, though a modest one. No rules governing the composition or method of selection of these councils were laid down; rather, villages and district heads were informally exhorted by British officers to "admit new blood". No executive powers or source of revenue were assigned to these councils. In fact, a subsequent proposal to advance them beyond the purely advisory stage proved abortive; a Government Circular recommending that the new councils be allocated a small sum of their own to work out of central native treasuries was coolly received by the Native Authorities, and the suggestion was not pressed.[16]

The Residents' and Chiefs' Conference of 1946 included the following among its resolutions: that General Orders for Native Authorities were desirable and should be called Native Authority Staff Regulations—(1) Native Authority Staff Regulations for Native Authorities should be prepared in the Secretariat; (2) where a number of Native Authorities combine to make an administrative unit a board should be appointed to accept responsibility for executive and disciplinary powers to deal with central staff and affairs; (3) Native

---

[15] C. W. Cole, "Village and District Council in the Northern Provinces of Nigeria", in *Journal of African Administration*, Vol. 3, No. 2 (1951), p. 93.
[16] *Ibid.*

Authority Staff Regulations should be issued by the Native Authorities with the approval of the Chief Commissioner.[17]

Rigorously implemented, such a resolution would have nullified the force of personalism within the traditional bureaucracy, a logical step if the Native Administrations were genuinely to achieve standards of modern administration. From previous accounts we know that, just as inexorably, to eliminate personalism would be to undo the mainspring of the entire traditional system. Hence the eventual fate of this proposal would mirror the course of reform as a whole, as we shall see it did. At this stage, the suggestion represented nothing more than that.

The 1947 Despatch and Macpherson's declaration doubtless added a measure of urgency to efforts to revamp the system. Certain proposals were thereafter renewed and extended. The gist of the Residents' and Chiefs' Resolution reappeared in the form of a document entitled "Model Conditions of Service for Native Authority Staff". The term "model" not only conveyed the idea that desirable standards in these matters were definable but also indicated that adherence to them on the part of the N.A. was to be voluntary. The title of the document was later changed to "Regulations Governing the Conditions of Service of Employees of the Native Authority", but the non-mandatory feature was retained. Apart from that qualification in terms of modern administrative criteria, the new code made few substantive inroads. It set up a schedule of grades of employees, with corresponding pay scales, efficiency scales, promotional increments, and the like. But minimal qualifications for entry and advance in the various grades were not established. Perhaps its greatest drawback lay in provisions regarding matters of discipline, which appeared to leave the way open to traditional machinations.[18]

Of these regulations, Abubakar Tafawa Balewa was later to say:

[17] *Summary of Proceedings*, p. 9.
[18] Section 2, Paragraphs 28-40. (a) The circumstances that might give rise to immediate interdiction seemed vaguely defined, i.e. when "the native authority considers that the public interest requires it". (b) Furthermore, in such cases, the N.A. could withhold as much as one-half the employees' pay, pending the outcome of an investigation. (c) The proceedings for these investigations, which could result in dismissal, were also loosely conceived, e.g. "The dismissal of an employee *may* be referred to a Disciplinary Committee [emphasis mine]—whose independent status was not provided for. (d) What protections in the nature of due process the rules did offer seemed largely negated by Paragraph 40: "If upon considering the report of the Committee the Native Authority is of opinion that the employee does not deserve to be dismissed, but that the proceedings disclose grounds for removing him on account of general inefficiency, it may remove him accordingly".

94

"They have been called 'model', Sir, and we do not know when they will become real. The Native Administration employees whom the model Regulations are to serve have no idea that they exist, and, Sir, though I do not wish to make a detailed criticism of the regulations as they stand, still I must point out, Sir, that they fall very short of our expectations".[19]

In 1948 something called the "outer council" made its appearance in Bornu Emirate, the forerunner of similar bodies throughout the upper North. The outer council, a name inspired by the desire to distinguish it clearly from the "inner" or emir's council, was conceived as the central counterpart of the new councils at the village and district levels. Unlike the latter, however, the outer council could only grow beyond the initial stage of an advisory organ at the expense of the emir's council's power, the persistence and expansion of which made the eventual atrophy of the outer council inevitable.

By contrast, a proposal to provide district councils with funds was again put forward, and in 1949 it was put into effect on a nominal scale; roughly two-pence per local taxpayer was allotted out of the central N.A. revenue. This sum permitted district councils to assume modest projects like constructing market stalls, wells, repair of rural feeder roads, and maintenance of local public buildings, which were formerly duties of local agents of the N.A. About the same time, the first Development Secretaries (later called Local Government or Local Government and Development Secretaries) were appointed. The primary functions of this new post, which came under central N.A. jurisdiction, were at first defined as guidance and supervision of the work of the new councils, i.e. physical development; later the emphasis was placed on democratic development. A not entirely incidental boon, from the point of view of the central N.A. authority, was that Development Secretaries naturally strengthened its grip on local affairs.

In early 1950 the Native Authority Ordinance was amended to make it possible for Native Authorities to appoint committees to deal with matters they might be willing to delegate, as well as "joint committees" that might coordinate some of the work of two or more neighboring Native Authorities. The decision to make use of this amendment was again left up to the Native Authorities themselves.

[19] *House of Assembly Debates*, 11th December 1950, p. 112.

Until 1950 a remarkable aspect of these stirrings in the field of local administration was that official actions alone had induced them, especially remarkable if one bears in mind the internal political ferment then surrounding the subject in other African territories. As it later emerged, a small number of Northerners had been very much concerned with many of the issues at stake. For example, one Malam Abubakar Imam had poured out his criticism of Native Administration in private letters to the retired Lugard; also thinking about these matters were the members of clandestinely political "friendly societies" and "discussion circles" (which had cropped up in several Northern centers), who were, however, constrained to keep their own counsel. But apart from such glimmerings, outwardly the North seemed to be living up to that reputation for tranquility which had long earned the high marks of many observers, British colonial officials not least among them.

In fact, the apparent concord had long served to justify the rationale of indirect rule; it now reinforced the policy of gradualism in local government. That is, both policies leaned heavily on the argument that the ultimate proof of the worth and legitimacy of the traditional political system was its evident "acceptability" in the eyes of the ordinary mass of subjects, a recurrent theme in both official literature and commentaries.[20] The reliability of such a test, however, turns on the procedure by which "acceptability" was defined and established. It takes no feat of reasoning to perceive that in the absence of institutionalized channels through which the popular judgment could be peacefully and periodically expressed, the only available test of "acceptability" boiled down to whether or not the peasants were on the point of, if not in a state of, physical revolt. But considering the impressive coercive apparatus at the disposal of traditional authority, and the virtual defenselessness of the peasantry in the face of it (of which Smith speaks), an element of self-fulfilling prophecy was inherent in these policies. The distribution of power in the system tended to thwart the exercise of the only means of protest the system afforded, while the absence of protest was taken as a mark of its soundness.

Thus, when on August 19, 1950 Abubakar Tafawa Balewa

[20] Perham, *Native Administration in Nigeria*; Sir Donald Cameron, *Principles of Native Administration and Their Application*, Lagos, 1934, *passim*; *Provincial Annual Reports*, Northern Nigeria; R. E. Robinson, "Why 'Indirect Rule' Has Been Replaced by 'Local Government' in the Nomenclature of British Native Administration", in *Journal of African Administration* (April 1950), pp. 12ff.

launched a frontal attack on the state of Native Administration in the Northern House of Assembly, his setting was dramatic and his opening remarks captured the moment:

> Mr. President, Sir, first I must crave the indulgence of the House and make my apologies to you, Sir, for constantly referring to my notes. My line is direct and the words I have written are frank; and I consider the motion of such fundamental importance that I can take no risk of missing one point or of weakening one statement by impromptu diversions into which I might be led by the strength of my feeling. You will see that the motion concerns the North alone; and as the other Regions are dealing with the same Problem in their own way, I hope I shall not be called upon to move this resolution in the Legislative Council: for it is here and now that a remedy for our disease must be found and applied with the least possible delay.
>
> Let there be no misunderstanding. I have no axe to grind and wish for no heads to roll in the gutters. I do not wish to destroy; I call for reform.

Balewa's formal motion called upon the government to appoint an independent commission of inquiry.[21] In retrospect, the substance of the motion is overshadowed in significance by the content of the supporting speech, which struck at almost all the critical issues— popular participation, the position of the emirs and the N.A. staff, the relationship between regional and local authority, the composition of the Native Administration Councils, bribery and corruption. Certain portions are so illuminating for my purposes as to warrant citing verbatim. On the role of the peasants, Balewa complained:

> . . . in practice in the past their views have never been sought, their welfare seldom regarded and their helplessness shockingly abused. And in the Native Authority Ordinance they hardly find a place. Far from the chiefs having well-defined duties, one of the biggest defects of the system is the complete ignorance of everyone from

[21] "Be it resolved that this House respectfully recommends to His Excellency the Governor that he be pleased to appoint as Independent Commission to investigate the system of Native Administration in the Northern Provinces and to make recommendations for its modernization and reform; and that the Northern public be given the fullest opportunity to discuss and criticize the report and the recommendations of the Commission before their final acceptance by the Governor". These remarks, as well as the quotes following, are taken from Northern Nigeria, H. C. Debates, August 19, 1950, p. 4 of the speech.

top to bottom about his rights, his obligations and his powers. This ignorance must somehow be removed and the people made to realize that they too have a share in their own government. First, it is necessary for everyone in authority to understand that he is a public servant, fed and clothed by the public and to act accordingly. . . . The illiterate mass of the people recognize no change in their status since the coming of the British. They are still ruled by might and administration is still none of their concern. . . . And for their part they should understand that the North enjoys freedom of speech and freedom of action within the law. It is not so today.

In the administrative area, Balewa drew attention to the structure of official recruitment and the official career, arguing that "improvement is impossible as long as Native Authorities continue in the practice of putting square pegs in round holes". He suggested that the Sole Native Authority was based on conceptions that were nontraditional and un-Islamic, as well as out of tune with current precepts, and proclaimed for all these reasons that "democratisation of Native Authority Councils has now become a necessity". But his most trenchant words were reserved for the last of his targets:

Finally, Sir, I come to the sting in the tail. One feature of Native Administration above all demands the immediate attention of the Commission. It is as all of you are well aware, the twin curses of bribery and corruption which pervade every rank and department. It is notorious, Sir, that Native Administration servants have monetary obligations to their immediate superiors and to their sole Native Authorities. It would be unseemly for me to particularise further but I cannot overemphasize the importance of eradicating this ungodly evil. *No one* [Balewa's emphasis] who has not lived among us can fully appreciate to what extent the giving and taking of bribes occupies the attention of all degrees to the exclusion of the ideals of disinterested service. Much of the attraction of a post lies in the opportunities it offers for extortion of one form or another. Unless the Commission fully realizes the gravity of this problem, and tackles it with courage, any recommendations they make for superficial reforms are bound to fail. It is a most disturbing fact that few officials can afford to be honest.

There was one other notable aspect of Balewa's speech, the part concerning the relationship of traditional and new elites. For despite

Balewa's uncompromising assault on the abuses he alleged, and despite his seemingly implicit avowal of faith in democratic norms, his remarks on that score offered a glimpse of an incipient groping on the part of the humbly born but educated "critics" (whom Balewa epitomized) for a modus vivendi with the aristocracy whose deputies largely made up his audience: "The Natural Rulers of the North should realize that Western education and world conditions are fast creating a new class of people in the North. That this new class must exist is certain, and the Natural Rulers, whom the North must retain at all costs, should, instead of suspecting it, try to find it proper accommodation. . . . I . . . personally prefer to see such changes coming first from the Natural Rulers rather than from the new class. Things are rapidly changing and much trouble and bitterness could be avoided if those in high positions of authority would keep their eyes open and agree to move with the time."

Practically all the activities in reform over the next few years may be traced to points in Balewa's historic speech. It will be appreciated, however, that the prospect of "outsiders", i.e. nonofficial British and nonnative officials coming in to help investigate[22] (which would have entailed direct intercourse with the peasantry) and then to make recommendations on democratization a priori, was thoroughly repugnant to all the canons of accepted policy. Thus, notwithstanding the fact that Balewa's motion carried,[23] the government (then wholly British) simply ignored the motion's express reference to an independent commission.

In lieu of investigative activities on the part of the proposed commission, the government assigned two District Officers to conduct a survey of existing conditions in Native Administration, while residents were instructed to set up provincial conferences to recommend appropriate actions. In other words, the controversies were to be aired entirely within the system. In fact, the Resident's instructions stipulated that the "convenors and prime movers" of the conferences should be the Native Authorities themselves.[24] These two moves re-

[22] Balewa proposed to include in his Commission a Professor of Political Science from an English university, someone with "up-to-date knowledge" of local government in East Africa, and "a trusted friend of the North"—he proposed Dr. Walter Miller, the missionary and critic of indirect rule!

[23] By a vote of 20 to 19, with all of the officials on the nay side and all voting nonofficials on the affirmative side, the first and only time this was to occur in the phase of parliamentary experience under colonial rule in the North.

[24] Other noteworthy stipulations were that the conferences were to be divided into separate sessions, one consisting of emirs, councillors, and other high officials,

sulted in the publication of the Maddocks-Pott Report, and a series of unpublished Resident's Reports. These provided working materials for a Joint Select Committee of the Northern Regional Council, whose recommendations, in turn, established the framework for the principal reforms that were implemented in the field of local government under the parliamentary regime. The major resulting innovations were redefinition of the status of chiefs, abolition of the Sole Native Authorities, and the Customary Presents Order. The committee also made suggestions concerning the proper composition for the various new councils, appropriate functions, and principles for delegating funds to them, and was instrumental in having the staff regulations drawn up.

The initial formal step in abolishing the Sole Native Authorities was the passage of a resolution, moved, significantly, by the Sultan of Sokoto, and followed by the enactment of the Native Authority (Definition of Functions) Law (in July 1952), which set forth the principles that were henceforth to govern the relationship between chiefs and councillors. The law provided for the existence of a wide variety of forms of Native Authority,[25] but the distinction it drew between (1) a chief and council and (2) a chief-in-council primarily concerns us here. In brief, the position of chiefs who came under the chiefs-and-council arrangements was to be a straightforward "constitutional one"; that is, they were to be bound by the majority vote of their councillors in all matters. This form generally fit prevailing political customs and institutions in the nonemirates, or southern areas of the Northern Region. The chief-in-council was conceived with the emirates in mind, although the law made a transition from that status to that of chief and council possible. The salient feature of the chief-in-council idea was this: an emir-in-council was obliged to consult with his councillors, but he could override them, provided that the Resident and ultimately the Governor was informed, and the latter chose not to intervene in the dispute in question. The law made no attempt to characterize circumstances which might give rise to such intervention, but from the form and wording of the relevant pro-

---

the other of a "larger and more representative" group, and that, in the latter instance "membership should tend to be by invitations from above . . . rather than by election from below". Circular No. 47946, dated September 29, 1950, from the Secretary, Northern Provinces.

[25] (a) Any chief or other person; (b) any chief or other person associated with a council either—(1) as a chief or other person in council, (2) as a chief or other person and council; (c) any council; (d) any group of persons.

cedure, it seems that a presumption of exoneration was intended to lie with the emir.[26] It is noteworthy that in the only recorded instance of an emir's having exercised a formal veto over his council under this provision, the government supported the emir.[27]

It is interesting that at this stage of development the "critics" among Assembly members were still vocal, and did not conceal their disparaging opinion of the evidently meager degree of democratic advance brought to pass by this change.[28]

The session of the House of Chiefs which resolved to do away with Sole Native Authority also went on record against "the twin evils of bribery and corruption", this time on a motion by M. Yahaya, Emir of Gwandu, which confirmed Balewa's estimate of the depth of the problem.[29] A special committee was formed, and its report illumi-

[26] "Whenever the chief acts otherwise than in accordance with the advice of council—

(a) he shall report the matter to the Governor or to the Divisional Officer for transmission to the Governor at the earliest opportunity, with the reasons for his action, and

(b) any member of the council may require that there be recorded in the minutes of the council any advice or opinion which he may give upon the question with the reasons therefore: When the Governor receives such a report he shall either:

(a) inform the chief that he does not intend to intervene, or

(b) call upon the chief to consult with the council further upon the question and if, after further consultation, the chief still considers it expedient for the purposes aforesaid that he should not act in accordance with the advice of the council, the Governor shall either:

(1) inform the chief in council that he does not intend to intervene further, or

(2) give such directions as he may deem expedient and the native authority shall comply with the direction of the Governor".

[27] In fact, in this instance government administrative officers had advised the emir to use his veto power. The incident occurred during 1957 in the Ilorin emirate; see *Provincial Annual Reports* for 1957, p. 54.

[28] Among those who severely criticized the report of the Joint Select Committee were M. Yakubu Wanka, M. Ladan Baki, M. Ahmadu Pategi, M. Abba Habib, and, of course, M. Ibrahim Imam. M. Yakubu Wanka is reported as having said that, "the present proposition to have Emir-in-Council changes nothing (cheers from some Members). It [is] very unsatisfactory and designed to suit N.A.'s and the Government. It does not satisfy us". M. Abba Habib, who later became General Secretary of the NPC and a Regional Minister (he, like all the above-mentioned, was also an employee of a Native Administration; the others were likewise NPC members), demanded that the report be rejected and debated further in the House. (See *Nigerian Citizen*, July 10, 1952, Supplement 1.) Balewa's own tone was mellowing noticeably: "Reforms that would disturb the happiness of the mass of the people should be rejected. I would like the House to accept the Report as a working basis". See Appendix A for profiles of these critics: Nos. 6, 3, 15, 106.

[29] "That this House, agreeing that bribery and corruption are widely prevalent in all walks of life, recommends that Native Authorities should make every effort to trace and punish offenders with strict impartiality and to educate public opinion against bribery and corruption". *House of Chiefs Debates*, February 26, 1952.

nated the fundamental implications of most "customary gifts". For example, on the tradition of exchanging presents on the occasion of Salla (the Muslim religious festival of *idl-fitr*, sometimes referred to as the *Lesser Beiram*), it pointed out that in order to fulfill his traditional obligations, the emir ordered his district heads to make requisitions from village heads, who solicited the hamlet heads, who made levies on the peasants. Since each of these subordinates were also expected to distribute largesse (the capacity to do so was also a sign of his political prospects), each exacted more than was forwarded to his superior. "It is clear", the report concluded, "that in the ultimate analysis the *talakawa* pay for everything".[30]

The Customary Presents Order followed. The pertinent excerpts from the order are included (in Appendix B) because they best document the myriad forms of corruption with which reformers inside and outside of government in Northern Nigeria were called upon to grapple. The Order itself had an uncertain impact. The categories of prohibited practices it embraced were very comprehensive and to the point,[31] although it should be noted that the Emir Yahaya, the originator of the legislation, refused to give his assent on the grounds that permitting exchanges of gifts on "family occasions" such as "the marriage of the chief or district head or village head or of a child of a chieftain [etc.]" furnished a new guise for continuation of the old offenses. More seriously, it might be said of the Order that it contained the seeds of its own innocuousness. M. G. Smith's account of the meaning and effect of this whole development is as follows: "In 1950 charges were being made quite openly that the Native Administration in the Northern emirates was corrupt. The British Administration was disturbed by such allegations. Finally, the Northern House of Chiefs established a committee to consider such malpractices. The conclusion reached by this committee revealed a wisdom like unto Solomon's. They decided that henceforward punishment for bribery and

---

[30] *Report on the Exchange of Customary Present* (Kaduna, 1954), p. 6.
[31] "All gifts and presents of all kinds passing to and from or between:
A. chiefs and their people
B. district heads and their people
C. village heads and their people
D. chiefs, district heads, and village heads and any of them
E. native authority officials and members of the public
F. officials of native authorities (other than subordinate native authorities) and subordinate native authority officials
G. superiors and inferiors as defined in this order"
First Schedule, N.R.L.N. 28 of 1955, p. 3.

other similar forms of corruption should fall equally on all parties involved. Thus, he who offers the bribe and he who takes it would suffer alike. This ruling put an end to further complaints of official corruption, and was heralded in Britain as a fundamental attempt by the Northern rulers at self-reform.[32]

While the deliberate effort to contain the political flux and controversy within the walls of the Northern household met with considerable success, the process of forging a common political institutional framework for Nigeria as a whole inevitably had implications for the plan of realizing continuity within change in the emirates. In particular, the proposal to introduce a ministerial system of government in each of the regions added complications to that perpetually delicate question of the relationship of the Northern regional government to the emirate Native Authorities. At the 1950 General Conference on Review of the Constitution, the Northern delegates, while giving their blessings to "the experiment" of putting executive powers in the hands of elected ministers in the south, pleaded that the North should be exempted from it for the time being. Throughout the conference they remained adamant in their resistance to pressures from southern spokesmen to alter their stand.[33] They finally gave in for the sake of keeping step with this fundamental, national constitutional advance. The remarks of the Northern delegates left unclear precisely what their objection was, but plainly it stemmed from anxieties about the possible consequences for the local political order. Ministers seemed to imply persons in direct authority over emirs, and the duty to control, hence potentially to intervene in, such local affairs as concerned the business of the ministers.

Feelings came out in the open, when within a few months of the inauguration of the new constitution the perennially testy Mallam Ibrahim Imam tabled a motion calling for the addition of a minister of local government to the Regional Executive Council! The government brought its full weight to bear and the motion was defeated.[34] It appears in retrospect that the government came to regard the defeat of

[32] *Government in Zazzau*, pp. 278-79. The recommendation to which Smith refers can be found in *Report on the Exchange of Customary Presents* (Kaduna, 1953), Para. 31, p. 7. See Appendix II for how the wording of the Order accomplishes the intentions of the committee in this regard.

[33] See *Proceedings*, esp. pp. 20-31, 67-68, 87, 96, 112.

[34] By vote of 56 to 25. M. Abba Habib and M. Yakubu Wanka were again among the "critics" who voted against the government; M. Abubakar Tafawa Balewa, now Central Minister of Transport, abstained. See *House of Assembly Debates*, July 7, 1952, pp. 26-33.

the motion as something of an embarrassment, because the action was thought by some to reflect on the government's ability to govern. Also, the younger more radically inclined elements within the Northern Peoples' Congress were pressing for a revision of the policy.[35]

Within a year the government itself successfully sponsored a bill to introduce the post, explaining that it was reversing its previous position, "because the matter has been approached from a different angle; because since that time there have been rapid developments in the field of Local Government; and because we can now see how the duties of a Minister for Local Government can be clearly and more narrowly defined, that the Government considers that there is a useful part for such a Minister to play.[36]

The last reason given confirmed the original misgivings about the scope of authority of such a position, or the severe restrictions on local autonomy it might give rise to. It also indicated the way in which the government proposed to resolve the potential impasse. A recent government white paper had similarly given an indication in stating that, "if any single Regional Minister were to be associated with local government . . . the large measure of autonomy enjoyed in accordance with accepted principles by Native Authorities must be preserved".[37] The insipid character of the functions the government now laid down for this ministry was clearly in keeping with the dictum.[38] Lest there be any doubt about what was meant by "accepted principles", the Civil Secretary asserted specifically that: "A Minister for Local Government would not, under any circumstances —(a) give orders to Native Authorities as to the management of their affairs, (b) concern himself in any way with the appointment or removal of Native Authority Office Holders or staff, still less with appointment, etc., of Chiefs, (c) interfere in the day-to-day administra-

---

[35] *Nigerian Citizen*, April 4, 1952, p. 1.

[36] *House of Chiefs Debates*, February 14, 1953, p. 76.

[37] *Recent Trends and Possible Future Developments in the Field of Local Government in the Northern Region*, p. 4.

[38] (a) To tour and observe the progress and development of N.A. Councils and Committees to report thereon to the Executive Council, (b) to carry the suggestions of the Lieutenant-Governor and his Executive Council to individual Native Authorities, (c) to carry ideas from Province to Province and from Native Authority to Native Authority in order that the new ideas and the experience of individual Native Authorities may be made available to all, (d) to encourage and advise in those areas where the Local Government system is backward and organization weak, (e) to let the public in this country and elsewhere know of the progress that we are making. This is most important for the peace and contentment of the Region and, more important still, for its reputation elsewhere. See *House of Chiefs Debates*, February 14, 1953, p. 76.

tion of the Native Authorities at any level, (d) concern himself with complaints against Native Authorities or their office-holders".[39]

Such definitions of ministerial power naturally were reassuring to most emirs who, led by the Sultan of Sokoto, now endorsed the revised innovation. (The Emir of Kano was a notable exception.) Revealingly, the late Emir of Zaria, Malam Ja'afaru, fixed the status of the prospective minister in his own mind by likening him to the traditional figure of the Waziri of Sokoto who customarily advised and represented the Sultan "but did not consider himself superior". "We used to say that Waziri was the ambassador of the Sultan, so this Minister", Ja'afaru concluded, "will be a sort of ambassador or messenger".[40] In this light, the choice of the reigning Sultan's cousin, the Sardauna of Sokoto as the first occupant of the new post must have seemed to Ja'afaru, and no doubt others, as singularly propitious.[41] (The English student of African politics, Thomas Hodgkin, remarked apropos of the Sardauna's appointment that it was "rather as though in England of the 1830's, the Marquis of Herfford had been made Minister of Local Government, on the distinct understanding that he was not to touch the Justices of the Peace!"[42])

Several further minor developments, which came about during the period through administrative action rather than by formal legislation or resolution, should be noted. In 1953 the government advised Native Authorities that they should no longer include *Alkalai* (Native Court Judges) in the membership of N.A. councils, in deference to the accepted modern political principle that executive and judicial authority should be separate.[43] Similarly the government demurred

---

[39] *Ibid.*

[40] *Ibid.*, p. 78.

[41] The Sardauna comments on this episode in his autobiography, as follows: "After many searchings of hearts and with much doubt a Ministry of Local Government was created in that same April. The other Regions had had such Ministries for some time, but Sir Bryan Sharwood-Smith, then Lieutenant-Governor, Northern Nigeria was uncertain of the effect such a Ministry and would have on the great Emirs. In the end, however, they took it in stride as a necessary coordinating body". Ahmadu Bello, *Autobiography*, p. 95.

[42] "Disraeli on Northern Nigeria", *West Africa* (May 9, 1953), p. 413.

[43] There is evidence to indicate that the Emir's Council had traditionally been wholly judicial in its focus. In 1943, for example, the district officer in charge of Katagum Division of Bauchi Province wrote to his Resident that, "The Emir's Councils here are still based on the idea of the judicial council and their functions are in practice solely those of Native Courts". (No. 2257/7, July 9, 1943, deposited in the Archives, Kaduna.) To the extent that this was true, the observation serves to reinforce the conclusion that the recent assumption of executive powers by Native Authority councillors is a departure from, not a reassertion of, the traditional pattern.

from prescribing by law the composition of N.A. Councils, but it had for some time been urging the Native Authorities to admit some educated nonpatrician elements to their ranks. Tafawa Balewa himself owed his appointment in 1946 to the Council of the Emir of Bauchi to this effort. It is estimated that by 1950 nearly all Native Authority Councils included at least one literate member.[44] Following Balewa's motion, recruiting educated traditionally low-status members by the process of cooptation was accelerated, although almost everywhere such members continued to comprise at best a small minority of N.A. councillors. In like vein, Native Administrations were increasingly encouraged to allot more responsibilities and funds to district and village councils. Late in 1953 the government announced that it would convert the Clerical Training College at Zaria into an Institute of Administration which would add to previous training functions that of acquainting N.A. officials with modern democratic government.

Measures in the delicate area of urban local government should also be noted. Recognizing that internal pressures for democratization were likely to come faster and more insistently in the towns, the government appointed a special committee to study and advise on urban local government policy. The report of the committee,[45] emphasized the propriety of relatively liberal policies in regard to popular representation (e.g. property qualifications were ruled out) and delegation of functions and financial responsibility (i.e. relative to current practices with respect to rural village and district councils).[46] It also outlined a plan by which town councils should progress by stages to a point of substantial autonomy from the Native Authority. On the other hand, from the point of view of these councils' ultimate growth into effective organs of democratic local government, some of the recommendations of the committee imposed some important restrictions, all of which were adopted. The first of these was that the President of the Town Council should be nominated by the Native Authority and should usually be the district head of the district in which the town was located. Second, the Native Authority, through the President, could exercise a veto on the decisions of the

[44] *Lecture Notes*, Institute of Administration, p. 9.
[45] *Report of the Committee on the Future Administration of Urban Areas* (Kaduna: Government Printer), 1953.
[46] The stages of development suggested were: (a) establishment of Town Council with delegation of financial responsibility; (b) Town Council to become subordinate Native Authority preparing own budget incorporated in Native Authority estimates; (c) subordinate Native Authority to have own separate estimates.

council. Third, all staff concerned with carrying out the functions of the council would "belong" to the central N.A. and would "be supervised by the President in accordance with the decisions of the council, which would, however, have no control over appointments, promotion, or dismissals". Finally, as in previous cases, the decision as to when, whether, and to which areas any or all of the committee's recommendations would apply, was left to the discretion of the central Native Authority. (Similar principles were already operative in relation to the rural councils.)

Some General Observations

It is possible to discern a pattern running through these various developments, proposals, procedures, and actions in the name of reform in the period just reviewed. The pattern consists of certain principles or artifices on the basis of which the government systematically went about local government reform under the label of gradualism. One of them may be identified as the separation of power and participation; instead of placing the central Native Authority Councils (which had extensive legal, administrative, financial, and staff resources) on a popular representative footing, opportunities for participation by the heretofore politically inert and locally disenfranchised peasants was largely circumscribed at the level of subunits, where the new representative councils lacked resources and operated under central N.A. surveillance. As the Minister of Local Government put it in 1960, such councils operated "in miniature and without doing irreparable harm by mistakes".[47]

A second such principle can be characterized as voluntary initiative or permissive guidance. Institutional innovations, which were conducive to the achievement of the major objectives and principles of a system of modern democratic local government but potentially disruptive of traditional institutions, were formulated by the regional government. But each Native Authority was in effect given the right to decide when, whether, or to what extent they should have effect. The device of "model staff regulations" was perhaps a prime example. It will be noticed that in general this principle was an extension of the old colonial conception of traditional authority as simultaneously agent and object of change. The regional government's preference for informal, administrative action (as against institutional or legal change) was implicit in the idea of permissive guidance, which leads

[47] *House of Assembly Debates*, April 26, 1960.

to a third principle: informal government pressure should be brought to bear in proportion to the degree of manifest political unrest or agitation. The stepping up of action in the aftermath of the Balewa speech was an indication of this. This principle also involved a tendency to use the elusive criterion of "accceptability" to set the pace of change.[48] The fundamental thing about all these principles was that each of them served to *avoid* any direct confrontation in the emirates between the norms of modern democratic local government and those of the traditional political system.

The Native Authority Law of 1954

In 1954 a bill promulgating a Native Authority Law to supersede the Native Authority Ordinance of 1943 was introduced and passed in the Northern Legislature. As government spokesmen pointed out, the new law was essentially a compilation and consolidation of previous reforms, a culmination of the developments that had occurred since the war. It may also be said that the guiding principles of reform identified above were also incorporated in the new law. The law did feature certain further modifications, but the Legal Secretary rightly predicted that: ". . . members will search in vain for anything revolutionary in the provision, because what we have sought to do is to build new improvements on to an old structure and to make allowance for other extensions and improvements when we require them".[49]

Specifically, the law confirmed existing arrangements concerning the powers of chiefs vis-à-vis their councils (notably that of "chief-in-council"), the relationship of outer, village, district, and town councils to the central Native Authority, the procedures for establishing Native Authorities and determining their composition. The principal "extensions and improvements" relevant to local government were to be found in Sections 35 and 60 of the law.

Section 60 had to do with the composition of subordinate councils (outer, village, district, and town councils), and the new rule introduced was this: when a Native Authority gave a subordinate council legal status (the technical terminology for this was "establish by instrument"—instrument being the legal document), it was ob-

---

[48] The Minister for Local Government in 1960 revealed the persistence of this attitude in explaining why elected central N.A. councils were not necessarily desirable: "The proof of the pudding", he mused, "is in the eating. The evidence of good local government is to be found in its ability to retain the confidence of the people and its ability to maintain law and order, providing those essential services which the people need and desire". *Ibid.*

[49] *Ibid.*, February 19, 1954, p. 226.

liged to provide that a majority of the members of that council be elected. It should be emphasized here that since there was nothing in the law that required the Native Administrations to promulgate such instruments, Section 60 did not remove the initiative from the Native Administrations; rather it simply established a formal procedure by which the Native Administrations were to democratize their subordinate councils insofar as they saw fit to do so. As the Legal Secretary reassured the House: "It is not intended to create any particular sort of subordinate councils at any particular time for all Native Authorities. Each will develop in its own way at the right time. The only requirement is that when a Local Council is created, elected members shall form a majority on the Council".[50]

In this context, two additional aspects of the law, some practical consequences of which we shall see later, are pertinent. One is the perhaps self-evident fact that the requirement of a majority of elected members left the composition of the remainder of any subordinate council to the discretion of the central N.A.; the other is that under the law the right to prescribe the method of election was likewise consigned to the central N.A.[51]

Section 35 provided that all appointments of Native Authority office-holders at a salary of £350 per year or more (the minimum figure was later amended to £390) were subject to the written approval of the governor—a power later delegated to the Premier, as eventually were most important powers of approval exercised by the government.

This brings us to a significant feature of the N.A. law as a whole, namely its bearing on the relationship of the central government and Native Authority. The essential point has already been noted: that the law provided for a variety of legal controls over the affairs of the N.A.; but the point deserves to be reiterated and emphasized. In fact, a reading of the law correctly gives the impression that theoretically the regional government can make, break, or dictate the policies of Native Authorities in every important area of administration of government, individually or in a group.[52] The conclusion to be

[50] *Ibid.*, p. 227.

[51] Section 38, Para. 19 and Section 60, Para. 1. The section numbers refer to the revised edition of the Native Authority law. See *The Laws of Northern Nigeria*, Chap. 77, Native Authority, Rev. Edn. (Kaduna, 1965).

[52] The relevant controls are dispersed throughout the law, but can be summarized as follows: the power to constitute and appoint Native Authorities and their councillors (Sections 3, 4, 6, 16, 20, 21, 24), powers over financial affairs (Sections 81, 91, 92, 93-104), staff (Sections 35, 36), in relation to internal disputes (Sec-

drawn from this is not that the autonomy and power of the Native Authorities are unreal, but that they are a product of deliberate political volition on the part of the regional government rather than the necessary consequence of the law in force.

It is merely a seeming paradox, then, that the law also strengthened the power and overall political role of the Native Authorities in several respects—the loosening of restrictions on certain classes of Native Treasuries, formalizing the strictly advisory role of administrative officers,[53] and the inclusion under the jurisdiction of the Native Administrations of persons formerly not subject to them. Other instances are the several provisions that tightened the Native Administrations' power of discipline in relation to their subjects,[54] and those granting them "powers to invest monies, to lend money for development and welfare and for general Native Authority purposes and to guarantee loans for the purpose of furthering development and welfare".[55]

One final observation about the passage of the N.A. law: its acceptance by the "critical" wing of the NPC in the Northern House of Assembly probably marked the culminating point of its drift toward an accord with traditional authority or its waning of appetite for undiluted democracy. Appropriately it was Balewa himself, in a speech that contrasts markedly with his earlier oratory, who sounded

tion 7), with respect to the legislative powers of the Native Administrations (Sections 40, 43, 44, 45, 153[1], 154). An additional control is provided in the power of the government to make and withhold grants to Native Authorities.

[53] On the other hand, Section 158 also formalized their powers of inspection and investigation in Native Authority affairs.

[54] These are contained in Part VI of the law, which confers some rather sweeping authority. Section 108 makes it a duty of all persons to assist the Native Administrations in the performance of their lawful duties as required and to "carry out such lawful instructions as he may receive from the Native Authority". Part VI further stipulates that the N.A. may empower any of its employees to "do all that may be reasonably necessary to give effect to any lawful order given by such authority". Section 109 gives the Native Authority the right to summon any person within its jurisdiction at any time. The penalty prescribed for neglect of these duties and for anyone who "obstructs or interferes with the lawful exercise by a Native Authority of any powers conferred by law" is a fine of £100 or six months imprisonment or both. Section III states: "Everyone who conspires against or in any manner attempts to undermine the lawful power and authority of any Native Authority shall be liable to a fine of four hundred pounds or to imprisonment for one year, or to both such a fine and imprisonment". Section 114[2] gives Native Authorities the right to make arrests without a warrant, "where time does not permit or where for any reason it is otherwise impracticable to obtain a warrant". All these powers were in addition to those in force at the time by virtue of customary law (which were revoked with the enactment of the Penal Code in 1959).

[55] "A review of the state of development of Native Authority system in the Northern Region of Nigeria on the first of January, 1955", *Journal of African Administration*, Vol. 7, April, 1955.

the new commanding note. Rebuking the few detractors of the law, he said:

> I find it difficult to understand what is really meant by democracy, Sir, hard to translate. It can be translated "as practiced by a particular place". In America, Sir, the people practice democracy; in the United Kingdom there is democracy. France is democratic, Sir, but there are all different kinds. So maybe, Sir, our democracy in Nigeria may be yet another kind of democracy (hear, hear). . . .
>
> What is our aim as regards Local Government in the Region? The aim, Sir, is to bring new ideas to the people, to give them the chance to take part in the discussion of their own affairs and also to introduce changes to them in such a way that their happiness and peace should not be disturbed. Sir, we can only introduce these changes and still maintain the happiness and the peace of the people if the changes are not too drastic.
>
> We seem, Sir, always to regard the Chiefs in the North as a completely distinct group and more or less as a group, Sir, quite cut off from the people. I think this is wrong, Sir; it is our intention as many Members have said often in the House that the people will grow with Chiefs, and that it is our wish in this Region that our progress should be based on the old and the new being brought together. The young legislators require the experience of the older people. . . .[56]

BETWEEN the effective date, 1954, of the Native Authority Law and the end of 1965, a few refinements were added along the lines of development and within the principles of action which we have indicated. Most were in the direction of increasing the controls *available* to the regional government. In 1956 a clause was added to Section 35 which provided that, "The Governor *may* [emphasis mine] direct a Native Authority to establish a committee for purposes connected with the appointment and dismissal of staff". In 1958 the Section was further amended to permit the Governor (at his discretion) to allow an N.A. employee to "appeal to the Governor from any decision of the Native Authority or member thereof in relation to any matter affecting the appointment or terms of service of such officer

[56] *House of Assembly Debates*, February 20, 1954, p. 243.

or member of the staff".[57] And in 1962, a government order stipulated that all Native Administrations had to form establishment committees, except for those which, under approval by the Minister for Local Government, were too small to form them and whose councils normally handled staff matters themselves.[58]

Two other developments in this later period are noteworthy. The Adult Education Section of the Northern Ministry of Education sponsored publication of a booklet in 1958 called *You and Your Country* which was designed to disseminate knowledge about, among other things, the constitutional and legal rules under which local and regional government in the North operated, and about the rights and obligations of citizens. In 1959 the government announced a plan to assign two regional government civil servants to act as Provincial Local Government Instructors, to assist Native Administrations in developing conciliar institutions.[59]

THE PRECEDING account of the process of reform in the period under discussion shows that the policy of gradualism yielded several concrete modifications of the local political system in the direction of the values of modern democratic local government. It also reveals that these reforms provided an equivocal test of the ability of traditional institutions to absorb the principles and objectives of modern democratic local government, for the simple reason that the relevant innovations were either not introduced into the heart of the system— the central N.A.—or they were advanced so as to make their ac-

[57] Lest the implication of this development be misconstrued, it should be pointed out that this latter amendment was occasioned by events in connection with Ilorin N.A., the single instance of an emirate Native Authority whose central Council was composed of a majority of elected members loyal to a radical political party. While the amendment is theoretically applicable to any N.A., it grew out of circumstances not having to do with the actions of a predominantly traditional N.A., but with those of a newly and democratically constituted N.A. Council which was embroiled in a dispute with staff members left over from the old regime. For further amplification see Chap 3.

[58] Ministry for Local Government Circular No. 56 of 1962 to all Provincial Commissioners and Native Authorities, cited in M. J. Campbell, *Law and Practice of Local Government in Northern Nigeria* (London and Lagos, 1963), pp. 124-25.

[59] Although it is too early to judge the effect of this measure, it is important to note that in 1955 a private member's motion to appoint Provincial Local Government Inspectors was defeated in the House of Assembly, with help from the government bench. See *Debates*, August 9, 1955, pp. 73-76. At that time the idea was looked on disfavorably as an instrument of "inter-position"; hence its acceptance in 1959 may have marked an important change of attitude in this regard by the government. On the other hand, the government took pains to point out that its Instructors would be confined to dealing with "junior employees" of the N.A. See *Daily Times* of Nigeria, July 21, 1959.

ceptance optional and therefore problematical. What would have happened if a more extensive program had been pursued is a most critical question that the above discussion leaves unanswered.

Significantly, however, there were three instances in this period when more thoroughgoing reforms were tried and rejected. The rejections strongly suggest how far reform could go "within the framework" of a potent traditional emirate system, and where the critical limits lay. One of these instances was the dramatic experiment in Ilorin Emirate with a fully democratized central Native Authority, to which justice can only be done in a separate chapter. The two others may briefly be related here.

The reflections of early British Residents regarding their experience with corruption under the indirect rule system, which Miss Perham has recorded,[60] reveals that above all it was the prospect of a breakdown in administration that had earlier deterred the British from imposing a decisive solution. This reticence continued into the terminal phase of British rule. As then Lieutenant-Governor Sir Bryan Sharwood-Smith expressed the point to the House of Chiefs in 1953, "The elimination of corrupt practices and the punishment and removal from office of corrupt servants cannot be permitted to involve inference with, or damage to, the whole structure of Government and administration from top to bottom. Individuals come and go, the State and the machinery of the State must endure".[61]

In principle, however, the Customary Presents Order represented a break with this tradition of official forbearance, although there was a serious question as to whether some of its provisions had not vitiated its impact. In the spring of 1956 the government was disquieted by disturbances involving peasants and local officials in northern parts of Zaria Emirate, eastern Sokoto, and possibly other areas. In eastern Sokoto the disturbances were associated with religious conflict between rival Islamic brotherhoods or confraternities—the *Tijanniya*, which in that part of the North had a militant following among *Habe Talakawa*, and the *Khadiriyya*, closely identified with

[60] See Chap. 1.
[61] *House of Chiefs Debates*, March 28, 1953, p. 4. See also, 1953 *Provincial Annual Report*, p. 9, where the Resident reported regarding an effort to stamp out official corruption in one emirate, Bauchi, as follows: "The imprisonment of two District Headmen and later the Head of the Native Authority Medical Department, followed by a public declaration of the Emir of reform and his determination to stamp out corruption, brought further investigations to a close, which, if pursued, might well have involved too many senior officials and have seriously disrupted the administration".

the ruling house of Sokoto). At one point, it was actually feared that the incident might be the beginning of a concerted *Habe* revolt.[62]

The government believed the commotions were partly attributable to excesses on the part of Native Authority officials and concluded that strong measures were in order. Very probably the responsible British officials were fortified in this conclusion by the knowledge of their impending withdrawal. On March 20, 1957 action was set in motion by Governor Sir Bryan Sharwood-Smith through his customary Speech From The Throne to the Northern House of Chiefs, which contained, in sharp contrast to his remarks quoted above, probably the most bluntly censorious words ever publicly addressed to that body.[63] In effect, the Governor admonished the chiefs to carry out an immediate and full-scale house-cleaning of their administrations.[64] His recommendations to the Chiefs were followed by directives to the Native Authorities and government officers in the provinces, which set forth the specific areas of local administration requiring attention and authorized them to take action accordingly.

[62] A telegram dated June 6, 1956 was sent to all Residents and signed by then Governor Sir Bryan Sharwood-Smith:

> Recent religious disturbances in Eastern Sokoto now shown to be deliberately organized with a view to the ultimate overthrow of established authority . . . it could degenerate if not contained into a Habe revolt. . . . Orthodox Tijanniya have obviously no part in this debased version being employed to incite peasantry. . . .
>
> Keep yourselves informed in consultation with local chiefs and leaders who themselves have equally to lose if movement spreads. . . .

Document in possession of the author.

[63] "My Government views with the utmost concern examples of failure on the part of the District Administration and the local Native Courts in various parts of the Region to carry out their duties justly and efficiently and their apparent inability or unwillingness to safeguard the interests of ordinary citizens. We are also gravely concerned with the scale of fraud and peculation, particularly in the larger Native Treasuries. . . . Not only do inefficiency, maladministration and nepotism cost the Administrations responsible the good will of the people as a whole; they also cost them the respect and confidence of the younger educated generation. . . . There are too many individuals in positions of authority or trust, office holders and officials alike, who feel that the increasing participation of the people as a whole in the affairs of the Region constitutes a threat to their own personal interests and comfort and that by using their official positions to repress and victimize, they will succeed in securing those interests against the popular will".

[64] "My Government is convinced that what is urgently required throughout the Region is, firstly, that the structure of each Central Administration be scrutinized and if necessary modified . . . secondly that the District Administrations are themselves overhauled with the utmost vigour, immediate disciplinary action being taken to chasten or dismiss those whose betrayal of their trust has led to the state of affairs which I have just described".

By July of the same year the government found it necessary to reverse its order suggesting a general purge of wrongdoers on the grounds that (a) so vast was the scale of corruption thus far revealed that to implement the order would lead to a general breakdown of administration, and (b) the discovery that the directive was being used by certain factors as a pretext for weakening or eliminating traditional rivals.[65] In sum, the government had quickly been obliged to resort to its old strategy of making stern examples of extreme cases accompanied by a warning to others.

The second incident, which clearly indicated limits to change within continuity in the emirates, was the failure to adopt the recommendations of the Hudson Commission. The background of this commission and its report[66] can be filled in briefly. Beginning about 1951, government was considering plans to establish a major "third", or "middle", tier of government (i.e. one between Northern regional government and Native Authorities) at the provincial level, the twelve Northern Provinces being "artificial" units of administration originally created solely for the convenience of the colonial authority. Initially provincialization appears to have been conceived as an alternative way of achieving that coordination and rationalization of local services which might otherwise have been accomplished through amalgamation of the smaller Native Authorities. Instead of altering the existing boundaries of traditional units, the idea was to create at the level of the larger nontraditional units of administration, new structures of local government to which some of the more complicated and expensive N.A. services (e.g. primary schools) could be transferred.

The idea was not immediately pursued in this form. In time, however, provincialization came to be thought of more as a means of realizing other major interests or objectives, which in fact involved a fundamental inversion of the original inspiration. The policy-makers later envisaged provincial structures not as instruments for centralizing local power, but as mechanisms for decentralizing or "devolving" (as the process was to be called) the power of the regional government.

There were two major objectives and interests that led to this shift of emphasis. There was the problem of growing unrest in the pre-

[65] Government Circular 4092/32, July 13, 1957, from the Governor of the Northern Region to all Residents.
[66] Provincial Authorities, *Report by the Commissioner*, Mr. R. S. Hudson (Kaduna, 1957).

dominantly non-Moslem provinces in the southern parts of the region (the "Middle Belt") which stemmed from the apprehension that self-government—that is, the withdrawal of the British—would mean domination and ill-treatment at the hands of the Moslem majority. Indeed, opposition political parties advocating secession of those areas from the Northern Region were building a following on such anxiety that was increasingly difficult to ignore. Thus, reallocating some of the powers of the regional government to the provinces seemed one way to reassure the Northern minorities and thereby cut the ground out from under threatening separatist organizations. At the same time, those who looked forward to the survival of traditional institutions in the emirates perceived that under existing arrangements an "unsympathetic" regional regime could emasculate these institutions "with a few strokes of a pen". It was appreciated that provincializing some central powers would not guarantee the future of tradition, but the prospects, it was reasoned, could at least be considerably enhanced. This conception of provincialization was tantamount to a proposal to create a federal system, i.e. to enumerate to the provinces certain powers which the Northern Region possessed as residual powers under the Constitution of the Federation of Nigeria. In this form the plan came to be referred to within official circles as the "twelve pillars" policy.[67]

Probably the "fissiparous tendencies" (an official euphemism) emanating from the Middle Belt encouraged the government to make haste with its provincialization scheme, but the other considerations remained an integral part of it. In any case, at the 1957 Nigeria Constitutional Conference, where various representatives of Nigerian minorities were pushing hard for some form of autonomy (notably separate "states" or regions), the Northern delegates announced the Northern government's intention to constitute Provincial Administration in each of the Northern Provinces, and requested that the constitution be amended to allow for this step.[68]

To this end, Mr. R. S. Hudson of the Colonial Office had been

[67] The released issues were disclosed at the Residents' Conference in Jos, May 16-21, 1955, which was addressed by Premier Sir Ahmadu Bello who strongly supported the idea at this stage.

[68] "Having regard to the great size of the Northern Region of Nigeria and to the widely differing customs and traditional systems of local government practices within the Region, to advise how best a measure of authority can be developed on provincial authorities so as to provide an acceptable link between the Regional Government and the native authorities, and to make recommendations regarding the composition and functions of such authorities". *Report by the Commissioner*, p. 1.

appointed in 1956 to draw up detailed proposals for provincialization in the North. The Constitutional Conference, as well as the commission to investigate "the fears of minorities and the means of allaying them" which the Conference had set up, were apprised of Hudson's work. To what extent the Hudson Report may have influenced the Minorities Commission's decision not to recommend any form of greater autonomy for the Northern "Middle Belt" area is an interesting but moot point. Two months after the Minorities Commission Report appeared, the Northern delegates to the Resumed Nigeria Constitutional Conference informed that body that the Northern Government "had not so far found it possible to establish Provincial Administrations in the form for which permissive provision was made in the constitution". Subsequently the idea of creating Provincial Administrations along the lines laid down in the Hudson Report was simply dropped.

Some observers suggested that the fate of the Hudson Report was to be understood solely as a function of the government's strategy for its Middle Belt problem. The crux of this interpretation is that the government had held out provincialization as a counter to the separatists, but once the crisis represented by the Minorities Commission investigation and other related pressures had subsided, the government found it convenient to withdraw its proposals. Be that as it may (I have no evidence to confirm or refute the argument), this explanation is not completely satisfying, for the simple reason that it ignores the other major objective provincialization was designed to serve. Furthermore, there is evidence that the Hudson Report foundered for other reasons.

The Hudson Commission's formal terms of reference reflected only the two most recent considerations underlying the provincialization idea.[69] The report produced by the commission, however, shows that of the original conception of provincialization as a road to greater local administrative efficiency and economy via the indirect route of superimposing larger local government units on the traditional administrations, had not been lost sight of. The plan Hudson advanced would not only have accomplished that objective, it also included certain proposals directly affecting the Native Administrations themselves. And while these proposals were a logical extension of the idea of securing greater efficiency and economy and were perfectly in keeping with the long-term objectives of local government reform, they were

[69] *Ibid.*, p. 33.

also potentially fatal to the traditional political structure of the emirates.

In the first place, virtually all of the powers and functions which, Hudson found, might be profitably "devolved" onto provincial administrations, turned out to be not regional government powers in the main but mostly ones belonging to the Native Authorities. Specifically, he proposed that the largest share of such local services as agricultural aid, animal health, forestry, education, health and social welfare should be transferred to the provincial level along with the staff members and revenues necessary to support them. Under his scheme, at least three of the N.A. portfolios (Agriculture, Veterinary, and Forestry) would have been entirely dissolved. In terms of the traditional system, the meaning of the proposition was clear: drastic reduction of the number of posts, the offices and titles, available for dispensation.

Since the representation in the new provincial unit of local government was to be based on population (in proportion to which Native Authorities, as well as the population at large, would have the right to select representatives) this aspect of the scheme was more disturbing to the smaller than to the larger emirates, which would naturally dominate the new provincial institutions. From the point of view of the smaller emirates what was being proposed was the surrender of some of their salient prerogatives to a super state in which they would wield little influence. In that light, their opposition to the Hudson Report was perhaps a foregone conclusion. But in fact the large Native Administrations were equally adamant against it.

Another particular of Hudson's proposed innovation was that the staff of the provincial administrations previously employed as regional civil servants under the control of the Public Service Commission would remain as before, while those transferred from Native Authorities would join them in that status. Hence the fortunes of the provincial staff, whatever their origin, would be beyond the influence of the officials of large and small emirates alike.

And for each emirate there was suggested a further and related change which was doubtless the unkindest cut of all. Section 74 of the report recommended that provincial authorities establish Native Authority Staff Standard Boards—in other words, a local equivalent of a Public or Civil Service Commission. Not surprisingly, the stand of the Native Authorities against the idea of Provincial Administration was uniformly adamant. Nor were they likely to have been assuaged in their hostility by the salvo that the section was intended to include in the arrangement *only* "Alkalai, heads of Native Authority councils, and all posts carrying Native Authority salary scales of Grade E or above", nor by the intended reassurance that "the Board would not appoint staff, but only act as a sieve to eliminate unsuitable candidates".[70]

The protests of the Native Authorities did not go unheeded by their auxiliaries, sympathizers, and dependents within the government. Thus the bill to establish Provincial Councils introduced and passed in the Regional Legislature in 1959 bore the slightest resemblance to what had been Commissioner Hudson's vision of a Provincial Authority. There was no real authority in the bill at all; the new Provincial Councils, like their postwar cousins in their fledgling days (outer, village, district councils, etc.), were strictly confined to an advisory capacity. They remained in this stage throughout the period covered in this book.[71]

THE ESSENCE of the doctrine of gradualism was a belief that the possibility of continuity within change in the emirates was virtually limitless, that traditional and modern democratic local institutions could ultimately be reconciled or fused in one coherent system. The abortive ventures in reform recounted in this chapter simply reinforce a conclusion which the whole pattern of postwar Northern reform sustains: that the expectation is a house built on sand. Efforts to bring off the feat of institutional synthesis in the emirates could and did yield reforms, but only insofar as those reforms passed over or absolved the basic practices, motives, and norms of behavior which—though at variance with modern democratic structures—gave meaning to traditional institutions so that it caused people to attach importance to them. The faith in gradualism supported the movement along the way to reform until it promised to erode the vital springs such as patronage and personal influence, which propelled the traditional system. But at precisely that point the faith became untenable; given the implicit priority of continuity over change, it was predictable that further efforts in the same direction would be repudiated.

It is unnecessary to conclude that professing the faith was sheer

---

[70] *Ibid.*

[71] This is still true as of July 1967. Cf. John D. Chick, "The Structure of Government at the Regional Level", in L. Franklin Blitz, ed., *The Politics and Administration of Nigerian Government* (London, 1965), pp. 102-103.

cant, and mistaken to suppose that the reforms it produced are without any significance. The conclusion, on the other hand, that the whole gradualist conception of the process of change was born of wishful thinking, seems inescapable. But to say that having the best of two worlds is impossible is not to say that the impossibility has not been imagined or desired. On the contrary, for some, at least, the doctrine of gradualism would appear to be a case of the wish having fathered the thought. The fascinating story of reform in Ilorin, which is told in the next chapter, will confirm and illustrate these themes.

CHAPTER 3

Ilorin: Revolution, Counterrevolution

IN THE preceding chapters I have recounted how the various Northern policy-makers arrived at the idea of developing modern democratic local government in the emirates through a gradual fusion, or synthesis, of traditional and modern political institutions. The discussion also showed that the inevitable results of this policy were alternately innocuous measures of reform and recoil from potentially more decisive steps.

In one notable instance, however, the Northern government, in defiance of the logic of its own policy, countenanced the rapid introduction of a fairly thoroughgoing modern and democratic political structure into an emirate. That instance was the "reform" of the Ilorin Native Authority. No discussion of postwar local developments in the Northern emirates would be complete, therefore, without an analysis of this particular experience. Indeed, perhaps more than any other single episode of this period, the saga of democratization in Ilorin dramatically illustrated the implications and limits, so far as local government development was concerned, of "continuity within change" in the Northern emirates.

In 1953 the representatives of the regional government in Ilorin embarked with the government's knowledge and approval on the first stage of an escalated plan whereby all councils in Ilorin, including the all-important "central" or "Emir's" Native Authority council, would eventually be reconstituted to contain a majority of popularly elected members. At this point, there reportedly was much talk in official circles of the possibility that the Ilorin plan might furnish the model for the future development of all the emirates, although in fact no immediate move was made elsewhere to emulate it. The implementation of the Ilorin reforms culminated in May 1957, when a newly constituted central council, with a majority of popularly elected members (the plan had made provision for 15 nominated or "traditional" members out of a total of 65, met to take up direction of the affairs of the Ilorin Native Administration. The climax of this protracted conciliar transformation coincided with the unforeseen ascendency of a radical political party—the Ilorin *Talaka Parapo* (ITP; *"Talaka parapo"* means "commoners' party" in the Yoruba language), to which a majority in the Central Council, as well as the majority of all subordinate coun-

121

cil members, belonged. For 15 months, until August 1958, Ilorin experienced genuinely representative local government, under a regime that was determined to obliterate the last vestiges of the traditional political order and usher in a new era of modern democracy. In that August, the regional government, having experienced a stormy period of relations with the ITP-controlled Central Council, officially dissolved it. This action brought to a premature end the life of the sole specimen to date of a truly democratically composed, and politically radicalized Native Authority in the Northern emirates.

Why, of all the emirates, was Ilorin the pilot site of such fundamental and far-reaching innovations in the established Northern system of local government? An answer is that the pressures for change were stronger in Ilorin Emirate than in any other. These pressures fall into four broad headings: (1) historical contingencies underlying the origin of Ilorin Emirate and special features of its traditional political system resulting from them, (2) early British influences, (3) southern Yoruba influences, and (4) the views of certain highly placed British officials in the post-Second World War period. As is virtually always found to be the case upon close examination of the current political dynamics of any emirate, the traditional and modern strands had intertwined to produce the contemporary Ilorin political configuration. Only to facilitate analysis are they to some extent separated here.

Pre-British Ilorin

Until 1817 the territory of what is now Ilorin Emirate formed the northernmost part of Yoruba domains, under the political authority of the Alafin of Oyo,[1] in what is now the Western Region of Nigeria. The Alafin's governor, or *are*, in Ilorin was one Afonja, the *Kakanfo* or senior war-chief, who in that year hatched a plot to become ruler of Ilorin. Probably to lend respectability to his cause and help secure the sufferance if not approval of the powerful Fulani emirs to the North, Afonja invited a reputedly pious Sokoto Fulani Malam, Alimi, who was then sojourning in Yorubaland, to join the conspiracy.[2] Alimi not only accepted, he summoned other Fulanis and

[1] The Yoruba people traditionally regard the *Oni* of Ife as their spiritual head.

[2] My account of Ilorin history before the advent of the Europeans is based on several published sources plus files in the Provincial Office of Ilorin, and my field notes. Among the published sources are two gazetteers of Ilorin Province: K. V. Elphinstone, *Gazetteer of Ilorin Province* (London, 1921); H. B. Herman-Hodge, *Gazetteer of Ilorin Province* (London, 1929), S. J. Hogben, *The Muhammadan Emirates of Nigeria* (London, 1929), pp. 151-64. *The Report of the Commission*

some Hausa and other Muslims, including his own four sons, all of whom were instrumental in Afonja's successful claim to independence from Oyo.[3]

The best published accounts disagree as to whether it was Alimi himself, or his son Abdusalame, who thereafter overthrew Afonja, had him slain, and became the first Fulani Emir of Ilorin.[4] But the important consideration here is simply that from 1831 (the death of Alimi), at the latest, on, Ilorin has been under the reign of a Fulani dynasty—although now, as always, at least 90 percent of the people of Ilorin are Yoruba in origin. The present Emir of Ilorin, like many of his predecessors and most of his present-day counterparts in Hausaland, speaks no Fulani. In his case, the first language is Yoruba.

It was noted before that Fulani rulers generally anticipated the British in the practice of indirect rule in Northern Nigeria, which holds true especially for Ilorin, where several prominent Yorubas (who, some claim, actively participated in unseating the Afonja) were incorporated into the official hierarchy, their descendants continuing in high office down to the present. An important case in point is that Abdusalame appointed four *Baloguns*, or warlords, known respectively as the *Baloguns* Fulani, Gambari (Hausa), Ajikobe, and Alanamu, the last two being Yoruba. The four *Baloguns*, who, with the *Liman* Ilorin, originally made up the Emir's Council, all remained powerful political figures; the more recent ones invariably traced descent to the first holders of their titles. Indeed, in precolonial Ilorin, de facto control of the emirates sometimes passed into the hands of a *Balogun*, or several together, which reduced the Emir to a puppet role. Inevi-

---

appointed to enquire into the fears of Minorities and means of allying them, 1958, pp. 74-85, contains a useful thumbnail sketch. For a general account of internecine Yoruba conflict, see J. F. Ade Ajayi and R. S. Smith, *Yoruba Warfare in the Nineteenth Century* (Cambridge, Eng., 1964). Also see Hogben and Kirk-Greene, *Emirates of Northern Nigeria*, pp. 282-306.

[3] According to Hogben the event was marked by an exchange with the newly enthroned Alafin, Maju, whose cryptic message to Afonja, "The new moon has appeared", received the curt rejoinder: "Let the new moon quickly set". *Muhammadan Emirates*, p. 152.

[4] Elphinstone points the finger at Alimi, while Herman-Hodge leans toward Abdusalame. Hogben states that it is the Oyo version of the story that makes Alimi the conspirator and usurper, while the Ilorin view is responsible for the legend which has Alimi, somewhat in the manner of dan Fodio himself, disdaining any power for himself personally and retiring without ever having assumed the throne. According to the latter story, Abdusalame is to be reckoned as the first Fulani Emir of Ilorin. The Minorities Commission adopted the "Ilorin version", *Report of the Commission*, p. 74. Cf. Hogben and Kirk-Greene, *Emirates of Northern Nigeria*, pp. 285-87.

tably, however, the Fulani triumph suppressed other formerly influential Yoruba leaders, the heirs of Afonja not least among them.

The Fulani rulers of Ilorin did not establish a uniform system of administration throughout the emirate. In the northern two-thirds of Ilorin, inhabited mainly by Oyo Yorubas, they modeled their administration on the dominant pattern of the Hausa-Fulani states, with jurisdiction over "districts" or fiefs being parcelled out to appointees of the Emirs—in this case, usually Fulani princes. This northern area became known as metropolitan Ilorin; Ilorin Town, the emirate capital, was located in the center of it. The Fulani emirs of Ilorin regarded metropolitan Ilorin as *dar al Islam* (the domain of the faithful) and the conversion of its people to that religion went hand in hand with their political subjugation. On the other hand, the southern third of the present domain of Ilorin emirate, or nonmetropolitan Ilorin, contained distinct segments of subgroups of the Yoruba people, mainly the Igbolo, Igbomina, and Ekiti Yorubas, but also including such smaller offshoots as the Offas.

Contrary to accounts long extant, the so-called nonmetropolitan districts are themselves highly heterogeneous both ethnically, in terms of identification and loyalties vis-à-vis Ilorin and the old patriarchs of southern Yorubaland, and politically.[5] Though the Igbomina, for example, have usually been assumed to owe their primordial allegiances as a group outside Ilorin, many of them in fact have from the early days of the emirate voluntarily recognized Ilorin as their sovereign—preferably distant—in opposition in this respect to other Igbominas who just as willingly regard their Ilorin-associated kin with disdain and Ilorin itself as anathema. These intraethnic cleavages apparently stemmed from different patterns of migration and political relations with rival powers in the eighteenth and nineteenth centuries, which are beyond the scope of this book. I would like to note, though, that consequently affairs in this area were always sufficiently fluid to allow for considerable political maneuver and intrigue in pre-British and contemporary times.

Despite the heterogeneity it is probably accurate to say that the Ilorin Fulani customarily regarded most of nonmetropolitan Ilorin as *dar al harb* (the domain of the infidel), hence as grounds suitable for slave-raiding. Many of its people were constantly subject to as-

[5] I am indebted to correspondence with Mr. C. W. Michie, and to paragraphs 14-23 of his unpublished report to the Resident, Ilorin, entitled "Local Government Reform in the Igbomina Area", 1953, a copy of which he kindly placed at my disposal.

sault from the north. But administratively the corollary of the complicated situation was that insofar as orderly government could be sustained under the circumstances, the nonmetropolitan Ilorins were left to their own devices, devices that resembled the comparatively decentralized, limited, conciliar-oriented, constitutional processes of government found in the Yoruba kingdoms to the south.

The long-term implications for the character of the traditional system of Ilorin can be summed up in the words "chronic instability"; it was this condition that helped set Ilorin apart from other emirates. In the last analysis, all the Fulani Emirs of Ilorin owed their positions to a palace coup. Consequently their authority was never as imposing as that of other Fulani emirs, whose position ultimately rested on military conquest rationalized in terms of sacred religious obligations. In sheer numbers, the Fulani's presence in Ilorin was particularly meager. Though all the Fulani dynasties in Northern Nigeria ruled an ethnically alien majority to whom they assimilated themselves culturally and linguistically, in Ilorin the assimilation proceeded less easily and effectively than in the Hausa states, where the Fulani political rise was preceded by a substantial period of peaceful Fulani cohabitation with the conquered people, among whom Islam had also penetrated more deeply.

In addition to disadvantages pertaining to political legitimacy and socio-political cohesion internally, an external difficulty confronted the Fulani regime in Ilorin. This difficulty was perhaps the most consequential of all. First, there was Oyo's, and later Ibadan's (both are southern Yoruba kingdoms), frequent campaigns to regain what he regarded as his "lost dominion". Again, comparable difficulties historically threatened other Fulani regnancies, notably Katsina, which over a long period was constantly beset with attacks from the ousted *Habe* regime which had reestablished itself elsewhere. But an important difference was that by virtue of superior technical resources, manpower, and deeper political roots, Oyo and Ibadan enjoyed a comparatively solid base of operations from which to harass their rivals.[6]

Chronic instability and its causes are reflected in the recorded history of Ilorin throughout most of the latter two-thirds of the nineteenth century. The history of the period is a chronicle of the vacillating fortunes of the Ilorin throne in defending itself against three recurrent

[6] Oyo's and Ibandan's closer proximity to European trading posts on the coast gave them an important edge in supply and skill in using modern weapons. Cf. Hogben, *Muhammadan Emirates*, pp. 158-59.

and interconnected menaces: (1) the onslaughts of the armies of Oyo, Ibadan, and other Yoruba states; (2) rivalry and intrigue by the influential Ilorin Yoruba lieutenants and political outcasts; and (3) rebellious and subversive activities in the nonmetropolitan area.[7] This history also indicates strongly that the Fulani authority in Ilorin was not maintained without propitious interventions by armies of the Emir of Gwandu, who, being in charge of the western portion of the Fulani Empire, was responsible for Ilorin affairs. In sum, it is evident that even in the pre-European, traditional era proper, Ilorin represented the "soft underbelly" of the Fulani Empire.

Early British Influences

As was true elsewhere in the Northern emirates, European colonizing efforts did not dissolve the sources of instability. Rather, they tended to contain them, indeed, bottle them up, while at the same time introducing fresh sources of differentiation and friction. In other words, factors determining the traditional balance of power were altered without this bringing to an end the old power struggles.

The most immediate consequences of the British intrusion were cessation of hostilities between Ilorin and its southern adversaries, confirmation of boundaries (roughly as they stood—inclusive of the nonmetropolitan area), and administrative reorganization. These steps,

---

[7] (1) For the complex strands of the wars between Ilorin and the southern Yoruba kingdoms, particularly Oyo and Ibadan, between 1831 and 1897, see especially the accounts of Hogben and Herman-Hodge. Ilorin had also to contend occasionally with the expansionist designs of the Nupe state as it existed under the Etsu Nupe, Masaba. The effectiveness of the Yoruba forces was considerably vitiated by spasmodic internal hostilities between Oyo and Ibadan, which Ilorin turned to advantage. (2) The above-mentioned accounts are full of direct references and allusions to instances of Yoruba chiefs in Ilorin making secret alliances with Ilorin's foreign enemies during these wars, a tendency that was confirmed by my inquiries in Ilorin. The families of Baba-Isale and Magaji Are, heirs of Afonja's house, which seem to have intrigued against the throne almost continuously, exemplify the impact of vindictive political pariahs on Ilorin traditional politics. Probably the best example of the persistence of rival ambitions toward the throne even on the part of Yoruba members of the Ilorin governing hierarchy is furnished by the career of a *Balogun* Alanamu, who succeeded in unseating one emir (Moma—he was succeeded by another member of the Fulani royal house) and virtually, in Hogben's words, "ruled Ilorin for nearly twenty-five years". (3) The Ekitis, Igbolos, Igbominas, Offas, and others seldom let pass opportunities presented by Ilorin's military embroilments to assert themselves or to help out the effort to bring about Ilorin's downfall. A legendary instance of this was the rule of the Offa contingent of an Ilorin army during a battle with the Ibadan forces, in which thousands of Ilorin troops lost their lives attempting to cross the Otin River. The Offa detachment is thought to have engineered the disaster by destroying the bridge across the river in the rear of the Ilorin army. A war lasting 10 to 13 years between metropolitan Ilorin and Offa ensued (see Hogben, *Muhammadan Emirates*, p. 157).

in turn, brought the appearance in many of the nonmetropolitan districts of formal headmen effectively controlled by the central authority. The district heads were usually locally recruited and at first appeared to adhere to the Yoruba norms governing the relationship of rulers and subjects.

Eventually, however, administrative centralization encouraged the district heads to imitate the metropolitan chiefs. Thus in time the British were compelled to abolish the institution of district headship in the nonmetropolitan area, having recognized that the erosion of constitutionalism there had entirely alienated the people from their chiefs. Meanwhile in metropolitan Ilorin, the British administrative reorganization followed its usual course of buttressing the position of the emir in relation to that of other rulers. Elphinstone observes of the aftermath of the British conquest that: "The Emir, finding himself backed up by the Resident, broke away from the constraining hand of (the *Balogun*) Alanamu and other chiefs and commenced to act up to his position; no longer was he a figurehead shaking in his shoes with dread of a sudden death, but an Emir supported by the Government who insisted on the payment of tribute. Alanamu's time had come; at an enormous meeting outside the Emir's palace he was judged to be unfit to hold his position, was publicly deposed and stripped of his farms; he left Ilorin for Ogbomosho where he lived until his death in 1910".[8]

By the same token, shaking up and streamlining the traditional administration inevitably added to the number of important persons in Ilorin who felt sorely aggrieved. Apart from the *Baloguns*, generally, an example was the so-called *Babakekeres*. Traditionally a *Babakekere* (literally, "little father", in Yoruba) acted in the judicial process as a kind of middleman between the judge and the litigants—peddling his influence with the court. At the same time, he customarily enjoyed the position of absentee fief-holder through the beneficence of the Emir. The new territorial administrative set-up, based on resident chiefs or heads in the districts, deprived the numerous *Babakekeres* of their fief-holding prerogatives and thereby earned their enmity.

In theory, the parallel reform of the judicial system left no place for a *Babakekere*'s proprietary rights in this sphere either. But in fact, the rights continued to be exercised, the practices involved being less conspicuous and hence more difficult to control than those of fief-

[8] *Ibid.*, p. 19.

holding. It may well be that the British reforms intensified the practice, as it is likely that a *Babakekere* tried to recoup from one function what he had lost through effective suppression of the other. In any case, the purge of the *Babakekeres* turned out to be a highly mixed blessing for the British, in that it spawned troublemakers for the new administrative set-up without ridding the Ilorin people of the *Babakekeres'* parasitic influence.

The legacy of other important, subterranean, aspects of the British presence were: (1) the cleavage between the nonmetropolitan and metropolitan Ilorins, previously based on ethnic and traditional political-cultural factors, was exacerbated by (a) affiliation to divergent "universal" religions (animism and Christianity were dominant in the south; the North was overwhelmingly Islamic), and (b) thanks to the activities of Christian missionaries in the south, differences in educational experiences and hence different receptivity to modern Western ways and values; (2) a nontraditional, politically frustrated, embryonic Ilorin "middle class" was created, consisting of various sorts of new entrepreneurs and Western-educated persons who, owing to the socially "indiscriminate" recruitment policies of the Christian missions, were far less apt to be of patrician origin than their counterparts in the "upper north"; (3) there came into being an external model of an alternative socio-political order (i.e. that of the southern Yoruba in Western Nigeria), which, in terms of modernity, tended to be well in advance of Ilorin. The impact on Ilorin of continuous exposure to and relations with a kindred people to the south would seem to constitute a classic case of what some social scientists have termed a "demonstration effect"—a facilitation of change through visible example. Here the impact was manifold, and it deserves emphasis.

Southern Yoruba Influences

The contribution of the southern Yoruba to political tension in Ilorin in the pre-British period has been noted. Under the British the struggle of the southern Yoruba to "recapture" Ilorin assumed the new form of petitions (followed by pro status quo counter-petitions) requesting the British to revise Nigeria's boundaries so as to place the kingdom within southern territory. The first in a long series of such requests was considered and rejected by Lugard in 1904. The agitation continued, however; in 1917 Lugard appointed a Boundary Commission to reconsider the case of one small enclave in the Ekiti area. The commission also confirmed existing boundaries. In 1936 one tiny fragment was transferred to what became the Western Region of Nigeria. With that negligible exception, however, all such efforts failed throughout the period of colonial rule, although the whole question received two more major reviews—that of the Governor-General Sir John Macpherson whose findings were published in 1952,[9] and finally that of the Minorities Commission whose 1958 Report has already figured prominently in previous chapters.

The very process of petition and review had significant ramifications. It occasioned political ferment and gave rise to nascent political organization at the Ilorin grassroots, especially in those nonmetropolitan districts that proved relatively receptive to revisionist overtures. At the same time, the later investigations growing out of the process helped convince some British officials that internal reform was an urgent necessity. I will return to these points.

If interregional boundaries remained nearly stationary, the store of social ideas in Ilorin most emphatically did not, for currents originating in southern Yorubaland were continually transmitted northward. Ilorin is geographically situated astride Nigeria's main north-south routes of communication and trade, and this alone was bound to be an impetus for change. In not only trade and commerce, however, but also in religious and educational matters, the close physical and ethno-cultural proximity of Ilorin and southern Yorubaland greatly enhanced the taste for change in this particular emirate above all others, as detailed observations of the Minorities Commission and other sources reveal.[10]

[9] *Extraordinary Federal Gazette*, September 3, 1952.

[10] (1) The Minorities Commission estimated in 1958 that Ilorin was 64% Muslim and 8% Christian, with the adherents of the former religion concentrated in the northern districts, and those of the latter in the southern districts. *Report of the Commission*, pp. 80-81. Christianity is particularly strong among the Ekiti, Igbolo, and Igbomina Yorubas, who at the time accounted for about 180,000 out of the total Ilorin population of over 400,000. (2) Ilorin occupies a unique educational position among the Northern Emirates. The Report states that "there are more educated young men from Ilorin than from the other Provinces of the Northern Region". This estimate is fully borne out by statistics I have gathered. Thus, of the 36 secondary schools in 1960 in Northern Nigeria, 5 were in Ilorin, including the first and only school at which Northern girls had completed a secondary course, the Queen Elizabeth School (cf. "Some Problems of Girls' Education in Northern Nigeria": an interview with Miss F. I. Congleton, *Overseas Educated*, Vol. 30 [July 1958]). Three of the five secondary schools were "voluntary" schools, established either by a mission directly or by communities (like Offa) under heavy missionary influence. According to statistics provided by the Northern Ministry of Education, Ilorin Emirate has more schools of all kinds than all of Bornu, Bauchi, Adamawa, and Sardauna Provinces put together. My survey in 1959 of the registration cards of the 51 Northern students then attending the University of Ibadan (then the only Nigerian university) found that 10 were from Ilorin. (3)

Politically these aspects of the "demonstration effect" might be said merely to have rendered Ilorin latently susceptible to the kind of modernizing nationalism the major southern political parties represented, but which was to find new sympathetic echoes in most of the land of the Northern emirates. But external pressure on Ilorin also had a highly deliberate aspect in the form of the Action Group. This major southern-based and Yoruba-dominated party, beginning about 1955 assiduously and sometimes ruthlessly tried to harness Ilorin social and political frictions to the wider causes of pan-Yoruba nationalism and anti-colonialism.

From the Ilorin perspective, the Action Group's remarkably well-financed and tightly efficient machine meant that internal discontent could now feed on generous and effective independent resources. As will be seen, this support came at the price of involvement in and

---

The different auspices of education and its significance in the metropolitan and nonmetropolitan districts, respectively, were pointed up by page 63 of the *Provincial Annual Reports* for 1957: "As regards Education the province is divided into two by a line running East and West through Ilorin Town. The population is almost equal on either side of that line. To the south of this line there are only five Native Authority Schools. North of it there are only a handful of Voluntary Agency Schools. In general, education south of the line is by Voluntary Agencies and to the north, by Native Authorities. Out of 121 pupils in the Provincial Secondary School, only eight live to the north of the line. Since selection has been by competitive examination, these figures indicate the qualitative and quantitative superiority of Voluntary Agency education . . . it is unrealistic to expect the Ilorin Yorubas . . . to compete on equal terms with Igbomina, Ekiti, and Igbolo. The latter peoples have many incentives to acquire education, the most notable being economic pressure". (4) *The Provincial Annual Reports for 1955* recorded that "in economic affairs the Province has continued to fulfill its traditional function of growing and selling foodstuffs and of exporting labour to the cocoa-growing and industrial areas of the Western Region and the colony. The continuing but somewhat reduced prosperity there has provided good markets for yams, maize and guinea corn . . . the high wages and payments in kind offered by the cocoa growers of the Western Region and the 5s minimum wage offered by the Government of the Western Region have continued to denude a large part of Ilorin Division of many of its able-bodied men. In the South and East of the Division the percentage . . . appears to be in the neighborhood of 40 percent. In one village area the figure was found, in 1954, to be 75 percent. Many of these absentees have cocoa farms of their own in the Western Region, particularly in the Ife division of Oyo Province. . . . The social and political, as well as the economic effects of the population movement, play a vital part in the life of the Province today." *Report of the Commission*, p. 54. (5) Of the general attraction exerted on Ilorin by the West, the *Minorities Commission Report* observes that, "Toward the West there is, first, the attraction of the language and customs which they have in common with the Yorubas of the West; that is at present said to be slighter in the northern part of the Division, and what there is has probably been aroused from outside. In the southern half of the Division there is a trade connection with the West; there is everywhere, particularly in the southern part of the Division, some impatience with government in general; this acts at present as a somewhat negative pull to the West". *Ibid.*, p. 82.

service to interests which transcended the objectives that had originally induced large numbers of the dissident Ilorins to accept outside support. In particular, a primary preoccupation of the Action Group was the annexation of Ilorin (along with Kabba) to Western Nigeria,[11] a fate that appealed only to segments (notably some of the nonmetropolitan people) of those Ilorins who sought structural reform within the emirate. Once the alliance was struck, however, the one cause became inextricably bound up with the other; this circumstance was to deeply affect the fate of the Ilorin experiment in democratic local government.

It is easy to see why Ilorin might be considered ripe for radical political reform, in light of the discussion above. But in the period in question, this assessment of the situation could not have become official policy without the support of persuasive voices among the British colonial policy-makers, not all of whom at the time perceived the situation this way. This brings us to a final, brief but important, point—"why Ilorin?".

IN THE chapter, "Perspectives on Reform", it was observed that after the Second World War, British officials concerned with colonial policy held significantly divergent assumptions about the future of the emirates of Northern Nigeria, even if in the end these differences were resolved into a common rationale about reform. Two important points on which these different assumptions turned, it was pointed out, were: (1) whether the basic social structure of the emirates would or should survive the introduction of representative institutions, and (2) what relative emphasis was to be given the importance of fostering Nigerian unity as against upholding the integrity of the emirates' social and political fabric. In terms of the official personalities of the moment, it was stated that the principal advisor to the Colonial Office in London (Hailey) inclined toward the priority of Nigerian unity and advocated democratization within the emirates, officers stationed in the North maintained a protective attitude toward the established order within the emirates, while Governor-General of Nigeria Bourdillon occupied the middle ground—indecision about the fate of emirate

---

[11] See *Proceedings of the General Conference on Review of the Constitution,* 1950. The Kabba Division of Kabba Province in Northern Nigeria is also overwhelmingly Yoruba in origin and Christian. Kabba was never organized as an emirate and its general history, political, social, and economic composition is otherwise unlike that of Ilorin. The controversy over boundary revisions naturally included Kabba, however.

internal structure and hopefulness that Nigerian unity would prove compatible with whatever might come in the emirates.

It is reasonable to surmise that a similar line-up of views was reflected in deliberations on the course of policy for Ilorin, except that the counsel of democratization appeared far more persuasive there than elsewhere. Official investigations connected with the Ilorin boundary dispute served especially to alert officials to the incendiary political situation within Ilorin.

In 1952 Governor-General Sir John Macpherson's review of the boundary issue had preserved the status quo ante, but probably he was much more impressed by other considerations such as the case in favor of change in the Northern emirates for the sake of the future of Nigeria as a whole. Following the publication of the 1952 *Extraordinary Federal Gazette* dealing with Ilorin, the man who previously had acted as Principal Assistant Secretary (Political) in the Nigerian Secretariat (i.e. to Macpherson) was posted to Ilorin. Under the direction of this officer, C. W. Michie, a survey of conditions was undertaken which culminated in an official report to the Resident, Ilorin Province, entitled "Local Government Reform in the Igbomina Area", dated April 4, 1954. This document gave the recommendations on which Ilorin's subsequent venture into democratic local government was based and with which the name Michie would become synonymous. To judge by the major relevant documents, this personification of the cause of fundamental change was not completely misplaced, for in them were prominently reflected Michie's own perspectives. For example, his 1954 report to the Resident of Ilorin began with a quote from the *London Times*: ". . . the aristocratic factions remain, but they no longer divide the country between them. There has grown up a third element—the public—which is neither with them nor of them, but which has become infinitely more powerful. . . ." Perhaps still more revealing and in longer perspective, in the first blush of Ilorin's "great experiment" of 1957-58, Michie, who by then was himself the Resident of Ilorin, penned another trenchant quote, this time from the English social historian of the nineteenth century, Trevelyan:

No one in 1835 foresaw the day when the new local government councils would not only light and pave the streets, but control the building of houses, the sanitation and health of the people; convey the workmen to and from their work; provide public libraries; carry on great municipal trades and industries; and finally educate the people.

The immediate change that excited contemporaries was the transference of authority to the dissenters and shopkeepers, in place of the co-optive oligarchies of Tory lawyers, churchmen and noblemen's agents who had enjoyed a close monopoly. . . . There was not much "sweetness and light" in the new style of politician, but they had a certain rough vigour, and were disposed to welcome "improvements" while the fact that they were chosen periodically by a real democracy kept them up to the mark in those matters in which the electors themselves felt any interest.[12]

THE EVOLUTION OF THE ILORIN NATIVE AUTHORITY COUNCIL, 1900-57

1900-50: The very fact that there were important modifications in the composition and structure of the Ilorin Native Authority Council long before the onset of concern about modern local government as such, is indicative of the inflammatory political material so deeply woven into the Ilorin system.[13]

Starting as early as 1907, the British and the Emir were obliged to deal with groundswells of political discontent, aggravated by various traditional figures whom the Pax Brittanica had disadvantaged and who were now bent on undermining the new order of things. Elphinstone and Hogben each draw attention to wider implications of such subversive activities. Hence, of the attempt by the ex-*Balogun* Ajikobi, Magajin Gari, and Ajaji Ogidilou (all Yoruba) to incite a band of Ilorin hunters to raid the British Residency, Hogben remarks, "there can be little doubt that the whole affair was in the first instance engineered to throw discredit upon the Emir. There is also no room for doubt that it was partly due to the old struggle between the Yoruba and Fulani, stage managed from over the border".[14] Elphinstone emphasizes the ex-*Balogun* Ajikobi's strategy of provoking "disaffection amongst democratic and anti-Fulani Yoruba sections".[15] Matters became serious in 1913 when the administration attempted to introduce a tax and met with rioting by the peasants, again, "egged on by Biala, ex-*Balogun* Ajikobi", and others. British troops were re-

[12] *Provincial Annual Report*, 1956, p. 49. The quote was taken from Trevelyan's *Between the Two Reform Bills: 1832-1867*.

[13] I wish to acknowledge the contribution to this section of an unpublished paper prepared by the Ilorin Central Native Authority Office, entitled "Constitution of Ilorin Native Authority Council", which outlines the development of the Native Authority since 1913.

[14] Hogben, *Muhammadan Emirates*, p. 163.

[15] Elphinstone, *Gazeteer of Ilorin Province*, p. 21.

quired to restore order.[16] The British concluded that the turmoil was attributable basically to the persistent political influence of Ilorin's pre-European (i.e. Yoruba) *ancien régime*; in 1913 they made the first major change in the Native Authority Council by appointing as salaried members two representatives of the house of Afonja—the Magajin Are and Baba Isale—and the principle was laid down that henceforth the old dynasty would always be included.

The occurrence in 1937 of fresh disturbances, in which the same Baba Isale as well as a *Balogun* Gambari were implicated, led to the second major overhaul of the Emir's Council. This time, in addition to appointing still another scion of an old traditional family (Magajin Gari), it was felt wise to admit two products of the new European education, Malam Muhammadu Gobir (who afterwards acquired the title of *Waziri*) and Malam Yahaya (later called Yahaya Ilorin), a teacher and later headmaster of the Ilorin Middle School.

The next major reconstitution, which took place in 1947,[17] yielded a greatly expanded, 27-member Council designed to accommodate, among others, representatives of the outlying districts, including for the first time several indigenes of the nonmetropolitan area (two Ekitis, three Igbominas, three Offas). Indeed, within six months an additional Ekiti and Offa representative each were added at the urging of the Resident.

The early beginning, frequency, and extent of the renovations in the structure of the central Native Authority Council contrast with the static condition over the same period of the Emirate Councils of the "upper North".

Table 1: Composition of Ilorin Native Authority Council, 1945

Emir of Ilorin	*Magaji Area*
Balogun Ajikobe	*Baba Isale*
Balogun Alanamu	*Imam Imale*
Balogun Fulani	M. Muhammadu Gobir (Visiting Teacher)
Balogun Gambari	M. Yahaya Ilorin (Headmaster, Ilorin Middle School)

[16] Hogben, *Muhammadan Emirates*, p. 163.

[17] In 1945 a Yoruba Imam, the Limam Imale, succeeded the deceased Limam Fulani; upon the death of the incumbent Baba Isale, his title and its holder's seat on the Council were not renewed.

1950-57: After 1950 there was a significant departure in official policy regarding the composition of the Council—the adoption of the principle of election. Heretofore, nontraditional members of the Council had been chosen exclusively by the method of nomination from above (i.e., the governor acting in consultation with local British officials and the leading members of the Council itself). The main impetus for this change evidently came from Macpherson's investigations in connection with the boundary issue, local officials having been apprised beforehand of some of the important conclusions in his published report, notably that there was a "body of opinion dissatisfied with the traditional Native Authority system of local government", especially in the southern area, which underlay much of the "secessionist" sentiment in Ilorin—the antidote to which, it logically appeared, was popular representation.

In December 1951 the Council resolved to extend its membership. The result was a new council of 14 nominated and 34 "elected members", whose official tenure dated from November 1952. Quotation marks belong around this term because the electoral procedure followed was actually indirect election, utilizing the subordinate village and district councils as electoral colleges. Since the composition of these subordinate councils was at this date wholly traditional in character, the "elected members" who emerged were in fact all traditional figures (12 district heads, 15 village heads, and 6 court members)[18] who, in effect, had nominated themselves. It also deserves to be pointed out that a "quorum"—dominated by the older, more experienced, but also nominated, salaried, and traditional hands within the Council—tended in practice to conduct the business of the Native Authority pretty much as before. Participation on the part of elected members was confined to infrequent and formal Council sessions that performed more of a ratifying than a deliberating role. Nonetheless, the germ of elective representation had now been admitted to the body of principles regulating Ilorin's local government system; this served to lower Ilorin's resistance to further extensions of the idea, if it effected nothing else.

A year after the formal inauguration of this Council, a committee of five Native Authority officials under Michie's chairmanship began a comprehensive review of conditions and policies (precursory to making recommendations for further reform of local government) which lasted until May 1954. A District Officer completed this re-

---

[18] "Constitution of Ilorin Native Authority Council", p. 2.

view between October of that year and February 1955. In substance, the reforms were two-fold, and they were significant: (a) direct elections (employing adult manhood suffrage and the voting device of a show of hands in the villages) to all district and village-group councils in the emirate; (b) thence selection of representatives from those councils to the central N.A. Council. A remarkable feature of the plan was its complete omission from several of the lower councils of any traditional or nominated members, although their inclusion in other lower councils assured traditional representation in the Central Council (see Tables 2 and 3). This selected elimination of traditional members was unprecedented as far as the Northern emirates was concerned.[19] Indeed, it is noteworthy that this step has never been repeated elsewhere (nor for that matter retained in those areas in Ilorin itself, where in the wake of the dissolution of the ITP-controlled Central Council, traditional representation was reintroduced in all district and village councils).

Before Michie's committee had set to work, a further reform of the Central Council had already produced a new overwhelming majority of indirectly but formally elected members (i.e. based on the use of legally prescribed electoral regulations). But because this election (which also used subordinate councils as colleges) took place (in October 1953) *prior* to the inauguration of the Michie rules of election to subordinate councils (legally in effect in December 1955), the political composition of the 1953 Central Council was in fact very little different from its predecessor (that is to say, because the electing subordinate councils had not themselves been popularly elected).[20] No revolution could occur, therefore, until the old Coun-

---

[19] The complete omission of traditional members went beyond prevailing practices in Western Nigeria, where local government councils even today provide for a substantial measure of traditional representation. "In every village area 'Michie's Committee' advised the electorate to give their traditional representatives at least one-third of the representation on the new councils. Sometimes— and particularly where the local 'Progressive Union' was powerful—this advice was rejected in favour of the 'one man one vote' system". Letter from C. W. Michie to the author, November 16, 1966.

[20] The main difference was in the fact that two subordinate councils, the Ilorin Town Council and the Offa District Council, had previously been reconstituted to consist predominantly of nontraditional members, and they were responsible for the appearance on the Central Council of the first elected members, who lacked traditional office, title, or high birth. But these were still in a small minority there. On page 58 of the *Provincial Annual Reports* for 1953, it is observed: "In Ilorin Emirate, where speed was of the essence, the first elected members of the Native Authority were returned by subordinate councils as they stood. Their membership, however, is largely confined to the wealthy or otherwise privileged and cannot be said to represent the tax-paying community as a whole. To bring them into

cil's term was up in 1956 and a new council could be formed on the foundation of popularly elected subordinate councils. That term was in fact extended to 1957 to permit the necessarily lengthy process of new elections (initially to some 300 subordinate councils) to be completed. This was finally accomplished in May 1957, the month in which the ITP-controlled Council began.

THE RISE OF THE ITP-AG GRAND ALLIANCE

THE FINAL stages of constitutional reform of Ilorin local government were accompanied by a mounting tide of political protest emanating from various political strains and tensions beneath the administrative surface. It appears from official descriptions of Ilorin's political mood "on the eve" that institutional reform came not a moment too soon.[21]

The increased restlessness was undoubtedly attributable in part to the fact that by 1956 the general political malaise in Ilorin had found highly organized political expression. It has been pointed out that the transformation of local government in Ilorin was not conceived with this development in mind. The typical British policy-maker's attitude was that "party politics", especially if its main concerns extend beyond the local level, is essentially inappropriate to the nature and functions of local government, and therefore regrettable if it occurs

line, a thoroughgoing inquiry is now being undertaken by a strong N.A. committee with the advice and assistance of a senior Administrative Officer, and though only in its infancy has already revealed a considerable measure of discontent with the existing order and a demand for representation by the 'commons' ".

[21] The *Provincial Annual Reports* for 1956 concerning Ilorin is particularly striking for its tone of alarm: ". . . reference was made to the signs of a breakdown of law and order in the previously inert 'metropolitan districts' lying around and to the north of Ilorin Town. Intensive touring of these areas by the Native Authority and Administrative staff showed that in certain Districts the people were refusing to obey the legitimate orders of the Native Authority . . . defiance of constituted authority was coupled with the illegal opening of markets and an anti-tax campaign. . . . Later it became known that a shadow N.A. had been 'appointed' and that the leading 'members' were widely known to the people of the disaffected areas. There was no doubt that a large percentage of the people in these districts no longer had confidence in their Native Authority", p. 53. With regard to the nonmetropolitan area, the appraisal was equally ominous: "In the preceding *Report* it was observed that the most far-reaching change in the field of social relations had been the incipient development of tension between the followers of Islam and Christianity. The effects of the schism are unfortunately to be found everywhere in the Province in different forms". "This disturbing trend was however foreshadowed", the *Report* continues, "by an even more fundamental change, namely, the increasing relegation of illiterate title-holders to an honorary position in local Yoruba society. This process has been going on for some years, but it has been accelerated by the local government reforms which began in 1953 and which are now gaining momentum", pp. 55-56.

in that context.[22] But in retrospect it is easy to see that the very conditions pressuring the government to make formal institutional changes were also bound to offer a highly favorable climate for the growth of a vigorous political party.

The Ilorin *Talaka Parapo* (ITP) was founded in 1954. Its origin, growth, and ideological development has been analyzed in R. L. Sklar's *Nigerian Political Parties*,[23] so a detailed discussion of the party is unnecessary here. But a comment on his account is relevant. Sklar's study, as well as official commentaries,[24] draw attention to a certain fundamental ideological ambivalence in the original political direction of the ITP, and remark on the apparent later conversion of the party into a clearly articulated organ of democratic social and political change. These observers perceived this initial ambivalence and its eventual resolution in terms of a basic conflict within the party between contradictory tendencies of "traditionalism", on the one hand, and "modern democratic radicalism", on the other.[25]

[22] In holding this attitude they were sharing the opinions of a long line of British protagonists and students of local government. The crux of the argument would appear to be that for local citizens to get together, take responsibility for providing themselves with services, and see that they are administered impartially, economically, and efficiently, is the proper business of local government—participation by political parties destructively introduces the spirit of partisanship, causes the injection of "extraneous considerations" into the decision-making process, and reduces the impact and role of the individual local citizen. This view, of course, is not exclusively British; it appears to be shared by some students of local government in the Western democracies.

[23] Sklar, *Nigerian Political Parties*.

[24] Notably the Minorities Commission's *Report* and the 1955 and 1956 *Provincial Annual Reports*.

[25] Sklar states that, "the first mass political party in Ilorin, the Ilorin Talaka Parapo . . . [originally] leveled criticisms against the reformed Native Administration in the name of tradition" and that it "coupled its commitment to tradition with such popular causes as tax reduction and the suppression of extortionary practices by sanitary inspectors, forest guards, and other party officials of the administration. . . ." *Nigerian Political Parties* (Princeton, 1963), pp. 351-52. "In 1956", he indicates, "the Commoners' Party entered into an alliance with the Action Group; thereafter, its criticisms of the Native Administration became more vigorous and its ideological line diverged irrevocably from traditionalism to radicalism", p. 352.

The 1955 *Provincial Annual Reports'* account of the ITP in its first year similarly reflects the party's apparently paradoxical program: "The Parapo's political objectives have not yet been fully defined, but it is already clear that they aim at 'restoring the former power and authority of the Emir and Chiefs' and at reducing direct taxation. They strongly oppose the present Ilorin Native Authority Council, which they claim is not responsive to public opinion". The following year the *Annual Reports* offered this analysis: "Their movement [i.e. that of the ITP] was born in 1954. At that time it was timid and traditional in outlook, resisting the demands of the directly elected, anti-N.A. Ilorin Town Council. . . . In November 1955 *Ilorin Talaka Parapo* speakers were still protesting their loyalty to the *Baloguns*, the hereditary leaders of the N.A. but their attacks on pro-Northern

The historical background to Ilorin politics sketched above may shed additional light on what at first glance seems to have been a rather puzzling phenomenon of an extremely rapid and basic, indeed chameleon-like transformation of a political organization. Perhaps the crux of the matter can be suggested immediately by reporting that many of my knowledgeable informants in Ilorin insisted that the ITP was "thoroughly radical" right from the beginning. On reflection, it turns out that this view of the party and the previously mentioned interpretation are quite compatible.

The proposition that from the start the Ilorin Commoners' Party stood for the betterment of Ilorin's nongoverning classes vis-à-vis the position of those whose interests were centered around the authority of the Emir (and the resources he commanded), is evidenced by three undisputed facts—the name of the party, certain of its originally proclaimed objectives, and the socio-economic and political status of most of its founders. Sklar's data on the party founders' occupations shows that the core consisted of new entrepreneurs, a class which in Ilorin (as elsewhere in the Northern emirates) was excluded from the traditional ruling class.[26] The party's initial aims and concerns included items that indicate the party's antagonism to the Native Authority and its intention to champion "popular" causes.[27] On the other hand, the facts that make the genesis of the

---

Peoples' Congress officials of the N.A. increased in intensity. They still remained critical of most of the measures of local government reform which they regarded as overrapid democratisation. . . . In January 1956, the *Ilorin Talaka Parapo* shed remnants of its traditionalism and demanded that elections to the Ilorin Town Council should be conducted by secret ballot. . . . *Ilorin Talaka Parapo* views and demands were changing and increasing. . . . By February *Ilorin Talaka Parapo* speakers were taking the line that they were the party of the 'have nots' and that the Northern Peoples' Congress stood for unearned privilege and the spoils of office. Above all, it was becoming clear that the *Ilorin Talaka Parapo* movement saw itself as a revolt of those who felt themselves to be underprivileged and of an emergent middle class against the concentration of political and administrative power in the hands of the traditional leaders of the N.A. and their families". Pp. 50-51.

[26] Alhaji Sulaiman Maito, cattle dealer; Jimoh Adelabu, trader and contractor; Saliman Baruba, barber and trader; Yahaya Kannikan, cattle dealer; Yakubu Olowo, cattle dealer; Bodinrim Tinko, machine sewer; Salau Gedele, motor park agent; Adebimbe Oniye, cloth seller; Dogo Agbogi, cloth seller; Jima Gorosa, Koranic Malam; Alhaji Aremo, trader. Sklar, *Nigerian Political Parties*, pp. 351-52, note 51.

[27] The Minorities Commission, to which the ITP's early manifestos were made available, states baldly that the party "stood for the interests of the common man as against the chiefs, officials, title-holders, and men of property. . . . Its objects are set out in a letter to the Native Authority, dated June 1 of that year [1955], and they are directed to domestic problems, social, political, and economic. It hoped above everything else for a more democratic system of local government". *Report of the Commission*, p. 77.

organization enigmatic are equally incontrovertible: (1) the party initially proclaimed its affinity for "tradition", with emphasis on the institution of chieftaincy, and (2) at first the party actually secured the sympathy and support of many chiefs, some of whom were very prominent in the established system of government, e.g. Yoruba *Baloguns.*

Against the background of Ilorin's traditionally volatile political system, the concomitance of these two sets of objectives is not surprising. First, it can be appreciated that at the time of the ITP's assay into politics the notion of "tradition" itself was ambiguous. There were, in effect, no less than three political traditions in Ilorin—the pre-Fulani Yoruba state; pre-European Fulani rule; and that which had been modified by the colonial system. In other words, appealing to "tradition" did not necessarily mean affirming the status quo; on the contrary, the affirmation of "tradition" could, and did under the aegis of the ITP, connote a demand for political change, a demand based on an image of an antecedent, pre-Fulani, traditional order. Second, it has been shown that under all three Ilorin "traditional systems" there was constant friction within the ruling hierarchy; members of the "ruling class" were always to be numbered among the enemies of the throne.

The caveat to which all of this leads is that the ITP's advocacy of tradition and its consorting with certain traditional rulers was, up to a point, perfectly consistent with its character as a protagonist of democratic change. Nor is that terminal point hard to locate. As long as the ITP remained purely a vehicle of *protest*, against the Native Authority as it existed in 1954, various "traditionalists" represented a natural source of support. These traditionalists were classifiable as follows: (a) ambitious "lieutenants" in the N.A. such as (especially) the Yoruba *Baloguns*, whose normal objective seemed to have been to gain the upper hand in relation to the Emir; (b) benighted political leaders or outcasts of the official ruling hierarchy, such as the *Babakekeres*;[28] (c) subchiefs or district heads who desired to increase their power and authority over their territory in relation to the central N.A.;[29] (d) peasants or commoners who in their glorifica-

[28] It is interesting to note that of the founders of the ITP, one—Saliman Baruba, barber, trader—was identified as also having been a *Babakeker*, while another—Yakeba Olowa, cattle dealer—was also a dismissed *Balogun* Fulani.

[29] One of my informants who characterized the ITP as being radical from the beginning commented on the party's traditional Chiefly support: "They were for tradition all right, but the tradition they favored was decentralization".

tion of traditional chieftaincy had in mind a reassertion of the pre-Fulani, Yoruba "constitutional" norms of government. To what extent the top leadership of the ITP deliberately appealed to these divergent groups, I do not know; but an answer to this interesting question is not necessary to the contention that for these diverse elements to find themselves making common cause in 1954 was a perfectly reasonable, even predictable, situation.

None of this is to say, however, that this mélange produced ideological coherence. On the contrary, the grounds on which objections were being raised against the central N.A. stemmed from certain mutually exclusive political aims or values. For example, it has been stated that the ITP opposed the 1953 ("pre-Michie") reformed N.A. Council; but while some were evidently critical on the grounds that it did not provide a sufficient measure of nontraditional representation, others saw in it the unwelcome ascendancy of the educated and administratively trained young councillors over the "old guard".[30] There are numerous examples. This situation would lead us to expect a parting of the ways within the ITP should circumstances arise that would require the party to progress from a protesting stage to that of devising and expressing a positive political program.

That these developments did operate as expected is indicated by the interconnected sequence of events that accompanied the breakup of the original ITP coalition and its blossoming forth into a conspicuous purveyor of radical democracy in Ilorin. These were the launching by the Action Group and Northern Peoples' Congress of competing drives for support, the onset of the Michie reforms, and, bound up with both of these occurrences, the initiation of mass elections.

Thus, shortly after the formation of the ITP, the Western Region-based Action Group made initial overtures to the new Ilorin party, probably with an eye to obtaining an ally for its campaign for the

---

[30] "In April 1955, the traditional and illiterate members of the Native Authority Council 'revolted' against the whittling away of their powers and privileges by the younger and literate councillors, some of whom were members of their own families and some of whom were elected members of traditional standing. The spark that set things off was a proposal that only literate councillors should be appointed chairmen of committees. At that time there is no doubt that some of the important traditional members of the Council temporarily cast their lot with the then conservatively-minded Ilorin Talaka Parapo. . . . The fact that educated young men must be paid more than their traditional leaders is causing great strain in the local body politic and the solution of the problems it raises is not yet clearly in sight". *Provincial Annual Reports* for 1956; cf. the objects of the ITP as reported by the Minorities Commission, cited in note 27.

transfer of Ilorin to the West in connection with the Federal Elections later that year. In order to counter the Action Group threat, some Ilorin citizens organized a local branch of the Northern Peoples' Congress, which easily won the two Ilorin seats in the 1954 election. Subsequently, the Action Group pressed its suit to the ITP, whereupon Alhaji Yahaya (he may be remembered as one of the first two Western-educated appointees to the Emir's Council in 1936, who, despite his position as a Minister in the NPC-controlled Northern Regional government, had remained aloof from the Ilorin Branch of that party and had instead identified himself with the ITP) made an abortive attempt to negotiate an alliance between the ITP and the central NPC.[31] The central NPC's rebuke of the ITP accentuated the differences between the two parties on the local level, which in turn was not unrelated to the ITP's stepped-up attacks on the Ilorin Native Authority.

Hereafter, the ITP's basic ideological impulses became clear enough in the kind of issues which these attacks involved. One involved the Ilorin Urban Water Supply system, which had been planned and set up by the regional government to operate under the management of the Native Authority. It was inaugurated in 1955 and immediately became the ojbect of a crippling ITP-inspired boycott ("90 percent effective"[32]) on the grounds that the Ilorin people had been led to believe that a recent increase in taxation (from a flat rate of 13s to £1) would cover the costs of the new system. A variation on this contention was to the effect that the "Northern Peoples' Congress-dominated Ilorin N.A. had received most of the cost of the supply as a free gift from the Regional Government".[33] In either version, the inference was that the imposition of a half-penny per four gallons charge

[31] Alhaji Yahaya's local political affiliation was reportedly bound up with the existence of a personal rivalry between himself and the President of the Ilorin NPC, Alhaji Sa'adu Alanamu, who was said to have been more influential than his rival in the Ilorin Native Authority Council at the time. Since the Ilorin ITP and the NPC branch could not reconcile, the central NPC leaders were presented with the delicate choice of either having to harbor this enmity within its fold or to reject the one's support for the sake of the other. In rejecting the application for affiliation from the ITP, the *Sardauna* is reputed to have declared that the ITP could not expect the deal with the "father", i.e. the central NPC, if it would not deal with the "son", the local branch. In light of the close ties of the Ilorin NPC with the Ilorin Native Authority, this decision and that anecdote, apocryphal or not, speaks volumes about the intimate nature of the relationship, which, we shall see, is generally true between that party and the emirate Native Authorities.

[32] *Provincial Annual Reports for 1956*, p. 51.

[33] *Ibid.*

on water indicated unethical practice on the part of the Native Authority at the expense of the public.[34]

Charges against the N.A., imputing maladministration and corruption, now increasingly earned the party's chevron. The ITP regulars trained their guns on the three customary but now detested practices known as *Babakekeres, Ishakole,* and *Aroja. Ishakole* is the Yoruba term for the tribute, traditionally rendered in kind, from peasant farmers to their overlords. *Aroja* refers to the same transaction between market men or women and officials. The destination of the proceeds of *Ishakole; Aroja,* and *Babakekeres* payments was invariably the private pockets of the recipients (or those of official patrons), not the public treasury. These customs were therefore particularly vulnerable to political agitation, and the ITP seems to have gained strength from its opposition to them.

It is significant that all observers seem to point to the events surrounding the 1956 electoral contests for control of the Ilorin Town Council as the occasion, if not the cause, simultaneously of a decisive internal fission and of an outward ideological crystallization of the ITP.[35] These events were: Originally the ITP "had espoused the right of chiefs to sit in the Ilorin Town Council, indeed to constitute a second chamber of that council".[36] Meanwhile the NPC had been making strenuous efforts to convince the pro-ITP chiefs that it and not the ITP was the better bulwark of their interests; indeed, that the basic objectives of the latter party were inimical to those interests. The recent conclusion by the ITP of a formal alliance with the Action Group (in April) hardly militated against this argument, since the prospect of transferring Ilorin to the West ("Where the Action Group Government was known to deal harshly with old-style natural rulers"[37]) was anything but congenial to many of the chiefs. In June the ITP (with considerable help from the Action Group) won a slight majority in the primary stages of a three-phase election arrangement. Before the next stage could be executed, the ITP, seeing that its margin of victory over its opponents was tenuous and apparently persuaded that a marriage between them and the chiefs was in the offing, "demanded the elimination of all nominated

---

[34] "The Native Authority strengthened them [the ITP leaders] in their determination by letting out contracts for selling water from the standpipes only to its Northern Peoples' Congress supporters". *Ibid.*

[35] See Sklar, *Nigerian Political Parties*, pp. 352-54; *Provincial Annual Reports for 1956*, pp. 51-53; my interviews corrobrate this view.

[36] Sklar, *Nigerian Political Parties.*

[37] *Ibid.*

traditional members from the primary and secondary electoral stages and all but the six senior and traditional ward heads from the Town Council itself".[38] An ITP boycott of the latter stages eventually induced the regional government to accede to most of the party's demands, to the great consternation of traditional leaders.[39] In the end, the ITP secured an outright majority in the Ilorin Town Council.

The conclusion to which the foregoing discussion points is that at bottom it was not ideological confusion on the part of the architects of the ITP that underlay the party's seemingly irregular origin and rise. Rather, the phenomenon can be attributed to the playing out in the context of Ilorin's peculiar political milieu of an otherwise not unfamiliar predicament: a discrepancy between the kind of appeals which help to nurture a political movement and the character of the substantive goals which its progenitors eventually aim to achieve. As we shall see, this assessment not only throws light on the party's beginnings, it helps explain the party's subsequent conduct as pilot of the Ilorin Native Authority.

One more aspect of the ITP's development requires mention. The party made no effort to project itself within the southern or non-metropolitan districts.[40] The Islamic affiliation of the principal founders and the core membership of the ITP doubtless partly accounts for this omission. But it is worth noting that the official British view partly attributed it to the fact that the district head system had already been abolished in southern Ilorin (as early as 1945). The implication here was that this earlier action had had the effect of obviating any clash *within* that area of rulers versus subjects, hence of making irrelevant an ITP-type appeal[41] (an interpretation that would seem to confirm that the thrust of that appeal had always been essentially anti-hierarchical, or pro-democratic change). The period under review did, however, see the sprouting of political parties in the nonmetropolitan area, each more or less centered on one of the indigenous

---

[38] *Provincial Annual Reports for 1956*, p. 52. The Report points out that, "As the instruments provided for a 37 percent injection of traditional members in the primary stages and for a 31 percent injection at the secondary level, the play soon became deadly serious".

[39] "At the end of August the Regional Government decided to send three Ministers to Ilorin for further consultations on the Town Council issue. They made a second agreement, acceptable to both political parties, but at first the N.A. Council, led by the six traditional Ward Heads, made it clear that they would rather have no Town Council than one directly elected and consisting of themselves and fifty-one elected members. They did eventually agree to most of the Ministers' proposals with foreboding, but flatly refused to accept any increase in the number of elected members". *Ibid.*, p. 53.

[40] See *ibid.*, p. 50 (Para. 4), p. 51 (Para. 7).

[41] *Ibid.*

Yoruba subgroups (Edge-Igbomina *Parapo*, Ekiti Federal Union, etc.), among whom animism and Christianity, as well as a republican spirit, were strong. While these parties shared the ITP's distaste for the autocratic traditions of the central N.A., they put much more emphasis on reunification with their Western Yoruba brothers than did the ITP, which had at first declined to make that objective an article of its alliance with the Action Group.[42] But, appreciating the other politically kindred aspects of these organizations, the ITP had come to a political understanding with them at the outset of popular electioneering in Ilorin. Hence these organizations were subsumed in the "Grand Alliance" which in May 1957 came to power in the Ilorin Native Authority. (The party composition of the central council and that of the subordinate councils at this date is shown in Tables 2 and 3, respectively.)

WHAT WENT WRONG? In an effort to justify or condemn the act of dissolving the ITP-controlled Council in August 1958, the Northern regional government and the ITP spokesmen tried to compile the most telling possible indictment and defense of the council. The result is the existence of two conflicting accounts, both of the conduct of that body and of the reasons for its dissolution, both versions disseminated by interested parties and hence unacceptable at face value.[43] The object here, of course, is not to condemn or justify the events in question, but to understand them. Fortunately there exists other material, which has made it unnecessary to rely on these interpretations[44] (and as might be expected the findings do not completely tally with either of them). Furthermore, for the most part, not facts but their meaning and significance, are disputed in the relevant versions; hence they too are useful sources of data. The best avenue of approach is to consider the record of the ITP Council in terms of the local government reform objectives set forth in the last chapter, starting with the council's indubitable accomplishments in these respects.

Table 2 gives the occupational backgrounds of the elected members of the Ilorin N.A. Council of 1957. It indicates that thanks to the

[42] See Minorities Commission *Report*, p. 77.

[43] The government's case is set forth in its white paper: "Statement of the Government of the Northern Region on the Report of the Committee of Inquiry appointed to investigate allegations about Ilorin N.A." (Kaduna, 1958). The ITP's arguments are scattered, but see especially, Northern House of Assembly *Debates*, August 5, 1958, pp. 431-42, *passim*; and *Daily Times* of Nigeria, December 27, 1957, p. 5; *Daily Service* of Nigeria, June 18 and July 29, 1958.

[44] *Minutes of the Ilorin Native Authority Council*, May 8, 1957 to August 1958 inclusive, mimeo.; "Provincial Annual Reports for 1957", by Mr. J. G. Davies, unpub., Provincial Files, Ilorin; field interviews by the author.

Table 2: Composition of Ilorin Native Authority Council, May 1957-August 1958

Tradition and Nominated members (15 + 1)
  Emir of Ilorin (ex-officio)

  Balogun Ajikobe
  Balogun Alanamu
  Balogun Fulani
  Balogun Gambari
  Magaji Are
  Magajin Gari
  Imam Imale
  Olaffa of Offa
  Elese of Igbaja
  Olobo of Obo Aivegunle
  Olupo of Ajasse
  M. Muhammadu (*Waziri*)
  M. Yahaya Ilorin (*Madawabi*)
  M. Saadu (local government secretary)
  M. Okin (provincial supervisor of accounts)

Elected members (50)	*ITP/AG Grand Alliance* (36)[b]	*NPC* (14)
Ethnic Origin		
Yoruba	35	9
Fulani	—	3
Hausa	—	1
Nupe	1	1
Religion		
Muslim	18	12
Christian	18[a]	2
Occupation		
farmers	14	5
business (trade, livestock, etc.)	6	1
school teachers	5	—
village and district heads	—	5
N.A. employees	1	1
firm employees	1	—
cycle repairers	1	—
gown decorators	1	—
politicians	4	—
carpenters	2	—
blacksmiths	1	—

[a] All elected from nonmetropolitan districts.

[b] Includes 19 Ilorin *Talaka Parapo*, 10 *Egbe Igbomina Parapo*, 3 Ekiti Federal Union, 3 Action Group members, and 1 "Independent".

Source: "Constitution of Ilorin Native Authority Council" (based on Ilorin Provincial Office Files P.C.J. 2329/s.1, C. 69), and my field notes.

Table 3: Party Affiliations of Members of District and Town
Councils in Ilorin Emirate

District	Membership			Party affiliation					
	nomin.	*elect.*	*total*	*N.P.C.*	*Ind.*	*A.G.*	*I.T.P.*	*E.I.P.*	*E.F.U.*
Afon	2	18	20	3	2	—	(13)	—	—
Owode	2	16	18	(14)	2	—	—	—	—
Oniro	2	12	14	—	2	—	(10)	—	—
Paiye	2	11	13	—	2	—	(9)	—	—
Malete	2	12	14	3	2	—	(7)	—	—
Oloru	2	20	22	4	2	—	(14)	—	—
Ejidogari	2	16	18	4	2	—	(10)	—	—
Lanwa	1	20	21	(13)	2	5	—	—	—
Igponrin	2	19	21	(12)	2	5	—	—	—
Akanbi	2	11	13	2	2	—	(7)	—	—
Idofian	1	12	13	(9)	1	—	2	—	—
Omupo	—	16	16	1	1	—	—	(14)	—
Ajasse	—	16	16	—	1	—	—	(15)	—
Esie Arandum	—	6	6	—	—	—	—	(6)	—
Agunjin	1	5	6	(2)	1	—	—	(2)	—
Ora	1	6	7	(5)	1	—	—	—	—
Igbaja	1	22	23	(10)	1	—	—	(11)	—
Oro	1	11	12	—	1	—	—	(10)	—
Share Yoruba	1	18	19	(17)	1	—	—	—	—
Oke Ode	1	15	16	5	—	—	—	(10)	—
Ile Ire	—	5	5	2	—	—	—	(3)	—
Isin	1	13	14	1	1	—	—	(11)	—
Omu Aran	1	10	11	—	1	—	—	(9)	—
Oko Ola	—	4	4	—	—	—	—	(4)	—
Oro Agor	1	7	8	—	—	—	—	(7)	—
Ilofa	—	8	8	2	—	—	—	—	(6)
Ekan	—	7	7	3	—	—	—	—	(4)
Idofin	—	5	5	(5)	—	—	—	—	—
Osi	—	12	12	—	3	1	—	—	(8)
Obo Eruku	—	5	5	—	1	—	—	—	(4)
Offa	8	23	31	1	8	(14)	—	—	—
Odo Ogun	6	15	21	9	6	—	—	—	—
Ilorin Town*	8	57	65	23	6	—	(28)	—	—
Totals	51	453	504	150	54				

* August 1958
Numbers in parentheses equal working majorities. 25   100   102   22

ITP, people who traditionally were excluded altogether from participating in the government of the emirate (ordinary farmers, petty traders, schoolteachers) got the opportunity to do so at the highest level.
None of the ITP councillors came from genuinely patrician families,
and at least a third represented nonmetropolitan peoples whose active share in Ilorin government previously had been minimal.

The elected NPC councillors, by contrast, were mostly heirs of the old regime, as were the bulk of the N.A. staff members, a circumstance that gave rise to a great deal of trouble, as we shall see.

An extensive organizational revamping to facilitate effective control by the popularly elected ITP majority was immediately carried out. The departments of the Native Administration were regrouped into eight divisions (finance, establishment, development, local government, education, public health, general tax advisory, and urban water supply), each under a "Head of Division" who exercised executive powers. But policy-making powers were placed in the hands of eight committees (corresponding to the administrative divisions) composed of elected councillors to which the Heads of Divisions were directly responsible. During the first three months, only ITP members were included, but thereafter the party conceded the right of the minority to have representation on these committees, albeit under pressure from British administrative officers.

In addition, a General Purposes Committee, consisting of the leading ITP councillors, functioned as a kind of grand policy-making body for N.A. affairs as a whole, although it tended to specialize in village and district administration, judicial and police affairs, and appointment and discipline of major officials in all categories—matters which previously were the exclusive preserve of the Emir and his closest traditional associates. A policy of recruitment and promotion on the basis of objective qualifications and demonstrated ability was adopted in principle for all posts; so far as the Heads of Divisions were concerned, it was definitely adhered to, with the result that the occupants of these new posts were among the ablest men in Ilorin. To this extent, an enhancement both of administrative efficiency and integrity of popular conciliar authority was achieved at the center.

Comparable strides were made at the level of the subordinate council. The Central Council showed a far greater willingness to delegate powers to these organs than had been typical of the nonpopularly controlled emirates. Among the more important services handed over were adult education, local public roads and buildings, and sanitary services. Functional delegation was backed up by the grant of a significant measure of financial autonomy. Certain sources of central Native Authority revenues in the past (e.g. bicycle licensing, slaughterhouse, and building permit fees) were reallocated to district and village area councils, which were also empowered and encouraged to levy "rates" to provide money for services introduced on their own initiative. By the end of 1957 over 20 subordinate councils had done so (the incidence of the "rate" varied from six pence to five shillings per ratepayer), compared with only one in the previous financial year. The total amount (over £11,500) for all subordinate councils in Ilorin from this source was tops in that year for the Northern emirates, as was the percentage of total central N.A. expenditures budgeted for support of subordinate councils generally. A comparable number of subordinate councils undertook responsibility for drafting their own budgets (or "estimates" in British parlance), which had officially been regarded as a great milestone in the progress of an emirate toward effective democratic local government.

A successful campaign to strengthen and reform the administrative hierarchy at the lower rungs through recruitment of abler people was virtually ruled out by the scarcity in supply, but the Central Council ordered the transfer of large numbers of district and village functionaries away from their customary area of residence, and sometimes into different administrative departments as well, all in an effort to dissolve those traditional bonds of personal loyalty between officials which encouraged favoritism and maladministration. At the same time, removals were made of some high officials widely reputed for engaging in supposedly prohibited practices, notably in the celebrated cases of the District Heads of Afon and Paiye.[45] The ITP Central Council informed the district councils of its intention, when it made a new appointment to the post of district head in the future, to solicit their preferences between the traditionally eligible candidates beforehand (which in the metropolitan districts was a fundamental departure from the customary procedure).

It can be said of the ITP Council's behavior toward subordinate councils that it went a good way toward closing that division between power and participation which was identified above as a major soft spot in the reform program devised by the government for the emirates as a whole. As a result, government officials in Ilorin reported markedly increased interest in, and even enthusiasm for, local govern-

[45] In its 1958 white paper on Ilorin these cases were cited as examples of political "victimization" on the part of the ITP Council. It is noteworthy, however, that the official *Divisional Annual Report* for 1957 commented on them as follows: "One of the major events of the year was the suspension of the District Heads of Afron and Paiye. In both these areas there had long existed an unsettled feeling and in September . . . a fact-finding committee . . . decided that the two D.H.s should be suspended and replaced until the end of the financial year. The D.H.s complained of political victimization but, whatever the truth of this, there was no doubt that their administration had been at fault".

ment in the districts and villages, particularly in the nonmetropolitan areas.[46]

It was observed that the ITP rose to power partly on the strength of specific promises to eradicate certain popularly reviled customs and to make definite improvements in the realm of local service. This provided a concrete test of the ability of the Council to act as an effective channel of grievance and interest articulation. The Council's first triumph in this regard was the suppression of *Ishakole* payments, a feat which, as British officials acknowledged, the colonial administration had tried and failed to accomplish for 50 years.[47] *Aroja* and *Babakekere* succumbed next. These officials further credited the reforms with bringing about what one described as a "magical drop in tension" compared with the political conditions in Ilorin during the previous year.[48]

Through the vigilance of its committees and the work of its new heads of divisions, the Council no doubt improved the quality of existing services; on the other hand, it does not appear to have materially advanced the level of services or development projects.[49] The ITP's campaign promise to do so without raising the rate of general taxation was mainly responsible for this disappointment. Another factor was the Council's action in regard to the water scheme, which it operated at a £16,000 loss for the year rather than repudiate the ITP's commitment to supply water without a levy at the standpipes. Eventually the Council would have had to be more realistic about the relationship between the level of public services and that of public revenue if it was to make any real headway (reportedly by the end of the year, the ITP councillors were preparing their constituents for the reimposition of a per-gallon water tariff).

Under the circumstances, a substantial achievement of the Council was to balance its budget in 1957, thanks largely to the councillors' personal efforts to increase the number of tax-payers through a more effective count. The net addition of 10 percent to the tax rolls in 1957 may have been a comment on the greater diligence and public acceptance of the new councillors or a reflection on the efficiency or fiscal integrity of the old regime; most likely was a little of both. In one ward of Ilorin Town, the increase was 40 percent.[50] Consider-

[46] See Ilorin, *Divisional Annual Report for 1957.*
[47] See also, *Provincial Annual Reports for 1957*, p. 53, para. 23.
[48] Davies, *Biu Book*; cf. *Provincial Annual Reports for 1957*, p. 51.
[49] See *Native Administrations and Townships Estimates, 1956-57* and *1957-58* (Kaduna, 1956, 1957), Items X through XV, and XIX.
[50] Davies, *Biu Book.*

ing, too, that overestimated revenue items and underestimated expenditure items had been a recurrent defect in the budgets of its predecessors, it seems fair to say that the relative overall performance of the ITP Council on the area of financial management of public services was respectable if not spectacular.

The government white paper, which incorporated the findings of the government-appointed Commission of Inquiry, censured the ITP Council for conduct which, however deplorable in itself, now seems irrelevant to the Council's performance as an organ of modern democratic local government. Thus the Council was criticized for "bad manners" and "rudeness" in its dealing with traditional chiefs, and administrative officers.[51] Other conduct, which is not usually officially condemned in relation to other Native Authorities, was condemned in regard to Ilorin—notably the Council's ignoring the advice of administrative officers on matters within the competence of the Council. Indeed, it was pointed out above that the N.A. Law nowhere provides that the Native Administrations are obliged to accept administrative officers' advice (except, of course, when they are conveying the directions of the regional government). On the contrary, administrative officers who had worked with various other Native Administrations since the war reported that on occasion other N.A. councils rejected their advice and invoked this feature of the law in support of their stand. It was also noted before that since the war the government itself had emphasized the essentially advisory status of administrative officers in relation to Native Authorities.[52]

A study of the white paper's bill of particulars reveals that the weight of the government's case centers on only one area seriously relevant to the primary objectives and principles of local government reform outlined in the last chapter—namely, the ITP Council's conduct toward the N.A. staff (18 of the 27 charges come under this heading).[53] Significantly, this is an area in which the evidence indicates that the Council did run afoul of the accepted canons of impartiality and impersonality. The analysis in the last chapter suggested that the character and structure of staff relations posed a fundamental difficulty for the policy of developing modern democratic local government within the framework of traditional institutions in

[51] The deeper significance of this behavior is discussed below. *Statement of the Government on Ilorin N.A.*, p. 8.

[52] *Duties of the Administrative Officer in Northern Nigeria.*

[53] Government of the Northern Region, Section 5, para. i-xvi, Section 6, para. iv, vi.

the emirates. A brief examination of the circumstances and influences underlying the ITP Council's transgressions on this score will show how this fundamental difficulty was manifested in the particular case of Ilorin.

The ascendancy of the ITP in the policy-making bodies or councils did not automatically effect any change in the ranks of the policy-executing administrative staff, which had routinely consisted largely of the relatives and clients of traditional authorities. As the system had previously operated, policy and administrative roles were combined; for example, many of the outgoing central councillors had at the same time been paid officials of the N.A. In the realm of political leadership, the logic of the government's policy of fostering continuity, or gradualism, meant that traditional officials had to be able to compete politically on equal terms with commoners. Hence we have the anomaly in Northern Nigeria, from a modern Western standpoint, that the right of officials or staff of the Native Administrations (the public servants of the local authorities, in Western usage) to participate in local politics was not restricted, as it was the West, to voting in elections.

On the contrary, the newly elected, radical-minded ITP councillors at all levels in Ilorin found themeslves with an administrative staff that was not only by origin a creature of a regime it had despised and ostensibly defeated, but a body of men free to continue working politically for its own ideas and interests against those of its nominal new masters, even to the extent of taking an active role in local opposition political parties. The result was that the ITP-controlled councils, especially the Central Council, started off with an attitude of distrust and suspicion toward its administrative staff, an attitude fortified in the first instance by the common knowledge that the bulk of these people were, as one would expect, members of the NPC.[54]

The councillors' most immediate fear was that their programs would be sabotaged, or at best not wholeheartedly implemented. The first response was a reluctance on their part to delegate even routine executive functions to the staff. Indeed, had it not been for the fact that a quorum of the ITP central councillors were professional politicians or otherwise in a position to work full-time on N.A. affairs, a serious overall decline in administrative efficiency would probably have occurred in 1957. British officers in Ilorin at the time judged that the industry of these councillors did succeed in offsetting this

[54] Davies, *Biu Book*, remarks on p. 7, "Nearly all of the staff is solidly N.P.C."

danger, but neither did the situation allow for any substantial improvement.[55]

Given the size of Ilorin emirate (2,647 square miles, with a population of nearly 400,000), and the complexity of operations involving over £200,000 annually, not to delegate executive functions was an unsatisfactory, if not ultimately unfeasible solution. A second response was to insist on the political neutralization of the Ilorin staff in accord with Western norms. ITP leaders were quick to point out that one of the arguments used to justify the regional government's policy in this matter—namely, that to disqualify officials from taking part in local politics would be to forfeit the only source of educated political leadership—was not valid in Ilorin, where missionary activity had produced more than an adequate number of reasonably educated nonofficials. The government's answer is said to have been that Ilorin could not be treated in isolation.[56] The government did not, in any case, alter its policy. It was perhaps predictable, then, that a third response of the ITP Council would be to replace as many of the existing staff as possible with personnel deemed more politically reliable. In doing so, the ITP Council itself departed from the norms of impartiality, impersonality, and bureaucratic "merit".

However extenuating the circumstances might seem to an outside observer, the government invoking these administrative norms found much to censor. Thus, item four of the findings of the Commission of Inquiry cited in the government white paper reads:

> The Native Authority gave notice of dismissal to 8 temporary scribes in July, 1957, and to another 6 in January, 1958; at least half of these were below the normal retiring age. It is recorded that the reason was to improve efficiency and that in future a minimum educational qualification of Middle IV would be required for such appointments. No records, however, exist about the qualifications of those dismissed or about other specific reasons for their dismissal. Records show that of the 22 temporary scribes engaged since then, only 3 had a Middle IV qualification.[57]

Other instances included one in which vacant posts that were supposed to be advertised were filled without such advertisement, while other applicants were turned away on the grounds that there had

[55] *Ibid.*
[56] See the article by J. S. Olawoyin in the *Daily Times* of Nigeria, December 27, 1957, p. 5. Cf. Davies, *Biu Book.*
[57] "Statement of the Government of the Northern Region", p. 3.

not been sufficient advertising; another in which an appointee-designate to the office of Chief of Police, returning after having successfully completed a training course at a recognized school, was harassed by being placed on probation at less than the regular minimum salary (he had once contested an election under the NPC banner), and several in which less objectively qualified personnel were favored over some who were more so.

Such actions further alienated the old staff members from the Council, whose distrust was thus reinforced, and so on in a vicious circle that generated the very discord the Council sought to stifle. Within a few months councillors and staff members were locked in open political combat. The latter petitioned the regional government and inspired letters to the newspapers airing grievances and seeking support and in turn were disciplined by their employers on grounds of disloyalty. Their next move was to demand that the Native Authority give recognition to an Ilorin Native Authority Workers' Union which would serve to protect the interests of staff. The N.A. Council took the position that it would grant such recognition only on condition of a government order rescinding the right of staff to engage in organized local political activity. It is interesting to note that a federal government labor officer, called in to help settle the issues between the N.A. Council and staff, withdrew precisely on the grounds that the questions were essentially political, not occupational.[58] Rather curiously in this light, the Council's refusal to recognize the Union forms the substance of one of the charges in the white paper, and even more so in light of the fact that, as an opposition member recalled during the parliamentary debate on that document, a few years before, another (conservative) N.A. had made a similar refusal with impunity.[59]

There has been sufficient discussion here of the issues ostensibly involved in the government's decision to dissolve the ITP Council—issues and principles of modern democratic local government—to suggest that they do not satisfactorily explain the decision. Indeed, it is noteworthy that after reviewing the Council's performance in these terms and listing its liabilities, the senior administrative officer

[58] "The Labour Officer reported that in his view there was no doubt that the issues were almost entirely political, that the union was at fault for viciously attacking its employers and that normal industrial [sic] relations could not be expected in Ilorin as long as the workers' organization so openly and actively associated with the Council's political opponents." Davies, *Biu Book.*

[59] Northern House of Assembly *Debates*, pp. 441-42.

for Ilorin Division (who presumably had been a target of ITP "rude-ness") in 1957 seems to have concluded that the Council's balance was healthy.[60] (On February 4, 1958 the regional government an-nounced that it was considering dissolving the Council.[61]) Yet not all of the ITP's "liabilities", or "misconduct", can be dismissed as self-defense against the danger of treachery by its staff. Such consid-erations do not explain, for example, why one staff member was ap-parently invidiously denied the privilege of an N.A.-financed auto-mobile; nor why even at the innocuous level of road laborers and masons, personnel were replaced with political faithfuls; nor why on occasion the powers of the N.A. were used to embarrass, penalize, or harass ordinary peasants (for example, the threat to shut down the markets of certain villages whose inhabitants were identified with the opposition).[62] Evidently the criteria of modern democratic local government somehow became a secondary consideration in the eyes of *all* the principals in the Ilorin controversy.

The truly crucial dimensions of this controversy can be seen only if one focuses on the impact of the ITP regime on the traditional struc-ture of authority. First, the ITP road to power was in electoral con-tests in which traditional rulers frequently suffered what to them was the extreme indignity of defeat at the hands of opponents who were commoners. Conversely many commoners had the novel experience of thwarting the magisterial will. The power of the ruling classes was further emasculated when the ITP assumed the powers of the central Native Authority, in particular, powers over district administration and appointments at all levels. If by virtue of these powers, commoners had occasion to dismiss or demote some district or village heads out-right, they summoned several more before the Council or its General Purposes Committee and ordered them to give an account of their administration. Superiors in the traditional hierarchy found themselves increasingly powerless to protect their auxiliaries or injure their rivals

---

[60] "The over-all picture, then, is one of enthusiasm for a reform that has caught the people's imagination in nearly all areas of the Emirate and of a relatively satisfactory first year that has strained the resources of the N.A. and of the Administration. The year has been one of the greatest possible interest. A social revolution is in progress, but it is not yet complete and much depends on the guidance and help received from the Administration in the next few years as the struggle of the common people against the previously privileged classes continues. In this respect Ilorin is in the forefront of the North, and the democratisation that is taking place here today can be expected to produce similar results in many other parts of the Northern Region in future". Davies, *Biu Book*.

[61] See *Statement of the Government*, cited in Appendix A.

[62] *Ibid.*, p. 10, para. x, xi.

in the bureaucracy. By the same token, political supplicants learned that loyalty to their old patrons was not as rewarding as before. Worst of all, the loss of patronage power and the abolition of forms of customary tribute had cast a cloud over the economic future of the traditional ruling classes, who fully appreciated the indivisibility of their economic and political prospects.

Menacing traditional authority seems to have been anything but uncalculated on the part of the ITP. Indeed, few opportunities seem to have been lost to fly in the face of traditional claims. In the minutes of the Ilorin N.A. Council for 1957, there are frequent instances of traditional officials, including the Emir, being publicly upbraided for some reason. On one occasion, he was threatened with dismissal. ITP councillors openly flouted customary rituals of deference to traditional authority, such as taking off one's shoes before entering the presence of royalty and nobility. Outraged at the appearance of an ITP leader in shoes at the Emir's palace, one incensed subject resorted to violence,[63] whereupon the ITP ceased to convene meetings there, a move which traditionalists probably rightly feared would suggest symbolically a break in the continuity of Ilorin's political institutions. When vacancies occurred in territorial chieftaincies the councillors sometimes beturbaned a candidate from one of the competing lineages of a local dynasty, thereby displaying the power to act as arbiter between the fates and fortunes of traditional ruling groups. In other cases, for example in Ora (a metropolitan district), the ITP demonstrated its willingness to go outside hereditary dynasties altogether to pick successors of whom it approved.

From the standpoint of the basic interests and sensibilities of Ilorin's ruling classes, perhaps the ITP Council's most serious moves came in the form of two related resolutions. One congratulated the Western region Yoruba society called *Egbe Omo Oduduwa* on its anniversary. This society was not only closely identified with the Action Group, which had come to be regarded by the Northern government as potentially poisonous to all the Northern Region stood for, but it was also a particularly zealous exponent of an Ilorin-West merger. The second resolution, passed on the eve of the Minorities Commission hearings—and significantly, less than a month before the Northern government declared that it might dissolve the Council —expressed the view of the Council majority that the Northern and

---

[63] Malam Ahmadu Rufai, who was sentenced to two months' imprisonment for assaulting Mr. J. S. Olawoyin. See *Daily Times of Nigeria*, December 27, 1957.

Western Regional boundaries ought to be redrawn so as to place Ilorin within the latter's territory, a move which, as the historically minded Resident C. W. Michie noted: "The Traditional leaders of Ilorin had been countering for one hundred and twenty-five years".[64] As this resolution lacked any legal force (interregional Nigerian boundary revision being a subject beyond the competence of any local authority), it probably smacked all the more of a gratuitous affront to traditional leaders.

These actions, and others that might be cited, are indicative of the ITP councillors' attempt to do something far beyond providing services in accordance with the principles and ancillary objectives associated with "modern democratic local government". The greater objective was to consummate a revolution, to uproot permanently the sources of traditional influence and authority, a result which institutional reforms had made possible rather than actual. The political power inherent in the new local government structures was put to use as an instrument, hopefully, of substantive political and social change.

The rather slim margin with which the ITP controlled the central N.A. doubtless intensified the councillors' awareness of the inconclusiveness, from their point of view, of the reforms thus far instituted. Considering the number of nonelected traditional members of the Central Council who invariably voted on the side of the NPC during the tenure of the ITP majority, the margin consisted of a mere seven seats in a council of 65 members (see Table 2). Indeed, a comparable situation within the Ilorin Town Council accounted for the curious fact that after four ITP members transferred their allegiance to the NPC, the ITP was reduced to a de facto minority there, despite its continued majority in elected seats.[65] Furthermore, traditionalists were still entrenched in the bureaucracy, which for all its desire, the ITP could not succeed in transforming overnight. Above all, there was the councillors' uncomfortable knowledge that probably the bulk

[64] *Provincial Annual Reports for 1956*, p. 50.

[65] Following the Ilorin Town Council election of 1957 the Council's composition was 32 ITP members, 19 NPC members and 6 traditional members. After the four ITP members "crossed the carpet", the NPC had 23 elected seats to the ITP's 28, but with the votes of the six traditional members, the NPC controlled the Council—a situation immediately reflected in the replacement of the former ITP Chairman of the Council by Malam Suleman Olokoba who was *Mogaji Agbadamu* (a traditional title) and a prominent NPC-er, and in a reconstitution of the eight committees of the Town Council, which reduced the ITP membership in them to a minority. See *Daily Times of Nigeria*, September 1, 1958 and the article by Malam Adelodun Yusuf in the same newspaper, November 24, 1958.

of Ilorin's predominantly peasant electorate, which had voted the ITP to power, did not fully share nor completely understand the essentially secular social and political values the party was seeking to promote. For, as we have observed, the ideological sights of the peasantry were fixed on a "return" to the political ideals antedating the Fulani coup d'etat, on a reinstating of the earlier traditional order.

The upshot was political insecurity of the ITP, which made their road to revolutionary change all the more rugged and their efforts to get there all the more feverish. The essence of the "revolutionary task" was communication with the peasantry—ultimately to "lift their sights" to the political and social objectives of the ITP leaders. But the most immediate problem was to "make an impression", to inculcate an awareness of the authority and power of the new regime. Yet victory in the long run presupposed success in the short, especially in view of the party's slim majority. The greatest difficulty was that for the moment the peasants' understanding of political power and authority derived exclusively from their traditional forms and expressions, such as patronage power or the ability to grant or withhold from a village the prerogative of operating a market. From this it can be seen how the ITP might be drawn into committing acts that, however effectively they conveyed the message of ITP power, were plainly more in keeping with the traditional system the party denounced than with the party's own goals—a predicament which paralleled the one underlying the party's obscure origin. In this light, the ITP councillors' seemingly compulsive tendency to assail and humiliate traditionally eminent persons in public is also comprehensible.

A willingness of political opponents to adhere to rules that functioning political institutions necessarily involve presupposes, as political scientists have often pointed out, agreement on certain fundamental issues: a minimum definition of a common political authority and legitimacy—what and who are worthy of ultimate loyalty. This generalization did not exclude Ilorin, where the differences between the ITP councillor and the traditionalists involved precisely such fundamental issues and where, consequently, neither side accepted the working principles of modern democratic local government as binding. The regional government, for its part, had countenanced the reforms in Ilorin on the assumption that they were compatible with the survival of the authority and influence of traditional rulers. But every day under the ITP regime made the assumption more untenable. Toward the end of the year district heads, as an act of protest began threatening to withhold from the Council the taxes they had collected. On May 17, five days before the government set up the Commission of Inquiry, the Emir, along with other traditional Ilorin notables, sent a petition to the government urgently calling on the government to intervene. It eventually became clear to the government that it either had to sustain traditional authority and abandon the democratic reforms in Ilorin, or to permit the opposite result. That it was this consideration, above all, behind the government's decision to dissolve the Council is noted in the remarks a government minister directed to the ITP Council leader, J. S. Olawoyin, during the parliamentary debate on the White Paper: "Honourable members will have noted in the Report of the Committee of Inquiry that our member for Offa is quite prepared to hurl insults at his traditional ruler, but is not prepared to apologise for them. . . . He does not apparently realize that it is against all Northern tradition for Emirs and hereditary titleholders to bandy insults with ill-mannered upstarts. . . . It is only proper therefore for the Honourable Member to be told here on the floor of this House how heartily we despise his actions toward his Emir".[66] (Two minutes of silence were observed in the House of Assembly on this occasion in commiseration with the Emir of Ilorin for the "abuses" he had suffered.[67]

The solicitude for tradition was based on more than sentiment, however; nor did it stem from concern only for Ilorin. From the beginning, traditional rulers in other emirates had followed closely the Ilorin "experiment", all the more so for its having been presented to them as a model for the future. In the House of Chiefs' first session following the inauguration of the ITP Council, misgivings were uttered;[68] as the full implications of what was happening in Ilorin sunk in the Chiefs made their apprehensive feelings known to the government. At bottom, the fear was that the message being transmitted in Ilorin—that traditional authority could be defied with impunity—would in time reach subjects elsewhere. The destiny of traditional authority everywhere in the emirates was bound up with its fate in Ilorin.

[66] Mr. Michael Audu Buba, Northern Minister of Social Welfare and Co-operatives, in the *Northern House of Assembly*, August 5, 1958, p. 447.
[67] *Ibid.*, p. 449.
[68] See, for example, p. 146 of the House of Chiefs *Debates*, August 12, 1957, where the Emir of Pategi comments: "In 1952, when the Ministerial system was introduced into this Region, we Chiefs had grave doubts lest this system would not work as it should. One example of this is the Ilorin Native Authority Council which introduced some subversive measures against the administration of the native rulers".

Full appreciation of why the policy of maintaining traditional authority was so basic to the current regional government must await an analysis of the dynamics of political institutions at the regional level. But the government's intervention in Ilorin may be taken as a demonstration both of the great importance which the government evidently attached to the policy, as well as of the fundamental limitations this emphasis necessarily imposed on the process of modernization and democratization of local government in Northern Nigeria. Exactly how fundamental and how immediate these limitations were to turn out to be in the case of Ilorin, the government probably never anticpated, however.

IN PLACE of the ITP Council the Northern government appointed what it termed a "caretaker council", presumably to suggest its interim character. To judge by official statements at the time, the government apparently expected that this step would allow Ilorin to retain much of the substance of the recent reforms in its system of local government while extracting the political rancor from it. Thus the Minister of Local Government was quoted as having "urged members of the newly constituted Ilorin caretaker committee to put politics aside in their deliberations, and to do only what they considered best for the people"; he "warned that local government councils should be devoid of politics because politics had nothing to do with the repair of roads, building of offices, provision of water supply and the education of children".[69] At the same time, it would appear from the number of members with traditional titles selected for the caretaker council that the government had acted under considerable pressure from its political supporters in Ilorin, traditionally eminent ones in particular, to restore the status quo ante (see Table 4). Furthermore, of the 20 members of the caretaker council, seven were illiterate, one was literate in Yoruba only, and one in Arabic only, while the elected members of the dissolved ITP-controlled Council included a B.A. and an L.L.B. In line with the policy of "depoliticizing" Ilorin local government, it was announced, however, that "in order to insulate Native Authority staff matters from political influence the Regional Government has also decided to take over responsibility for the Ilorin Native Authority staff and to set up an independent Establishment Committee for this purpose".[70]

[69] *Daily Times* of Nigeria, October 1, 1958.
[70] See "Statement of the Government of the Northern Region of Nigeria on the Report of the Committee of Inquiry appointed to investigate allegations about Ilorin Native Authority", printed in *Daily Tribune of Nigeria*, August 29, 1957.

Table 4: Composition of Ilorin Caretaker Council July 1959[a]

M. Sule Gambari,[b] Emir of Ilorin
M. Tukur Ayao (*Balogun Ajikobi*)
M. Belloh (*Balogun Alanamu*)
M. Yahaya (*Balogun Fulani*)
M. Aliyu (*Balogun Gambari*)
M. Zubieru (*Magaji Are*)
M. Mohammed Beeloh (*Magajin Gari*)
Mr. Arowolo, *Oba Oloffa* (the village head of Oloffa)
M. Olayila, *Elese Igbaja* (the district head of Igbaja)
Mr. Fahbemi, *Olobo of Obo Aiyegunle* (district head of Obo-Aiyegunle)
M. Mustapha Keji, *Essa of Offa* (district head of Offa)
M. Aliyu Folayan, *Olupo Ajasse* (district head of Ajasse)
M. Salihu Ayinla, *Imam Imale*
Alhaji Kamal Deen (trader)
Mr. J. O. Daniel (Native Treasurer)
M. A. K. Oba (local government secretary)

[a] Cf. Table 5, Table 6.
[b] Succeeded to throne in July 1959 upon death of M. Abdulkadiri.
Titles in parentheses are traditional and nominated members.
Source: field notes.

A conclusion of the discussion above is that the controversy in Ilorin revolved around fundamentally opposing conceptions of the proper basis and objects of political authority, a conflict that could not be resolved within the framework of principles or rules normally governing an operative system of modern and democratic local government. It might therefore be expected that, given a chance, the traditional rulers of Ilorin would seek to reimpose their own conceptions of political authority, notwithstanding any ground rules of modern and democratic local government which this might require flouting in the process. It might further be predicted specifically that this effort would involve an attempt to recover the key to the traditional structure of power in an emirate—the power of patronage. Moreover, the government, notwithstanding its stated intentions, would be constrained to give over that key in deference to its policy of upholding the authority and influence of traditional rulers. Just as the institutions of local government had taken on an instrumental significance that transcended their functions under the ITP, so the caretaker council would use its position to reassert the overriding claims of the traditional rulers' right and capacity to govern. In sum, it might be anticipated that the reaction to the revolutionary inroads of the ITP regime would take the form, not of a neutralization of political power, but of counterrevolution. And the record of the caretaker council in the year following its appointment indicates that what occurred in Ilorin was just that.

Almost immediately the caretaker council set about undoing much of the work of the ITP Council. In the new council's first month alone, seven decisions of the ITP were reversed. One major instance was the reinstatement of the District Head of Igbaja, whom the ITP had dismissed on grounds of maladministration. The reinstatement of the notorious District Heads of Afon and Paiye followed about a month later. This action was accompanied by a verbal exchange among them, the Emir, and the Resident, which was particularly interesting considering that the suspension from office of the District Heads had been cited, in connection with the government's dissolution of the ITP Council, as a prime example of the misconduct of the Council. The exchange was recorded in a Minute of the new Council:

> The Resident suggested that before the Council resolved into committee, the District Heads of Afon and Paiye should be called into the meeting to be addressed by him and, he hoped, the Emir would like to address them.
>
> The District Heads were then called in.
>
> The Resident told the Council that the District Heads of Afon and Paiye were to be reinstated by order of the Regional Government because the former Council only suspended them and that they should in justice be reinstated. He recalled that the failure to reinstate these District Heads led to the appointment of the Mant Committee of Inquiry and thus the present Council was obliged to rectify matters.
>
> He said that as Resident of the Province, he wished to make it quite clear that both the District Heads of the Afon and Paiye were bad District heads. He said that in view of this, they were suspended as a warning to them and it was up to them to learn a lesson from what had happened.
>
> The District said that they should therefore return to their Districts humbly, quietly, without rejoicing, and with gratitude to the Native Authority and the Government who reinstated them.
>
> He revealed that he intended to instruct Administrative Officers to look closely into their administration and that if there were any reports of oppression or victimisation he would look into the affair himself.
>
> The Resident warned that if there were any injustice in their administration, he would recommend their removal. He said that this

was their second chance so that they should learn to cooperate with their people and their Council too. Continuing, he said that he would expect to see minutes of their District Councils fully kept every time they met and that they (District Heads of Afon and Paiye) would be watched carefully.

The Emir spoke next. . . . He added that unless they (District Heads of Afon and Paiye) improved they would be removed as District Heads.

The two District Heads who had in their reply stated that they were unpopular with their people for political reasons were warned by the Resident to desist from giving lame excuses and were advised to listen to the words of the Emir so that all might be well with them.

The two District Heads then promised that they would reform.[71]

Another notable step was the abolition of the post of Native Authority Education Officer, then held by Alhaji Yahaya, the ex-government minister whose connection with the ITP was noted above. The *Waziri* of Ilorin, M. Muhammadu Gobir, the man who, along with M. Yahaya, had been a "first" Western-educated appointee to the Council in 1936 and a Head of Division under the ITP Council, was publicly chastised by the caretaker council.[72] A motion was introduced and carried in the Council's first month which reaffirmed the customary right of a district head to collect a portion of his people's cash crops. One of the councillors argued in support of the motion that the District Head of Malete "used to collect the crops until party politics came and people started agitation. The D. H. Ballah concluded that the D. H. Malete should be left to collect the cash crops as he used to do".[73]

As far as Ilorin's traditional rulers were concerned, having had the affairs of Ilorin Town, the traditional seat of authority in the emirate, under the control of the ITP was probably second in repugnance only to the ITP's power over the central bureaucracy. The circumstance responsible for the ITP's loss (by one vote) of control in the Town Council did not render the new political balance in the council

[71] Minutes of the Ilorin Native Council, Minute 157, 23rd of September 1958, Ilorin Native Authority Council, mimeo.

[72] See the Resident's comment in the Ilorin Provincial Annual Report for 1958, p. 53.

[73] Minutes of Ilorin Native Council, Minute 17, 5th and 6th of August 1958.

very secure. After two months, the caretaker council resolved to reconstitute the Town Council, reducing the number of elected members from 51 to 34 and raising the number of traditional members from 6 to 18. The caretaker council also decided not only that the alteration of the Council's elected membership called for new elections, but that it was an occasion for regrouping the existing electoral units of the town—which the caretaker council proceeded to do amid open and unrefuted charges of gerrymandering.[74] In the ensuing election, the NPC emerged with 21 of the 34 new seats, to the ITP/AG's 13.

As agents of the regional government in Ilorin, administrative officers were responsible for implementing the government's depoliticization policy. Hence, several of the decisions taken by the caretaker council entailed rejecting the advice of administrative officers whose opprobrium that council, in turn, incurred. The tone of the Resident's *Annual Report* on events in Ilorin emirate in 1958 would seem to represent among such documents the most sweeping condemnation of the role of a group of Northern traditional rulers:

It has always been the fear of the leading traditional titleholders in Ilorin Town that modern political developments would strip them of their authority and privileges, and in the past they have resisted these developments by every legal and illegal method. Prior to the election in 1957 they had used the whole Native Authority machine, including the police, the courts, and the officials of the Forestry and Health Departments for this purpose. It was, therefore, only to be expected after so sudden a reversal of their fortunes that they would not always act with absolute impartiality. . . .

Encouraged by the victory the traditional members of the caretaker council quickly shook off the last shreds of the lethargy that had overtaken them in the ITP/AG controlled Council, and showed themselves more and more disinclined to take advice. The power which had been exclusively theirs in the past had again been placed within their avaricious grasp and with it they sought to dominate the other members of the Council. Motions were brought in decrying the formation of the Government controlled Establishment Committee; they called for enhanced powers for themselves and

[74] For example, the Action Group organ, *Nigerian Tribune*, editorialized in the issue of October 10, 1959 that "Fulani settlements outside the boundaries of certain local councils have been incorporated in these council areas for the purpose of this election. That is gerrymandering of the highest order".

for the granting of large loans for the enlargement of their already big houses. A political procession was held without a permit, the leaders being convicted, fined, and bound over in the Magistrates Court. A scurrilous and unwarranted attack was made on the Waziri, a trusted official with forty years' service in the Ilorin Native Administration. . . .[75]

The nub of the counterrevolutionary movement was the Council's recapture of the power of appointment and supervision of N.A. administration staff which the government had initially vested in the four-member "Independent Establishment Committee".[76] The first, and decisive, move was made in the caretaker council's second meeting. An official Minute of the Council relates the story:

(*Minute* 52, 5th and 6th of August, 1958)

The Oba of Ileffa, through the Chairman, moved that the Council should ask the Resident to pray the Governor that—

1) Since the appointments of the title holders were not like ordinary appointments and since it always entailed some complications known only to special people, the Governor should please take away the power on all matters concerning title holders from the Establishment Committee and give it to the Emir and his Chiefs as was always the practice.

2) That the membership of the Establishment Committee should be increased by 6 to be appointed from among the Councillors.

The Resident said it would be improper for him to approach the Governor at this time with the request of the Council. The Caretaker Council and the Establishment Committee was appointed about three weeks ago. However, if the Council conducted its business properly and gained the confidence of the people then the request might be considered and put before the Governor. But that would be after a period of about three to six months.

(Magaji Are, Balogun Fulani, the Olupako spoke, asking that the Resident inform the Government anyway.)

The Resident said if the Council so wished he would convey the wishes to the Governor. The Resident, however, was not prepared

---

[75] *Provincial Annual Report on Ilorin*, 1958, by C.J.L. Reynolds, Senior Resident, mimeo.

[76] The members of the Committee were: (Chairman) Mr. J.N.C. Parmenter—Mr. Parmenter was then Senior District Officer, Ilorin Division; Malam Muhammadu Gobir; *Wazirin Ilorin*; Malam Saidu Aloa, District Head of Ballah; Mr. J. O. Daniel (Native Treasurer).

to recommend any change yet. And the Governor was determined that the appointments of title holders should be made on merit and devoid of political and personal interest. Hence the composition of the Establishment Committee.

Balogun Ajikobi thanked the Resident and said the argument really was that only 4 Councillors had been put on the Establishment Committee. The Council had confidence in these four. But the Resident should not apply the English way of doing things with the people here. According to the present setup, it appeared that a part was greater than the whole, the 4 on the Committee were greater than other Councillors. People were talking about it already and if the Resident refused the motion, then people would conclude that the 4 were the fathers of the Council. . . .

The Resident said the Council had just been appointed and yet one of the first things it wanted to do was to ask the Governor to make more appointments. The Governor would not be pleased to receive such a recommendation.

The Chairman said that in view of all that had been said and explained, was the Oba Iloffa willing to withdraw his motion?

The Oba said no.

The Acting Local Government Secretary then explained that there were two motions before the Council.

The Chairman then called for votes.

10 voted in support of the Oba Iloffa's motion.

4 voted against it.

The denouement was dryly recorded in the last paragraph of the Resident's Report quoted above: "In December, the Regional Government decided that the Establishment Committee had fulfilled the purpose for which it had been formed, confidence in staff appointments having been restored. It was accordingly dissolved and its power transferred to the caretaker council".

In light of what has been said here about the basis of the controversy in Ilorin during the reign of the ITP, it is interesting to note the apprehensions which the *Balogun* Ajikobi expressed in connection with the Oba of Iloffa's motion—that under the independent Establishment Committee setup it "appeared that a part was greater than the whole", that "the 4 on the Committee appeared greater than other Councillors", that "People were talking about it"—the allusion being to difficulties with "the English way of doing things with the people here". For quite apart from the more obvious reasons why they should want control over staff matters, the reinstated traditional rulers, like the ITP councillors before them, were evidently concerned with communicating their political reascendancy to the Ilorin people in ways they would understand. Without the power of appointment, the caretaker council's authority might, to the popular mind, seem ineffective. With the power, the claims to omnipotence, to an ability to arbitrate the destinies of friends and enemies, to superiority over any other claimants to authority—all claims integral to the authority of traditional rulers—would again be credible. One former Establishment Committee member recounted to me an experience in the aftermath of the caretaker council's assumption of the Committee's powers, which seems clearly to reflect this reality: "We have been hooted in the streets for decisions we took contrary to the desires of the Caretaker Council. When the powers of appointment were transferred to the Council, everyone in Ilorin cried to us, 'you see that our traditional Councillors cannot be defied'. The Councillors openly ridiculed us for having dared challenge their will".

The concern with communicating power in the prevailing milieu of Ilorin helps to explain what otherwise would seem purely petty acts reversing quite minor decisions of the ITP Council. For example, one of the motions passed in the caretaker council's first month was to suspend a grant of £600 the ITP Council had made to the Ilorin Football Association.[77] Another cancelled an order to locate a new N.A. Court Registrar's office away from the premises of the Native Court. The substance of such issues were obviously less important than the opportunity they afforded to demonstrate that what the ITP Council had wrought, the caretaker council could put asunder.

An intriguing aspect of this whole matter of, as it were, symbolic communication of power, was the Ilorin people's apparent readiness to construe things strictly in terms of power events which had other more available explanations. For example, C. W. Michie, under whose guidance the reforms that led to the ITP's rise to power had been introduced, was in 1958 transferred to the post of Permanent Secretary to the Minister of Agriculture. In terms merely of the regular British public servant career pattern, the transfer represented a well-earned promotion. According to the same source quoted above, however, the people of Ilorin had their own interpretation of the change, which

[77] See *Nigerian Citizen*, August 12, 1958.

one of them characterized with: "Behold Michie, the constitution-maker, dealing with fertilizers!"

But the act which more than any other represented symbolic communication of political power was the alteration of the site the ITP had selected for the construction of new office buildings for the Ilorin N.A. This minor episode shows the basic struggle which, as I have tried to show, extended beyond the surface of local government values per se, and inevitably subordinated them. This phase of the account may fittingly conclude with a brief description.

When the ITP came to power in 1957, one item of N.A. business urgently requiring its attention was the construction of new office buildings to house the secretariat of the Native Authority, whose expanded operations had long since outgrown their old quarters. The old buildings were adjacent to the Emir's palace, there they represented a monument of political continuity amid changing times. Existing space near the Emir's palace was not adequate, however, to accommodate the needed additions in office facilities. The ITP thus presented the traditional members of the Council with a choice between three alternatives, each anathema to them. One alternative was to build the new secretariat on the site of a market in Ilorin Town known as the Emir's Market, which had stood for over a hundred years. To the traditionalists, the elimination of a landmark that had been so long associated with the name of Ilorin's Emirs was an extremely distasteful prospect. (Furthermore, the ITP's proposed new site for the old Emir's market, *Apata-Onomi*, was in the heart of an ITP stronghold.) A second alternative was to locate the new secretariat far out on the edge of the traditional capitol, which would also destroy the image of direct political continuity with the distant past. The third alternative was to demolish the customary compound or residence of Ilorin's *Magajin Gari* (one of the most eminent traditional titles in Ilorin) to make room for the secretariat near the Emir's palace. The traditionalists dreaded all three alternatives because they anticipated that any of them would offer the ITP a chance to boast of its power to nullify an arrangement sanctified by tradition.

Apparently the traditionalists were not mistaken. They made their Hobson's choice in favor of the Emir's market site. It is said in Ilorin that the ITP Council exploited to the hilt the opportunity to point out to the people of the emirate the magnitude of what it had brought to pass. By the time the caretaker council was appointed, this plan for the new secretariat was well advanced, though the Emir's market was still in existence. It is also said in Ilorin that the dissolved ITP councillors had publicly consoled themselves with the thought that its authority would "live on" in the location of the new secretariat. In turn, the caretaker council, or rather its traditional member majority, came to believe that its authority depended on the fate of the Emir's market. Again, excerpts from the caretaker council's minutes best tell the story of the confrontation (for purposes of following the discussion in the Council excerpted below, it should be pointed out that one week previously, the Council had voted, on the strong advice of the Resident, to proceed with the previously accepted plans for erecting the new secretariat on the site of the Emir's market):

> The Balogun (Gambari) said it was true that the Council took a decision last week but they were not pleased with it although they did not want to reject the advice of the Resident. However, the townspeople were saying that they did not like it and that the Secretariat should be built on the vacant site originally intended (i.e., near the Palace).
>
> Mr. Daniel pointed out that according to the Council's Standing Order No. 16, a decision once taken could not be reviewed until 3 months had passed.
>
> The Emir said it was true that people were talking and wishing the Secretariat not to be built in the new market. If the Standing Order did not allow a change, nothing could be done until the 3 months expired.
>
> Balogun Gambari retorted that by then considerable work would have been done on the building.

The Emir said he knew that and would not fail to listen to what people were saying and wishing particularly when it was remembered that the Council existed only to cater to the interests of the people. The fact that this matter kept cropping up showed the amount of interest people had in it. It would therefore be good to reconsider the matter.

The Emir admitted that the matter affected him too and therefore he did not want to talk too much about it. The Emir then asked if the Resident had anything to say and if he would not mind reconsidering the matter.

The Resident said he had said what he had to say on the subject and Mr. Daniel was quite right about the Standing Order which the Council had approved. . . . However, the Resident's private opinion was that the Caretaker Council should not revise the previous decision because public money had been expended on the building. If the building were stopped someone would have to pay the £1200 that had been spent on the work so far. This would be wasted and about another £300 would be spent in removing the building materials from the site. The Council would have to pay compensation to contractors who had contracts to build the Secretariat on the site. The Resident asked the Council if it could stop the building wholeheartedly in view of all these facts; if the Council liked, however, it could. But the Council must wait for 3 months to expire.

The Resident told the Council that earlier in the day, he had a letter from the Permanent Secretary, Ministry for Local Government, in which it was stated that members of the Council might be surcharged by the Director of Audit for breach of contract. For a contractor if he had received a contract for say £20,000, he would naturally require heavy compensation for such a breach of contract. What the Council would have to pay in compensation the Resident did not know, but it was certain the Council would have to pay something.

The Resident then told the Council that the matter was in the hands of the Council.

Balogun Alanamu greeted the Resident and said that they had no interest in the market save for the townspeople who were regular users of the market. . . .

The Resident asked the Council to bring up the item after 3 months.

Balogun Alanamu said since the contractor was not being supervised, it should be possible to tell him to stop work in the meantime.

The Resident did not deny this, but the Standing Order must be followed.

Balogun Ajikobi would like to know if compensation was to be paid for asking the contractors to change the site of working or stop working entirely.

The Resident explained that the contract was made for the site in the Emir's market. It would still be a breach of contract if the site were changed.

Balogun Fulani thanked the Resident. He said it was a pity it appeared they were troubling the Resident but they would like the work to stop whatever money it cost. . . .

Balogun Ajokobi asked if the Standing Oorder did not allow the Chairman to waive this order.

The Acting Local Government Secretary read and explained Standing Order No. 16 to the Council.

The Resident said the matter could not be rediscussed except at the absolute discretion of the President who could allow the subject to be reopened . . . the Resident then asked the Emir if he allowed the matter to be reopened.

The Emir said since a lot had been said already about it, he would allow the Council to continue to debate it. [Italics in the text]

Balogun Gambari then moved that the Secretariat should be built on the originally proposed site and not in the market. The market should remain as it was.

The Magajin Gari and Balogun Fulani supported. . . .

The Resident told the Council that it was his duty to say that before the Council put the motion, Councillors should know how much had been spent so far because it would be an act of irresponsibility to pass the motion without this information. The Resident would like Councillors to know too that it was the taxpayers' money that was being spent. . . . The Resident said the Council may have to pay several thousand pounds in damages. Councillors should have all figures on the amount spent at their finger tips before they could speak confidently on the matter.

Balogun Gambari said that he could not find out for himself. The Resident told the Balogun to ask the Provincial Engineer. The Balogun said he could not because he never did.

The Resident said about £200 had been spent but there were other contracts. These should be found out from the Provincial Engineer.

The Emir then put the motion to the Council.

The motion was passed by a vote of 15 to 1.[78] The curtain was finally rung down on the episode a few weeks later when, as Minute 136 of the 16th of September recorded, "Amidst applause from both Coun-

[78] The only vote cast against the motion was that of Mr. J. O. Daniel. Four Councillors were absent. See *Minute* 38 of the Ilorin Native Authority Council, August 26, 1958.

cillors and spectators the Chairman ordered that work on the new central office building be stopped". The alternative eventually adopted was the demolition of the *Magajin Gari's* compound—an alternative with which the power of the ITP was not so popularly identified.

THE INSTITUTIONALIZATION OF COUNTERREVOLUTION

DEVELOPMENTS in Ilorin local government in the period between the above events and the fall of the civilian political regimes both regional and federal in January 1966, in effect, represented a process of consolidation, institutionalization, and to a certain extent, containment, of the counterrevolution of 1958. In ways similar to the caretaker council's conception and application of its authority in its first weeks in power, the resurgent traditional elements of Ilorin sought to ensure themselves against any recurrence of the grand experiment of 1956-58. In this effort they were greatly aided by the NPC, as was only to be expected in light of that party's general policies and its intimate local interconnections with these same elements. Thus, for example, the *Provincial Annual Report* for 1959 observed that, "Certain Senior NA officials who, in the eyes of the [Caretaker] Council, had been either lukewarm in their opposition to the [AG/ITP] or also had actively supported it, were retired. There was, in fact, throughout the year a steady swing of the pendulum away from the stand of the Alliance towards that of the traditional members and of the NPC with which they openly and enthusiastically associated themselves."[79]

Another such measure was the judicious delegation or redelegation of relevant powers on the part of the NPC Government in Kaduna (e.g. control of local police which initially had been handed to the Nigeria Police was returned to the N.A.). In turn, the enhanced powers of the Council were put to use penalizing recalcitrant opposition and reinforcing those not inconsiderable numbers of the opposition who were made to perceive the merits of conversion. Similarly the local NPC branches, themselves capitalizing on the return of sympathetic forces to power in the Central Council, were persuasive in drawing former opposition supporters in the (temporarily dissolved) subordinate councils into the official fold.

The caretaker regime continued until October 1961, a longer period than might be justified strictly in terms of emergency conditions in the conventional sense. For purposes of consolidating and institutionalizing counterrevolution, however, the timing was salutary. An

[79] *Provincial Annual Report*, 1959, p. 54.

"elected" Central Council was "reinstituted" at this time, but the step had awaited not only the informal marshalling of political realignment through the manner of means just suggested, but also felicitous alterations in the formal arrangements: the rules of the game. In this respect, there had been conspicuous retrogression in the direction of the pre-ITP system of election and representation, including substantial reweighting of the composition of both central and subordinate councils in favor of traditional membership, a return to a more conservative use of subordinate councils as electoral colleges to higher councils,[80] and the redrawing—or, in effect, gerrymandering—of certain subunits of representation and administration.

Appropriate care was taken over the appointment of new chiefs when such opportunities arose: as in the former ITP stronghold of Offa, where a cooperatively disposed new Oloffa took office on June 5, 1959 (the same day the old Oloffa fled to the Western Region, having correctly been informed that a detachment of Nigeria police was being dispatched to back up a government order of exile). Between 1962 and 1964 the new Oloffa ruled his district with a council possessing only advisory powers, because the rump ITP members of the old council (50%) were sufficiently strong in this area to sustain a boycott of any council composed on an elected basis. Indeed, in general it is fair to say that the use of boycott by the ITP in several instances in the period after 1958 ironically facilitated the institutionalization of counterrevolution.

It is important to observe, too, that the counterrevolution, as such, was not total, in that many members of the newly elected council majorities after 1961 represented a segment of the NPC that was traditional neither by background nor by outlook. Equally notable is the fact that in the latter years of Northern civilian government the Ilorin N.A. Council was frequently chastised (but less often disciplined) by Kaduna, which discovered that those of its instructions the Council found uncongenial were apt to be ignored.[81] The outer limits of the counterrevolution on each side basically were set,

[80] Under the "Michie system" only elected members of the lower or subordinate councils could stand for election to the central N.A. Council. Under the new system any member could, including traditional members. The change meant that power-wielding traditional officials could once again virtually dictate their own election to the N.A. Council.

[81] See the *Provincial Annual Reports,* 1961, 1962, and 1963. These Reports are conspicuously more superficial than earlier editions, with regard to Ilorin and elsewhere, no doubt owing to the increased political sensitivies of Kaduna-emirate relations. Even so, there are clear hints of friction with respect to Ilorin.

however, by fundamental political considerations: the NPC's self-interest in the continuing efficacy of traditional authority, on the one hand, and on the other hand, the Council's appreciation of the leverage wielded by the NPC on the otherwise politically uncommitted. Above all, the situation was held together by mutual and absolute dread of a return to the revolutionary upheaval indelibly associated in Ilorin with "democratic local government". The "Ilorin experiment" had inspired the regional government to apply firm brakes on the progress of democratization in the emirates generally,[82] and it was never to fully release them again.

Undeterred by such considerations and evidently unedified by the performance and claims of any of the political factions in Ilorin, the Military Government in May 1966 brought the course of "local government development" in Ilorin full-circle. It dissolved the Native Authority Council and reconstituted Ilorin as a "Sole Native Authority", with the (civilian) Divisional Officer of Ilorin in charge. The reasons cited for this action included "the continued refusal of the N.A. to obey Government instructions and to follow the advice of the Government officials posted to the province" and that "the councillors had been more interested in factional feuds than in the welfare of the people", all of which had "resulted in unpleasant and wasteful expenditure of N.A. funds".[83]

[82] Circular No. 16, 11th April 1958 (to all Residents) from the Permanent Secretary, Ministry for Local Government, Kaduna:

> . . . I am to say that experience in some Native Authorities has indicated that the sudden introduction of elected majorities is not always the best method of introducing sound democracy. An elected majority can behave in just as autocratic manner as any despot of the past and often with less judgment due to lack of experience in handling public affairs and people, and particularly staff.
> It is therefore the policy of the Government preferably to introduce elected minorities first at the Native Authority level while giving special attention to District and Town Councils which must have elected majorities. The latter Councils are more easily guided and controlled and have not the legal powers which make the training of a Native Authority with an elected majority so difficult". . . .

[83] New Nigerian, May 3, 1966, Vol. 1, No. 102, p. 1.

PART TWO

The Local System in Action

CHAPTER 4

A Survey of the Central Bureaucracies

DURING the two decades 1946-66 there were in Northern Nigeria 34 units of local government or Native Authorities officially classified as emirates.[1] Although the pre-European traditional political system of these emirates possessed at least most of those features previously described as characteristic of the type, important variations and differences existed among them, some of which, as in Ilorin, had a critical bearing on political development. As Table 5 shows, the existing 34 emirates vary greatly in area, population, and wealth. Such basic conditions as the level of modern Western education, communications (in both the British sense of facilities for the physical movement of goods and people and in the American sense of media for conveying information and ideas), and the degree of cultural and social cohesion, were not uniform. Hence important common elements and problems, as well as significant patterns and variations, are singled out for discussion in this and the next chapter. The discussion is based primarily on data gathered in 12 of the emirates, initially chosen for study with an eye to encompassing the major relevant variables.[2] These chapters will show how far and with what results the measures of local government reform which the policy-makers devised were implemented. The discussion begins with a general account of the framework of central administration and government in the emirates—organizational features, powers and functions, and financial position.

ORGANIZATIONAL PATTERNS

AS IN THE RECENT colonial past, the main elements in the administrative structure of an emirate were the territorial subunits (districts and villages) under resident heads or chiefs, the technical services depart-

[1] This figure excludes the historical emirates of Jema'a and Biu, which in recent years have become parts of wider units of local government formed through federation (the official term) with one or more nonemirate units, which together have assumed the names Jema'a Federation and Biu Federation, respectively.

[2] The 12 emirates I visited in 1959 for periods of from one to six weeks each are: Adamawa, Argungu, Bauchi, Bida, Bornu, Dikwa, Gwandu, Kano, Katsina, Kazaure, Sokoto, and Zaria. This was in addition to the three months spent in the capital and shorter periods of time in other parts of the region. Material to update this initial survey was gathered in 1963 and December 1966 on return visits to the region.

Table 5: Scope of Emirate Native Authorities

Native Authority	Area (sq. miles)	Pop.	Taxpayers	
			1959	1966
Abuja	2,237	101,000	17,508	19,000
Adamawa (old)	18,558	779,000	146,421	70,000
Agaie[b]	875	25,962	7,174	15,000
*with Lapai				
Argungu	3,335	171,000	37,116	40,000
Bauchi	14,516	432,204	96,955	113,000
	*with Daas			
Bedde	2,000	45,000	13,942	19,000
Bida	4,867	172,085	51,701	54,000
Borgu	10,908	76,000	15,826	19,000
Bornu	32,995	1,005,775	279,800	345,000
Daura	see Katsina	143,127	38,005	41,000
Dikwa	5,149	265,202	66,349	51,000
Fika	1,669	114,632	29,625	32,000
Gombe	6,481	378,330	69,802	82,000
Gumel	1,205	148,361	30,681	33,000
Gwandu	6,207	316,579	90,787	98,000
Hadeja	2,492	275,637	68,316	73,000
Ilorin	2,647	398,569	116,710	107,000
Jama'are	149	20,358	5,130	5,000
Kano	12,933	2,973,350	756,572	810,000
	*with Kazaure			
Katagum	7,000	309,612	79,525	89,000
Katsina	9,466	1,339,998	358,685	395,000
Kazaure	see Kano	86,632	25,636	29,000
Keffi	see Nassarawa	73,938	16,720	20,000
Kontagora	9,132	122,993	29,919	34,000
Labiagi	1,713	22,973	7,701	9,000
Lafia	3,949	114,973	23,716	35,000
Misau	890	105,416	25,010	26,000
Muri	10,684	260,280	55,796	59,000
Nassarawa	5,563			
	*with Keffi	88,865	24,425	27,000
Pategi	2,451	55,580	5,829	6,000
Sokoto	25,108	2,020,340	828,516	886,000
Wase	2,227	—	7,333	8,000
Yauri	1,306	72,319	18,590	20,000
Zaria	16,488	796,000	144,880	161,000

* Combined figure(s).

Sources: *Nigerian Yearbook*, 1959 (Lagos, 1958), pp. 203-11; *Report of the Constituency Delimitation Commission* (Lagos, 1958); C. R. Niven, *Our Emirates* (Lagos, n.d.); author's field notes; Northern Nigeria, *Local Government Yearbook*, 1966 (Kaduna, 1966), pp. 10-11.

ments with headquarters in the emirate capital and agents in the outlying areas, the judiciary or "native" courts, the police, and the
"native" treasury—all operating under the direction of the central
council presided over by the Emir. After 1952 the distribution of
power within the central councils of most emirates changed significantly, in the direction of collective decision-making and away from
the monocratic rule of the Emir. As will be demonstrated later in
Chapter 6, the extent and implications of this change differed from
one emirate to another; even where the change was greatest, from the
point of view of democratization and modernization, change was limited. The structural variation appears in the three distinguishable
organizational forms found among central councils—small councils,
usually of less than 12 members who regularly met in plenary session; large councils in which some business is normally conducted
through committees; and very large councils in which committees
handled most of the day-to-day council work. A vigorous committee
system was usually present in councils composed of a majority of
elected members; this was the least common form. The most common form, and the most traditional, was the first; it was found in the
largest and politically most important emirates, Sokoto, Kano,
Bornu, and Katsina. Thus a small council did not necessarily corre-
spond to the scale of administration.

In this period the central councils, of all types, tended to adopt
what was often loosely referred to in Northern Nigeria as a "cabinet" system. In most councils direct responsibility for a particular subject was assigned to one councillor; usually such a councillor's
portfolio actually included several subjects, each corresponding to an
administrative department, the executive head of which was directly
responsible to that councillor ("N.A. Minister", as the analogy had it).
There was no uniformity in how the subjects or departments were
grouped in different emirates, except that responsibility for central
and district administration, the nerve centers of the traditional structure, invariably was kept in the hands either of the Emir or a close
and subordinate associate holding the second highest traditional title
in that emirate—usually *waziri*.[3] For similar reasons the *wakilin
yandoka*, or chief of police, a departmental head, was in almost all

[3] In the pre-European era only Sokoto Emirate used the title and office of
waziri (from the Arabic *Vizier*), the chief minister or principal advisor to the
Sultan. The British encouraged the introduction of a comparable post in each of
the other emirates, and most of them followed Sokoto in titling its holder *waziri*,
although *Madawaki* (in Kano) and *Magajin Gari* (in Kazaure) also used.

cases a member of the ruling family. Table 6 shows the allocation of responsibilities in one council of the small noncommittee-system type.

The impetus for this organizational trend was the growing number and complexity of functions which Native Authorities were called

Table 6: Example of a Small N.A. Council Organizational Plan

Divisions	Councillors	Departments	Head of Departments
Administration and Judicial	Emir	central adm.	
		district adm.	Wakilin Ofis
		village adm.	
		native courts	Chief Alakali
Natural Resources and Cooperatives	Ciroma	veterinary	Sarkin Shanu
		agriculture	Mardanni
		forestry	Sarkin Daji
Works, Local Government Medical and Health	Wambai	works	Magaji Jisambo
		survey	Magaji Jisambo
		district Council Funds	Wakilin Raya Kase
		medical	Wakilin Asibiti
		health	Sarkin Tsapta
Police and Prisons	Sarkin Yaki	police	Wakilin Yandoka
		prisons	Yari (Treasury Ma'aji)
Education	dan Iya	provincial sec. school	Wakilin Makaranta
		3 senior primary schools	Their Headmasters
		adult education	Wakilin Yaki da Jahilci
Finance	M. Adama B. Diko	Treasury	Ma'aji

upon to perform. The general expectation was that specialization would increase the councillors' technical competence and fix responsibility more clearly, thus enhancing administrative efficiency. It was indicative of the continued importance of traditional considerations, however, that they often determined the success or failure of the formal arrangements, as Zaria's experience illustrates. In Zaria, as in other emirates, the British had long encouraged the assignment of "ministerial" responsibilities, or "portfolios", to those councillors who displayed superior educational qualifications, aptitude, and experience. But serious administrative difficulties arose in Zaria because the councillors' traditional standing was not always commensurate with the status that their new modern role implied, or, in other words, because traditional and modern lines of authority were not in accord. The following observation was made by a committee appointed in 1957 to inquire into the causes of the difficulties: "Most of the heads of Departments, especially in the case of important Departments, are all 'Sarauta Holders' appointed by the Emir. As such they may have little real interest in or usually no real experience in the detailed affairs of their Departments. The peculiar status of these 'Wakilai' (Department Heads) places Councillors responsible for these Departments in a most embarrassing position since the 'Wakilai', owing to their right of direct access to the Emir, are in a position to by-pass the Councillor and in effect to countermand and nullify any decisions of the Councillors in this direction. No Councillor would be prepared to run such a risk. Thus, the present system involving Wakilai mitigates against the efficient operation of the system of Councillors with portfolios".[4]

The committee's recommendation was that the prestige and status of the portfolio-holding councillors as assessed by *traditional* criteria—title, remuneration, access to the Emir—should be upgraded. In 1963 it was reported that the problems were yet to be solved, which was hardly surprising, considering the difference between the bases of traditional relationships within the administrative hierarchy and that which the British-inspired plan of organization envisioned. By the same token, where different considerations were mutually accommodated, the "cabinet" system appears to have enhanced administrative efficiency.

The appropriateness of applying the terms "cabinet" or "ministers" to the plan of council organization was qualified by the fact that, except in the few cases in which the majority of the council was elected, the portfolio-holding councillors were not constitutionally responsible to any wider representative body; they usually comprised the whole council, or formed a majority. In those not infrequent cases in which nonportfolio-holding councillors were also heads of departments, the anomaly in nomenclature was compounded.

The hope that the new, "outer councils" would in time assume the

---

[4] Report of the Committee of the Zaria Native Authority on the Reorganization of the Native Authority Council and of the Native Authority's Central Administrative Structure, mimeo., 1957, p. 5, para. 19 (b).

role of a popularly elected representative chamber to which the N.A. "cabinet", or "Inter council", would be accountable, never materialized in any emirate.[5] Indirect election of members to the outer council, using the district councils as electoral colleges, were almost universally employed. But more important, none of the outer councils ever enjoyed any legal power beyond that of advising an inner council. In 1955 the government made clear its intention with respect to the outer councils, in introducing an amendment to the Native Authority Law of 1954 which reads: "The outer council shall have no executive powers or functions and shall not form part of the Native Authority".[6] What is more, in practice the outer councils served as a channel for the transmission of views, information, and policies *to* rather than *from* the lower councils in the districts and villages. District and village officials (local chiefs or N.A. departmental functionaries) who won election to an outer council (as they frequently did) owed this position either to members of the inner council, to Department Heads responsible to those councillors, or sometimes even directly to the Emir himself. Not having any real political power or influence over central officials, nonofficial peasants who were elected were not encouraged to abandon their traditional posture of awe and deference to authority. By 1959 the outer councils were no longer even officially heralded as the institutional foundation of future democratic development; rather the dominant motif had become the democratic evolution of the inner or traditional central council, and of councils at the district and village level.[7]

One final point about the cabinet system plan is that the peculiarly powerful role of many N.A. councillors in it undoubtedly reinforced the traditional character of their relationship to subordinate members of the bureaucracy and to ordinary subjects. In the English system, any paid official of a local government body is legally barred from also becoming a councillor. It was seen in Chapter 4 that to prevent the coalescence of administrative and political roles in local government was, in principle, fundamentally contrary to the Northern Government's policy. The portfolio-holding central N.A.

[5] R. E. Wraith, "Local Government", in John P. MacIntosh, *Nigerian Government and Politics* (Evanston, Ill., 1966), p. 246, note 1.

[6] Subsection (2) of section 57 of the Native Authority Law of 1954 (as amended by Native Authority [Amendment] Law, 1955), Revised Edition, 1965. Previously this subsection simply read: "The outer council shall not comprise or form part of the Native Authority". All references to the Native Authority Law in this chapter refer to the 1965 Revised Edition, unless otherwise noted.

[7] *Institute of Administration Lecture Notes*, L.G. (59) 79, January 1959, mimeo., p. 9, para. 24.

councillor was nearly always a salaried official of the N.A., combining a share in decision-making authority (including legislative authority—i.e. in regard to local rules, bylaws, and orders) with executive or administrative functions—he both formulated and directed the implementation of policy. The result was a figure whose nominal designation as a local government councillor completely failed to convey, to anyone having in mind the English or any comparable system, the wide range and manifold sources of power and influence at this councillor's disposal.

The Range of Powers and Functions

As ANOTHER observer once remarked, "In the Northern Region, for most of the people 'Government' means 'Local Government'.[8] The division of powers between the Regional Government and local authorities is such", the same observer goes on to say, "that the Emirate constitutes a state within a state". To this high estimate of the degree of power concentrated in the central bureaucracy of an emirate, the assessment of the *Sardauna* of Sokoto himself, during his tenure as Minister for Local Government, may be added: "The Native Authorities in this Region have developed into complicated administrations which carry out much of the work of Government. They provide the policy for almost the whole Region. They construct our buildings, they build and maintain our roads. They collect taxes. They administer justice and perform a thousand and one other tasks. This is often not realized either inside or outside this Region. There is nothing, Sir, to compare them to the other Regions or indeed in West Africa".[9]

A glance at some of the more important specific functions and powers which the Native Administrations exercised confirm these assertions. They fall under the principal categories of maintenance of law and order, provision of public services trade and commercial undertakings, agency work (on behalf of the regional government), and licensing and regulatory authority.

From Lugard's time on, Native Authorities in Northern Nigeria were the primary source and instrument of public order and security. Under the post-independence constitution, police forces were in principle an exclusively federal responsibility; regional governments, as such, were not permitted to maintain their own. However, local authorities

[8] *Report of the Commission appointed to enquire into the fears of Minorities and the means of allaying them*, p. 55.
[9] Northern House of Assembly *Debates*, 19th February 1954, p. 225.

were allowed to retain their own small contingents. Fewer Federal or Nigerian police were deployed in the North than in the other Regions of Nigeria, no doubt partly because there was less need for them there. But whether this was the cause or the effect of the adequacy of the N.A. police, they and not the Nigeria police continued to be the dominant law enforcement agency in the Northern Region (in 1965 the ratio was 2 to 1, or 7,000 N.A. police to 3,500 Nigerian police).[10]

But the effectiveness of the Native Administrations as guardians of the peace did not derive solely, nor perhaps even primarily, from their possession of an organized police arm. The real secret of their success was the automatic obedience ordinary subjects of an emirate customarily paid to anyone in a position of authority, including especially the district and village chiefs and their minions. The account of law enforcement in a Sokoto district, found on the second page of the *Sardauna*'s autobiography, is descriptive of the emirates: "My father [the District Head of Rabah] was responsible for some sixty villages in eight village areas, containing about thirty thousand people. . . . He was responsible to the Sultan for the supression and prevention of crime and here again he worked through the Village Heads. There were no police in these rustic places, any more than there are now. He had to use his followers and servants to arrest criminals, and so did the Village Heads".[11] This is the situation which made it possible for the Northern Region to get along with an average total police strength of less than one officer for every 2,000 persons.[12]

Equally impressive is the array of public (technical) services with which the Native Authorities were concerned.[13] In allocating responsibilities to Native Authorities in Northern Nigeria, the superior government, whether colonial or indigenous, appears always to have been concerned as much with upholding or reinforcing the Native Administrations' authority and role as with augmenting its own range of influence and power. Invariably there was a division

[10] See Alan Milner, "The Maintenance of Public Order in Nigeria", in L. Franklin Blitz, *The Politics and Administration of Nigerian Government* (London, 1965), p. 193.

[11] *Sardauna: My Life* (Cambridge, Eng., 1962), p. 2.

[12] Based on a population of 20,000,000 and including the Nigeria police stationed in the Northern Region, the N.A. police, and the *Dogari* (the traditional "palace guard", now largely reduced to ceremonial functions), which totaled less than 10,000 men.

[13] For a comprehensive list of technical services provided by the Native Authorities, see *Local Government Yearbook 1966*, pp. 34-37.

of labor between the government and the Native Administrations, but rarely did it rest on the principle of preemptive jurisdiction. The result was that there existed scarcely any category of public services in which the Native Administrations did not play a vital role.

In other words, the division of technical labor between government and Native Administrations was not compartmental but hierarchical; both performed functions with respect to each major public service on different echelons of an integrated administrative structure. Generally the government had overall policy-planning and supervisory duties and direct responsibility for tasks and personnel involving professional or relatively high-level technical skills. The Native Administrations handled the more routine aspects of the service concerned or those requiring a relatively modest degree of technical proficiency. Table 7 provides the organization of medical and health services as an illustration.

Table 7: Organizational Plan for the Administration of Public Services

Regional Government	*Native Administration*
(a) General—establishment of the Medical Department, administrative, professional, higher technical and clerical; training of staff, both government and Native Administration, for all branches of medical and health services; Research, experiments and investigations	Cooperation in all medical and health activities in their areas, e.g. facilitation of sleeping sickness clearance schemes, surveys and treatment campaigns, subsistence and fees, if any, of staff in training
(b) Medical—construction, equipment, maintenance and staffing of all hospitals other than "cottage" hospitals (i.e. rural hospitals having not more than 25 beds); care of lunatics; leprosy control; sleeping sickness control including research and training of workers, surveys and intensive treatment campaigns	Construction equipment, maintenance and staffing of dispensaries, lying-in wards, small maternity centers, child welfare centers, ambulances and ambulance services; support of destitute leper patients; establishment of dispensaries for treatment of residual sleeping sickness cases after mass treatment campaigns
(c) Health—sanitation in townships and government stations (residential areas); health propaganda; prevention and control of epidemics	Sanitary inspectors and other staff working with them in their areas; sanitary materials and structures; health centers in association where possible with dispensaries; vaccination; reporting of outbreaks of infectious disease; cooperation in control including, if necessary, construction of temporary hospitals

Source: *Administrative and Financial Procedure Under the New Constitution: Financial Relations between the Government of Nigeria and the Native Administrations* (Lagos, 1947), p. 116.

The administrative responsibilities of the education, veterinary, forestry, public works, and agricultural services were all apportioned in like manner. For our purposes, the important point about these arrangements is that while performance of the N.A. functions clearly presupposed the government's performing its functions, the N.A. functions were such that they brought the Native Administrations into contact with the people much more frequently and regularly than did those performed by a government operating only at the "commanding heights" of administration. Indeed, I was assured in 1959 that it was quite possible that a Hausa peasant might live out his entire life, lengthened thanks to modern public medical and health services, without ever encountering a government medical department officer or employee. In general, it may be said that the peasants seldom realized that the government's role made possible what was dispensed to them through their N.A. It must be kept in mind that it was a deliberate stratagem of indirect rule, especially with regard to modern services, which were likely to meet with popular resistance and suspicion (inoculation, conservation, etc.), to rely on the traditionally disciplined and relatively intimate relationship of rulers and subjects to facilitate administration. The traditional authoritarian structure of society generally worked to assure a degree of popular acceptance of modern practices which the level of education or of popular commitment to the government per se could not be counted on to provide. It was, to this extent, a highly convenient substitute for understanding and consensus in furthering a modernization process. The special efficacy in Northern Nigeria of the provision for compulsory or "communal" labor for certain types of public projects under the Nigerian Labour Code undoubtedly owed much to that same relationship.[14] These considerations help explain (but not completely) why the government was content to have the role of the Native Administrations remain more viable than its own. (A full explanation must await an analysis of political dynamics in Part Three.)

A related aspect of the government's policy was the practice of

[14] Section 120 of the Nigerian Labour Code provides that if a majority of the inhabitants of a town or "their direct representatives" agree, communal labor may be exacted from each, for specific purposes in stated locations. Native Authorities are empowered to exercise this power. Its most common uses in the emirates appeared to be *kashin yawo* (noxious weed eradication), digging wells, rural road construction and maintenance, and bush clearance. Political controversy has surrounded the practices of the Native Administrations, which, the NEPU has alleged, have involved nonpublic projects.

"engaging" Native Authorities to undertake development projects on its behalf. For such projects, the Native Authorities recruited the necessary local staff, paid wages and other charges (for which they were reimbursed), handled the accounting involved, and performed various other tasks. A study primarily of the financial aspects of this practice, made by a British employee of a government ministry in 1959, reached the conclusion that the practice was "difficult to commend", and recommended its termination. But this analysis overlooked the other special advantages, which I have suggested accrued to the government from the Native Administrations playing a prominent part in the development process (to say nothing of the regime's political stake in maintaining the influence, prestige, and power of the Native Administrations); his recommendations were not accepted.

Native Authorities were also permitted to engage in their own economically remunerative activities, classified in official estimates as "Commercial Undertakings". Examples included partial financial participation in small-scale or "cottage" industries, full initiation and management of a public utility (a bus service, water supply scheme, or electricity system), and short-term commodity trade (an activity which could also be justified as a public service, since it provided a means for the N.A. to stabilize the local market price of staple foodstuffs. This price might otherwise by ruinous for the farmer who, having sold his crops to private speculators while the supply was plentiful and prices lower, later on found himself having to buy on the market to feed himself and his family.) The more than doubling of N.A. revenue from this source in the decade of fiscal years 1949-50 and 1959-60, from £127,835 to £458,274 for all Native Authorities, represents a marked expansion in such activities. However, in more recent years there was a tendency for Native Administrations to hand over complex commercial undertakings to the government or to public corporations. But an enterprise like the Kano N.A. Electricity Undertaking (begun in 1959 at a cost of about £300,000; it presently supplies most of the electricity to Kano) attests to the financial and managerial capacity of the wealthier emirate Native Authorities to operate impressive and complex schemes.

The activities over which the various Native Administrations exercised licensing and/or regulatory powers are too numerous to list in full, but an idea of their range is conveyed by the following list of items: advertisements (posters, billboards, etc.); domestic animals; rental of bicycles; commercial vehicle stations; fishing; ferry charges; groundnut marketing; irrigation; leprosy and malaria control; production and sale of liquor; markets; registration of births, deaths, and marriage; school attendance; and carrying of weapons. Not the least of the items usually found in the list were some having directly or indirectly to do with political activity, for example, assemblies and processions, loudspeakers, and conduct likely to cause a breach of the peace.[15] It is to be noted that in exercising such licensing and regulatory powers, the Native Administrations were deeply influencing Nigeria's entire political system. Similarly, in regulating such matters as groundnut and cotton marketing, the Native Administrations indirectly affected the nation's economy.[16]

Such vital and extensive functions imply copious legal powers and authority, and these the Native Authorities definitely enjoyed, under Part III of the Native Authority Law of 1954 as amended. These encompassed all three spheres of governmental activity—executive, legislative, judicial. In addition to authorizing specific duties and functions, Part III generally conferred on Native Administrations the power to engage and regulate staff; to legislate on matters within their competence (make bylaws and rules and issue orders); make arrests; make determinations concerning the allocation, use, and alienation of land; to control strangers (including explicitly the power to expel strangers from the Native Administration's jurisdiction); and to fix the liability of persons to its jurisdiction. The exercise of most of these powers was subject to the regional government's approval. It is highly significant, however, that a general power to issue orders (Part III, Section 43) did not require the approval of any other authority. Until it was superseded by the Northern Penal Code Law of 1960, Paragraph 9 of this section provided that such an order could be issued: "prohibiting, restricting, or regulating or

---

[15] Circular No. MLG 501/183, Ministry for Local Government, Kaduna, 6th June 1957 (Index of Local Government Subsidiary Legislation). See also N.A. Law, Revised Edition, 1965, Sections 38 and 42.

[16] Perhaps the most notable instance of the government's delegating powers of great importance for the whole Nigerian economy to the Native Administrations was the so-called Native Authority Cotton Examination Service that operated from 1954 to 1957. Under this system N.A. officials weighed and graded cotton. Official assessments determined the price paid to the farmer. Since the world market for Nigerian cotton depended on the integrity and reliability of this grading procedure, the Native Administration's role was critical. The Service appears to have operated with little or no supervision from above. In 1957 it was abolished and its functions were assumed by the government.

requiring to be done any matter or thing which the native authority, by virtue of any native law or custom for the time being in force and not repugnant to morality or justice, has power to prohibit, restrict, regulate, or require to be done". The full significance of the provision if appreciated when considered in conjunction with Section 49, which expressly vested the Native Authorities with the power to declare what native custom is, and to modify it. These same provisions, taken together, corresponded to the category of traditional criminal offense in the emirates known as *kin umurci* (disobedience, to chiefs or N.A. officials), which represented a prodigious weapon of coercion in the hands of the Native Administrations.

Arrest, imprisonment, and fines were applicable under the N.A. Law to any person who failed to appear before a Native Authority when so directed, when he obstructed or interfered with the lawful exercise of powers by the Native Authority, assumed them, or falsely "held himself out to be a chief".[17]

Perhaps more than any other single power or function, the power of taxation has over the years buttressed the authority and influence of emirate Native Administration. In the early days of British rule Lugard established the principle that the right to tax, as well as the proceeds, belonged exclusively to the government. This principle has been law since then (although in the 1920s it had to be reasserted against the desire of high British administrative officials in the North to surrender the taxing authority to the Native Administrations.[18] It will be remembered, however, that one of the cardinal attractions Lugard saw in traditional emirate government was its long-standing system of taxation, which he in fact proceeded to adopt with modifications for the sake of greater simplicity, efficiency, and "justice". Not only the types of taxes imposed (principally the *haraji*, or general tax on income, and the *jangali*, or tax on cattle), but the procedures for collecting them in Northern Nigeria were rooted in tradition. So far as the mass of people in the emirates were concerned, the obligation to pay taxes continued to be viewed as deriving from membership in an emirate. Moreover, since the government from Lugard's time on, relied on the Native Administrations as principal tax-collecting agencies, traditional officials enjoyed the guise if not the legal status of levyers. The guise was reinforced by the fact that N.A. officials were charged with determining individual assess-

---

[17] Sections 109-110.
[18] See *Report* by S. Phillipson, pp. 55-56.

ments,[19] and by the fact that the government always permitted the Native Administrations to keep a large share of the proceeds as N.A. revenue (originally at the percentage rate of 50% of the total, the share varied over the years; the latest arrangement was that government retained a flat 5 shillings per taxpayer). For the subject of an emirate, the results were therefore very much the same as if the tax formally "belonged to the Native Administrations—one in which deference and awe of authority was sustained through the knowledge that N.A. officials had, among the other formidable powers and sanctions at their disposal, the ability to influence the amount of his retained earnings. This situation was not materially altered by the introduction in 1962 of a new personal tax law.[20]

FINANCIAL RESOURCES AND THEIR USES

To TAKE ACCOUNT of the level of financial resources and expenditure yielded by this system of taxation, along with other sources, is to ap-

[19] The method of tax assessment in the emirates has been described by S. Phillipson as follows: "The unit of assessment is the village. As and when opportunity offers, Administrative Officers prepare detailed Assessment Reports based on a close investigation of selected areas in respect of the average yield per acre cultivated, market price of produce, annual value of livestock and earning capacity of tradesmen and craftsmen. A total income for the unit is computed from these statistics and a certain percentage (not exceeding 10 per cent) is fixed as the total tax payable by a unit. The Village Head is informed of the total tax assessment of his area and apportions it, in consultation with his council of elders, according to the ability to pay of individual taxpayers. . . . As Assessment Reports can only be prepared at long intervals, the tax assessment of a unit is calculated in the intervening years (a) by dividing the tax assessment of the latest Report by the number of taxpayers living in the unit at that time, which yields the basic "incidence of taxation", and (b) by multiplying the figure of incidence by the total number of taxpayers then living in the area as ascertained at an annual census". *Report*, pp. 66-67. The important point in these paragraphs is the discretionary authority which rests with N.A. officials to determine the amount of tax payable on the part of the individual at the village level.

[20] R. E. Wraith comments on the negligible impact of this innovation so far as the N.A. role in taxation was concerned: "Although native authorities have rating powers for general or specific purposes, the bulk of their revenue comes from a direct tax known as the 'community tax'. The Personal Tax Law of 1962 established a government income tax on people with ascertainable incomes of more than £350 a year, but this does not affect the native authorities unless the Commissioner of Revenue appoints an N.A. as his tax-collecting authority, in which case the N.A. would retain 20 per cent for its services. Under this Law, however, the great bulk of the population now pay community tax which is levied and collected by the N.A.'s. It is a graduated tax, legally determined by the Provincial Commissioner though in practice assessed in the traditional manner by district and village heads. Variations in its amount are considerable from one N.A. to another, though the majority of assessments lie between 40s and 45s. Of this tax, 12½ per cent is paid to the Regional Government, and the 87½ per cent retained by the N.A.'s constitutes the major source of revenue". "Local Government", pp. 246-47.

preciate fully the strategic position of the Native Authorities in the parliamentary era.

During the world depression of the early 1930s the rate of increase in N.A. revenues fell off considerably; otherwise it has been officially estimated that the rate was in excess of 10 percent per annum, starting from a total figure of £10.5 million. As may be calculated from Table 8, over 12 percent of that sum came from govern-

Table 8: Expansion of N.A. Revenue, 1949-66 (in pounds)

	1	2	3	4	5	6
	Local revenue	Commercial under-takings	Grants from govt.	Grants from other sources	Capital works	Total
1949-50	2,752,336	127,835	217,938	99,252		3,197,361
1950-51	2,832,168	155,392	279,137	112,294		3,378,991
1951-52	3,451,102	340,555	537,433	190,241		4,520,331
1952-53	4,248,375	216,759	700,104	227,823		5,393,061
1953-54	4,643,436	220,942	830,543	219,754		5,914,675
1954-55	5,170,174	266,444	1,015,916	291,339		6,743,873
1955-56	5,921,022	292,771	1,095,158	210,408		7,519,359
1956-57	6,713,705	303,549	1,153,731	293,066		8,464,051
1957-58	7,281,463	368,980	1,197,941	279,854		9,128,238
1958-59	7,371,282	447,762	1,212,179	325,852		9,357,075
1959-60	8,187,319	458,274	1,345,034	448,287		10,438,914
1960-61	9,466,275	380,368	1,430,556		143,840	11,421,039
1961-62	10,140,013	330,316	1,413,910		206,015	12,090,254
1962-63	10,386,141	384,812	1,551,554		155,397	12,477,904
1963-64	10,722,794	293,360	1,721,002		230,035	12,967,191
1964-65	13,324,111	490,100			356,080	14,170,291
1965-66	11,494,055	445,435	2,311,225		377,815	14,628,530
Percent increase						
1949-50 1959-60	297.4	258.4	517.1	351.6		226.4
1959-60 1965-66	14.4	17.4	15.3		17.8	46.0

ment grants. In later years it was normal for the amount that the government gave in this form to Native Authorities to exceed that which the Native Authorities paid to the government as its share of total income tax receipts (the largest part of the regional government's revenue was derived not from income tax but from a share of taxes on Nigerian imports and exports, plus grants from the federal government). In the years between 1949-50 and 1958-59, at least, Native Administrations received 50 percent more than they paid.

N.A. expenditure was classed under the conventional fiscal headings of recurrent and capital expenditures (listed as Works Extraordinary and Special in the relevant tables). One of the restraints which the government imposed on the use of N.A. money was the requirement that no more than 45 percent of the total expenditure was to be spent on Personal Emoluments—salaries, pensions, etc. Another was that no more than 25 percent could be spent under the combined headings of Law and Order, Central Administration, and District Administration. Although these limits on administrative overhead may seem generous by Western standards, and although the actual expenditures in this category have normally run close to the permissible maximums, nevertheless, the policy worked fairly well in assuring that most of the increase in economic standards of the region was devoted to expanding services and projects of general public benefit rather than to swelling the incomes of officials. Thus in the 10-year period 1949-50 to 1959-60, the rate of increase in expenditures for purposes other than Personal Emoluments was more than double that for Personal Emoluments. Under the "other purposes" were included such items as medical, agricultural, forestry, and veterinary services, development of natural resources, public building construction, roads, and other capital development projects.

The system of making grants to Native Authorities provided another means which the government used to influence the direction of N.A. expenditure. After the adoption of recommendations made by S. Phillipson in 1947,[21] such grants were earmarked for specific purposes, which allowed the government not only to encourage the expansion of services and development projects generally but to influence the relative emphasis which was placed by the Native Administrations on various items. It is interesting to note, for example, that the item on which the Native Administrations over the 10-year period referred to spent more than on any other—education—was also the item that drew the largest percentage of Regional Government grants (see Table 10 for the statistics for 1959-60).

The formulation of Native Authority Five-Year Development Plans, the first of which covered 1949-54, further facilitated the guidance of N.A. expenditures. The plans consist of estimated expenditures on the part of Native Administrations exclusively in the nature of capital development. Table 9 gives a breakdown of such special expenditures under the various headings of ordinary expenditure for the

[21] Phillipson, *Report*, pp. 90.

Table 9: Expansion and Uses of N.A. Expenditures, 1949-60
(in pounds)

	1	2	3	4	5	6
			Commercial	Works		
	Personal	Other	under-	extraor-		
	emoluments	charges	takings	dinary	Special	Total
1949-50	1,273,049	954,066	225,112	484,327	49,235	2,985,787
1950-51	1,329,387	1,098,370	365,699	447,381	57,337	3,300,174
1951-52	1,571,707	1,443,107	344,892	525,263	63,845	3,948,814
1952-53	1,735,461	1,748,424	277,522	754,593	228,073	4,744,073
1953-54	2,101,030	2,144,854	250,233	1,135,103	161,855	5,793,075
1954-55	2,242,320	2,582,568	334,299	1,286,590	362,766	6,808,543
1955-56	2,618,324	2,918,429	391,911	1,257,268	684,426	7,870,358
1956-57	3,036,795	3,121,125	348,546	1,153,410	157,578	7,817,454
1957-58	3,272,158	3,632,204	398,702	1,110,976	110,613	8,524,653
1958-59	3,438,202	4,019,617	427,666	522,741	33,470	8,441,696
1959-60	3,648,831	4,408,862	454,651	1,832,287	154,827	10,499,458
1960-61	9,292,475		407,841	1,834,130	330,050	11,864,496
1961-62		9,292,475	411,704	1,544,210	132,163	11,803,452
1962-63		10,021,241	342,038	1,199,090		11,562,369
1963-64		10,002,407	307,168	1,155,755		11,465,350
1964-65*†	11,359,393		464,557	1,738,148	141,703	13,703,747
1965-66*	12,672,675†		450,107	1,840,497		14,963,279
			Percent increase			
1949-50						
1959-60	186.6	362.1	101.9	213.3	278.3	251.6
1959-60						
1965-66	55		106.6	12.4		45.5

* Estimates only.

† "Estimates in 1964-65 as presented have not been revised to take into account the wages and salaries increases following the Morgan Commission", p. 41, Note 1.

Source: 1949-60, G.R.I. Dees, p. 12; 1960-66, *Local Government Yearbook*, p. 41.

second five-year period 1954-59, and for the projected third plan. This table also reflects the particular attention education received, an emphasis again partly attributable to the use of Government Capital Development Grants to help support and shape the substance of the Five-Year Plans. Under the First Plan total expenditure was in the neighborhood of £4 million; the Second Plan reached nearly £6.5 million; and according to the projected Third Five-Year Development Plan, inaugurated in April 1959, approximately £11 million was to be spent. This plan was superseded, however, by the adoption of a National Six-Year Plan (1962-68) with which N.A. spending was coordinated.

Four observations may be draw from this brief look at the financial affairs of the Native Authorities. The first is that the total revenue and expenditure (not counting grants) indicates that as a whole the Native Administrations were not only solvent, but became increasingly wealthy, and relatively self-sufficient. Withdrawal of government grants might have in most (but not necessarily all) cases forced drastic curtailment of an emirate's expenditure on the service or project affected, but the general administration of almost all of the Native Administrations could have survived pressure of this sort. The second is that the course of N.A. financial development was concrete proof of the regional government's desire to maintain the Native Administration's effective institutions, and even to increase their role in the political and economic life of the region. The third is that an annual recurrent expenditure of £10.5 million to £12.5 million in years when the region's total budget was approximately £14 million to £16 million (1959 to 1964) suggests that in terms of the development of the overall regional economy, the resources of the Native Administrations as a whole were significant, and became more so as development progressed. Fourth, it would appear that the government successfully followed a policy of "induced modernization", through which it was not only able to involve the Native Authorities in efforts and schemes of economic development generally, but to orient their economic activities toward the fulfillment of specific priorities, such as education and roads, which were set in light of the region's overall needs. That this success was achieved with minimal alterations in the realm of the central N.A. political structure will be seen in the political aspects of some of the major problems and issues of the central bureaucracies to which we now turn.

Some Major Problems and Issues

Popular Participation: According to the particular manner in which members were selected to participate, six principal types existed among the 64 central Native Authority councils in Northern Nigeria: (1) chief and traditional members; (2) chief, traditional, and nominated members; (3) chief, traditional, nominated, plus a minority of elected members; (4) 50 percent elected members;

(5) chief plus a majority of elected members; (6) chief and all elected members.

However, as reflected in Tables 14 and 15 which shows the proportion of elected members in the emirate central Native Authority councils alone (as of October 1959 and July 1962), the types featuring most of the elected N.A. councillors were concentrated in the non-emirate, or Middle Belt, area. In 1954 only 9 out of 34 emirates had elected majorities; significantly, only one (Bida) was a First Class Emirate. In other words, the larger, more populous, and more his-

Table 10: Regional Government's Contribution to N.A. Expenditure, 1959-60 and 1965-66

Heading	Total estimate	Percent of grants	1959-60 estimate	Percent of grants	1965-66 estimate*	Percent of grants*
Education	£1,040,376	66.3	£153,935	81.6	—	62.8
Medical	208,311	13.3	24,375	12.9	—	6.2
Water supply	61,880	3.9	—	—	—	—
Communications	161,088	10.3	3,450	1.8	—	—
Building	6,330	0.4	2,330	1.2	—	—
Misc.	91,973	5.8	4,550	2.5	—	—
Total	£1,569,958	100	£188,640	100	£2,126,690	100

Source: 1959-60, G.R.I. Dees, "Papers on Native Authority Finance," No. 3, mimeo, 1959, p. 12; 1965-66, *Local Government Yearbook 1966*, p. 54.
* Not included or not computed in yearbook figures.

Table 11: Regional Government's Contribution to N.A. Capital Development Projects

	1954-59		1959-64	
	Grant	Percent of total	Grant	Percent of total
Agriculture	£240,602	3.7	£343,129	3.1
Education	1,258,868	19.5	2,373,803	21.7
Forestry	80,068	1.2	162,222	1.5
Medical	475,291	7.4	806,726	7.4
Veterinary	171,145	2.7	237,597	2.2
Communications	1,094,763	17.0	1,728,539	15.8
Public Buildings	868,360	13.4	1,780,030	16.3
Urban Development	417,941	6.5	876,955	8.0
Rural Development	664,916	10.3	1,335,338	12.2
Public Utilities	713,207	11.0	922,389	8.4
Miscellaneous	233,750	3.6	370,507	3.4
Unallocated	239,083	3.7	873	—
Grand total	£6,458,000	100	£10,938,108	100

Source: G.R.I. Dees, "Papers on Native Authority Finance," No. 2, 1959, p. 43.

Table 12: Projected Regional Government Contribution to N.A. Capital Development Projects under 1962-68 Development Plan

	Grant	Percent of total
Agriculture	£ 620,123	4.9
Education	4,546,715	36.1
Forestry	327,299	2.6
Medical	997,605	7.9
Veterinary	519,896	4.1
Communications	1,357,753	10.8
Public Buildings	1,273,282	10.1
Urban Development	1,080,204	8.6
Rural Development	1,048,168	8.3
Public Utilities	470,512	3.7
Miscellaneous	336,590	2.7
Unallocated	—	—
Total	£ 12,578,147	100

Table 13: Traditional Status of Councillors

	Emirate	Sarakuna					Talakawa	Un-known	Total[*]
		(r)	(n)	(m)	(c)	(v)			
1.	Adamawa	1	8	1	2	2	5	—	19[a]
2.	Argungu	3	3	—	1	—	—	—	7
3.	Bauchi	3	6	2	—	1	2	6[b]	20
4.	Bida	3	7	—	2	3	6	—	21
5.	Bornu	2	7	—	1	1	4	—	15[c]
6.	Dikwa	3	4	—	—	—	1	—	8[d]
7.	Gwandu	2	5	1	—	—	1	—	9
8.	Kano	3	10	—	—	1	1	—	15
9.	Katsina	3	5	—	3	—	2	—	13[e]
10.	Kazaure	3	2	—	1	—	—	—	6
11.	Sokoto	3	4	—	2	—	—	1	10[f]
12.	Zaria	10	3	—	—	—	1	3[g]	17
	Total	38	60	4	10	8	24	9	160
				120					

Symbols:
- (r) royalty
- (n) nobility
- (m) marriage
- (c) clientage
- (v) vassalage

[*] includes emirs
[a] 1 vacancy
[b] six elected members not available for interview during author's visit
[c] 7 vacancies
[d] 5 vacancies
[e] 5 vacancies
[f] 5 vacancies
[g] 3 elected members from southern Zaria districts not available for interview during author's visit

torically or traditionally important the emirate, the less the *degree* of formal democratization attained.[22] The only significant change was in the number of councils with a minority of elected members, which doubled from 10 in 1959 to 20 by 1962. After 1962 all Native Authorities were required to have at least some elected members;[23] but the number of emirates with elected majorities remained the same. Clearly the government's policy of leaving the timing and extent of democratization to the discretion of the Native Administrations generally yielded quite unspectacular results even with respect to the central council's formal composition. Yet the continuity in formal structure does not fully convey the measure of substantive political continuity that was discovered on closer examination of the membership composition of these institutions.

Table 14: Balance of Representation in the Central Councils, 1959[a]

Emirates with elected majority	(Ratio)	Emirates with elected minority	(Ratio)	Emirates without elected members
Abuja	(5-1)	*Adamawa*	(6-13)	*Argungu*
Agaie	(36-33)	*Bauchi*	(6-14)	Bedde
Bida	(12-10)	*Bornu*	(3-12)	Daura
Borgu	(15-7)	*Dikwa*	(3-5)	*Gombe*
Jama'are	(5-4)	Fika	(4-11)	Gumel
Keffi	(14-7)	*Kontagora*	(4-9)	*Gwandu*
Lapai	(36-20)	Lafia	(5-10)	Hadeja
Nassarawa	(10-7)	Muri	(3-7)	*Ilorin*
Pategi	(22-13)	Wase	(7-9)	*Kano*
		Zaria	(6-11)	Katagum
				Katsina
				Kazaure
				Misau
				Sokoto
				Yauri
Total 9	(150-101)	10	(47-101)	15

[a] Italicized emirates are First Class emirates. Jema's and Biu emirates, which have been federated with nonemirate Native Authorities, are not listed.

Source: field notes.

An analysis of the central councils of 12 emirates in terms of the traditional status backgrounds of the members as investigated in 1959 is presented in Table 13. As stated in the introduction, traditionally

[22] The grade of the emirate (First, Second, or Third Class), which is synonymous with the grade of the emir concerned, was originally determined by the British, based on a combination of criteria—principally size of territory and population and "historical" prominence.

[23] M. J. Campbell, "The Structure of Local Government", in Blitz, *Politics and Administration of Nigerian Government*, p. 119.

Table 15: Balance of Representation in the Central Council

Emirates with elected majority	(Ratio)	Emirates with elected minority	(Ratio)	Emirates without elected members
Abuja	(5-4)	Adamawa	(6-19)	Bornu
Agaie	(36-33)	Argungu	(2-6)	Gombe
Bida	(12-8)	Bauchi	(6-10)	Gumel
Borgu	(15-7)	Bedde	(2-6)	Hadeja
Ilorin	(32-16)	Daura	(2-10)	Kazaure
Jama'are	(5-4)	Dikwa	(8-9)	
Lafia	(18-9)	Fika	(4-11)	
Lapai	(36-20)	Gwandu	(2-8)	
Pategi	(22-13)	Kano	(5-18)	
		Katagum	(4-9)	
		Katsina	(5-21)	
		Keffi	(14-18)	
		Kontagora	(5-9)	
		Misau	(6-8)	
		Muri	(5-10)	
		Nassarawa	(10-20)	
		Sokoto	(5-15)	
		Wase	(7-9)	
		Yauri	(2-5)	
		Zaria	(6-10)	
Total 9	(181-114)	20	(106-230)	5

a Italicized emirates are First Class emirates.

Source: M. J. Campbell, *Law and Practice of Local Government in Northern Nigeria* (London, 1963), pp. 66-68.

membership in the ruling class (*sarakuna*) of an emirate was attainable through one or more of several routes—agnatic kinship, marriage, vassalage, and clientage (for further discussion of these terms see Chapter 9). The backgrounds of councillors traditionally of the *sarakuna* class are broken down in these terms in Table 13, which also distinguishes between royal birth (i.e. kinship with a family or dynasty from which emirs may be chosen) and nobility (kinship with other hereditarily titled families). The status placement of councillors was determined by fixing the father's identity (except that current marriage relationships of the councillors themselves were also taken into account). The figures indicate that notwithstanding the particular method of selection, the vast majority of central councillors belonged to the class of *sarakuna*. They or their kin would have formed the political leadership of an emirate even had there never been any alteration in the methods of selecting that leadership. Very few of those who were by traditional criteria excluded from political leadership gained participation at this level by virtue of the "democratic" reforms.

In this context, it is interesting to note the preponderance of non-royal over royal members of the *sarakuna* class in all the councils except two, Kazaure and Zaria. To this extent, the distribution of membership corresponds, by and large, to traditional principles, which also accords with the modern conciliar idea of distributing power among various social segments. In other words, it seems likely that the traditional recognition of the norm facilitated the incorporation of additional nonroyal members of the *sarakuna* class, in accordance with the objectives of reform. (The reasons for the two exceptions in the table are similarly traceable to traditional conditions—the political structure of these emirates was more than usually centralized; furthermore, Kazaure and Zaria traditionally were obliged to accommodate vigorous intradynastic lineage and interdynastic rivalries, respectively.[24]

As might be expected, in most councils concerned, there was a correlation between the ratio of councillors who were commoners, or *talakawa*, on one hand, and the ratio of elected to nonelected members on the other. For example, the Bida Council had a majority of elected members and at least six members who were *talakawa*. The Kano Council had few elected members and only two commoners, both traders.

It would be incorrect to assume, however, that elections necessarily resulted in the selection of more *talakawa* to a central council than did other means. Almost as many (10) of the 24 *talakawa* councillors in the 12 emirates had attained that position by virtue of nomination as through election. In effect, the electorate most frequently used the vote to confirm in power their preestablished traditional leadership. A prime example of this was Zaria, where each of three elected councillors from the Northern preponderately Muslim districts belonged by birth to one of Zaria's three royal dynasties.[25] More often, the elected *sarakuna* councillors enjoyed the traditional status of noble or vassal (e.g. M. Kaigama Zubairu of Bornu, M. Umaru Nassarawa of Gwandu, M. Ndaliman of Bida, etc.

These results were partly attributable to the imperfect proce-

[24] For Zaria see Smith, *Government in Zazzau*, esp. pp. 6, 102-23.
[25] M. Usman Shehu, *Madakin Zazzau* (the District Head of Makarfi) is a *Bornawa*, the dynasty of the Emir (Malam Ja'afaru) reigning at the time he was elected: M. Mohammed Aminu, *Iyan Gari* (now Emir of Zaria) of the *Katsinawa* dynasty, and Malam Nuhu Bamalli (now also a Nigerian senator) who, as his name implies, is a member of the *Mallawa* dynasty (the singular of *Mallawa* is *Bamalle*).

dures (from a modern democratic point of view) that characterized elections to central councils. Typically the conservatively weighted subordinate and outer councils served as electoral colleges. Until 1962 voting was by show of hands or "whispering" (into the ear of an officer who was usually either a government or a Native Authority official). After 1962 the secret ballot generally was used; however, the use of indirect methods of representation was not abandoned.[26] However, as we shall see, the fact that the more "advanced" procedures applied in regional and federal elections have yielded much the same results suggests that there was more to it than procedural factors. The *sarakuna* class, as far as the peasants were concerned, remained the preferred reservoir of political leadership. On the other hand, an emir and his traditional councillors, albeit initially acting under the influence of colonial officials, themselves chose in several instances to elevate qualified and able *talakawa* to their ranks, after appreciating the talents they brought to new administrative tasks. Similarly, some *talakawa* in central councils (especially traders) were there because traditional rulers thought it desirable to add members to represent this useful special interest.

It would be equally incorrect to conclude from the fact that leadership tended to stay within the ruling strata that elections had no broadening effect on representation. Many men of noble or vassal status who were elected to a central council would not otherwise have found a place there. In general it may be said that by virtue of new procedures, the central councils geographically if not socially became more representative than they had been. Particularly in the case of emirates with a traditionally centralized political structure and a culturally heterogeneous or pluralistic ethnic makeup, the presence of an outlying district's chief in the central council was an important development.

Extending formal representation was at best only half the battle of genuine democratization. Election to a council did not necessarily mean *effective* participation for the councillor. There were several factors limiting the effective participation of new men.

Responsibility for day-to-day council business rested with full-time salaried councils which rarely were elected but if so even then were holdovers from an earlier time. Elected councillors usually attended council meetings only at long intervals—every month (Zaria)

[26] Campbell, "Structure of Local Government", p. 132.

to every three months (Bida and Adamawa). To a certain extent, this situation stemmed from the combination of the great distances and the poor communications (roads, etc.) between the capital and the outlying districts in which the elected councillors often resided. To mention one admittedly extreme case, an elected N.A. Councillor from the Mambilla Plateau area of Adamawa Emirate, in order to attend Council meetings in the capital of Yola, had to trek five days and make a 4,500-foot descent on foot, then journey 240 miles over a motor road before reaching a council meeting.[27]

Yet even those elected councillors whose constituency was a capital territory, or one easily accessible to it, were seldom as effectively involved in the conduct of affairs as others. That the de facto exclusion of elected councillors was often deliberate was reflected in the existence of what was appropriately if caustically termed the *"majalisar dare"*, literally "council of the night"—an inner clique of councillors who did their deliberating outside the regular council meeting (which in the same idiom was disparaged as *taron banza*—the "useless meeting"—in contrast to the assemblies that lacked formal status but whose decisions counted). The *majalisar dare* was later able to confront the larger body with more than one fait accompli. Often, the introduction of elected members had been a reform pressed on the established councillors from above, against their own profound inclination to hold power exclusively in their hands; the *majalisar dare* was their answer.

Ironically the same initiation of a system of committees which in the context of a fully democratic conciliar institution might rightly be regarded as a step toward more effective democratic control—as it was in Ilorin—tended to produce within the prevailing conciliar structure much the same effect as the *majalisar dare*. So far as could be determined, only eight elected councillors in the 12 emirates were active members of key committees. As it was with extended representation generally, the impact of an active committee system was to enhance the effective participation of certain members of the pre-established ruling strata, rather than of those traditionally outside this group.

[27] Route described in connection with the Lamido of Adamawa's tour of the Mambilla area in 1951, in *Northern Regional Daily Press Service* (Release No. 555), March 3, 1959. The construction of a new road onto the plateau, and the inclusion of this area within the boundaries of the new Sardauna Province, had considerably relieved these obstacles by 1965.

As the committee system operated in practice, a further limitation stemmed from the marked tendency of councils to make of the General Purposes Committee what amounted to an executive or permanent steering committee, controlling the whole range of N.A. activities. (In British practice a general purposes committee was one that assigned various ad hoc tasks from time to time. Membership might fluctuate according to the skills and interests of the different councillors. Its function was not general administrative oversight.) The Northern Nigerian adaptation not only curtailed the participation of the council; it also detracted from the effectiveness of other committees.

As for the ability of the general public to influence the decisions of the central councils, it may be doubted whether any substantial progress was made. This was not only because of the limited nature of the constitutional modifications and the shortcomings of the electoral system, but also to the fact that adequate information was rarely available to the public. The lack of a press continuously publicizing local issues that were before the councils was important, but the playing out of the logic of the "cabinet system" analogy was perhaps even more serious. Thus, applying the norms of secrecy and collective responsibility otherwise appropriate to the central councils tended to stifle informal public debate prior to and after making decisions.[28] This intensified a proclivity for secrecy already inherent, as we have seen in the traditional politics of an emirate.

The plural emirates: To the British practitioners and sympathetic critics of indirect rule in the emirates of Northern Nigeria, the existence within the boundaries of certain emirates of substantial numbers of people who historically, ethnically, culturally, and religiously, are alien to the society of their Fulani overlords posed a dilemma. Prior to the coming of the British, several larger groups of such people had successfully evaded, through constant movement or retreat into inaccessible hills, or withstood, through military prowess, incorporation under Fulani rule. Others paid formal allegiance while retaining substantive autonomy. The crux of the issue this situation posed for the British was whether to recognize or foster Fulani he-

---

[28] One piece of official publicity asserts the principle of collective responsibility: ". . . having voted, he [the local government councillor] must support in public the action of his council. To criticize it outside the Council Chamber is only to weaken its authority. If he feels that he cannot in all honesty support it, then he should resign and criticize from outside". *Citizen of the North*, Part II, issued by the Ministry of Education (Kaduna, n.d.), p. 7.

gemony among such peoples. On the affirmative side were such considerations and rationalizations as administrative convenience, the growth of a more enlightened and benevolent attitude on the part of the Fulani rulers, the salutory ("civilizing" and "unifying") effect of Islam, and the relative superiority under modern conditions of a more centralized and disciplined form of administration and government over that to which the non-Hausa-Fulani peoples were accustomed. The differences between the Hausa-Fulani traditional patterns of government and those of most, but not all, of the groups concerned roughly corresponds to the now well-known distinction drawn by Fortes and Evans-Pritchard between African political systems of types "A" and "B", or between "state-type" and "segmentary-type" systems.[29] In an earlier day, the conciliar processes of government which most of these latter groups followed was regarded as no blessing.

On the negative side were such considerations as the demonstrated inclination of these groups to resist Fulani rule and the possible future penetration of the civilizing and unifying influence of Christianity. Above all, there was the nagging realization that to encourage their assimilation to the emirate form was, as Margery Perham put it, "really a negation of indirect rule".[30] In theory, the British solution was to uphold the institutions, customs, and autonomy of the native peoples. In practice, Miss Perham observes, "this policy was not strictly carried out".[31] Indeed, my own research revealed that there was a tendency during the last half-century of Fulani ruling families associated with the central bureaucracy to assume the headships of preponderately non-Fulani districts.[32]

The outstanding "plural emirates" include Adamawa, Bauchi, Bedde, Biu, Fika, Jema'a, Ilorin, Lafia, Nassarawa, Zaria, and to a lesser extent, Bida. In recent years these emirates have experienced growing unrest and demand for change by various minority groups, stimulated by all the talk of "self-" and "local" government. The demand variously and sometimes simultaneously took the form of agitation for greater autonomy and for a fairer share in the government and administration of the entire emirate. It is generally con-

[29] See *African Political Systems* (London: Oxford University Press, 1940), pp. 5-23.
[30] *Native Administration in Nigeria*, p. 135.
[31] *Ibid.*, p. 134.
[32] Particularly in Bauchi, Adamawa, and Zaria emirates.

ceded that emirate minority groups were more grossly underrepresented in the ranks of administrative staff than in the central councils.

As in the nonmetropolitan districts of Ilorin, a particular object of dissatisfaction was the Fulani District Head, or worse, the local chief who had adopted the manner and political habits of one, contrary to the more egalitarian and conciliar norms of his own people.[33] Such dissatisfaction often went hand in hand with resentment over being derided as *kafiri* (unbeliever), for adherence to Christianity or animistic worship. Until recently—1948—many non-Muslim peoples in emirates were perforce subject to the Muslim judicial and legal system which embodied standards of justice often uncongenial to their own.

The unrest not infrequently erupted in revolt, sometimes violent. For example, in 1949-50 the Hill Jarawa people, concentrated in a rocky terrain on the fringe of the Jos Plateau, were chafing under the regime of a district head appointed from the royal family of Bauchi (which happens to be of the Gerawa, a non-Fulani people of this area; Fulani dominate the ranks of the Bauchi nobility). In pre-British days the Emirs of Bauchi practiced their own brand of indirect rule vis-à-vis the Jarawa, recognizing the chief appointed by the Jarawa from among their own. In 1949 the Jarawa mounted a campaign to have a local man substituted as district head; the campaign included a refusal to pay taxes directly to the Emir.

Riots over similar issues were staged at different times by the Sayawa of the same emirate (Lere District), and the peoples of the Madagali, Mubi, Michichika, and Kilba districts of Adamawa. Kindred sentiments, if not the same techniques, were manifested among such peoples as the Katah and other related peoples in southern Zaria province, the Chamba and Batta people of Adamawa, the Arago of Lafia emirate, the Ngizim and Karekere of Fika. Organizations using constitutional means also appeared, e.g. the Habe Tribal Union, the Kilba State Union, the Pan-Jarawa League, the Pan-Sayawa League. It is noteworthy that the leadership of these groups was drawn mostly from associates of Christian missionary groups,[34]

---

[33] The demeanor of one such local chief, whose people were in the forefront of a movement for secession from the old emirate, into which they were absorbed subsequent to the British pacification, was described in a British Administrative officer's words as follows: "To walk through the market with [the district head] is reminiscent of a Royal Garden Party, as the ranks of people bow and bend in graceful salutation to the royal progress".

[34] For example, the President of the Pan-Jarawa League in 1959 was Mr. Dogon Yaro of Fusaru, a Sudan Interior Mission (S.I.M.) parishioner; and the

from whom they were widely believed to have at least received moral, if not organizational and financial support. Much quicker than Hausa peasants to complain about and expose any irregularity by a regime in which they had little stake, more articulate (thanks to missionary training), and more adept at grassroots political activity, such minority groups were a thorn in the side of ruling classes of the plural emirates even when they were not working for formal institutional changes.

The response to these pressures took various forms. In one district, Fika Emirate, the death of a royal district head was seized on as an opportunity to do away completely with the institution of district head, as in some of the Ilorin nonmetropolitan districts. The Bauchi Hill Jarawa's campaign succeeded in obtaining a chief of local origins, who in 1959 appeared to be firmly in the clutches of his village heads. Toro District was dissolved and the Jarawa people afterwards constituted a district (Jarawa) unto themselves. In Lere District of the same emirate, there was instituted a system of "District Head-in Council" along the lines of the Emir-in-Council reform —an innovation that was adamantly resisted in other emirates. But perhaps the most significant outcome is the fact, corroborated in the tables above, that the regimes in the plural emirates were obliged to introduce elected representation more fully and rapidly than the others. In other plural emirates a similar result was accomplished through co-optation.

In the old Adamawa and Dikwa Emirates there occurred a drastic and unique reaction to minority discontent, growing out of the peculiar historical status of most of the minority districts concerned, which were part of what was formerly the United Nations Trust Territory of the Northern Cameroons. In November 1958 the UN conducted a plebiscite to determine the wishes of people living in the territory about their future disposition (against, it is interesting in retrospect, the advice of its preliminary Visiting Mission, which had concluded after a preliminary tour of the area that the people's desire to remain part of the Northern Region was so evident as to make a plebiscite unnecessary). The questions posed in the plebiscite was (1) "Do you wish to join with the Northern Region as

---

Secretary was Mr. Anyam, a Sudan United Mission (S.U.M.) schoolteacher. The President of the Pan-Sayawa League, Mr. Gwonto Mawru, was an S.U.M. lay preacher, while the Secretary and Chief Organizers were employed as schoolteachers under the same mission. Both groups also included animists among their officers.

part of an independent Federation of Nigeria?" and (2) "Do you wish to remain under British Trusteeship, pending a final settlement?" The overwhelming majority vote for the latter, which came as a shock to the Northern Regional Government, the Visiting Mission, and most British observers.[35]

In the months preceding the plebiscite, I witnessed part of the vigorous campaign by local political parties, interpreting the plebiscite as a chance for minorities who felt suppressed under the regime of the Adamawa and Dikwa Native Authorities to repudiate and escape it. Thus the Plebiscite Commissioner's report to the UN Trusteeship Council would seem to have been correct in concluding that the "voters had made use of the opportunity offered by the plebiscite to register what was in effect a protest vote against the system of local administration prevailing in the Northern Cameroons and a desire for the introduction of reforms in the system of local government".[36]

The indeterminate option represented by the second alternative necessitated a second plebiscite, in which a choice between remaining part of Nigeria or joining the neighboring, formerly French-administrated Trust Territory of Cameroon was offered. In the interval between plebiscites, the Northern regional government assiduously sought to win over the people with an unprecedented program of reform.[37] One of its first steps was to excise the Trust Terri-

[35] See West Africa, November 14, 1959, p. 1.

[36] Quoted in Northern Nigeria Daily Press Service (Release No. 2871), December 3, 1959.

[37] Soon after the first plebiscite the government appointed a commission of inquiry, to whose report it responded in March 1960 as follows:

The Northern Regional Government has finished consideration of the Report of the Commission of Inquiry which was appointed by the Premier to make recommendations for local government reforms in the Northern Trust Territory. Very far-reaching proposals have been made by the Commission and these have, in the main, been accepted by the Regional Government.

An outline of the impending changes has been given to the native authorities concerned and during his recent visit to Yola the Premier discussed with the Adamawa Native Authority, the necessary re-adjustments which will be required in its organisation after the excision of its Trust Territory areas.

The most significant aspect of the reforms to be introduced is that as from 1st April 1960, new Divisions and Native Authorities will be created in the Trust Territory. Two new administrative divisions, staffed by the Northern Region Administrative Officers, will be created out of the area of Adamawa Trust Territory.

The other Division from the Adamawa Trust Territory will be known as THE NORTHERN TRUST DIVISION . . . at Mubi.

These two Divisions will from April 1, completely cease to have any ties with Adamawa Emirate. However, the area of Dikwa Division will remain as it is,

tory districts from the jurisdiction of the traditionally constituted emirates, forming new Native Authorities which gave the minorities the local autonomy they sought. In February 1961 the second plebiscite was held; this time the people voted to join Nigeria. They

but the District of Gwoza will be constituted into a new Gwoza Native Authority completely independent of the Dikwa Native Authority. For Dikwa Native Authority itself very important changes will be made in the composition of the Native Authority Council and district administration.

The Government has decided that the area of United Hills Subordinate Native Authority will not be included in any Division of the Trust Territory, but it will stand by itself as an independent Native Authority. The Government will consider how best to organise the administrative supervision of the area.

As a preliminary to the formation of the new Native Authorities and the reorganisation of the Dikwa Native Authority, all district, town and outer councils will be dissolved and new elections for district and town councils held throughout the Territory with the exception of the United Hills area. The system of outer councils will be abolished.

The newly elected district and town councils will elect their members to form the respective Native Authority Councils and to widen the elected membership of the Native Authority Council in Dikwa. The District Councils when formed will be asked whether to confirm their present district heads or to nominate new persons to be appointed by the Native Authorities.

In Dikwa Emirate new village heads will be elected. The instruments establishing new Native Authorities will include a provision for safeguard of minority interests . . . all the necessary arrangements for the local elections which will be conducted on the basis of adult male suffrage under the secret ballot system.

The Government is convinced that customary courts in Southern Adamawa, known as the Siyasa Courts, have become unpopular and it has accordingly been decided to abolish them. In accordance with the wishes of the people they will be replaced by Alkali's courts which will have assessors to represent non-Moslem interests. The present customary courts will continue until suitable persons to be appointed as Alkalai are forthcoming.

The best solution regarding courts in the Northern Trust Division is not clear and a further investigation will be conducted by the Divisional Officer to determine the judicial system which will be most acceptable to the people. In Dikwa, the Native Authority is being instructed to pay more attention to the efficient administration of justice and to ensure that only qualified persons are appointed as Alkalai and their assistants.

The Government has also adopted the recommendations of the Commission for the division of capital and movable assets, and financial reserves which are based on a principle ensuring justice to all the parties involved.

On the question of staff the Government agrees that those employees who are not wanted by the new native authorities or who justifiably feel they cannot carry on under the changed conditions, will be retrenched. A scheme for paying compensation and pensions in deserving cases, is being recommended to the Native Authorities concerned.

These measures which will shortly be introduced are in full accord with the freely expressed wishes of the people. They will give the largest measure of democratisation and autonomy in the local government system of the Trust Territory. They will also prepare the Northern Cameroons for the period of separation during which the area will stand apart from Nigeria.

It is hoped that the people of the Cameroons will realise the importance of these reforms and act responsibly in the task of establishing their new Native Authorities. It will be necessary for the people not to make much of their differences if they want the new changes to succeed.

did so as a new Province of Northern Nigeria—Sardauna, named after the Premier. The area previously known as the Southern Cameroons voted for fusion with the Cameroon Republic. The cause of minorities in the other plural emirates, however, happened not to enjoy the historical good fortune of UN trusteeship status.[38]

In the long run, the surging minorities must confront the remaining plural emirates with a choice of (a) serious dilution of traditional standards, particularly in regard to employment and regulation of Native Administration staff, a challenge not really begun to be met; (b) an explosive political situation; (c) resort to stringent repression. The reaction to the choice made will ultimately determine the political future of the plural emirates, which is likely, no matter what choice is made, to help set a pattern for the other emirates. In the short run, the apparent consequence of having to reconcile culturally centrifugal forces—surprising as it may seem to those who assume that the communal conflict, or "tribalism", is always inimical to democratic development in Africa—was an acceleration of reform in the direction of democratic patterns which placed the plural emirates ahead, in that respect, of their culturally more homogeneous neighbors.

Rational unit size: As may be seen in Table 5 above, the Northern emirates are enormously varied in population, territory, and wealth. In population each of two emirates—Kano and Sokoto—exceed such African nations as Dahomey, Liberia, Libya, Togo, Somalia, Congo (Brazzaville), and the Central African Republic. Kano, the most populous of the two, also surpasses Guinea, Senegal, Niger, Sierra Leone, and Chad. Kano Emirate covers over 12,000 square miles, while Sokoto is twice that area. Kano's revenue in 1965 (almost two and a half million pounds) was slightly larger than that of the Cameroon Republic, Somalia, Gambia, and several of the smaller ex-French African territories. At the other extreme are found such

---

The Government wishes to emphasize that the reforms being introduced have not departed in any way from the ascertained wishes of the people.

The members of the Commission, of which M. Muhammadu Tukur, Emir of Yauri, was the chairman, were M. Gwanma, Chief of Kagoro; Alhaji Shehu Ahmadu, Madawakin Kano; Mr. D. H. Lloyd-Morgan, Acting Permanent Secretary to the Ministry of Health; and Alhaji Ali Akilu, Senior Assistant Secretary, Premier's Office (secretary).

Nigerian Citizen, March 5, 1960, pp. 1, 12.

[38] For an account of the historic transfer of the Cameroons from German colonial rule to the League of Nations Mandate Commission, and thence to the UN Trusteeship Council, see Kirk-Greene, *Principles of Native Administration*, pp. 79-87; and Hogben and Kirk-Greene, *Emirates of Northern Nigeria*, pp. 445-46.

emirates as Bedde (population 45,000, area 2,000 square miles, revenue £72,000) and tiniest of all, Jama'are (population 20,000, area 149 square miles, revenue £20,635).[39] Hence the magnitude of some emirates is such that the appellation "local" seems hardly to apply, while that of others drastically limited the scale of services and development they could support.

At either extreme the cause of modern democratic local government would have been better served had existing unit boundaries been altered, by either splitting up the giants or consolidating the midgets. Colonial administrators recognized the economic waste and inefficiency in operating the smaller Native Authorities, but to have shut them down would have been contrary to the tenents of indirect rule, and, more practical, detrimental to cooperation among fellow emirate rulers. Amalgamation and subdivision of emirates also ran against the grain of the government's policy in local government; in this respect, the desideratum of rational unit size and that of the integrity, authority, and cohesion of traditional communities were clearly at loggerheads.

Year after year the problem found expression in the *Provincial Annual Reports*. In the 1951 Report it was noted that the "continued resistance to the amalgamation of the Pategi and Lafiagi Native Treasuries makes progress difficult when money is perennially tight".[40] In 1953, "The current financial year brings to an end the first five-year plans of such treasuries as could afford them (Lafiagi and Pategi could not)",[41] in 1955, "the absorption of this tiny emirate (Jama'are), the size of a small district, by Katagum, would be to the advantage of the people";[42] in 1957, "the financial history of both Lafiagi and Pategi has always been that of the poverty attendant upon small administrative units. The capital expenditure heads of both Native Authority were frozen for the third successive year due to lack of funds";[43] in 1958, "The Agaie N.A. is so financially weak that no realistic progress will be made until agreement is reached on some form of sharing services with its neighbors", and ". . . the future (of Lapai Emirate) depends on sharing services with neighboring N.A.'s . . . or subsidy from the regional Government to support the dignity of this tiny Emirate".[44]

[39] See *Local Government Yearbook 1966*, pp. 42-43.
[40] *Provincial Annual Report 1951*, p. 30.
[41] *Provincial Annual Report 1953*, p. 59.
[42] *Provincial Annual Report 1955*, p. 18.
[43] *Provincial Annual Report 1957*, p. 57.
[44] Unpub. manuscript.

The identity of the emirate Native Authorities as states inevitably came into play here. The authority and prestige of any emir whose domains would have been reduced or dissolved into some larger entity would suffer serious damage in the eyes of his people, perhaps irretrievably; for one of the traditional tests of an emir's political strength is an ability to hold, if not extend, the territory of his kingdom. Recognizing this, the British, in the days of pacification, used territorial dismemberment as a means of humbling recalcitrant emirs.[45] It is significant here that each of the three instances of amalgamation in recent years (Bussa-Kiama, the Biu, and Jema's Federations) involved an emirate whose ruler lacked valid traditional claims over the dominion he had been controlling.[46]

In lieu of the amalgamation of small emirates, the stated policy of the Regional Government was to encourage the establishment of common, or "Joint Services" between different Native Administrations, an innovation for which legal provision is made in Section 10-80 of the Native Authority Law. The fact, reflected in the observations made in the *Provincial Annual Reports*, is that use was not actually made of the provisions to any extent. By 1965 only five emirate Native Administrations had promulgated instruments.[47] It must be recognized that from the point of view of the emirate N.A., the closest analog of what emirate rulers were asked to do when urged to combine control of major services was not, say, cooperation between an English parish and a county council, but more the surrender of vital resources by a sovereign national power to a superstate. The proposal was certain to be met by all the well-springs of resistance that have always greeted such visions—historical sentiment, pride, and, above all, vested interests in various offices and perquisites. If an emirate's slight population was detrimental to economic viability or development, the large populations of emirates like Bornu, Kano, Sokoto, and Zaria were unconducive to realization of some of the political advantages ideally associated with local government—intimate public knowledge of problems and leaders, community initiative and participation, greater sensitivity of governmental institutions to local needs and conditions.

[45] For Zaria see Smith, *Government in Zazzau*, pp. 201-202; and Hogben, *Muhammadan Emirates of Nigeria*, p. 89. For Kontagora see *ibid.*, p. 136. Accounts of other instances are found in the various provincial gazetteers.

[46] See Smith, *Government in Zazzau*; and Hogben, *Muhammadan Emirates of Nigeria*.

[47] *Index of Subsidiary Legislation Made Under the Native Authority Law* (*Cap. 77*) (Kaduna, 1966), p. 69.

The lack of adequate communications within almost all the emirates reinforced the desirability of unit reduction in some cases. For example, one proposal was to transfer Nguru district of Bornu emirate to Bedde emirate, the capital of which, Gashua, is only 42 miles away. A Grade "A" tarred road connects the two points. But Nguru is 230 miles from Maiduguri, the capital of Bornu Emirate, and most of the road between these two points was untarred, and reputedly treacherous. However, deliberate fission of emirates was even more obviously contrary to the whole rationale of the government's policy than fusion, in that it would release far larger numbers of people from the discipline and influence of traditional society which was the political and administrative foundation of the whole Northern Nigerian regime. Nothing, moreover, would have been more likely to incur the sharp opposition of the powerful local traditional rulers concerned. Nguru remained under Bornu.

N.A. staff standards: By 1964 all the Northern Native Authorities together employed approximately 42 thousand people who represented considerably more than half the total number of employed persons in Northern Nigeria (i.e. employed in organizations employing 10 or more persons) recorded in the 1952-53 Nigerian census. This number also represents many times the total numbers of Northern Nigerians employed in the same year in the Northern government service. Most Native Authorities had many unfilled posts for which provision had been made in their estimates, and the expected doubling of total N.A. revenues by 1970 implies a substantial capacity for expansion in staff. When these figures are juxtaposed against the average annual rate of leaving school, it may be appreciated that the specter that has haunted other African governments—an inability to provide employment opportunities for its expanding low and "middle level educated manpower"[48]—was greatly offset in Northern Nigeria by the absorptive capacity of the Native Administrations. In this respect alone, the contribution of the N.A. system to Northern internal political stability was enormous.

No systematic data regarding the educational level of N.A. staff are available, but as salary level can be assumed to have been related to the Native Administrations' ability to attract and hold qualified staff, it may be assumed further that the larger Native Adminis-

[48] See Frederick Harbison, "Human Resources and Economic Development in Nigeria", in *The Nigerian Political Scene*, Robert O. Tilman and Taylor Cole, eds. (Durham: Duke University Press, 1962), pp. 213-19.

trations were better off in this regard than smaller ones. The role of "objective" standards of recruitment and promotion in the N.A. services was complicated generally by the persistence of traditional patterns and norms.

The nature of the conflict between traditional and modern norms of administrative employment, and the failure to resolve the conflict through imposition of a comprehensive, legally binding, civil service type code and agency (local Government Service Board or Commission) for local government staff in the region as a whole has been discussed elsewhere.[49] In brief, Smith's summation of his data on Zaria in 1950—that modern educational qualification was "neither a necessary or a sufficient condition for appointment to the Native Administration"[50]—may be taken as applicable to the Native Administrations generally in the period of my study. My spot check on the backgrounds of N.A. staff members in two other emirates in 1959 (Bida and Gwandu) confirmed, as Smith's Zaria data indicates, that *sarakuna* predominated over *talakawa* in the ranks of N.A. service, and that the reigning royal dynasty, or lineage segment, predominated over the nonincumbent dynasty or lineage segment.[51]

In the case of Bida, I undertook to find out whether there existed in 1959 a distribution among technical department employees in terms of dynastic affiliation comparable to that Smith had found 10 years earlier in Zaria, which like Bida, has a royal dynastic structure consisting of three families (Masaba, Usman Zaki, and Magiji Umaru). To this end, I requested a cooperative senior official of the N.A. to gather tabulated data on the dynastic affiliations of selected departments, on a form supplied by me. Replies were received from all departments canvassed. The confirmative and revealing results of this survey, which parallel Smith's data, is contained in Table 16. Furthermore, not only had a comprehensive legal code and agency (which would have invalidated Smith's generalization) not been adopted, other developments may have worked to confirm it. Thus beginning in 1953, the government launched a policy of "northernization" of the regional public service (i.e. recruitment of Northern

---

[49] See Chapter 2.

[50] *Government in Zazzau*, p. 274.

[51] So far as the general level of efficiency was concerned, however, this development probably was offset to some degree by the growth since 1950 of specialized N.A. staff training facilities such as the Institute of Administration—for general administrative and clerical training and schools for police, agricultural, forestry, and veterinary department employees.

Nigerians to replace expatriates or non-Nigerians and southern Nigerians), the tendency of which was to syphon off many of the better qualified and trained personnel of all but the most affluent Native Authorities. This development was to be expected, if for no other reason than the superior inducements and conditions offered by government service. Moreover, for those beneficially affected, the desire to work under a legal British type personnel code employed by the government service was an additional motive for transferring.

Ruling out imposition from above, the government's stated policy was to encourage Native Administrations at the local level to approximate such a code, and more specifically, to set up local staff standard boards or civil service commissions to define and regulate policy in this area.[52] At least none of the 12 selected Native Authorities surveyed in 1959 adopted a regularized system of application and recruitment for their staff posts, or of contracts, nor established firm minimum educational qualifications.[53] The system of grading of posts outlined in the N.A. Model Staff Regulations appeared to be erratically applied. No government administrative officer at any time managed to sell the idea of a board or commission for appointments to any emirate Native Authority.

Another approach to a similar objective was the constitution of N.A. Establishment Committees (most of the 12 had them), the powers and functions of which were emphatically limited, however. These committees were formally delegated powers with respect to hiring, engagement, dismissal, and remuneration of staff. But the jurisdiction of the committees was confined to the categories of temporary and daily-paid workers, and permanent staff of Grade G or below only; the top six grades of the staff were excluded. Moreover, the Establishment Committees were subject to the provisions of Section 67 of the Native Authority Law, permitting the N.A. to impose any restrictions and conditions on committees it deemed proper, to appoint the chairman and all members, and to determine their terms of office. Under the rules of all 12 Native Administrations, the chair-

[52] See *Report of the Joint Select Committee of the Northern Regional Council*, 1952; and Ahmadu Sardauna, *Local Government Development in the Northern Region* (Zaria: Gaskiya Corporation, 1953), p. 18, where the Sardauna states, "Native Authorities are being encouraged to set up Appointments and Promotions Boards, which will be responsible for deciding between the relative qualifications of candidates for employment and promotion".

[53] Section 3(a) of the *Native Authority Staff Regulations* (*Amended up to 1st December 1964*), states that no appointments shall be made until an appropriate course has been passed; Section 24 says that a Native Authority *may* require an official to pass a departmental test.

Table 16: Dynastic Composition* of the Bida N.A.—1959

Department	Masaba		Usman-Zaki	Magiji-Umaru	unaffiliated	Total
Agriculture	no.	3	4	3	1	11
	%	27.3	36.4	27.3	9.1	100.1
Education	no.	2	4	7	3	16
	%	12.5	25.0	43.8	18.8	100.1
Judicial	no.	5	6	9	—	20
	%	25.0	30.0	45.0	—	100.0
Prisons	no.	6	—	4	3	13
	%	46.2	—	30.8	23.1	100.1
Veterinary	no.	2	2	4	—	8
	%	25.0	25.0	50.0	—	100.0
Works	no.	4	6	5	3	18
	%	22.2	33.3	27.8	16.7	100
Misc.	no.	2	5	8	1	16
	%	12.5	31.3	50.0	6.3	100.1
Total	no.	24	27	40	11	102
	%	23.5	26.5	39.2	10.8	100

*Includes clients and kin.

man of this committee could be removed at any time during his term of office at the discretion of the N.A. Council. In practice, most of the members of the establishment Committee were drawn from the inner circle of traditionally prominent, titled, full-time, salaried councillors, or those having client relationships with the emir. Finally, there was the general limitation stemming from the role of the General Purpose Committees.

Concerning the very top Native Authority offices, there were legal controls from above in the form of a provision of the N.A. Law requiring Native Administrations to seek the approval of the Governor (who had delegated the power to the Premier) for any appointment it made in this category. Out of the total number of persons employed by Native Authorities, only three percent were in this category in 1959, however, and it is doubtful whether the percentage distribution increased dramatically thereafter. Furthermore, except in the case of Ilorin, neither this provision nor that generally allowing the government to disallow or revoke the creation of any office or any appointment was ever invoked in relation to the 12 Native Administrations surveyed. It is probable, however, that knowledge of the provisions acted as a restraint and that the government issued some warnings based on them.

It is not to be inferred that Native Administrations were indifferent to modern administrative and technical talent. Educational qualifications, efficiency, and experience were valued, preferably in conjunction with proper traditional credentials. There were few complaints of refusals by an N.A. to engage a promising nonaristocratic graduate of the Western schools (his relative chances of promotion and remuneration were another matter). Skill and talent appeared to have been appropriately used. Tenure in such posts by educated and administratively able personnel depended on past receptivity of families to Western schooling. In some cases this was notably high and in many others conspicuously low. Native Authorities seldom denied the claims of families in the nobility or vassalry to territorial offices, and the government ordinarily did not interfere, partially on the grounds that there is "more to ruling than schooling". Significantly, however, the government more than once directed its local administrative officers to make known its rising expectations in this respect.

Two additional points about the use of talent are noteworthy. The first is that, since, often, members of the *sarakuna* class had acquired Western education in advance of and to a greater degree than their *talakawa* subjects, modern and traditional criteria were not necessarily self-exclusive. The second—and one that is equally significant —is that the traditional institution of clientage (through which commoners were sometimes elevated to the *sarakuna* ranks long before concern about Western education entered in) sometimes permitted a use of new talent within the framework of a traditional relationship. As was true of prominent *talakawa* who were central councillors in such emirates as Bida, Katsina, Adamawa and the one in Sokoto (and no doubt in other instances), "new" men sometimes assumed a clientage relationship with the person responsible for their recruitment. Absorption of modern values and maintenance of a traditional institution were, to this extent, compatible. (These themes will be pursued more fully in a later chapter dealing with regional political leadership.)

The incidence of corruption: The susceptibility to evasion of the one major piece of postwar legislation (the Customary Presents Order) to deal with what the Northern Nigerian-born prime minister of Nigeria called in 1950, "the twin curses of bribery and corruption", the extent of which he asserted, "no one who has not lived among us can fully appreciate", was noted previously. 15 out of 34 emirate Native Authorities had not as of 1965 enacted the order.[54] At the same time, self-help (*Bincikin kasa*) was interpreted by Native Courts, at least up until 1959, as a punishable offense against customary law or as a violation of the precept against "assuming the powers of the Native Authority".

On a brief return to Zaria in 1959 Smith observed a "striking" decline since 1950 in extortionary forms of corruption at the village level, such as unauthorized grain and market requisitions, fines on individuals suffering from certain diseases, and underpayment of labor (which he attributes in part to attempts at exposition on the part of NEPU, the radical political party).[55] On the other hand, another anthropologist working in Bornu Emirate in 1956-57 reports that "tribute was referred to as normal by the population at large, by junior Native Administration officials, and among several close associates of District Heads throughout the Emirate".[56] Allegations to the same effect were also freely forthcoming to me in 1959, 1963, and 1966. At least one case, resulting in the dismissal of a district head in still another emirate in 1957 indicate that outright extortion had not totally disappeared from the region by 1959, the apogee of NEPU influence.[57]

Both Cohen and Smith also draw attention to irregularities in tax collection.[58] The combination of (a) the method of lump-sum assessment of villages, with individuals' shares being allotted by Na-

[54] The 19 subscribers are Abuja, Adamawa, Agaie, Argungu, Bida, Borgu, Daura, Gombe, Gumel, Gwandu, Hadeja, Kano, Katsina, Kazaure, Lafiagi, Muri, Pategi, Yauri, Zaria. See *Index of Subsidiary Legislation*, p. 34.

[55] "Historical and Cultural Conditions of Corruption Among the Hausa", Smith's initial observations on corruption are in the chapter, "The Economic Aspects of Political Activity", of his unpub. diss., "Social and Economic Change among Selected Native Communities in Northern Nigeria" (Department of Social Anthropology, University of London, 1951).

[56] Ronald Cohen, "The Analysis of Conflict in Hierarchical Systems: An Example from Kanuri Political Organization", in *Anthropologica*, Vol. 4, No. 1 (1962), p. 96.

[57] Charges on which the District Head of Jibya, Katsina Emirate, was dismissed in 1957 included the following unauthorized levies: six pence for school children's uniforms from every taxpayer, whether the donor had a child attending school or not; one shilling for the Red Cross from every taxpayer; three shillings for Cassava plant (which District Heads were supposed to distribute without charge) from householders, whether or not they received an allotment from the plant; one shilling from every prostitute living at Jibya Town, followed by collections of six pence and three pence separately from each of them; *kudin ruwa* (literally, "money for water") on the eve of the *Sallan Azumi* [Muslim holiday for the id-el-Fitr]—i.e. one shilling from anyone who sold water in kerosene tins and six pence for anyone selling water from earthen pots.

[58] Smith, *Government in Zazzau*, pp. 282-83; Cohen, "*Analysis of Conflict*", pp. 100-101, 103.

tive Administration officials, (b) those officials' discretionary power to exempt from taxation the infirm, the over- and the under-aged (usually below 16 and above 55), (c) the inability of most peasants to read tax receipts, and (d) the general lack of on the spot supervision by the government—would appear to have made tax-collecting a particularly exploitable source of peculation. This typically took the form of registering fewer than the number who actually paid tax. Smith noted a discrepancy of over 210,000 between the adult population of Zaria Emirate in 1951, registered on the basis of tax returns (540,000 persons), and that revealed by the Nigerian census conducted in the same year (in excess of 750,000 persons).[59] In 1959 a financial specialist in the Northern Ministry for Local Government made what was probably a conservative estimate of the total discrepancy (for the whole region) revealed by comparing registered taxpayers in 1958-59 with the number of adults who registered for voting in the federal election of 1959.[60] The estimated discrepancy (attributed to laxness or inefficiency in the count) was 772,666, which represented a probable loss of revenue per annum of over one million pounds. Taking into account those findings alone, the magnitude of corruption, especially in light of the total N.A. revenue for the year of less than 10 million pounds, had to be considerable.

Recurrent instances of other forms of corruption, e.g. embezzlement and defrauding of Native Treasuries, are recorded in the *Provincial Annual Reports* and the vernacular paper, *Gaskija Ta Fi Kwabo*, throughout the period under study.[61]

It is not to be lost sight of, of course, that cases of dismissal from office and criminal conviction were evidence not only of the existence of corruption, but also of the regional government's concern with

---

[59] Smith, *Government in Zazzau*, pp. 282-83.

[60] The assumption was made on a 2% annual increase in the number of possible taxpayers; Smith asserts a 2.5% annual population increase for Zaria (*ibid.*, p. 283). The 1959 comparison does not take into account *jangali* (cattle tax), which in 1958-59 represented 10% of total collections.

[61] A Ministry for Local Government publication, *Magilisarku*, No. 5 (1958), p. 15, states that "losses of cash and stores through theft and embezzlement from Native Authorities during the past five years have amounted to more than £100,000 . . . and that unproved losses by contributor negligence and extravagance could well total another £100,000". According to a responsible official in the Government Audit Department, this figure was conservative. Also see *Daily Times* of Nigeria for September 10, 1959, which carried on page 3 the story of the suspension from office of two Kontagora N.A. Councillors in connection with the destruction by fire of the Kontagora-Wushishi Native Treasury following an unannounced visit of a government auditor. For other reported examples of fraud and peculation see *Provincial Annual Reports*, 1952-63, *passim*.

corruption and hence of its being liable to punishment. The increasing publicity given to such cases might furthermore have stimulated new expectations on the part of the public vis-à-vis officials, thus acting as a deterrent. Yet cognizance of the realities of traditional politics could complicate public interpretation of punitive action against officials. That the pervasiveness of local administrative irregularities obliged the government to follow a policy of selective enforcement has been noted.[62] The traditional role of an emir and other patrons entailed the obligation to protect and advance his dynastic interests against those of his rivals. Hence the exposure and dismissal of a culpable individual official was more often than not attributed to that traditional exigency rather than to general enforcement of impersonal standards.

A celebrated instance of this was the dismissal of Alhaji Nuhammadu Lawal, MHA, the district head of Dutsin Ma in Katsina, who held the title of Yandaka. The Katsina Yandaka's family, the Yerubawa Fulani (who have prescriptive right to the title) is historically a rival center of power to the throne of that emirate—the first Yandaka having been one of two persons in addition to the founder of the original royal dynasty (the Dallazawa, after the founder, Malam Umaru Dallaji) to have received from Sokoto a green flag, which elsewhere is an exclusive symbol of paramount authority in an emirate. (This historical situation appears to have been unique to Katsina.) The British, however, deposed the last Dallazawa emir and replaced him with Malam Dikko (of the nonroyal Katsina Sulebawa family) whose son, Nagogo, is the present emir. The Yandaka's family is known in Katsina to have at first refused to recognize Malam Dikko and to have later preferred a Dallazawa successor upon Dikko's death. Under the new regime the reputation of the Yandaka for resistance to the authority of the throne continued. The ex-Yandaka's administration initially came under scrutiny in the wake of investigations set in motion by the Governor's 1957 speech from the throne. For two years the outcome was in doubt while, reportedly, the Yandaka was presenting his cause to Kaduna. Whether or not justifiably, the Yandaka's eventual dismissal was in Katsina almost universally and inevitably interpreted as a triumph of the throne over a rival, and as a sign of the Emir's relative influence in Kaduna. The moral is that "selective enforcement" was bound to have, at best, deeply ambiguous meaning. Under this policy there was often no

[62] Cf. Cohen, "Analysis of Conflict", *passim.*

perceptible difference between reform and plain old internecine strife among the aristocracy.

Students of emirate society appear to agree that at bottom its apparently high incidence of official corruption stems in large part from conflicting pressures and expectations regarding social and official positions, rather than from any singular aptitude for venality on the part of those who occupy them. Cohen describes these pressures:

> Not all pressures exerted upon the District Head originate from his superior in the political organization. The District Head is a local potentate and must act like one. He lives in a much larger compound than other people in the District, and supports a large number of dependents and their families. He must maintain his own band of praise-singers and his own group of Koranic *mallams* (teacher-priests). Periodically he feeds the local Native Administration personnel and gives out money to wandering players who come into his town to entertain the populace and to sing his praises. His dependents, many of whom he supplies with horses, must have dress costumes for ceremonial occasion and gifts from him at times of *rites de passage* in their family and at annual religious festivals. All these things must be done and done "well" if the District Head is to be judged by himself and others as a successful chief. Common people, Native Administration personnel in the bush, and District Heads often discussed or made allusions to the relative merits of one District Head's chiefly attributes as opposed to another. Since widely known cultural values define what is meant by "good" District Head behaviour, the person in this role constantly feels pressure, both from his own values and the demands of those under him, for proper chiefly activity.

> In sum, it should be realized that the salary given to the District Head does not allow him to maintain his social role.[63]

While all this suggests the inappropriateness of viewing the problem of corruption in the emirates in terms simply of moral turpitude, it also indicates an inherent difficulty in regional government policy. The root of the malady the government ostensibly aimed to eradicate lay in the very condition it sought to promote—continuation of the prestige, symbols, influence, and bonds of traditional authority.

A note on the role of native courts: The legal and judicial sys-

---

[63] *Ibid.*, pp. 103-104.

tems in force in Northern Nigeria had a bearing on virtually every important aspect of local no less than regional government and politics in the emirates; conversely the development of these systems was deeply influenced by emirate institutions. The promulgation in 1959 and 1960 of the new Penal and the Criminal Procedure Codes of law, respectively, introduced apparently major politically significant changes in the role of the so-called native courts, which long formed in the emirates the principal vehicle for the administration of justice. The implication of the reform of 1959-60 must therefore be viewed against the background of the traditional and colonial judicial institutions that gave rise to it.

From the standpoint of modern conceptions of justice, conditions in the emirates before 1959 were alien and antagonistic in several respects. The key to the situation was the pervasive use of classical Islamic law (the *shar'ia*), in this case of the Maliki school, as enforceable criminal law. Several peculiar features of this law and the coalescence of judicial and executive authority which the law envisages are germane here.

In the first place, the *shar'ia* is not merely a code of law in the Western sense, but a prescription for every aspect of the believer's individual and social life, derived from an ideal conception of Islamic faith and practice. Nothing pertaining to human conduct lies beyond its authority, and its dictates are, in theory, immutable.[64] Northern rulers could thus plausibly interpret Lugard's initial pledge not to interfere with religion as implying a commitment neither to alter nor deny the force of Islamic law. The British prohibited those *shar'ia*-prescribed punishments deemed repugnant to "natural justice", e.g. stoning to death for adultery, mutilation for theft, etc., but otherwise accepted and honored this interpretation. British backing also helps explain why Northern Nigeria represented, prior to the 1959-60 reforms, the only land outside of Afghanistan and the Arabian Peninsula clinging to the orthodox *shar'ia* in the domain of criminal law.[65]

Paradoxical as it may seem, the *shar'ia* also allowed the Northern

---

[64] See Reuben Levy, *The Social Structure of Islam* (London, 1957), pp. 150-91; Gustav von Grunebaum, "Islam: Essays in the Nature and Growth of a Cultural Tradition", Memoir No. 81, *American Anthropologist*, Vol. 57, Part 2 (1955), pp. 127-40; J.N.D. Anderson, *Islamic Law in Africa* (London, H.M. Stationery Office, 1954).

[65] "Native Courts and Native Customary Law in Africa"; Report of the Judicial Advisors Conference, 1953, *Supplement, Journal of African Administration* (October 1953), p. 35.

Nigerian expositors enormous scope for legal invention, owing to the fact that, as a leading scholar of Islamic law has pointed out: "In the Islamic law there are some six or seven offences, meticulously defined in the classical texts, which carry prescribed punishments—most of them exceedingly severe. For the rest, however, the texts merely prescribe that all other wrongdoing shall be suitably punished. This gave the native courts an almost unfettered discretion both in the definition of the alleged offences—even those with a political flavour—and also in their punishment".[66]

Many of the doctrines laid down in the orthodox legal texts are at variance with corresponding Western tenets. Probably the most glaring instance is the law of homicide. The Maliki doctrine in particular does not recognize provocation as a mitigating circumstance; it defines "deliberate" homicide in terms of the aftermath of hostile acts without regard to the probable intention as reflected in the means employed (a classic illustration being the death of a person following a hostile attack on him with a feather). It also makes the penalty for homicide variable according to the wishes of the heirs of blood (who may decide whether death, blood-penalty, or no penalty at all is imposed). In certain circumstances, the word of the blood heirs, as registered in oath-taking, is taken as conclusive proof of the defendant's guilt, whether or not supported by firsthand knowledge of the crime.[67] The murder of a nonbeliever by a Muslim was not punishable by death (the victim's blood heirs were entitled to only one-half or one-fifteenth the compensation due those of a Muslim, depending on whether the victim was a Christian or pagan). The definition of acceptable witnesses, in homicide and other criminal causes alike, expressly excludes any "interested party", women, and non-Muslims, all in a region the population of which is one-third non-Muslim. In general, the rules of evidence in Islamic law are far more concerned with, and depend on, assigning roles of litigants in the trial than with findings of facts.[66] Thus not only is the Islamic criminal procedure invidious in the distinctions it makes in the status

[66] J.N.D. Anderson, "Criminal Law Reform in Nigeria: A Major Advance", *Modern Law Review*, Vol. 24, No. 5 (September 1961), p. 617.

[67] See J.N.D. Anderson, "Conflict of Laws in Northern Nigeria: A New Start", *International and Comparative Law Quarterly*, Vol. 8, Part 3 (July 1959), pp. 443-44.

[68] In a trial under Islamic law a great deal depends on whether the accuser or accused or which supporting witnesses are first given the opportunity to swear oaths. In certain circumstances, swearing of oaths is ipso facto grounds for acquittal or conviction, without any opportunity for counteroaths being extended.

of litigants; from a modern Western standpoint, in the hands of a partial judge it is highly susceptible to interested influence (as is, of course, the wide area of discretion in defining offenses and ascribing penalties).

This brings us to the second aspect of discrepancies between traditional and modern conceptions—judicial organization. The power to appoint and dismiss the chief judge (Hausa, *alkalin alkalai*) is invested in the Emir (or in more recent times in him and the councillors of the Native Authority). Indirectly, through the *alkalin alkalai*, or directly, appointment, dismissal, and promotion of other judges was also controlled by the N.A. In Kano the executive seems to have done so directly; in Zaria, the subordinate judges owe their career to the Chief Judge, the Emir exercising control through manipulation of the chief judgeship. Traditionally the factors governing a judicial career were comparable to those underlying a traditional administrative career: relationships of kinship, marriage, and clientage, lineage or dynastic rivalry, etc.

Most offenses under Islamic law are not within the category of the six or seven crimes (*hadd*) singled out in the Koran for specific punishments. In the last resort, the rest of the offenses are subject to the determination of the executive acting in a judicial capacity (this area of discretionary executive or administrative judicial authority is known in Islamic law as *siyasa*). The domain of *siyasa* was accorded recognition and institutionalized in the Anglo-Northern Nigerian set-up in the form of courts presided over by the emir and operating alongside the so-called *alkali* courts. Within this domain the division of labor between *alkali* courts (the duties of which in the other, or *hadd*, category of punishments were all but eliminated by British prohibitions, plus the rigorous requirements of proof laid down in the *shar'ia*[69]) and the emirs' courts were usually a matter of practical convenience and prestige. Certain of the more weighty and significant cases were frequently reserved to the latter. Native Courts graded "A" (sometimes referred to as "A" "unlimited"), among which several of the emirs' courts were numbered, had the power to impose the death penalty.

Side by side with native courts, the British established a separate set of courts presided over by British jurors and applying a Nigerian code incorporating the substantive and procedural essentials of British criminal law; this rendered none of the foregoing

[69] Two eye witnesses to adultery, etc.

any less anomalous from a modern or Western point of view. Thus, to which of two widely divergent sets of institutions, with their conflicting standards of justice, a defendant in a criminal case became subject, was largely determined through chance circumstances e.g. the location of the crime, whether the arresting officer was a Nigerian or an N.A. policeman, whether a British administrative officer chose to exercise his power to confirm or transfer the case to another jurisdiction. In practice, 90 percent or more of all litigation was handled by the native courts.

Links between these two worlds of justice were uncertain and, from the point of view of aggrieved litigants, unreliable. Ordinarily appeals from native courts of Grade "B", "C", and "D" did not go to a British court (and never at all in cases involving a penalty of £25 or less or six months' imprisonment or less). Before 1956 the appellate court for the higher grades was normally a British court, but that year a Moslem Court of Appeal was introduced (a move which, in the view of some English legal scholars, enhanced the stature of the *shar'ia*).[70]

Another blow against integration of the two worlds of justice was the withdrawal of the applicability of prerogative writs (save that of habeas corpus) to native courts, formalized in the High Court Law of 1955. Furthermore, the Moslem Court of Appeal Law explicitly forbade the High Court and Moslem Court of Appeal from interfering with the judicial process in native courts on grounds of technical defects.[71] At the same time, no professional legal practitioners were allowed to appear before the native courts.

In lieu of the customary protections of a British court system, British administrative officers' powers of transfer and review were relied on for relief against the discriminatory features of the Islamic law, and some of the other grosser violations of British standards. This unusual arrangement (representing in effect reliance on the executive arm of government as the guarantor of justice) was justified on grounds of convenience, the unavailability of adequate

[70] See A.N. Allot, "The Moslem Court of Appeal", *West Africa* (August 10, 1957).

[71] Clause 23—"No proceedings in the native court or in the Moslem Court of Appeal, and no summons, warrant, process order or decree issued or more thereby shall be varied or declared void upon appeal solely by reason of any defect in procedure or want of form but the Moslem Court of Appeal and the High Court when respectively exercising powers of appeal under this law shall decide all matters according to substantial justice without undue regard to technicalities". Quoted in *Northern House of Assembly Debates*, 13th March 1956, p. 454.

Western-trained judicial personnel, and fairness (the assumption was that as between "natives" the British officers would be strictly impartial). Independent observers and students of the Northern legal institutions of this period have generally credited the effectiveness of the "saving grace" role of administrative officers; as far as strictly private litigation was concerned, the assessment would seem for the most part to have been justified. Usually overlooked in the assessment, however, was the inevitable pressure on British officers, in litigation involving Native Authority officials (especially high-placed ones), to uphold the efficacy of traditional authority, the sine qua non of indirect rule. Not to embarrass the N.A. could be a compelling injunction, especially if, as increasingly happened after 1952, such cases involved radical politicians avowedly seeking to undermine traditional authority.[72]

The structure of justice was a highly important adjunct to that of political authority in two major respects. The first, as suggested above, was the advantages it offered in the suppression of radical political agitation. The second, which Smith's Zaria study stresses, was the indispensable contribution it made to the ability of superiors in the administrative bureaucracy personally to protect their kin or client subordinates from the danger of conviction and dismissal stemming from charges of maladministrative behavior.

On the eve of Nigerian independence the Northern regional government announced its acceptance of recommendations for reform of this legal and judicial system in the direction of more internationally accepted principles. The recommendations were made by an expert panel of jurists the Northern government had appointed for the purpose. Significantly, one of the members of the panel has speculated that among the specific considerations that may have prompted the government to take this action was the emphasis the (British-composed) Minorities Commissions' Report placed on the necessity for "a full recognition of the fundamental right of equality before the Law", exemplary developments in other modern Islamic countries, and the "need to attract foreign capital"—hence the imperative of "a legal and judicial system which would give confidence to foreigners".[73]

October 1, 1960 marked the effective inauguration of a coordinated program of legal and judicial reform which included the

---

[72] For a discussion of "Legal Limitations on Political Liberties" in Northern Nigeria in the postwar period, see Sklar, *Nigerian Political Parties*, pp. 355-65.
[73] Anderson, "Conflict of Laws", pp. 450, 452.

Penal Code, the Procedural Code, the Native Courts (Amendment) Law, and related legislation establishing a so-called Shar'ia Court of Appeal and a Native Courts Appellate Division of the regional High Court. This program was addressed to all of the controversial problem areas indicated above—(1) conflict between traditional and modern standards and norms of justice, (2) duality in the systems of law and courts, (3) the status persons before the law, (4) the quality of judicial administration, and (5) the relationship of the judiciary to other local institutions.

The meaning and effect of the adopted reforms became a subject of considerable controversy, not only within Nigeria,[74] but in the pages of professional law journals abroad,[75] where it has been contended by one side that the reforms were a "new start" and a major advance, and by the other that their net effect was "retrograde". A full airing of the points in contention is beyond my scope and competence here, but certain issues particularly pertinent to the themes of this book deserve attention.

The heart of the reforms were the new Penal and Criminal Procedure Codes. The codes were deliberately modeled on the corrresponding laws in the former British Sudan, on the grounds that, although British in origin, they had already been modified to fit special needs in that predominately Islamic and African country and therefore were particularly suited to Northern Nigeria.[76]

The effects of adopting these codes on the preexisting situation in Northern Nigeria were threefold: (1) elimination of the duality of codes, hence of the "conflicts" of law that stemmed from it; (2) equalization of the status of all persons before the law; (3) abolition of the category of "offenses against native law and custom", the authority of the *shar'ia* being confined to personal and family matters.

Significant as these inroads were, clear traces of the earlier norms of justice were to be observed in the subsequent arrangements. It is evident that an attempt was made to approximate certain

---

[74] See Northern House of Assembly *Debates*, August 13, 1959, Coll. 2052-2081; and John West, "The North Has No Need for a Martial Law", *Daily Service*, September 12, 1959, p. 7.

[75] See *Modern Law Review*, Vol. 24, No. 5 (September 1961), for a symposium; "Criminal Law Reform in Northern Nigeria", "Retrograde Legislation in Northern Nigeria?" by Justin Price, "The Northern Nigerian Codes", by Olu Odumosu; and J.N.D. Anderson, "A Major Advance", pp. 604-25. In his book Schwarz calls Price's article "unfair" without stating his reasons for that judgment. *Nigeria*, p. 257, note 21.

[76] The Sudan Codes were themselves originally based on the Indian Codes, which in turn represented an adaption of English law.

substantive features of the *shar'ia* in the new codes. Thus, not only is drunkenness a criminal offense under the new Penal Code (Section 401), but any drinking of alcohol by a Muslim (Section 403—punishment, one month imprisonment, five pounds, or both). Adultery is punishable by two years imprisonment, a fine, or both (Sections 387, 388). Breach of contract, under Section 381, is made a criminal cause (instead of falling under the category of a tort, as in English and American law). Section 393 of the Procedure Code reads: "A native court having jurisdiction over capital offences shall before passing sentence of death invite the blood relatives of the condemned person, if they can be found and brought to court, to express their wishes as to whether a death sentence shall be carried out and shall record such wishes in the record of the proceedings." Section 394 reads that such declaration of blood heirs may properly be part of a decision as to the exercise of the prerogative of mercy.[77]

Other clauses in both codes reflect an aim to incorporate provisions that would sustain the authoritarian character of official relations with the public. To wit, Sections 136, 137, and 138 of the Penal Code make it an offense to fail to (a) heed a "summons, notice order or proclamation" requiring the attendance of a person before *any public servant legally competent* to issue the same [italics added], (b) produce a document as directed in the same way, (c) or supply any information so requested, respectively. Section 10 of the Penal Code defines "a legally competent public servant" to include everyone appointed by the regional authority (not excluding the officials of public corporations) or any local government authority. In other words, any Native Administration official was given the power to so command anyone in the jurisdiction of the N.A. Section 393 of the same code defines criminal defamation in conspicuously broad terms: "Whoever, save as hereinafter excepted, by words either spoken or reproduced by mechanical means or intended to be read or by signs or by visible representations makes or publishes any false statement of fact, intending to harm or knowing or having reasons to believe that such false statement of fact will harm the reputation of any person or class of persons or of the government or of any native authority in the Northern Region or of any local government authority in the Northern Region shall be punished with imprisonment for a term which may extend to two years or with fine or with both".

[77] Cited in Price, "Northern Nigerian Codes", p. 611.

In the procedural domain, lawyers continued to be forbidden to assist any party before native courts, which were also still immune from the application of ordinary prerogative writs. The reasoning which justified these features, namely that competently trained judges of the native courts were unlikely to be available for some time in sufficient numbers to operate all the courts under the usual Western restraints, also led to that proviso, which, prima facie, was the most serious, even if initially accepted as a temporary expedient:

> In any matter of a criminal nature a native court shall be guided in regard to practice and procedure by the provision of this Criminal Procedure Code (Section 386).
>
> The fact that a native court has not been guided or properly guided by the provisions of this Criminal Procedure Code shall not entitle any person to be acquitted or any order of the court to be set aside. (Section 386, 3).

Subsection 2, of the same Section, did, however, qualify this permission of latitude with respect to certain technical requirements, not all of them to the advantage of the litigants.

With respect to the problem of duality in the system of courts, full, if indirect integration, was virtually achieved. The Native Courts (Amendment) Law introduced new Provincial Courts (the appointment, discipline, remuneration and promotion of whose judges were the responsibility of the Regional Government rather than Native Authorities) to which appeals from all criminal judgments of the native courts could be brought in the first instance. Higher appellate jurisdiction in such cases rested with the High Court, a special Division of which was created to deal with cases originating in native courts (the Division consisted of two ordinary High Court judges, plus a *Shar'ia* Court Judge—the latter was a feature not accepted without challenge in the Federal Supreme Court[78]), and thence with the Nigerian Federal Supreme Court. Later, the scope of the *Shar'ia* Court was restricted to cases to which relevant Islamic personal law only applied (previously the *Shar'ia* Court could hear any case of personal law as long as all the litigants concerned consented). In criminal jurisdiction courts above the provincial level, professional legal representation was available, though lawyers continued to be excluded from native courts that continued

---

[78] See Olawoyin *v.* Commissioner of Police, cited in Keay and Richardson, *Native and Customary Courts*, p. 75.

to handle over 90% of all litigation in Northern Nigeria, little of which ever reached the appeal stage. (There is no provision for automatic appeal; it depends on the litigant's initiative.) In principle, nevertheless, these innovations did not give everyone access on an equal footing to the same or equivalent courts.

Furthermore, the disadvantages of prohibiting professional legal representation in the lower courts was somewhat alleviated through establishment of an Inspectorate section of the Northern Ministry of Justice. In effect, the duties and powers of the inspectors, who were responsible to a Commissioner of Native Courts, represented a continuation in a new form of the old process of administrative review. On the initiative of an inspector, appeals and "transfers" of jurisdiction could be instituted. Moreover, the High Court of the Northern Region was empowered "to order that a Provincial Court should try a case at first instance if it appears at any time that it is necessary to secure a fair trial or in the interests of justice generally that a native court having jurisdiction should not dispose of any particular cause or matter".[79]

In regard to the quality of judicial administration in native courts, the foundations of improvement were laid in the introduction of specialized local training courses for *Alaklai*, including a formal academic diploma course for a very limited number of them.[80] Given the large number of personnel involved and the limited educational facilities available, however, these training programs were a long way from realizing a fully professional quality of judicial administration. By 1965 qualification and performance according to modern criteria in the judicial sphere was still no more a necessary or sufficient condition of employment than in the administrative realm.

Nonetheless, it is clear that the judicial reforms were much more far-reaching than anything achieved in the administrative and political structures, perhaps partly because independent expert advice in this field was more palatable, and no doubt also more imperative in terms of the requisites of attracting to the region the desired foreign investment capital. The program of reform closely followed the recommendations of the distinguished international panel of jurists, who visited the region for the purpose on two occasions within a three-year interval, each time submitting reports to a Northern govern-

[79] *Ibid.*, p. 283.
[80] *Ibid.*, p. 76; also S. S. Richardson, "Training for Penal Reform in Northern Nigeria", *Journal of African Administration* (1961).

ment at its invitation.[81] At least one member of the panel believes that the panel had made a radical impact on the whole traditional order.[82] It is clear, however, that even the panel was obliged to come to grips with political realities which favored the persistance of some traditional norms. The substantive accommodation in significant respects of the new Penal Code to conceptions of the *Shar'ia* has already been noted; they were not eliminated. There appears to be no good judicial reason, moreover, why the panel could not have recommended a system of rotation of native court *Alkali* among the various emirates, which would have gone far toward achieving an independent relationship of the judiciary to executive and legislative authority which other panel recommendations seemed concerned to accomplish.[83] But such an arrangement would have seriously impaired the political leverage native authorities had traditionally enjoyed in relation to the native courts, and no such recommendation was forthcoming. Furthermore, the panel never broached at all the issue of the fusion of executive, legislative, and executive functions represented by the existence of Emirs' Courts. For its part, the government made plain that it had no intention of allowing judicial reform to be carried to the point of fatal injury to a vital source of the Na-

[81] See the white papers, "Statement of the Government of Northern Region of Nigeria on the Reorganization of the Legal and Judicial Systems of the Northern Region" (Kaduna, 1958); and "Statement made by the Government of Northern Nigeria" (Kaduna, 1962). The panel members were Sayad Mohammed Abu Rannat, Chief Justice of the Sudan; Mr. Justice Mohammed Sherif, Chairman of the Pakistan Law Commission; Professor J.N.D. Anderson, School of African and Oriental Studies, University of London; Alhaji Shettima Kashim, then Waziri of Bornu and afterwards Governor of the Northern Region; and M. Musa, Chief *Alkali* of Bida emirate.

[82] See Anderson, "Criminal Law Reform", p. 617.

[83] In accordance with agreements reached at the 1958 Nigerian Constitutional Conference which met after the work of the panel was completed, a judicial Service Commission was introduced into Northern Nigeria under the Native Courts (Amendment) Law of 1960. The law invested in this commission the power of approval of appointments to higher grade native courts, which were otherwise the prerogative of the native authorities. Under the 1960 law, however, approval was to be exercised *subsequent* to the act of appointment by native authorities, and *how* subsequent (that is, how long after the appointment was approval necessary) was conveniently left unspecified. Hence, the efficacy of this provision was problematical. The 1962 recommendation of the panel was that the approval be *prior* to the appointment, though all courts below Grade A and Grade A limited continued to be exempted. This recommendation was ostensibly accepted by the Northern Government. A few months later, however, NPC delegates to an All-Nigeria party conference were agreeing with their southern counterparts on plans to abolish the Judicial Service Commission in all regions, which was in fact done less than a year after the implementation of prior approval. Thereafter, approval reverted to political control—exercised by the Northern Ministry of Justice.

tive Authorities' influence and control.[84] Indeed, despite the fact that previous policy had been to "freeze" the number of Emirs' Courts with capital jurisdiction, it was bestowed on at least two more Emirs after the program of reform had been accepted.[85] Thus, in general, it must be said that in judicial institutions, as in the entire structure and operation of the central bureaucracies generally, reform yielded a functioning system that represented not a decisive break with the past, but a complicated matrix of traditional and modern influences.

[84] "We must never forget that the native courts are part of the native authority machine, and that *alkali* and native court judges are employees of the native authorities and serve the people of the native authority". Statement by the Honorable Attorney General of Northern Nigeria, *House of Assembly Debates*, April 6, 1960, Col. 514.

[85] For a statement regarding the government's decision to extend the power of capital punishment to the Emir's Court of Bida and Kontagora emirates, see Northern Nigeria *House of Assembly Debates*, May 3, 1960, Col. 764.

CHAPTER 5

The Subordinate Councils

THE VAST MAJORITY of local government councils in Northern Nigeria were officially designated subordinate, that is, legally and administratively subordinate to the Native Authorities within whose area and jurisdiction they operated. Subordinate Councils existed at each

THE NETWORK OF LOCAL COUNCILS

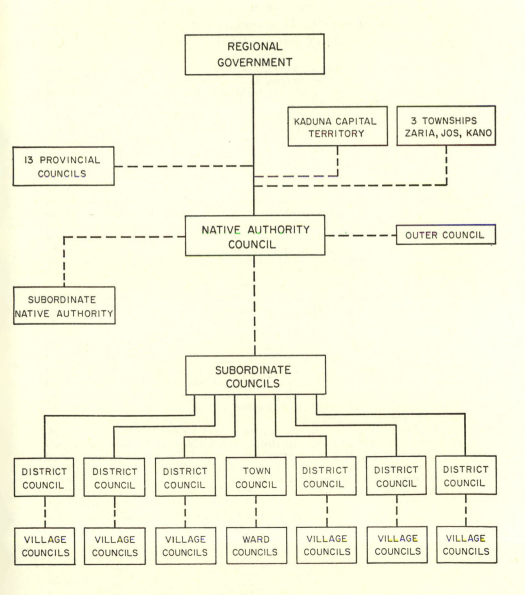

administrative level below that of the central bureaucracy village, district, ward, and town. Unlike the central councils, almost all of them owed their origin to recent, mostly postwar, efforts to develop popular organs of local government at those levels.[1]

The existence of similarly "new" institutions, the outer and provincial councils, has been noted, along with the fact that they were deliberately kept in the status of strictly advisory bodies having no executive powers and functions or spending authority. Ward councils and village councils, except, again, in a few plural emirates, notably Ilorin, were in the same position. Hence these bodies and certain other special local arrangements need not detain us further in this discussion of conciliar local government as it has operated between 1954 and 1965.[2] Of primary interest here are the district and

[1] The principal exceptions encountered were at the village level, where in some cases a rudimentary conciliar structure in the form of village elders and hamlet heads advising the village head was traditional. Except in certain districts of plural emirates, in which the chief was of local origins and might formally or informally make a practice of consulting with elders and village heads (a situation usually denoting adherence to a form of government antecedent to that of the emirate), district councils and all town councils were nontraditional bodies.

[2] In 1965 five local units known as Townships were functioning in Northern Nigeria. Two (Bussa and Bacita) were set up after 1962 to accommodate new communities centering around new development projects, the Niger Dam and a sugar factory. The other three—Kano, Jos, Zaria, not identical to the Townships of those names but adjacent to them—were survivors of a much larger number in an earlier day. In general, Townships represented a policy of isolating from the N.A. system urban areas in which services were relatively sophisticated and/or mixed populations of Europeans and African "strangers" (i.e. nonlocals) were especially numerous. Their legal position was formalized in the Townships Ordinance (Cap. 131 of the Laws of Nigeria) of 1963. In principle, Townships were separated into First, Second, and Third Class, but in fact, all five were Second Class. Second Class Townships were administered by a Local Authority who in each case was actually a government administrative officer, with whom an advisory council of varying composition might consult. On the origin of the Township arrangement see R. E. Wraith, "Local Government", in John P. Macintosh, ed., *Nigerian Government and Politics* (London, 1966), pp. 203-205.

Between 1956 and 1962 Kaduna, the regional capital, was also specially administered—directly by the Governor-in-Council, whose authority was exercised by an administrator. Four local councils, which represented ethnically distinct quarters of the town, advised the Administrator, who alone (with the approval of the Premier) determined which powers were delegated to them. Kaduna was then officially known as the Kaduna Capitol Territory, and it was sometimes interpreted as an arrangement combining desirable features of the so-called Canberra and Washington systems, after the Australian and United States systems of administration in their capitals, respectively. Other observers in Northern Nigeria suggested, however, that the arrangement was a device to spare the regional government the embarrassment of having Kaduna affairs under the control of political opposition elements; Kaduna was won by NEPU in the regional election of 1956, and in the 1959 Federal election the NPC eked out a victory over NEPU, although the combined votes of NEPU and Action Group exceeded the NPC total. These parties also made a relatively strong showing in the regional election of

town councils, of which by 1965 there were approximately 317 and 35 examples, respectively, in the emirates. The total for subordinate councils in the Region as a whole was over 850.[3]

Like the central bureaucracy, district and town councils were the fruit of the Northern Government's policy of gradualism. As such, they were a product of conflicting impulses—to accommodate democratic norms, on the one hand, and protect and reinforce traditional authority on the other. To some degree, these impulses could be simultaneously pursued, either by confirming traditional institutions in their customary powers while acknowledging but limiting the right of popular participation in them, or by creating new political institutions which substantially extended the right of the masses of people to participate, while denying them many sources and levers of power that traditional authority enjoyed. From the point of view of fully democratic local government (and for that matter from that of a purely traditional system) either course was a good deal less than satisfactory. The central bureaucracy embodied the essence of the first alternative and the subordinate councils, in effect, represented the second. Thus the effects of a separation between power and participation were to be observed in various aspects of these councils.

Table 17: Growth of Subordinate Council Revenue

Year	Total amount (all Native Authorities)
1949-50	£ 69,000
1950-51	78,000
1951-52	83,000
1952-53	98,000
1953-54	133,000
1954-55	161,000
1955-56	185,000
1957-58	344,500
1958-59	477,200
1959-60	488,300
1960-61	602,300
1961-62	669,300
1962-63	677,400

Source: *Native Authority Estimates*, 1949-50—1956-57; *Statistical Yearbook, 1964*—1957-58—1962-63.

1961. In 1962 the Kaduna Capitol Territory was abolished and Kaduna became legally and in every other important sense, the Kaduna Native Authority. In 1964 the NPC federal candidate for Kaduna was elected by an overwhelming margin.

[3] See *Northern Nigeria Local Government Yearbook 1966* (Kaduna, 1966), p. 10, Table 5.

DISTRICT COUNCILS existed in all emirates and in at least one town council in the majority of them (including all but Kazaure and Dikwa among the selected 12). Under the Law of 1954, Native Authorities were authorized, but not required, to place their subordinate councils on a legal footing. This step was accomplished through an N.A. legislative act, officially styled an "instrument", which set forth the composition, functions and powers, sources of revenue, electoral and operational rules of the council or councils concerned. Normally the instruments followed "models" of such legislation prepared in the Ministry for Local Government, a practice that resulted in a large measure of uniformity in the legal provisions governing all subordinate councils. It is worth noting that the process of providing subordinate councils with instruments received considerable impetus from the work of the Hudson Commission, which recommended that only legally constituted subordinate councils be allowed to serve as electoral colleges for the projected provincial councils. By 1959 only three emirates (all graded first-class—Argungu, Gwanda, and Zaria) still had some subordinate councils without instruments; most were brought into line by 1965. By 1965 there were in the emirate a total of 151 district councils, 32 Town Councils, and 21 Outer Councils with instruments.

These instruments generally stated that the councils might "tender advice to the Native Authority on any matter of public importance within its area". Provision was also made for subordinate councils, such as Native Authority councils in relation to the Regional government, to act as agents on behalf of the Native Authority in connection with public projects and services. In addition, subordinate councils could in principle establish services of their own for which the N.A. might make money available. (Subordinate councils were also generally given the right to raise revenue through imposition of "rates", a term for tax taken from English local government; the quite different meaning of the term in Northern local government is noted below.) Otherwise, none of the other major powers and functions (control of police, courts, tax-collecting, etc.) which made the council of the central bureaucracy such a formidable institution were ever shared with subordinate councils. And lacking independent legislative or rule-making powers of their own (ostensibly in conformity with the conventional precept that delegated authority—i.e. that delegated to the N.A. by the Regional government—should not be delegated), subordinate councils were largely without the means to augment the powers and functions laid down in their instruments.[4]

The various services that were assigned to subordinate councils taken as a whole numbered approximately 30,[5] but seldom was one council assigned them all, nor were all the legally allocated services necessarily performed. The legal phraseology used in his connection was: "the council may and if so required by the Native Authority shall establish, provide and maintain the following services". The mandatory option permitted an N.A. council to rid itself of services it preferred not to operate itself (e.g. cemeteries and burial of paupers, pest control, and at least until recently, attendance of pupils at junior primary schools). At the same time, allocation of a service, or any other function or power, to a subordinate council did not legally prohibit the N.A. from regulation or independent activity in respect thereof.[6]

As in the case of the Native Authorities vis-à-vis the Regional government, the practical division of labor between Native Authorities and subordinate councils was hierarchical; the functions and services which were allocated to subordinate councils involved relatively small expenditures of funds, limited technical facilities, and few if any trained personnel. Unlike the first case, however, this arrangement did not allow subordinate councils to enjoy the compensating political

[4] The legislation governing the functioning of subordinate councils is found in sections of the Revised Edition of the N.A. Law, 1965, as follows: District, Village Group, and Village Councils—Sections 56, 59, 60, 61 and 66; Outer Councils——Sections 57, 59, 60 and 61; Town Councils—Sections 55, 59, 60, 61 and 66.

[5] For example, (1) reading rooms and libraries, (2) parks, gardens and open spaces, (3) markets and slaughterhouses, (4) motor parks, (5) lodging houses, (6) the entertainment of official guests, (7) roads and drains which are declared by the Native Authority to be the responsibility of the Council, (8) footpaths, footbridges and ferries, (9) buildings, (10) water supplies, (11) the fencing of animal tracks, (12) grazing grounds, (13) animal pounds, (14) tsetse control, (15) dams and ponds, (16) arrangements for the attendance of pupils at Junior Primary Schools, (17) school meals at Junior Primary Schools, (18) adult education, (19) town and village planning and improvement, (20) village medical dressing stations, (21) feeding of pauper patients, (22) leprosy clinics, (23) sanitary services, (24) cemeteries and burial of paupers, (25) pest control, (26) distribution of planting material, fertilizers and plant protection products, (27) forestry and fruit tree nurseries, (28) amenity planting, (29) maintenance and protection of communal forestry areas, (30) maintenance of district council vehicles.

[6] Section 4(2) of the Adamawa Native Authority local Councils Instrument, which states that "Nothing contained in this section shall be deemed to prejudice or derogate the Native Authority's right to exercise any power or function vested in it by law".

advantages of greater public exposure and the appearance of autonomy. The essential difference was that the instruments invariably forbade subordinate councils to hire their own salaried staff. They could employ only such people as might be engaged on the basis of monthly allowances or wages paid daily—that is, unskilled personnel. For the rest, subordinate council services had to be carried out through the central Native Authorities' departmental staff, whom subordinate councils were expressly denied any authority to command, supervise, dismiss or, apparently, even criticize.[7] In the nature of the case, the unskilled employees generally worked under the direction and supervision of the salaried technical departmental staff of the central bureaucracy.

The official rationale for these prohibitions were: (1) additional trained personnel at the district level were generally not available, (2) those available were needed in the service of the central N.A., and (3) subordinate councillors lacked enough technical knowledge and experience to direct trained staff competently. But the first argument should have logically made it unnecessary to legislate against employment of salaried staff on the part of subordinate councils, and the third was to some extent as much the effect as the cause of the policy; for under it councillors had no incentive to acquire the appropriate knowledge nor opportunity for relevant experience, as they well might have had full responsibility had the services been theirs. The second argument amounted to saying that the efficiency and/or prerogatives of the central N.A. must take precedence over the objective of a conciliar process of government at lower levels—which is precisely the situation which the separation of central N.A. and subordinate council levels of jurisdiction was supposedly designed to avoid. No part of this rationale would appear to have justified denial of the right of subordinate councils to criticize N.A. staff for conduct in relation to services for which those councils were ostensibly made responsible. There is little doubt that the existing low level of literacy in the rural areas limited the governmental capacities of subordinate councils. At the same time, it is difficult to avoid the conclusion that the deliberate proviso against an independent subordinate council staff or service partly reflected a desire to keep this politically significant

---

[7] "Departmental officers are the employees of the Native Authority not the Council and therefore they cannot be criticized for the policy they carry out". *N.A. Office Guide Part III, Subordinate Councils*, Chapter 13, p. 5.

prerogative where it traditionally resided. In any case, the fact that subordinate councils lacked their own staff must be counted a very serious handicap to their mission to become effective units of democratic local government. The same may be said of the financial arrangements through which the business of subordinate councils was conducted.

IT HAS BEEN noted that subordinate councils were dependent on the central N.A. for most of their revenue. This arrangement was officially termed "delegation of financial responsibility", i.e. on the part of a central Native Authority councils. Most of this delegated revenue took the form of a certain proportion of the *haraji,* or general tax (calculated on a per capita basis) collected within the boundaries of a district or town, which the subordinate council of the area was allowed to "retain" (e.g. two shillings for each taxpayer). In addition, an N.A. could designate the proceeds of some of its activities as sources of N.A. revenue (licensing fees for bicycles, beggar minstrels, native liquor vendors, fees for operating bakeries, markets, slaughterhouses, lorry parks, and animal pound fees). The smallest amount of any subordinate council's revenue came from "rating", which in Northern Nigeria was not, as it is in England, a levy on the value of real estate. In England, rating normally provides the greatest single source of local government revenue, but a local addition to the *haraji* or *jangali* taxes which a subordinate council was permitted to impose for specified local purposes (a most popular one was the purchase of an ambulance).

While aggregate subordinate council funds did grow steadily over the periods between 1949-50, 1959-60, and 1962-63, the average total sum for the whole period was still modest indeed, about 5% of total central N.A. revenues. Table 18 shows the percentage of total expenditure each emirate N.A. "delegated" to all its subordinate councils in 1959-60, the minimum and maximum amounts given to particular councils, and the average amount so allocated. (D.C.F. stands for District Council Funds; it included the funds of town councils.)

An official blueprint for the gradual attainment by subordinate councils of adequate financial resources and substantial self-reliance in financial management envisaged three stages, in the last of which the subordinate council was to prepare its own budget, or estimate, and enjoy an ordinary, or recurrent, revenue in excess of

Table 18: Financial Delegation to Subordinate Councils, 1959-60*

Native Authority	Total Revenue	Total Expenditure	Total D.C.F.	% D.C.F. of Expenditure	Status of D.C.S.	Range of Allocation		Av. Per Council	No. D.C.S. £3000 or more
						min.	max.		
Adamawa	£471,971	£493,124	£19,232	8.1	D.F.R.	139	5,006	1,031	1
Muri	122,052	121,957	4,290	4.1	D.C.F.	105	815	390	none
Bauchi	289,347	286,832	5,325	2.1	D.C.F.	150	754	380	none
Combe	217,115	226,711	7,087	4.0	D.C.F.	214	5,370	1,181	1
Katagum	211,431	240,542	11,702	6.6	D.F.R.	200	3,267	1,702	1
Misau	75,202	77,784	1,712	2.8	D.C.F.	54	408	285	none
Jama'are	14,977	18,335	253	2.0	D.C.F.	30	78	51	none
Lafia	67,973	74,973	4,186	7.2	D.F.R.	30	811	70	none
Nassarawa	57,795	59,418	1,609	3.2	D.C.F.	42	299	195	none
Keffi	46,390	42,266	1,565	4.2	D.C.F.	180	430	261	none
Bedde	39,019	45,378	1,280	4.0	D.C.F.	80	800	320	none
Borgu	952,413	923,068	15,952	2.5	D.F.R.	248	1,058	725	none
Dikwa	162,706	188,384	1,670	1.3	D.C.F.	60	445	209	none
Fika	87,619	90,087	7,214	10.2	D.F.R.	703	2,569	1,031	none
Borgu	53,060	51,331	3,167	7.0	D.F.R.	89	785	176	none
Ilorin	314,704	343,601	47,729	17.0	D.F.R.	67	9,489	1,491	2
Pategi	18,642	16,624	144	1.0	D.C.F.	44	50	48	none
Kano	1,845,741	1,629,886	195,485	16.1	D.F.R.	2,215	58,020	7,240	22
Gumel	78,580	76,511	4,800	8.4	D.C.F.	781	1,616	976	none
Kazaure	57,262	48,512	1,850	4.8	D.C.F.	270	660	462	none
Daura	86,076	86,879	3,135	4.4	D.C.F.	193	479	627	none
Katsina	771,509	797,333	64,612	10.0	D.F.R.	750	6,347	3,072	8
Abuja	54,281	54,733	900	1.9	D.C.F.	80	345	225	none

238

Table 18 (continued)

Native Authority	Total Revenue	Total Expenditure	Total D.C.F.	% D.C.F. of Expenditure	Status of D.C.S.	Range of Allocation min.	Range of Allocation max.	Av. Per Council	No. D.C.S. £3000 or more
Agaie	21,872	21,646	351	1.7	D.C.F.	—	—	117	none
Bida	169,240	170,198	2,650	1.8	D.C.F.	210	510	331	none
Kontagora	89,331	84,303	1,088	1.4	D.C.F.	37	348	121	none
Lapai	20,113	17,893	387	2.3	D.C.F.	38	261	129	none
Wase	20,084	17,315	615	3.5	D.C.F.	76	194	154	none
Argungu	86,902	96,933	3,057	3.8	D.C.F.	101	268	437	none
Gwandu	225,567	227,780	7,752	4.1	D.F.R.	122	1,334	456	none
Sokoto	1,047,277	1,073,543	39,836	5.4	D.F.R.	75	1,607	829	none
Yauri	48,886	43,707	4,793	11.0	D.C.F.	173	996	799	none
Zaria	435,706	431,730	7,117	2.0	D.C.F.	193	817	444	none

Key: D.C.S.   District Council Service
D.C.F.   District Council Funds
D.F.R.   District Financial Responsibility

* Figures for Hadejia and Lafiagi were not available.

£5,000.[8] Councils in the next to last stage normally had less than that to spend; their estimates were incorporated into those of a central Native Authority, but they received grants-in-aid from the N.A. in addition to ordinary revenue, and were authorized to impose "rates". These two stages together were officially called D.F.R. (District Financial Responsibility). Generally speaking, only D.F.R. councils employed personnel even on the basis of allowances or daily wages. The initial, and least developed stage was called D.C.F. (District Council Fund). It represented the fact that the sole source or revenue was the per capita proportion of general, or cattle, tax and that expenditure of funds was controlled closely by the central N.A. In practice, the total amount available to such a council was rarely more than £1,000. The funds of councils in the D.C.F. stage were earmarked for specific purposes and projects that required the advance approval of the N.A. Table 18 shows that less than one-third of the emirate Native Administrations had subordinate councils developed to the D.F.R. stage in 1959. Only two—Kano and Katsina—appeared to be in the advanced phase of the D.F.R.

If the figure of £5,000 is officially regarded as the dividing line between developing and advanced councils, I have estimated that the figure of £3,000 represented some kind of take-off point in the establishment and growth of subordinate councils as functioning institutions of democratic local government. For roughly this sum appears to have been necessary to a combination of salutory advances— the initiation of services requiring long-term, or recurrent, expenditures, the ability to support the nucleus of a trained staff, even if the council was not permitted to engage it, and hence achievement of noticeable improvement in the level of local amenities—all of which also meant the council might hope to impress the community as being an effective instrument of public welfare. Of the 381, subordinate councils in the emirates in 1959, the one year for which the relevant data is available, 35 councils in Kano emirate had 22; apart from Kano, only six emirates had at least one such council—Adamawa, Gombe, Katagum had one each; Ilorin had two, and Katsina had eight. Even if the take-off point is set two-thirds lower than the one estimated (£1,000 per annum), only six more Native Authorities

[8] See *Delegation of Financial Responsibility to District Councils*, N.A. Office Guide (n.p. and n.d.), Part II, p. 3.

could have joined the last group, and the vast majority of all subordinate councils still would have fallen well below the mark.

For subordinate councils at all levels, having adequate funds did not mean that they could be spent purely at the council's discretion. A variety of central N.A. controls applied to subordinate expenditures. Except for some councils in Kano and Katsina, the estimates of subordinate councils formed part of those of the central N.A., affording the latter opportunity not only to assist the subordinate councils to avoid accounting errors, but to regulate the direction of expenditure. Rarely were there banking facilities at the district level; consequently subordinate council funds were usually left "on the deposit account" in the central N.A. treasury. (There was more than one instance in which the N.A. denied a subordinate council the privilege of using an independent banking facility, even though it was in a nearby town easily accessible to it.) A universal, and the most effective, financial restraint exerted on subordinate councils, however, was the N.A. practice of limiting the amounts which could be withdrawn from the "deposit account" without the Native Administration's express approval. The figure varied, from £250 in the case of the Kano council to that of the Mambilla district council of the old emirate Adamawa, which in 1959 was forbidden to spend "so much as an aninini [1/10th of a penny]", as the Adamawa N.A. treasurer pointed out, without first clearing with him. But the most common figure appeared to be £50. Such tight control served different purposes; it prevented a strictly economic indiscretion or waste through ineptitude or dishonesty at the subordinate council level. On the other hand—and this was particularly apt to be feared, with good reason, by subordinate councils whose members' political views were unsympathetic to the N.A. and to the Regional Government— it sometimes frustrated a project whose only drawback would have been stealing the political thunder of the central N.A. In either event, the councils were clearly deprived of the experience of fully responsible management of public funds.

The fact of a significant variation in the financial position which subordinate councils obtained, between different emirates and within the same emirate, is worthy of note. As may be seen in Table 18, the range in the amounts "delegated" to subordinate councils was considerable (from £30 to £50,000); the degree of autonomy in financial management also varied widely. The government's policy of leaving it up to the Native Administrations to decide how much they delegated made this variation possible of course.

It will be observed that wealthy Native Authorities, such as Ilorin, Kano, and Katsina, were among those Native Authorities spending the highest percentage of their total expenditure on funds for subordinate councils (17, 16.1, and 10%, respectively). Conversely, some of the smallest allocations were made by some of the poorest Native Authorities, e.g. Pategi, 1%, Jama'are, 2%, Agaie, 1.7%, Lapai, 2.3%. The extremely low council expenditures of the smallest Native Authorities probably indicated that an N.A. revenue level existed below which an N.A. could not finance its central administrative apparatus and essential services and also have enough left to support subordinate councils adequately. Larger or more wealthy Native Authorities could afford to do both. But among Native Authorities whose revenue was above the minimal level, there does not appear to be any obvious explanation for the occurrence of a wide variation in the *percentage* of revenue delegated. Yet it can be seen in Table 18 that there was hardly any direct relationship between total N.A. revenue and percentage of financial delegation. Thus the percentage of total N.A. revenue allocated by the dwarf emirate Jama'are was approximately the same as that delegated by a neighboring giant —Bauchi (which had almost 20 times more revenue). Zaria did no better than Jama'are, either, despite having 30 times more revenue. The total revenues of Abuja, Borgu, Kazaure, and Yauri Emirates were roughly comparable in 1959, but Abuja spent 1.9 on subordinate councils, Kazaure, 4.8%, Borgu, 7%, and Yauri, 11%. The last named, with a total revenue of under £50,000, surpassed Katsina, with a total revenue of over £771,500 in allocating funds to subordinate councils. Two emirates, Kano and Sokoto, had revenues in excess of £1 million; Kano delegated 16.1%, Sokoto only 5.4%. Clearly more than financial capacity determined N.A. policy in this regard.

The explanation usually advanced in Northern Nigeria was simply that some Native Authorities were more "progressive" than others. However, the fact that a significant part of the definition of "progressive" was "willingness to delegate funds to democratically constituted subordinate councils" obviously renders that hypothesis very unsatisfactory. If the definition of "progressive" is reduced to, say, relatively greater exposure to Western education (a common reduction), difficulties are also encountered. It is true that a central council like that of Katsina, which was noted for its high proportion of councillors educated in Western-type schools was also in the category of those Native Authorities which allocated a high percentage to subordinate councils, but so is Fika which was not so noted, while again, Argungu, which is so noted, was among those Native Authorities that delegated a very low percentage (3.8). The experience of Western education alone did not make for financial liberality, nor its absence, for cautiousness.

We have already seen that culturally plural emirates faced special problems in relation to minority districts. Again, however, there was no direct correlation between cultural plurality and extent of financial delegation. But the fact that the plural emirates were found at either extreme in this regard may indicate one factor of underlying alternative policies. For example, up to 1959 the old Adamawa N.A. harbored profound apprehensions that allocation of substantial money to minority districts would merely further whet their appetites for autonomy. The specific argument the Adamawa N.A. apparently used, against the contrary advice of certain British administrative officers, was that if the "pagan districts" got the idea that they could financially generate their own services, the last thread of unity would be broken. In any case, subordinate councils in Adamawa were kept relatively impoverished (more so than is indicated in Table 18, because Adamawa N.A. was notorious for inflating this item in the estimates, while spending little in practice). Centrifugal forces in Zaria and Bauchi may similarly help account for those emirates' below-average allocations.

On the other hand, Fika, Lafia, Borgu, and Yauri are plural emirates which allocated above the average percentages; it is perhaps significant that they are small (in population, territory, and resources) plural emirates, hence doubly susceptible to pressures from below as well as from the Regional government above. It is further interesting to note that these emirates were in former years all well below the average. Nor is it unreasonable to suppose therefore that a special pattern in certain plural emirates was strong resistance to the demands of minorities for a greater share of the emirate's resources up to the point where discontent threatened the stability of the central regime; then a sudden and rapid decentralization and delegation of funds occurred in an effort to stem the tide and salvage as much of the original situation as possible.

In nonplural emirates the traditional structure had something to do with policies of financial delegation. For example, it is doubtful whether the Katsina N.A. could have politically afforded to refuse substantial delegation to districts whose chiefs had always considered themselves nearly the equal of the emir and who always prepared to make trouble if they felt their rights were being trampled on. By way of contrast, a highly centralized N.A. like Kano, which delegated even more extensively than Katsina, could be confident that no allocation to subordinate councils would be confused with a grant of independence. Indeed, not only in Kano, but elsewhere, it was suggested to me that often disproportionate allocations to certain subordinate councils followed the higher traditional status or personal standing of the chief of that district (the observations below on the position of district heads will amplify this further). It is highly unlikely, given the nature and vigor of traditional policies in an emirate, that in exercising discretionary authority to delegate funds, Native Authorities would totally ignore the cardinal traditional rule that followers should be compensated and rivals should be given no more than can be avoided.

POPULAR PARTICIPATION

UNTIL the 1954 Native Authority Law, a subordinate council Instrument had to provide for a majority of elected members. Hence only some of the few remaining uninstrumented councils were without an elected majority in 1959. All such instruments stated that elections were to be held every three years. In 1959 the electoral system governing most subordinate councils had progressed from the use of village and ward councils as electoral colleges returning several members to a direct procedure using village or ward areas as single-member electoral units. Almost everywhere the method of voting that was used was either that of a show of hands, the so-called whispering vote, or (less commonly with the decline of electoral colleges) that of each elector physically lining up behind the candidate of his choice. (The secret ballot was rarely employed.) With these methods, how an individual voted was readily ascertainable by those in authority. Suffrage was enjoyed by resident sane males 21 years or over who were taxpayers.[9]

Participation in subordinate councils of village heads and some-

[9] I.e. those who had either paid tax in the electoral area for three years immediately preceding the election, or were born in the electoral area and paid tax there in the year immediately preceding the date of the election or were not liable to pay tax in the period by reason of being exempted.

times certain local title-holders was assured through designating in the instruments (by office or title) up to one-third of the council membership as traditional or ex-officio members. In addition, the N.A. was empowered to nominate as members of a subordinate council representatives of "interests or sections of the community which in the opinion of the Native Authority were not otherwise adequately represented on the council"; the power was commonly used to appoint nomad Fulani, Hausa *muguzawa*, or pagans, or in the plural emirates, representatives of particularly small minority groups. The fact remains, however, that the requirement of an elected majority—and it may be seen that seldom was there more than a technical majority—afforded the masses of *talakawa* with the novel opportunity to be represented and act as representatives in local political institutions with executive authority.

I undertook no systematic investigation of the personal backgrounds of rural district council members. If the products of town, N.A., regional, and federal elections are any guide, however, it may be assumed that a good portion of elected members were by birth members of the *sarakuna* class. Nor is it unlikely that among elected members were to be found clients, servants, or courtiers (*fadawa*) of local notables. However, if for no other reasons than that members of the *sarakuna* class are less numerous in the countryside than in the towns and, more importantly, that election to a district council holds relatively little attraction for them, it is also likely that more *talakawa* were actually in district councils than in any other representative body. Most observers of the local government system seemed to agree that the main problem confronting the democratic development of nonurban subordinate councils was not so much one of getting *talakawa* onto the councils as that of making their presence felt once they "arrived". The voting methods in force and the heavy weighting of traditional and nominated members doubtless contributed to maintaining the reticence and deference of *talakawa*, as did dependence of councils on the central bureaucracy for funds, authorization to spend them, and staff whose conduct was expressly made none of the council's business. But in this respect, the greatest single source of political continuity was the position of the district head.

The Position of the District Head

THE CRUX of the district head's position was a duality inherent in his role and the conflicts that necessarily resulted from it. This duality, in turn, made it profoundly difficult for ordinary members of subordinate councils to maintain a relationship to the district head that was consistent with a democratic structure of authority.

All subordinate council instruments, including those governing town councils, stipulated that the chairman of the council would be the district head of the area. As chairman, the district head was not only the presiding officer in subordinate council meetings, but also the chief executive officer of the council. Thus N.A. financial regulations prescribed that the officer controlling district council fund expenditure was the district head.[10] This meant that the district head was, among other tasks, responsible for that of employing whatever day labor the council needed; the council could initiate no action except through him. It was to and through the district head as chairman, moreover, that grievances or criticism directed to the Native Authority were to be expressed.

But the district head was also the appointee of the Native Authority and its chief representative and agent in the district. As such, he was charged with carrying out the directions of his superior, to whom he was expected to be loyal. He was also expected to be able to prevent the N.A. from being troubled by agitation in his district. Furthermore, he was to maintain law and order, in the absence of adequate police, by means of an autocratic relationship with his subjects. That the Native Authority controlled his appointment, tenure of office, prospects of promotion, and pension rights was clearly ample inducement for the district head to fulfill these expectations.

The incompatibility between this aspect of his role and what is normally expected to be the position of the chairman of a democratically constituted council is obvious. The chairman could not be removed or disciplined by members of the council, to whom, in fact, he was in no way accountable for his actions (save, perhaps, verbally), even when these were carried out in the council's name. Grievances or criticism of administrative superiors were supposed to be expressed through a chairman who had a vested interest in maintaining the appearance if not the substance of tranquility, and failing that, in bringing troublemakers to the attention of those superiors. It would have been a temerarious councillor indeed who would have embarrassed the man partly responsible for assessing his taxes, who allotted usage of farming land, supervised the dispensation of medical, agricultural, and veterinary services and advice, who was author-

[10] See *Notes on District Council Funds* (Kaduna, 1955), p. 5.

ized to apply a multiplicity of rules, regulations, and orders—violations of which were tried by an *alkali* or native court judge to whom the district head was apt to be linked. Clearly the position of the district head vis-à-vis that of the subordinate councillors did not encourage the use of the council as a channel for public expression of grievances; nor did it make the district head think and act as first among equals.

It should be noted here that reportedly there were several instances of subordinate councils that requested permission to select the chairman from among the elected council members; but as far as I know, no Native Authority ever consented to such a proposal. The nearest thing to an exception to the practice of imposing the chairman from above was the unique Ajiya-in-Council set-up in Bauchi, noted above, but this arrangement called for local discretion in selecting the person to occupy the position of district head, not the council chairman as such. As simultaneously chairman and agent of the central N.A. in the district, even the Ajiya presumably remained subject to some of the same cross-pressures which were exerted on others in that position.

Rather inconsistently—considering that ultimately it was Regional government policy that upheld the position of the district head—the Regional government encouraged Native Authorities to counter autocratic tendencies within subordinate councils. Thus, in addition to supervising the mechanics of subordinate council proceedings (drafting and use of standard orders, recording of council minutes, preparation of agenda, etc.), local government, or Development Secretaries, were charged with helping to educate subordinate councillors to "know their rights and duties" and with generally instructing local communities in the ways of modern conciliar local government. But like other officials, the development secretary was subject to the authority of the district head when operating in his district. In keeping with the government's reluctance to interpose its own authority between traditional rulers and the people, the government established no direct administrative link between itself and subordinate councils, although after 1960 local government instructors, working out of the Institute of Administration (a government institution later incorporated into Ahmadu Bello University), offered courses in democratic local government in the districts; the scheme was financed through a grant from the Ford Foundation. As a means of overcoming the limitations which the structural relationships between subordinate councils and the central N.A. imposed, these instructors suffered in practice from much the same circumstance that characterized the old Development Secretaries. Conceivably another means might have been organized political parties, but these never effectively penetrated the district councils. In response to surveys carried out by the administration or by the central N.A., district councillors invariably described their party affiliations as NPC or "independent". However, no real NPC organizations existed within these bodies, and in reality a district councillor's describing himself as an NPC adherent was tantamount to a declaration of his loyalty to the district head, who was almost automatically regarded as the party's chief local representative.

Town Councils, Parties, and Participation

Town councils were established in at least 20 emirates. The legal powers of town councils were identical to that of district councils, as were most of their functions, except that they sometimes operated certain services only towns could support—a piped water supply, fire services and street lighting, and urban planning. The Bida and Katsina town councils, among others, were distinguished for their introduction of the secret ballot. Otherwise, the critical differences between the town councils and district councils stemmed from the peculiar economic and social features of the urban milieu.

Whereas the overwhelming preponderance of district councillors were farmers, many town councillors were craftsmen, small traders or *attajirai* (wealthy merchant traders), employed semi-skilled laborers, and minor N.A. functionaries (*ma'aikitan en e*). The towns concerned were often not only populous centers of trade and cottage industry, but several (Kano, Zaria, Funtua, Gusau) were also railheads; these and others were sometimes modern administrative or manufacturing centers as well. At the same time, the towns were strongholds of Islamic cultural, religious, and educational activity. The people of the towns were subject to influences, reactions, and needs unknown to the rural peasant, or not known to anything like the same extent. That all this was conducive to the growth of popular political consciousness is indicated in the fact that in at least 10 of the 20 town councils opposing political parties at one time or another confronted each other. By 1959 the radical NEPU party enjoyed a majority over the NPC in only one town council—Potiskum —although in previous years it had held a majority in the Kano, Zaria,

Funtua, Jega, and Mubi town councils (as well as in the Jos and Minna town councils lying outside the emirates). Although just as legally subordinated to the N.A. as the district councils, town councils were often politically turbulent.

The Zaria town council became politically aroused in 1957 over the issue of a water supply system for Zaria City (NEPU had won an overwhelming majority in the Zaria town council elections of 1955). The Native Authority's campaign proposals for a water system had provided for financing the service through a local rate. The NPC supported the Native Authority's plan, but the NEPU members of the council argued strongly that levy of a penny and a half per gallon at the standpipes would produce sufficient revenue and would constitute a more equitable arrangement than one in which each adult inhabitant of Zaria City would be obliged to pay the same amount without regard to how much water he consumed. When the issue was finally brought to a vote, the NEPU scheme received a clear majority. Insisting on the council's right to make decisions in regard to a function delegated to it in the council instrument, the NEPU councillors put the scheme into effect. The relative popularity and success of the NEPU plan was suggested by the fact that although the NPC gained control of the council at the end of 1957, that party thereafter made no move to alter it.

In general only in towns was there any real degree of separation of identity between the local NPC party and the N.A.—a circumstance which relatively effective opposition on the part of NEPU helped to produce.[11] In both the Zaria and Kano town councils, the NPC, on occasion, joined NEPU in protesting against N.A. restrictions on the councils' freedom of action. The Kano town council (in which the NPC in 1959 held a narrow majority of 26 seats against NEPU's 24), as a whole, once petitioned the N.A. for authorization to spend its "own" revenue (which was considerable by Northern standards—about £46,000 per year) entirely at its own discretion, instead of having to seek the approval of the N.A. for each withdrawal of £260 or more from the council's account in the N.A. treasury. A lesser but no less indicative conflict occurred over the question of whether the Kano N.A. or the Kano town council should be responsible for the installation of kola-nut stalls in the city market. Authority over the kola-nut stalls is a traditional perk of a

---

[11] Kano, Zaria, Mbui, Potiskum, Yelwa, Jega, Gusau, Katsina, Malumfashi, and Funtua.

minor titled official called the Wakilin Goro, however, and the N.A. refused to take it away from him. The Kano town council also objected to the Native Authority's withholding from it jurisdiction over the staff of the Kano city hospital (which in theory it controlled), on the grounds that since the council's instrument did not allow for employment of salaried staff, to transfer those affected to the jurisdiction of the council would be to deprive them of their pension rights. In this case, the N.A. did not deny the councillors' contention that they were technically competent to assume control over the hospital staff, yet the N.A. was not willing to amend the council's instrument accordingly.

The Zaria town council at various times found itself chafing under the Native Authority's paternal yoke, for the reasons indicated in the following item, which appeared in a Northern newspaper:

> All members of the NPC-controlled Zaria Town Council have threatened to boycott all future meetings of the Council, unless the previous decision taken by the Council are implemented by the Zaria Native Authority. . . . Among the decisions taken by the Council and forwarded to the Native Authority for implementation are: that Zaria City and Tudan Wada be provided with street lights for which the Council voted the sum of £1,000, and the decision that roads and bridges in Tudan Wada be repaired and drainages constructed on both sides of the roads, for which a sum of £850 was voted by the Council. The letter in which these remarks are contained concluded by saying that since the Native Authority did not care to carry out the decisions of the Council, made by elected representatives of the people, the party controlling the Council felt that it had not been allowed by the Native Authority to exercise its power and for that reason its members would not attend any of the Council's meetings in the future.[12]

Table 19 shows that while the largest group of NPC candidates for the 1958 elections to the Zaria town council were drawn from the ranks of the N.A. itself, the majority of them had other traditionally nonruling-class occupations; all but one of the NEPU members were in the latter category. A more extensive breakdown of the Kano town council (1960), by occupation, ethnic affiliation, and tra-

[12] See *Nigerian Citizen*, November 21, 1959, p. 1. The boycott failed to materialize however.

ditional class shows that there were more persons outside traditionally participant categories than inside, although these categories were heavily represented among NPC members (Table 20). Even so, for the NPC this represented a significant broadening, in terms of social background, over the party's typical composition.[13] Recruit-

Table 19: Occupational Backgrounds of Candidates in the
1958 Zaria Town Council Elections

Occupation	NPC	NEPU
N.A. employee	16	1
teacher	1	—
business agent	7	1
craftsman and shopkeeper	3	7
trader	14	25
farmer	6	6
politician	1	1
Total	48	41

ment from the ranks of the urban *talakawa*, on the part of the normally aristocratically dominated urban branches of the NPC, was encouraged by effective competition from NEPU, the conscious exponent of a political upsurge of the *talakawa*. Accordingly, one would expect to find the aristocratic, or *sarakuna*, class substantially more in evidence in wholly NPC town councils. And if the background of members of one such town council—that of Sokoto as elected in 1955—is any indication, the validity of that expectation is substantiated.[14] The record of town councils in which com-

[13] The NEPU members of the Zaria town council elected in 1955 included 13 craftsmen and shopkeepers, 11 traders, a small businessman, a farmer and an Arabic teacher. The 16 NPC members were employees of the N.A. That only two of these 16 ran for reelection in 1958 was an indication of a tendency for notables and aspirants in the Native Authority to leave the field of membership in local councils to the less eminent. Most of the NPC ex-councillors were reported to have been promoted to higher N.A. posts, however.

[14] Of the 22 members elected to the Sokoto town council in January and February of 1955, I determined that six were members of the royal Fulani family of Sokoto called Toronkawa (M. Cigari, M.A. employee; M. Altine Samfur, M.A. employee; M. Ibro Gidadawa, Gidan Waziri, M.A. employees; M. Garba Jabo, M.A. employee; M. Shehu Mudal'a and M. Haruna, M.A. employees). Five were members of noble Fulani families (M. Ahmadu Wali, M.A. employee; M. Mai-Wurno Tela, tailor; M. Ahmadu Danbaba, M.A. employee; M. Yahaya Assasa, M.A. employee); at least three others were *fadawa* (M. Mamman na Hakimi, M.A. employee; M. Gadon Burwa, tailor; M. Shehu, trader). One (M. Haliru Giye) was a member of a cattle Fulani family, and one was a member of the southern Nigerian community resident in Sokoto Town (Mr. Oghibe, M.A. employee in the Works Department); and one's background was undetermined (M. *Marafa* Hassan, a name which suggests ruling class membership; Marafa is a Sokoto title). In other words, probably only two out of the 22 were Habe *talakawa* by origin.

Table 20: Kano Town Council, 1960

Occupational Composition

		N.A. employee	teacher	politician	trader	tailor	Total
Council as	no.	10	1	2	10	4	27
a whole	%	37.0	3.7	7.4	37.0	14.8	99.9
NPC members	no.	10	1	—	1	2	14
	%	71.4	7.1	—	7.1	14.3	99.9
NEPU members	no.	—	—	2	9	2	13
	%	—	—	15.4	69.2	15.4	100

Ethnic Composition

		Fulani	Habe	Total
Council as	no.	8	19	27
a whole	%	29.6	70.4	100
NPC members	no.	6	8	14
	%	42.9	57.1	100
NEPU members	no.	2	11	13
	%	15.4	84.6	100

Traditional Class Composition

		Sr	Sn	Sv	Sc	S	T	J	Total
Council as	no.	4	4	2	2	12	13	2	27
a whole	%	14.8	14.8	7.4	7.4	44.4	48.1	7.4	99.9
NPC members	no.	4	2	2	2	10	3	1	14
	%	28.6	14.3	14.3	14.3	71.4	21.5	7.1	100.1
NEPU members	no.	—	2	—	—	2	10	1	13
	%	—	15.4	—	—	15.4	76.9	7.7	100

Key:
- Sr Sarakuna royalty
- Sn Sarakuna nobility
- Sv Sarakuna vassalage
- Sc Sarakuna clientage
- S   Sarakuna
- T   Talakawa
- J   Judicial class

Note: Only one member of the Council, an NPC man, held a traditional title (3.7%).

peting political parties were active suggests that they stimulated popular participation as well as debate on local problems.[15]

[15] In regard to popular political participation, control of a town council by a political party also usually carried the advantage of councillors' having access to the party organization as a channel for venting grievances, canvassing attitudes, and disseminating the councillor's programs. As for other aspects of local government, however, the participation of partisan members of political parties did not always prove salutary, as some British officials and scholars of local government would have predicted. For example, one of the town councils under the control of NEPU

It would be a mistake, however, to assume that concern with the modern secular political objectives and values of local government alone accounted for the vibrancy of the town councils. As might be expected, political parties whose paramount interest was in regional or national power used local elections to test or demonstrate their political strength. Even this, however, does not do justice to the intensity of political feeling which elections to town councils sometimes stimulated. Unlike districts, the towns, and especially towns that are capitals of emirates, contain a high proportion of people who by birth or through other channels are directly connected with the emirate's rulers.[16] Consequently the politics of town councils must be understood partly in terms of urban social and political cleavage which antedated the new institutions and interacted with modern forces and conditions. This is best illustrated in the experiences of the Zaria and Jega (of Gwandu Emirate) town councils.

The old walled city of Zaira (*Birnin Zazzau*) is divided for purposes of local government administration into four wards: Kwarbai,

---

proposed a salary increase for ward heads of the town. NEPU leaders admitted that part of their motive was to try and win the ward heads' support in the next election. The increase, which was long overdue, had previously been favored by NPC members of the council; but divining NEPU's strategy, they joined certain traditional and nominated members in defeating the motion.

Perhaps the most important general instance, however, was the record of party organized councils on the question of urban tax assessment. The system of lump taxation applied in rural areas was an expedient justifiable in terms of the general unavailability of a trained revenue-collecting agency and written records with which it might work even if it existed. But conditions in the towns are different, and the under-assessment of the salaried employees and the wealthy merchant traders, whose resources were scientifically determinable, had long been a recognized defect of the Northern tax system. Even where such persons were taxed at an appreciably higher rate than farmers in the villages, the prevailing system was still unprogressive, in that a uniform levy (for example, £8 in one emirate) tended to be imposed without due regard for the varying financial capacities among individuals within this economic category. Apart from that, even the higher uniform rates were known to be extremely low, considering the group's capacity to pay. For various reasons, Native Authorities were reluctant to increase the rate of assessment of wealthy traders. In a few instances, however, Native Authorities have suggested that the function might be assumed by party controlled town councils. But the parties turned out to be unwilling to accept such offers or to demand the function in other cases. There is little doubt that the reason was fear of loss in political popularity to party opponents.

On the other hand, it should be pointed out that had parties had greater control over expenditure, which might have allowed them to initiate popular projects in a way that might offset any political odium attached to the assessment function, they would have had more incentive to assume it.

[16] Smith, *Government in Zazzau*, p. 222, that about one in every four compounds in Zaria City contained an official of the Native Authority.

Table 21: Analysis of Results of 1955 and 1958,

Zaria Town Council Elections by Wards

Ward	NPC		NEPU		Composition of Ward
	1955	1958	1955	1958	
Kwarbai	11	11	—	1	Mainly persons related to the three Fulani ruling houses of Zaria, N.A. employees, and some employees of business firms
Kaura	—	5	13	7	Mostly independent Habe traders and farmers, but about a third of these are also servants or *fadawa* of the ruling houses
Juma	2	4	3	2	Traders, Koranic mallams and farmers: Mixed Fulani and Habe
Iya	—	—	6	6	Predominately independent Habe traders and craftsmen having no connection with royal or noble families
Tudun Wada	3	6	5	6	Mixture of various Northern tribes and occupations, mostly Muslims

Kaura, Juma, and Iya. These, together with the area just outside the city walls inhabited by Muslim strangers (i.e. Muslims not indigenous to Zaria Emirate), formed the electoral units of the town council. The Kwarbai ward contains the offices and palace of the Native Authority, and the overwhelming proportion of the residents are members of aristocratic Fulani families or are their retainers (and by occupation, N.A. employees). Table 21 shows that the Kwarbai ward gave overwhelming support to the NPC in town council elections. Iya Ward, primarily populated by independent small traders was staunchly NEPU. Significantly, a difference between Iya and Kaura wards is that a segment of the people in the latter area were also personally attached to one or the other of the Zaria ruling houses as traditional clients, followers, or *fadawa*, and the ward was accordingly divided politically. Similarly, the influence of Koranic Malams probably contributed to the NPC's support in Juma Ward. Probably only in Tudun Wada was party competition based on social groupings derived solely from nontraditional factors and conditions. Otherwise the parties to a large extent relied on their ability to stimulate traditionally divergent social class identities and interests in order to engender partisan popular political participation in the institution of the town council (a manifestation in local government of a pattern which we shall later see underlies much of the dynamics of party competition vis-à-vis regional institutions, as well). Perhaps this whole phenomenon was even more clearly illustrated in the evolution of the Jega town council, of Gwandu emirate.

The population of Jega town is approximately 9,000, most of which engages in trade and other commercial activities in the Jega market. Situated near the confluence of the Zamfara and Niger Rivers, and therefore astride the major trade routes running between southern Nigeria and Nupe (Bida), Kano, and Sokoto, Jega was a flourishing entrepôt long before the coming of Europeans.[17] Jega has also been the capital of Jega District since it was first selected as such by M. Buhari of the originally emigrant Gimbanawa clan—which enjoys hereditary rights to the district headship with the Sarkin Kebbi.[18] The people indigenous to the area of Jega Town and District are known as Gobirawa.

By 1956 NEPU had succeeded in winning a considerable following among the Jega Gobirawa under a local Bagobiri party leader, M. Sa'adu. The local NEPU platform appears to have consisted largely of attacks on alleged acts of maladministration (especially in connection with market fees and tax collection) and on the manipulation of the "Yan Commission" (agents of large-scale traders who are paid on the basis of a certain percentage of each transaction they make). About this time, Jega was one of the scenes of religious agitation inspired by the so-called Yan Wazifa wing of the Tijanniya brotherhood, a puritanical and reformist group. The Jega Yan Wazifa bolstered NEPU in its attacks on people in authority, who in the eyes of the Yan Wazifa, were guilty of impiety and sacrilege. The combination of the traditional cleavage between the

---

[17] On the history of Jega see E. W. Bovill, *Caravans of the Old Sahara* (London, 1933), pp. 254ff.; and E. J. Arnett, *Gazetteer of Sokoto Province* (London, 1920).

[18] M. Buhari or Bohari was the son of Abdu Salame, a prominent figure in the Fulani Jihad, whom Arnett identifies as a native of the Ariwa Mantu tribe (whom he states are identical with the Arewa people of the old kingdom of Kebbi and of present-day Argungu emirate). Gimbana was a district of Kebbi in which Abdu Salame settled for a time. The Gimbanawa are the descendants of Abdu Salame, who later migrated to Jega, of which his son Bohari became the first chief.

Gobirawa and Gimbanawa, friction between the *Yan Wazifa* and ordinary Muslims, official abuses, and commercial exploitation produced the political discontent that brought NEPU to power in the town council via the election of 1958 (NEPU won seven out of 10 elected seats). This is reflected in the backgrounds of the parties' candidates, as shown in Table 22.

Table 22: Backgrounds of Candidates in the
Jega Town Council Elections, June 21, 1958

Traditional origin	NEPU	NPC	IND
Gimbanawa	—	8	1
Gobirawa	7	2*	—
Other	3	2	—
Occupation			
petty trader	3	2	1
Koranic mallam	—	1	—
commission agent	1	3	—
kolanut seller	3	—	—
farmer	1	—	—
fisherman	1	—	—
servant of District head	—	2	—
politician	1	—	—
N.A. driver	—	1	—
contractor	—	3	—
"Yan Wazifa" Tijanniya	7	—	—

* Both *fadawa* of the district head.
Source: field notes.

This rise of NEPU in Jega Town was regarded on all sides as a challenge to the authority of the District Head and therefore ultimately to the authority of the Emir-in-Council. The experience suggested that such challenges could induce the central N.A. to make greater concessions to town councils than to district councils—though only concessions permissible within the existing framework of legal and administrative restrictions operating on subordinate councils generally. Thus, taking to heart the counsel of British officers who feared a further deterioration of traditional authority, the Gwandu N.A. (which was one of the few Native Administrations having no instrumented district council in 1959) promulgated the Jega town council instrument which provided for an elected majority and secret balloting under which the 1958 elections were held. Thereafter, the town council was given the largest financial allocation (£ 1,000 in 1958-59; the estimated figure for 1959-60 was £ 1,334) of any subordinate council in Gwandu. (It is noteworthy that the average financial allocation to the 10 town councils previously singled out was substantially above that of district councils.) It is interesting to note, too, that the £8,000 loan which the Northern Regional Development Corporation made to the Gwandu N.A. for construction of a new market in Jega Town was reportedly made not without consideration of the probability that credit for the project would be shared by the local NPC. That in the Jega Council by-elections of January 1959 the NPC gained two new seats and retained control of a third, while NEPU lost two, was no doubt gratifying to the official strategists of "liberalization". Thereafter, Jega town council remained NPC.

The various forces at work in the towns would seem to have represented a high potential for popular political action and demand. The subordinate council system never allowed the full development of this potential, however. The inherent difficulties were summed up in the following remarks contained in an administrative officer's report on the progress of two town councils:

> The position of the Town Councils (X and Y) is as unsatisfactory as it is difficult of solution. However, their future remains a major problem. Careful review and drastic reform might prove the answer. Composed of well-meaning but largely ignorant members, granted powers that remain unacknowledged by the District Head, circumscribed by too heavy a subordination to the Native Authority, the meetings simply develop into a clash of wills between the Chairman and elected members. I believe that the real solution could be found were the District Head to be excluded from membership and the Chairman to be elected from among elected members only. Such a drastic reform would probably prove unacceptable to the Native Authority and would be useless unless it were coupled with an equally courageous financial reform. . . . A real responsibility for the management of local affairs would, I believe sincerely, prove a salutary thing for members who are frustrated by membership of a council that by its very composition and instrument can only be a forum for the expression of grievances.[19]

IT IS IMPORTANT to emphasize again that in terms of a fully modern and democratic system of local government, the problems and

[19] Document in possession of the author.

limitations of the subordinate council system, like those of the central bureaucracy, derived in the last analysis from the deliberate perpetuation of a set of functioning traditional political institutions, relationships, and values, which were both historically and normatively alien to modern and democratic forms. As was pointed out before, and as this and the last chapter illustrate, Northern gradualism did not merely represent a notion of the preferability of slow against rapid political change (albeit this is how the policy was most often presented); rather it was also grounded in the desire to see political and economic change combined with the survival of important preexisting political patterns and conditions. Given the inherent antagonism of these objectives, it was inevitable that institutional arrangements designed to realize them both should have succeeded in realizing neither completely.

By the same token, however, the subordinate council system, like the present state of the central bureaucracy, could not be satisfactorily accounted for without recognizing that the conflict of values was "genuine"—in the sense that both traditional and modern democratic patterns of government were in fact modified or qualified in order to attain something of each. The net result was a set of institutions in which elements of both patterns, however logically or normatively incompatible, in fact coexisted. In this regard, the difference between the district councils and the town councils represented only a difference in the degree to which friction was involved. Friction is not the same thing as mutual exclusiveness or total disruption, however. Subordinate councils, including town councils, like the central bureaucracy, constituted parts of a functioning system, notwithstanding the alien origin and normative variance of the elements which comprised them.

CHAPTER 6

The Position of the Emirs

So FAR in this discussion of the administrative and political system of the northern emirates in action I have dealt with the system as a whole, examining it from the perspective of a modern Western, and specifically British, system of local government. In this chapter I have singled out one institution within the complex of institutions which constitutes the traditional system of emirate government and tried to show how it affected and was affected by the various forces of political change up to 1965. Since emirship is the pivotal traditional institution, through tracing its development in this period we can expect to gain further insight into the sources and limits of change and of resistance to change in the emirate system.

To analyze that development it is necessary to examine two separate yet interrelated aspects of the emirs' position: (a) vis-à-vis central councillors and subjects within the local states, and (b) in relation to the new system of regional government and politics. The specific topics included in the discussion below are the motivating forces and changing functions of emirship, the standards of recruitment to the office, the various sources of the emirs' power, its extent and limits, and the impact of party politics. The discussion should properly begin with some observations on the institution of emirship as it existed prior to European contact.

THE TRADITIONAL POSITION OF EMIRS

A COMMON THEME in criticism directed at the system of Native Administration after the war was that under British rule emirs had attained a position of power far exceeding their actual traditional role. This line of argument has been pursued by a northern scholar, Abudakar Imam, in a notable exchange of letters between himself and Lord Lugard over the years preceding Lugard's death in 1945.[1] In essence Imam argued that the power of the emir under

[1] Alhaji Abubuakar Imam was born in Kagara, Niger Province, into a prominent judicial family of Katsina origin. He entered the Katsina College in 1927, a year before the Northern Premier and a year after the Federal Prime Minister. In 1939 he was chosen by Dr. R. M. East of the Gaskiya Corporation for training as the first Northern Nigerian journalist. Imam wrote for *Gaskiya Ta Fi Kwabo*, the Northern (Hausa) vernacular newspaper which began publication in 1939. He is generally credited with having given the newspaper its name. In 1943 he was the sole Northerner to join the West African Press delegation to the United

British rule exceeded traditional bounds because British recognition and support became a sufficient condition of his control in the state, whereas in pre-British days various internal restraints, including the influence of traditional councillors, had acted to limit an emir's freedom of action. "It is commonly believed by peasants as well as by the educated", Imam complained in 1943, "that nowadays if an Emir wants to injure you he simply tells the Resident you are a bad man, or that you do not show him respect. It is believed that sooner or later this has its effect, and that it is no good to appeal to the Resident direct, because he will simply pass you on to the Emir, and thus create enmity between you." The answer Lugard is said to have given seems to express perfectly Lugard's tendency to confuse the ideal with the reality of indirect rule—"So they [the emirs] do not know that the best way to please the Resident is to please the peasant?"[2]

As an avenue of criticism, the argument made by Imam and others was a particularly persuasive one among Northerners, in that it combined an appeal to tradition with a reproach to colonialism in the interest of reform! The argument doubtless facilitated the abolition of "Sole Native Authority" in favor of "Chief-in Council". At the same time, the British could assure themselves that this change represented a reaffirmation of their fundamental policy—a correction of the law to conform with the "true" traditional position of the emirs.

The argument also appears to have given rise in Northern Nigeria to the misleading conclusion that the traditional Fulani Emir was at one time a constitutional monarch. That suggestion would appear in turn to rest on a confusion between the nature of constitutional limitations on the one hand, and *effective* or *de facto* limitations on the other. The crucial point is the traditional absence in the Fulani system of any legitimate and institutionalized procedures through

Kingdom, where he was taken by Mr. Hans Vischer, British Director of Education in the North, to meet Lugard. Invited by Lugard to state his views on the system of indirect rule in the North, Imam set forth criticisms, but expressed sympathy for the idea that traditional institutions should properly form the basis of Northern government. Cf. Zanna Ibrahim Shehu, "Meet Alhaji Abubakar Imam, One of the Architects of the Richards Constitution", *Nigerian Citizen*, June 27 and July 1, 1959.

2 "The Problem of Northern Nigeria as the Natives see it: An account of an interview with Lord Lugard by Abubakar Imam; Editor of *Gaskiya Ta Fi Kwabo*, and a member of the African Press Delegation to the United Kingdom in 1943", August 1943 (deposited in the Nigerian Archives Kaduna, under Kaduna: Governor's Office General #1088, Item 8).

which the subjects of an emirate could depose an emir. (It is the availability of such procedures which in the same period fundamentally set apart certain other traditional West African monarchies, such as that of the Yoruba, or that of the Akan people of Ghana.[3]) Once installed in power by the council of electors or by kingmakers, a Fulani Emir was assailable only through extralegal means—assassination, civil war, usurpation, sabotage, etc., or through the intervention of *external* authority—the suzerain of Sokoto (who, being concerned with the stability and interests of the Hausa-Fulani state system as a whole, was naturally reluctant to intervene unless, on balance, an emir's activities were more of a peril to those objectives than intervention itself). Furthermore, Sokoto itself was obviously not subject to legitimate external limitation.

The 12 emirates closely surveyed in 1959 all had traditional councillors who traditionally could offer advice and apparently even criticism. Such was theoretically the role in particular of the religiously learned men, or *Malams*, who were sometimes members of the traditional council (who tended to be displaced, under Fulani rule, with *sarakuna*, often over the opposition of judges who undertook to uphold the established constitution).[4] Nothing, of course, prevented emirs from heeding their councillors' advice or even from leaning heavily on it at all times. In fact, there are indications that the influence of councillors varied not only between different emirates but within the same emirates, and that, particularly in times of crisis, an emir was hesitant to act without their agreement.[5] But the political style or practical circumstance of an emir is not to be con-

[3] On the Yoruba see Lloyd, "Yoruba Traditional Rulers", The authoritative study of the Akan monarchy is K. A. Busia, *The Position of the Chief in the Modern Political System of Ashanti* (London, 1961). See also David E. Apter, *The Gold Coast in Transition* (Princeton, 1955), p. 84 and *passim*.

[4] M. G. Smith, personal communication.

[5] See, for example, "Translation of Arabic Letter from Sultan of Sokoto to Colonel T.L.N. Morland", in H.F. Backwell, ed. tr., *The Occupation of Hausaland* (Lagos, 1927), p. 14, which records a reply from the Sultan of Sokoto to an ultimatum issued by a British officer on behalf of Lord Lugard at the time of the British conquest. The reply gave as the Sultan's reason for delaying an answer his desire to confer with his councillors. Since it may have been a convenient way of stalling for time, however, this is obviously not an ideal piece of evidence. In both Kano and Katsina, historical circumstances originally placed an unusual degree of influence and power in the hands of nonroyal lineages. Thus, in Katsina until 1903 there were three districts not directly under the control of Katsina; their rulers were directly responsible to Sokoto. In Kano representatives of nonroyal lineages have normally formed part of the traditional Kano Council of Nine, but the representation and influence of these councillors varied at different times according to the character and interests of the Emir and other conditions of his reign.

fused with his legal authority. Many instances were also cited by informants knowledgeable about the pre-British era, of emirs who chose to rule contrary to their councillors' advice, and did so with impunity. The ultimate power of decision was the emir's alone and his position as a *de jure* dictator was recognized and taken into account by assailants or rivals. Chronic conflict with his councillors might portend trouble for an emir, but such trouble did not take the form of anything remotely comparable to a vote of no confidence.

That effective limits to an emir's power traditionally existed is indicated in the fact that emirs were sometimes successfully intrigued against by rivals and that the threat of such intrigue appears to have been a constant royal preoccupation. The absence of any rule of primogeniture was an important source of restraint. Not surprisingly, the comparatively rare instances of a downfall of an emir were often associated with conditions of war, which might weaken or distract the throne. Maintenance of the large and loyal armies, on which an emir ultimately depended for his own security and that of his realm (and for the wealth to be had from slave-raiding), required delegation and sharing of power, as did the sheer inadequacy of roads and other physical facilities to allow complete control of territorial subordinate chiefs. Like the emir's councillors, however, territorial chiefs and military commanders ultimately owed their appointment and tenure of office to the emir. Their base of power might on occasion be effectively but never juridically independent. And the emir's autocratic authority was at all times subject to reinforcement through that supremely compelling proposition that disobedience to an emir was abnegation of the faith of Islam.

If the internal structure of the monarchy was autocratic in form if not always in substance, it is clearer still that the traditional relationship between the monarchy and the masses of *talakawa* was in form, if not always in substance, despotic. Upon the death of an emir, various segments of the ruling class could, through representation in the kingmakers' council, try to bring about the choice of a successor likely to be congenial to their ideas and interests. Neither this opportunity nor that presented in official exercise of the delegated authority of the state, directly afforded *talakawa*, by definition, any influence or protection, however. Such results a *talaka* might secure indirectly through an especially abject form of that institution which was generally an expression of essential powerlessness—clientage—the personal dependence and loyalty of a subordinate in relation to a superior. But the prospects of a *talaka's* forming a useful clientage relationship normally presupposed possession of the very attributes which only acquiescence made possible: economic resources (usually gained through farming land to which access was controlled ultimately by the emir or through some kind of licensed craft, or trade in which in the patronage of *masu-sarauta* was desirable), and demonstrations of respect, loyalty, usefulness, and reliability.

THE IMPACT OF BRITISH RULE

IRONICALLY, the Pax Britannica eliminated important sources of resistance to the power of emirs in putting a stop to wars and slave-raiding, in substituting British suzerainity for that of Sokoto, by protecting "legitimacy" against subversive intrigues by rivals to the throne, by accepting "official" interpretations of religious dicta. At the same time, however, the British sought to impose certain limitations of their own. Specifically, the colonial administration sought to make appointment and tenure of the office dependent in part on ability, training, performance, and integrity (by British standards). Extortion, nepotism, bribery, confiscation of rivals' wealth and office (*wasau*), etc., became forbidden practices. As overseers of the traditional system, British administrative officers were to guide emirs to enlightened ideas and practices of government.[6]

[6] An intriguing and revealing glimpse of the relationship of the British colonial administration to emirs is provided in the text of the *Speech By His Excellency The Governor at the Installation of the Head Chief (Estsu) of the Nupes at Bida* on 19 March 1935 (copy of original typewritten and unpublished manuscript in possession of the author), which reads:

I salute the Etsu Nupe, Councillors, Chief and people of Nupe. I have come here today to administer the Oath of Allegiance to the new Etsu Nupe and to hand to him his letter of appointment and staff of office.

You all know that there are three ruling families in Bida, those of Osman Zaki, Masaba, and Umaru Majigi, all descended from Mallam Dendo, a prominent figure in Nupe history. The late Etsu was of the House of Masaba and his predecessor Mallam Bello was of the House of Osman Zaki. The Council of Electors have now selected a member of the house of Umaru Majigi, Muhammadu Ndayako, a son of Muhammadu Lth Emir of Bida who died in February, 1916, after having reigned for fifteen years.

I understand that the electors have selected a trustworthy man who in their judgment is capable of guiding the progress of the Nupe people under the more modern conditions in which we all live now. If so, that is good.

I congratulate you Muhammadu Ndayako on your appointment as Etsu Nupe. I have heard good reports of you, and it is with pleasure that I am about to recognise you as the Etsu Nupe by handing you a letter of appointment and the appropriate staff of office.

There are several reasons why the formal limitations imposed by the British failed to change the autocratic character of emirship or, for that matter, the objectives and norms of the institution. Several such factors have already been noted elsewhere. Thus the influence the British could exert on traditional institutions was neces-

You should all know that the state of affairs in Nupe land in recent years has caused me grave concern. The prevalence of intrigue, pawning of human beings, and the dark events of 1932, when three unfortunate women were stoned and burnt to death in the middle of Bida Town in broad daylight, cannot quickly be forgotten. I trust that such things will never happen again. They bring the Native Administration into grave disrepute and my administration also, because the Etsu is my representative in Nupe land.

It is my earnest endeavour to further the policy of administering the people through their own Chief, but I feel strongly that in the past enough has not been done to train the Chiefs in the art of administration. An Administrative officer is trained and only after long training and experience becomes a Resident. A Chief requires training and guidance in no less measure.

The people are becoming more enlightened day by day; the desire for progress is multiplying. The clouds of fear and superstitions are lifting and the light of knowledge is becoming increasingly strong. The acts of a Native Administration are now, quite properly exposed and open to public criticism and, if we are to preserve this system of administration through the Chiefs, those who exercise authority must be fitted to rule in accordance with modern standards of civilised society.

In order that the Native Administration may grow in strength and advance along these lines it is my wish that the Resident and District Officer should take an active part in the direction of the day to day affairs of the Native Administration and attend the Council meeting of the Chief regularly so that they may constantly advise the Chief and his Council and guide them in their deliberation. The Chief must never hesitate to seek the advice of the Resident or District Officer when difficulties and problems arise. Orders and instructions, except on routine questions, should be carefully considered by the Chief and Council and the approval of the Resident or District Officer obtained before they are issued in the name of the Chief so that his authority may be maintained. The Resident and District Officer will not deal with the people direct and the greatest care will be taken to ensure that the religious beliefs and racial characteristics of the people are not interfered with.

Etsu Nupe, you have a Council which I am told is representative of all classes of the people. You must never fail to take counsel with these advisers in your responsible task of ruling, as required by your own native law and custom, and, as I have said, you must always seek the guidance of the Resident or of the Administration Officer representing him. You and your Council may be assured of my strongest support in your efforts to promote the welfare and the prosperity of your people. Your primary duty and obligation; that all obtain justice and fair play especially in your Courts; and so you and your work will be judged. Let it be your care that dark happenings such as occurred in 1932 are never repeated in the history of your country.

I rely on your loyalty, good faith and ability, Muhammadu Ndayako and enjoin you to read carefully the terms of your letter of appointment wherein you are appointed to be the representative of the Governor amongst your own people. A copy of this address will be furnished to you in your own language; the instructions which it contains should be regarded as being in extension of those in your letter of appointment.

From the bottom of my heart I wish you, your Administration, and your people the greatest success, prosperity, and happiness.

sarily restricted by the small numbers of available administrative personnel on which effective supervision depended.

Much more important, given the decision to preserve indigenous institutions as viable instruments of rule even while modifying certain of their characteristics, the British administration was always cautious lest overfrequent deposition of emirs destroy the authority of that institution and thus undermine its own position. In other words, there was a disposition to treat sympathetically emirs' accounts of what the maintenance of their authority required (which often amounted to what their interests were). "Efficiency" and "stability" tended to be the operative criteria for evaluating an emir's performance, the first quality being more readily identifiable than "integrity" and the second a more immediate requirement than "progress".

As the emirs appreciated that in the last analysis it was the British governor who controlled succession and tenure, they naturally responded to this situation by cultivating the support of the administration through exhibition of the qualities most immediately likely to impress and endear. Having won British support, the emir then faced his councillors and people with the additional, indeed crucial, backing of British authority. Established in law as "Sole Native Authority", he then retained and further secured legal sanction for disregarding advice tendered by his councillors. It is therefore understandable how observers like Abubakar Imam and Tafawa Balewa could feel, with many others, that the net effect of colonial administration until the end of the war had been not just the maintenance of arbitrary and autocratic chieftaincy but its intensification.

Another paradoxical point to be noted is that even effective British regulation of emirs did not necessarily promote the modernization of the institution of chieftaincy. Indeed, to the extent that effective control was supplied by external forces, there was no need for the traditional system to develop internal means of control. This reality is reflected in the fact that although emirs were not infrequently disciplined under colonial rule,[7] punishment was seldom if ever ini-

[7] If the degree of "constitutionalism" characteristic of the pre-British traditional system is questionable, the extent to which the British administration acquiesced in arbitrary emirship can also be exaggerated. In theory, the Nigerian governor (later the lieutenant-governor, then the Northern governor) could only approve or veto a candidate for the throne proposed by the traditional electors. In practice, the governor, acting on the advice of his subordinates (especially the Resident who submitted annual confidential reports on the conduct of emirs in his province) could and often did select and depose emirs as he saw fit. Some notion of the

tiated from within. Growth of genuine conciliar sanctions was almost totally inhibited.

A related feature of colonial control of chiefs was that administrative action was nonpublic. A correlary to the axiom that deposition must not be imposed too frequently lest it undermine the institution, was that it should be done, when necessary, with a minimum of publicity. For the public, the first indication that an emir had fallen into disfavor was usually his removal or "retirement". The public did not participate in the process through which specific misdoings leading to this ultimate penalty were exposed and criticized. The emir's faults remained "decently buried between the covers of a confidential file".[8] Consequently, purely traditional expectations regarding the performance of Emirs tended to persist in the popular mind uninformed by the considerations on which British administrative action was taken.

If the British did not eradicate autocracy or entirely change the motivation and objectives of kingship, they were more successful in modifying the characteristics of those who held the office. Since the traditional rules of succession did not involve the principle of primogeniture, competition among hereditarily eligible candidates was an essential attribute of the institution. When possible, the British took advantage of this situation to "encourage" the selection of traditional candidates who gave evidence of possessing the qualities the British desired. These efforts were backed up with an educational policy of giving priority to the training of the ruling class, particularly the sons of emirs, a policy that resulted in gradually raising the educational level of traditional emirs.

Again the attainable results within the framework of indirect rule were limited. The educational attainments of a given candidate had to be balanced against his acceptability by traditional norms, and the two principles were frequently in conflict. The irreducible traditional criterion of acceptability was selection by the traditional electors. These were often men who did not themselves possess, nor highly value in others, the qualification of Western education. Certain factors which enhance, indeed traditionally define, a "good candidate"—such as the amount of cash or kind (*kudin su-*

---

frequency with which Northern emirs were deposed early in the pre-war colonial era is provided by Hogben, *Muhammadan Emirates of Nigeria*, Part II, pp. 68ff; and Smith, *Government in Zazzau*, pp. 199-238. Also see *Provincial Gazetteers* and *Provincial Annual Reports*, 1901-1909.

[8] Perham, *Native Administration in Nigeria*, p. 118.

rauta) a candidate was able to offer to the electors, or the number of followers or clients he could boast—frequently outweighed educational prestige in the eyes of the electors. Moreover, in order to attain the necessary advantages in the traditional competition, a prospective candidate was frequently drawn into practices of maladministration (such as the selling of offices, extortion, etc.) which were the very antithesis of what the British were attempting to introduce as the characteristics of a good ruler. It would be no exaggeration to say that in the era of indirect colonial administration, acceptability of a candidate in traditional terms was almost prima facie evidence of undesirability according to certain British goals. Although the development of the educational system made possible the availability of more and more candidates with the desired educational prerequisites and modern administrative experience, these qualities became neither necessary nor sufficient conditions for attaining the throne, much less for retaining it.

Indeed, a candidate's educational and administrative competence and integrity provided little guarantee of his subsequent performance as emir. Administrative records provide numerous examples of the British having made great efforts to influence the traditional competition on behalf of a "promising" candidate only later, to their distress, finding themselves seeking his dismissal as emir. For regardless of their personal inclinations or attributes of character, emirs were products of and prime participants in a complex of traditional institutions of which their role and prestige as emir was a part. Ineluctably, they tended to act in accordance with the main principles and basic political dynamics governing those institutions. I will return to this point.

Finally, it is appropriate to be reminded again that apart from considerations of expediency, "indirect rule" had the aura of philosophy. Upholding chieftaincy was desirable as well as prudent. Preservation and protection of tradition were *positive* objectives of the British along with "progress" and "enlightenment". To the British almost as much as for the indigenous people, the words tradition and emir had connotations of moral excellence.

SOURCES OF THE POWER OF EMIRS

IT IS AS NECESSARY to understand the basic sources of the emirs' power as to appreciate the forces which limited and influenced its use. In the postwar period, these sources, like the relationships and values they supported, derived from aspects of the original political system which persisted and from contingencies of British colonial administration.

A very important source of power was mastery of coercive force and techniques, which the Fulani originally demonstrated in the religious war of *jihad* of 1804. Possession of an effective military establishment and their subjects' awareness of its superiority over all available means of resistance was a cardinal asset long before the arrival of the British. In standing behind indigenous authority, British authority (itself established by virtue of conquest of the Fulani conquerors) naturally reinforced the peoples' estimate of their rulers coercive potential, and justifiably so in light of the refinements in organization and technology which the British might bring to bear.[9]

The conquest of the Hausa states having been justified by the religious objectives of purification and reform, the emirs' secular power continued to be augmented by appeals to the ideals of Islam, which combine temporal and religious authority in the person of the ruler. The much remarked attitude of obedience toward emirs shown by the Hausa, as expressed in the phrase *"addinimmu addinin biyyaya ne"* (our religion is a religion of obedience), followed naturally from the belief that the authority of emirs is divinely sanctioned. Although, in theory, obedience is enjoined only in the case of orders which are lawful according to the divine law (*shar'ia*, in practice, commands of the emir were customarily obeyed without regard to or knowledge of their lawfulness.[10] To the theocratic definition of authority as inculcated by Islam, there must also be added the un-Islamic, less articulated but no less real, belief of most subjects in

[9] Historians of the colonial penetration of Northern Nigeria have emphasized the relatively "peaceful conquest by the British". Indeed, the military action required to subdue the emirates seems to have been minimal. At the same time, the resort to troops against the "recalcitrant" Emirs such as Sokoto, Kano, and Kontagora, made it clear that conquest was the basis of the British sovereignty like that of the emirs before them. Indirect rule probably further minimized the factor of violence in the functioning of the colonial system of administration. Nonetheless, the coercive potential of the European power was an ultimate sanction of which indigenous rulers and subjects alike were aware. Further, after the fall of Sokoto, which marked the establishment of British authority, the use of force was not unknown. A rebellion against taxes imposed in the early years of administration in Katsina is said to have been sharply put down by the British, and *mahdism* and other quasi-religious forms of revolt were usually dealt with severely.

[10] See Smith, *Economy of Hausa Communities of Zaria*, p. 10.

the supernatural powers of rulers, a phenomenon which antedates the acceptance of monotheism but persisted beyond it.[11]

The pledge of Lord Lugard to the emirs, that the religion of the people (that is, Islam) would not be interfered with (redeemed in such policies as excluding or later tightly restricting Christian missionary activity in the emirates), obviated the damaging effects on the religious claims of Islamic religious rulers that might otherwise be expected as a result of their subordination to an alien Christian power. In recognizing Islam as "native law and custom", and in meticulously observing formal doctrines and protecting Muslim sensibilities, however, the British encouraged a degree of religio-political orthodoxy that an unfettered traditional order hardly possessed.

Under the *shar'ia*, "supreme executive and judicial power is vested in the sovereign, and by the process of delegation each and every official of State becomes his representative. Judicial competence results only from appointment by the ruler".[12] Enormous legal scope derived from the power of administrative discretion (*siyasa*), which was duly recognized by the British. Thus the competence of the executive in the system of justice was not only a matter of the appointment of judges, but extended to the power of intervention and direct adjudication. The power of *siyasa* was formalized by the establishment of courts of justice presided over by emirs themselves. The more important Emirs' Courts (called Grade A, or Grade A unlimited Native Courts) were given capital jurisdiction.

A great range of powers derived from the emir's position as head of a bureaucratic system of territorial administration. As administrative offices and titles (*sarautu*) were held at the pleasure of the emir, their holders were obliged to demonstrate their loyalty or forfeit not only those advantages but the general protection and support of the emir. These obligations of loyalty at once derived from, were expressed by, and gave rise to the personal bonds between officials and the emir which have been summarized as rela-

---

[11] In 1959 an organizer of a local opposition political party commented to me that organization was made extremely difficult because of the belief, among rural folk especially, that "if the emir pronounces a curse, there is no escape for his victim". For a discussion of the survival of animistic beliefs and practices among certain Muslims in Northern Nigeria, see Greenberg, *Influence of Islam.*

[12] N. J. Coulson, "The State and the Individual is Islamic Law", *The International and Comparative Law Quarterly* (January 1957), p. 57; cf. sections 136, 137, and 138 of the *Northern Penal Code.*

tionships of kinship, marriage, and clientage. Since office and title represented the main avenues to wealth and social prestige, competition for office and title generated the political system. In controlling appointments and tenure of office, the emir was truly dominant politically. When, as Sole Native Authorities under the British, emirs were empowered to make bylaws, rules, and orders having the force of law, the circle of executive, legislative, and judicial authority was complete. Yet there was another, less conspicuous but no less important adjunct of the emir's power which should be noted.

Before the arrival of the British, an emir's control over his territory rested to a considerable extent on his superior command of sources of information. The political system over which an emir reigns was (and is) one whose complexities it would be difficult to exaggerate. It was beset by rivalries and tensions at every level, which the emir was compelled either to manipulate to his advantage or to see work against himself. Tensions existed between the various dynastic groups eligible to compete for emirship, between palace agents and territorial chiefs, between title-holders and those seeking title and office, between the subject population and subordinate chiefs and officials. Effective rule presupposed the ability to assess accurately the strengths of various parties and to time accordingly recognition of competing claims. To this end, the emir employed a variety of persons whose primary duty it was to imform him on all happenings of potential or present significance in his emirate. These included agents called *jekadu* (messengers), *yan labari* (literally, "sons of information"), and *yaran sarki* (literally, "the emir's boys or menials"), who circulated in outlying territories, and the various types of *fadawa* (courtiers) who supervised avenues of communication in the emirate capital.

The British immediately grasped a certain importance in the emir's virtual monopoly of these networks of communications and information-gathering to the existing political system. British officers on tour were directed always to travel with *yaran sarki*, and *talakawa* were never interviewed except in the presence of these or some other representative of the emir. Although in principle the post of *jekada* was abolished (the institution of *jekadu* was associated with extortion in connection with tax-collecting), *yan labari*, *yaran sarki*, and *fadawa* continued to provide their vital services to the emir, making a substantial contribution to his continued personal influence and power.

The Impact of Local Government Reform on the Position of Emirs

In regard to the position of the emirs, the central feature of the changes designed to accommodate conciliar norms of local government was the abolition of their status as Sole Native Authorities in favor of the new status of Chief-in-Council introduced under the Native Authority (Definition of Functions) Law of 1952. Legally a Chief-in-Council was thereafter obligated to consult his council under normal conditions. Furthermore, official acts promulgated by a Native Authority operating the Chief-in-Council provisions were required to contain the joint signatures of the emir and certain designated councillors. However, an emir could overrule an opposing majority of his councillors provided he could secure the support of the Governor. These innovations were confirmed under the Native Authority Law of 1954. Only a few of the emirs were ever shifted from the status of Chief-*in*-Council to that of Chief-*and*-Council (which connoted lack of a legal power of veto); Chiefs-*and*-Council were mostly to be found in the Middle Belt Area of the Northern Region. Thus the potentially most far-reaching reform in the direction of democratization of the Northern chiefs' position was for the most part not applied to the emirs.

The Chief-in-Council idea constituted one of the more ingenious devices of Northern gradualism, in that it combined the possibility of structural change with an opportunity to avoid it without making either result certain or inevitable. Whether an emir's councillors gained control over him depended on their willingness and courage to assert their new legal prerogatives, and on whether the Governor would subsequently back them up. From an emir's point of view, this meant that insofar as he could continue to command the obedience of his councillors (through whatever means available to him, or simply through their political inertia), he might continue substantially as before. The procedure provided for in the case of a conflict between an emir and his councillors was in fact used only once (during the 1958 crisis in Ilorin). This is not to say that the reform was without consequences elsewhere. A clear indication of the fallacy of the contention that the reform represented no more than an adjustment of law to fit the traditional situation is the series of cases involving an emir's loss of his throne which soon followed its introduction.

THE "DEPOSITION" CASES, 1953-1965

DEPOSITION, or the forced retirement of emirs, did not begin in the postwar era. It was pointed out above that the British Administration took such action more frequently than has generally been realized. The significance of many postwar incidents lies in the fact that they were initiated either through action of the emir's councillors, or in Kaduna, instead of resulting purely from British administrative displeasure. Thus in the period between 1953 and 1965, there were at least seven instances of "dismissals" of emirs. The Emirs of Kano, Adamawa, Bauchi, Biu, Kaiama, and Argungu "retired" or "resigned", and the Emir of Dikwa was formally deposed.[13] In addition, there were cases (notably Gwandu and Zaria) of threatened dismissal, which failed to materialize.

These cases are obviously not numerous, nor did they typify the distribution of power that prevailed between emirs and councillors. But they do reflect one end of a range of distributions and as such were important.

The ex-emir of Dikwa, M. Mustapha Ibn Sanda, took office just about the time that the Chief-in-Council arrangement was being introduced in April 1952. The Native Authority Councillors accepted the choice of the traditional electors, but being aware that Ibn Sanda had a past record of maladministration (he had served a one-year sentence for embezzlement), they asserted that he must agree to be bound by a virtually defunct traditional Bornu Accession Oath pledging Emirs "to deal justly". The emir's refusal to do so, on the grounds that swearing on the oath administered by the British absolved him from taking any other, was a warning of the conflict between him and his councillors which raged during the next two years.

Relations became so embittered by 1954 that the councillors openly denounced the emir and appealed to the British to depose him, on the grounds of maladministration, abuse of office for personal ends, and defiance of his councillors on important matters of policy. The councillors also claimed that since the emir had refused to take the traditional oath, he had never truly become emir. This con-

---

[13] Formal deposition of Northern emirs is a rare event. It is nearly always found more convenient to force the resignation or retirement of a chief. For the emir's part, he avoids unnecessary embarrassment and usually wins a "pension" or *ex-gratia* allowance from the Native Authority on condition that he reside outside of his former emirate and refrain from political activity. Deposition is governed by the Appointment and Deposition of Chiefs Ordinance, Section 4.

tention was a shrewd effort to invest their action with the sanction of traditional political obligation; but for councillors to invoke it against the Emir's de facto control of the throne was an entirely new step, the success of which rested on its being taken in conjunction with the secular sanctions and principles introduced by the 1952 law. Another development associated with the Dikwa deposition case was the public expression of the principles underlying the act. The government's official announcement stated that the emir's faults were "his autocratic bearing, reliance on irresponsible personal favourites and his frequent refusal to consult his council".[14]

The case of the ex-emir of Kaiama, like that of Dikwa, is another in which traditional claims were joined with sanctions created by modern legal reform to produce a new political structure. Interestingly, the Emir of Kaiama had long enjoyed a good reputation with the British, who appreciated the fact that, though autocratic in his methods, the Emir had repeatedly shown himself willing to support innovations. Moreover, he seemed to eschew maladministration and self-aggrandizement. Yet in 1953 the Emir's resignation was forced by councillors who protested his autocratic behavior, citing in their cause the new conciliar principles of local government. Beneath the surface of these events, however, there were also traditional considerations which clearly influenced the councillors in their attitude to the Emir.

The Emirate of Kaiama was a unit of government the British had created for administrative convenience. Four districts, over which the ex-emir lacked any traditional claim to suzerainty, were placed under his jurisdiction as Sole Native Authority.[15] In effect, the Kaiama councillors, a majority of whom were the traditional hereditary rulers in these four districts, lost little time in reasserting their former independence vis-à-vis the Emir once the 1952 reform had strengthened their hand. The emirate was subsequently dissolved and the Kaiama districts now form part of the Borgu Emirate,

---

[14] See *Nigerian Citizen*, April 1, 1954, p. 1.

[15] Kaiama in the days before European penetration of West Africa, was merely one of five districts of the Emirate of Nikki. Most of Nikki Emirate, including the capital, was left on the French side of the line (which the British and French drew to mark their spheres of influence) that divided French Dahomey from British Nigeria. The British elevated Mora Tasuede, then chief of Kaiama, to the position of Sole Native Authority over the four districts left on the British side of the boundary as well as Kaiama district which gave its name to the new "emirate". Thus the Emir of Kaiama exercised over five districts powers which tradition gave him for only one.

which is said to be a closer approximation to the pre-British situation and more palatable to the four headmen concerned.

Councillors of the Bauchi Native Authority clashed with their emir in 1953, claiming the misappropriation of district council funds. At this point they were satisfied to require the Emir to sign a document pledging himself to rectify alleged abuses on his part.

When in April 1954 the Emir arbitrarily attempted to impose higher market fees in Bauchi Town, the councillors were considerably embarrassed by the arrival of a NEPU delegation headed by Aminu Kano, which proceeded to organize popular feeling against the increases. As a result, the increases were withdrawn. Later that year it was revealed that the Emir had imposed a cruel physical ordeal on a defendant in a civil case before his court (contrary to Section 208 of the Criminal Code of Nigeria) and the councillors thereupon disavowed him. By announcing his retirement, the Emir avoided the formal deposition which otherwise almost certainly would have followed these events.

In 1953 the councillors of the Adamawa Native Authority drew up an undertaking similar to that in Bauchi, which defined the standards of conduct expected of the *Lamido* ("Emir" in Fulani). Like the Emir of Bauchi, Ahmadu, the Lamido of Adamawa, proved incapable of conforming to the standards, and his resignation was forced in July 1953. Moreover a "detailed and comprehensive list of conditions" was imposed on the next Lamido, Aliyu Musdapha, upon his succession of Ahmadu.[16]

The Emir of Argungu's resignation in 1960 is of special interest, in that his dispute with his council involved popular demonstrations on behalf of both parties and also introduces us to the phenomenon and problem of chiefs in politics. In the Argungu controversy the ostensible issue was the Emir's tendency to seek preferential treatment for his sons and offices, which his Council claimed were undeserved on the basis of merit. I was in Argungu in August 1959 and thus was able to assemble the following brief account when the dispute erupted.

In 1935 the Emir of Argungu, Muhammadu Muza, agreed that the *sarauta* (title and office) of District Head of Baiyawa should be abolished and the territory amalgamated with the neighboring District of Augi. Ostensibly this arrangement was advocated on the grounds of administrative convenience; this was the explanation

---

[16] 1953 *Provincial Annual Reports*, p. 3.

of the British District officer who recommended the proposed change to his superiors. However, it was widely believed at the time that the Emir had made the proposal because he had at that time no adult male heirs to occupy the district headship of Baiyawa, which was traditionally reserved for the sons of Argungu emirs. Knowing this reason for keeping the *sarauta* vacant—and thus out of the hands of the Emir's dynastic rivals—would not be acceptable to the British, the Emir argued for it on the grounds of administrative efficiency.

Muhammadu Sheshe, who succeeded to the throne in 1953, had a young adult son to whom he wished to give an appropriate *sarauta*, namely that of district head of Baiyawa. By this time, however, the fact that amalgamation of the Augi and Baiyawa Districts made administrative sense was apparent, and the change had come to be generally accepted. The councillors made known their reluctance to re-create Baiyawa as a separate district simply in order to accommodate the new Emir's son. Naturally the Emir's dynastic rivals were especially cool to the idea. But the new Emir prevailed, and in 1955 his son, M. Muhammadu Fakkai, received his *sarauta*.

The next year, 1956, was the year of the "democratic" elections to the Regional House of Assembly, and the Emir sought to advance the position of his eldest son further by securing his election. He put pressure on the local branch of the NPC which succeeded in wresting the nomination from a M. Muhammadu Mera who had already been chosen as the local party's official nominee. Subsequently the Emir's son, whose title was *Sarkin Gobir*, also replaced Muhammadu Mera as President of the Divisional Branch of the NPC. These moves incurred the hostility of many people in Argungu, not the least of whom was Muhammadu Mera, himself a *dan sarki*, or son of a former Argungu emir, Muhammadu Sani.[17]

In 1959 history seemed about to repeat itself, as the Emir simultaneously sought to transfer the Baiyawa District *sarauta* to a second son who had by then come of age (the *Sarkin Gobir* in the meantime had become a member of the N.A. Council), and to get his client, the Magajin Gari, M. Hassan, the nomination as candidate for the Federal elections of 1959, again at the expense of M. Muhammadu Mera.

[17] References to the Emir's intervention in the Argungu NPC nominations later appeared in a report in the *Nigerian Citizen*, April 1, 1959, under the heading "Party Rift in Argungu?" which anticipated the coming events in August.

By 1959, however, considerable resentment against these actions and other alleged offenses of the Emir had crystallized within his Council, whose members boasted relatively high educational qualifications and modern administrative talent.[18] These councillors succeeded in blocking the nomination of the Emir's client, Hassan (who was also a councillor), by presenting evidence of an irregularity (in connection with an insurance policy) committed sometime previously by him; this not only secured his dismissal but got him a criminal conviction. Having thus openly defied the Emir's interests, the Council, consisting as it did of essentially the same personalities who supported Muhammadu Mera over the Magajin Gari in the NPC Executive Committee, was inevitably led into a split. On August 24 matters came to a head when a march of over 200 townspeople was organized. Shouting "*Ba mu so, Ba mu so*" (We don't want him [the Emir], we don't want him) the marchers proceeded to the house of the British District officer to demand the ouster of the Emir, while at the same time a majority of the Argungu N.A. Councillors declared themselves on strike against the Emir, refused to come to their offices, and undertook to dissolve the connections that had symbolized their political solidarity with the Emir.[19] The following day, the Emir called on his supporters from the villages to stage a counterdemonstration. Administration came to a standstill, and the matter was hurriedly referred to Kaduna. After restoring a temporary modus vivendi that permitted administration to continue, the government at Kaduna appointed a commission of inquiry, which ruled against the Emir in October 1959. The commission cited the division "between the Emir and his supporters on the one hand and the majority of Native Authority Councillors, District Heads and Departmental Heads on the other", and noted that those opposed to the Emir included "the great majority of

[18] Muhammadu Mera, who was then Councillor for Education, is a graduate of Kaduna College, where he attained Middle VI. The *Turakin Argungu*, Councillor in Charge of Finance is a graduate of Katsina College and a member of the Federal House of Representatives from 1954 to 1963. The Senior Councillor, in charge of District Administration and Taxation, Alhaji Umaru, the *Madawakin Argungu*, is noted as the first modern "administrative" councillor in Argungu (he was appointed in 1944). The other council member was the *Kunduda*, the title of traditional advisors to the Emirs of Argungu.

[19] The daughters of the Madawaki and the Kunduda were wives of the Emir; they immediately withdrew from the Emir's compound, while his daughter, who was married to Muhammadu Mera, was returned to the palace. These instantaneous "divorces" provide a striking confirmation of the political significance of marriage among the traditional aristocracy.

276

educated men in the Emirate".[20] Subsequently M. Muhammadu Mera, the young educated former Councillor for Education, who had been the prime victim of chiefly autocracy in Argungu, was installed as the new emir.

Emphasis on education was probably overdrawn in the commission's analysis. The disaffection of Council members due to maladministration by the Emir was inseparable from the dispute over *sarauta* matters. It should be noted that the *Kunduda* was not educated, but that he was the District Head of Augi, from which district territory he had been excised in order to re-create Baiyawa district for the benefit of the Emir's son. As a young *dan sarki* Muhammadu Mera (at 29 he was the same age as Muhammadu Sheshe's son; the *Sarkin Gobir* was a natural rival of the *Sarkin Gobir* in the contest for the throne which would have naturally ensued upon the death of the aging Emir). Rivalry for the NPC nomination was therefore an inseparable aspect of the traditional struggle for the *sarauta*. The succession of Muhammadu Mera as Emir of Argungu in 1960 had the effect of resolving the anticipated struggle for the Argungu *sarauta*.

The Argungu crisis highlights several points of general interest: (a) the new hazards for an emir who had bad relations with his Councillors under the circumstances created by the new definition of chiefly status; (b) the attempt of both parties in the dispute to mobilize at least the impression of popular support for their side; (c) the intervention of the Emir in modern party politics; and (d) the interplay between traditional and modern political objectives, especially interests pertaining to *sarauta* competition, on one hand, and the modern electoral process on the other (a phenomenon explored in detail in Chapter 9).

As an indicator of political change, all of these "deposition cases" are instructive on two principal counts. First, they illustrate that at least some emirs could be held accountable *within* the emirate political structure—in contrast to the previous situation in which the only power to enforce responsibility was outside the structure. Second, these manifestations of conciliar control were accompanied by public statements which rationalized the action taken. In this, deposition performed an educative function which under purely colonial "tutelage" it did not serve. Evidently the government now thought it proper to allow cases of deposition to be publicized

[20] *Northern Regional Daily Press Service Release* No. 2517, October 20, 1959.

although their approach seemingly still reflected an attitude of caution against telling the people too much.[21] At the same time, the series of cases were seized on as an opportunity to point up the moral in detail to other emirs.[22]

Another development in recent years is a tendency for newly enthroned emirs to make public promises to introduce or adhere to reforms which represented curtailment of the freedom of action enjoyed by emirs in days gone by. Such undertakings were entered into by the *Lamido* of Adamawa appointed in 1953, the Emir of Bauchi appointed in 1954, and the Emir of Dikwa appointed in 1953. In his inaugural, the Emir of Dikwa proclaimed: "there will be no room for a good number of old traditions in the new house I am going to build. There will be no room, and I repeat this, no room for bribery and corruption, and for illegal exchange of disguised gifts between senior and junior in public life. I shall make it my business to see that all promotions and appointments are by merit and qualification. Selfishness and short-sightedness are the enemies of progress. This must be eradicated".[23] Similarly, much interest and comment was aroused by the radio broadcast of the Emir of Kano's inaugural in 1953. Although there had been no overt evidence of any open rift within the Kano N.A. Council under his father, the deceased Emir, the new Emir, Muhammadu Sanusi, nonetheless promised administrative reform, specifying judicial and executive power and land tenure as matters that would be particularly affected:

> There have in times past been criticisms of the administration of Kano on the grounds that it was too centralized, too autocratic, too much in the hands of one family.
>
> I now solemnly promise to you, the people of Kano, that I will consult my council on all matters and shall welcome from them their frank and honest opinion. . . .
>
> I shall hold all judicial proceedings of my Court in a building allocated for the purpose outside my residence, until a new Court building can be erected.

[21] Accounts of cases of deposition in the vernacular newspaper, *Gaskiya Ta Fi Kwabo*, and in the English language paper, *Nigerian Citizen*, which were both indirectly controlled by the Northern government, contained few of the details recounted here. However, these accounts, together with communication by word of mouth, were doubtless effective in spreading the word that conflict with councillors was largely the cause of these Emirs' demise.

[22] A document discussing the background of the cases in some detail was circulated in 1957 and earmarked for the attention of the emirs.

[23] *Nigerian Citizen*, April 22, 1954, p. 3.

I shall ensure that the Court hears only cases brought before it in accordance with its jurisdiction.

As an earnest of my intention to make my Council fully representative of the people I have determined that I will never at any time appoint any close relative of mine to hold the posts in Wali, or of Council Member in charge of the City, or Council Member in charge of the Districts. . . .

There may be other parts of the Administration and Local Government which require review and I shall turn my attention to these shortly but those of which I have told you now are I believe the first essential to good government in the time in which we live.[24]

Such public declarations suggest, especially when they have occurred in the wake of a locally instigated deposition or official warning, that emirs were increasingly subject to the observance of conditions and rules imposed by central councillors. This, in turn, suggested the growth of some degree of contractual relationship between the two; it was precisely a contractual element that the traditional conciliar structure conspicuously lacked before.

THE SANUSI OF KANO AFFAIR

PRIOR TO 1963 it seems fair to say that most close observers of the Northern Nigerian scene were skeptical that under prevailing sociopolitical conditions any of the "Big Three" emirs would ever be brought down. I was no exception. The deposition cases discussed above primarily involved local instigation and support which, it was doubted, could be mustered solely from within the regimes of such internally well-entrenched rulers as Kano, Sokoto, and Bornu. At the same time, so long as basic internal solidarity was sustained, it seemed unlikely that Kaduna, deeply indebted politically as it was to the influence and machinery of the local emirate bureaucracies, would move directly against any of these three rulers of enormous populations. The forced resignation of the Emir of Kano in the spring of 1963, following the report of a Sole Commission of Inquiry into Kano N.A. financial affairs, was therefore a dramatic refutation of the previous estimate. That estimate had overlooked the possibility that there could arise between the Premier and a Big Three emir a personal enmity so severe as to oc-

[24] *Daily Comet*, December 31, 1953.

casion an ultimate test of wills, notwithstanding the serious political dangers for both parties which such a contest would inevitably entail. No one had fully assessed the inordinately proud personalities of the *Sardauna* and Muhammadu Sanusi, ex-Emir of Kano.

Some informed observers traced the beginnings of political jealousy between Sanusi and the Sardauna as far back as 1959, when at the official Northern self-government celebrations the Emir was not extended an invitation to be seated with the principal dignitaries and was rebuked upon trying to do so uninvited. Others believe the antagonism first arose in connection with the Emir's brief appointment in 1961 as acting governor of the Northern Region, during the temporary absence of the last British governor, Sir Gawain Westray Bell—a situation which inevitably involved delicate considerations of protocol with respect to the Emir and the Sardauna as Premier. Whatever the origins, there is wide agreement about other incidents and issues that contributed to strained relations. The Emir was an adamant opponent of certain key pieces of legislation sponsored by the Sardauna's government, including the Provincial Administration Bill of 1962, which introduced Provincial Commissioners, appointed from among the membership of the Regional House of Assembly with the rank of minister. In more than one respect, this constituted a blow to the lofty pretensions of Kano—not only were provincial commissioners placed over the Emir in official precedence, but the person appointed to this new ostensibly superogatory post in Kano was a titled member of a Sokoto royal slave lineage.[25] In the context of historic claims, that appointment conveyed the unmistakable message that the Emir of Kano was being put in his place by the Sardauna.

Against this bill and the later Land Tenure Law (which transferred certain highly lucrative functions from the Native Administrations to Kaduna), the Emir of Kano had unsuccessfully attempted to mobilize the NPC Kano contingent in the House of Assembly, an obvious provocation of some magnitude, considering the Sardauna's position as party head, as well as the head of the government. To make matters worse, the Emir's son soon thereafter divorced a daughter of the Emir of Gwandu, the Sardauna's cousin.

[25] Cf. Billy J. Dudley, "The Northern People's Congress", in John P. Macintosh, ed., *Nigerian Government and Politics* (Evanston, Ill., 1966), p. 398, note 3, where Dudley incorrectly states that Alhaji Aliyu, *Magajin Gari* of Sokoto, is a member of the Sokoto ruling family.

As in many other episodes involving change in this period, an immediate reaction to the Sanusi case was that it foreshadowed a break with the "politics of tradition", i.e. reciprocal cooperation and exploitation between Kaduna and the traditionally oriented emirate regimes generally. As time passed and radical reform, either in Kano or other emirates, failed to materialize, this view became increasingly untenable. The new Emir of Kano, Aminu, took office with a council from which very few of the old guard were absent. This was evident to all who appreciated the dynamics of these politics—that had more than issues of personal power been at stake, most of the continuing councillors would necessarily have shared the Emir's fate. Indeed, it seems obvious that without the cooperation of key Kano officials, some of whom, as Dudley notes, had their own scores to settle with the Emir, the Commission of Enquiry could not have uncovered the formally relevant evidence.[26] It is highly unlikely that such cooperation could have been obtained without the appropriate reassurance having been given such persons. The report of the government-appointed Sole Commissioner[27] has remained unpublished, no doubt in part because it is more broadly incriminating than was consonant with the degree of continuity in the membership of the pre- and post-Sanusi Kano N.A. Councils. Furthermore, the tenor of the Government's *Statement on Kano Native Authority Affairs* indicates that criminal indictment of the Emir, which as the Statement itself says was successfully instituted against lesser culprits, was warranted.[28] This clearly could not have been achieved, however, without the self-incriminating testimony of expert witnesses. The Emir was permitted to retire in exile.

A final clue to the meaning of the Sanusi of Kano case is that otherwise parallel investigations into the financial affairs of the Zaria and Gwandu Native Administrations were carried out at about the same time without resulting in their emirs having to resign. It was reported that in the case of the Emir of Zaria, an investigation, which "clearly led to the enhancement of his own position",[29] through dislodging dynastic rivals, was made by the Emir himself. Whether justifiably or not, the meaning of these episodes to anyone belonging to the traditional political culture of Hausaland was certain

[26] *Ibid.*, p. 398.
[27] D. J. Muffet, now on the staff of Duquesne University.
[28] See the text of the *Statement on Kano Native Authority Affairs* in the *Nigerian Citizen*, May 1, 1963.
[29] Dudley, "Northern People's Congress", p. 399.

to be that, like other rulers, the *Sardauna* had employed a customary technique for rewarding those loyal to him and punishing those who were not.

An unusual aspect of the Sanusi case, however, was that the *Sardauna* had succeeded in doing what some traditional heads of the Fulani empire had tried and failed to do—dethrone an Emir of Kano. The period of political unrest in Kano that followed the Emir's demise, however, showed that under parliamentary institutions this maneuver was politically very risky.[30] The risks help to account for the fact that not further upheaval in Kano, but return and adherence to normalcy everywhere, was the aftermath of the Sanusi case of deposition.

New Functions and New Emirs

THE LEGAL REFORMS that contributed to subjecting some Emirs to conciliar and ministerial control in the dramatic and decisive manner illustrated by the above cases of deposition, coincided with other developments, more long-range in origin, which reinforced the trend toward realizing the concept of emirship implied in the term "Chief-in-Council". One development was the increase in number and complexity of the functions which Native Authorities were called on to perform in the march toward economic development. Another and related development was the growing preference for candidates for emirship who possessed the assets of Western education and modern administrative ability.

Public goals shifted emphatically in the postwar period away from economic self-sufficiency and "basic" administration (i.e. the maintenance of law and order), to economic development and increased provision of social and welfare services. Consequently all levels of government were called on to perform additional functions and duties. At the same time, rationalization and coordination of policy between the regional government and local administrations became increasingly important. Native Authorities were employed more and more as instruments for implementing policy laid down by the regional government. Fewer and fewer public ques-

---

[30] In the wake of the Emir's resignation there emerged a new political party called the Kano People's Party (KPP), centered around dissident NPC members partisan to the ex-Emir Sanusi, who from his place of exile in another emirate, was able to receive and give encouragement to the KPP's activities. Anti-Sardauna feeling among the KPP adherents was intense. Not surprisingly, some NEPU agents fished in these troubled NPC waters, and for at least a year following the dethronement, the NPC organization in Kano was in a state of turmoil.

tions could be approached from first principles; instead, Native Authorities found themselves confronted with a growing body of administrative direction emanating from Kaduna.

Before 1959 at least, the extent to which the regional government intended to reduce the power of the emirs was in doubt, yet the increasing volume and complexity of instructions from regional headquarters alone tended to make the old singlehanded administrative autocracy of emirs impossible. Finding themselves burdened with responsibilities they could not meet without assistance, emirs perforce were led to acknowledge the principle of division of labor and to attract to their service councillors with the requisite skills and educational qualifications. Specifically, new functions were implicit in Native Authority and government Five Year Plans, Financial Directions, development projects and schemes, and the vast number of government circulars designed to achieve local administrative compliance and uniformity between Native Authorities. This, combined with reforms designed partly to foster progress toward democratization, made it possible for councillors in some Native Authorities to translate their new-found administrative indispensability into a voice in policy-making. The net effect was a perceptible shift, or dispersion, of power within Native Authorities, which represented not democratization, but, in historical terms, a reversion from autocracy to oligarchy.

It would be a mistake, however, to conclude that emirs always acquiesced in the "inevitable". Thus postwar developments hit hardest where the emir concerned was illiterate (in Roman script) and unequipped to comprehend the various new administrative operations or the opportunities these operations presented for the exercise of power. Yet many emirs, including some who were illiterate, made shrewd adjustments to the new situation, adjustments which minimized their loss of power. Sometimes such accommodations were effected by astute manipulations of the possibilities presented by the basic structural principles of the traditional emirate system that had persisted in the face of change. An excellent example of such an adjustment was afforded in Kazaure Emirate.

The aging Emir of Kazaure (his year of birth is listed as 1886, although he is believed to be as much as 10 years older) lacked basic Western learning, i.e. literacy in the Roman script. Yet observers in Kazaure emirate in 1959, who conceded that the Emir was personally inactive in the day to day administration of Kazaure because of his advanced age, lack of training, and the increased scale of administrative activity, insisted that his political grip on Kazaure affairs had relaxed very little. Inquiry into the decision-making process of the Kazaure administration substantiated this contention. How had the Emir managed under new conditions and his own personal disabilities to retain a preeminent position?

In 1944 the Emir of Kazaure, who understood well the power implications of "modernization of administration", wrote to a M. Muhammadu who was then working as a scribe in the Kano Native Treasury. M. Muhammadu is the descendant of the Kanuri slave lineage which traditionally served the ruling House of Kazaure. Son of the Tarno (slave title) of Kazaure, M. Muhammadu owed his employment in the Kano Native Authority to having been selected for education in the Kazaure primary schools, from whence he graduated to the Kano Middle School, where he attained the Middle IV standard (equivalent of two years of secondary education). His performance in school and in his job at Kano gave evidence of his aptitude for tasks in the "modern" milieu. At the same time, his family's position in the traditional structure of Kazaure emirate defined his personal traditional status and assured the asset of loyalty and service to the throne. The Emir's letter to M. Muhammadu was an invitation to him to return to Kazaure for service in the Kazaure N.A.

From 1946 to 1949 M. Muhammadu, having accepted the Emir's offer, was the Supervisor of the Kazaure Native Authority Works Department. In 1949 he was elevated to the Council of the Emir of Kazaure and given the title of *Magajin Gari* (principal councillor), which in Kazaure is the equivalent of the position of *Waziri* in other emirates. Thereafter the Emir placed the expanding responsibilities and powers of the Native Administration on the *Magajin Gari*, who was eminently suited to receive them, from the point of view of both the British Administrative officers and the Emir. The *Magajin Gari* soon became outwardly the most powerful man in Kazaure. A list of his duties and positions from 1959 to 1963 (in 1963 he was appointed Provincial Commissioner for Bornu Province, and left Kazaure) gives some indication of the scope of his activities in Kazaure public affairs.

In these years the *Magajin Gari* in Kazaure was the Senior Councillor and chief advisor to the Emir, District Head of the home or capital District of Kazaure, and in charge of the administrative portfolios of District Administration, Education, Works, and Co-Operatives. As the Kazaure Schools manager, he was also head of a department. The *Magajin Gari* was a member of all N.A. committees in Kazaure including the Tenders Board, Tax Assessment, and Finance Committees of which he was chairman. He was the representative of Kazaure in Kano provincial affairs, being a member of two provincial boards. He was also the member of the Regional House of Assembly from the constituency of Kazaure, and patron (formerly president) of the local branch of the Northern People's Congress.

The *Magajin Gari's* rise to power was at once confirmed and expressed by his marriage to a daughter of the Emir of Kazaure. It was hardly any exaggeration to say, as they did in Kazaure, that nothing happened there without the approval of (and usually by execution of) the *Magajin Gari*. At the same time, his personal origins in terms of the traditional emirate socio-political system, his client-patron relationship with the Emir, and his marriage made it clear to the people of Kazaure that the extraordinary powers of the *Magajin Gari* were exercised exclusively in behalf of the incumbent Emir. People in Kazaure were quick to point out that since the *Magajin Gari* was ineligible as a rival for the throne, he could act only to support it. His slave origin made his role of the Emir's man wholly acceptable and familiar to the people. In other words, since mobility and flexibility were features not unknown to the traditional ruling class (which included, it will be remembered, slaves), traditional socio-political principles obviated any impression of disruption or dislocation in authority, which the *Magajin Gari's* position might have otherwise suggested. As it was, his role was mutually advantageous. Without the Emir's patronage M. Muhammadu would not have enjoyed the position he did. In turn, the Emir retained his influence over the technical and administrative matters that affected his interests. What appeared to be delegation turned out to be a means of avoiding the more power-debilitating features to which the unavoidable "decentralization" resulting from assumption of new official functions might have otherwise given rise. It is also worthwhile adding, that, as the acknowledged head of the Kingmaker's Council, the *Magajin Gari* will have a decisive voice in choosing the next emir of Kazaure, and his support of the present Emir's house against its dynastic rivals may be expected.

I am not suggesting that the Kazaure situation is typical. The small territory (four small Districts), population involved (86,000), plus Kazaure's relative geographical isolation (Kazaure was virtually cut off from the outside world during the rainy season, which left its roads impassable), allowed a degree of concentration of power which was unusual. However, to the degree consistent with the scale of administration, and depending on the availability of suitable people, many of the emirs succeeded in cushioning the impact of change through skillfully manipulating traditional relationships. Officials approximating the role of the *Magajin Gari* were to be found in several other emirates.[31]

On the surface, some features of the organization of the Bornu Native Administration resembled that of Kazaure. Yet Bornu provided a convenient and interesting contrast; there the interaction between modernization and tradition worked out differently.

THE BORNU EXPERIENCE

IN 1959, the Shehu of Bornu was 88 years old and partially blind. He had withdrawn from an active public role, although he retained his titular position as head of the Bornu Native Authority. Responsibility for the actual work of administration of Bornu emirate rested with Shettima Kashim, the *Waziri* of Bornu, who had occupied this position and title since 1956. Shettima Kashim's educational attainments and administrative talents, his modern political career and influence in Nigerian affairs, taken together with his family background, placed him, like the late Premier of the Northern region, atop both worlds of traditional and modern leadership.[32] In 1960, as Sir

---

[31] Particularly Gumel, Adamawa, Zaria, Sokoto, and Katsina.

[32] Shettima Kashim was educated at the Bornu Provincial School and the famous Katsina Training College. Until 1938 he was a teacher at the Bornu Middle School, later Visiting Teacher, in which capacity he was awarded the traditional title of *Shettima*. He was one of four chosen by the government in 1949 to be the first Northern Nigerian Education Officers (posts in the Senior rank of Civil Service). Elected in 1952 to the Northern House of Assembly, he was in turn elected to the Lagos Legislature where he became the Central Minister of Social Services and later Central Minister of Education. He resigned his Central Ministry and returned, via a by-election, to the Northern House of Assembly where he was made a Minister in charge of Social Welfare, Cooperatives and Surveys. Shettima Kashim resigned his Regional Ministry in 1956 to become the *Waziri* of Bornu; subsequently he lost his seat in the House in the 1956 elections. Shettima Kashim has remained a member of the National Executive Committee of the Northern People's Congress. In 1957 he was advisor to the government party at the London Conferences on the Nigerian Constitution. He was also a key member of the Panel of Jurists, which in 1958 recommended basic reforms in the legal system of Northern Nigeria, of which he privately had long been critical. Shettima Kashim is the author of several educational textbooks in the Kanuri language and a member of the governing council of the University College, Ibadan. His wife, the daughter of the Katsina College-educated merchant-trader, Alhaji Ahmed

Kashim Ibrahim, this man became the first African to be appointed Governor of Northern Nigeria.

The Bornu Native Authority in 1959 had recently undergone important structural modifications, which seemed to signify a permanent reduction in the power of the throne. While Shettima Kashim's position of authority at least equalled that of the *Magajin Gari* of Kazaure, the former's traditional status was such that he could by no means be regarded as essentially a proxy of the Emir. After 1956 the Bornu *Waziriship* acquired an importance considerably in excess of its traditional role. The heightened position of *Waziri* Shettima Kashim, like that of others elsewhere, certainly owed something to the expanding functions of administration and the concomitant necessity for trained administrative talent. In this case the Shehu's physical handicaps and the great scale of the Bornu administration (Bornu, largest of all the Northern emirates, has a territory of 32,995 square miles, and a total population well over one million) doubtless added to the importance of these considerations. But Shettima Kashim's ascendancy also owed a good deal to the special conditions under which he became *Waziri*.

He had assumed the post following the second major administrative purge in Bornu in three years, occasioned by exposure of widespread official corruption which implicated all but a few of the highest Bornu officials. At this time it was feared that failure to carry out the reforms promised after the first purge might now so discredit the N.A. as to lead to a breakdown in administration.[33]

Thus Shettima Kashim took office with a virtual mandate (from

---

Metteden, is one of the few far Northern women educated to secondary school level. Shettima Kashim is a member of a distant branch of the family of Al-Kanemi, founder of the present ruling dynasty of Bornu, although his branch is not in the line which has heretofore furnished the Shehus of Bornu. As the first African to occupy the office of governor, which on the British model had become a "constitutional" position without direct power, he enjoyed great dignity and prestige.

[33] In 1953, the Resident of Bornu had written: "The year 1953 may well have marked a turning point in the annals of modern Bornu. It is always difficult to assess history while one is living in it but there can be little doubt that the great political and social reforms springing from the events of February are having and will have increasingly profound effects on the lives of every inhabitant of Bornu Emirate and indeed of the other Emirates within the Province". *Provincial Annual Reports*, 1953, p. 41. Following the second series of administrative scandals in 1956, the Resident wrote: "It is depressing to have to report that the promise shown in 1955, particularly in Bornu Emirate, has not been maintained. . . . These disgraces are even more disappointing when they follow so closely on the purge of 1953 and the Council re-organisation of 1954. One is driven to ask whether it is merely the face that changes and not the heart". *Provincial Annual Reports*, 1956, pp. 29, 31.

both the British Administration and popular sentiment) to transform standards of official conduct and modernize the administration. To these ends, the *Waziri* was allowed to assume crucial powers, including a decisive say in the selection and supervision of top N.A. officials. Subsequently the administrative elite in Bornu, while it still reflected the importance of traditional factors along with objective qualification and ability, actually owed its position not to the Shehu but to *Waziri* Shettima Kashim.[34] Keeping in mind that the power of appointment or patronage is one of the most important sources of the power of traditional emirs, it is not surprising to find that in Bornu, ceremonial ritual, praise songs sung by the young N.A. officials (including one which is simply the repetition of the words "Waziri Kashim, Shettima Kashim") and in general, the symbolic expressions of allegiance usually reserved for emirs only, had become centered on Shettima Kashim. At the same time, Shettima Kashim's great influence in the "new spheres of regional party leadership (which in this case was not rivaled by the reigning monarch due to his physical inability to participate) considerably augmented the *Waziri*'s local power and prestige.

It is important, of course, that the traditional origin of the title and position of *Waziri* made the role of Shettima Kashim in this period comprehensible and acceptable to the people in traditional

---

[34] Apart from the Shehu and the Waziri, there were 13 members of the Bornu Native Authority Council in 1959, of whom five were councillors with administrative portfolios. The Councillor in charge of Local Government, Community Development, Works, Surveys and Wells was Zanna Mustafa Laisu (Zanna is a Bornu title), who is descended from the prominent family of the Zanna Luntima who was a loyal and trusted lieutenant of the first Shehu of Bornu, Laminu. The Treasurer, Kachella Bornu (Kachella is a traditional slave title in Bornu), who was a member of the Council at the age of 22, is a descendant of the family of the Kaigama, title of the Bornu slave general in charge of the army of the first Shehu. The Wali (legal advisor), Adam, is of the traditional family of the Imams of Bornu (Imam = priest). M. Othman Idrisa, Councillor in charge of Social Services is a commoner. The other administrative councillor was Zanna Bukar Dipcharima, the Federal Minister of Commerce and Industries (see his capsule biography in Appendix A). Another influential member of the council was M. Muhammed Lawan, who is the government's Provincial Agriculture officer for Bornu province. The average educational qualification of the above mentioned people is over Middle IV. The superintendent of Prisons, Shettima Kagu is also a councillor without portfolio. There is one purely traditional councillor, Abba Yusuf a ward head of Yerwa Town, who is a member of the House of Ibrahim Waidama, another venerated family of a lieutenant of Shehu Laminu. Two District Heads had been elected to the council by the Outer Council, and one a trader and contractor, Alhaji Mala Garba, was elected by the Yerwa Town Council. The Heads of Departments in Bornu boasts an average attainment of Middle IV, while all but two of them are of royal or titled families. Almost all of these officials were appointed after the events of 1956.

terms. Yet, in fact, the extent of power, responsibility, and respect he then enjoyed in practice was unique. In this instance, the form of tradition facilitated the substance of change.

QUALIFICATIONS VERSUS ROLE

ALONG WITH new functions, the other long-range trend tending to reinforce legal reform in the position of Northern emirs was the increasing selection of emirs whose personal backgrounds included Western education and administrative experience.

Availability of eligible Western-educated candidates was the product of seeds sown many years ago by the British colonial policy, which gave initial priority to the education of "natural rulers." Educational and administrative ability increasingly became part of the popular image of a "good' emir, although the majority of northern emirs remained relatively lacking on this score.

One important indication of the trend was the declining role of the purely traditional members of the Kingmakers' Council. Membership in the council is prescribed by tradition, and usually includes persons holding titles originally given to prominent slave officials, Malams, or revered advisors of the patriarch of first emir of the dynasty concerned, subject to the rule observed in every emirate that a kingmaker may not himself be eligible to be emir.

Many of the traditional kingmakers even today are without educational or administrative qualification, due in part to the tendency in the past for the more remunerative offices (the number of which greatly declined under the British) to be reserved for those with the closest ties to the incumbent monarch. Such kingmakers sometimes have found themselves enjoying less and less influence in choosing an emir. In practice, the king-making proceedings became increasingly dominated by kingmakers who had the requisite qualifications, or, as happened in some cases, the nonroyal administrative N.A. councillors in effect became the de facto council of electors. Alteration in the composition of the kingmakers group facilitated the selection of emirs with *ilmin turawa* (literally, "European knowledge") in preference, for example, to candidates with *ilmin arabiya* (religious knowledge) only.

In Adamawa emirate as early as 1946, the Council of Electors was prepared to take the radical step of departing from the hereditary line of succession altogether in favor of the *Waziri* at the time (now retired), who was distinguished in his educational credentials, experience, and integrity, but who by birth was ineligible for selection. The councillors had reviewed all the candidates belonging to the royal family, and concluded that they were too old, of unsound mind, dismissed and/or convicted ex-N.A. employees, lacking any experience in public affairs, or minors. Since the council members, as a result, had lost confidence in the ability of the royal family to provide a successful Lamido, they, with the approval of the majority of the district heads, offered the name of the *Waziri* to the Resident for transmission to the Governor. The proposal was an embarrassment to the British, who feared the reaction from other emirs to such a precedent would be calamitous. It is an ironic but significant comment on the nature of indirect rule that the proposal to name the *Waziri* was rejected despite the fact that he possessed more so than any of the hereditary candidates those qualities the British were trying to instill in "natural rulers". The 10th Lamido, Ahmadu, who unhappily confirmed the council's worst fears (his resignation in 1953 was discussed above), was chosen instead. To my knowledge, the Adamawa proposal was totally unprecedented, in that it came from a majority of all the responsible traditional officials—the British themselves can be said to have instigated deviations from the established line of royal succession in only three cases—all in the early days of establishing their authority.[35] The Adamawa succession crisis of 1946 was there-

[35] Katsina was the only emirate in which the Administration went entirely outside the dynasty to select a ruler. In the wake of the Satiru uprising against British rule in 1906, the British installed a new emir from a branch of the ruling family in Gwandu that had not previously furnished a ruler. That emir (Haliru, the 14th Emir of Gwandu) was a descendant of Abdullahi dan Fodio, first Gwandu Emir, but neither Haliru's father nor his grandfather had been Emir and his selection broke with traditional rules of succession in Gwandu. All subsequent Gwandu Emirs (including the incumbent) have been from the *Gidan* Haliru. In Bida the troops of the Royal Niger Company in 1897 deposed the recalcitrant Etsu Nupe, Abubakar (the fifth Fulani Emir of Bida), a member of the *Masaba*, one of the three Bida dynasties. The appointment of Muhammadu (sixth Fulani Etsu Nupe), which was confirmed by the administration in 1901, was in conformity with the principles of dynastic rotation in that Emirate; but the Masabas are said to harbor enmity to this day against the British for dispossessing their house and against the Umoru Magaji House for what Masabas say was a conspiracy with the British. The grounds for these departures from legitimacy in all three cases were irreconcilability with or disloyalty to British rule, rather than response to internal demands by councillors or others. All other depositions of emirs were followed by appointments that conformed to the broad rules of succession in the emirate concerned (except in Zaria, where M. G. Smith has shown that the British, over half a century of rule, inadvertently transformed the monarchy). The traditional order of rotation among the three dynasties of Bida was violated in 1962 with the appointment of M. Usman Sarki of Masaba out of turn. But this decision was an essentially internal one not associated with alienation or disapproval of the previous regime.

fore a striking early manifestation of the gradual development that tended to make objective achievement by Western standards an increasingly necessary if never sufficient condition of emirship.

Among rulers in the period 1953-1965 who were well qualified in terms of Western standards were the Emirs of Katsina, Abuja, Yauri, Gwandu, Dikwa, the Etsus Lapai and Bida and the Mai Bedde, all of whom, interestingly, were graduates of Katsina or Kaduna Colleges. It is probably no accident that they enjoyed reputations as progressive leaders in local and regional affairs.

In recent years the most famous of the "progressive" emirs was Alhaji Yayaha, the late Emir of Gwandu (1938-1954). *Sarkin Gwandu* Yahaya's reputation for *adalci* (righteousness) as a ruler is a modern legend in Hausaland. On gaining the throne, he set about to establish Gwandu emirate as a paradigm of good government. Paternalistic in his conception of his office, he is said to have made himself constantly accessible to the masses and to have ruthlessly exposed and punished official corruption. As a District Head, he discouraged the use of a retinue and toured his district on a motorcycle or drove his own car. During this time he decided to become monogamous, and gave up all his wives except one. (When Yahaya became Emir of Gwandu, he abolished the traditional title and function of the *Shantali*, or royal procurer, in Gwandu). The Emir's unusual religious piety seems to have been an important if politically disquieting source of his passion for social justice and reform.[36]

He applied this interest in reform with equal vigor to regional affairs. Long before Tafawa Balewa's historic motion in the House of Assembly, the Emir of Gwandu attacked the problem of the indebtedness of N.A. officials in his emirate which he thought to be the root of official corruption. He took the lead in urging on emirs

[36] About 1927, while he was the District Head of Kalgo, Yahaya was exposed to religious tracts published by the Sudan Interior Mission. His interest aroused, he went on to read the New Testament. Later he contemplated renouncing Islam for Christianity, thinking the latter religion embodied more fully the principles of social justice. Such a decision would have almost certainly disqualified him as a future ruler in Gwandu; for a Muslim, this would have been the supreme sin of apostasy. The prospect of such an important Muslim prince even voluntarily converting to Christianity caused the British Administration no little consternation. British officials encouraged him to enter the Katsina Training College where it was hoped exposure to Islamic texts and the influence of the religious *Malams* would lead him to reconsider the merits of Islam. Afterwards, apparently convinced that Islam also implied the code of ethics which attracted him to the Christian Gospel, Yahaya returned to Kalgu from Katsina having abandoned the idea of conversion, and was thereafter renowned as a devout Muslim.

the definition and prohibition of corrupt practices embodied in the Customary Presents Order of 1953. He is also thought to have been the decisive influence in persuading the emirs to accept the innovation of ministers in the North, although his advocacy did not imply abandonment of a paternalistic outlook.[37] The exemplary conduct of Alhaji Yahaya is said to have partly inspired several of the later group of young progressive emirs mentioned above. Such emirs, particularly the very youngest ones in this category, often found themselves in the curious position of being ahead of their councillors in the advocacy of modernization. Having been exposed to Western political and social ideals through education and to the advanced views of their associates in school and among the younger N.A. staff members, the young emirs apparently were in certain instances motivated to accept traditional office less for the glory (which was not in all cases commensurate with their abilities) than for the opportunity to exert influence on change.[38]

It sometimes happened in such cases that the very reform that tended to tie chiefs to the collective will of their councils had effects contrary to those intended. Thus, because councillors or other high N.A. officials themselves usually had a vested interest in the practice of patronage and self-interested use of public office, the "enlightened"

[37] "We know that there are Ministers of Local Government in both the Eastern and Western Regions but there is none in the North . . . in the first place we were too frightened when this proposal was first presented to us. . . . We did not oppose having a Minister of Local Government who would tour around and inspect the progress of various local administrations; what we opposed was that the Minister would be above the Chiefs. . . . We really do not like the North to be behind, what we do not like is to reduce the dignity and authority of the Chiefs, and that the Minister should be above them. That is our only objection". *House of Chiefs Debates*, February 14, 1953, pp. 78-79.

[38] A noted example is Mohammed Tukur, the present Emir of Yauri. Mohammed Tukur, born in 1923, was educated at Kaduna College (Middle VI) and afterwards received a scholarship for further study in the United Kingdom. From 1948 to 1951 he was a lecturer in Hausa at the School of Oriental and African Studies of the University of London. He returned to Nigeria in 1952, where he was appointed Clerk to the Nothern House of Chiefs. He had been appointed the first Nigerian Northern Commissioner in the United Kingdom when he received news of the death of his father, the late Emir of Yauri, and of his selection by the Yauri electors as the new Emir. He decided to give up the former appointment for the latter. Yauri is a small (pop. 72,000) and rather isolated emirate at the southernmost tip of Sokoto province. The Emir's salary of £1,100 is just over a third of what Mohammed Tukur would have received as Northern Commissioner (£3,000) in addition to the nonmonetary attractions and distinctions that go with being Northern Nigeria's principal representative abroad. Moreover, in deference to the sensibilities of his people, his wife has returned to *purdah* (seclusion) although she was with him in London where they could ignore the custom. Mohammed Tukur is widely known for his efforts toward "enlightened" rule in Yauri emirate since 1955.

emir was sometimes frustrated by the persistence of retrograde influences he could not escape. This situation was particularly apt to arise when emirs presided over councils of heavy traditional representation. That some lesser traditional title-holders should resist change, in opposition to the efforts of their "new emir", is understandable. They were more personally vulnerable to change. Even the most radical proposals regarding the future of emirs granted them security as ceremonial heads of local government units, while the talents of the young educated emirs would have alternative uses in politics, commercial enterprise, or the civil service. Lesser traditional figures who lacked these assets faced the prospect of total eclipse. This problem was illustrated by the experience of one Native Authority whose emir was not particularly noted for progressivism. The emir had, however, emerged as a supporter of the Resident's proposal to have an independent body appoint and control the N.A. staff, but his councillors were vehemently opposed and the suggestion was shelved.

Furthermore, the new emir remained subject to demands from his own family or lineage members, and the numerous dependents which custom dictates he inherit from his predecessor, who regarded their own protection and support as one of the emir's responsibilities. Such an emir always found it difficult wholly to disregard such claims no matter what his own convictions. He ruled within an institution and over a people who still evaluated his performance by traditional standards. Intrigue against his regime could be expected to befall an emir considered to be "mean"; especially was this a danger in the more fluid circumstances created by postwar reforms. Yet in attempting to protect or augment his authority by living up to such traditional expectations, even such an emir was unavoidably driven to practices that provided the necessary supplement to his statutory income, but which were incompatible with the objectives he had set out to achieve.[39]

Such a state of affairs reveals a dilemma that gradualism was ill designed for overcoming, namely that even the "successful" tutelage

[39] *The Daily Service* carried the folowing item about the new Emir of Ilorin appointed in 1959: "The Emir of Ilorin, Malam Sulu Gambari, has asked out of his palace the late Emir's servants because 'I have no room for idleness here'. In a circular letter sent to most of the servants, the Emir bitterly protested against idleness and warned those concerned to leave the palace and look for jobs elsewhere. He pointed out that the responsibility borne by the Emir [for] the servants was great, adding that as a modern Emir, 'I cannot tolerate it'. A spokesman [for] the servants later accused the Emir of violating the people's cherished custom by forcing out the servants from the palace". July 30, 1959, p. 1.

of the emir in the ways and values characteristic of a modern political system could be mitigated by other conditions that had not undergone change, or had done so to a lesser extent. Progressive emirship operated in and sometimes was powerless against the complex of related institutions of which emirship itself was only a part. Thus, although it is undeniable that a determined emir could do much to influence and encourage change, under prevailing conditions his freedom of action was limited. The irony that the development of conciliar rule should have in certain instances actually contributed to this limitation is another indication of the ambiguous results partial reform of well-entrenched institutions may have.

The Differential Impact of Change

It should be evident from the discussion thus far that the various forces working for change—legal reforms as well as longer range trends—did not have uniform effects on the position of all the emirs. A common legal framework for a large measure of conciliar control and certain supporting factors existed, but the actual response to the new legal circumstances varied widely. In each situation discussed above a complex interaction between forces of tradition and change produced an uncertain and indecisive result.

Thus far attention has been drawn to situations in which significant change was clearly manifested, albeit qualified or promoted by the forces of continuity, which, like change itself, may also be "dynamic". But some emirs seem to have experienced relatively little if any adverse change in their position as a result of political developments over the last two decades. Without attempting to deal exhaustively with every variable or trying to establish a universal relationship, factors which were positively correlated with a high degree of political continuity in the position of emirs may be singled out.

One salient factor was the composition of the Native Authority councils. In those councils in which there was a majority of elected members, the emir's position was clearly circumscribed. In most emirates, however, the majority of seats were not filled by elected members.[40]

While the importance of talent and education increased everywhere, the impact on the emir's position was not always disadvantageous. In some emirates a certain number of seats were traditionally reserved for members of prominent families. In these cases, membership in

[40] See Table 15.

the emir's council derived in part from hereditary prerogative. Although never completely independent of the need to enjoy the emir's support, such a hereditary councilor had enjoyed a certain security. Traditionally he represented the interests of his noble family; even if he displeased the emir he could only be replaced by another member of the same family. Insofar as appointments came to be governed by neither strict adherence to tradition nor by an independent body such as a local "public service commission", an emir's power of discretion often actually increased. Not surprisingly, some emirs took advantage of this "transitional" state of affairs to combine the criteria of "objective qualification" with loyalty to his person. The important point is that although emirs were required to work with a council, new principles of access to membership through the uncertain process of selection allowed the emir to continue to have a relatively docile and obedient group of councillors, whose position was informally subject to strictly traditional considerations.

The degree to which the previous power of the emirs survived was also partly a matter of religious sanctions. All of the Northern emirs are quasi-theocratic rulers, but, in fact, their importance as religious figures varies. One consideration here would seem to be the historic relation of the patriarch of the emirate concerned to the founder of the Fulani empire, Shehu dan Fodio, and to the religious war, or *jihad*, conducted by him. Thus no other emir enjoys quite the religious authority of the Sultan of Sokoto, the direct descendant of dan Fodio and inheritor of the traditional title of Sokoto Sultans—*Sarkin Mussulmai* ("King of the Muslims"). The Sultan is also the head of an important religious sect (the *Khadiriyya*). Similarly the Emir of Kano is a *mukkadim* ("high priest") of an Islamic sect which claims the allegiance of over half the Northern Muslims (the *Tijaniyya*). The Emirs of Gwandu are descendants of dan Fodio's brother, Abdullahi. The Emirs of Bauchi are descendants of a trusted pupil and disciple of dan Fodio, and so on.

The amount of judicial power enjoyed by an emir was extremely important. Again, most of the emirs presided over courts and dispensed justice. But not all of them had the same jurisdiction or powers, their relative legal responsibilities being designated by the grade of their court. These gradations corresponded to the gravity of the cases an emir might deal with and to the severity of the punishment which he had the power to mete out. It would be difficult to exaggerate the extent to which subjects were impressed by an emir who had the power to hand down a death sentence, compared with an Emir who could not. In short, judicial power was directly connected with political authority and power.

Finally, emirs were not all equal in their relationship to the regional government. Emirates differed in the degree to which effective control and supervision were exercised by the regional government and, conversely, in the amount of influence the Native Authority had vis-à-vis the government. We have seen that postwar legislation affecting emirs and Native Administrations (notably, the N.A. law of 1954) was largely permissive in form. The pace and extent of the reforms to be introduced was left to the discretion of the various Native Administrations. In practice, there was relatively little small emirates could do to resist pressure from the regional government. Large emirates, on the other hand, had certain advantages. The open hostility of their large populations could present serious difficulty for the administration of government policy; at the same time, the larger emirates were well represented in the legislature and cabinet which made the laws or were responsible for administering them. An emir who commanded a large bloc of seats in the Regional House was to be reckoned with, as the aftermath of the 1963 Kano episode revealed.

This brings us to the most important point about the differential impact of change. The factors that tended to maximize continuity, to protect and perpetuate the position of the emir as the most powerful figure in his kingdom, were not randomly or evenly distributed; on the contrary, they coalesced in the three largest of the Northern emirates.

Three emirs—the Sultan of Sokoto, the Emir of Kano, and the Shehu of Bornu—were important religious figures, enjoyed the greatest influence of all the emirs in regional government, and made the fewest concessions to "democratic" representation on their councils. They presided over Grade A Courts and over native administrations, of which they have remained the de facto as well as de jure head. And their degree of power under the parliamentary regime correlates well with their traditional ranking in historic Sokoto empire.[41] The internal position of some emirs, such as the Emir of Zaria, more nearly approximated that of the Big Three than of the other chiefs. But only these three could have been justified in saying of themselves between 1959 and 1963, as M. G. Smith remarks apropos

[41] The Order of Precedence in the Northern House of Chiefs, which is based (for the emirs) on the traditional imperial ranking, is as follows (I have deleted the nonemirate chiefs):

of the Emir of Zaria in 1950—"L'etat c'est moi".[42] After 1963 and the Kano case, they no doubt thought more modestly of themselves.

The preeminent position of these three emirs provides us with at least one contour of the whole landscape of continuity and change and helps to resolve the seemingly contradictory answers given in contemporary Northern Nigeria to the question of how much the position of the emirs had changed since World War II. In varying degrees the position of the majority of the emirs was altered by the developments of the last decade. For the Big Three emirs, the abolition of "Sole Native Authority" in law meant relatively little in reality. But of the total number of people who live in the Northern emirates, more than half live under the regimes of the three still very powerful emirs.

The Impact of the Regional Parliamentary System

ONE important reason why emirs as a group were able to resist pressures for change is that in many ways the course of postwar Nigerian constitutional development ran counter to the forces working for reduction of their power. In the Southern Regions the introduction of central parliamentary institutions led to the relative decline of traditional chiefs because popular, secular leaders aggressively assumed the power that fell on the new institutions of government. In the Northern Region, the sphere of influence of the emirs expanded in proportion to the scope of the new political units. The British government prescribed establishment of parliamentary institutions as the basis of Nigerian constitutional advance toward self-government. In the North, in the attempt to introduce the required changes without

		Emir of Misau
Sultan of Sokoto	Emir of Pategi	Emir of Hadeja
Shehu of Bornu	Emir of Yauri	Emir of Daura
Emir of Gwandu	Emir of Muri	Emir of Kazaure
Emir of Kano	Emir of Borgu	Emir of Gumel
Emir of Bauchi	Emir of Jema'are	Mai Bedde
Lamido of Adamawa	Mai Fika	Emir of Keffi
Emir of Katsina	Mai Biu	Emir of Nassarawa
Emir of Zaria	Emir of Ilorin	Emir of Jema'a
Emir of Bida	Emir of Kontagora	Emir of Lafia
Emir of Agaie	Emir of Dikwa	Emir of Abuja
Emir of Lapai	Emir of Argungu	Emir of Wase

Source, *House of Chiefs Debates*, Vol. 4, No. 1, 20 March 1957, p. vii. Cf. Hogken and Kirk-Greene, *Emirates of Northern Nigeria*, Appendix B.

[42] *Government in Zazzau*, p. 245.

dislodging traditional authority, British officials made every effort to closely associate the emirs with constitutional developments as they affected the North.

The initial reaction of the emirs was cautious and suspicious. The prospect of being subject to central Nigerian representative institutions was particularly odious. This had been foreseen by the wartime Governor of Nigeria and other British officials. Their solution was therefore to encourage the emirs to take a more aggressive view of the question of constitutional development and of their possible role under the new parliamentary institutions. The keynote of this approach was sounded by Governor Bourdillon: "To put it quite simply, has the time not come when we must persuade the Emirs, for their own good and that of their people, to say, not 'We will not tolerate Southerners advising the Governor in our affairs', but 'We insist that we and our people should have an equal right with the South to advise the Governor in Nigerian affairs?' "[43] The emirs were equally apprehensive about the implications of superimposing democratic institutions on the emirates, whether at the Nigerian or Northern Nigerian levels. Politically it was expedient to keep them from feeling alienated. Accordingly emirs were assured that constitutional changes did not mean they would be supplanted within their own domains by politicians. The first Northern Nigerian to be consulted by Sir Arthur Richards, the Governor whose name was given to the first postwar constitution, was the Sultan of Sokoto.[44]

The emirs were subsequently heavily represented in the series of local conferences held in connection with the second postwar constitution (the "Macpherson Constitution"); among Northern Nigerian representatives they sometimes occupied a dominant position.[45] At the Ibadan Conference of 1950, the Emir of Zaria emerged as a major spokesman for the North, demanding that the North be given 50% of the seats in the Nigerian legislature. Later, the Sultan of Sokoto helped organize the famous *Kudin Taimakon Arewa* ("money to help the North"), a collection that was to be used to continue the fight if the demand of 50% representation was not met. As parliamentary institutions and political parties emerged, the emirs retired to a less

[43] *A Further Memorandum on the Future Political Development of Nigeria* (Lagos, 1942), Part II, "The Northern Provinces", p. 1.
[44] Kalu Ezera, *Constitutional Developments in Nigeria* (Cambridge, Eng., 1960), p. 66.
[45] See *Review of the Constitution, Regional Recommendations* (Lagos, 1949), pp. 9-10.

conspicuous role in constitutional negotiations, but at every major juncture in constitutional development thereafter, in 1955, 1956, 1957, and 1958, meetings of the Northern Chiefs, usually presided over by the Sultan of Sokoto, were summoned to discuss and approve the next step in constitutional advance. These meetings, which sometimes took place apart from the regular meetings of the House of Chiefs[46] and were not publicized, gave the emirs an opportunity to express misgivings out of the public eye. The British officials in the North, in response, pursued a policy of saving the chiefs from a "constitutional revolution" right up until self-government. The culmination of the effort came in the extremely favorable position for the chiefs that was written into the constitution prior to the transfer of power to the regional government.

British policy in this respect was in accord with the view of the leaders of the majority NPC party who represented Northern Nigerians in constitutional negotiations leading to self-government. The reasons for this are discussed more fully in subsequent chapters, but they may be summarized as follows: the NPC was itself dominated by elements sympathetic to the emirs; the party largely relied on Native Administrations for organization and campaigns; and the support and cooperation of the emirs was considered necessary to the unity and strength of the North vis-à-vis the southern regions. Indeed, the NPC was scarcely less solicitous of the emirs' views on constitutional matters than it was of the British. Prior to the 1957 London Conference, at which the Northern Delegates announced their intention to accept regional self-government in 1959, the NPC Committee on Constitutional Revision met with a subcommittee of the emirs. The emphasis of the meeting was on reassuring the emirs that constitutional arrangements designed to protect their status would be upheld by the NPC. A minute of the NPC Executive Subcommittee on Self-Government held in Kaduna in the spring of 1956 states:

> Some members expressed doubts [about] what will be the position of Chiefs when a Party that has no sympathy for them comes into power, what will become of them when we become self-governing?
> It was resolved that the politicians have no power to commit the future generations; every Party in power can do what it likes once

[46] The composition of the House of Chiefs under the constitution in effect in 1965 was: (1) all First Class Chiefs ex-officio, (2) 95 other chiefs selected in accordance with rules determined by the legislature, (3) an advisor on Muslim law.

it wins the support of the majority. Nothing better can be put in the Constitutional Instrument other than the provision of the House of Chiefs and their share in the Executive Council. It is our hope to maintain this position as long as our party exists.[47]

Apart from questions affecting their status, the emirs were vitally interested in other substantive issues of constitutional deliberations. The direct influence of some of the more powerful Northern emirs on the shaping of the Nigerian constitution is a significant but little appreciated aspect of postwar Nigerian politics.[48]

The results of the policy of combining traditional and popular authority in the constitution were to be seen in the extraordinary position of power which chiefs in Northern Nigeria occupied under it. The Nigerian constitution gave the Northern House of Chiefs equal legislative powers, including power over financial appropriations, with the democratically elected House of Assembly. Technically, although

[47] Undated mimeo. copy of the author. Probably such assurances encouraged some emirs in viewing the achievement of self-government (not unreasonably) in terms of a reassertion of the traditional structure of authority—e.g. the speech of the Emir of Zaria (Ja'afaru) on the Northern Region self-government motion: "Mr. President, Sir, I rise to thank the Almighty God who has made it possible for me to live to see this day. I am one of the few old people in whose time the administration of this country was taken over and we have lived to see the day when it has been returned to us. It is not a surprise that this power which has been taken away from our leaders, the descendants of Shehu Dan Fodio, is being returned to them. (Applause) Therefore, we are sure that they will hold the power as it has been held by their ancestors, with honesty". *House of Chiefs Debates*, August 12, 1958, p. 86.

The Sultan of Sokoto, addressing a distinguished gathering of government and Native Authority officials who journeyed to Sokoto for the occasion following the formal surrender of regional powers in Kaduna, stated: "We celebrate today, Sunday, March 15, the fifty-sixth anniversary of the day the control of this country passed into the hands of the Europeans. It was here at the foot of the palm tree that the great events took place and here on this very spot we celebrate the return of power to the hands of the people of the Northern Region of Nigeria. Let us pray that God may return to us in full measure that which in His infinite wisdom He took from us". Northern Region Daily Press Service Release No. 647, March 17, 1959.

[48] During the meeting of the Northern House of Chiefs following the (Resumed) London Conference of 1958, the Premier revealed something of this influence by recounting this incidence of the Conference: "One day when I rose early in the morning, I found in my room a cable from Nigeria, and as soon as I opened this cable, I found it contained some unpalatable words from a brother of mine. Whom do you think it was? The Sarkin Mussulmi [The Sultan of Sokoto]! The words in this cable were— 'Sardauna, you have left the North united and you should not let an inch go from the North'. Although it is not customary for people to sweat in London, I did at that time. This encouraged me and all the Northern Delegates when I distributed copies of the cable to them. On that day the belt broke and Kabba and Ilorin remained in the North". *House of Chiefs Debates*, December 18, 1958, p. 128.

no conflict ever arose, the constitution placed the "Lords" over the "Commons", in that the last word formally rested with the Chiefs.[49]

The constitution further stipulated that at least two chiefs must be represented in the regional cabinet (styled Executive Council).[50] By virtue of this provision, no less than four were at any time cabinet members, invariably as ministers "without portfolio".[51] When these powers are combined with the prescribed procedure for amending the constitution,[52] the formidable position Northern Chiefs occupied in that document can be fully appreciated.

In effect, the constitution provided chiefs with the collective power of veto over all matters within the competence of the regional government, not the least of which was the power to pass laws affecting the status and powers of chiefs. Moreover, the position of the emir ministers was bolstered considerably by the fact that they could make policy and speak for themselves at the highest level of government. Thus entrenched in the constitution, these emirs were especially well protected against any proposals that might have worked against

[49] This can be inferred from the following constitutional provision. Section 28 of the constitution provides that in the event of a legislative impasse between the two Houses, the bill in question becomes subject to a special procedure. This special procedure, also laid down in Section 68, provides that the President of the House of Chiefs, or, in his absence, the Deputy Speaker (both of whom are emirs) shall preside over a joint sitting consisting of 20 delegates from each of the two legislative Houses (Chiefs and Assembly), which shall consider the bill. Paragraph (e) of subsection (5) of Section 28 states:

> Any question proposed for decision at the joint sitting shall be determined by a simple majority of the delegates present and voting; and the person presiding shall cast a vote whenever necessary to avoid an equality of votes, but shall not vote in any other case. . . ."

The Constitution of Northern Nigeria Law, 1963 (Kaduna), p. 15. Cf. John D. Chick, "The Structure of Government at the Regional Level", in L. Franklin Blitz, ed., *The Politics and Administration of the Nigerian Government* (London, 1965), p. 91.

[50] *Ibid.*, Section 34, subsection (4), p. 17.

[51] The "without portfolio" status was a practical arrangement and did not necessarily imply a subordinate position in the Executive Council as far as the emirs were concerned. The Sokoto Provincial Conference (on Constitutional proposals) recommended this arrangement "because the meeting, headed by the Emirs themselves, felt that it would be impossible for Chiefs to supervise a Department in Kaduna as well as rule an Emirate in the Provinces". *Report of the Resident,* Sokoto Provincial Conference on Review of the Constitution, August 3-4, 1949, p. 2 note.

[52] The "establishment of the Legislative Houses" is an "entrenched" provision of the Nigerian constitution. Entrenched provisions can only be amended by "a two-thirds majority of all the members of each House of the Legislature of the Region concerned, with the concurrence of all members of each House of the Federal Legislature". See *Report by the Resumed Nigeria Constitutional Conference*, held in London in September and October 1958 (H.M. Stationery Office), Cmnd. #569, 1958, p. 29, paragraph 62, for the background to this provision.

them. At the same time, their strategic position in regional affairs affirmed the impression commonly held in the emirates that the "new democratic" institutions at Kaduna were an extension of the authority of emirs, not their retrenchment.

THE COUNCIL OF CHIEFS

IN APRIL 1958 a constitutional amendment set up a new body to regulate Northern chieftaincy affairs. Formerly chieftaincy matters had been the responsibility of the Governor alone, acting at his discretion. The new body was called the Northern Council of Chiefs. In 1959 the Governor was designated chairman, but soon thereafter he relinquished this role, first to the Sultan of Sokoto and later to the premier. Use of the word "consult" instead of "recommend" in the wording of the amendment made it clear that the formal status of the Council of Chiefs was to be technically advisory.[53] In practice the council, its permanent membership consisting as it did of the premier and the three most important emirs, wielded considerable influence over matters affecting chiefs.[54]

One observation about the amendment is that the setting up of this body and the assignment to it of the exclusive power to discuss chieftaincy affairs precluded the airing of these matters in the Northern House of Assembly. It is difficult to avoid the conclusion that this was a deliberate device designed to minimize public criticism of chiefs by elected representatives. Moreover, in continuing the arrangement whereby the grading, discipline, and appointment of chiefs were matters not within the competence of any ministry, the

[53] *The Constitution of Northern Nigeria Law,* Section 75, subsection (3), p. 32. The relevant provision is as follows:

> The Governor shall act in accordance with the advice of the Council of Chiefs of the Region in the exercise of all powers conferred upon him with respect to—
> (a) the appointment, approval of the appointment or recognition of a person as a chief
> (b) the grading of a chief
> (c) the deposition of a chief
> (d) the removal of a chief or a person who was formerly a chief from any part of the Region; or
> (e) the exclusion of a chief or any person who was formerly a chief from any part of the Region.

[54] *Ibid.,* Section 75, subsection (1), p. 32:

> There shall be a Council of Chiefs for the Region, which shall consist of—
> (a) the Premier, who shall be chairman
> (b) those Ministers of the Government of the Region who have been appointed as such from among the members of the House of Chiefs
> (c) the persons for the time being co-opted as members of the Council in accordance with subsection (2) of this section.

amendment would seem to have short-circuited the assumption of these powers by the Executive Council as well. The premier's responsibility for chieftaincy affairs was thus exercised outside the Executive Council. Apart from him and the Governor, only chiefs could discuss authoritatively questions concerning chiefs, and the Governor was constitutionally bound to act in accordance with the advice of the premier.

EMIRS IN POLITICS: THE MYTH OF NEUTRALITY

WHETHER emirs should "participate in politics", that is, in the politics centering on the new institutions of parties and popular elections, formed one of the most controversial and illuminating issues regarding the position of emirs under the parliamentary regime.

During the first decade of this regime, British officials repeatedly urged emirs to remain aloof from politics for the sake of upholding the image and ideal of an emir as "the father of all his people". The appeal was coupled with a practical argument that to do otherwise would be to risk loss of popular respect and perhaps even retaliation at the hands of a rival party that might some day control the regional government. Initially at least, this argument was adopted by Northerners who apparently envisaged a future for the emirs corresponding to the present constitutional position of the British monarch. Political neutrality on the part of emirs, in any case, was the official government policy. This policy dictated that they should not publicly exhibit any preference for political parties, should refrain from using their considerable judicial and executive powers to persuade, coerce, or reward individuals in voting.[55] Neither were they to interfere in the internal affairs of political parties.

The actual behavior of the emirs belied official policy. The 1959 crisis in Argungu recounted above is one example. In general, the extent of partisanship on the part of the emirs merely varied from the overt to the thinly covert, from the case of the late Emir of Bida who openly canvassed his Districts on behalf of an NPC candidate

---

[55] It is difficult to reconcile political partisanship with the official Oath of Office for Chiefs in use in 1959: "I ——— do swear that I will well and truly serve Her Majesty Queen Elizabeth the Second and her representative His Excellency the Governor (General) of Nigeria, that I will obey the laws of the Federation of Nigeria and the lawful commands of His Excellency the Governor, provided that they are not contrary to my religion, and that if they are so contrary, I will at once inform the Resident; *that I will rule my people with justice and impartiality, and that I will do my duty without fear or favour, affection or ill will.* So help me God". Emphasis added.

in the federal election of 1959 to the more numerous examples of emirs who always maintained a formal posture of neutrality while making their influence felt behind the scenes through subordinates. The general factors that worked against the policy of neutrality were several.

(1) The constitution accorded equal powers to the House of Chiefs and allotted to the Chiefs seats in the cabinet. The cabinet, or Executive Council, was controlled by a political party, and in conformity with British practice operated under the rule of collective responsibility.[56] Chiefs in the cabinet were therefore bound to support the party controlling the government and were necessarily identified with it. The government party could hardly have selected chiefs as cabinet members other than those who were sympathetic and loyal without jeopardizing its base of support. Furthermore, only with the approval of the House of Chiefs were party programs translated into law.

(2) The local judicial and administrative powers of the emirs were far in excess of any enjoyed by a modern British monarch.

(3) Emirs who were not prepared to be relegated to a symbolic or ceremonial role naturally made alliances with political parties which upheld their established powers and opposed those which did not, with the means at their disposal. Considering that the government deliberately identified itself with traditional authority, while the ideology of the opposition parties embraced the principles of democratic radicalism, it seems idle to have expected that emirs would be indifferent to the fortunes of the political parties. Thus the Emir of Pategi's remarks during the debate on the motion for Northern self-government expressed the feelings of most of his colleagues: "Mr. President, Sir, administrative officers have warned us chiefs in the past that we should not indulge in political activities as we are the fathers of all the political parties in this Region. But in my own view, if all the children of this Region belong to you how can you support one who is disloyal and brings confusion to the whole community? It is also important to love whoever loves you and also support he who stands for honesty and justice, and oppose those who have been behaving themselves irresponsibly".[57]

[56] *Official Manual of Executive Council Procedure*, Chap. 1, p. 1: "All members of a cabinet are collectively responsible for policy decided in the Council . . . if any Minister feels conscientiously unable to support a decision taken by the Council, he has one course open to him and that is to resign his office".
[57] *House of Chiefs Debates*, August 12, 1958, p. 88. Specific public pronounce-

(4) The steadily dwindling prospects of NEPU's coming to power either regionally or at the level of the central N.A. Councils after 1957 meant that the risks of retaliation at the hands of a victorious opposition party were increasingly remote, compared to the immediate benefits to be gained from supporting the party in power.

(5) As the political struggle in Ilorin also suggested, the notion of a loyal opposition was totally alien to the traditional rulers of the emirates. The crucial political issue was the fundamental one of the nature and basis of authority. Parties which in effect declared their intention to transform authority from a traditional to a secular and democratic base were regarded by the emirs not as legitimate opponents but as heretical and subversive elements. Until very recently, the British Colonial Authority had taken a similar view.[58]

---

ments by the parties on their future intentions regarding the position of chiefs were infrequent and cautious. The 1959 Election Manifestos of both the NPC and the NEPU are silent on the issue. However, the 1956 election eve broadcast by the Sardauna stated for the NPC: "We believe in the institution of Chiefs and as long as we are in power we shall ensure that the Chiefs will have representation in the Regional Executive Council and that the House of Chiefs will continue to be a part of our legislature. We believe that the Emirs and Chiefs of Northern Nigeria can easily adapt themselves to modern democratic local practices. We are pleased with the way in which Chiefs are accepting the changing conditions in Nigeria". Aminu Kano's statement for the NEPU was: "We shall recognize the chiefs as agents for local government and their position shall be safe-guarded by law. We shall guarantee their dignity and respect outside politics". The main difference between these statements seems to be that NEPU opposed the present *regional* role of the chiefs while NPC pledged itself to preserve it. The difference regarding their intentions in the field of local government was less clear. When queried in 1959, officials of both parties repeatedly claimed that their policy in local government was to reduce the powers of the emirs and democratize their councils, leaving them in the position of "constitutional" rulers with largely ceremonial functions. For NPC this was, at best, a long-range goal to be realized gradually. NEPU stated that it would carry out its program immediately if it came to power. The crux of the issue would therefore seem to have been (a) the timing of reform in local government and (b) the place of the chiefs in regional government. It will be noted, of course, that there was a contradiction between the two parts of the NPC policy, in that so long as chiefs retained power in the region it would have been impossible to introduce fundamental changes in local government. In any case, NPC was not anxious to divorce itself from the emirs, while NEPU was regarded by the emirs as the *bête noire* of traditional authority.

[58] NEPU, for instance, was regarded as subversive first on account of its anti-colonial nationalism, and second because British authority, under indirect rule, was inextricably bound up with that of the emirs. Activities of nationalist parties were scrutinized in official reports under the heading of "subversive activities", while, without naming names, chiefs were officially warned of a conspiracy against their rule. See, for example, the speech of the Governor to the Northern House of Chiefs in 1954: "For some time now the Regional Government has had ample evidence of the ill effects of the abuse of liberties by groups of irresponsible persons, who, claiming to reform, try to impose their will on or undermine lawfully

(6) The policy of neutrality presupposed a lack of relationship between political issues and power in the "modern" or "democratic" sector and political issues and power in the "traditional" realm, which was obviously not the case. For example, as we shall see later, modern party competition and elections in the emirates sometimes turn on traditional issues (such as succession questions and dynastic rivalry) which were of immediate and intimate concern to any emir. To the extent that there was interplay between traditional and modern forces and conditions, emirs were inescapably "in politics".

(7) Finally, there was the reality of the government party's organizational reliance on and leadership integration with Native Authorities. This also precluded any real detachment of emirs from politics. The public tacitly assumed that locally the NPC acted with the blessings of the emir and seldom was an emir known to declare otherwise. In regard to interparty politics, an emir's authority was on more than one occasion deliberately used by the NPC to help resolve nomination disputes that threatened party unity, or to help select the "right" candidates. British conduct on this score was similarly inconsistent.[59]

In sum, the policy of neutrality was beset with contradictions. Emirs' de jure and de facto position in the constitution, regional government, and local government, their actual involvement with the mechanics and controversies of political party competition, and their

constituted authority. Please be assured that the Regional Government is fully alive to these developments. We have the matter in hand and we are adopting for our part measures to counter such activities whatever their source or inspiration and to prevent them from spreading". Quoted in *Nigerian Citizen*, March 4, 1954, p. 5. On the other hand, it is to the credit of the Administration that the proposal of an official in 1953 to suppress NEPU by outlawing it was rejected on the grounds of democratic liberties.

[59] Prior to the federal elections of 1954 the Governor of Northern Nigeria wrote to the Emir of Katsina:

> The second problem which will arise in connection with the selection of the new House of Representatives will be to ensure that the suitable representatives are fitted to the different constituencies. There is no knowing how many candidates may offer themselves in each constituency but presumably every one of them will have to find a proposer and seconder in the final electoral college of his constituency.
>
> You know better than I do the qualities required of members of the House of Representatives, and it will not be difficult to find suitable persons from Katsina. I hope it will be possible for at least one older man to get elected who has had previous experience either in the present house or in the Richards Legislative Council. Such a man is invaluable for advising the other members and giving them a lead, even if he does not make spectacular speeches in public.

Letter from the Governor of Northern Nigeria to the Emir of Katsina, April 26, 1954.

traditional reflexes as wielders of power and authority were all arrayed against neutrality. The emirs consequently found themselves constrained to give lip service to a standard which in fact was glaringly inconsistent with the role assigned to them. They also found themselves receiving divided counsel. For example, the regional government's instructions to administrative officers in January 1959, prior to the federal elections, were that chiefs should be persuaded to eschew indicating preference between the parties. In September, however, a government party official and minister challenged the opposition to cite any Nigerian law that forbade chiefs to participate in politics.[60] Other statements quoted in the Nigerian press similarly cast doubt on the extent to which local branches of the government party in particular understood or accepted the idea that chiefs should be neutral.[61]

That the institution of emirship was incapable of absorbing the norm of neutrality in relation to the politics of new institutions would seem to be another manifestation of the problem of partial or piecemeal strategies of change. In this case, government policy singled out one particular trait, or norm, associated with modern constitutional monarchy and exhorted emirs to emulate it, without taking into account the absence of conditions that were logically as well as historically antecedent to that trait or norm: (a) the monarch is symbolic of the authority of the state per se and not identified with a particular regime; (b) the authority of the monarch is derivative of and dependent on representative processes, or, in other words, that the monarch lacks sources of power independent of those processes; (c) the integrity of the monarchy is not a live issue in political competition; (d) rival political parties find the adherence of the monarch to neutrality mutually advantageous and acceptable. In this light, it is clear that political neutrality on the part of the Northern emir was pure myth.

ONE significant point which this discussion demonstrates was the inseparability of local and regional government and politics, for the position of emirs was affected by developments at both levels. Develop-

---

[60] See *Daily Service*, September 16, 1959, p. 13; *Nigerian Citizen*, May 21, 1963.
[61] E.g. "In a statement in Kano the NPC denied that chiefs and emirs supported the party. It added that they only supported what they felt were in the best interests of the people. On the other hand, the NPC said that the natural rulers for their own interests and that of their people should support the party that guided its continuity and existence in the North". *Daily Times*, September 15, 1959, p. 6.

ments at one level sometimes reinforced and at other times limited developments at the other.

The discussion also indicates that there was a significant decline in autocracy in the emirates without the occurrence of democratization or constitutionalization of the emir's position. Conciliar control of emirs was achieved in most emirates, but the structure of that control was oligarchic, not democratic. Usually this control was exercised over emirs in the name of values associated with modern democratic local government, but actually the motives were almost always mixed with considerations that were traditional in origin or which simply represented a personal bid for a greater share of political power. Those who exercised this control owed their enhanced positions mostly to a process of administrative cooptation rather than to representational or electoral processes. "Modernizing oligarchies", some of these central councils might in one sense be called, but they were oligarchies nonetheless.

Finally, a set of observations prompted by the materials of this chapter concerns the evident complexity of the interplay between forces of change and continuity, for the consequences and sources of conditions which affected the institutions of emirship were intricate indeed:

Significant changes in form (e.g. the abolition of "Sole Native Authorities") did not necessarily result in significant substantive change (as suggested by the cases of those emirs whose relationship to their councils continued substantially as it was before abolition).

Significant changes in substance (e.g. instances in which illiterate traditional kingmakers without administrative responsibilities in practice lost a voice in choosing the emir) were sometimes accomplished without changes of form (i.e. the emir continued to be chosen by the traditional council of electors).

"Tradition" sometimes facilitated resistance to change (e.g. the uneasy position of the educated and progressive emirs, or the role of the Magajin Gari of Kazaure).

"Tradition" sometimes acted to promote change (e.g. the ascendancy of the Waziri of Bornu, the deposition of the Emirs of Kaiama and Dikwa).

Power derived from "tradition" was sometimes used to facilitate change (e.g. the role of the Emir of Gwandu, Yahaya); conversely, power derived from "democracy" was sometimes used to perpetuate "tradition" (e.g. the NPC policy regarding the position of emirs).

Sometimes the short-range result of a long-range trend toward change (e.g. modification of the basis of recruitment to Native Authority councils from purely traditional criteria toward secular, modern criteria) was actually retrograde (i.e. new recruitment criteria gave some emirs more personal discretion in choosing councillors and other top officials and in this way strengthened his hand vis-à-vis rival factions).

Admittedly the complexity of interaction between forces of modernity and tradition are apt to be greatest where a duality of institutions exists, but probably the process of introducing social and political innovations into an established order is nowhere completely without similar complications and nuances.

Dynamics of Regional Politics

CHAPTER 7

An Anatomy of Parliamentary Leadership

THE FOCUS in the remaining chapters is on the regional political institutions that were introduced into Northern Nigeria in 1946. These institutions were modeled on the modern British system of parliamentary government. As in previous chapters, the context of Part Three is political change and continuity in that region as it existed up to the end of 1965, when civilian parliamentary government was overthrown. Part Three attempts to assess the extent to which these new regional institutions occasioned change in and/or fostered the maintenance of preexisting political patterns in the emirates. The assessment will take us further toward some general conclusions regarding the confrontation between modernity and tradition in Northern Nigeria.

A pertinent matter for study here is the characteristics and bases of regional political leadership as exemplified in the social backgrounds, relationships, attitudes and interests of the members of the lower house of the Northern parliament, officially called the Northern House of Assembly. As I observed in the introduction, students of the modernization process have thought one of the crucial differences between modern and traditional societies is the nature of political leadership. Indeed, change in the composition of political leadership has been assumed to be an important source as well as a result of fundamental or systematic political change. This assumption seems partly to rest on the expectation that because modern political institutions emphasize functions and skills unknown to or less important in traditional institutions, those outside any traditional group of political leaders will be better prepared to exercise or more willing to acquire them than those within. The new political figure pushed forward by this situation can be expected, so this line of reasoning goes, to use his position in ways that both sustain the new institution and promote the qualities (Western education, professional competence, etc.) to which he ultimately owes that position. He thus helps to spread throughout his society a process of modernization initially set in motion by an institutional innovation.

But what if persons drawn from segments of society which traditionally occupy positions of political leadership also assume modern positions of leadership, either by acquiring the appropriate functions and skills or despite them? At best, the process of change may lack a source of momentum. More seriously, might not the conduct of such leaders in new positions tend to reemphasize the traditional qualities and institutions to which they are accustomed and from which their prestige and influence at least partly derive, and in doing so limit the scope of modernization and imbue modern institutions with traditional values generally?

The following detailed examination of the backgrounds of members of the Northern House of Assembly elected from the area of the Northern emirates between 1956 and 1965 will show that they were drawn overwhelmingly from the political elite segment of traditional emirate society. Here and in the chapters to follow an attempt will be made to isolate sources and ramifications of this continuity of leadership and to show that the broad implications of this phenomenon were exactly as suggested in the last paragraph. The discussion must begin with a brief reiteration of the features of political leadership in traditional society.

THE THREE MOST salient features of traditional leadership in the emirates are stratification, hereditary legitimacy, and personalism. The traditional society of every emirate is divided into a ruling class (*sarakuna*) and a commoner class (*talakawa*). Membership in either is usually fixed at birth. The classification of individuals in these terms is complicated by the existence of the new regional and national positions of governmental authority which were not formally restricted to members of the traditional *sarakuna* class and which *talakawa* sometimes occupied. Yet Northern Nigerians who hail from the emirates continued with confidence and wide agreement to classify individuals into one or the other classes, based not on the individual's role in relation to modern institutions, but on his standing—or more frequently, on his father's standing—in the political hierarchy of the emirate of his origin. Thus sometimes high officials in the new regional or national institutions were given a general Hausa appellation—*manya-manya* ("important persons"; formerly this was virtually a synonym for *sarakuna*), yet they were still denoted as *talakawa*. Furthermore, in the eyes of the emirate peoples the individual's traditional status vis-à-vis the political hierarchy of his emirate continued to be the most important factor determining his social placement, even in the broader contexts of contemporary Northern Nigerian and Nigerian society.

Table 23: The Structure of Traditional Stratification

Sarakuna (rulers)

> reigning emirs
> sons of reigning emirs
> sons of former and late emirs
> grandsons of reigning, former, or late emirs
> other members of royal dynasties
> emir's councillors
> hereditary district head
> client district heads
> royal slave officials
> free courtiers (*fadawa*)
> village heads
> other employees of native administration

*Koranic malamai (teachers), imami (Islamic "priests"),
alkali (judges)*

Talakawa (commoners)

> wealthy merchant-traders (*attajirai*)
> lesser traders and contractors
> small traders
> farmers
> weavers
> blacksmiths
> mat-makers
> woodworkers
> dyers
> barber-doctors
> house servants
> musicians
> butchers

Quite elaborate and complex principles of stratification operate among, as well as between, the *sarakuna* and *talakawa* classes. In Table 23 an approximate social ranking of various major categories of emirate society is given. It will be noted that the ranking is based on a combination of factors—hereditary status, occupation, tenure of various kinds of political office, personal connection. This table, derived from inquiries in 12 selected emirates, roughly corresponds to the ranking previously recorded by M. G. Smith for the Zaria emirate.[1] This ranking is necessarily only approximate, because a combination of factors may offset the social rank-order an individual would occupy according to one factor alone. Thus a royal slave descendant who holds high office might be placed above a member of a royal

[1] *Economy of Hausa Communities of Zaria*, pp. 83-108.

dynasty who lacks any office, although their positions would be reversed were neither of them officials. An employee in the lower echelons of the Native Administration (*mai'akitan ene e*) might be regarded as *sarakuna* or *talakawa*, depending on the status of his father or his own personal connection (or lack thereof) with an emir.
Malams, Imams, and *Alkali* actually represent an intermediate
group, being seldom simply classified as *sarakuna* or *talakawa*. For a
member of a royal dynasty to be a merchant-trader was unheard of in
the past, but in my investigations the combination was sometimes encountered. Table 23 also ignores, as a subsequent statement by Smith
points out, "those distinctions between old and young, *Karda* and
shigege (hereditary as against acquired occupation), slave-born and
free, rural and urban, rich and poor, which do not escape attention in
Hausa society".[2] Yet, "other things being equal", the order of categories indicated in this table provides a guide to social stratification in the emirates, and it will be useful for the discussion below.

In every emirate eligibility for the highest office of state—emirship
—is confined to descendants of an emir whose mantle was attained
in more or less ancient times (usually but not invariably the first
emir inaugurated after the *jihad*). The hereditary principle also de-
termines access to the bulk of the other high offices of state, including those reserved for heirs of ancient free-born holders of certain offices and titles (nobles) and for descendants of titled slaves,
respectively.

Personalism traditionally pervaded all relationships among members of the ruling class hierarchy, as well as relationships between such
members and *talakawa*. The allegiance of persons to superiors in this
hierarchy is secured through and expressed in the receipt of patronage
ranging from gifts, the award of office and title, to full economic support and the privilege of marriage with the patron's female relatives.
Beneficiaries of such favors in return owe loyalty, in the form of gifts,
loans, and services such as information about matters affecting his
patron's interests.

This element of personalism is intimately bound up with the phenomenon of rival solidarity groups within the ruling class (invariably
encountered in every emirate), which form around the branching
lines of descent within the royal dynasty or around the existence of
multiple dynasties. For it is above all the prospect of benefit from a
patron's good fortune and of neglect or discrimination at the hands

[2] "Hausa System of Social Status", *Africa*, Vol. 29, No. 3, July 1959, p. 314.

of his rivals that generates these solidarities. But personalism also creates the element of interclass mobility present in the traditional structure of society. For through giving personal loyalty and service to a patron official, a *talaka* might acquire political office and title and hence membership in the *sarakuna* class, a social elevation which might be acknowledged in and further strengthened by marriage into an aristocratic family.

It is significant that these patterns reflect the principles or norms which students of the modernization process have stated as the essence of traditionalism. Loyalty to official superiors rather than an impersonal standard of official performance is one such principle. An aspect of this personalism is related to another such supposedly distinguishing principle—that the duties and obligations involved in the traditional relationships, on the one hand, and the rewards and benefits, on the other, are not precisely defined; they are characterized by diffuseness (uncertainty) of function and reward.

The concepts of ascription and achievement which scholars have frequently used to express differences in the modes of leadership recruitment in traditional and modern societies, also calls attention to the character of political leadership in an emirate. In an emirate the ascriptive nature of political leadership recruitment—that is, the predominant importance attached to "who a man is" as against "what a man can do"[3]—derives ultimately from the practice of restricting access to the highest office of state (to which all other state offices are subordinate and accountable) to a certain family or families. Yet it is also important to note that political recruitment patterns in the emirates traditionally were not wholly ascriptive, as is evidenced in the channels of interclass mobility. The substance of the "skills" and "talents" relevant to premodern society differed from that associated with those terms in the context of modern industrialized societies, but it would be a mistake to believe that a traditional emir was formerly oblivious to those qualities as such. Traditional recruitment criteria were never restrictive to the point of inflexibility.

The Social Anatomy of the Northern Parliamentarians

Appendix A contains detailed biographical sketches of all members of the Northern House of Assembly, from 1956-61 and 1961-65, elected from constituencies which lie within the emirates, including the Northern Regional Ministers, plus those of the ministers of the 1959-64

[3] See Marion J. Levy, *The Structure of Society* (Princeton, 1952), p. 251.

Table 24: Northern House of Assembly, 1956-61; Federal Ministers: Class Composition, 1959-64

		Sarakuna					Talakawa		Total	Trad. titles
		(r)	(n)	(v)	(c)	(m)*		(s)		
Northern House of Assembly as a whole	no.	39	26	8	5	—	23	2	103	60
	%	37.9	25.2	7.8	4.9	—	22.3	1.9	100	58.3
Regional ministers	no.	7	7	2	1	—	2	—	19	11
	%	36.8	36.8	10.5	5.3	—	10.5	—	100.7	57.9
Federal ministers	no.	1	4	—	—	—	4	1	10	5
	%	10	40	—	—	—	40	10	100	50
Opposition	no.	1	2	—	1	—	6	—	10	0
	%	10	20	—	10	—	60	—	100	0

Key: (r) royalty
(n) nobility
(v) vassalage
(c) clientage
(m) marriage
(s) slave descent

* See text for explanation of blanks in this column.

Table 25: Northern House of Assembly, 1956-61; Federal Ministers: Occupational Composition, 1959-64

		N.A. Councillor (1)	Dist. head (2)	Judicial (3)	Dept. head (4)	Village head (5)	Teachers (6)	Other N.A. employees (7)	Merchant traders (8)	Trader contractors (9)	Politicians (10)	Tailors (11)	Bicycle mechanics (12)	Farmers (13)	Company executives (14)
Northern House of Assembly as a whole	no.	25	23	4	12	2	3	11	11	5	2	1	1	2	1
	%	24.2	22.3	3.9	11.7	1.9	2.9	10.7	10.7	4.9	1.9	0.9	0.9	1.9	.9
Regional ministers	no.	7	3		3	1	2	2	1						
	%	36.8	15.8		15.8	5.3	10.5	10.5	5.3						
Federal ministers	no.	1	2		1		2	3							1
	%	10	20		10		20	30							10
Opposition	no.									5	2	1	1	1	
	%									50	20	10	10	10	

Table 26: Northern House of Assembly, 1956-61; Federal Ministers: Ethnic Composition, 1959-64

		(1) Fulani	(2) Habe	(3) Nupe	(4) Kanuri	(5) Yoruba	(6) Other	(7) Total
Northern House of Assembly as a whole	no.	50	25	4	12	4	8	103
	%	48.5	24.2	3.9	11.7	3.9	7.8	100
Regional ministers	no.	8	3	4	2		2	19
	%	42.2	15.8	21.0	10.5		10.5	100
Federal ministers	no.	3	2	1	2	1	1	10
	%	30	20	10	20	10	10	100
Opposition	no.	2	3		2	3		10
	%	20	30		20	30		100

Table 27: Northern House of Assembly, 1956-61; Federal Ministers: Western Education, 1959-64

		(1) Special[a]	(2) Unknown[b]	(3) 1st	(4) 2nd	(5) 3rd	(6) 4th	(7) 5th	(8) 6th	Middle II (9) 7th	(10) 8th	(11) 9th	Middle IV (12) 10th	(13) 11th	Middle VI (14) 12th	(15) none	Av. no. yrs. Western schooling	Katsina College
Northern House of Assembly as a whole	no.	4	2	1	5	6			11	1	4	2	19	1	30	17	7.5	28
	%																	27.2
Regional ministers	no.											1	6		11	1	10.6	10
	%																	52.6
Federal ministers	no.						1		1				2	1	7		11.5	7
	%																	70
Opposition	no.												1		3	4	5.6	2
	%																	20

(a) Specialized schools such as Kano School for Arabic Studies.
(b) Figures in columns 1 and 2 not included in totals and averages.

321

Table 28: Northern House of Assembly: Class Composition, 1961-65

		(r)	(n)	(v)	(c)	(s)	(?)	(S)	(T)	(J)	Total^a	Trad. titles^b	Total^c
House of Assembly as a whole	no.	47	32	7	6	2	5	99	14	3	116	77	138
	%	40.5	27.6	6.0	5.2	1.7	4.3	85.3	12.1	2.6	100	55.8	
Returned members	no.	29	18	5	3	1		56	7		63	45	63
	%	46.0	28.6	7.9	4.8	1.6		88.9	11.1		100	71.4	
New members	no.	18	14	2	3	1	5	43	7	3	53	32	75
	%	34.0	26.4	3.8	5.7	1.9	9.4	81.1	13.2	5.7	100.1	42.7	
Ministers	no.	13	10	2	3	1	1	30	3		33	25	38
	%	39.4	30.3	6.1	9.1	3.0	3.0	90.9	9.1		100	65.9	
Returned ministers	no.	12	9	1	2	1		25	3		28	20	28
	%	42.9	32.1	3.6	7.1	3.6		89.3	10.7		100	71.4	
New ministers	no.	1	1	1	1		1	5			5	5	10
	%	20.0	20.0	20.0	20.0		20.0	100			100	50	

Key:

(r)	royalty	
(n)	nobility	
(v)	vassalage	
(c)	clientage	Sarakuna
(s)	slave descent	
(?)	unknown	
(S)	total Sarakuna	
(T)	Talakawa	
(J)	judicial class	

a Total = total members whose class was known
b Trad. titles = members with traditional titles
c Total = total number of members

The class percentages are based on the total number of members whose class positions were known. The percentage of members holding traditional titles is based on the total number of members.

Table 29: Northern House of Assembly: Occupational Composition, 1961-65

		NAC	DiH	DeH	VH	tea	NAs	m-t	t-c	pol	far	?	Total
House of Assembly	no.	24	31	5	4	11	36	14	4	6	1	2	138
as a whole	%	17.4	22.5	3.6	2.9	7.9	26.1	10.1	2.9	4.3	0.7	1.4	99.8
Returned members	no.	20	16	3		3	14	5		1	1		63
	%	31.7	25.4	4.8		4.8	22.2	7.9		1.6	1.6		100
New members	no.	4	15	2	4	8	22	9	4	5		2	75
	%	5.3	20	2.7	5.3	10.7	29.4	12	5.3	6.7		2.7	100.1
Ministers	no.	15	2	1		6	8	1		4		1	38
	%	39.5	5.3	2.6		15.8	21.1	2.6		10.5		2.6	100
Returned	no.	14	2	1		3	6	1		1			28
ministers	%	50	7.1	3.6		10.7	21.4	3.6		3.6			100
New ministers	no.	1				3	2			3		1	10
	%	18				30	20			30		10	100

Key:
NAC N.A. Councillor
DiH district head
DeH department head
VH village head
tea teacher
NAs other N.A. employees

m-t merchant-trader
t-c trader-contractor
pol politician
far farmer
? unknown

Table 30: Northern House of Assembly: Ethnic Composition, 1961-65

		Fulani	Habe	Nupe	Kanuri	Yoruba	Other	Unknown	Total known*
House of Assembly as a whole	no.	57	19	4	12	2	10	34	104 (138)
	%	54.8	18.3	3.8	11.5	1.9	9.6		99.9
Returned members	no.	33	11	4	9		5	1	62 (63)
	%	53.2	17.7	6.5	14.5		8.1		100
New members	no.	24	8		3	2	5	33	42 (75)
	%	57.1	19.0		7.1	4.8	11.9		99.9
Ministers	no.	15	2	4	7	1	3	6	32 (38)
	%	46.9	6.3	12.5	21.9	3.1	9.4		100.2
Returned ministers	no.	14	2	4	5		2	1	27 (28)
	%	51.9	7.4	14.8	18.5		7.4		100
New ministers	no.	1			2	1	1	5	5 (10)
	%	20			40	20	20		100

* The percentages are based on the total number of members whose ethnic group was known. The number in parentheses in this column is the total number of members.

Federal Government of Nigeria who also fell within this category.[4] Most of this data are summarized in Tables 24-30. The 1956-61 data on every member were obtained in all but a few instances through administration of a uniform questionnaire containing the following items: name, occupation, place (emirate) of birth, date of birth, constituency elected from, religion, ethnic origin, education including number of years of Western schooling completed if any, political party, traditional title if any, any relationship with a royal family, membership in an emir's council or not, travels outside Nigeria if any, and occupation. The accuracy of most of the data was double-checked against the testimony of knowledgeable informants during my nearly year-long tour of the Nigerian provinces in 1959. For the 1961-65 membership the data are less complete and the method partly modified (a combination of the previous method plus questionnaire, published data, and information from informants was employed), due to the more limited time available to me for the purpose during briefer return visits in 1963 and 1966. Nevertheless, the data obtained for this period are more than adequate to permit generalization about the social composition of the 1961-65 House of Assembly. Where uncertainty exists concerning the veracity of particular items a question mark has been inserted.

Some general findings that emerge from an analysis of the tables are as follows: Out of the grand total of 103 members of the 1959 Northern House of Assembly who were elected from constituencies that lie within the emirates, 77, or roughly 75%, belonged to the *sarakuna* class, applying this term only to members whose *fathers'* position corresponds to one or more categories of membership in that class. If the term is extended to include also those whose own position alone placed them within one or more such categories (i.e. marriage or clientage relationships to aristocrats), the number of the total emirate members of the *sarakuna* class was 84, or roughly 82%.[5] Well over a third of the total emirate members were related

---

[4] Time and opportunities to the researcher did not permit a comparable survey of the backgrounds of Northern ordinary or backbench members of the Nigerian Federal House of Representatives. It may be said, however, that there is no reason to believe that such a survey would have yielded significantly different results, except that the slightly higher average Western school attendance reflected in the backgrounds of the Northern federal ministers may also hold true for all of the Northern federal representatives.

[5] This figure is arrived at by assuming that Native Administration employees who do not belong to the *sarakuna* class by birth or marriage have clientship relationships with those who do, an assumption which informants told me was a valid one. Doubt arises in the case of the trained N.A. employees who are com-

to royal families and another fourth belonged to the hereditary nobility. Twenty-five of the 39 members of royal families, or over 24% of all emirate members of the House, were sons of emirs (*yan sarakuna*)—the pinnacle of the traditional socio-political hierarchy and a stratum which forms but a negligible percentage of the more than 12 million people who (according to the 1953 census) live in the emirates.

Table 28 shows that this remarkable continuity of leadership in terms of traditional elite structure was not only generally sustained in the membership of the 1961-1965 Northern House of Assembly, but that in some aspects there was some intensification of the pattern. Thus the percentage belonging to the *sarakuna* class increased from 82% in 1956-61 to *at least* 85.3% in 1961-65 (the minimal nature of the latter calculation stems from the fact that it does not include marriage relationships, about which systematic data could not be collected for the latter group). Furthermore, within particular elite categories there were slight increases; the higher the category in terms of social structure the greater was the slight increase involved. Thus the percentage belonging to the hereditary nobility increased from 25.2 to 27.3%, while the percentage of royalty increased from 37.9 to 40.5%. Moreover, this augmented continuity occurred notwithstanding the addition of a considerable increment of newly elected members (i.e. those who were not also members of the 1956-61 House— 75 new members out of a total 138 members elected from emirate constituencies, or 44.3%. It may be seen by comparing Table 23 with Tables 24 and 28, that in general, the higher the traditional stratum the greater the number of *sarakuna* parliamentarians who belonged to it. It was previously pointed out that hereditary membership in the *sarakuna* class and possession of *sarauta* (traditional title) were not synonomous, birth conferring only eligibility to compete for certain titles. Yet 60 of the 77 *sarakuna* members of the 1956-61 Northern House and at least 77 of the 99 *sarakuna* members of the 1961-65 Northern House held traditional titles, a further mark of the steep elite structure of the group. Indeed, notwithstanding the minority of nonemirate members, and without the benefit of comparable figures for other countries, it yet seems unhazardous to speculate that the Northern House of Assembly constituted the most aristocratic parliamentary body ever elected. Breakdowns of the backgrounds of emir-

---

moners by birth; they have been employed primarily for their skills, but do they also enter into client-patron relationships once they are employed? My informants thought it axiomatic that they do.

ate members in terms of ethnicity and occupation, which further reflect the traditional elite composition of the group, are provided in Tables 25, 26, 29, and 30.

An equally significant observation, however, is that in terms of Western education and modern administrative experience the emirate members of the Northern House of Assembly constituted an elite in their community. Thus, according to the 1953 Nigerian census, less than 2% of the population of Northern Nigeria was literate in Roman script and less than 1% had attended Western-type schools. For the area of the emirates taken separately these figures are known to be lower, Western education having in the past been concentrated in the nonemirate or Middle Belt area of the Region, where Christian missionaries were most active. But 83.5% (86 out of 103) of the emirate members of the 1956-1961 Northern House of Assembly had from 2 to 12 years of such schooling (the average number of years completed at such schools for the House of Assembly as a whole was 7.5). Some of the remaining members were literate in the Hausa language written in *ajami*, or corrupted Arabic script, and a few in Arabic itself. Less than 15% were totally illiterate (compared with an overall illiteracy rate for Northern Nigeria in 1953 of around 93%).

It is also noteworthy that the level of Western educational qualification of members of the House holding ministerial rank was considerably higher than that of the rest—18 out of 19 Northern ministers having attended school for an average of 10.6 years. In the Federal parliament, where only English is spoken (Hausa is a second official language of debate in the Northern Assembly), and where Northern members had to debate with more highly educated southern members, no minister from the Northern emirates had less than 10 years schooling, and 7 out of 10 of these had completed secondary school (as compared with only 57.9% secondary school graduates among the ministers of the Northern regional government). But as may be seen in Tables 24 and 28 the proportion of traditional aristocrats within the circle of those of ministerial rank was not drastically lower than that of the Northern House as a whole. In other words, more often than not it was found possible to recruit better educated persons for the modern political offices which called for a higher degree of this kind of qualification without going outside the ranks of the traditional ruling class.

Opposition Members

The few parliamentarians who came from very humble segments of emirate society were mostly in the opposition parties. They included a tailor, a bicycle mechanic and several small-scale traders and contractors. It is not to be overlooked, however, that, notwithstanding the social-revolutionary orientation of these parties, 4 of the 10 opposition, 1956-61 members were also members of the *sarakuna* class, including one who was a member of a Zaria royal family (M. Ango Soba, whose father was the district head of Soba). The phenomenon of the "patrician radical" is one to be encountered again in connection with analysis of the dynamics of political parties and elections (Chapters 8 and 9).

Ibrahim Imam

The leader of the opposition[6] in the Northern House of Assembly, M. Ibrahim Imam, claimed descent from the Sefawa dynasty which ruled Bornu emirate for centuries before the rise of Al-Kanemi (also known as Shehu Laminu), who led the repulsion of the Fulani invasion of Bornu in 1810 (Al-Kanemi's descendants have occupied the Bornu throne since his death in 1835). M. Ibrahim's father, Hamsami Imam, was the late Chief Alkali of Bornu. Ibrahim Imam was formerly a member of his Shehu's Council and General Secretary of the NPC, in which role he was the architect of the NPC's famous eight-point program designed to secure the virtually complete political autonomy of the North vis-à-vis the southern regions. But his official positions did not deter him from a role of relentless critic of other NPC policies, particularly that perpetuating the power of traditional rulers.[7] Having recorded some of his controversial proposals for reconstruction of the party in a memorandum which the 1954 Jos NPC Convention rejected, he resigned his party post. Imam's de-

---

[6] No official opposition was recognized by the government in the 1961-65 House, where opposition members originally numbered only 10, none of them a native of any emirate except Imam who was returned from a nonemirate constituency.

[7] See the article, "Mallam Ibrahim Imam: Wizard or Windbag?", *Nigerian Citizen*, March 31 and April 4, 1956, in which the author observes: "In the House of Representatives, in spite of the fact that he was the General Secretary of the NPC Ibrahim always voted [according to] the dictates of his conscience, much to the embarrassment of his party supporters who numbered little less than 50 percent [of] the House. He sometimes voted with the Action Group, N.C.N.C. or at best remained neutral. I remember when a division was called on the lead-zinc bill introduced by an N.C.N.C. Minister. He voted along with the Action Group, leaving his party men, who were supporting the Government, to their fate".

tractors assert that a deeper reason for the resignation was disappointment over his not being chosen for ministerial office. His expulsion from the Shehu's Council soon thereafter was an indication that radical policies were equally incompatible with membership in that body.[8]

Imam subsequently became first the patron and later the president of the Bornu Youth Movement, a party devoted at once to fundamental political change within Bornu emirate and to exploiting the irredentist susceptibilities of the Kanuri (Kanuri people form the bulk of the Bornu population), whom constitutional development for the first time placed under regional political institutions dominated by Fulani in the Northern House of Assembly between 1954 and 1956, the year the other opposition members under discussion were elected, he literally formed a one-man opposition. The record of debates in those years and afterwards shows him to have been a consistent, trenchant, and usually well-informed advocate of political reform in the emirates, especially in matters involving civil liberties.

The Precedent of Islam

Ibrahim Imam was born into a family of the class of *alkali*, Imams, and religious teachers (or Malams). Several other leading critics of the emirate system seated on both government and opposition benches possessed a similar background (e.g. M. Sani Dingyadi, founder of one of the most politically contumacious of the organizations to which the NPC traces descent, and M. Ibrahim Mahmud, a NEPU adherent). At least three of the nine NEPU members elected to the federal House of Representatives in 1959 came from such families, including the most famous radical Northern politician of all—Malam Aminu Kano, member of a Fulani judicial lineage of Kano emirate called Genawa. In his politically formative years M. Aminu's mentor was the late Malam Sa'adu Zungur, the reputed Koranic scholar and son of the

---

[8] *Nigerian Citizen* for October 7, 1954 carried this account:

> The Shehu-in-Council considered M. Ibrahim Imam's conduct in his capacity as a Bornu Native Administration Council member, and in particular his non-attendance at certain Council meetings, his failure to co-operate and the public speeches allegedly made by him which reflected on the integrity of other members of the Council in connection with the recent inquiry into the affairs of the ex-Emir of Dikwa.
>
> An explanation of his course of conduct was called for, and the Shehu-in-Council have given careful consideration to his representations but have found them unacceptable, hence the recommendation to terminate his appointment in the Council.

late *Limanin* (Imam of) *Bauchi*. M. Aminu Kano's father, Malam
Yusufu, was at one time the Acting Chief Alkali of Kano; his grandfather was Hassan Abdulaz, a distinguished Malam; and his grandmother's reputation for Islamic learning earned her the respectful title
of *Modibo*.

A connection between a radical posture in modern politics and a
membership in a family of *alkali*, Malams and Imams may have been
in the role of these figures as interpreters of Islamic law and trans-
mitters of the moral and spiritual values of an Islamic society. As
others have pointed out, "Islam knows only one law, the divinely revealed Shari'a which holds sway over political no less than over social, economic and cultural life".[9] Hence those concerned with the
exposition and dissemination of the Shari'a, or the doctrines (including
those derived from the Koran) which make it up, are not only influential and respected members of the community in the emirates,
but they also represent the only legitimate source of criticism of the
conduct of the traditional state. To be reared in the tradition of the
judicial, scholarly, and priestly families, as was Aminu Kano and
others, was then to be exposed to the notion that the behavior of
traditional rulers may justify criticism or even censure. Clearly most
of the products of this tradition did not translate their learning into
the principles of radical democracy, yet in listening to the utterances
of Aminu Kano in particular at NEPU rallies and on other occasions,
it was difficult to resist the conclusion that his political outlook and
perhaps that of others like him owed a good deal to family heritage.[10] Other prominent onetime radical leaders with the relevant

[9] E.I.J. Rosenthal, *Political Thought in Medieval Islam* (London, 1958), p. 23.
[10] For example, Aminu Kano's article, "My Resignation", in the *Daily Comet*
of Nigeria, November 11, 1950, pp. 1, 4, in which he explains why he had recently resigned his post as a teacher and government servant to assume full-time
work with NEPU, reads in part as follows:

> I resigned because I refuse to believe that this country is by necessity a
> prisoner of the Anglo-Fulani autocracy or the unpopular indirect rule system.
> I resigned because there is no freedom to criticize this most unjust and
> anachronistic and un-Islamic form of hollow institution promulgated by Lugard.
> I resigned because I fanatically share the view that the native administrations,
> as they stand today, coupled with all their all too trumpeted "fine tradition" are
> woefully hopeless in solving our urgent educational, social, economic, political,
> and even religious problems. . . .
> I cannot tolerate these institutions because of their smell. I cannot tolerate
> them because they do not tolerate anyone. They even go to the extent of doom-
> ing the future of their critics. I am prepared to be called by any name. Call me
> a dreamer or call me a revolutionary, call me a crusader or anything you will.

> I have seen a light on the far horizon and I intend to march into its full circle
> either alone or with anyone who cares to go with me".

Quoted in C. S. Whitaker, Jr., "Three Perspectives on Hierarchy: Political

background including M. Saidu Zungur, M. Sani Dingyadi (later an NPC member), M. Lawan Danbazau, and in general according to M. Aminu Kano himself, the most reliable local NEPU leaders among the Kano Hausa.[11]

"NEW" ELEMENTS IN THE GOVERNING GROUP

IT IS IMPORTANT that among the members of the majority party and the survey group are also persons whose backgrounds would not have qualified them for positions of political leadership according to purely traditional criteria. These include specifically the group of merchant-traders, a few Western-educated upwardly mobile *talakawa*, and a few cases of the interesting special category of slave descendants.

Trade, however vast in scale and no matter how remunerative, was an occupation traditionally spurned by the *sarakuna* class. In the past, even the wealthiest merchant-traders were therefore *talakawa*; ethnically they were almost invariably *Habe*. Yet they helped to maintain the traditional political structure, particularly in the large and powerful states of Kano, Katsina, Zaria, and to a lesser extent, Sokoto. M. G. Smith's analysis of the peculiar traditional political role of the prosperous merchant-traders (*attajirai*) of Zaria was applicable to the emirates generally:

"Wealth carries great prestige, but little political weight in traditional terms; this means that a merchant, however successful, is debarred from investing his capital in the purchase of important political office. Equally, according to Maliki law, he is prohibited from investing his capital on interest bearing terms. Yet, as the customary rate of profit in trade is high, and the market conditions have been favorable, these merchants who have managed to raise their turnover above a certain level cannot fail to amass what are, by native standards, large sums. . . . Hence the wealth of those concerned with distribution, and the dilemma which faces them; for if Islam forbids investment at interest, and the political system prevents investment in status, the productive system, that is, the instruments of production traditional among the Hausa, has little room, since the abolition of slavery, for investment of capital on a large scale; while to import and maintain the

Thought and Leadership in Northern Nigeria", *Journal of Commonwealth Political Studies*, Vol. 3, No. 1 (March 1965), pp. 1-19.
[11] Interview with M. Aminu Kano, Kaduna, September 4, 1963.

productive apparatus of the Europeans might bring these merchants into economic competition with the European firms on whose goodwill their prosperity depends . . . although a more important restriction on such investment is the lack of technically skilled Hausa workers capable of operating or maintaining machinery, and reluctance to employ Ibo labor.

What then can these unfortunate merchants with surplus income do? One answer is to go to Mecca, preferably by the most expensive means—the aeroplane. . . . But since it is considered unnecessarily ostentatious to visit Mecca more than once, though some do, and the pilgrim, addressed as Alhaji after his return, has shown himself to be a man of affluence by the style of his pilgrimage, commercial confidence in him is increased and is usually expressed by an increasing volume of trade, with the consequence that he may soon become even wealthier than before. At this stage, the merchant, if his *arziki* or good fortune continues, often starts making loans on a more substantial scale than before, for which the salaried Native Authority officials, who habitually live beyond their means, provide an open market whose risks are covered by a high and irreligious rate of interest (25 percent per month). . . . It is probable that a large part of the surplus income of the Zaria merchants is still invested in the maintenance of the nobility at their accustomed standards of living, and hence we have an interesting situation in which that class of persons who could with ease indulge in conspicuous waste is constrained, because their culture forbids them to compete with the nobility in this way, to contribute to the expense of another class of whom their culture requires extravagance and display. These gift-debts form a valuable contribution, made by merchants, to the maintenance of traditional standards and culture.[12]

The presence of 11 *attajirai* in the Northern House of Assembly (one of them M. Musa Gashash as Minister of Land and Survey) shows that representative institutions gave the *attajirai* a measure of participation in government which traditional values did not allow them. However, that all 11 sat on the government side was indicative of the fact that this social segment did not challenge the dominant role of the traditional political elite.

Three of the 11 dismissed from offices in local Native Adminis-

---

[12] *Economy of Hausa Communities of Zaria*, pp. 100-101.

trations, were instances of the reality that aristocrats sometimes deigned to turn to trade when they were forced out of traditionally preferred occupations. One of these was Bukar Garbai, a son of a Shehu of Bornu; he was once a district head. Another was a district head in Katsina emirate and a third was the son of an *Alkalin Alkali* who entered trade after being ousted from his post in the Katagum N.A. Works Department. The fathers of two other *attajirai* were *fadawa* to an emir. These five are, strictly speaking, cases not of an upward mobility of *talakawa* but of a downward movement of *sarakuna*.

The others undoubtedly owed their membership in the House to changed political circumstances and to the special assets they brought to such circumstances (for other traditionally excluded social segments did not experience a proportionate recruitment of new political leaders from their ranks). The NPC appears deliberately to have chosen *Habe* merchants to contest seats against NEPU candidates who attempted to ignite the smoldering resentment of many *Habe* against the ruling descendants of the Fulani conquerors, as in Kano City. Thus in 1956 the late Alhaji Ahmadu Dantata, probably the wealthiest Kano merchant at the time, was chosen to oppose M. Aminu Kano in the constituency of Kano East, while one of M. Aminu's lieutenants was confronted in Kano City West with the opposing candidacy of another leading *attajirai*, M. Musa Gashash. In both cases the NPC strategy was successful. Alhaji Ahmadu Dantata's long-established custom of distributing alms to all supplicants at one of the gates of Kano City each Friday after attending Mosque doubtless helped his campaign, and in general it may be said that the practice of distributing largesse served the *attajirai* well in the role of modern political leader.

It was important that the entrance of these *attajirai* into active politics did not occur as a result of their demand for a share in governmental decision-making, but in response to overtures on the part of leaders in the NPC who perceived the assistance which *attajirai* could render in competition for the loyalty of the mass electorate. Both Dantata and Gashash insisted to me that initially they were extremely reluctant to run for office, which was confirmed by other party leaders. Presumably there later existed a greater appreciation among this group of the importance to their economic interests of being represented in government, for a growing trend in all the large emirates was for the roster of NPC candidates to include one or more *attajirai*.

In Northern Nigeria the government was the largest source of contracts. Governmental and quasi-governmental agencies provided a variety of economic services, formulated policies, and laid down economic regulations, all vital to businessmen. For example, each season the Northern Region Marketing Board purchased, at a price it officially set for the whole region, virtually the whole of the region's leading cash crops—groundnuts, cotton, beniseed. It accomplished this through middlemen officially designated as Licensed Buying Agents. Large trading operations like those of Dantata and Gashash functioned under official franchises, handling the bulk of the transactions with the farmers. Hence the Marketing Board at once determined who engaged in what represented the region's major commercial activity, and ultimately the level of profit the enterprise yielded as well. The Ministry of Trade and Industries served as a source of technical advice and as a clearinghouse for the organization of commercial ventures involving indigenous and foreign capital. (Such arrangement helped to overcome some of the previous obstacles to productive investment by the *attajirai*, which Smith points to.) As in the case of such new enterprises as the Nigerian Canning Company, Kaduna Textiles, Ltd., Northern Development (Nigeria) Ltd., etc., the Development Corporation was often a third partner. These economic institutions were politically controlled either directly or indirectly.

The significance of these and other links between the economic and political systems is not only that they helped to draw merchant-traders into politics and keep them there; it is that they promoted a degree of dependence of the Northern Nigerian "entrepreneur" on those who controlled government to an extent unknown to his historic counterpart in Western societies. Far from occasioning the emergence of a source of power outside the purview of an "ancient regime" of political leadership, economic development in Northern Nigeria tended to foster an interdependent relationship between the wielders of political authority and the agents of economic innovation; indeed, these roles were only analytically separable. And given the dominance of the governmental arm by persons whose political roots were embedded in the traditional order of society, to have expected the merchant-traders to bring about a transformation of the traditional leadership structure would be to make a false parallel of historical experience.

There was no indication that the *attajirai* rejected or resented a subordinate place in a leadership that embodied traditional presuppositions, while the signs of deference could clearly be observed. Even the wealthiest Kano merchant hesitated to put on a turban during meetings of the House (other members of traditionally humble origin freely affected this aristocratic style). The cloth of his gown remained conspicuously simple, though no doubt of superior quality; and similarly, his residence, located in the *Habe* quarters of the old city or outside its walls, was typically large and usually had a plush interior. But the exterior of the building revealed nothing of this. To the eye of the stranger, the one outward mark of his social distance from the masses was the American car he favored, along with the chiefs. If he sought to elevate his social position, his effort was likely to take a form which implied acceptance rather than departure from a traditional definition of prestige, notably marriage into an aristocratic family, which further cemented his political bond with traditional authority. Among the Kano *attajarai* in the 1956-61 House of Assembly, for example, one—Alhaji Nabegu—was married to a daughter of the Galadiman Kano, who was uncle to the emir; another, Haruna Kassim, was the brother-in-law of a Kano district head. Many, I was told, aspired to crown their commercial success with similar unions.

It may well be that the children whose education the *attajirai* increasingly insist on will grow up to be less politically acquiescent than their fathers, and with less stake in the status quo they conceivably could furnish leadership in a future movement to achieve fundamental change. It should be pointed out that there were a few notable instances of *attajirai* who were not members of the House of Assembly who openly lent their support to radical political parties.[13] Buttressing the existing culture of political stratification continued to be the chief political contribution which *attajirai* as a whole made during the period covered in this study, however.

As is discussed more fully below, the educational policy of the British colonial authority gave initial priority to the education of the

[13] Perhaps the most celebrated examples are the two brothers of Ahmadu Dantata, Jamil and Mahmudu. The former unsuccessfully contested a seat in the Federal House in 1959 under an Action Group banner; Mahmadu, reportedly a very popular spendthrift, was a NEPU backer until his conviction on charges of counterfeiting, for which he was still serving out a prison term in 1959. Alhaji Ibrahim Yayi, Alhaji Abduallahi Maradi, and Alhaji Dan Ladidi are other Kano merchants mentioned to me as having at one time or another supported NEPU.

sons of traditional rulers. This policy largely explains how the present generation of political leadership came to possess the dual attributes of high ascriptive prestige and well above average educational qualification. Even some apparently conspicuous exceptions to this generalization are not exceptions in reality, however. For aristocratic families are known to have been initially so distrustful or hostile to the idea of Western education that when pressed to send their sons to school they sometimes sent along instead the sons of servants or retainers (including slave-descendants) and kept the true identity of these pupils from the British. Others may have done so from more positive motives, but the important point is that politically prominent *talakawa* were often found to owe their initial educational opportunity to some personal link with such a family.

Alhaji Aliyu, Makaman Bida

A noteworthy example of a commoner by birth who rose to the heights of contemporary political leadership, thanks in no small part to the fortune of having been sent to school by his father's titled patron, was *Alhaji Aliyu*, Makaman Bida, formerly the Northern Minister of Finance. According to sources in Bida, M. Aliyu's father served as a Koranic Malam in the household of a Nupe nobleman who held the title and office of *Ma'aji* (treasurer) in that emirate. The *Ma'aji* was responsible for M. Aliyu's entrance into elementary school; thereafter ability and effort led to his advancement on an educational ladder which culminated at Katsina College, where he mingled with the sons of hereditary rulers, including one who became premier of the Northern Region (the Sarduna's first two years at Katsina overlapped with M. Aliyu's last two). M. Aliyu returned to Bida as a teacher in the Middle School, of which he later became headmaster. In 1942 it was decided that the traditional council of the *Etsu Nupe* (Emir of Bida) required the services of a Western-educated member to help cope with increasingly complex administrative tasks, and M. Aliyu was chosen. As the award of an important title, *Makama*, indicated, he became a valued and trusted member of that council, whose logical choice he was to represent Bida in the Northern legislative body introduced in 1947 under the Nigerian (Richards) constitution. The succeeding (Macpherson) constitution empowered the Northern legislative representatives to select from their members ministers of the regional and central governments. They chose M. Aliyu for one of the posts, probably not unmindful of the political importance of the Nupe minority.

Generally regarded as the Sardauna's closest colleague in the Northern government, Alhaji Aliyu regularly served as acting premier during the Sardauna's frequent travels abroad, as well as the principle liaison between the government and the party secretariat (in connection with the 1959 election campaign, for example, all the expenditures of the secretariat required his endorsement). He held his portfolio—the critical one of finance—throughout the life of the civilian regime. That he also generally reflected the views of the more conservative parliamentarians, particularly on matters touching the powers of the Native Administrations, suggests that upward mobility within a traditional predominantly ascriptive structure of leadership could engender belief in its validity and commitment to its preservation.

Prominent Slave-descendants

Alhaji Abudakar Tafawa Balewa, the Prime Minister of the Federation of Nigeria and Alhaji Yusufu Maitama Sule, the Federal Minister of Mines and Power, are two fascinating cases of slave-descendants who owed much to the fortuitous circumstance of having been selected by their fathers' masters[14] to be recipients of the new learning designed for the heirs of traditional rulers. Unlike A. Aliyu, however, both these men had a reputation within their party for being "radicals" or critics. They were not wedded to the idea of the inherent worth of the traditional order.

Maitama Sule is a royal slave-descendant or *bacucune* (plural, *cucunawa*), as this status is known in Kano emirate, even today.[15] He

[14] It was previously pointed out that Lord Lugard's method of abolishing slavery in Northern Nigeria was intended to provide a period of transition before the traditional ruling class should cease to command the labor of slaves from which their wealth at that time was essentially derived. Hence Lugard's abolition proclamation provided that all persons born after April 1, 1900 were free. It also provided that slaves born before that date were free to apply to the courts for manumission, an application which the court would be bound to honor. By deliberate implication, those who made no such application were confirmed in their existing status.

[15] Slave ancestry persists as a distinctive Hausa social classification, although slavery as a legal institution does not. Again Smith's account of the Zaria situation is elucidating: "Hausa society no longer contains an explicit status of slavery (bauta; slave-*bawa.*, f. baiwa, pl. bayi); but Hausa emphasize the status of a person's parents and grandparents. The grandchildren of slaves are described as *mantankara.* . . . Facial marks indicated the slave status of *dimaiai* as well as captives. These facial marks are no longer common; but in many respects the old *dimaiai* relation persists between slave-owners and the issue of their former slaves. The emphasis which Hausa place on parental status as slave or free has

graduated from the Kaduna College, successor institution to Katsina College, which was reconstituted as the capital around 1940. The college was later moved again to Zaria and now functions as one of the two special Northern Nigerian government colleges. One of the founding members of NEPA—the organization from which the radical NEPU derived much of its political program, along with its name, reportedly at the suggestion of M. Maitama himself—once wrote political tracts advocating democratization of the institution of emirship. Later he joined the NPC and became chief whip of the party in the federal House of Representatives and a leading party spokesman, valued particularly for his ability to hold his own in debates with the formally more educated southern politicians.

The circumstances surrounding his elevation to the rank of federal minister following the 1959 election constitutes an interesting vignette of the phenomenon of continuity and change. Theoretically a minister of the government of Nigeria enjoyed precedence over a chief, although in practice Maitama Sule's ministerial portfolio—Mines and Power—provided him with little occasion to exercise his authority in Kano (which has no extractive industries and its own electricity corporation). Nevertheless eyebrows of Kano traditional officials were reputedly raised at the prospect of a *bacucune* becoming a minister. That the incumbent emir, Sanusi, was widely regarded as being the proudest and most jealous of his authority of all the emirs, made the situation all the more delicate. But misgivings about the impact of Maitama Sule's appointment on the emir's authority and prestige were averted when a short time before M. Maitama became minister, the Emir turbanned him *Dan Masani* of Kano, an action which at a stroke had the effect of expressing the Emir's sanction of his appointment, dramatizing the connection between modern and traditional leadership prestige, and emphasizing the loyalty the new minister was expected to retain toward his king and benefactor.

Alhaji Sir Abubakar Tafawa Balewa

It was frequently stated in Northern Nigeria that some of the NPC

---

the function of maintaining these *dimaiai* relations. This emphasis does not contradict Lugard's rule that persons born after 1 April 1900 are free, but simply ignores it, and it also modified the effect of self-redemption by slaves". *Government in Zazzau, 1800-1950* (London, 1960), pp. 253-54ff.

It should be added that Maitama Sule and the late Abubakar Tafawa Balewa bore the facial marks Smith refers to. Apparently the distinction between slave and slave-descendant is not always observed, perhaps especially in Hausa elderly persons' speech—an old British Resident's messenger more than once referred to one of them as "bawa".

leaders, who in earlier days were attracted to the NEPU cause, altered their views as a result of a realistic reassessment of the forces of change compared with those working to sustain the traditional order. Such a reassessment, it was previously suggested, partly accounted for the marked difference in attitude toward local government reform displayed in Tafawa Balewa's second major parliamentary speech on the subject, compared with the first. Yet Balewa opposed the NEPU from the start; it is also clear that his views were never wholly satisfactory to the leading elements in that party nor to those of the NPC, all of which indicates a thread of consistency in those views, stemming from premises shared by neither group.

Traditionally all slaves in Bauchi emirate, unlike some in Kano, appear to have formed an essentially menial estate—which may help to explain why, in that yet highly ascription-oriented Northern Nigerian milieu, Maitama Sule publicly emphasized his parental origin while the Prime Minister was content to see his obscured.[16] Balewa's career was a classic case of success based on personal ability and achievement. Initially encouraged scholastically by a British official, Balewa became a teacher and one of the first from Northern Nigeria to earn a diploma in education at the University of London. He was then a headmaster; later, he was one of the first four Northern Nigerians given a status and salary equivalent to that of a member of the (previously wholly British) senior public service. The same qualities led to his selection as a member of the Bauchi Emir's Council, and hence to his selection as a parliamentarian and minister.

If the experience of upward mobility instilled Alhaji Aliyu Makamam Bida with faith in the traditional hierarchy, the same experience permitted Balewa to maintain a critical detachment (it is noteworthy that Balewa had no traditional title; the honor is said to have been proffered more than once). But this experience was probably also an underlying factor in his having been repelled by the NEPU, with

[16] It has been recorded in various publications that Abubakar Tafawa Balewa is a son of a late *Ajiyan* Bauchi, District Head of Lere. See e.g. *Who's Who in Nigeria* (Lagos: Nigerian Printing and Publishing Company, 1959); Thomas Melady, *Profiles of African Leaders* (New York: Macmillan, 1961), pp. 150-51, Ronald Segal, *Political Africa* (New York: Praeger, 1961). In fact, his father was originally the Ajiya's slave, with the title of *Shamaki*, or Garkuwan Shamaki (this slave *sarauta* is now held by the late Prime Minister's son-in-law and private secretary, M. Ahmed Kyari), meaning literally "shield of the horses", which indicates the nature of this servitor's traditional function in battle. Most younger Nigerians appeared to be unaware of these facts, while there was an inclination on the part of more senior people who did know them to keep them hidden, especially from foreign researchers.

its populistic or mass democratic assumptions concerning the proper structure of authority. Two recurrent themes in his speeches during the decade of constitutional advance toward Nigerian self-government were fear of demagogy and concern for the leadership prospects of "deserving", or qualified, persons. Thus, in one speech he expressed the opinion that, "even when Nigeria is ripe for responsible government, leadership should not be granted through the medium of its people who are agitating",[17] and in another his anxiety that "There are men, as I say, Mr. Chairman, who can shoulder these responsibilities, but do we all believe that it is [that] type of people whom I have in mind who will be given the opportunity of shouldering these responsibilities?"[18]

I am suggesting here that the legacy of Balewa's experience of mobility was a professional or bureaucratic conception of leadership, based on demonstrated ability and objective achievement, a belief in, to use a recent coinage, meritocracy, which was equally in opposition to the aristocratic principles embraced by the NPC and to the NEPU's brand of democracy.

SOME SOURCES AND DYNAMICS OF LEADERSHIP CONTINUITY

WITHOUT LOSING sight of the important fact that the parliamentary institution in Northern Nigeria allowed persons to attain a position of political leadership which an untrammelled traditional structure is unlikely ever to have allowed them, the holding sway of persons with superior traditional credentials was by far the more conspicuous reality. To suggest some of the causes and ramifications of this reality is in order here. One point is that a new institution injected into a society was in itself powerless to eliminate its members' notion of the qualities needed for leadership. In the case of the emirates we are dealing with a people who had long evinced a "general preference for social continuity and for stability in the status order", who, in other words, admire *karda* over *shigege* (heritage versus acquired occupational role).[19] Faced with having to decide suddenly who should occupy a new kind of political office, it was perhaps only reasonable to have been concerned more with a primary qualification for political office in general—the capacity to issue legitimate and binding commands—than with demands which were peculiar to the new office

[17] *Proceedings of the General Conference on Review of the Constitution* (Lagos, 1950), p. 47.
[18] *Nigeria Legislative Council Debates*, February 20, 1954, pp. 244-52.
[19] Smith, "Hausa Systems of Social Status".

and therefore unfamiliar. In this sense, the Northern electorate's preference for aristocrats may have deserved the label, "the wisdom of the ignorant".

British Educational Policy

A history of modern education in Northern Nigeria awaits (and warrants) study, but it may be stated here that whatever other characteristics and results the British educational policy may have had, it respected and reinforced the traditional bias in favor of ascribed political leadership roles.

British educational policy was a natural concommitant of the doctrine of indirect rule. As Sir Donald Cameron, a former governor of Nigeria, put it, "If indirect rule is to be truly tribal [in Northern Nigeria], we must educate from the top down, and not as in Southern Nigeria from the bottom upwards".[20] This precept governed the selection of pupils to the government-sponsored schools in the emirate area of Northern Nigeria from their earliest days until very recently (certainly up to the passage of the 1956 Education Act of Northern Nigeria). The first of these institutions were the three so-called Nassarawa schools, which were inaugurated in Kano City by the colonial educator, Hans Vischer. One was for the sons of chiefs; another was for the children of the *malamai* class who were expected to supply the teaching staff of the first, plus clerks and surveyors for the government service, while the third was a craft school designed to attract "the right class of native artisans".[21] Of the schools for the sons of chiefs Vischer wrote: "The object of this school is to train the sons of Chiefs with a view to [making] them physically and mentally better fitted to assist the Government in the Administration of the country, to bring them into closer contact with the Government, to acquire for them a better understanding of the policy pursued by the Government, to acquire for them an elementary knowledge of sanitation and hygiene and above all to open their eyes to the commercial possibilities of the country".[22]

"The intention", remarks an official of the Northern Nigeria Ministry of Education in a pamphlet published in 1959, "was to produce a

[20] Sir James Currie, "Indirect Rule and Education in Africa", in *United Empire* (November 1932), p. 614.
[21] *Quarterly Report: Education Department (Quarter ending June 30th, 1910), submitted to H. E. the Governor at Zaria, July, 1910 by Hans Vischer.* Archives, Kaduna #3666, 1910.
[22] *Ibid.*

literate ruling class so that the new administration with its rules, regulations, and associated office routine could be carried on".[23] The enrollment in the first year reveals the fact that the Nassarawa Sons of Chiefs School was meant to serve the emirates, not the offspring of chiefs in the Middle Belt or riverain region.[24]

The Nassarawa Sons of Chiefs School also served as a prototype for similar schools established later in other provinces. In endorsing a proposal to set up one of these in Bornu in 1937, an administrative officer gave expression to the aim underlying all of them: "My own view is that provision of such a school would meet a want which will become increasingly necessary as the country advances. However much political acumen one of the ruling classes may have by inheritance, it will always be of advantage if he has a broader and more educated knowledge than his subjects".[25]

The need referred to was explicitly given a priority higher than maximum exploitation of talent *per se*.[26]

These were elementary schools. At the secondary school level Vischer's objectives were embodied in the decision to create Katsina College to which (in principle) traditional rulers' children were recruited. "The object of the course of training", we are told, "was to provide as far as possible, all the essentials of a good English public school".[27] Katsina College not only provided training; it also offered the unprecedented opportunity for future officials of the ruling hierarchies in the emirates to mix with each other. This opportunity was extended beyond school days by the Katsina College Old Boys

[23] D. H. Williams, *A Short Survey of Education in Northern Nigeria* (Kaduna, 1959), p. 9.

[24] *Ibid.* "The pupils come from the following Provinces and towns: Kano 12, Katsina 28, Kazaure 3, Katagum Division 9, Bida 12, Gombe [Bauchi] 2". In an unpublished memorandum dated 29 May 1914, Vischer asserts, "no Pagan pupils have been admitted to the Schools at Kano".

[25] File marked "Schools for the Sons of Chiefs", File 2856 (Bornu) 1937048, Item #244, Archives, Kaduna.

[26] For example, in a Memorandum (No. 51/1942, dated 9 September 1942) from the Secretary Northern Provinces to Resident Kano Province, concerning government Education Department schools recruitment policy: "It would be disastrous to disregard entirely the wishes of a Native Authority. Local considerations [such as local prestige, influence, or character] must sometimes involve the second best man, *qua* scholastic attainment, filling an appointment; but before this is allowed satisfactory evidence must be provided in every instance to show that local considerations are of sufficient weight to justify Government accepting a proposal which falls short of the best".

[27] Williams, *Short Survey*, p. 26. Because of the political parallel Katsina College has been referred to as "the Eton of Northern Nigeria", but the educational model for the school was Winchester.

Association. The political fruit of the Katsina College experience may be observed in Table 27, which shows the high percentage of the school's graduates who were among Northern ministers and even members of the Northern legislature as a whole.

Table 30 is also worth noting in this connection. It shows that while complaints heard in Northern Nigeria about "Fulani domination" of the new political offices were not without foundation, in fact the Northern ministers and legislators were ethnically a far more heterogeneous lot than might be expected. In the new realm of regional leadership, social class solidarity transcended ethnic affinities. This development, which was crucial to the success of the present regime, owed much to history, Islam, the Hausa language, and the political good sense of certain top NPC leaders (Fulani ones not among the least of them); but Katsina College must also be included in any list of contributing factors.

Other measures which followed naturally from the principles of indirect rule and which initially helped to assure the old elite's mastery of the new institutions were the use of pyramided electoral colleges, a rule allowing emirs personally to select 10% of the membership of the final colleges in connection with the first "popular" election in 1951, the declaration of Hausa as a second official language in the Northern House of Assembly (this permitted non-Western-educated or even illiterate members to follow the proceedings), and the decision *not* to impose on the employees of Native Administrations the usual British prohibition against seeking elective office while employed as a public servant.

Living up to the Traditional Image

ALL THE FACTORS so far mentioned, helpful as they may be to an understanding of the origins of the present pattern of leadership, belonged essentially to the earlier years of leadership recruitment. But there were dynamic forces at work that made for the resilience of the pattern. The point here is that parliamentarians with high traditional status tended to act in ways that confirmed and perpetuated their society's preconceptions regarding the basis and characteristics of political leadership.

One example was the deference the parliamentarians, ministers, included, constantly displayed in their contacts with emirs and others high up in the traditional hierarchy. During sittings of the Northern House of Chiefs in Kaduna, deference was clearly visible. On the first day of the session ministers who were members of the lower house (i.e. all but four—the lower house ministers were also ex-officio members of the upper chamber) could be seen at the entrance to the chamber greeting the arrival of important emirs with the customary deferential gestures (a bowed back, the arm raised with a clenched fist, and the standard verbal formulas—*Ranka ya dade*, "may your life be prolonged"; *Allah ya kyara masa girma*, "may God increase your greatness"). Enthusiasm was shown at the appearance of the ruler of a minister's own emirate. Later in the evening each minister showed his respect for his emir by visiting the latter's Kaduna residence (an axiom of traditional protocol in emirate society is that a superior never calls at the house of a subordinate)—hence the emirs had their own compounds in Kaduna, and they did not return any minister's visit.[28]

These fine points of protocol are of more than interest, for the emirate peoples always assumed that they reflected the relative political power actually in force between people. For the aristocratic-minded minister who was also sensitive to the constitutional dignity of his office, how to behave toward his emir when on official tour in his emirate was a delicate problem. One of the Northern federal ministers gave this account of how he dealt with it: "Whenever I have to visit the Emir on official business, I make it a practice to call on him twice; once in my official capacity as a Minister and once in my role as the Emir's subject. When I arrive in town, I drive to the Palace and enter the outer Council Chamber where the Native Authority meets. There I shake hands with the Emir and while discussing my business I sit on a chair. I do not prostrate myself. Later that same day I send a message to the Emir saying that I would like to pay him another visit. This time, the Council is not in official session. I prostrate myself when I approach him and I leave my shoes outside. I do not sit on a chair, but take my place with the other councillors on the floor, and I keep my head reclined when the Emir speaks".

Apparently not all the ministers were as careful to distinguish between roles as this one was. In Kano ministers made a practice of removing from their cars, before entering the city, a flag which signified ministerial rank because the Emir of Kano's car bore the same

---

[28] This rule was observed regardless of how intimate the relationship was. Thus an emir might periodically have travelled long distances to the capital where his son lived as a minister, parliamentary secretary, or civil servant, but in such cases I was assured that the emir never appeared at his son's residence.

flag by virtue of his position as minister without portfolio. Their justification for this practice was expressed in the words of a Hausa proverb, *Ba a hada sarki biyu a gari daya* ("one must not have two kings in his own town!").

More obvious ways in which the parliamentarians showed their attachment to a traditional definition of leadership were to court the honors, cultivate the manner, and acquire the trappings associated with it. By 1965 no fewer than 10 persons holding ministerial rank had resigned their modern offices to take up posts involving traditional titles in their local Native Administrations.[29] It was generally believed that any of the ministers eligible to succeed an emir would have resigned in order to do so, given the chance. There was at least one case of a government official, a parliamentary secretary no longer holding local office, who without success proposed his name to the traditional electors of his emirate when the throne fell vacant, despite the fact that he was not a member of a royal dynasty.

It not previously a holder of a title, a member of parliament usually sought to exalt his elective office by winning one, usually with the help of the augmented financial resources he enjoyed thanks to his electoral success. Or, if already titled, he might try to exchange a lesser title for a more prestigious one. Several ministers (and probably several more backbenchers) received important titles *after* being elected to a legislature. Indeed, in one case, Farouk, his title was created to accommodate him. Examples of already titled parliamentarians who attained higher title during their parliamentary careers include Alhaji Isa Kaita, who became *Wazirin Katsina* after having been *Madawaki*; M. Mohammadu, formerly *Magajin Gari* who became *Dangaladima* in Borgu; M. Hassan Abuja, who became *Sarkin*

---

[29] M. Bello Kano, now Makaman Kano, resigned his ministerial office to become the district head of *Dawaki Ta Kofa* in Kano, with the title of *Dan Amar*. Two *Waziris* of Bornu—(A. Muhammadu, now an officer in the Nigerian foreign service and M. Shettima Kashim, the present *Waziri*)—gave up government ministries to accept this prestigious traditional appointment. Alhaji Laden Baki, formerly Parliamentary Secretary of the Minister of Works, became the *Wazirin* Ayyuka ("*Waziri* of Works") in his native Katsina. And in 1960 the Minister for Local Government, Alhaji Maikano Dutse, left that office to succeed his deceased father as *Sarkin* Dutse, of Dutse District in Kano. M. Shehu Usman Sarki resigned his federal ministership to become *Etsu* (Emir of) Nupe. M. Muhammadu Bashar, formerly *Wombai* of Daura and a Northern Minister, became Emir of Daura; Umaru Abba Karim, the *Wali*, or first councillor, in Muri, was previously a parliamentary secretary and Minister of State. M. Sani Gezawa became a Kano N.A. councillor upon resigning as Parliamentary Secretary, Federal Ministry of Establishment. A. Maje Abdullahi, *Turakin* Kano resigned as Parliamentary Secretary to the Northern Premier to become District Head *Waje* in Kano emirate. A. Ado Bayero resigned as Nigerian ambassador to Senegal to become an Emir of Kano.

Abuja after having been the *Makama*; Alhaji Usman of Katsina, a minister, who became *Sarkin Maska* after being *Galadiman Maska;* and Alhaji Ahmed of Zaria, whose lesser title of *Sarkin Tsapta* was exchanged for a major one—*Dallatu*. Similarly appointment to an emir's council often marked the rise of a parliamentarian (and encouraged him to identify himself with the council's interests), as did marriage into a socially superior family.

Few parliament members who lacked *sarauta* professed to have no interest in acquiring one. In my survey, a frequent reply to the query, "Do you hold a traditional title?" was "not yet". Another indication of concern with traditional office was the employment most ministers arranged with their Native Administrations. A minister had to resign his post in order to take up an active post in a Native Administration, but an N.A. office-holder who became a full-time government minister (i.e. *with* portfolio), did not resign; rather he officially went "on leave without pay". His post was retained in the estimate (budget) and was filled by an "interim" or "acting" appointment. This arrangement was regarded as insurance against the uncertainties of elected office. "An election to the House takes place every five years", explained one minister, a hereditary noble in 1959; "My *sarauta* is for life". (In light of the developments after 1965, this remark now smacks of truly prophetic insight.)

The crux of the above observations is that the members of parliament, in honoring a traditional pecking order in relation to local rulers (and among themselves as well), in assuming the trappings of traditional status and rank and in actively pursuing traditional office and title (sometimes to the exclusion of a rewarding career in modern office), in effect *reinvested* the resources and prestige of their modern offices in the culture of traditional stratification. They did not undermine traditional popular conceptions regarding the basis and characteristics of political leadership; they sustained and renewed them.

Alhaji Sir Ahmadu Bello, Sardauna of Sokoto

The late Alhaji Sir Ahmadu Bello, *Sardauna* of Sokoto, the Premier of the Northern Regional government, was at once the prime example of Northern parliament members' continuity with the traditional structure of leadership, and the key instrument of a conscious effort to maintain this continuity.

A member by agnatic descent of the imperial ruling family of Sokoto (known as the Toronkawa clan of Fulani), the *Sardauna* (as he continued to be most commonly referred to—for people of Hausa culture, this traditional title was not only more familiar but probably more prestigious than being called Sir Ahmadu) was a great-grandson of Sultan Bello, the son of Shehu dan Fodio. On his maternal side he was related to the Kano dynasty, his grandmother being the daughter of the Fourth Emir. The reigning Sultan of Sokoto, Sir Abubakar, was a first cousin.

The *Sardauna's* deep personal involvement in the dual worlds of the traditional and the modern political systems was mirrored in an interesting career. Graduating with a superior record from Katsina College in 1931, he became a teacher in the Sokoto Middle School. In 1934 he resigned to assume his deceased father's office and title —*Sarkin Rabah* (the District Head of Babah, in Sokoto). In 1938 the Sultan of Sokoto Hassan died, and the usual succession contest ensued. Traditionally the Toronkawa of Sokoto are divided into two principal rival lineages, the Bellawa (after Muhammam Bello, the first Sultan) and the Atikawa (after Abubakar Atiku, the Third Sultan). The winning candidate was the present Sultan, Sir Abubakar, who is a member of the Bellawa. Amhadu was one of the unsuccessful aspirants, although he, too, was of the Bellawa lineage (thus he adopted the name of his ancestor Bello as his second name upon receipt of his British knighthood in 1959). It is probable that these rival Bellawa candidates represented an incipient process of segmentation within the lineage based on proximate lines of descent, as usually happens to a royal lineage which succeeds, as had the Bellawa, in monopolizing the throne throughout a series of successive reigns.

Ahmadu's candidacy in 1938 is said to have marked him as a potential threat to the power of the new sultan, who soon posted him to Gusau, a town at the eastern extreme of the Sokoto emirate, where he was officially responsible for general administrative supervision of the surrounding districts. About this time, the Sultan awarded him a title of *Sardauna*. But apparently his energy and efficiency as an administrator were such that his personal influence in the kingdom as a whole increased rather than diminished. In 1943 he was brought to trial in the Sultan's court and convicted of misappropriation of *Jangali* (cattle tax). At the time, it was unheard of for a Sokoto subject to appeal to the secular British magistrate against a decision of the court of the *Sarkin Musulmai* (traditional title of all Sultans of Sokoto, whom the Muslim faithful in all the emirates recognized as their spiritual leader), but the *Sardauna* did so successfully, with the help of a southern Nigerian Christian lawyer (the late Chief Bode Thomas)!

Having won judicial acquittal and reinstatement, the *Sardauna* neither became a critic of the traditional system nor challenged the authority of the Sultan, but instead assiduously cultivated his confidence and friendship. This response, which at the time puzzled European observers,[30] seems, in retrospect, to have been a profound expression both of the *Sardauna's* acceptance of the traditional system as fundamentally legitimate, and of his personal ambition to succeed in terms of its values rather than through defiance of them.

Again to the bewilderment of Western observers, the *Sardauna's* rise to the top in the modern institutions of party and regional government did not reduce his often publicly stated desire to one day become Sultan of Sokoto. His chances from the start were complicated by his proximity in age to the incumbent sultan; only seven years separated them. Clearly, to have acted in a way that would reduce or impair the lofty position of the sultanship would have been inconsistent with this desire to ascend to that office. Thus, quite apart from other considerations, the *Sardauna* had a considerable personal stake in upholding the power and prestige of traditional rulers, and also in associating his modern institutional role with traditional leadership. In this connection, it is interesting to note that as late as 1954 the *Sardauna* was contemplating the possibility of reviving Sokoto as the seat of regional political authority.[31] The Nigerian constitution provided that in the Northern Region, unlike in any of the other regions of the federation, the premier could be a member of the House of Chiefs (of which the Sultan of Sokoto was automatically a member) instead of having to belong to the popularly elected House of Assembly.

Meanwhile, the premiership was conducted in a style which suggested nothing so much as it did a traditional political leader. It was the *Sardauna* who chose March 15th, anniversary of the fall of the Sokoto forces to Lugard's troops in 1903, as the day on which self-government was granted to Northern Nigeria. The deliberateness of this choice is indicated in the fact that the official celebrations actually took place the following May. The *Sardauna's* speeches frequently touched on the past glories of the Fulani empire, the desirability of

[30] See "Strong Man of the North", *West Africa*, January 3, 1953, p. 1,233.
[31] *Minutes*, NPC Executive Committee, January 3, 1954, No. F. 7 (mimeographed document in possession of the author).

preserving tradition, and the religious sanctification and duties underlying political office. In defending the provision of the new Northern Nigerian penal code which made any drinking of alcohol by a Northern Nigerian Muslim a criminal offense, the *Sardauna* gave his assurance that, "as long as my party, the NPC, is in power in the Region, it will not legalize what God has forbidden".[32]

The image of piety was further projected in annual pilgrimages to Mecca in the company of prominent emirs, selected ministers, and other dignitaries (whose inclusion in the premier's airplane was assumed to indicate their enjoyment of his personal favor), and in the occasion of his evening meal, taken daily with the ministers, government civil servants, and other luminaries who regularly showed up at his house (indeed, prolonged absence was a matter for adverse comment), and sat on the floor, often around large bowls of food they shared, in a manner strongly reminiscent of dan Fodio and his followers.

In the period 1963 to 1965 the *Sardauna's* bid for religious glory, which seemed an obvious means of extending and reinforcing his political power, became increasingly more overt and aggressive. The intensified effort took such forms as restoring or founding impressive new mosques, especially ones in Kaduna and Sokoto, which also served as occasions to demonstrate solidarity with the wider Islamic world;[33] convening conclaves of Islamic scholars and educators, at which he sought not only a personal impact (partly with lavish gifts to all in attendance), but presided over discussions of points of doctrinal and ecumenical controversy; sponsoring publications of classic religious texts, some with strong political overtones.[34] Undoubtedly the most striking and significant manifestation of this open indulgence in religious leadership, particularly so in light of the ostensibly secular nature of the premiership and its presumed function as a source of Northern regional unity, was the series of "Islamic conversion tours" which the *Sardauna* undertook to lead through remoter areas of the region in which non-Muslims were numerous and historically resistant to Islamic penetration. In this single activity, if in no other, the *Sardauna* forfeited even the pretense of strictly

[32] Quoted in the *Daily Times* of Nigeria, September 3, 1959, p. 3.

[33] See *Speeches Delivered at the Historic Ceremony of the Opening of The Rebuilt 100,000 Sultan Bellow Mosque on Friday, 5th July, 1963 at Sokoto* (n.p., n.d.).

[34] See especially the Hausa edition of Sheikh Abdullahi Ibn Fodio, *Liya'ul Hukkami (Hasken Mahukumta)* (Zaria, n.d.).

"modern" conceptions of political leadership. Whether he was motivated by overweening personal ambition or sincerely inspired by religious fervor is less important than the simple fact of his insistence on
associating his office with sectarian religious ends.

In general, the quality of personalism in the relationship between
the *Sardauna* and his ministers bore a traditional stamp. The scale of
gifts that regularly flowed from him to his ministers was sometimes
lavish (extending in some cases to Cadillac automobiles) and always symbolic of the ties between them. In January 1961 the
Nigerian Citizen reported the convening of a meeting of the Northern cabinet at the *Sardauna*'s Sokoto residence, where each was presented with a horse—that deeply tradition-laden symbol of power
and allegiance. Ministers were known to leave their shoes at the door
of the premier's office upon entering, to say nothing of the prevalency
of the practice at his house.

The *Sardauna*'s dress (typically a gown of exquisite fabric, an
elaborately brocaded cloak, crowned with a high turban), and
his physical bearing cultivated the public's image, as did studied allusions to inherited greatness. For example, in a 1959 campaign speech
in Bauchi Emirate, home of Prime Minister Abubakar Tafawa Balewa, he observed that with the latter acting as the Northern premier's
"biggest lieutenant in the present day set-up of Nigeria", the relationship between Sokoto and Bauchi remained as it had been "since the
beginning of Fulani rule in the Region", the First Emir of Bauchi
having been a pupil of dan Fodio and a "lieutenant of Sultan
Bello".[35] In a similar vein he seized the occasion of a post-election
party rally in Kaduna to announce his decision (later rescinded) to
retire from politics in 1961, comparing his action with that of dan
Fodio, who at the completion of the Fulani *jihad* divided the empire
between his son Bello and his brother Abdullahi. "When the current political battle is over", he stated, "I, too, will divide this country between my two trustworthy lieutenants"; he then presented an
alkyabba (traditional cloak signifying bestowal of authority)—in
manner of investiture by an emir—to his "lieutenant in the south",
Tafawa Belawa.[36] On another occasion, responding to congratulations
from members of the House of Assembly on his performance as premier, he affirmed that he personally strove "to follow in the footsteps of my ancestors".[37]

[35] *Nigerian Citizen*, November 11, 1959, p. 16.
[36] *Ibid.*, December 19, 1959, p. 1.
[37] See Northern Nigeria, *House of Assembly Debates*, April 16, 1960, Col. 291.

Such appeals to traditional legitimacy by the *Sardauna* were more than matched by the terms in which his political colleagues frequently chose to express support, expressions which at times sounded almost like oaths of fealty.[38] But perhaps the most eloquent, if silent, manifestation of the texture of the relationship of the *Sardauna* and other Northern political leaders was revealed, by accident to me during my first return visit to the Region in the summer of 1963. Riding in an automobile with a knowledgeable Northern friend who was a senior civil servant, I remarked offhandedly that we had just passed a certain government minister from Kano Emirate who was alone in a car with a Sokoto license plate, and asked whose car it was. My friend promptly informed me that it was in fact the minister's car and that his sporting a Sokoto license plate was a matter of what he called *"fadanci"*, i.e. a symbol of his individual allegiance to the person of the *Sardauna* of Sokoto. Afterwards he was able to show me that the practice was followed by several other non-Sokoto ministers.

All of the foregoing suggests that the office of Northern Premiership was in the process of becoming a kind of grand emirship, which is the way many people not unreasonably regarded it already in 1959. By 1963 the *Sardauna* was widely and with deliberate irony being referred to as *Sarkin Arewa*—Emir of the North.

The *Sardauna's* autobiography, *My Life* (reportedly largely ghosted by a former British high civil servant), confirms the indications here of a man of towering ambition and ego.[39] In life respected and feared, admired and envied, cultivated and despised by Northerners, the assassination of the *Sardauna* by a military officer and a member of the southern Ibo tribe (a man who in fact had grown up in Kaduna and was later a frequenter of the circle at the *Sardauna's* residence in Kaduna, where he was stationed), promises to establish the *Sardauna* in local legend as a powerful personification of those attitudes of cultural pride, inward regarding self-sufficiency, and taste for command and hierarchy, which for better or worse may well remain ingrained indefinitely in the patterns of political leadership in the world of the emirates.

[38] Cf. Billy J. Dudley, "The Northern People's Congress", in John P. Macintosh, *Nigerian Government and Politics* (Evanston, Ill., 1966), p. 382.

[39] In his autobiography, *My Life*, the *Sardauna* claims direct maternal and paternal descent from the Prophet Mohammed, illustrated by a diagram to this effect. The merits of the claim need not detain us here; its importance lies in the attempt to establish a pedigree. The book is permeated with similar expressions of self-glorification. See *My Life* (London, 1962).

Yet it is a mistake to reduce this complex figure to a wholly traditional dimension. His background in Western education, his administrative talents, the unconventionality of his resort to British justice in 1943, have been noted. His desire to see economic development in the Northern Region was unquestioned even by those who complained of an insufficient sense of urgency in the way his government went about the task. As premier he presided over important reforms in local government and administration and in the area of legal and judicial organization in many instances contrary to the express wishes of influential traditional rulers. It was perhaps his very desire to buttress the power and prestige of the traditional ruling class that often led him to take action, both remedial and preventative, against members whose behavior he felt might be prejudicial to the interests of the whole. As ex-officio Chairman of the Council of Chiefs, he took the lead in imposing dismissal or discipline in some of the more extreme cases of official misconduct on the part of chiefs, and more than once warned that his government "would not hesitate to remove any chief who is found guilty of oppression or of neglect of his duty"[40]—a threat he later made good in the case of the Emir of Kano, though not simply for these reasons. Informally he is known to have cautioned aristocratic families against the risks of neglecting Western education for their sons (a number of whom were sent to English public schools in response to such exhortations).

The *Sardauna* accepted the parliamentary framework, new goals and functions of government, and the desirability of skilled and talented leadership. But what he would not allow was that these circumstances made the emergence of an entirely new set of rulers either inevitable or desirable ("if my friend might live for centuries", he said to the southern nationalist Mbonu Ojike at the 1950 Ibadan Conference—after Ojike's speech alluding to the universal decline of monarchy in the 20th century—"he might still find natural rulers in the North").[41] Appropriately, he recorded his gratitude to the founders of Katsina College, whose graduates, he once noted with satisfaction, "hold almost all the key positions in the administration of the Region today."[42] The vision that inspired the Katsina College survived in the

[40] *Daily Times* of Nigeria, January 30, 1961, p. 1.
[41] Proceedings, p. 142.
[42] *Northern Nigeria's Day of History: Speeches made by H. E. the Governor, Sir Gawain W. Bell and the Hon. Premier, Alhaji Sir Ahmadu Bello, on Sunday, 15th March 1959* (Kaduna, 1959), p. 2.

Sardauna's efforts to encourage sons of the aristocracy to enter new and potentially influential occupations including the Nigerian army and the Nigerian police, although until very recently *yan sarakuna* generally scorned these vocations in favor of more traditionally prestigious jobs in local administration. Thus the first military governor-general of Nigeria, the late Maj. Gen. Aguiyi-Ironsi, was able to appoint as military governor of the Northern Region Maj. Hassan Katsina, who is a son of the emir of the emirate from which his last names derives, in an obvious gesture of deference to Northern sensibilities about proper leadership.

Officials concerned with the civil service personnel informally estimated that at best only a very small percentage of Northerners in the top echelons of the senior branch of the service came from *talakawa* families, although the interesting papers by Kirk-Greene on this subject produce a sharply different picture of the composition of the lower rungs.[43] As in the case of earlier British educational policy, an argument which northern officials generally presented in defense of socially favored recruitment policies was that participation of traditionally high status persons was required to build up the prestige of the new occupations, and further, that the respect such persons generally commanded was an objectively relevant asset in performing these functions.

Apparently the *Sardauna* had envisioned the continuance of a regime of predominantly aristocratic composition which he was prepared to operate, as he in fact did, under conditions and restraints imposed by the pursuit of economic development and the framework of democratic procedures. When he remarked to Prime Minister Macmillan during Macmillan's visit to the Northern Region elections of 1959, that, "The Conservatives won in England and the conservatives also won in Nigeria",[44] he very likely had the parallel in social history in mind, rather than a comparison of party platforms. The relatively flexible traditional patterns of political leadership recruitment, the head start of the aristocracy in Western education, the fact that its members controlled access to strategic new loci of power, together with the special advantage they had in being conscious of the historic

---

[43] A.H.M. Kirk-Greene, "Bureaucratic Cadres in a Traditional Milieu", in James S. Coleman, ed., *Education and Political Development* (Princeton, 1965); and "Qualification and the Accessibility of Office: Perspectives on Traditional Criteria for the Selection of Public Servants in Northern Nigeria and the Growth of the Principle of Merit", in Arnold Riukin, ed., *Nations by Design: Institution Building in Africa* (New York, 1968), pp. 253-332.

[44] *Northern Nigeria Daily Press Service*, No. 87, January 16, 1960.

political implications of economic advance in the West—all increased the possibility that the longevity of the British aristocracy might be matched if not surpassed in Northern Nigeria under democratic forms. The reality of these prospects was expressed in a dilemma which Aminu Kano, the NEPU leader, told me faced his party in 1959 and what it stood for: "If there were a revolution tomorrow and nepotism was stamped out, the revolutionary government, if it chose officials on the basis of their education and modern administrative experience, would still discover its ranks filled with the class it meant to dethrone".

CHAPTER 8

The Dynamics of Political Parties

THIS CHAPTER examines the impact of traditional emirate institutions, behavior, and norms on the development of the two major Northern political parties of the period, the Northern Peoples' Congress (NPC) and the Northern (later Nigerian) Elements Progressive Union (NEPU). The dynamics of the parties, in terms of political continuity and change, are revealed through a comparative analysis of specific aspects of their activities—party organization, mobilization of party membership and support, particular strategies and techniques of political action, and ideologies. First, however, it will be helpful to place this subject in historical perspective.

From the beginning, political nationalism in the upper North followed two divergent courses. One course was an attempt to harness a program of revolutionary internal political change to the new political forces released by the Nigerian nationalist movement and changing British colonial policy. The other tendency entailed efforts to contain and manipulate these same forces within the bounds of the traditional political order. The key to an understanding of the experience of interparty competition in this period is to appreciate that in this sense, *both* these parties were ambivalent, despite the profound differences between them in ideological orientation which each claimed for itself. This assertion must be elaborated in the context of the parties' origins and responses to the developments of the period.

Nationalistic political consciousness in the Northern region was first expressed at the time of the inauguration of the College Old Boys Association by graduates of Katsina College in 1939. Given the nature and original purposes of the Katsina school, it was inevitable that members of the traditional ruling class would dominate the ranks of the Old Boys. However, the Old Boys actually constituted an elite in two senses, high status in traditional society and relatively superior achievement in Western education and administrative skill. In organizing an association, the Old Boys sought to enhance their own prestige and influence vis-à-vis three rival claimants, British colonial power, autocratic emirs, and the more highly Western-educated men of the southern regions of Nigeria—in other words, all whose interests intruded on their own claims to leadership or threatened to frustrate their desire for reform or both. As one of them later put it, their aims were "(1) to ooze out imperialism, (2) to break down the idea of sole Native Authority, and (3) to prevent domination by Southerners".[1]

At this time, political organizations based on nontraditional principles were suspect in the eyes of emirs and British officials alike, despite the fact that the status origins of most Old Boys disposed them to favor moderate reforms that would accommodate their special talents without precipitating a fundamental upheaval of traditional socio-political institutions. Because nearly all its members were employees of the colonial government or of Native Administrations, the Association could do little to overcome the obstacle of determined official hostility. Consequently it became moribund within two years of its inauguration.[2]

Former members kept the ideas of the Association alive during the 1940s, by helping form discussion groups of educated young men in several Northern towns: the Zaria Friendly Society and the Zaria Provincial Progressive Union, the Sokoto Youth Circle and the Citizens' Welfare Association of Sokoto, the Bauchi Discussion Circle, the Bauchi General Improvement Union, and the Kano Citizens' Association. Groups that displayed prudence and moderation were tolerated by the Native Authorities and the British, who nevertheless watched their activities closely. Those which came under the influence of radicals did not survive: the Zaria Friendly Society and the Bauchi Discussion Circle, for example.

The Zaria Friendly Society was forced to disband when its founder, *Malam* Sa'adu Zungur, a Koranic scholar and noted nationalist (one of the handful of Northerners to take the bold step of joining a southern nationalist party—the NCNC—of which he was general secretary from 1948 to 1951) used its platform to attack the system of Native Administration. Similarly, official recognition was withdrawn from the controversial Bauchi Discussion Circle by the British Resident who had helped initiate it, when his salary and that of the Emir of Bauchi came up for discussion in the presence of both. The person in charge of the agenda for the Bauchi Discussion Circle was Zungur's protégé, M. Aminu Kano. Other ostensible nonpolitical or-

[1] M. Nuhu Bamalli, "The Northern Peoples' Congress", 1959, mimeog.

[2] "The Problem of Northern Nigeria as the Natives See It: An Account of an Interview with Lord Lugard by Abubakar Imam, Editor of *Gaskiya Ta Fi Kwabo*, and a Member of the African Press Delegation to the United Kingdom in 1943", August 1943 (deposited in the Nigerian Archives, Kaduna: Governor's Office General 1088, Item 8).

ganizations served as forums for political discussion. Meetings of the Northern Teachers Association, for example, were not limited to discussion of matters of professional interest, but also took up larger political questions.

In 1948 the continuing ferment among the Old Boys elite, represented by the rise and fall of these scattered relatively informal groups, crystallized into a region-wide organization called the Northern Peoples' Congress (*Jami'iyyar Mutanen Arewa*), the NPC. This event actually represented the merger of two groups founded earlier the same year (the *Jami'iyyar Arewa* at Zaria and the *Jami'iyyar Mutanen Arewa A'Yau* at Kaduna). Officers of the NPC included Dr. R.A.B. Dikko (a Fulani convert to Christianity who was the North's first medical doctor), President; M. Abubakar Iman (the editor of *Gaskiya Ta Fi Kwabo*), Treasurer (these two representatives of the conservative strain in Northern political thinking), as well as those with a radical bent such as Sa'adu Zungar, Advisor on Muslim Law, and M. Aminu Kano, Joint Auditor. The continued vulnerability of the majority, who were dependent on official employment, led the new organization to describe itself disingenuously as a "purely cultural one, the object of which is to afford Northerners the opportunity of meeting together to discuss common social problems".[3] The pursuit of more overtly political objectives was implicit, however, in the NPC motto—a declaration of intention to war against ignorance, idleness, and oppression (*yakin jahilci, lalaci, da zalunci*) in the North. Surviving discussion groups at Sokoto, Kano, and Bauchi were transformed into local branches of the NPC.

A year before this, a group of young men with noticeably different social backgrounds had established an organization called the Northern Elements Progressive Association (NEPA), whose avowed purposes were more openly political.[4] The founders of NEPA, although of better than average education, were mostly either employed by commercial firms or in the secondary, clerical rank of official employment. A son of the Emir of Kano was secretly a member, but none of the others had high traditional status. Most members

---

[3] Bamalli, "Northern Peoples' Congress".

[4] In a letter from M. Raje Abdullah, President of NEPA, to the Resident, Kano, dated April 24, 1947, Abdullah explained that the object was "to study conscientiously and objectively the various problems, educational, economic, social, and otherwise—facing the common man of the North with a view to making representations where necessary to the authorities. This we of the Association have solemnly pledged ourselves to do with neither fear (either of the Authorities or of our own people) nor bias".

were *Habe* commoners; there were few Old Boys among them. Several came from outside the area of the emirate system, i.e. from the lower northern or the Middle Belt region.

The founders of NEPA were distinguished by another characteristic that continued to mark the development of radical Northern nationalist organizations—connections with southern nationalist parties. Dr. Nnamdi Azikiwe, the president of the then dominant Nigerian Nationalist Party, the NCNC, had encouraged the foundation of NEPA during his tour of the North to solicit funds for a delegation to the Colonial Office in 1947. The president of NEPA, *Malam* Raje Abdullah, later became president of the revolutionary Zikist movement. Other Zikists and NCNC members of southern ethnic origins acted as informal "consultants" to NEPA, and its public meetings were sometimes addressed by prominent NCNC leaders such as Mbonu Ojike.[5] Details of NEPA's organization and program were handled secretly, but its Arabic motto hardly concealed the boldness of its motivating spirit: *Man Lam Yakhful Laha, Yakhafu Kulla Sha'in Man Yakhful Lah Kullu, Sha'in Yakhafu* ("He who does not fear God fears everybody, but he who fears God is to be feared by some"[6]). The intended innuendo was not mistaken by the alarmed authorities; key NEPA members were abruptly dispersed from their posts in Kano, and the organization folded in 1949.

The establishment of the first Northern organization to declare itself a political party was left to the enterprise of eight people, again mostly *Habe* commoners, who founded the Northern Elements Progressive Union (NEPU) in Kano on August 8, 1950. Reportedly the name was suggested by M. Maitama Sule[7] who thought the affinity to the title NEPA was justified by the revolutionary ideology that inspired the new group. A declaration of principles issued in October 1950 proclaimed the existence of a "class struggle between the members of the vicious circle of the Native Administrations on the one hand and the ordinary *talakawa* [commoners] on the other", and announced that the NEPU was to be dedicated to the "emancipation of the *talakawa* from domination by these privileged few" through

---

[5] "This association", stated an address welcoming Ojike to Kano, "is . . . out to bridge—Allah helping—the chasm that divides the North from the South". *West African Pilot*, April 14, 1947.

[6] The translation was given to me and confirmed by former NEPA members. I am informed, however, that the Arabic is unorthodox and probably reflects local adulteration of the language.

[7] See Appendix A.

"reform of the present autocratic political institutions".[8] *Malam* Abba Maikwaru, the president of another largely *Habe* group, called *Taron Masu Zumunta* which organized outside the walls of Kano traditional city in the *"Fagge"* district,[9] was elected president of NEPU. He brought members of this group with him into the new party. Several prominent members of the NEPU also belonged to the Kano branch of the NPC, holding that the nonpolitical status of the NPC made simultaneous membership in both groups proper.

A showdown between radical and conservative elements in the two strains of the Northern nationalist movement came with the Jos convention of the NPC in December 1950; the convention proscribed dual membership in the NEPU and NPC and insisted on the elimination of radical elements, especially Zungur and Aminu Kano, from the NPC executive. NEPU adherents in the Kano delegation countered with a proposal to convert the NPC into a political party, and the rejection of this proposal signaled a final rupture between the two factions. Soon thereafter, M. Aminu Kano, then headmaster of the Maru Teachers' Training College in Sokoto, resigned his position and returned to Kano to devote himself fulltime to politics. His newspaper article explaining his resignation made it plain that he intended to develop the NEPU into an instrument for challenging the established order.

In April 1951 Kano was elected vice-president of the NEPU and early in 1953 was elevated to the position of president-general. After 1959 he bore the title of life-president.

1951-1965

The promulgation of the Nigerian Constitution of 1951 altered the political situation in the North, with profound consequences for the development of political parties there. Whereas colonial policy and the interests of traditional authority in the North were previously hostile to the idea of political parties, provisions of the new constitution, such as those prescribing elections, ministerial government, and re-

[8] NEPU, *Sawaba Declaration of Principles* (Jos: Baseco Press, 1950).

[9] The population of the *Fagge* district of the Kano metropolitan area is composed largely of "strangers", or immigrants from the more northerly areas of the Sudan, e.g. "Damagaramawa" (people from Damagaram in Niger) or "Buzaye" Tuareg serfs from the Sahara and commercial traders from Arab, Levantine, and North African countries. The cosmopolitan atmosphere is receptive to radically minded political parties; while, unlike the behavior of the Nigerian communities of the *Sabon Gari*, the culture and Muslim identity of *Fagge* people permit them to have close relationships with and therefore greater influence on the indigenous people of the traditional city.

gional powers, necessarily made parties officially acceptable, legitimate institutions. The federal character of the constitution, which called for both Central and Regional African ministers, and legislatures composed of African majorities, also prompted the Northern educated elite and traditional authorities to close ranks against the southern nationalist parties.

At the Ibadan Constitutional Conference of 1950 the traditional Emirs of Gwandu, Zaria, Katsina, and Abuja joined prominent educated commoners such as *Malam* Abubakar Tefawa Belewa in the defense of Northern interests, including financial reforms allocating a greater share of revenue to the North, regional control of electoral procedure, a bicameral regional legislature with equal powers for the Northern Houses of Assembly and Chiefs, and parity of representation in the central legislature. When it appeared that the last demand might not be met, the Sultan of Sokoto used his influence to promote *Kudin Taimakon Arewa* (money to help the North) in order, had it been necessary, to carry the "Northern" case to London. The Ibadan Conference and the fund-raising campaign first established the pattern of successful collaboration between traditional authorities and the younger, educated elite that became the hallmark of the NPC.

The workings of the new electoral system induced the NPC to convert itself into a formal political party; this decision, in turn, led to a new balance of power within the NPC. Electoral regulations, as they applied to the North under the 1951 constitution, stipulated a series of indirect "tier" elections to the Northern House of Assembly, extending from village and ward units up to the final stage of provincial colleges. Members of the Regional House, in turn, were to select the Northern members of the central legislature from its numbers. Native Authorities were given the right to "inject" into the provincial colleges 10% of the total reaching that stage through the protracted elections at lower levels.[10] Like many other aspects of institutional change in the North, the system was a compromise between the principles of traditional authority and democratic representation, which yielded some peculiar results.

At the primary and intermediate stages of elections at Kano City, Jos, Kaduna, Maiduguri, and Kabba, victories were registered for candidates running on the platform of the NEPU. It appeared for a

[10] On the electoral procedure used in the Northern Region for 1951 see C. R. Niven, "Elections in Northern Nigeria", *Corona* (May 1952), pp. 179-81.

time that NEPU, to the great consternation of NPC leaders, might capture the Northern House of Assembly.[11] Hastily certain NPC executive committee members met and decided to convert the organization into a political party as of October 1, 1951. The announcement declaring the new status of the NPC suggested the party's intention to act as a progressive but moderate counterweight to the NEPU.[12]

The step was taken too late to permit the party, as such, to present candidates. However, the susceptibility of the electoral college arrangement to manipulation allowed the Native Authorities to rally forces on behalf of their favored candidates in the subsequent colleges. The colleges employed the method of the "whispering vote". Moreover, the "ten-percent injection" device enabled an undetermined number to take seats in the Northern House despite their having been defeated at lower stages of the election by NEPU candidates, not one of whom was eventually successful. Conspicuous among those who won, thanks to the injection device, were four N.A. officials at Kano, including M. Inuwa Wada and M. Bello Dandago, who later became federal ministers, and M. Isa Kaita, later Northern Minister of Education.[13] In the North as a whole, candidates who were Native Au-

[11] "It is reported from Kano that quite unexpectedly, the Northern Elements Progressive Union [allied for the purposes of election with the NCNC] have gained seventeen seats in the City elections. That in itself may not be very important but if, and it is quite possible, NEPU gains several district seats, the position might arise that NEPU will have complete control of the final Kano electoral college and will be in a position to elect twenty of its members to the House of Assembly. If they but capture one or two other Provinces they might well gain control of the House of Assembly."

"If the farcical position at Kano, where [it looks like a minority group will get] control against the declared interests of the overwhelming majority of the people, is repeated elsewhere in the North, there must be the most stringent heart searching particularly at the top, to find the cause. In the meantime, the red light is showing—may its warning be heeded before it is too late".

Editor, *Nigerian Citizen*, October 25, 1951, p. 6.

[12] Its declared aims were: "(1) regional autonomy within a united Nigeria; (2) local government reform within a progressive emirate system; (3) the voice of the people to be heard in all the councils of the North; (4) retention of the traditional system of appointing Emirs with a wider representation on the Electoral Committee; (5) a drive throughout the North for education while retaining and increasing cultural influences; (6) eventual self-government for Nigeria with dominion status within the British Commonwealth; and (7) one North, one people, irrespective of religion, tribe, or rank". Manifesto for the Northern Peoples' Congress, October 1, 1951, quoted in *Report on the Kano Disturbances* (Kaduna, 1953), p. 45.

[13] In the 1954 elections the ten-percent injection device was discontinued. An electoral reform committee under the chairmanship of Mr. C. R. Niven, then Resident of Plateau Province, explained: "We feel that by now the country and the leading citizens concerned, have gained sufficient political knowledge to be

thority officials triumphed in all but a few cases; afterwards the overwhelming majority of members elected to the House declared for the NPC.[14]

Upon the declaration of formal political status by the NPC, the government invoked its General Order No. 40, which prohibited participation in politics by government civil servants, thereby forcing members employed by the government to resign. These regulations were not applied to Native Authority officials, however. The net result of the moves was that a rump of the original organization, composed of a majority of traditional, aristocratic elements and a few wealthy self-employed merchant-traders, was left in control of the party. The stage was then set for a shift in the locus internal party power away from an extra-parliamentary "congress" of self-styled moderate "progressives" primarily concerned with political reform,[15] to a parliamentary caucus, equally, if not more interested in the defense of traditional authority and prestige, on which it was to rely for electoral support from then on.

The fundamental structural shift in the NPC, the signs of which became more and more evident as time passed, was remarkable for the fact that practically everywhere else in West Africa at comparable stages of constitutional advance, successful nationalist parties were being transformed into agencies of almost the opposite social and ideological tendencies. The immediate answer to "what was different" about party development in Northern Nigeria is to be found in the particular underlying socio-economic and political conditions discussed throughout this book, as well as in the specific legal and constitutional expedients just described. The constitutional reorganization of Nigeria in 1954, as a Federation with residual powers in the regions, further supported the trend toward a separate course of Northern development; clearly the emergence of the *Sardauna* as president-general of the NPC and northern premier also contributed substantially. However, to understand fully how this course of devel-

---

relied upon to return responsible people to the new House without any artificial stimulation". *Report on Electoral Reform in the Northern Region* (Lagos, 1953), Section A, Paragraph 1.

[14] Thus the new Northern House of Assembly was not originally organized on a party basis, nor were ministers so appointed. The House remained in this state until the government acknowledged control by the NPC in December 1953.

[15] One of this group, M. Abba Halib, has recorded that others, "who were considered radicals and were the backbone of the new party", included A. Abubakar Imam, A. Inuwa Wada, A. Ibrahim Imam, M. Yakubu Wanka, A. Nuhu Bamali, M. Yahaya Gusau, and the late A. Abdul Kadiri Makama. "How I Became a Politician", *Sunday Post* of Nigeria, October 14, 1962, p. 4.

362

opment was sustained through a series of ever more democratically organized elections (those of 1959, 1961, and 1964 involving male suffrage, direct voting, and the use of the secret ballot) requires a closer examination of party structure and dynamics. As we shall see, a key to Northern political continuity was that the cardinal objective of modern democratic political parties—the winning of mass electoral support—was achieved by the NPC through astute manipulation of traditional forces and institutions.

Democratization of the rules governing party competition also affected the nature and fortunes of the NEPU. A comparative analysis of NEPU's experience—its largely unsuccessful efforts to mobilize a mass political movement based on the principles of democratic radicalism—of the methods the party employed, of the obstacles it encountered and its limited successes, will further reveal the impact of emirate tradition on Northern party politics.

PARTY ORGANIZATION

The NPC

The second item of the NPC manifesto was "Local government reform within a progressive Emirate system". Within a year it was amended to read, "Local Government reform within a progressive Emirate system *based on tradition and custom*," it being explained that the change was "directed at maintaining a balance between the radical and the conservative elements in the Congress".[16] The implication of the amendment was that the party had decided not to disturb the basic emirate structure, but to work within it. Apart from its obvious ideological implications, that decision had significant consequences in terms of party organization.

In the upper North the Northern Peoples' Congress installed itself squarely on the boundaries of traditional emirates. The lines of local administrative and party organization became virtually coextensive. At the local level branches of the party were set up to coincide with the subunits of the emirate—hamlet, village, rural district, ward, and town. One result of this arrangement was that traditional-administrative and party authority tended to be exercised by the same personnel, especially in rural districts. Thus among 68 rural district branches investigated in 1959, in 60 the party chairman was also the district head. The majority of the branches were created on the initiative of the district head, usually acting under encouragement

---

[16] Emphasis added; see *Nigerian Citizen*, August 18, 1952, p. 1.

from above. The inducement to organize locally seems to have been more in the nature of a summons than an appeal. Actual meetings of rural district branches were in general highly infrequent, and many such units were merely "paper" branches.

As in the case of the subordinate local government councils, the presence of the district head in the top position of leadership had the effect of reversing the direction of control that one might expect to obtain under conditions of interparty democracy. Instead of serving primarily as the source from which demands and interests were communicated to higher party authority, rural district branches primarily functioned a means of transmitting the directions of higher party authority downwards. There was no evidence that this relationship was ever challenged in word or deed by the rank and file of these branches themselves, a development which would have been tantamount to a redefinition of the traditional relationship of peasants to their district head, to say nothing of that to his superiors. One progressive district-head-NPC-president complained to me that his efforts to sound out the rural branches on party proposals (during the late postwar phase of constitutional conferences) were received at first with dismay and after four years of meetings with obvious skepticism and caution. "If a *talaka* wants something he might come to me personally or through a *bafada*", he added, "but not to a party meeting". Indeed, Tafawa Balewa, himself a commoner, lamented the reluctance by the peasantry to speak up through the party: "I once visited a village and tried to tell the people about the party and also to elicit the views of the people", he told a party convention. "All they could say was that *goggo* [baboons] were threatening them".[17]

Since district heads were nearly always empowered to exercise the authority of the Native Authority in matters vitally affecting party organizational efforts, including granting or withholding permits for party campaign rallies and stipulating conditions under which the rallies could be held, the fusion of administrative and party authority facilitated the organization of the party. By the same token, it had the negative but potent advantage of allowing harassment of the opposition in myriad ways. One district head explained, for instance: "When the opponents of my party receive a permit to stage a public lecture in my district, I am always careful to allow them a most solitary place to which nobody would care to go, apart from indirect

[17] *Minutes, NPC Emergency Convention,* November 21, 1953 (mimeo. in Hausa).

364

pressure which I assert to make the lecture a total failure, and I do succeed".[18] Similarly a few timely arrests by N.A. policemen operating under orders of a district head immediately after such meetings, naturally impressed the crowd with the power available to one party and the disabilities of membership in the other, even were charges not pressed. In this situation, British administrative officers, whose job it was in principle to uphold the right of free and open party competition, were in practice frustrated because of their equivocal role via-à-vis the Native Administration, as an anguished letter from one of them to a colleague makes clear.[19]

In conformity with the party's close relationship to the emirate system, NPC party structure was highly decentralized. Like the major parties of the United States, the national party effectively operated only at election time. On NPC organizational charts, the key unit was normally located at the level of the division (like the province, divisions were originally the units of colonial administration; divisions were usually coextensive with traditional emirates). Significantly, however, in those divisions that included more than one traditional emirate, the latter became the focus of decision-making. For example, it would have been unthinkable for the Kano Divisional Party Executive to nominate NPC candidates for Kazaure emirate, although the latter represents only a tiny portion of the territory, population, and wealth of Kano division. The reason was that NPC organization reflected and acknowledged the traditional identity of emirates as quasi-sovereign "autonomous" states, and adjusted accordingly.

For this reason provincial executive committees of the NPC tended to be what their name literally implied—committees of various divisional executive bodies concerned with matters of common interest

[18] Letter from Bello Dandago, *Sarkin Dawakin Kano*, M.P., to the Party Manager, September, 1957, Secretariat Files, Kaduna, quoted in R. L. Sklar, *Nigerian Political Parties* (Princeton, 1963), p. 363, note 81.

[19] "The District Head of ———— is a known rogue, but a strong one, and therefore indispensable: a fact of which he is all too well aware. The NEPU and other party backers are all experienced jailbirds, whose intention is to get the District Head in that place. The result is that life in ———— is a series of complaints and counter-complaints by rude and angry people who know all the rules. As the police are not too wonderful, one has to prevent any possible cause for complaints since complaints are invariably insoluble. If a District Head is proved to have been oppressing NEPU he gets an increment: if the NEPU complain of a District Head, and are sent away because the complaint is mendacious or embarrassing to the Native Administration, then the A.D.O. gets reprimanded. At the same time, the last instructions given to the A.D.O. were that the N.A. was not to be embarrassed, for all its faults. The District Head can do what he pleases, under cover of this support, provided that he does it first and is discovered afterwards". Letter, October 30, 1955, in possession of the author.

rather than a higher authority to whose decisions divisions of emirates were subject.[20] It was also indicative of this situation that efforts on the part of NPC central secretariat officials to achieve greater organizational coherence, implying central direction and control, were repeatedly rebuffed by the elected party leadership.[21] Indeed, central secretariat officials, who often represented the thinking of the more radical elements of the party,[22] exercised little if any influence on the formation of policies, which was a great source of dissatisfaction with their role, especially when they contrasted it with that of their counterparts in other Nigerian parties. Another consequence of centering party authority at the emirate level was to subordinate and thus reduce the influence of the less tradition-bound urban branches of the party, which formed the core of NPC local organization before 1951, and continued to attract the relatively more radical and assertive local NPC members.

The organizational link between the NPC and the emirates had concrete advantages. The influence of the emir was used informally (where his own choices were not at odds with the party's) to settle intraparty disputes over nominations, thus contributing to party discipline. More importantly, once official candidates were chosen, an emir, by merely "passing on" their names, through the ordinary administrative channels, to district heads and other officials in outlying areas (which perforce vested the nominees with traditional sanction)

[20] An exception revealing in this respect until 1958, Zaria emirate was the only emirate in Zaria province, the other administrative units being "independent" non-Muslim Native Authorities. Not only do Zaria Native Authority officials dominate the Zaria divisional and provincial executive; the latter normally makes the decisions (including nominations) for the whole province. This could occur originally because there was no other emirate in the province to provide a counterweight to Zaria. In 1958 Jema'a emirate was transferred from Plateau to Zaria province. The transfer had not, however, produced any notable change in the provincial structure of the party, in part, as officials explained, because Jema'a was a vassal state of Zaria emirate in pre-British times. See Smith, *Government in Zazzau*, pp. 77-78, 202.

[21] In 1953 Ibrahim Imam, then general secretary of the NPC, submitted proposals for greater centralization which were rejected by the party. This, he contends, was the major reason for his resignation expulsion from the party. In 1958 the party manager, M. Rafih, a founding member of the NPC in 1948, resigned his position after similar organizational measures were not accepted. The secretariat's memorandum had called for the establishment of four zones, comprising three provinces each, with supervisory authority to be placed in the hands of national organizing secretaries. The memorandum also pleaded for a greater role for the central secretariat and deplored the practice of local party branches "going around to the leaders of the party in absolute ignorance of the central secretariat".

[22] Another item in the ill-fated 1958 reorganization memorandum proposed that, "Where we find an N.A. unfavorable to its people within its jurisdiction, the NPC should also oppose the role being played by that N.A."

automatically marshalled the support of all these officials on behalf of the official party candidates.

The contribution of the traditional emirate structure to the party was not limited to the upper echelons of the bureaucracy. This helps explain some initially puzzling aspects of NPC organization. In 1959 the organizational strength of the party per se probably reached an all-time high. That year the NPC stationed two permanent organizing secretaries in each division, and one or two temporary field secretaries or foot campaigners per division were recruited for the duration of the federal election campaign. These workers constituted the total field force paid out of national party funds. It was not the practice of the NPC to use voluntary party organizers. Thus, for approximately every 58,666 people living in emirates, there was one NPC party worker. It is impossible that a team of that size could have effectively canvassed such a large population, especially when one takes into account the vast territorial scope, the poor communications system, the lack of any party newspaper, and an illiteracy rate of 75%. (It is inconceivable that the much smaller party staff existing prior to 1959 could have done so.) Yet even in remote villages party flags, emblems, and sloganizing were much in evidence. It is officially estimated that over 90% of those eligible registered and voted for the NPC in the emirate provinces in 1959. Even considering the fact that here and there divisional or provincial branches of the party paid for a few additional organizers out of their own funds, the over-all results constituted a highly improbable feat of party organization.

Actually the party relied primarily not on its own efforts in organization but on the numerous staff of the Native Administrations, which provided the party with continuous and direct access to the area and people under their jurisdiction. The NPC early recognized that Native Administration employees represented virtually a ready-made local party machine. Thus a party organizational manual written in 1953 states: "The party must make every effort to have one member at least in every village of fair size in the Region. This is possible if the party can win the hearts of village and District scribes, school teachers and N.A. employees *whose work concerns touring*, e.g. agricultural, veterinary, medical, and forest *mallams*. The services of such officers to the party are most important".[23]

[23] Emphasis added. "Sake Tsarin Jam'iyyan Mutanen Arewa", NPC Secretariat, Kaduna, December 13, 1953, p. 4, paragraph (3) mimeog.

In light of the organizational assistance given the party at every level by the Native Administration, on the one hand, and of the defense of traditional emirates constantly waged by the party, on the other, the nature of the relationship between the administrative apparatus of traditional emirates and the NPC party machinery is best characterized as symbiotic—one sustained the other.

The incidence of tradition in party organization at the national or regional level was no less evident. Under the constitution of the NPC, the annual convention of the party theoretically enjoyed "absolute power to decide major policies of the party".[24] However, the prescriptions of the party constitution seldom provided a guide to actual practices and arrangements. The constitution stipulated annual conventions, but no ordinary conventions were held in 1951, 1953, 1957, 1959, or any year thereafter (emergency conventions were held in July 1952 and September 1957). It also provided for annual election of party officers. However, in 1953, one year after the *Sardauna* assumed the presidency, the convention voted to freeze the slate of officers then selected for five years (and even this time limit was thereafter ignored). As it happened, these five years coincided with the crucial period of negotiating terms for the transfer of colonial power to the federal and NPC regional governments, which eliminated any role for the convention in these crucial dealings.

The realities of party structure reflected the ascendancy of the parliamentary party, dominated, as we have seen, by aristocratic elements, over the extraparliamentary convention (originally the focus of reformist sentiments)—open to anyone selected as a delegate by local branches, each of whom was entitled to one vote.[25] This process of parliamentary party control began in 1951 with the transfer of the party secretariat from Zaria to Kaduna, where it could be closely supervised by the new ministers, and might be said to have culminated in 1959 when a group composed exclusively of parliament members met at Kaduna to draft and adopt the party's electoral manifesto, which no other party organ formally considered at all prior to its publication. On no occasion after 1951 did the rank and file outvote the platform on issues discussed in the convention. Existing records show that discussion was perfunctory, and that formal voting was rarely a part of convention proceedings.[26] This remarkable

[24] *Northern Peoples' Congress: Constitution and Rules*, p. 3.
[25] *Ibid.*, p. 4.
[26] See *Minutes* of the following conventions: Kaduna, December 1952 (in Hausa); Kaduna, July 1952 (in English); Jos, April 1954 (in Hausa); Maiduguri,

control of the rank and file of the extraparliamentary party was never legislated. Rather it appears to have represented a spontaneous manifestation of the hierarchical relationships and expectations vis-à-vis established authority that stemmed from acceptance of premises of traditional society.

Policy discussions, when they occurred, were concentrated in the parliament caucuses of the federal and regional legislatures, where the principle of decentralization prevailed. At caucus meetings, customarily held at the premier's house in Kaduna during sessions of the Northern House, in principle two delegates from each province represented the other members from their area. A minister from each province served as a permanent chairman of his delegation. In contrast to proceedings at annual conventions, the atmosphere of parliamentary party meetings was one of relatively free give and take. Discipline was sometimes invoked on motions of importance to the government, but the principle of decentralization was honored in the right of a representative not only to assert the views of his constituency, but to submit private legislative motions that were disapproved by a majority of the caucus and would therefore be voted down in the House. One apparent reason for this permissive climate was that, compared to open conventions there was uniformity in the social composition of the caucus. There, traditional notables could deal with each other on an equal plane.

NEPU

NEPU organization was at first highly centralized and geared for change. Local organizational patterns varied widely, but usually they initially cut across traditional boundaries. The superior local branch was located at the provincial level (provincial annual conferences were particularly important), but occasionally large urban branches such as Kano and Zaria NEPU were paramount. The women's and youth subsidiary organizations of NEPU were much more vital to party organization than their counterparts in the NPC. NEPU parliament members did not automatically assume prominent positions in their local branches, and they were most inconspicuous in the National Executive Committee (the life-president himself only succeeded in becoming a parliament member in 1959).

Until 1963 annual provincial conferences elected all the members

June 1955 (in Hausa); Kaduna, August 1956 (in Hausa); Zaria, September 1957 (in English); all mimeog.

of the various provincial executives, which in turn elected working committees to run the day-to-day party business. Paid organizers (allocated on the basis of one per province, plus an additional one for large or important divisions), unlike their NPC opposite members, usually held decision-making positions; e.g. they were chairmen of the provincial committees that nominated party candidates. The position of the organizer made him a link in a direct chain of command which extended from national headquarters in Kano to the local units. NEPU officials extolled the work of an "informal unpaid army" of Hausa traders who traveled widely, touching a large network of markets in rural areas.

Supreme authority at the central level was vested in an annual conference which met regularly and was attended by delegates of local branches and women's and youth sections. Four of the party officers were hand-picked annually by the life-president, and others were chosen by a committee consisting of one representative from each of the 12 Northern provinces, plus Kano City, over which the life-president presided. He also submitted a list of candidates for membership in the national executive committee to each annual conference for its approval. A great deal of party business was in practice conducted by subcommittees, the most important of which were Elections and Finance (both chaired by the life-president).

In this period breaches of discipline were rare, probably because of the powerful position of Aminu Kano as life-president. The only notable instance of a conflict between the extraparliamentary party and a parliament member was resolved by expelling the latter. A further indication both of the degree of central control exercised by the national party and of the NEPU's comparative disregard for traditional demarcations was that in 1959 several NEPU candidates were selected to run in constituencies of which they were neither natives nor residents, an electoral hazard never risked by the NPC.

This high degree of centralization, in contrast to the organizational structure of NPC, held true at least on paper until approximately 1962. Thereafter the emphasis of NEPU organization was clearly on decentralized control. Provincial and even new divisional executive committees assumed decisive importance in such critical matters as the nomination of the party's candidates for elected office. This change of organizational style reflected tactical decisions to concentrate almost exclusively in the area of the emirates, i.e. to disengage from the Middle Belt, and to engage more in the exploitation of local community issues and traditional socio-political cleavages. The pressures underlying these decisions are indicated below. For the moment, it is enough to note that these pressures drew NEPU, organizationally and otherwise, willy-nilly, further and further into the social and political order as it existed and away from the world of change which the party leaders had imagined at one time they would soon be governing.

LEADERS, MEMBERS, AND SUPPORTERS

The NPC

The interlocking directorate of modern regional (especially NPC party) and traditional leadership was the subject of a previous chapter. Here it is only necessary to observe that the patterns described therein were duplicated at the level of local NPC branches. For example, in Sokoto province at least 33 of the 38 members of the executive committee between 1958 and 1964 were Native Authority personnel, and roughly the same proportion were either regional or federal parliament members. To illustrate the same phenomenon in another way, 7 of the 9 members of the Sokoto Native Authority Council were NPC members of the regional or federal legislatures. Rarely was there a Native Authority Councillor who was a NEPU member or supporter. In most places, my inquiries on that point were considered absurd. It is also important to note that at the provincial and divisional levels of party organization, wealthy *Habe* merchant-traders, who constituted a major breach in the continuity of established political leadership, were usually less well represented and exercised far less influence than in the regional and federal parliamentary parties. The power they enjoyed varied inversely to the proximity of the party unit to the central bureaucracies of the emirates, which was another indication both of their limited party role and of the limits of change in the character of the Native Authority.

On the other hand, in Bornu, Bida, and Zaria emirates, merchant-traders, as Richard Sklar has observed, tended to comprise a relatively high percentage of the executive committee membership. Significantly, those emirates experienced relatively effective NEPU activity, which in turn induced the NPC to push *attajirai* to the fore. In both Bornu and Zaria, however, decisions about nominations and other important party strategies were nevertheless determined by high officials of the Native Authorities operating behind the scenes. In these situations the local party branches hoped that such discretion would reduce the potential damage to the NPC of NEPU criticisms of the N.A.—innocence by disassociation—without actually dislocating party authority.

Another example of NPC arrangements calculated to provide a certain flexibility of leadership and thus to offset NEPU criticism with a minimum of sacrifice in traditional structure was the dual party organization that operated in towns such as Katsina and Zaria. In Katsina Town one branch of the party drew its leaders and supporters from the section of the town primarily inhabited by *Habe* commoners, while a second branch controlled the area in which the compounds of the *sarakuna* class predominated. In Zaria City a coordinate executive committee operated in the stranger settlements (*sabon gari, Tudan wada*) located outside the walls of the traditional city. This dualism of organization was resolved by the subordination of all town branches of the party to the divisional or emirate executive above them, where the social composition of leadership was for the most part, as already noted, safely aristocratic.

As was true at the regional level, the local leadership of NEPU, on the other hand, reflected the party's ideological aspiration—a radical democracy in which the ordinary *talakawa* would have a fair share. Certainly by any relevant measure—occupation, education, or traditional status—the majority of local NEPU leaders were drawn from lower social strata, as data previously summarized in a published study by R. L. Sklar and C. S. Whitaker, Jr. shows.[27] NEPU recruited its leaders substantially from the categories of small trade, crafts, shopkeeping, laboring, and arming. Unquestionably, however, a good many educated teachers, salaried clerks, and technical workers employed by Native Authorities covertly sympathized with NEPU's program, but were prevented from assuming leadership positions by considerations of career.

It is also true that the incidence of NEPU leaders of high traditional status was greater in local and extraparliamentary units than at the parliament level. The patron of the party, for example, was M. Abubakar Tambawal of Sokoto, a great-great-grandson of Shehu dan Fodio. The NEPU Muslim Legal Advisor and Organizer in charge of Sokoto province was M. Lawan Danbazau, who is a member of the patrician Fulani clan of Kano, called the Danbazawa. A member of the Masaba, one of the three ruling dynasties of Bida emirate, was the secretary-general of the party, Abubakar Zukogi

---

[27] "Nigeria", in Coleman and Rosberg, *Political Parties*, pp. 612-15.

Zukogi, like Aminu Kano, typified the presence in the party of "patrician radicals" whose ideological convictions led them to identify with the *talakawa*, but whose high ascriptive status was an advantage in mobilizing radical political support in a highly ascription-conscious society. Some others of comparable status, such as Abubakar Tambawal, were products of chronic friction within the aristocracy,—a phenomenon explored more fully in the next chapter. They are men who became politically disaffected as a result of losing their positions in the N.A., either because some of their administrative transgressions were prosecuted or because they fell victim to the intense competition for *sarauta* or both, since, thanks to the dynamics of traditional politics, the two causes were often related. For the disaffected, NEPU represented an alternative channel of political activity and a chance to recoup some influence and stature. Because formerly powerful officials always retained some following, the party, in turn, counted on gaining support through being associated with them. This expectation was epitomized in the 1959 elections in the candidacies under NEPU's banner of two deposed emirs, the former Emir of Dikwa, Mustapha Ibn Sanda, and Ahmadu, ex-Lamido of Adamawa.[28]

In effect, the active membership of the NPC represented a coalition of interests that included hereditary rulers, traditional notables, the higher Western-educated elements, the *ma'aikata* (N.A. clerical and technical workers), and well-to-do merchant traders. The coalition was steeply structured, with traditionalists in the upper echelons of the hierarchy.

Clearly, however, after the institution of formally democratic procedures in the elections of 1959, 1961, and 1964, the Northern Peoples' Congress could not have remained the dominant party were it wholly or even primarily dependent for support on this coalition, which for all its power, numerically comprised a small minority of the electorate. Ultimately the triumph of the NPC came from the support of the peasantry; it is in this connection that a traditional institution probably made the greatest contribution to the NPC's steadily increased political hegemony (see Table 31).

It was previously stated that clientage is a key traditional political institution, indeed, a major social adhesive of the emirate system. "Clientage", as M. G. Smith observed apropos of Zaria in 1950, "is coterminus with Hausa political society . . . [it] incorporates such dif-

[28] See Chap. 6.

373

Table 31: Northern Nigeria Election Results, 1951-65

	Constituencies Won			
Election	NPC	NEPU	Action Group	Other[b]
1951	[a]	—	—	—
1954	79	—	1	10
1956	107	9	4	11
1959	134	8	25[c]	7
1961	156	1	9	—
1964	162[d]		4[e]	1

[a] Among the seats occupied by declared party members, all were NPC. This declaration of NPC membership came *after* the election; however, the seats were not contested under party labels.

[b] Small (provincial) parties and independents.

[c] In alliance with United Middle Belt Congress (UMBC).

[d] Contested under the banner of Nigerian national alliance (NNA), a coalition including several smaller southern parties but dominated by the NPC.

[e] Contested under the banner of the United Progressive Grand Alliance (UPGA), which included the NCNC and AG/UMBC.

ferentiating factors as ethnicity, occupational status, lineage, and rural-urban distinctions and defines the boundaries of the political society of Zaria emirate".[29] The crux of the clientage relationship in all the emirates is that patronage, economic security, and protection can be exchanged for personal loyalty and obedience. For the *Habe talakawa*, clientage represented the principal channel of upward mobility, toward and within the ruling circle. For those outside that sphere, lesser forms of clientage relationships provided virtually the only defense against such eventualities as arbitrary tax levies, injurious treatment in judicial proceedings, discrimination in allocation of farming land or in administration of public services, to mention the most common perils.

The efficacy of traditional clientage within an emirate lies in the ability to exercise influence in proportion to the rank and position in the socio-political hierarchy. Typically an influential official enjoys the allegiance of less influential persons below him and owes allegiance to a more influential person above. The structure of the NPC fits conveniently into this structure of traditional relationships in at least two important aspects. First, by virtue of powers it exercised through control of the government, the party was a principal agency of patronage offices, loans, scholarships, contracts, and other opportunities sought by the upwardly mobile. This could be accomplished either directly and formally or indirectly and informally through the medium of the party or ex-party men who dominated the pub-

[29] Smith, *Government in Zazzau*, p. 260.

lic boards, corporations and commissions. Second (and of the greater consequence in terms of winning *mass* support), the interlocking directorate of local administrative and party personnel inescapably bound humble persons to traditionally august figures in their capacity as party men. The dependency that derived from the vast network of clientage relationships inherent in traditional society were transferred to the party. Loyalty to the NPC became a way of defraying traditional political obligations.

The NEPU

Theoretically, of course, the right to choose and reject political parties by secret ballot offered a remedy for the condition of personal servitude. But in the upper North, after the first experiments with the secret ballot seemed to portend revolutionary results, the electoral fortunes of the NPC instead increased, while those of its opponents diminished even as the use of direct voting and secret balloting spread. Thus in the regional elections of 1956, 19 urban seats were contested on this basis and opposition parties won six, or 31% (see Table 32). In the 1959 federal elections all 110 Northern constituencies

Table 32: Results of the First Direct Elections Held in
Northern Nigeria, November 1956

Constituency	Party	No. votes
Kano (East)	NPC	2,119
	NEPU	1,776
	NPC majority	343
Kano (West)	NPC	3,252
	NEPU	1,229
	NPC majority	2,023
Kano (South)	NPC	2,928
	NEPU	499
	Ind.	74
	NPC majority	2,429
Kano (Waje)	NPC	2,082
	NEPU	1,793
	NPC majority	289
Kaduna	NEPU	1,845
	NPC	1,433
	NEPU majority	412
Zaria	NEPU	4,754
	NPC	3,611
	Ind.	1,601
	NEPU majority	1,143

Constituency	Party	No. votes
Ilorin	ITP-AG Alliance	3,710
	NPC	3,226
	ITP-AG majority	490
Jos	NEPU	4,070
	NPC	2,406
	AG	616
	Ind.	51
	NEPU majority	1,664
Offa	AG	2,588
	NPC	1,758
	AG majority	830
Sokoto (East)	NPC	2,400
	NEPU	383
	NPC majority	2,017
Sokoto (West)	NPC	1,285
	NEPU	732
	Ind.	651
	NPC majority	553
Katsina	NPC	
	NEPU	
Gusau	NPC	1,281
	NEPU	1,053
	Ind.	1,039
	AG	208
	NPC majority	228
Yerwa (North)	BYM	2,416
	NPC	2,060
	BYM majority	356
Yerwa (South)	BYM	2,558
	NPC	1,691
	BYM majority	867
Okene	ITU	3,716
	NPC	893
	Ind.	331
	AG	98
	ITU majority	2,823
Bida	NPC	1,545
	NEPU	750
	NPC majority	795
Nguru Town	NPC	2,054
	NEPU	1,234
	NPC majority	820
Kaura	NEPU	2,901
	NPC	1,378
	Ind.	1,266
	NEPU majority	257

situated in emirates were won on this basis; NEPU (the only opposition party to win any of these) captured only eight of the emirate
seats, or 5.5% all other opposition victories being scored by the Action
Group outside the emirate area, except for two seats in Adamawa
emirate. Finally, in the 1961 and 1964 regional and federal elections
NPC candidates were returned in every emirate constituency without
exception. Considering that neither the essential features of NEPU
nor those of the society at large substantially changed in this period,
and assuming that mere opposition ineptness was not responsible,
what accounts for these disappointing results? Why, far from produc-
ing the reversal of traditional Northern political structure ostensibly
implicit in the adoption of this formal democratic device, did use of
the secret ballot help confirm that structure in being? In retrospect,
part of the answer lies in the inherent limitations of competitive parties as an instrument for fundamental socio-political change, under
such conditions as existed in the North.

Fundamental change of a political system through mobilization of
support for a political party which seeks that objective yet must operate within the existing system, necessarily entails a protracted development. A radical political party, like any other conscious challenge
to a *functioning* social and political order, initially occupies a highly
defensive position. The favorable response of the electorate depends
on the party's first successful incursions into the established order,
political skirmishes which demonstrate, or at least suggest, its ability
to produce desired results. Where preexisting political institutions are
fragile or limited in scope, the task of such a party is proportion-
ally easier. Even so, at some point, or at various points, the party
must demonstrate that it is an effective and relatively desirable alternative to the institutions it means to supplant. Had the traditional
emirate system lacked any effective means whatsoever of "articulat-
ing interests" or securing redress, NEPU might have encountered less
resistance. As it happened, however, the traditional institution of clientage effectively competed with the potential functions of radical
opposition. Thus realized, NEPU's program would have offered
far greater results than anything the *talakawa* achieved through traditional means. Without opportunities for exercise of power, however,
the NEPU could implement none of its proposals. In this regard,
NEPU's experiences were frustrating. Its initial successes were nullified by electoral vagaries. Subsequent electoral victories in regional
contests fell far short of the majority needed to gain control of the

government or even to influence legislation very much; the subordination of town councils to Native Authority councils turned the winning of majorities in some of the former into pyrrhic victories. Even the politically aroused peasantry were left with no recourse but to continue to rely on the old methods of personal clientage, which provided some measure of relief and satisfaction, but which were incompatible with partisanship for the NEPU.

Another related limitation was that the inherent gradualism of the electoral process tended to automatically expose the peasantry to the possibility of initial retaliation, a fear not altogether removed by the later use of secret voting devices. The fact that electoral support for NEPU tended to follow highly visible geographical lines within constituencies meant that the political sympathies of a particular hamlet, ward, or *layin* (residental street or block) could be easily identified. This might very well have led peasants to conclude that the potential risks were not even approximately worth the possible gains.[30] It would be the baldest speculation to assert that had it been possible for a majority of the peasantry to "rise as a man" and vote against the NPC they would in fact have done so. On the other hand, it is clear that precisely the inherent "gradualism" of the electoral process seriously qualified its political efficacy even for those who did desire or perceive the advantages of structural change.

None of the above analysis is intended to obscure or minimize the importance of outright suppression of political opposition of the regime, numerous specific cases of which have been documented in detail by Sklar, Post, Schwarz, and Dudley.[31] It is well to be reminded, however, that social and political history suggests that the devices of even the most repressive of regimes may only serve to stimulate determined and eventually effective opposition, provided certain other conditions are present. It is in an effort to suggest of what such conditions at least partly consisted in the Northern Ni-

[30] In fact, the exercise of the secret ballot permitted ample opportunities for political surveillance. In at least one constituency observed in the 1959 elections, NPC "counting agents" were instructed where possible to record the tally of each ballot box, the number of which corresponded to a small geographical location. It was not possible to know exactly how individuals cast their votes, but it was possible to determine in some cases how small street-blocks did.

[31] See Sklar, *Nigerian Political Parties*, pp. 355-65; K.W.J. Post, *The Nigerian Federal Election of 1959* (London, 1963), pp. 292-95; Frederick A. O. Schwarz, Jr.; *Nigeria: The Tribes, the Nation, or the Race—the Politics of Independence* (Cambridge, Mass., 1965), pp. 145-46; B. J. Dudley, "Federalism and the Balance of Political Power in Nigeria", *Journal of Commonwealth Political Studies*, Vol. 4, No. 1 (March 1966), pp. 25-26.

gerian case that primary stress has been laid here on aspects of the social, economic, and political environment that handicapped and eventually overcame NEPU.

In this context the frequently encountered suggestion that the allegedly subservient habits of the Hausa peasant accounted for his failure to avail himself of the ballot for the redress of grievances is not persuasive. There is evidence, both historical and contemporary, that this inference is unwarranted. The hypothesis could not easily account for the early successes of NEPU; in any case, it should be evident that there are grounds other than those of temperament on which to base an explanation of the political behavior of the Hausa peasantry.

The socio-economic identifies of the NEPU activists suggest another angle. NEPU activists, those who openly recruited other and proclaimed their partisanship by inscribing the party initials or symbol (the star) on their doorways, and shouting to the world the party slogan, *Sawaba*, were precisely persons in a socio-economic position to ignore or to conceive alternatives to the relationships and assumptions which tied others to the NPC. Most of the activists were in the towns. The core consisted primarily of unemployed youths, independent small traders, and artisans. Small traders, especially, were apt to find that attachment to eminent persons was neither inevitable nor necessary to their livelihood. Small-scale sale of popular trade-items released them from pressures that constrained others in relationships of dependency, while neither the source of supply nor the magnitude of their turnover nor the social position typical of their customers gave them any vested interests in the maintenance of the existing social structure. To this lack of restraint to be added various grievances (e.g. against taxes levied on their activities). Furthermore, official irregularities in the towns were more easily exposed, social and economic life was less disciplined, and the inhabitants were typically more sophisticated in the awareness of and the willingness to assert their rights under law.

Similarly, urban youths had not yet entered the normally adult relationship of clientage. They were employed only intermittently, for example as *yan tebur* ("sellers of daily incidentals," combs, soap, ballpoint pens) or *yan haya* ("bicycle renters"), were psychologically receptive to cosmopolitan influences, and were readily drawn to NEPU. A related group, which was important as a source of NEPU activity, were the *Gardawa* or "pupils engaged in memorizing the

379

Koran". *Gardawa* travel extensively from town to town and remain unattached to local, settled, social hierarchies. In many cases, urban youths had migrated from villages on their own initiative because they were unwilling to endure the work, discipline, or subservience that peasant status demanded (such youths were derisively referred to by the more substantial part of the community as *yan iska*, ne'er-do-wells", literally, "sons of the wind"). A British district officer expressed an allied aspect of the appeal NEPU held for the youths in an assessment of the performance of that party in the towns of southern Katsina during the regional 1956 election: "[NEPU's] main strength is provided in this area at least, by relatively normal young men who are purely and simply bored and enjoy any escape from the humdrum—flags, passwords, badges, planning at night, fast cycles down the bye-ways, a delicate frisson from seeing yourself in opposition to your elders and a sense of belonging to an organization bigger than your village". These groups, however, were not sufficiently numerous nor always even of the appropriate age, to provide the electoral support required by a major party in a predominately rural society. For the NEPU, as for the NPC, any substantial support had to come from the rural adult peasantry.

In the villages, one of the first and most successful of NEPU's early activities was a campaign against compulsory communal labor for non-communal purposes, which in the North was a custom that survived the enactment of a Nigerian labor code. Party agents effectively instructed the rural *talakawa* on the purposes for which compulsory communal labor could be legally used. The labor was to be restricted to such projects of general benefit as removal of *kashin yawo*, a weed grass injurious to crops. The law forbade the use of unpaid labor for tasks which produced purely personal return to individual officials. This was typical of NEPU's approach to the peasantry—the indirect advocacy and defense of their interests through informal campaigns of enlightenment which informed the peasants of their rights and encouraged them to assert the rights. It is in this respect, rather than in electoral results, that the NEPU probably had the greatest impact on Northern political development, which is one of the reasons that it was always taken far more seriously in the emirates than its electoral strength as a party indicated.

While NEPU's activities had an effect, they did not necessarily result in votes. Knowledge of the law was one only aspect of the problem; another was the readiness of individuals to assert themselves. In colonial days British officials employed the administrative rule that complaints of official misconduct were to be entertained only if made personally by the accused persons. Third parties, including party organizations, could not themselves bring complaints, a rule which also obtained in judicial proceedings. The African successors followed suit. NEPU action of this kind therefore depended strictly on the initiative of the individual peasant, who usually, and for good reasons, preferred to refrain from action or to rely on the channels and procedures of clientage, rather than to challenge the authority of influential persons.

On the other hand, at least one rural area of the upper North—the northern districts of Zaria emirate—which was consistently a NEPU electoral stronghold, was also the scene of serious unrest that threatened to reach the proportions of a full-scale insurrection during 1957. I did not investigate this area, but a speculation (for which there is in fact some evidence) consistent with the above interpretation of NEPU is that the ordinary clientage mechanisms failed to work, or worked so imperfectly that the peasantry felt that on balance they had nothing to lose through acts of defiance.[32] The implication here is that NEPU thrived only at the highest pressure points of the system; votes for NEPU served as a protest in situations of extreme duress. Some thoughtful emirs themselves acknowledged to me the contribution that NEPU, in performing this safety-valve function, had made to the maintenance of the system.[33]

Probably the most significant source of NEPU voting strength was the traditional structure of socio-political differentiation. NEPU made its greatest inroads among the conquered indigenous population—the *Habe*, who remembered a past in which they ruled themselves, free of Fulani overlords. The impact of the traditional cleavage between Fulani and *Habe* on modern politics is best illustrated with respect to Zaria and Kano Cities, where the phenomenon was particularly important.

[32] One clue to the situation in Northern Zaria was the proliferation of village and ward heads at very low salaries, which led them to commit excesses in order to supplement their incomes. Thus the 1959-1960 N.A. estimates list 842 village and ward heads at a total cost of £10,368, or an average income of just over £12 per year, a figure approximating that reported by M. G. Smith in 1950, although the cost of living during the ensuing 10-year period increased substantially. This figure also appears to have been well below the regional average for emirate village heads. See *Native Administrations and Townships Estimates*, 1950-60 (Kaduna, 1960).

[33] Interviews with M. Ja'afaru, Emir of Zaria, March 31, 1959; A. Umar Ibn, Ibrahim Al-Kanemi, Emir of Dikwa, June 22, 1959; A. Haruna, Emir of Gwandu, September 17, 1959.

Within its mud walls, old Kano City (*Birni*) is divided for administrative purposes into four large sectors or areas: North (*Fuskar Arewa*), South (*Fuskar Kudu*), East (*Fuskar Gabas*), and West (*Fuskar Yamma*), each of which contains several subdivisions or wards.[34] Beneath this fourfold modern administrative division is an older traditional line bisecting the city, which runs roughly from a point between the Wambai and Mata Gates of the eastern wall westwards to the vicinity of the *Goron Dutse*. South of that line down to the southern wall, an area which includes the *Fuskar Kudu*, are located the Emir's palace, the Central Mosque, and the offices of the Native Administration; it is a part of the city inhabited almost wholly by Fulani. North of the line is the section (comprising most of *Fuskar Gabas* and *Fuskar Arewa*) inhabited overwhelmingly by *Habe*. It is said that in former times the sense of differentiation and deference was so acute that *Habe*, on crossing the line to the Fulani side, habitually removed their shoes. Today this geographical division remains a manifestation of the deep traditional social division in Kano City. To a certain extent, the traditional divisions are associated with occupational categories; typically the Fulani engage in administration, while the *Habe* are concerned with trade, commerce, and crafts, which the Fulani eschew. The political ramifications were reflected in the fact that NEPU enjoyed substantial support from the *Habe* side in every election—local, regional, and federal from 1950 to 1965. Thus the NPC only narrowly won the Kano City constituencies, which included the *Habe* areas, in the elections of 1954 and 1956. Significantly, M. Aminu Kano, the NEPU candidate, was defeated in both cases by opposing *Habe* NPC candidates, M. Maitama Sule and Alhaji Ahmadu Dantata, a wealthy and popular merchant-trader. For the 1959 elections, the almost completely *Habe Fuskar Gabas* was combined with the highly cosmopolitan area of *Waje*; Aminu Kano was promptly elected to the House of Representatives, defeating in the process the *Wakilin Waje*, N.A. official and member of the prominent Fulani clan, the Yolawa. A subsequent "re-

[34] In the case of Kano, these patterns of affiliation also may reflect a historical situation unique to the emirate. Some say that at the time of the *jihad* some Hausa of Kano supported the Fulani who in turn thereafter distinguished between them, as *Hausawa* and *Habe*, who either opposed the Fulani conquerors or remained neutral. Throughout the 19th century the Fulani regimes apparently ruled with support from these *Hausawa*; it is therefore just possible, should all this be so, that some or all of those reported as *Habe* with NPC affiliations actually belonged to this special category of *Hausawa*. Such a distinction between *Hausawa* and *Habe* has not, to my knowledge, been reported for other emirates.

delimitation" (in effect, gerrymandering) of this constituency split up the electoral combination of *Habe* and strangers, and NEPU failed to win any Kano City seat in 1961 or 1964.

The boundaries of the fourfold administration division and those of the twofold traditional division in Kano, coincide approximately but not perfectly. Thus small enclaves are found in certain wards which by tradition should be elsewhere. A further indication of the impact of traditional groupings was that the enclaves tended to be pockets of each party's strength in the other's territory. For example, the sub-wards of the *Fuskar Kudu*, located immediately south of the city market (e.g. Zango and Alfindiki), contain mostly *Habe* small traders who voted NEPU, while the Yola sub-ward, in which Yolawa Fulani are concentrated, was heavily NPC.

That the *Habe*-Fulani split was to be regarded as a phenomenon of social class rather than tribal allegiance or ethnic affinity or dissimilarity, is confirmed by observing political partisanship in Kano City more closely. Thus the residents of the Warure ward of *Fuskar Yamma* were mainly *Habe*, but they were also *fadawa* (courtiers) to royalty and nobility. Warure was NPC. However, the preponderance of the *Habe* in certain other wards of *Fuskar Yamma* (e.g. Sabom Sara, Gyaranya, Kaigama, Yelwa) are small traders. These areas voted NEPU. The lines of potential "tribal" or communal conflict were blurred by those of class allegiance, which took precedence. It was really the *Habe talakawa* of Kano (i.e. those without official position) who were the bedrock of NEPU support.

The *Habe* factor was not strictly a matter, either, of occupational class, which it also transcended. In Zaria a number of *Habe* members of the town council were in the same occupational category as their Fulani colleagues, but these Fulanis tended to belong to the NPC, while their *Habe* occupational counterparts were NEPU. Both the *Habe* and Fulani in question, moreover, were *talakawa* who enjoyed neither royal nor noble status nor political-administrative office. It is not necessary to conclude that the phenomenon of ethnic parochialism, rather than that of social stratification, was at work here; the phenomenon indicated that *subjective* as well as *objective* identifications help to determine Hausa-Fulani class placements, and thus political preferences. Political identification with the commoner class of *Habe*, on the one hand, or the ruling class, on the other, was apparently a partly psychological matter, which up to a point was more important to some than other (objective) factors, such as ethnic affinity, ascribed status, wealth, or occupation.

The NEPU struck responsive chords in other traditional conquest states that were ethnically and historically peripheral to Hausaland. One example was the Fika emirate in Bornu province, where a political association based on the subject peoples of the state, the Ngizim and Karekare Union was allied at the regional level with NEPU, while the ruling tribe, the Bolewa, were identified with the NPC.[35] Similarly, in the Lafia emirate of Benue province, the Arago people, to whom Lugard at first gave emirate status (in Doma and Keana emirates, now abolished), but who chafed under the regime of a numerically superior and ethnically dissimilar "ruling tribe", were at one time attracted to the banners of opposition parties. In general, the important point about such situations as have been described in the last few pages was that latent and manifest feelings of social differentiation and friction—which derived not primarily from recent Western contact or internal socio-economic change, but rather inhered in traditional structure—were transmuted into forces in the interplay of modern political party competition.

STRATEGIES, TECHNIQUES, AND RELATIONSHIPS

The NPC

The NPC attempted to foster a belief in the unity and sanctity of the community as traditionally constituted, and to represent itself as essential to the community's further preservation. Insofar as there was popular adherence to traditional conceptions and values, these represented weapons in the interparty competition, and were exploited accordingly. Thus NPC party "lectures", or campaign speeches, frequently dwelt on the sacred qualities, glories, and virtues of the past, stimulating sentiments of loyalty to that past and to its contemporary exponents. Both the NPC and NEPU chose strategies and techniques that invoked and manipulated certain forces and reactions

[35] A complex history lies behind the constitution of the present Fika emirate. The Bolewa, said to be of Kanembu origins, are thought to have migrated to the area of the present Fika emirate, where they subjugated the established Ngamo people and enthroned a Bola chief. Similarly the Ngizim originally gained control over the Karakare and organized Potiskum, next door to Fika. As a result of various intrigues and maneuvers in the early days of the protectorate, the British amalgamated Potiskum with Fika, placing the Ngizim and Karakare of Potiskum under the jurisdiction of the *Mai* Fika. See "Notes on the History of Fika and Potiskum", *Gazeteer of Bornu Province*, compiled by H. R. Palmer (Lagos, 1929), pp. 34-35.

which had persisted along with the traditional order. At the same time, each party sought to control the new forces and reactions generated by incipient modernization. Flexibility in using secular and traditional approaches to the electorate was the essence of party competition. It was no coincidence that the NPC party flag color—green, which was also a prominent motif on governmental artifacts, party vehicles, poster handouts, and even the clothing of partisans—is also the color of the flags Shehu dan Fodio presented to his followers who in 1804-1810 waged *jihad* and later became emirs of the Hausa states. In the same vein, to instigate conflict within the community, to be *in opposition* to the hallowed and time-honored political order, was stigmatized by the NPC as heresy and treasonable to the community. Patriotism and unity were synonymous with Islamic harmony in the community (the NPC slogan was *salama*, "peace").

An inseparable part of NPC strategy was the use of religious themes and values. In a society as highly differentiated as an emirate, some ideal that stresses integrative values was essential to a strategy of communal solidarity. In emirate society, Islam virtually alone provided such an ideal. Thus the NPC attempted to establish itself as a defender of the *dar es Islam*. It extolled the bonds of the community of the faithful and the wisdom of Islam's strictures against dreaded schism.[36] The party's defense of emirship, by definition a quasi-theocratic institution, was cited as a reason for supporting the party on the grounds of piety; party, faith, and community were portrayed as ultimately one. The argument that NEPU's alliance with a predominately non-Muslim party, the NCNC, entailed an allegiance incompatible with fidelity to Islam, was a corollary of NPC's doctrine of unity which it relentlessly and effectively propagated: "NPC is the party of the Sardauna, the party of Shehu Usuman dan Fodio, but that party, NEPU is the party of Zik (Azikiwe), *Sarkin Inyamilai* ('chief of the—derogatory Hausa term for 'Ibos'). Ask the men of the village, who is NEPU's leader? Tell them Zik is the leader and that they should not play around with religion".[37]

The close relationship of some religious teachers and learned men to the NPC was both cause and effect of this stratagem. The *malla-mai* are the main vehicles in the emirates for the popular dissemination and interpretation of religious knowledge; as such, they have enormous influence. Probably the largest number and certainly the

---

[36] Cf. Smith, *Government in Zazzau*, p. 249.
[37] *Minutes*, Kano Provincial NPC "lecture", August 1947 (mimeo. in Hausa).

most influential *mallamai* identified and were popularly identified with the NPC. They tended to be reactionary in their outlook on the modern world.[38] To lend authority to the party's religious dictums, the NPC cultivated the *mallamai*, whose counsel reinforced the predilections of NPC's more tradition-bound and orthodox-minded leaders, members, and supporters.

The identification of the party with such highly charged cultural meanings and values may account in part for the occasional eruptions of extreme violence, and the intermittent appearance of strong-arm gangs, associated with the party and prepared to vindicate by coercion a social order they professed to regard as sacrosanct. NEPU adherents taunted and disparaged some eminent traditional personages embarking at the Kano airport for the 1953 London Constitutional Conference. In response, a group called the *Yam Mahaukata* ("sons of madmen") sprung up in Kano after a British judge failed to convict the accused offenders. Branches of the *Yam Mahaukata*, which was openly associated with the NPC, have appeared in Bida, Lafia, and Chafe districts of Sokoto emirate, among other places. Eventually outlawed, for months the *Yam Mahaukata* terrorized local members of NEPU. It was succeeded by the now defunct Alheri Youth Association, an NPC affiliate. Following the rise of the *Yam Mahaukata*, an informal band called the *Yan Akusa* (after the helmet-like hat made of tin which they wore) operated in Kano City. Less formally, in September 1958 a member of the Shehu of Bornu's household was killed in an interparty brawl that occurred near the home of M. Ibrahim Imam, the leader of the opposition in the Northern House and patron of the Bornu Youth Movement. The next day six members of that party met violent deaths.[39]

Another effect worth noting in passing, of employing strategies and techniques based on traditional institutions, was that they precluded the use of certain others that are often regarded as endemic to African political parties. Tribal unions, which played important

[38] Prior to the federal election of 1954, at a time when interparty tension was particularly high, influential *mallamai*, on being asked officially for possible solutions, suggested that NEPU be banned, or both the NEPU and the NPC. (See *Nigerian Citizen*, December 16, 1954, p. 3.) The former reluctance of the NPC to enter into entangling alliances with southern parties, its later attempt to appear as little associated with them as possible, and the inclusion of religious taboos such as the drinking of alcohol by Muslims in the definition of criminal offenses in the 1959 Penal Code, are areas in which the conservative *mallamai* are said to have wielded influence in the formation of major party policies.

[39] See *General Report and Survey on the Nigeria Police Force for the Year 1958* (Lagos: 1959), p. 13.

roles in the growth of African nationalist movements and often serve today as allied or ancillary party organs elsewhere, including southern Nigeria, played virtually no part in modern politics in the upper North.[40] This would seem to be partly attributable to the fact that the span of the traditional Fulani empire is multi-tribal and to the insistence of Islam on the unity of all believers.[41] Thus traditionalism and tribalism, in the sense of ethnic affinity or antagonism, were in these circumstances not synonymous but in fact mutually exclusive socio-political proclivities.

Although it is evident that the vital, probably crucial, advantage of the NPC in the upper North was its interconnection with traditional structures and institutions, this by no means exhausted the assets at its command. On the contrary, the innovation of modern structures and functions at the Regional level tended to buttress the position of the party. Insofar as the party acted in concert with or in support of traditional forces, the impact on these of such innovation was either neutral or actually beneficial.

Given the circumstances of a fundamentally nonplural "modern" economy, together with the relatively strong position and initiative which the public sector characteristically assumes in the development of non-Western, pre-industrial economies, the advantages that followed from being the party in power in such a system are considerable. It is a commonplace that concentration of the resources and techniques necessary to the economic modernization process in the hands of government enhances the power of the "government party". But

[40] In 1959 the NPC secretariat listed 10 tribal unions as affiliates; all of them, however, were in the Middle Belt area. It is indicative of NEPU's attitude on this subject that its 1959 electoral manifesto proposed that all political parties "organized on a tribal basis" be banned from Nigeria. See *West African Pilot*, October 2, 1959, p. 1.

[41] Difficulties arose for the NPC because of the fact that just a little less than half of the Yoruba population of the Western Region are Muslims, and that large numbers of them belong to the Action Group in that region, a problem that did not arise in the case of the Eastern Region whose inhabitants are nominally Christian or animist. The Action Group attempted to counter the particularistic overtones in Northern propaganda directed against it by emphasizing these statistics. At the same time, the fact that the Action Group was regarded by many NPC strategists as having far greater potential appeal in the upper North than would the NCNC without its NEPU ally was related to this situation. The accession of D. S. Adegbenro to the national presidency in 1962 was intended to stress the Action Group's debt to Muslim support. On the other hand, the great imbalance of Christians over Muslims among the top leaders of the Action Group was a weak point which the NPC did not fail to exploit. Sklar identified only 11% of the Action Group National Executive Council as Muslim in 1958, while 75.6% were Christians. Sklar, *Nigerian Political Parties*, pp. 247-51.

such concentration also renders more open to choice the basic purposes for which economic power may be exercised. This situation stands in contrast to Western political economies in which, at a comparable stage of development, the innovative function was more fragmented among agencies and economic institutions outside public jurisdiction. Concentrated power is by definition more amenable, more susceptible to direction, than power that is diffuse. To the extent that the NPC managed to muster economic sources of power for itself that elsewhere transformed traditional political systems, it is accurate to say of the modern political party institution that, had it not existed, the continuity of the Northern political system would have required its invention.

The extent to which the NPC succeeded in controlling the new structures and functions arising from development programs was indeed considerable. Apart from those "politically responsible" ministries directly concerned with development, the major Northern economic development institutions were the Regional Marketing Board and the Northern Region Development Corporation, both of which were nominally autonomous. Established under the Constitution of 1954, the Marketing Board provided investment and loan capital for the statutory Northern Region Development Corporation. The most important functions of the NRDC were the provision of loans to persons for schemes and projects "designed to further the economic development of the region", the formulation and administration of such schemes and projects, and the investment of funds in productive agricultural and industrial projects. The rationale for vesting such important powers in these corporate bodies was insulation from political party influence.[42] In reality, their composition allowed for ample party control.[43] The chairman of the Marketing Board in 1959 was an expatriate; the NRDC Chairman was Alhaji Aliyu, *Turakin Zazzau*, a former NPC Minister and party Executive Committee member.[44] The civil servants appointed to these boards normally received instructions on matters of interest to their ministers. Those appointees who were not civil servants were either party members, known sympathizers, or reliable emirs and chiefs. Under the NRDC law, the powers of the corporation with respect to the making of loans were

---

[42] See *Second Annual Report of the Northern Region Development Corporation* (Kaduna: Government Printer), p. 7.

[43] See *Development Corporation Amendment Law*, 1956, Section 2.

[44] It is a common practice in Nigeria, north and south, to award public corporation chairs to party stalwarts who lose out in electoral contests.

vested in a loans committee which consisted of all members of the corporation minus the official (i.e. civil servant) members. This left a committee of 10, of whom at one time six were members of the NPC (five of the six were also title-holders of Native Authorities), two were emirs (the Lamido of Adamawa and the Emir of Lapai), and two others, who listed themselves as independent of any party affiliation, were high officials of their respective Native Authorities.

In a manner not altogether foreign to the practice of political parties in Western countries, the "indirect" party control of these institutions was far-reaching. Just prior to the 1959 federal election the loans committee of the NRDC authorized a total of £550,000 in loans to individuals (including a large sum to an NPC official in a closely contested constituency), while the Marketing Board a little earlier had authorized an increase in the minimum price paid to primary groundnut producers of 50 shillings a ton—an increase that did not reflect any corresponding change in world market prices for that crop. Such judicious timing of economic measures was an obvious manifestation of party influence in economic structures,[45] or so it appeared at the time.

The association of traditional leadership with modern secular structures was secured through the power to appoint members to such bodies. Aside from the presence of traditional figures in such strategic positions as membership on the Loans Committee, the powers of that particular body were exercised with the advice of local provincial Loans Boards in which the incidence of traditional leadership was even more marked.[46] This pattern of membership was approxi-

[45] During a political campaign tour in Katsina emirate in December of 1959, the premier, apparently abandoning the fiction of nonparty management of the NRDC, "warned his party supporters not to be misled by the propaganda of the NEPU which claimed that it would increase groundnut prices. His own Government had already increased the ground price by 50 shillings this season. He appealed to the farmers to seize the opportunity to market their crops." *Daily Times* of Nigeria, December 7, 1959, p. 24.

[46] The chairmen of the boards in the upper Northern provinces in 1959 were: Adamawa, the *Malladkin Adamawa*, M. Bello Malabu, MHA; Bauchi, M. Garba, *Madawakin Bauchi* (former MHR); Bornu, the Emir of Dikwa, M. Umar Ibn Ibrahim El Kanemi; Ilorin, M. Salihu Fulani, District Head of Afon; Kano, A. Abubakar, *Dokajin Kano*, MHA, District Head of Kuru; Katsina, Alhaji Abubakar, *Magajin Garin Katsina*; Niger, the Emir of Abuja, M. Suleimanu Barau; Sokoto, the Emir of Gwandu; Zaria, *Sarkin Yakin Zazzau* (former MHA). All are either emirs or emir's councillors. In addition, the Emir of Lafia is the chairman of the Benue Provincial Loans Board. Over 70% of the membership of these boards in the provinces cited were Native Administration officials and/or of traditional aristocratic social status, as the term is employed in Chapters 4 and 7. See C. F. Dudley, "The Northern People's Congress", in John P. Macintosh, *Nigerian Government and Politics* (Evanston, Ill., 1966), p. 390.

mated by such other major modern institutions as the Gaskiya Corporation Board of Control, the Northern Region Scholarship Board, and the Northern members of the University College (Ibadan) Council, the Nigerian College of Arts, Science and Technology Council, the University College (Ibadan) Hospital Council, and possibly other agencies not investigated.

The foregoing assessment of the role of the NRDC (and its Provincial Loans Board in particular) was made on the basis of information informally gathered several years before the publication, under the auspices of the Nigerian Military Government, of a white paper which confirms and documents the myriad ways and surprising extent to which the financial resources of this public institution were used to further the purposes of the NPC *and* the privileged maintenance of the traditional elite, which formed the basis of the party's local leadership and support.[47]

A few comments should be made here concerning the Regional Public Service, or rather its "Northernized" segment. As of October 1, 1959, only 12.5% of Northern senior civil service posts were occupied by Northern Nigerians, and all but two of the remaining posts were manned by expatriates; by 1965 Northerners outnumbered southern Nigerian and expatriates together. The selection, regulation of conditions and terms of service, discipline, etc., of all Northern civil servants were in the hands of the Public Service Commission, ostensibly an independent body, the legal status, functions and procedures of which were molded after its British prototype. Throughout the period the Northern PSC was under the chairmanship of a Northern Nigerian, Alhaji Abubaker Imam.[48] By 1965 it was still too early to say whether the norms of political impartiality under which the PSC operates had actually produced the desired politically unfettered indigenous public servant. One difficulty was that many of those who had reached the senior ranks had been associated with the NPC prior to the enforcement of General Order 40, 1951. As a result, there was a tendency for such officers to identify themselves with the

[47] A *White Paper on the Military Government Policy for the Reorganization of the Northern Nigeria Development Corporation* (Kaduna, 1966), *passim.*

[48] Alhaji Abubakar Imam was formerly an editor of *Gaskiya Ta Fi Kwabo*, a foundation member and officer of the Northern Peoples' Congress in 1948, and a famous disputant in an interchange with Lord Lugard on the system of indirect rule in 1943. Born in Niger province, Alhaji Abubakar Imam is thought of as a commoner, but he was born into a distinguished judiciary family. His father, M. Shehu Usman, was *Alkali* in Katsina emirate, and his elder brother M. Bello Kagara was later the *Wali* of the same emirate.

fortunes of the party. Party officials, on the other hand, often tended to look on certain civil servants as loyal operatives, expecting them to cooperate, beyond their professional liability, in political control of departmental administration.[49] Another more subtle and largely unanswered question was the extent to which equivocation occurred extemporaneously as a reflex ingrained by the traditional political culture such as loyalty. The practice of many civil servants stationed in Kaduna of personally presenting their respects to the premier at his house on Sunday mornings, in a manner that smacked of the forms of customary relationships, was one manifestation of a traditional influence. Such behavior might have eventually characterized the form more than the substance of the relationship, yet it would be rash to assume that the Northern Public Service was immune from such influences, especially, but not necessarily exclusively, when civil servants had backgrounds of service in Native Administrations.[50]

Clearly the nonpartisan civil service would have become effectively established only as a result of change in party regimes. During any party's tenure a British model of the civil service is always a fundamentally intractable instrument, implementing, as is its constitutional duty, the policies and directions of the party in power. As such, the Northern Public Service could not have served as a counterforce in the process of NPC hegemony, notwithstanding the fact that the service itself owed its origin to concepts that are alien to the traditional structures and values in which that party was immersed.

The NEPU

We have seen that the NPC strategy was to stimulate favorable mass reactions through appeals to solidarity and harmony in the community; the strategy also attempted to bring within the purview of

[49] For example, the ill-fated 1958 party secretariat memorandum, cited above, included the recommendation that a Northern civil servant within each government department be designated to serve as an informal listening post for the minister concerned, to assure that party policies were sympathetically received and administered. For a fair and illuminating treatment of this issue see A.H.M. Kirk-Greene, "Qualification in and the Accessibility of Office: Perspectives on Traditional Criteria for the Selection of Public Servants in Northern Nigeria and the Growth of the Principle of Merit" (unpub., 1967).

[50] P. H. Canham has observed that the problem may be particularly acute in situations where "the politician concerned . . . has spent a large part of his life in a State or Chiefdom where the 'permanent staff' are closely attached to the Chief, often by ties of blood, and are only 'permanent' so long as their patron retains his chieftancy". "Parliament and the Civil Service in West Africa", in *What Are the Problems of Parliamentary Government In West Africa?* (London, 1958), pp. 91-92.

the party the modernizing structures that affected the community's material welfare and progress. The logical, and to a large extent actual, outcome of this approach was the identification of the party with the state, in terms of its traditional and modern boundaries. The NEPU strategy, by contrast and in response to that of the NPC, was to generate social class solidarity and a feeling of deprivation among the peasantry against an established order which it sought to portray as an edifice of privilege. Part of the NEPU's technique was to convince the peasantry of the liberating possibilities of political change, to induce them to assert their interests and desires through the institutions which the new democratic government in principle provided. The NEPU constantly emphasized that the new institutions of government were meant to supplant traditional methods and objectives of government and to transform traditional authority relationships. Thus in one of Aminu Kano's early speeches for NEPU, delivered before an amazed audience at Sokoto in 1952, he argued that present emirs were no better than public servants who should defer to the *talakawa,* whose taxes paid emirs' salaries, rather than the other way around. But faced with the persistence of popular expectations vis-à-vis political institutions, and the fact of their control by allies of tradition, NEPU also employed extraconstitutional techniques of opposition. In the early days of NEPU, Aminu Kano tried to inculcate in his followers the doctrines of satygraha, or nonviolent civil disobedience as developed in India.[51] The principle of nonviolence seems not to have taken hold among NEPU supporters, but in some instances resort to action against constituted authority was occasionally endorsed by the party. Upon the appearance of the *Yam Mahaukata,* NEPU organized the PAW (Positive Acting Wing) to retaliate in kind. In Kano City in 1959 the *Yan Kwaria* (so called after their helmets, which are made from calabashes) were the NEPU strong-arm counterparts of the *Yam Akusa.*

Fundamentally, however, NEPU operated as a constitutionally legitimate political party which pursued political and social change through the electoral process. In mobilizing electoral support NEPU also had to cope with the existence of socio-political continuity, to meet the peasantry where it was, as well as to prod them with a vision of

---

[51] An announcement of a decision to adopt *satygraha* as a technique by the Kano (fagge) Branch of NEPU in 1951 cited as its justification, "Letters, petitions, resolutions, and honest criticisms have been given no due consideration". *Daily Comet,* October 2, 1951, p. 1.

what the party wanted them to become. "We discovered", said Aminu Kano in 1959, "that NEPU could not be effective by preaching Laski to the *talakawa*.[52] Instead, NEPU, as well as the NPC, tried to reach the peasantry by invoking values and exploiting susceptibilities that inhered in the traditional political culture. Of course these sentiments were not given the same interpretation; in some cases they stressed themes greatly different from those of the NPC.

In the social distinction between *Habe* and Fulani, and the over-lapping *talakawa* and *sarakuna*, traditional political culture offered NEPU a potentially prime antidote to NPC's manipulation of traditional forces. By stressing traditional themes, NEPU hoped to encourage comprehension of its program by the people and to put the potency of tradition to work in its own behalf. An example was the organization of the Askianist movement which existed as a NEPU off-shoot from March 1951 to about 1955, when it collapsed after irregularities in the management of its funds disillusioned its followers. The movement took its name from the famous Muhammed Askia, who usurped the throne of the medieval Western Sudanic empire of Songhai, initiated a period of rule renowned for its cultural and religious renaissance, and marched against the Hausa states, conquering Zamfara and Gobir (roughly the territory of what is now Sokoto province), Zaria and Kano. To a group of young *Habe* adherents of NEPU who served as officers of the organization,[53] Muhammed Askia seemed a perfect symbol[54] for projection of NEPU's program and leader—M. Aminu Kano. Hailing Aminu Kano as the Askia of modern times—occasionally the NEPU leader was referred to as "Muhammed Aminu" and the organization as the Northern Askianist (Aminiyya) Movement[55]—the Askianists meant to suggest that the revolutionary exploits of Askia (literally "usurper") would be repeated

[52] Interview with Aminu Kano, Kano City, May 7, 1959.

[53] The charter officers of the Askianist movement were: Mudi Spikin, president; Mustapha Dambatta, secretary; Kaula, treasurer; Magaji Dambatta, publicity secretary. In 1952 Sabo Bakinzuwo became secretary, Ahmadu Chomodo (alias Bida) was treasurer, Muhamamadu Dodo, publicity secretary, and Uba Na Alkassim took the post of information officer. All were identified as being of *Habe* origin. M. Aminu Kano acted as patron.

[54] Lady Flora Lugard describes Muhammed Askia as a man of "liberal principles and large views, naturally humane, and disposed to temper justice with mercy, more than usually cultivated, active, wise and firm. . . . He had the courage frequently to disobey the unjust orders of his master, and thus, while he risked his own life, stood between the Monarch and the defenceless people over whom he ruled". *A Tropical Dependency* (London, 1905), pp. 171-72.

[55] See *Daily Comet*, March 22, 1951, p. 4.

393

in their time.[56] By 1959 they described him as Aminu Shehu (cf. Shehu dan Fodio).

The Askianist movement does not seem to have made much of an inroad, but it represented an intriguing example of NEPU's constant efforts to stimulate revolutionary political responses thoroughly evoking the memory of a traditional political order that antedates Fulani rule and was therefore a source of latent anti-Fulani feeling. The special relevance of NEPU's appeal to the *Habe* consciousness of the peasantry was that inference of rebellion and reference to tradition went hand in hand. In a similar vein, NEPU propagandists sometimes argued that later Fulani rulers had betrayed the ideals of the revered founders of the empire. Thus Shehu Usman dan Fodio, Sultan Bello, and dan Fodio's brother, Abdullahi, the first Sarkin Gwandu, were often described as "great Muslim democrats" who would abhor the regime of their successors.

As with the NPC, the NEPU's tactic of turning traditional myths and themes to its own advantage involved an attempt to place the stamp of Islam's approval on its own political program. NEPU's motto, *Girman-Ubangiji, Gama-Kai, Taimakon-Juma* ("To glorify God, association, and service to the community") struck this note. The popular association of the party symbol—the star—with the star and crescent of Islam, and the wearing of the red fez by many NEPU militants, were at least as propitious as the NPC's use of the symbolic color green. Party leaders told me that initially NEPU's interest in the political implications of Islam was aroused in self-defense against the damage done to it by NPC propaganda.[57] Passages of the Koran, and sayings of the Prophet favorable to Christians, doctrinal affinities between Islam, Christianity, and Judaism, and certain historical indications of practices and attitudes of tolerance by the early Muslim Caliphs of religious minorities[58] were themes commonly cited by NEPU "lecturers" in support of the party's alliance

[56] British officers did not fail to perceive subversive overtones of the Askianists; the Hausa editor of the *Daily Comet* was arrested on a charge of publication of seditious matter, for reproducing their manifesto. The government later dropped its charges. See *Daily Comet*, April 21, 1951, p. 1.

[57] NEPU leaders recount a meeting with the Emir of Kano in which the Emir challenged the party's program on the grounds of heresy. Finding themselves ill-prepared to answer a number of the Emir's specific doctrinal contentions, they resolved to make their own studies of the Koran and other texts to find support for the party's position on major social and political issues.

[58] See Alfred Guillaume, *Islam* (London, 1956), pp. 33-34, 53, 73; Reuben Levy, *The Social Structure of Islam* (London, 1957), pp. 3, 66. For example, NEPU speakers and sympathetic *Mallams* emphasize the levying of a special poll

with the NCNC and its advocacy of "one Nigeria". It also became NEPU's practice to seek Islamic doctrinal support for wider aspects of the NEPU ideology, particularly the value of egalitarianism, and to intersperse political speeches with religious allusions and justifications. M. Lawan Danbazau, NEPU's advisor on Islamic law, was the party's specialist in these matters, and large NEPU political rallies often included a performance of his speciality. The innumerable NEPU political verses and songs were notable for their use of apocalyptic language and parables depicting the eventual outcome of a class struggle between the forces of NEPU and its opponents, in terms of the salvation and deliverance of the former and the eternal damnation of the latter:

> We shall reach the time when he who is all-powerful will
>   become just like a moth round a candle
>
> We beg the Lord God Almighty to see that the commoners (men
>   from villages or wherever they live) of the world are not
> plagued for the sake of homage,
>   sitting around like skewered meat before the fire . . .
>
> O God, Nigeria has been left
> with no money and no surfeit of well-being
>   thousands of her people have been overwhelmed.
> NPC, the ruin of the world,
>   none can save you from the fires of hell . . .
>
> NPC's ambition has perished,
> they have appropriated the whole of the people's property
> to pay their own fares to Mecca
> to pray for glory;
>   but in fact they have overlooked that they are really
>   praying for hell-fire.[59]

Several groups variously associated with or allied to NEPU were in turn associated with Islam. An example of such a loosely associated group was the Sharifai Union of Kano. In Arab lands, Sharifai (Arabic, *Ashraf*) are people who claim direct descent from the Prophet,

---

tax on non-Muslims (*jizya*) by the first Caliphs as an indication of their privileged status as protected peoples, and play down the apparent invidiousness of the distinction.

[59] "The song: We recognize those who have wronged us", by M. Abba Maikwaru (undated private printing), in possession of the author.

and commonly enjoy the special esteem of Islamic communities.[60] Kano Sharifai are said to be actually descendants of the agents of Shehu Magili, a descendant of the prophet who visited Kano to advise Muhammadu Rumfa, the fourth Fulani Emir (1463-1499) on his duties as a ruler. These descendants of Magili's associates have remained in Kano as a somewhat separate and distinct community; they presently make up a ward of the city and have their own ward head (the *Sarkin Sharifai*). The Northern Sharifai inherited something of the reputation of their ancestors: learned and blessed men. The Sharifai Union was organized in 1952, with such declared objectives as "opposition to extortion by the *sarakuna*", "championing of the *talakawa's* interests", etc. These were clearly in line with those of NEPU, which members of the Sharifai Union supported.

Several groups having Arabic names which especially concerned themselves with Muslim education were other examples of ancillary NEPU bodies in this general category. They included *Zaharal Haq* ("the truth is revealed"—the revelation was NEPU's interpretation of Islam as being opposed to authoritarianism); *Tab'junal Haq* ("the masses will rule those now ruling"); *Nujumu Zaman* ("start of the day"); and *Muftalhairi*. They reflected NEPU's realization that it had to counter the charge that the party's objectives were odious to Islam. Their programs were designed principally to provide religious training, especially for young people, with NEPU's own political slant. The *Jami'iyyar Islamiyya*, or Northern Moslem Congress, which founded Arabic schools in the towns of Kano, Maiduguri, and Jos, was also said to be sympathetic to NEPU.

The most notable instance of a link between the party and sectarian religious sentiments and affinities, however, was the connection between NEPU and the religious brotherhood called *Tijaniyya*. Probably the majority of the *Tijaniyya* adherents in Northern Nigeria voted for the NPC and were politically quiescent. Certainly a majority of the Northern emirs who identified themselves with any brotherhood were *Tijanists* (Arabic, *turug*; pl. *tarigua*). However, what may be called a left wing of the *Tijaniyya* in Northern Nigeria—commonly known by the term *Yan Wazifa*[61]—was a radical influence in both

---

[60] Reuben Levy comments that the *Ashraf* "have been acknowledged by all Arabs since the seventh century as persons of the highest nobility, and the proudest Bedouin chief kisses the hand of the poorest of them". *Social Structure of Islam*, p. 67.

[61] Those who practice the litany of the *Wazifa*. For this and other doctrinal and practitional aspects of *Tijaniyya*, see J. Spencer Trimingham, *Islam in West Africa* (Oxford, 1959), pp. 99-100.

religion and politics. Religiously the *Tijaniyya*, and especially the *Yan Wazifa*, is a reformist, puritanical, missionary-minded sect which rivals the *Khadiriyya*—the other major *turug* in Northern Nigeria—which is closely identified with the ruling house of Sokoto.

Politically in Northern Nigeria the *Tijaniyya* stands in relation to the *Khadiriyya* and orthodox Islam as a non-conformist to an established church. Often, where the head of an emirate follows the *Khadiriyya*, but *Tijaniyya* is strong as in Sokoto, the latter is regarded as a threat to existing authority and treated accordingly. More orthodox *Tijani* emirs look on the *Yan Wazifa* in much the same way. Moreover, the puritanical zeal of the *Yan Wazifa* creates fearless assailants of rulers who stray from the path of *adalci* (righteousness). This fervor is combined with a high degree of organization, and these are qualities that make them both a highly volatile, and seriously disturbing element to any established regime. Hostile emirs, however, merely intensified friction between the traditional ruling class and members of the *Tijaniyya*, the greatest number of whom are *Habe* commoners. The result was that although there was no formal or organizational tie between the *Tijaniyya* and the party, a "natural alliance" existed between the *turug* and NEPU in certain parts of the upper North, especially eastern Sokoto, southern Katsina, Argungu, Gombe, and Adamawa emirates, where membership in the two organizations was usually reciprocal.

NEPU strategies, tactics, and relationships are reflected in the results of elections in which the NEPU achieved minor victories against the political citadel of the NPC. NEPU won 15 seats in 2 elections (7 in the regional elections of 1956, 8 in the Federal elections of 1959) of the six regional or federal electoral contests held in the North up to 1965. Of the 15, 6 were won in urban constituencies (3 others were won in constituencies that include urban centers),[62] 3 seats were won in heavily *Tijaniyya* areas.[63] Two were won by NEPU candidates in the category of disaffected members of the traditional ruling class,[64] 1 seat in a contest which otherwise turned on

[62] The six urban constituencies were Jos (2), Kaura Namoda Town, Zaria Urban, and Kaduna in 1956, plus Kano East in 1959. The three mixed constituencies were Katsina South-Central (which included Malumfashi) in 1956. Chafe-Gusau (which includes the town of Gusau), and Kaura Namoda (which includes the town of Kaura Namoda), in 1959.

[63] Kaura Namoda Town in 1956, Kaura Namoda and Chafe-Gusau Districts in 1959, all in eastern Sokoto.

[64] Katsina South-Central (M. Abdulmumuni), and Misau (M. Ibrahim Mahmud) in 1956.

issues of traditional rivalry,[65] and the remaining 3 were won in that area of acute peasant unrest, northern Zaria.[66]

Again, the important point is that the NEPU strategy that produced these results was not confined to efforts to indoctrinate the electorate in the new and relatively unfamiliar values usually associated with democratic institutions, nor to enlighten the electorate about the new political possibilities presented by the adoption of such institutions in Northern Nigeria. On the contrary, NEPU attempted to use almost any element in traditional political culture that would serve to mobilize political opposition.

To an extreme degree among the important contemporary political parties of Africa, the NPC proclaimed the preservation of traditional political values and culture to be one of its long-range goals. The *Sardauna*, who was personally committed to this objective more than any other top leader, was the party's most articulate spokesman on the subject. His broadcast during the 1956 election campaign on behalf of the NPC made clear the party's intention to seek a permanent place for traditional authority in the future of the region:

> The NPC does not believe in the total abolition of everything that is old, though we do believe in adapting our ways and ideas to suit the times.
>
> We believe in the institution of Chiefs and as long as we are in power we shall ensure that the Chiefs will have representation in the Regional Executive Council and that the House of Chiefs will continue to be a part of our legislature. We believe that the Emirs and Chiefs of Northern Nigeria can easily adapt themselves to modern democratic local government practices. We are pleased with the way in which Chiefs are accepting the changing conditions in Nigeria.
>
> No lasting progress can be achieved without their fatherly, spiritual, and moral support. Our attitude to Chiefs and elders is one of respect and co-operation because we believe that they have a very important part to play in the administrative, social, and economic development of our people.[67]

On several occasions during the events marking the attainment of

[65] Kankara-Kogo.

[66] Zaria North in 1956, Ikara-Makarfi, Kubau-Soba in 1959. The Zaria North seat was won by M. Anga Soba, who is a "patrician radical".

[67] *Nigerian Citizen*, September 19, 1959, p. 6. Cf. the *Sardauna*'s statement in the Northern House of Assembly quoted earlier.

Northern Regional self-government in 1959, the *Sardauna* took special pains to express his party's affirmation of traditional culture. On self-government day, March 15, a date deliberately chosen to remind the world of Northern political continuity (this was also the date of the fall of Sokoto to Lugard's troops in 1903, and the *Sardauna's* speech was made on the historic battle-ground) he observed: "When we survey all the phenomenal changes that have occurred in our recent history we are gratified with an important factor in our way of life, that quality of the Northern peoples—an ability to absorb, adapt, or renovate new ideas without completely discarding [our] social inheritance, even despite the attractions of glittering alien systems. In so doing we are proud to follow the old Hausa saying 'It is better to repair than to build afresh'. I am told that this belief has helped other nations to greatness and I have a firm conviction that, God willing, it will do so for us". Subsequently, "respect for all traditional institutions, chiefly or otherwise, and their maintenance" was reaffirmed as a major principle in the party's 1959 election manifesto.

On the other hand, the NPC manifesto heartily subscribed to programs of material development and administrative modernization that promised to "lift Nigeria from the status of an under-developed country".[68] This program included most of the familiar items of a plan for African progress: expansion of Western education ranging from higher education to adult literacy, increase in agricultural productivity, an assault on disease and infant mortality rates, development and exploitation of natural resources, sponsorship of technical research and training, creation of conditions conducive to foreign aid and investment, and encouragement to indigenous industry.[69] Within the limits of available resources, the record of the NPC-controlled Northern government, as well as that of the NPC-dominated federal government, gives no cause for doubting that the party was serious about economic development. The question inevitably arises, however, as to how and to what extent the party proposed to combine its pursuit of secular goals with support of a social structure and traditional culture in the upper North, which appeared in many ways uncongenial to such a program.

A good answer may be that the party was never forced to reconcile its two commitments. The modest level of actual economic de-

---

[68] *Ibid.*
[69] See text of the NPC manifesto, *ibid.*, pp. 6-66.

velopment was no overwhelming difficulty, but there were handicaps involved. The party was able to convince itself, and perhaps the people, that its policies were compatible and could remain so indefinitely.

But this optimism was not universally shared within the party or even among the party leadership. Members of the party could readily identify internal factions in the rank and file and among the cabinet ministers which held different assumptions about the future and/ or priorities. In general, those most optimistic about maintaining the present state of affairs were the same persons who most wanted to perpetuate the existing social structure, although there were also pessimists in the ranks of the defenders of tradition who saw themselves as fighting a rearguard action to hold off the inevitable within their lifetime. There were also those, especially prominent among the group of younger ministers, who lacked pretensions to truly high traditional status or office and who were essentially secularist in outlook. They regarded the neo-traditionalist structure of political leadership and the high valuation of tradition as regrettably expedient tendencies, to be abandoned as quickly as political conditions would permit. This group was apt to complain bitterly of N.A. inefficiency and corruption. The voices of both the latter two groups, however, were publicly muted, or were heard only within the party. The voice of the party was in effect the *Sardauna*'s, who personified the dual commitment.[70]

An example of the party's desire to combine secularism with tradition was the decision to place the administration of a new public housing program under Native Authorities. The decision was not a departure from past practices, since it was also British colonial policy to use Native Authorities as agents for schemes or projects introduced and paid for by the government. The decision did show that the NPC government continued to want to make the Native Administra-

[70] The *Sardauna*'s political outlook comes closest to representing a rationalization, indeed, to making an ideology of what in fact has been taking place in the upper North since the war—a process of institutional and functional change amid structural continuity. When the *Sardauna* said to a southern Nigerian nationalist at the Ibadan constitutional conference of 1950 that, "If my friend might live for centuries he might still find natural rulers in the North", he was not conceding that the fulfillment of his prophecy would rule out progress. Rather, the statement reflected his belief that the traditional ruling class can survive by accepting, as he has done, the challenge of the new functions and formal restraints brought about by modern democratic government. Apparently the *Sardauna* believes that the aristocracy will *earn* its right to continue ruling and that the electorate will gratefully acknowledge its contribution. See my "Three Perspectives on Hierarchy: Political Thought and Leaderships in Northern Nigeria", *Journal of Commonwealth Political Studies*, Vol. 3, No. 1 (March 1965), pp. 1-19.

tion an integral part of development efforts where possible. Development programs were drawn up with Native Authority participation in mind. Even relatively large foreign commercial firms found it necessary to obtain official local favors (e.g. allocations of plots for their retail outlets) from Native Authorities. In order to operate within the territorial jurisdiction of the Native Authorities managers of foreign firms learned that without the cooperation and goodwill of the Native Authorities they could not conduct their businesses smoothly, with the result that they were often as solicitous of the sensibilities and demands of the Native Authorities as the NPC government itself. Reportedly ministers informed representatives of firms that on certain matters they had to deal with the Native Authorities and Native Authorities certainly expected ministers to proceed in that spirit.

The party's dualistic aspirations had other less obvious but perhaps more far-reaching implications. One involved the NPC's attitude toward contacts outside the Northern Region. The attitude was one of desiring a minimum of intercourse with any external power that might attempt to intensify the extent or pace of northern change.

An instance of this attitude was the NPC policy of "northernization". The northernization policy was originally meant to apply to the Northern public service and was designed to replace as rapidly as possible the expatriates and southern Nigerians, who were overwhelmingly predominate in the service, with "qualified Northerners". Accordingly, new recruitment was based on an order of preference that stipulated "Northerners first, expatriates second [on the grounds that they could be employed on 'contract terms' that would permit the government to replace them at the first opportunity], southern Nigerians last". The policy was justified on the grounds that open recruitment would perpetuate the disadvantageous position of Northerners who in the past enjoyed fewer educational opportunities, and therefore lack as yet the formal qualifications possessed by large numbers of southerners. It is now abundantly clear, however, that the policy also reflected the party's fear of an alien and potentially politically disruptive element in the North. First enunciated in 1954, northernization was gradually extended to include economic enterprise within the reach of government;[71] it became increasingly evident long before the tragic events of 1966 and 1967 that the ultimate intention was to prevent the "southern community" from having any

[71] See Sklar, *Nigerian Political Parties*, pp. 327-31.

401

influence, if not to expel it from the North altogether.[72] The implications of this objective in terms of the goal of national integration in Nigeria are by now too sadly apparent to require elaboration.

For similar reasons, the NPC remained a staunch advocate of retaining the regional set-up in Nigeria, i.e. one in which residual powers (including the crucial ones affecting chieftaincy affairs, local government, the public service, and the judiciary) were vested in the regions, with the North being the largest region in population and territory. Federalism not only greatly helped the party to effectively combat attempts at penetration of the North by the more radical southern political parties; it permitted the NPC, since it dominated the North, to command the lion's share of power in the federal government, and thereby to neutralize the latter's influence in Northern affairs. (The NPC never directly contested a seat in any other region of Nigeria, although it gained additional seats in the Federal House by virtue of individual carpet-crossings and alliances with minor southern parties.) By winning almost all the seats *within* the Northern Region, the NPC emerged as the largest single Nigerian party. Alone among the major Nigerian parties, all of which had their strength in a region, the NPC by itself could theoretically have formed the government of the federation as early as 1959 by capturing seats wholly within its own territory. Table three shows how the distribution of constituencies between the regions of Nigeria were such that the NPC's increasing hegemony in the Northern Region automatically meant ever greater NPC control of the federal government, much to the frustration of the southern parties. The table also shows the growing north-south political polarization brought on by this situation. Alteration of the constitutional distribution in favor of the south would have enhanced the ability of a successful non-Northern party (or parties) bent on rapid or thoroughgoing change to shape the destiny of the North.[73]

[72] In 1958 the premier made a statement in the Northern House of Chiefs on behalf of his cabinet, as follows: "The Atta of Igala has asked that everything within the law should be in the hands of Northerners, down to market stalls (which must be licensed by Native Authorities). I would like to assure the Atta that the policy of Northernisation is like a charm within our pillows which are always under our heads, and we sleep and rise with this question in our minds and by the grace of God the people of the South will leave the North". *House of Chiefs Debates*, August 12, 1958, p. 94.

[73] Even without amendment of the constitution the Action Group in 1959 made no secret of its intention, if it won the election, to use the powers of the federal government to induce social and political change in the North. The gist of the Action Group's plan was to establish minimum national standards in education, wages, etc., thereby forcing the hand of the Northern government.

The same fear was probably partly the reason for the NPC's unwillingness to endorse any plan for West African political unification.[74] The party was especially cool to nongovernmental organizations for promoting "pan-Africanism" such as the All-African Peoples Conferences, to which the NPC never sent a delegate (unlike the major southern parties and NEPU, which were represented at all of the meetings of the conference between 1959 and 1965). It is also likely that the NPC's attitude was to some extent responsible for Nigeria's policy of remaining aloof from either of the inter-African groupings of states, e.g. the "Casablanca" or "Brazzaville" powers, which flourished unofficially from 1959 to 1964.

The fact that the NPC was conducting a kind of holding operation on behalf of traditional society had other ramifications in the field of foreign relations. Party leaders were not unmindful of the potential danger to their policies of, say, recruiting technicians from the Soviet Union or other foreign leftist governments which are vigorous exporters of their ideologies. Thus attachment to tradition provided a powerful motive for maintaining close relations with the West, which the party associated with the old relatively sympathetic British policy of respecting indigenous authority and political culture. As the *Sardauna*, when asked whether he would seek Soviet aid, put it: "That is not our policy. We have to work with those we are accustomed to. If we were to bring in Soviet technicians we do not know how they would get on with the Nigerian people".[75] The party's electoral manifestos explicitly repudiated a policy of neutralism.[76] On the other hand, party leaders assiduously increased contact with the "Moslem world", of which they considered the North to be a part,[77] partly to offset the impact of the Western influences on the religious aspect of traditional culture. Pakistan, Saudi Arabia, and Egypt especially inspired Northern confidence.

Traditional religious sensibilities also produced effective opposition from NPC members of the Northern House to a proposal or accept-

[74] The *Sardauna* thought any such plan "premature", because "our own homes are not yet consolidated". See *Daily Times* of Nigeria, January 19, 1960, p. 1.

[75] *Ibid.*

[76] See *Nigerian Citizen*, September 19, 1959, p. 6. The repudiation may account for the fact that the prime minister, although he has stated the policy of Nigeria to be one of nonalignment, never uses the term "neutralism," but has substituted instead the rather awkward phrase of nonalignment "as a matter of routine". (See *Debates*, Federal House of Representatives, August 20, 1960.) A perceptive study of the contrasting foreign policies of the major Nigerian political parties is Claude S. Phillips, Jr., *The Development of Nigerian Foreign Policy* (Evanston, Ill., 1964).

[77] See e.g. *Daily Times* of Nigeria, November 1, 1960, p. 1.

Table 33: Regional Distribution of Constituencies and Victories
in Nigerian Federal Elections, 1954-65

	(1) Total Nigerian constituencies	(2) Northern Nigerian constituencies won by NPC	(3) Southern Nigerian constituencies
1954	181	79	91[a]
1959	312	134	138[b]
1964-65	312	162[d]	145[c]

[a] Victories in southern constituencies were distributed among four major parties and miscellaneous small parties and independent candidates, as follows: NCNC, 56; AG, 23; United National Independence Party (UNIP), 4; Kamerun National Congress (KNC), 5; miscellaneous small parties and independents, 13.

[b] Victories in southern constituencies were distributed among three major parties and miscellaneous small parties and independent candidates, as follows: NCNC, 81; AG, 48; miscellaneous small parties and independent candidates, 9.

[c] Victories in southern constituencies won by an alliance of parties (UPGA) composed of the NCNC, AG, NEPU, and UMBC.

[d] Nominally won under the banner of a national alliance of several parties (NAA), but actually the NPC accounted for all of them.

Note: The difference between the figures in column (1) and the combined figures in columns (2) and (3) represent non-NPC victories in northern constituencies.

ance by the federal government of a loan from Israel. The hostile reaction to the question seemed a clear indication of how religious considerations affected practical ones. Similarly the *Sardauna's* thinking about social problems was sometimes colored by assumptions not conducive to formulating public programs to alleviate them, as when he stated his view during one electoral campaign that, "poverty was an act of God", to which the proper Islamic response was almsgiving.[78] The *Sardauna's* continued opposition to female suffrage, in fact apparently to any important public roles for women,[79] was another indication that the reconciliation of secular and traditional values did not come easily to him, or to the party, which followed his lead.

By contrast, the *content* of NEPU's *program*, as distinct from the party's methods of propagating it, made few concessions to traditional culture and values. Ostensibly the only major exception was the party's undoubted devotion to Islam and Islamic culture; except that, unlike the NPC and traditional authorities, the NEPU interpreted Islam as cherishing the ideals of social equality and libertarian government. In part, because of the British administration's tendency

[78] *Nigerian Citizen*, May 18, 1959, p. 1.
[79] *Ibid.* "Woman's place is in the home and not in politics".

to support accepted, purportedly orthodox, opinions, however, NEPU made little headway toward wider acceptance of its religious views.[80] Politically the NEPU leaders, especially Aminu Kano, who enjoyed a reputation for being devout, came close to fitting that relatively rare breed of active Muslims who believe the Islamic ideal to be a secular state.[81] It might be pointed out that NEPU was an enthusiastic supporter of the decision to introduce an essentially secular Northern penal code, and that party leaders sanctioned what from a religious standpoint was the rather desperate action by NEPU defendants summoned before native courts of denying their faith (in Islam apostasy is the supreme offense) in order to be tried instead by British magistrates using a Western code.[82]

[80] A typical example of the British role in such controversies is an exchange between NEPU officials and the Acting Resident of Kano in September 1958. NEPU objected to an order of the Kano Native Authority that prohibited women from participating in public ceremonies, including political meetings. Under the order, women who did so could be arrested. NEPU requested the intervention of the British Administration, arguing that:

> According to Islamic Law, the husband is solely responsible for the moral and social behavior and associations of his wife, not an Emir.
> Some of us are determined to emancipate our wives from the shackles of outmoded customs and degradation, and an interference by an external hand on marital life goes beyond Islam and common sense.

The Resident replied:

> The arrangement to which you object was made some two years ago. It was designed to arrest progressive deterioration in moral standards amongst the community, and was made on the advice of a committee comprising, amongst others, the most prominent religious leaders in the city. . . .
> In view of the composition of the Committee to which I have referred above, I am surprised that you contend that the terms of the announcement offend against Moslem law and tradition. This is not the view of those who are most qualified to advise on this point, and I am sure that I should be unwise to intervene in the sense which you require.

NEPU Files, Secretariat, Kano.

[81] Professor Wilfred Cantwell Smith has observed this tendency in Pakistan. He also points out that certain Christian theologians have posited just such a view, and that, of course, many Christian Protestants accept such a position. *Islam in Modern History* (Princeton, 1959), p. 254.

[82] Prior to the adoption of the penal code, the Northern House passed a bill which provided that non-Muslims would be allowed to "opt out" of courts presided over by Muslims, following the recommendation of the Minorities Commission in 1958. The recommendation was primarily designed to meet the fears and objections of Northern Christians living in the jurisdiction of Muslim emirates (although the law also permitted Muslims to opt out of non-Muslim proceedings). NEPU and other opposition party members who distrusted the impartiality of native courts, began to use the law to avoid being tried by them. The practice produced a stormy reaction from the government, which passed an amendment intended to put a stop to the "abuse". See *Debates*, Northern House of Assembly, May 3, 1960, Col. 753.

So far as the goal to economic development was concerned, there appears to have been no important differences between the two major parties concerning immediate concrete measures. NEPU's proposals incorporated nearly all the items of the NPC manifestos listed above. NEPU claimed, however, that it would pursue development more wholeheartedly and with greater urgency than its opponents. The real issue dividing the NEPU from the NPC was ideological. It involved precisely those matters of socio-political structure that were most significant in the upper North.

I have already noted the prominent themes of social class interest and class conflict in the NEPU's propaganda. The themes reflected the party's desire to create a social and political order that would maximize popular participation in government and provide the widest possible access to social roles and rewards. This, rather than the narrower, more doctrinaire meaning of "public ownership of the means of production", is what the party had in mind when it proclaimed a belief in "socialism". (Given the overwhelmingly agrarian, small-holdings, agrarian economy of the North, the relevance of socialism in the classic industrial sense would have been questionable in any case.) Thus Aminu Kano's election broadcast for NEPU in 1954 proffered a "Socialist Commonwealth . . . in which there will be equal opportunities for all men and women and [which will] do away with vested interests and privileges".[83] Not only doctrinally, but tactically (in light of NEPU's important small trader constituents, any other of the conventional conceptions of socialism would have been misplaced).

Certain of the party's statements and policies do reveal that NEPU's concept of equality went beyond the notion of mere "equality of opportunity", however, to something approaching substantive social equality.[84] In this spirit the party in 1956 denounced the NPC for extravagance in the construction of ministers' residences, and promised it would convert them into hospital wards on coming to power. In the same election year the party also recommended reducing the salaries of legislators by almost half,[85] and in the following year expelled one of its own parliamentarians for proposing in the Northern House of Assembly that the government give members advances for

[83] *Nigerian Citizen*, December 16, 1954, p. 5.
[84] See the NEPU *Sawaba* Manifesto, 1956, esp. p. 3, para. 3; p. 11 (4); p. 13, para. 3; p. 14; p. 15 (9).
[85] "Northern Elements Progressive Union Views on the Nigerian Constitution" (typescript, 1956), p. 2.

the purchase of cars.[86] NEPU political verses and songs denounced sharp discrepancies in wealth and exhibited the propensity, common among self-conscious revolutionaries, to condemn any kind of intemperance.[87] In the political realm the NPC's concept of a properly hierarchical structure of leadership and participation was rejected in favor of reliance on what is best characterized as pure democracy. Aminu Kano stated the NEPU proclivity this way: "We interpret democracy in its more traditional radical sense, and that is the rule of the common people, the poor, the illiterate, while our opponents [the NPC] interpret it in its more modern Tory sense, and that is the rule of the enlightened and prosperous minority in the supposed interest of the common people.[88]

Since NEPU's devotion to modernism was essentially unqualified by any desire to retain a traditional system, which the party regarded as archaic and unjust, its positions on Nigerian and African issues were free of regional or national particularism. It long espoused as an ultimate goal a unitary form of government for Nigeria, and the alteration of the federal structure through reversion of residual powers to the center as a more immediate objective.[89] The party was in al-

[86] *Debates*, Northern House of Assembly, March 6, 1957, p. 605.
[87] For example:

Come hither, people of Nigeria,
I call you to have done with yesterday's ways . . .
greed and gambling and drinking,
and running after women of the world
These won't get us to our goal.

. . . . .
Follow NEPU, it is its aim to stop us
from living a life of pleasure, or relying
on membership of a particular tribe, and to prevent conceit,
and "sniffing the air", which prevents the ambitious
man from reaching his goal.

. . . . .
Here is one with a whole trunkful of clothes, i.e.
he has eaten and drunk and sits cross-legged (like a prince)
while here is another without a covering
his evening meal is a mouthful of cassava flour
And in the morning he does nothing but shiver.

"The Song: We recognize those who have wronged us", by M. Abba Maikwaru. I am indebted to Dr. David Arnott and his assistants in the School of Oriental and African Studies, University of London, for the translation of this highly colloquial poem.
[88] From the *Presidential Address to the Fifth Annual Conference of the Northern Elements Progressive Union*, 1955, quoted in Sklar, *Nigerian Political Parties*, Vol. 2, p. 372.
[89] *Views on the Constitution* (N.P.N.D.), pp. 1-2.

liance with the southern-based NCNC from 1953 on and, indeed, contested all elections under a common banner; Aminu Kano was a a vice-president of the NCNC.

The outlook for the party was enthusiastically pan-African, although preliminary unification on a regional basis (West Africa, East Africa, etc.) was generally regarded as a more realistic immediate goal.[90] Although there was no indication that NEPU was basically less oriented toward the West than was the NPC, its leaders were more outspokenly critical.[91] In principle they welcomed economic assistance from eastern countries and unreservedly subscribed to "neutralism" as a foreign policy for Nigeria.

I UNDERTOOK the discussion in this chapter to reveal the imprint of traditional political culture on the salient aspects of the two major indigenous Northern political parties, their historical growth and development, structure, organization, tactics, ideological orientations, policies, and programs. The tatoo seems to have been indelible, whether one examines the internal features of the parties or the characteristics and results of interparty competition. Much of the formal structure and rules of the parties corresponded to Western prototypes, yet the way the parties actually operated in the upper North would be incomprehensible without reference to the particular traditional political system and culture with which the parties interacted at virtually every point. An understanding of the role of political parties is necessary, in turn, to a comprehension and assessment of the impact on the Northern political system as a whole, and on all the innovations experienced by the emirates between 1945 and 1965.

The relationship between the organizational machinery of the NPC and the administrative apparatus of the traditional Native Authorities was characterized above as symbiotic. In fact, the term is suggestive of the whole relationship of the Northern political parties to the traditional system. This characterization most clearly fits the Northern Peoples' Congress, which achieved political dominance largely by utilizing and fostering traditional institutions. But we have also seen that NEPU, which was built on a reaction against these institutions and an intention to transform them, in practice found it

[90] Interview with Aminu Kano, New York City, October 1960.
[91] See Homer A. Jack, "Mallam Aminu Kano—A Profile", in *Africa Today* (September 1959), p. 10; and Phillips, *Nigerian Foreign Policy*, pp. 86-87, 101-107.

prudent to express its objectives and adapt its tactics to conform to traditional political understandings and interests in order to be politically effective at all.

The crucial juncture in Northern party development would seem to have been the response of the parties to the progressive extension of the suffrage in the period 1951-1959. Affording the peasant masses the right of participation, a right wholly foreign to both the traditional and colonial systems of rule, altered the formal rules governing the acquisition and retention of political power. Mass enfranchisement meant the right of the peasantry to choose between political parties organized to attract the support of the electorate by whatever means worked. The NPC soon discovered that traditional institutions and behavior could not only largely survive this formal constitutional change, but in fact could facilitate the process of mass political induction as required by the new democratic procedures. Traditional themes and values appealed to the peasantry; traditional bureaucratic structures provided the framework for organizing and directing appropriate political action. To be sure, the dominant group of NPC leaders regarded the perpetuation of tradition as desirable per se, but this discovery added a persuasive note of realism that could not be denied even by those less attached to traditional values. It must be recognized that a powerful source of political continuity in Northern Nigeria was the simple and practical consideration that, for the NPC at least, the politics of tradition were demonstrably successful politics in terms of the practical exigencies of the new democratic institutions.

If the maintenance of tradition proved to be beneficial to the NPC, that party in turn, greatly contributed to the maintenance of tradition by politically mediating and controlling the economic development process. The system of party government placed the power to dispense and allocate the major resources, rewards, and offices available for development in the hands of the party capable of winning elections. Directly or indirectly, the Northern government commanded all the most important sources of new wealth and opportunity. In such a situation, party "patronage" inevitably constituted an even more important source of political power that it typically does in societies where the control of wealth and opportunity is more diversified. Furthermore, the more determined and impatient individuals were to better material conditions or the chances for more attractive and creative types of work, willy-nilly, the more important the power of patronage was. Moreover, in addition to offering the prerogatives of patronage in the sense of ability to offer rewards for support, party government also allowed the party in power to choose such means of furthering the economic general welfare which at the same time subserved its particular, tradition-oriented political and social policies. Similar observations might be made with respect to some of the Western democratic welfare-state politics, but the fact remains that they applied with particular force in Northern Nigeria. There the distinctive ability of the party-in-power to exercise political discretion in dispensing the economic power of government was its use to impede the emergence of the very kind of social and political order that Western democratic institutions were designed to serve.

In Northern Nigeria there appears to have been at work a magnetic cycle of power in which the economic power of government buttressed the NPC, which reinforced traditional institutions, which helped the party gain access to the economic power of government, and so on, almost irresistibly. Thus, if functional and institutional innovations in Northern Nigeria largely resulted not in the undermining of traditional institutions and behavior but in their reinforcement, as seems apparent, part of the explanation must be found in the dynamics of the new institutions of competitive party politics and party government as they functioned in the environment of Northern Nigeria.

The unhappy experience of NEPU in attempting to break through the magnetic cycle of privilege and power to achieve fundamental change in the socio-political order illuminates important aspects of the problem of political change or lack of change. It can be seen that basically only two courses of action were open to NEPU. On the one hand, the party could seek to manipulate the traditional system to its own advantage, by exploiting internal conflicts and strains. On the other, it could try to convince the peasantry that the NEPU in power would bring about a better life, a substantial improvement in their condition not being possible under NPC/traditional rule. The party did in fact try both kinds of approach. Welcoming to its fold disaffected aristocrats who had lost out; intensifying the consciousness of traditional differentiation and conflict between *Habe* and Fulani and between other traditionally conquered and ruling groups; capitalizing on the existence of rival sectarian tendencies within the Islamic "community of the faithful" (*Tijaniyya* versus *Khadiriyya*); recruiting elements only partially or imperfectly integrated into traditional society (independent traders, *yan iska, gardawa*)—all these were NEPU activities typical of the first approach. The party's efforts to gain control of local government councils, its attack on "communal labor", its exposure of instances of maladministration and corruption by Native Authorities, its educational programs and propaganda activities designed to present attractive promises of change for the peasantry in general were typical of the other approach. Judged by electoral results, neither course of action led to victory for NEPU which in the last two elections of the period failed to win any emirate constituencies.

The failure of NEPU to convince the peasantry that voting the party into power would lead to a better life suggests some interesting if negative conclusions about the process of socio-political change. Political parties had not grown out of a search on the part of the peasantry itself for better ways to satisfy its demands and needs. The institution was constructed in accordance with developments (changing colonial policy, nationalism in the south and among the Northern educated elite) in which the peasantry played no part. The essence of NEPU's task, therefore, was to *create* among the peasantry a conception of an attainable alternative social and political order, fundamentally different, yet more desirable than the existing one. The obstacles were indeed formidable. Historic insularity and an extremely low level of literacy were two such obstacles. Another was the centralized and hierarchic structure of untransformed Native Administration, which tended to nullify the impact of NEPU majorities at any level below the emirate (i.e. in the subordinate local government councils), and to render futile electoral victories short of the number required to form the government at the regional level. The net result was the absence of any opportunities for NEPU to provide positive and immediate incentives for desiring change, or even to provide visible examples of the prospective fruits of change. Insofar as it tried to be positive, NEPU was reduced to presenting a case for fundamental change that was merely abstract and problematical. Such a program was no match for the competing opportunities of participating in a functioning system, the possibilities as well as the disabilities of which were well known to the peasantry and firmly in control of the NPC.

Simply by identifying itself with a viable organization of society, the NPC could offer blandishments that were real and immediate. Thanks to the new skills and resources imparted by the colonial rule,

and extended through participation in an expanding and modernizing national economy, the NPC itself was able to lay claim to having
actually realized, through the existing system, some of the improvements (increased social services, incomes, goods, etc.) merely projected by NEPU to a utopian future. At the same time, thanks to the
party's rapport with traditional authority, the NPC simultaneously
profited by the peasantry's very real fears of various day to day official
harassments by their reluctance to forfeit that measure of commonplace protection and relief which open defiance of traditional authority would have precluded.

The general inference here seems to be that for institutional innovations to result in systemic change the innovations must be accompanied by a process of what might be called the "concretization of
alternatives". For it was the ability of a functioning system, in the
form of the emirates to continuously provide immediate and concrete
inducements and dissuasions, that placed its challengers at a tre-
mendous disadvantage. This ability rendered uneconomical or irra-
tional initial departures from established patterns, however rational
or economical such departures might have been in the long run. In the
absence of socio-economic catastrophe the efficacy of institutional
change for basic or systemic change was at best slight, because it
was unaccompanied by the awareness of concrete alternatives that
meaningful choice requires. This awareness conceivably might have
come from substantial new knowledge or information (more intense
communication or contact with other systems), or from experience
(sub-systemic experiments), but institutional innovation per se did
not, and could not, provide these opportunities.

Several factors apparently minimized the impact NEPU was able
to achieve by manipulating internal tension, although, as we have
seen, much of what success it had may be traced to efforts in this
direction. The results attained through attracting "disaffected aristocrats", for instance, were limited because that source of discontent, in
the nature of the case, was confined to a small segment of the electorate. Moreover, the substance of this discontent was such as to
otherwise restrict its usefulness to NEPU. Aristocrats drawn to
NEPU out of a reaction to reversals in their personal fortunes did
not usually share the party's desire to construct a new social and political order from which invidious distinctions and privilege would
be absent. More often than not, they were motivated by the
chance they saw in NEPU to recapture something of the lofty sta-

tion from which they had fallen. They did not so much reject the old game as they sought to play it in a new way. So motivated, they tended to make unconvincing bearers of the revolutionary message NEPU sought to convey. (Their brother aristocrats in the NPC derided this element in NEPU with a not inappropriate epithet—"disgruntled". Some, as might be expected, adhered only temporarily and opportunistically to the party. Having demonstrated an ability to retain a substantial following as NEPU politicians, they readily heeded overtures to return—with the following—to the NPC fold.[92]

The latent hostility of the *Habe* toward their Fulani overlords involved the majority of the electorate, and was therefore potentially a more promising source of internal dissension. Apart from the inability of the party either to reward the *Habe talakawa* or to provide them with protection, other obstacles lay in the way of channeling the traditional enmity into modern political expression. The traditional system of leadership recruitment, with its use of *Habe* vassals, slaves, and clients, provided precedents for extending opportunities to the subject class. Moreover, the proliferation of offices occasioned by increased economic activity and new institutions increasingly enabled the traditional ruling class to admit even greater absolute numbers of *Habe* than ever to the ranks of leadership. While the added degree of mobility amounted neither to displacement nor to repositioning of the traditional elite, it was sufficient, when combined with the fluidity of traditional recruitment, to help contain a political movement that relied heavily for its leadership on the development of a sense of individual frustration or alienation. Ambitious *Habe* had no reason to feel that advancement was impossible.

It must also be said that the NEPU seemed to have backed away from totally opportunistic tactics. For example, the party did not very actively or openly encourage either the Askianist movement nor the *Tijaniyya-Yan wazifa* unrest, and was never comfortable in accepting such support. In the latter case, the initiative for the de facto alliance came from the *Yan wazifa*; in both of the cases it is clearly seen that the particular political party refused to acknowledge any official connection between these groups and the party, or officially to approve the ideas that inspired them. Aminu Kano, in particular, remained aloof from the Askianists; he maintained a formal neutrality in the

[92] The best known example is M. Abdulmumuni, a former district head and local NPC leader in Katsina emirate, turned NEPU from 1956 to 1959, when he crossed over to the NPC side of the House of Assembly. Details of his political career are recounted in the next chapter.

413

Tijaniyya-Khadiriyya controversy. There seem to have been two sources of these inhibitions. First, there existed a feeling that to exacerbate communal tensions of that kind was contrary to NEPU's secular and universalistic ideology[93] and inconsistent with NEPU's objective of broadening the *talakawa*'s psychological perspectives from traditional to modern issues and problems. The other inhibiting factor was the party's fundamental attachment to Islam, especially its ideal of unity. The party might unhesitatingly invoke the blessing of Islam on the ideals of egalitarian democracy and, under duress, even justify the use of ruses in judicial proceedings that called for false declarations of nonaffiliation (apostasy). But there is no indication that the *Yan wazifa*'s extreme tendencies toward fundamentalism and intolerance, which extended to regarding non-*Tijanists* as *khafiri* (unbelievers in Islam), were anything but repugnant to the top NEPU leaders in particular. Moreover, there was the practical consideration that to endorse such tendencies in the areas where Tijaniyya predominated would be to alienate party supporters in areas where the *Tijanists* were weaker in numbers or less militant. The result was that NEPU could ill afford to even accept support spontaneously engendered by extreme sectarianism, and even less afford to commit itself to the propagation of such sentiments.

Finally, an observation made about the relationship of institutional change and behavioral continuity in this study generally, deserves reiteration in the context of this chapter. It is that democratic institutions would appear to be sufficiently elastic in form to accommodate a remarkable range of social and political behavior and norms, apparently including (under the right conditions) behavior and norms alien to the societies in which the institutions originally developed. Far from automatically occasioning the emergence of new basic social and political values, the institution of the political party in Northern Nigeria proved perfectly serviceable as an instrument of a type of *ancien regime* whose demise elsewhere is associated with the growth of that institution.

[93] It is indicative of NEPU's outlook that the party's 1959 election manifesto— "Forward to Unity, Freedom, and Prosperity"—proposed the outlawing of all political parties "organized on a tribal basis". See *West African Pilot*, October 2, 1959, p. 1.

CHAPTER 9

Popular Elections and Neman Sarautu: A Case of Institutional Convergence

IN THE two previous chapters I contended that in Northern Nigeria under parliamentary government the key political positions were occupied mostly by the traditional ruling class, and that the formal structure of a "modern" political party facilitated this situation. Consequently, the entire political system was one of traditional values and responses. Far from having led inexorably to a profound political transformation, the introduction of modern political institutions resulted, to a significant extent, in their being assimilated into the political habits and norms of the traditional society.

This chapter deals with another facet of the same themes. In it I attempt to show how two very specific and mutually alien political institutions—one modern, the other traditional—became virtually inextricable, and to elucidate the impact of this admixture on the process of political change. The term "institutional convergence" is assigned to this general phenomenon; in the particular case to be discussed I argue that the distinctive structure of political power was responsible for its particular manifestations. Dominated by members of a traditional elite, one of the most characteristic modern political forms—popular elections—came to be perceived, interpreted, and adapted in terms of the preconceptions and interests of that elite. More specifically, popular elections served as a new framework for a form of traditional political competition called, in Hausa, *neman sarautu* (literally, "pursuit of office and title"), for which members of the traditional elite customarily vie.

This discussion must first describe the salient features of the institutionalized system of traditional political competition. I will then draw attention to some of the forces and factors that tended to promote a linkage of this institution with that of modern electoral competition. Various aspects of the interplay of these two institutional complexes may then be identified and illustrated by reference to specific instances. In conclusion, it is observed that "institutional convergence" reflected and influenced the political system of Northern Nigeria as a whole, and that this reality suggests revision of a widely accepted general proposition regarding political change.

415

Neman Sarautu

THE KEYSTONE of the traditional politics of every emirate in Northern Nigeria is the fact that bureaucratic titles and offices are always attained through competition. Since eligibility to compete for the most important of the offices and titles is determined by heredity, the vast majority of citizens of the emirates are barred from participation. Certain *sarautu* may, however, be obtained through the channels of clientage or marriage relationships with the hereditary elite. No rule of primogeniture or any other principle of automatic succession operates in this system. And this fact, plus the widespread practices of polygamy and concubinage by the royal and noble families, explains why there are always several, and usually numerous, candidates for even those *sarautu* reserved for high birth, including that of *sarki* (emir). Thus no matter what the special criteria for any given *sarauta* it invariably invokes an intense contest.

The intensity is increased by the fact that possession of a *sarauta* customarily brings the highest social prestige and the greatest perquisites of wealth and power. Formerly the equally relevant but negative side of this attraction was, as M. G. Smith remarked of one emirate in 1950: "The alternative to participation was obscurity and poverty, since manual labor in this status group is regarded as a sign of poverty, and with poverty there is loss of social effectiveness".[1] After 1952, however, modern political, commercial, and regional civil service employment provided alternate sources of reward. Yet both the material and psychic satisfactions of traditional office-holding continued to rival those of modern occupations. In fact, in some notable instances, the attractions of the former proved to be greater. In all periods, those who lacked the requisite hereditary eligibility or connections might serve as retainers to the powerful. Ordinary *talakawa* apparently have always derived satisfaction from the pageant and drama of *neman sarautu*;[2] after 1952 they remained just as fascinated as those more directly involved. Thus, either intimately or vicariously, *neman sarautu* was a preoccupation of the entire society.

There are three basic types of *sarauta*. The highest office, the emirship, is to a certain extent a type apart. In addition to the universal rule that only members (i.e. agnatic descendants) of the royal family or families can become an emir, often only the sons or sometimes sons and grandsons of once reigning emirs may gain the throne. Re-

---

[1] *Economy of Hausa Communities of Zaria*, p. 93.
[2] *Ibid.*, pp. 94-95.

cently there has been a tendency to relax the latter restriction,[3] but the son of an emir (*dan sarki*) or the grandson (*jikan sarki*) still occupies a favored position within royal families. A further advantage is prior tenure of some lesser bureaucratic office and title. Commonly, too, successful candidates will have previously held certain specific titles more frequently than others. Prior tenure of the title *ciroma* or *dan Galadima* (literally "heir apparent") is a notable instance of this, although being *ciroma* or *dan Galadima* does not insure automatic succession.[4] In every emirate the choice among candidates for the throne rests with a small council of electors whose composition is fixed by custom, which invariably prohibits any royal kinsman from being a member of the council.

A second class of *sarautu* consists of those reserved by tradition for certain noble families, usually Fulani, but sometimes also including the descendants of Habe *sarakuna*, who during the jihad and afterwards volunteered allegiance to the Fulani conquerors.[5] The emir is obliged in such cases to make his choice from among that

[3] Examples of presently ruling emirs of states where this rule once obtained, who are neither sons nor grandsons of former emirs, include the Sultan of Sokoto, the Emir of Zaria, and the Emir of Bauchi. There are probably other examples.

[4] An exception to the traditional rule of no predetermined succession held true in Gwandu, where the *dan Galadima*, who was always appointed to that *sarauta* by the incumbent emir, almost automatically succeeded to the throne upon the latter's death. Under the 15th Emir of Gwandum, M. Basheru (1915-1918), the custom, together with the title, was abolished at the instigation of the British administration, so that another candidate could be elected. A similar custom formerly prevailed in Bida.

[5] Random examples of titles reserved for Fulani nobility are *Madawakin* Kano (Yolawa Fulani), *Sarkin* Maska of Katsina and *Galadiman* Katsina (Danezawa Fulani), *Yandakan* Katsina (Yarubawa Fulani), *Dambon* Katsina (the District Head of Ingawa—Yarimawa Fulani), *Magajin Garin* Sokoto. As is apparent in the case of Katsina (it is also true of Sokoto), hereditary tenure of district headships and other titles by noble families is a prevailing practice. Originally all but two of the district headships were held by Fulani in the Adamawa emirate were held by nonroyal Fulani clans (the Gudu'en, Wolarbe, Jangi'en, Daware'en, Illag'en, etc.).

Some examples of *sarautu* held hereditarily by Habe families are *Sarkin* Kogo of Katsina, *Sarkin* Kebbi, *Sarkin* Illo, *Sarkin* Giro, *Sarkin* Aliero, ali of Gwandu. In Sokoto the important *sarautu* traditionally held by the descendants of Haben *Amana* ("living in peace", i.e. loyal to the *Sarkin Musulmai*) include *Sarkin* Zanfara of Anka District, *Sarkin* Burmi, *Sarkin* Donko (district head of Bukwimu), *Sarkin* Mafara (district head of Gummi), *Sarkin* Gobir (district head of Sabon Birni—the district which contains the majority of the old state of Gobir), *Yandoto* (the district head of Chafe), *Sarkin* Kotorkoshi, *Sarkin* Kwianbana (the last three named being Katsina *Habe*), *Sarkin* Adar (the district head of Dundaye), *Yari* (district head of Gandi), *Sarkin* Kebbi (district head of Kebbe), *Sarkin* Burmi of Tureta.

Note: except for the *Habe* territorial titles in Sokoto, the examples above are illustrative rather than an exhaustive listing.

family which collectively enjoys a hereditary right to the *sarauta* concerned.

The third major class of *sarautu* consists of those wholly "in the gift" of the emir. Some of these are customarily awarded to members of his dynasty (*dangin sarautu*); others may be given to free clients, cognatic kinsmen, or slaves. The number or proportion of these *sarautu* varies widely (Zaria, where almost all important appointments fall within this definition, is one extreme; Sokoto would appear to exemplify the other.) But all other Fulani emirs exercise this "unrestricted" power of patronage to some extent.

The primary means by which individuals vie for all types of traditional title and office is, in the Hausa euphemism, *gaisuwa* ("greeting")—actually the practice of plying those having the right to make appointments with gifts in cash or kind. In this sense, *gaisuwa* is at once the accepted method of resolving the conflicting claims of all the many candidates and a reward for holding office—which usually implies the right to make subordinate appointments and thus enjoy in turn being the object of *gaisuwa*. The reason why having previously held a senior *sarauta* constitutes an advantage in the competition for emirship should now be evident. For those eligible, holding any *sarauta* provides an opportunity to acquire some of the income necessary to compete successfully for the throne. To the exigency of *gaisuwa*, Hausa commonly add that of possessing *isa* (influence) as a source of success. But since the degree of an individual's influence is largely measured by such attributes as the pedigree of his wives, the number of his followers and retainers, and his connections with other influential people (all acquired principally by distributing material largesse), the ability to wield "influence" turns out to be indistinguishable from the capacity for effective *gaisuwa*. In former times such were *the* means of candidacy for office; if the reports of numerous observers and participants are to be believed, the recent association of modern qualifications and functions with the attainment and duties of *sarauta* has not at all diminished the efficacy of the old methods. Indeed, from a traditional perspective, the result of "development" has been to further narrow the base of selection, rather than to have introduced new means of reducing the competition.

One further important aspect of the institution of *neman sarautu* must be pointed out as a prelude to the following discussion. Usually traditional competition is not merely a matter of a contest between individuals. Rather it tends to take the form of rivalry between corporate or solidified groups, a feature which is most conspicuous, perhaps, in those emirates, like Zaria and Bida, that have a tradition of rotating the emirship among their hereditarily separate ruling houses. But the tendency to form rival units is endemic to the political system of any emirate, even if its structure is formally unidynastic. In the latter case, lineage segments based on more finely differentiated principles of kinship, rank, and interest tend to emerge within the dynasty. A common pattern is for the sons of a former emir to compete with the emir's brothers. Another is for the sons of one former emir to oppose the sons of another emir; or frequently the line may be so finely drawn as to pit sons of the same father by different mothers against one another. The concrete interest binding together the members and supporters of a solidarity group seeking the *sarauta* of emirship is the expectation that the successful candidate will reward his cohorts with offices and titles which come under his control. And since important *sarautu* are necessary steppingstones to the emirship, besides being desirable in their own right, they, too, tend to be objects of solidarity-group rivalry.

In some cases the origin of intradynastic lineage-splintering may be located several generations back. In Sokoto, for example, the Toronkawa are split primarily between the direct descendants of Sultan Muhammadu Dello (1817-1837), who are known as the Bellawa, and the direct descendants of Abubakar Atiku, the third Sultan (1837-1842), known as the Atikawa.

Variation of the lines of rivalry is also common, usually resulting from the failure over a prolonged period of a previously successful competing line to furnish an emir. In such cases new divisions within the ranks of the dominant lineage group can be expected to develop eventually. A prime current example of this process was observed in Gwandu, where the *Gida* (literally, "house", corresponds to *dangin sarauta*), or descendants of the third *Sarkin* Gwandu, Halilu (1833-1858), have nearly been eliminated from the competition by a series of successive appointments from the rival *Gida* of Haliru, the 14th *Sarkin* Gwandu (1906-1915) who was installed at the instigation of the British. Popular speculation in Gwandu is that the *sarauta* rivalry will henceforth concern only those sons of the three sons of the Emir Haliru who had served as emirs—Muhammadu Basheru, the 15th *Sarkin* Gwandu (whose son is the present emir), Shehu Usuman, and Yahaya, the 16th and 17th emirs, respectively.

That more than a single individual's fortunes are at stake helps to explain the extreme intensity of traditional competition. Indeed, both a cause and an effect of this intensity is the tacit assumption that any emir, having gained the throne, will attempt (within certain limits) to remove from office those identified with his dynastic lineage rivals to make room for his own kinsmen and clients. Much of an emir's power rests on his ability to do this. Nowadays one of the important "limits" is that appointments and dismissals must usually be justifiable on grounds of minimal administrative qualifications, performance, and integrity (or lack thereof.) But even that limit is far from strictly observed; furthermore, objective bases for evaluating performance can usually be found, or sometimes invented (a possibility increased by an emir's legal powers and judicial influence). Thus the expectation remains that within given limits an emir will show the appropriate preferences regarding appointment and supervision of subordinate officials. This naturally reinforces the keenness, indeed bitterness, with which traditional rivalry is often waged.

These, then, are the attributes of political competition, or *neman sarautu*, as it operates in the traditional system. This institution and the total complex of customary norms, rules, and behavior (as only slightly modified by colonial rule) that revolve around it, were actively functioning when a modern system of democratic elections was introduced into Northern Nigeria. Along with other aspects of the traditional system, it continued to flourish as a part of the system of local administration, side by side with the modern system.

POPULAR ELECTIONS

PERIODIC, popular democratic elections are also a kind of political competition. However, the purposes served by elections in the Western societies with which it is commonly associated diverge fundamentally from those of the institution of *neman sarautu*. In such societies a democratic election ostensibly allows political leadership to be drawn from a wide social base, promotes rational political debate, allocates political power according to the judgment and interests of the majority (political consensus), and forces political leaders to behave according to that consensus (political accountability, in the terminology of democratic theory). In at least these respects, the institution of popular elections is radically at odds with that of *neman sarautu*. *Neman sarautu* is relatively exclusive in its social criteria of leadership recruitment, in its definition of the boundaries of participation; and it produces a privileged class of political leaders who exercise power without having to account for it in the democratic sense.

Yet the two institutions share superficial features. Both are used by a society to choose political leadership and place authority. In both cases, the outward and immediate objects of competition are usually remunerative, highly respected public offices. Each institution gives rise to political rivalry and to solidarity. These similarities were not easily obscured by differences in terminology—representatives and political parties, on one hand, kings and noblemen and dynasties on the other. On the contrary, the similarities of form, if not of function, encouraged those confronted with the two institutions in Northern Nigeria to respond to one in terms of the other. In retrospect, it would have been surprising to find that a time-honored pattern of behavior centering on the notion of political competition in one context had been totally divorced from the same idea in another context. Rather, it might have been expected that two institutions, operating concurrently, both involving collective political action and each frequently featuring as contenders the very same men, would inevitably exercise reciprocal influence. In fact, as we shall see, the two institutions interacted dynamically in a number of fascinating ways, and the course of political action within the one institution was frequently inseparable from the political exigencies of the other.

IT SHOULD be noted that the rules governing the selection of modern representative leadership in Northern Nigeria were deliberately fashioned to assign a prominent role to traditional authorities. This doubtless gave some initial impetus to the tendency for concern with *sarautu* and with modern elections to become intermixed.

The Constitution of 1946, the Richards Constitution, stipulated that nonofficial members of the Northern House of Assembly were to be nominated directly by Native Authorities (the governor then appointed the nominees), on the basis of one per province—except for Sokoto and Kano provinces, which were allotted two and three nominations, respectively. Consequently, the large emirate Native Authorities were in a position to dominate the nominations in the far northern provinces. Since at that date an emir was legally a "*Sole* Native Authority", the House between 1946 and 1951 was composed almost entirely of traditional notables personally handpicked by the most important emirs.[6] (Two of these Assembly members joined two emirs from the Northern House of Chiefs to form the Northern representation in the Legislative Council at Lagos.)

The Constitution of 1951, the Macpherson Constitution, introduced a system of elections which, though substantially more democratic than the old procedure, still permitted Native Authorities to control it indirectly. The electoral regulations under the new constitution, it may be recalled, provided for a series of indirect five-tiered elections extending from village and ward units up to the final stage of provincial electoral colleges. Voting was by show of hands, except in certain urban areas where the final colleges used the whispering vote method. The use of these methods (justified in the opinion of the colonial administration by the overwhelmingly illiterate and politically inexperienced electorate) meant that voters' choices were virtually public knowledge, at least at the lower stages; this probably encouraged, if encouragement were needed, the *talakawa* to choose local officials who tended in turn to vote for their superiors in the traditional administrative hierarchy. Moreover, Native Authorities were empowered to make an injection of up to 10% of the total membership of the final college. The upshot of all this was that the final colleges in the upper Northern provinces were largely composed of district heads, other important traditional office and title holders, and lesser N.A. functionaries, who were loyal to an emir.[7] Since political party organization was then in a very rudimentary state, as well, emirs had a free hand in determining who would become representatives from their areas in Kaduna and Lagos, and they appear to have made good use of it. At the time, a correspondent for *West Africa* noted the tight control of the emirs with this anecdote: "In the Zaria election . . . popular men were defeated while N.A. nominees got through. Before the election I was shown a list giving the names of the four to be elected. If my informant could give such a tip, 100 percent correct, by guesswork only, it is a safe bet that he

[6] For a list of members of the Northern House of Assembly as of August 1950, see *Northern Debates*, August 19, 1950, p. 12.

[7] The composition of the final electoral college at Zaria was typical: out of a total of 68 members it included 12 district heads, 4 Alkalai, 3 N.A. councillors, 5 other important traditional titleholders, 7 village heads, and 11 minor officials of the N.A.—a total of 48, or 72 percent, who were official appointees of the emir. This figure does not include nonofficial clients, etc., whose relationship with traditional authority was not officially recorded. See Zaria Provincial File, ELE/5, p. 12.

can be relied on for the next Derby or Grand National".[8] Not surprisingly, the voters tended to draw the appropriate conclusion—that traditional and modern institutions were inseparable. One British official summed up the response of the *talakawa* in 1951 to the idea of popular elections, in saying, "after all, *sarautu* matters are none of our affair". Despite the subsequent growth of political parties and the democratization of electoral procedures, the habit of elections and *neman sarautu* inexorably coalesced in the popular mind, and in fact, persisted.

Apart from the more or less officially sanctioned role of the emir in early elections, other factors later helped to keep the two institutions linked. One was that of financial remuneration. Membership in the House of Assembly and the Legislative Council initially provided a substantial salary, £400 a year. The figure was raised in 1955 to £800 for ordinary members. Members were also entitled to an interest-free loan of £1,000, payable in two years, for the purchase of an automobile to facilitate attendance at legislative meetings; to an automobile maintenance allowance of £140 annually, plus one shilling and three pence per mile on trips to and from regular meetings. In addition, parliament committee members received three guineas per night while they met in committee. Those appointed parliament secretaries or ministers in the government received much larger basic salaries—£1,500 and £3,000 per year, respectively—and allowances for chauffeurs, entertainment, and maintenance of residences (provided by the government), in addition to those perquisites granted ordinary members. The range of the base salaries alone represented incomes of from 26 to 100 times the per capita average for Nigeria.[9] Nor did a subsequent Nigeria-wide austerity cut in parliament salaries much alter the situation—£720 per year for regional legislators, £1,350 for parliamentary secretaries, and £2,700 for a minister.

The significance of these salaries is that those elected to modern legislatures were able to command a standard of living and adopt a style of life, including distinctive habits of dress, comparable only in terms of traditional images, to the demeanor of the most lofty title-

[8] February 9, 1952, p. 103; cited in Smith, *Economy of Hausa Communities of Zaria*, p. 290.
[9] See *Economic Survey of Nigeria*, Lagos, 1959, p. 17. Regional breakdowns are not given in this study, but it is known that the average income of the Northern region was lower than the national average. Thus the figures given above are a conservative estimate.

holders (*masu-sarauta*) in the wealthiest emirates. The added wealth implied the ability to pay a higher "bride-price", which might open the way to marriage into a traditionally influential and prestigious family. Possession by a member of the legislature of an automobile— a perquisite which in his emirate was previously confined to the emir, a few top district heads and councillors, and perhaps a very few affluent traders—by itself might well have led the populace to associate the two kinds of positions. Furthermore, an elected member was entitled to honorific distinctions, e.g. the initials M.H.A. (Member of the House of Assembly) placed after his name, reminiscent of the use of titles. He was often greeted with phrases and gestures which expressed traditional attitudes of social and political deference, such as "May your life be prolonged". All this helped convey the aura of traditional office.

As the remark of the British officer quoted above indicated, the popular identification of institutions disposed the far Northern electorate, its rural segment especially, to regard elective office as a mere appurtenance of traditional authority. In turn, those whose high status in the traditional order had accustomed them to enjoy or to have the expectation of some day attaining such perquisites and symbols were inclined disproportionally to offer themselves as candidates.

Another highly practical reason for the coalescence of these institutions was perhaps the most important of all. As already noted, the traditional political system functioned concurrently with the modern one; *sarautu* continued to attract the eligible powerfully. Significantly the means of obtaining these much-coveted *sarautu*, i.e. wealth and influence and the special advantages to be had through membership in a modern legislature, were the same.

In the case of a member of a royal family who was eligible for the throne, for example, the monetary rewards of elected office were sometimes invested in the cultivation of *isa* (influence), or, probably more often, saved as *kudin gaisuwa* (money for "greeting") against the day when the kingmakers would meet to choose the next emir. If that day or his particular chances appeared remote, his extra income was helpful in acquiring some lesser *sarauta* (or, if he already had one, in moving up to a more important one), which at the same time advanced his competitive position in the long run. Those eligible only for offices open to the nonroyal (e.g. nobles, royal in-laws, or even ambitious commoners) were similarly able to improve their situations within respective traditional rank-orders by winning an election to a modern legislature. In one rare instance already cited, a parliament secretary who was definitely ineligible by blood even attempted (unsuccessfully) to induce the kingmakers to make him an emir. In general, it was true that the commonly shared rewards of wealth and prestige made for a dynamic and mutually beneficial interplay between modern electoral and traditional office-holding—the more fortunate one was in the one sphere, the better off he was likely to be in the other. Precisely this situation partially explains why, even in the absence of effective competition between political parties as such, or of political controversy about public issues in the ordinary sense, nomination and election to modern parliamentary bodies were highly desired and strenuously sought after throughout the era of parliamentary government.

It should also be noted in passing that this interplay was not confined to elective modern office, although there it tended to be greatest. Attainment of any prestigious and remunerative modern position—e.g. in the civil service or the management level of important commercial firms—could and sometimes did have similar implications. Nor was this interplay always voluntary. One example was the standing gained by Alhaji Umaru Gwandu, the speaker of the Northern House of Assembly, in his native emirate. The first Northern Nigerian to hold the office of clerk of the Northern House of Assembly (a senior civil service post), Alhaji Umaru Gwandu is also a member of Gwandu emirate's ruling family.[10] During my visit to Gwandu early in 1959, Alhaji Umaru Gwandu's appointment as the first Northern Speaker of the House of Assembly was widely rumored (he assumed the position toward the end of that year). Consequently, as it was explained to me, Alhaji Umaru Gwandu was certain to stand high in the running for emirship in the event of a vacancy. My own surprise at his being mentioned was on the grounds that his particular branch of the ruling house had not furnished an Emir of Gwandu since 1868, that he was already highly placed in the modern government service, and that he had not appeared to me to be interested in

---

[10] A branch of the royal Toronkawa family of Sokoto. The first *Sarkin* Gwandu was Abdullahi, a brother of Shehu Usman dan Fodio. Thus the Sardauna of Sokoto (premier of the Northern Region), along with other Sokoto Toronkawa, is Umaru Gwandu's cousin. The latter was educated in Gwandu and Sokoto schools and at the Katsina Higher College. Prior to his appointment as Clerk of the House, he had variously served as the Emir of Gwandu's private secretary, as secretary of the Gwandu N.A., and as scribe to the Emir's (M. Yahaha) judicial court.

becoming an emir. To all this the answer was, Alhaji Umaru had now become so prominent, well-known, and well-to-do, that his inclusion in the list was just naturally to be expected. The idea that he might not desire the position was summarily dismissed.

If success at the polls paid off in the quest for *sarautu*, the reverse was also sometimes true. That is, the higher an individual's standing in the traditional hierarchy of title-holders, the greater was his influence over the traditional administrative apparatus, which in turn could be instrumental in success as a candidate for modern elective office. Even had he not desired *sarauta* for its own sake, the popular office-seeker did well to be drawn into the arena of traditional competition for the tactical advantages to be derived for the purposes of modern electoral contests.

Still another factor linking the two spheres of political action was that the modern regional government, formed on the basis of popular elections, possessed powers that inevitably affected the traditional balance of power in the emirates. The regional premier's crucial influence over chieftaincy affairs (namely, the appointment, grading, discipline, and dismissal of chiefs), the Minister of Local Government's responsibility for approving Native Administration appointments involving annual salaries in excess of £390 (which included the most important *sarautu* in most emirates), and the general exercise of the discretionary power of appointment to important statutory boards and corporations, were only the most obvious levers. Even the ordinary member, as a part of the parliamentary caucus, became at least a small part of the decision-making process which influenced the fate of traditional ambitions. When election led to executive modern office (the cabinet), he was, of course, still better able to protect or to pursue interests of a traditional nature, in relation to his own emirate.

Perhaps the most interesting interrelationships of these modern and traditional institutions was a function of the traditional cleavages within the ruling class, particularly its royal segment. Just as traditional competition occurred along the lines of dynastic or lineage-group solidarity and rivalry, so this tendency was transferred in some cases to modern elections. In other words, instead of transcending the traditional lines of cleavage, as might be expected, the structure of modern interparty competition and intraparty factionalism paralleled them. Thus the antagonisms of *neman sarautu* often were discovered beneath the surface of the modern electoral process, affecting the modern competition in significant if sometimes subtle ways.

This transference of traditional political rivalry to the domain of the modern political system can be illustrated by reference to specific postwar electoral contests in certain emirates. The most clearcut case I know of, that of Kazaure, an emirate whose compactness and small scale have previously afforded a birdseye view of other significant phenomena in this book, will serve again here.

ELECTIONS IN KAZAURE

THE RULING DYNASTY of Kazaure was established in 1924 by Malam Dambo, a member of the Fulani clan called Yerimawa. According to legend, the Yerimawa derive their name from the clan's early location in Bornu, where for a time they enjoyed the protection of an important title-holder called Yerima. Legend has it that, being more independent than other settled Bornu Fulani families, the Yerimawa migrated westward to Kano rather than pay homage to the Shehu of Bornu. Their arrival, about 1804, coincided with the raising of the jihad by Shehu Usman dan Fodio of Sokoto. Dan Tunku, a leader of the Yerimawa, sent greetings and a pledge of allegiance to dan Fodio, who in turn acknowledged dan Tunku's support by giving him a turban and religious instructions.

After the completion of the jihad and the establishment of the Sule-bawa Fulani as the ruling dynasty in Kano, friction developed between that house and the Yerimawa. In the early 1820s, acting on the advice of Dambo, his son, dan Tunku led his kinsmen and followers from the area of Dambatta district in Kano emirate northeast to the village of Kazaure. There ensued an historic battle between the Yerimawa and the Kano forces, led personally by the Emir of Kazaure, in which the outnumbered Yerimawa triumphed. Thus secured in Kazaure, the Yerimawa petitioned Sokoto for support. Subsequently Sultan Bello intervened, forbidding further fighting and presenting Dambo with a flag, the symbol of Fulani sovereigns. As the first flag-holder (in contrast to his father, who was only given a turban by Sokoto), Dambo is reckoned as the first Emir of Kazaure and his direct descendants have occupied the throne ever since. Kazaure, like Sokoto and most other emirates, is therefore formally uni-dynastic.

Dambo was succeeded by Muhammadu Zangi, whose line became

extinct for lack of a male heir. The last three Emirs of Kazaure have all been the immediate descendants of Muhammadu Maiyaki, the third *Sarkin* Kazaure. True to form, however, the descendants of Maiyaki have tended to split up into rival lineage groups. In the first instance this rival grouping was threefold, revolving about the three sons of Maiyaki, Muhammadu Tura (fourth Emir of Kazaure), Magaji Abdu, and Yarima Abdullahi, the last two having failed to attain the Kazaure *sarauta*. In the period 1956-1965 the son of Magaji Abdu, Adamu, was the emir. His predecessor was a son of Muhammadu Tura, one Umaru. Since no offspring of Maiyaki's third son, Yarima Abdullahi, has yet succeeded and since this is still technically possible, it is not yet certain whether the Kazaure competition will ultimately crystallize into two or three lineage group patterns. However, while the Yerima Abdullahi line cannot yet be fully counted out, there is a strong tendency to look on the sons of Umaru and Adamu, respectively, as the next principal contestants to the throne. Therefore, the hottest traditional rivalry in Kazaure is a two-cornered one—the *Gidan* Umaru versus the *Gidan* Adamu.

For several reasons serious modern electoral activity developed relatively late in Kazaure. In 1946 the Emir of Kano nominated (under the procedures of the Richards constitution) all the representatives from Kano province to the Northern House of Assembly, and his choices did not include anyone from Kazaure. In 1952 the *Magajin Gari*, whose nomination is said to have been personally secured by the Emir of Kazaure, Adamu, was returned unopposed to the Assembly by the provincial electoral college. For the federal election of 1954, Kazaure had to share a seat in the House of Representatives with Dambatta district of Kano, a situation that was resented, and not surprisingly, in light of Kazaure's historic association with that area.

Perhaps the first prefigurement of things to come arose in connection with the 1956 elections to the Northern House of Assembly. The official candidate of the Northern People's Congress for Kazaure was Alhaji Muhammadu, the *Magajin Gari*, whose intimate political relationship to Adamu, the emir, is described in another chapter.

In 1956 M. Zakari Yau, the *Mutawalli* or treasurer of Kazaure, who was a son of Muhammadu Tura (the fourth Kazaure emir) and therefore a brother of Umaru (the fifth emir), also announced his candidacy, as an independent, but decided at the last minute to withdraw. The *Magajin Gari* was again elected unopposed in that year. Had the *Mutawalli* run against the *Magajin Gari*, it would have been the first Kazaure electoral contest featuring opponents identified with the *Gidan* Umaru and the *Gidan* Adamu, respectively.

Until 1959 party opposition to the NPC was unusually feeble, and it has remained so, probably as a result of a combination of factors having to do with Kazaure's physical isolation, poor communications, low educational development, and, consequently, an extremely limited degree of modern political exposure. Kazaure was a striking example of the persistence of centralized autocracy under conditions of institutional change. The NPC in Kazaure therefore had a virtual monopoly of modern party support in all elections. In 1959 opposition parties secured little more than a thousand votes (608 for NEPU and 580 for the Action Group) out of a total of some 18,000 votes. In 1961 there was no NEPU candidate; the AG's nominee received 295 votes out of 15,312. The NPC candidate in the 1964 federal election was elected unopposed. But despite anemic opposition party activity, at least two electoral campaigns (1959 and 1961) in Kazaure were among the bitterest waged in Northern Nigeria. The primary source of this acrimony was not ideological or policy disagreement between the parties or even within the NPC, but the persistence of rancor ingrained in the pattern of traditional politics and projected onto the electoral stage.

When I visited Kazaure in May 1959 (the elections were in December), Malam Zakari Yau was once again contemplating running as an independent against the official NPC nominee. This time, the official NPC candidate was Alhaji Ibrahim, the son of the Emir of Kazaure and holder of the important title of *Wombai*.[11] The *Wombai* was an N.A. councillor, with responsibility for police, prisons, and medical and health services; with the *Magajin Gari*, he also sat on the key N.A. committees—Finance, Tax Assessment, and Tenders. In the exercise of these duties, as in his blood-connections, the *Wombai* epitomized the interests of the *Gidan* Adamu.

Significantly Malam Zakari disavowed any disagreement with the program or interests of the national organization of the NPC. He openly stated his intention, should he run and be elected, to sit on the NPC side of the House of Assembly. His self-proclaimed motive was that he simply thought he would make a better representative of Kazaure than the official party nominee. It is difficult to say con-

---

[11] Originally this was a slave title in Kazaure, as is true in most emirates that have used it. The Kazawa *Wombai* was always powerful, however, and the title was no longer considered the exclusive preserve of slave-descendants.

fidently whether or to what extent Malam Zakari was at this stage actively animated by a desire to thwart the *Gidan* Adamu, whose votaries dominated the local NPC executive; or whether and to what extent he consciously sought to profit from the traditional solidarity of members and supporters of the *Gidan* Umaru vis-à-vis their rivals. What can be said with certainty, however, is that the Kazaure NPC strategists were deeply anxious lest Malam Zakari's candidacy activate the traditional cleavage and jeopardize the party's chances for success. Accordingly Kazaure NPC officials, especially the *Magajin Gari* (then patron of the party) and *Wombai* (official candidate and president of the party) made repeated efforts at this time to bring M. Zakari into the official party fold, where, of course, he would have been subject to party discipline. M. Zakari's persistent refusals merely intensified the party leaders' anxiety and made them increasingly suspicious of his intentions. It is also significant that Zakari's reaction was being widely interpreted in Kazaure as a sign of the likelihood of an electoral contest along the lines of *sarauta* competition. In May it was even being predicted that a member of the third group of *sarauta* eligibles—the *Gidan* Yerima—would enter the lists, a speculation which further suggested the special meaning the coming federal election was assuming to people of Kazaure.

As it turned out, M. Zakari once more inexplicably decided (as he had in 1956) not to run. The *Gidan* Yerima failed to produce a candidate. But except for alterations in the anticipated cast, Kazaure's election drama took place as expected: the main theme and central plot was traditional rivalry. M. Zakari's projected role as symbolic standard-bearer for the interests of the *Gidan* Umaru was taken up by Malam Ibrahim Na Maitama, a teacher in the Senior Primary School at Kano, and a son of the late emir. Faithful to the script, his official NPC opponent was to be the *Wombai* of the *Gidan* Adamu. The two candidates' positions in the traditional structure of Kazaure lineage can be seen in Table 34 which is an abbreviated genealogy of the Kazaure royal dynasty. As election day approached, antecedent political sympathies mounted, and by April there was no doubt that the election was to be the occasion of a test of strength between the two main branches of the ruling family.

Early in the campaign official NPC forces placed great emphasis on the record of the NPC regional government in providing new social services and development for Kazaure, as well as the promise of continued progress under an NPC-controlled federal government.

Table 34: Genealogy of the Emirs of Kazaure

(showing relationship of rival candidates in the federal election of 1959)

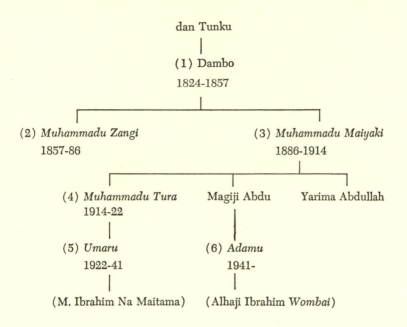

At this initial stage, the party's appeal to the electorate was part secular and part modern, and its focus was on regional and nationwide institutions. At the same time, the Kazaure party, like NPC branches elsewhere, stressed its identification with the traditionally legitimate authority of the local throne and its subordinate bureaucracy, the Native Administration. Predictably the regional party's championship of traditional chieftaincy was trumpeted as the indissoluble link between the two kinds of interests.

M. Ibrahim Na Maitama's interpretation of what was at stake in the elections was quite different. Since he, like M. Zakari, pledged support for the NPC programs in Kaduna and Lagos, the merits of that party were declared not to be at issue. He, too, professed support of economic and social development and of the continued dignity and authority of emirs. The important question, in his view, was who, or more precisely which, of the royal factions in Kazaure, would better bear the mantle of both traditional legitimacy and progress in public welfare? To the interested parties—the blood kin, inlaws, clients, and camp followers of the *Gidan* Umaru—the answer was obvious. With little effort on Ibrahim Na Maitama's part they were enlisted in his cause. Together these partisans now concentrated their efforts on convincing the disinterested bulk of the community, the enfranchised *talakawa*, that they too would profit by defeating a son of Adamu in favor of one of Umaru's heirs.

This delineation of the issues clearly directed the major focus away from the wider regional and national political systems to the local political system of Kazaure, and consequently from secular to more or less traditional considerations. Both the official and independent candidates were thereby confronted with problems. The efficacy of the local party organization's appeal to the power of the NPC (national or regional) to achieve development and to uphold traditional chieftaincy tended to presuppose the existence of a unified traditional community at the local level. In a divided community, however, this power of the party had negative as well as positive ramifications, for it inevitably gave rise to the fear that the popularity and influence of the NPC might unduly strengthen one traditional faction at the expense of the other. Why should the *Gidan* Adamu-Kazaure NPC coalition be allowed to lay exclusive claim to the sanctity of tradition? And hadn't the *Gidan* Adamu, by taking credit for the successes of the NPC government, become more firmly, indeed dangerously, entrenched? Such anxieties tended to vitiate the effect of the official NPC line (namely, defense of the Kazuare community as a whole) and compelled the local NPC official forces to defend the particular merits and interests of the incumbent ruling faction, a defense that inevitably worked to Ibrahim Na Maitama's advantage. For on this level of argument, the *Gidan* Umaru-independent supporters had only to protest that the official NPC-*Gidan* Adamu adherents were deficient or undesirable *as rulers of Kazaure*, to proclaim their own comparative virtues, and to leave aside the record of the NPC-controlled government in Kaduna and Lagos.

Compared to this approach, the objections raised against M. Ibrahim Na Maitama's contentions turned out to be rather ineffectual. The nub of his contentions was that a victory for him would lead to desirable reforms in Kazaure. The NPC countered that this claim was patently fraudulent in light of the fact that the federal government (unlike the regional government) had no jurisdiction over chieftaincy matters or local administration; thus the outcome of a federal election, as such, could not affect either the tenure of Kazaure traditional offices or the conduct of administration. To Ibrahim Na Maitama (and doubtless to the general Kazaure, which was hazy about the provisions of the Nigerian constitution) this consideration was a mere nicety. The heart of the matter at issue, Ibrahim Na Maitama argued, was the balance of power between the royal lineages. To place another member of the *Gidan* Adamu in the federal legislature —a source of money, influence, and patronage—could only increase the prestige and power of that royal house at the expense of its rivals, which no issue of formal constitutional jurisdiction could alter.

The result was a campaign in which both sides sought to manipulate the tensions and strains inherent in the structure of traditional competition. The election became a mock battle over the Kazaure *sarauta*; as such, it was waged bitterly and wholeheartedly. On this point, some of the promises made by Ibrahim Na Maitama are revealing, including those to dismiss the emir, the *Magajin Gari*, the N.A. councillors and most district heads, and to make new appointments to these posts. For the *talakawa*, Ibrahim Na Maitama's platform contained the condemnation of practices of maladministration and corruption on the part of the N.A. and the prospect of drastic tax relief. All this was fervently promised, considerations of constitutional jurisdiction to the contrary notwithstanding. Admittedly many other lesser issues, charges, and countercharges were raised on Ibrahim Na Maitama's behalf (including purely personal controversies about the private conduct of the candidates). This account does not purport to provide a comprehensive coverage of all the issues involved or of all aspects of the election. My interest here is in the *alignment of political forces*. The important point is that Ibrahim Na Maitama's campaign was clearly designed to mobilize and combine two kinds of discontent vis-à-vis the incumbent rulers: (a) the frustrated and anxious royals "outs" and (b) the hapless *talakawa*. The further significant fact is that the former elements took the initiative and bore the thrust of this effort.

Ibrahim's decisive victory over the *Wombai*, who suffered the ultimate electoral ignominy of losing his deposit,[12] precipitated a

---

[12] The returns were officially tabulated as follows:

Ibrahim Na Naitama (Ind.)   12,896
Ibrahim *Wombai* (NPC)   4,670
Musa Dan Ginjaje (AG)   580
Musa Disina (NEPU)   608
    Independent majority   8,826

major internal political crisis in the emirate of Kazaure, which continued from the federal election of 1959 through the regional election of May 1961 and afterward.[13] In the aftermath of the 1959 election, adherents of the *Gidan* Umaru publicly construed the results as having placed in question the legitimacy and power of their traditional rivals, and as a sign of their own imminent rise to prominence. Conversely, the Emir and high officials of the Native Authority regarded the outcome as nothing less than a revolt against its authority; accordingly they castigated and treated as subversive elements those who had been associated with Ibrahim Na Maitama's cause. The marked intensification of the climate of conspiracy, intrigue, and counterintrigue which now characterized the atmosphere in Kazaure could only be understood in terms of the dynamic interrelationship of modern elections and the traditional politics of *neman sarautu*. The conduct of the Native Administration itself during this subsequent period would be inexplicable without knowledge of the deeper implications of the 1959 federal election. For in reaction the full power of the incumbent regime became bent on breaking the local influence of their rivals, who were playing their new hand to the hilt.[14] Of what that "full power" consisted may be inferred from previous accounts in this book of the scope, techniques, and norms represented by the apparatus of "Native Administration". Thus, as might be expected, there were changes in key administrative personnel. Powers over taxation, the dispensation of social services, the judiciary, the police, and the prisons were all at the disposal of the Kazaure Native Administration. The victory of the Emir's trusted chief lieutenant, the *Magajin Gari* (see Chapter 6), against still another son

[13] My comments on the post-election (1959) period are not based on observation and interviews in the field. I had the good fortune, however, of being able to have interviews with reliable and knowledgeable Kazaure informants following the period of field work.

[14] Following the defeat of the *Wombai* (given in February 1961 the more prestigious title *Galadima*) by the *Gidan* Umaru candidate in 1959, pressure was brought by the administration (regional government) to appoint another representative of that House to the Emir's council in recognition of its popularity demonstrated in the 1959 election. The person chosen, after considerable negotiation between the two dynastic factions, was M. Yusufu, now titled *dan Iya* and made Councillor for Education, having previously been a teacher in Kano. For his turbanning ceremony (according to my informants), he rode from Kano into Kazaure in triumphant procession, afterwards donned an *alkyabba*, tied "ears" in his turban after the manner of royalty, carried a staff to council meetings, and at one point introduced a motion that the Emir should retire because of old age.

of Umaru, J. Maitama Na-Iro, in the 1961 regional election,[15] at once reflected and further assured a dramatic reversal in the fortunes of the Kazaure dynastic factions.[16]

In one sense, the case of Kazaure may be taken as a paradigm of the phenomenon of institutional convergence being discussed here. But it was not a completely typical example. For several reasons the relationship between traditional and modern political competition in the Northern emirates was seldom so pronounced or so clearcut as in Kazaure. Apart from the factor of its insular geographical location, Kazaure also represented one of the relatively uncommon instances in which the boundaries of the traditional emirate and those of the modern electoral constituency coincided perfectly.[17] More often than not, two or more constituencies were to be found within

[15] The returns were:

> Alhaji Muhammadu, *Magajin Gari* (NPC) 8,622
> Malam Maitama Na-Iro (ind.) 6,395
> Malam Musa Biu-Ibiyaru (AG) 295
> NPC majority 1,942

[16] Some months after the appointment of *dan Iya* as Kazaure Councillor for Education (see preceding footnote) a commission of inquiry into the affairs of its Education Department was launched at the request of the Kazaure Native Administration. The commission was chaired by Malam Maitama, the new *Mutawalli* (and a member of the *Gidan* Umaru). It included the *Galadima* (*Gidan* Adamu). This body found irregularities in the conduct of the department, but not sufficiently damaging to warrant dismissals or prosecutions. At this point, the Kazaure N.A. requested that the commission be reconstituted and inquire further, on the grounds that the first commission had failed to unearth all the relevant evidence due in part to the reluctance of certain members, notably the *Galadima*, to appear to be acting with partiality. The duly reconstituted commission was chaired by Malam Muhammadu (the *Magajin Gari*) and a British administrative officer, Mr. Timothy Brierly. This commission uncovered evidence adequate to justify *dan Iya's* dismissal for gross negligence (he departed for Lagos) and to sustain criminal convictions against the headmasters (both *Gidan* Umaru) of the Kazaure junior and senior primary schools, respectively. By 1963, of the five remaining serious hopefuls of the *Gidan* Umaru, three were living outside of Kazaure, one (M. Maitama Na-Iro) was working quietly in Kazaure as a teacher, and the fifth, M. Ibrahim Maitama (the *Madaki*, formerly the *Mutawalli*) remained on the Emir's council. Other new assignments included the *Galadima's* assumption of the duties of chief councillor (upon the appointment of *Magajin Gari* as provincial commissioner for Bornu) and a new member of the Kazaure council, who was identified as a slave descendant, related on his maternal side to the *Gidan* Adamu. The title of *dan Iya* was awarded to M. Abdullahi, formerly *Wakilin* Gona, and a son of the Emir Adamu. In the federal election of 1964 the (*Gidan* Adamu) NPC candidate was elected, *unopposed*.

[17] For the 1959 federal election there were seven such cases in all—the constituencies of Misau, Keffi, Nassarawa, Bedde, Potiskum, Kazaure, Yauri—each of which fit exactly within traditional boundaries. A few other emirates dominated in population the constituencies in which they were included, i.e. Lafia, Borgu, Pategi, and Abuja.

the traditional unit.[18] The availability of more than one constituency meant that conflicts of interest within an emirate could be resolved more readily through compromise on a basis of equitable distribution of opportunity than by waging a pitched battle for a single prize. Furthermore, in large multiconstituency emirates, the consequences of a melee were potentially far graver from the point of view of the NPC regime, which was therefore more inclined to take active steps to prevent this happening, as we shall see. The specific case of Kazaure, then, even though atypical, nevertheless constituted a concise and highly transparent example of what was a widespread but usually more subtle tendency. Thus various elections in several emirates involved antagonisms deriving in part from sources of traditional rivalry and cleavage, often obscured beneath the surface of party politics.

The forms this phenomenon took varied: (1) instances of the ambitious title-holder or seeker jostling, free-lance, as it were, to improve his *individual* position in the traditional hierarchy; (2) cases of ousted traditional title-holders looking for revenge and recovery of prestige and wealth; and (3) manifestations of more enduring antagonisms which reflected discontents and schisms inherent in special historical and structural features of particular emirates.

EXAMPLES of contests arising primarily out of individual attempts to ascend the competitive ladder of traditional prestige and power abounded in every election. One notable case was the struggle over the Assembly seat for Gwandu North in the regional election of 1956. In that contest four different members of the *Gidan* Haliru branch of the Toronkawa dynasty opposed each other, although each was an adherent of the NPC. All four were *yan sarki*, sons of former emirs. Certain additional aspects of this contest were especially interesting. The winner of the seat, the then *Sarkin* Gabas, district head of Gwandu, was the son of the late Muhammadu

---

[18] Thanks to the Constituency Delimitation Commission's terms of reference, constituencies were so drawn as to avoid wherever possible any amalgamation of emirates for electoral purposes. Thus, although most emirates contain more than one constituency, only a few were submerged in a larger nontraditional unit. To quote the commission's report, "In all cases where [administration] boundaries are not involved and the size of constituencies is not compromised we have tried to include people with a community of interest in the same constituency". (See *Report of the Constituency Delimitation Commission* [Lagos: Government Printer, 1958], paragraph 13, p. 9.) This observance of the integrity of traditional communities undoubtedly contributed to creating the phenomena discussed in this chapter.

Basheru, the 15th Emir of Gwandu. His three opponents—the *Ubandoma*, district head of Birnin Kebbi; the *Sarkin* Gobir, district head of Kalgo, and M. Aliyu, an organizer in the N.A. Adult Education Department—were all sons of the Emir Haliru, but each was born of a different mother. The fact that all of the contestants were members of the *Gidan* Haliru, the ascendant branch of the dynasty, placed the competition in a different category from that of the Kazaure affair—i.e. no challenge to the throne was implied. It would appear that an incipient process of lineage differentiation, or segmentation, operated in the formation of these rival candidacies. Indeed, in Gwandu this configuration was assumed to indicate the future lines of competition for the Gwandu throne, an assumption no doubt stimulated by the probability of a re-formation of those lines for other reasons suggested earlier in this chapter.

In the same emirate and the same election, the constituency of Gwandu Central was the scene of a triangular contest between Alhaji Dalhautu Bida, at the time the son-in-law of the Emir Haruna, Malam Kakale, a dismissed chief scribe of the Native Administration and reportedly a member of a traditional *fadawa* (courtiers' family, and M. Aliyu, *Sarkin* Kudu, the District Head of Dakingari, who was a member of the *Gidan* Halilu branch of the Toronokawa and thus a representative of the "out" faction of the Gwandu royal house. All three were members of the NPC. The first named ran as the official NPC candidate, while the other two called themselves "independent". The belief in Gwandu was that support of his son-in-law by the Emir was largely responsible for Dalhautu Bida's victory.[19]

In another emirate the 1956 regional election in Katsina North featured a close contest between two candidates associated with *sarauta* interests. Katsi North was a constituency primarily composed of two important districts of Katsina emirate, Mashi and Kankiya. The rivals for the seat, both NPC members, were Alhaji Muhammadu Sada, a brother of the Emir (Nagogo), who had just been promoted to district head of Kankiya, and M. Aminu Iro Mashi, son of the district head of Mashi, who happened to be married to a daughter of Nagogo, the Emir. In the final electoral college, there were 16 Mashi members who had pledged themselves unwaveringly to M. Aminu, five members from the minor districts of Mallamawa and Dankara, whose intentions were uncertain, and 20

---

[19] The couple was subsequently divorced.

members from Kankiya whose unanimous commitment to their new chief was not assured. Again, the alleged intervention of the Emir is popularly credited with tipping the balance in favor of the district head of Kankiya. The Emir's emissary for this purpose is thought to have been Alhaji Muhammadu, the *Sarkin* Musawa, brother to the Emir and chief whip of the NPC in the Northern House, who suddenly appeared at the scene of the electoral college the night before the election.[20]

Kaura Namoda (in Sokoto emirate), won in 1956 by a NEPU candidate, also experienced dual candidacies based on divergent traditional claims. In this case the district head of Kaura Namoda was the official NPC standard-bearer. He was challenged by an "independent" who was a member of a different segment of the *sarauta* family. Other examples in the general category being discussed occurred, in the federal election of 1959 and the regional election of 1961, in such constituencies as Daura West, Bauchi South East, Gombe Central, Nafada (also in Gombe emirate), Nassarawa, Kontogora South East, and Rabah-Wurno (in Sokoto emirate). Indeed, it is fair to say that wherever a modern election within an emirate produced one or more independent candidates, the strong likelihood was that some aspect of traditional ambition was at stake.

The nominally independent status of certain candidates, it should be observed, was of the essence of the coalescence of institutions. For, as we have seen, such independents were invariably dyed-in-the-wool adherents of the NPC, whose official nominees they opposed. They were not necessarily alienated from either the traditional political regime or the modern government party. On the contrary, they simply took modern elections to be an appropriate forum for the pursuit of comparative advantage vis-à-vis other traditionally eligible seekers after socio-political prestige and power.

By way of corroboration, this phenomenon is sufficiently common to have been repeatedly, if obliquely, alluded to in various British administrative officers' official comments on electoral contests in several different emirates.[21] One of these comments seems particularly to the point. In discussing the course of the federal election of 1954 in the constituency of Lafia emirate, Mr. C. W. Cole, British Resident, concluded: "Though the rival camps adopted new nomencla-

[20] *Provincial Files*, Katsina, No. DS/1/35.

[21] See, for example, Northern Region, *Provincial Annual Report*, 1951, p. 54; 1954, pp. 15, 32, 77; 1956, pp. 14, 23, 117.

tures the divisions between camps and the platforms upon which they argued their merits still centered around the old, unchanging issues".[22]

The full extent of this situation did not show up in the election contest itself, it must be added. Increasingly over the years, with the growing appreciation by the government regime of the virtue of party discipline, the preliminary stage of selecting the official NPC nominee was the occasion of this kind of controversy. The impact on the nomination process was in the nature of the case less visible than the conduct of public elections. As in the British system, there were no open primaries; ostensibly the local "party organization" designated its official candidates, and detailed information was correspondingly less easy to come by. Undoubtedly, however, the traditional factor was frequently at work in the nominating process.

Occasionally, the ensuing difficulties of adjudicating competing traditional claims allowed a glimpse of their presence, however. The controversy over nominations in Sokoto in 1959 was such an affair. Early in that year, the executive of the Sokoto division (which is coextensive with the emirate) branch of the NPC appointed a subcommittee to make recommendations to it on personnel suitable to contest the 21 seats allotted to Sokoto division. The subcommittee was instructed to submit three or four names for each constituency. Predictably the subcommittee's choices consisted primarily of titled officials of the Native Administration, and other traditional notables. However, from the party's point of view, the results threatened to be catastrophic, for as the deadline for posting official nominations approached, most of those being tentatively considered announced their intention to run as independents if they were not given the official nod.[23] Reportedly, premier and NPC president-general, the *Sardauna* of Sokoto, subsequently advised the Sokoto NPC executive (itself composed overwhelmingly of the higher traditional officials of the N.A.) to rescind previous instructions and make its own determinations. It is interesting that in the actual election in only one of the 21 Sokoto constituencies (Rabah-Wurno) did any independent oppose the official party choice, a feat the executive is said to have accomplished in part through the good offices of the Sultan of Sokoto.

That emirs and other highly placed traditional figures were often,

[22] *Ibid.*, 1954, p. 32.
[23] Interview with M. Usman D. Bugudu, Federal Electoral Officer, Sokoto province.

officially or unofficially, concerned with party nominations is more than incidentally related to my theme of institutional convergence. First, those aspiring to modern elective office and to a *sarauta* at the same time often found that the door to advancement in both realms of competition was manipulated by the same clique of men, or even a single man, where the emir himself was personally active. Itself a mark of convergence, the overlapping directorate of party and traditional bureaucracy stimulated the tendency in other respects. Thus, to resolve the competition for the party label, the same method as applied to the dispensation of *sarautu*, namely, *gaisuwa* (plying a superior with gifts of cash or kind) was widely employed. In one emirate there was remarkably consistent agreement on a standard fee commanded by the emir for securing a nomination; the figure mentioned was £300.

That emirs did play an active role in the nominating process, at once a cause and effect of the dovetailing of institutions, was confirmed by an NPC official: "In previous elections, the emir can be said to have been *the* nominator in most places. Now he does not pick the candidates directly. In that respect there has been an important change. However, the emir is still the most powerful single influence in the selection of candidates. To make his influence felt, he must work through the nominating machinery set up by the party, instead of doing it directly. It is still possible, even probable, that he will be successful in this, but it is not invariably so".[24]

The qualifying phrase at the end of the statement is perhaps as important as the rest of it, for one of the reasons, that "independent" candidacies persisted in spite of party efforts to enforce discipline, was the encouragement they sometimes received from an emir, particularly if his own choices had been disregarded by the local party. Such a situation arose in the 1959 elections in Gombe emirate which contained four constituencies—Ako, Duku-Kwame, Gombe Central, and Nafada. In each, an independent candidate identified with the NPC opposed the party's official nominee. Two of the independents were sons of the incumbent Emir of Gombe; one was a younger brother; and the fourth a district head and the Emir's client. All enjoyed the backing of the Emir against the party's official candidates.[25] (All lost, including one who lost his deposit.)

[24] Interview with Malam Abba El Ansari, National Organizing Secretary, Northern People's Congress, Kaduna, November 14, 1959.
[25] *Ibid.*

The potential implications for the traditional system of modern electoral contests pushed an emir into an active role. It might be, as in Kazaure, that dynastic interests and the interests of his regime were at stake. Or, considering the assets that an elected member brought to *neman sarautu* and vice-versa, together with the fact that an emir's traditionally assigned role was to reward his loyal allies and punish his enemies, emirs could not afford to be indifferent to the outcome of elections. Yet an emir's intervention naturally reinforced the tendency of the modern institution to become caught up in the workings of the traditional one.

THE SECOND CASE in the threefold categorization, that of the ousted traditional official, had somewhat different implications. The ambitious patrician characteristically remained, at least in spirit, within the fold of the government party and the established regime of his emirate. But traditional notables who found themselves discharged from title and office (due either to dynastic or lineage rivalry, or to administrative misdeeds, or, most likely, to both reasons together) were more apt to be drawn to organizations out of sympathy with both the NPC and traditional authority. (Less commonly, dismissed title-holders retained or recovered enough influence to win the official NPC nomination. Examples include M. Abdulmumuni, the ex-*Galadima* of Katsina, A. Aminu, or ex-*dan Iya* of Kano, and the ex-*Yandaka* of Katsina.) In general, however, since their career in the traditional bureaucracy was at an end, the ousted *masu-sarauta* had little to lose by an affiliation with NEPU. But they were able to regain something of the prestige, influence, and wealth that the possession of *sarauta* formerly imparted, or at least to try.

The political career of M. Abdulmumuni of Katsina emirate was another pertinent instance. M. Abdulmumuni was once district head (with the title of *Galadima*) of the Malumfashi district of Katsina, traditionally a hereditary dominion of the Danezawa clan of Fulani, of which M. Abdulmumuni is a member. In 1954 Abdulmumuni was charged with corrupt practices and dismissed from his *sarauta*. Subsequently, in the regional election of 1956 he entered the contest in his home area (the constituency of Katsina South Central) as an independent, against his brother (same father, different mother), the NPC candidate, who had succeeded him as *Galadiman* Malumfashi, and another *mai-saraut a Sarkin* Pawa, the district head of Kankara. By Abdulmumuni's own account, his motive in contesting was that he "resented losing [his] *sarauta*", and not receiving the nomination as the NPC candidate. That was "the sole reason for [his] running, and for [his] joining NEPU".[26] An especially interesting feature of his success was that the composition of the final electoral college for Katsina South Central was 36 NPC members, 6 NEPU, and 9 Independents. As the ex-*Galadima* received 27 votes, at least 12 officially NPC members voted for him rather than the party's candidate, which would suggest that to at least a third of the NPC members loyalties other than party ties were transcendent. Soon after the election, Abdulmumuni announced his adherence to NEPU.[27] In 1959 he crossed over to the NPC side of the Assembly and as an official candidate of that party ran for and won the regional election of 1961.

M. Yahaya Sabo of Lafia, who was a NEPU National Executive Committee member from 1958 to 1963, was a candidate in 1954, 1956, 1959, and 1961. A member of the *Gidan* Ari of the Lafia royal dynasty and an ex-N.A. employee, his opponent in the first of those elections was a member of the *Gidan* Dallah branch of the dynasty which then controlled the throne.

In the 1959 elections the case of Malam Mudi of Argungu emirate is particularly illuminating. In August 1959 M. Mudi was slated by the Action Group opposition party to be its candidate in the constituency of Argungu, although he withdrew before the election.[28] A dismissed N.A. policeman, M. Mudi is the grandson of a former Emir of Argungu. During the month of August 1959 that emirate was undergoing a crisis over its throne, the occupancy of which eventually changed hands. At that time, the Emir of Argungu, Muhammadu Sheshe, was suspended, pending a government investigation into the affairs of his administration, and the final outcome of the controversy was uncertain. What is interesting about all this is the fact that M. Mudi's avowed hope was to emerge from this crisis as the new Emir of Argungu (being eligible by blood), and that he freely announced his belief that a victory in the federal election would augment his claim.[29]

26 Interview with M. Abdulmumuni, Kaduna.
27 NEPU naively expected to benefit from his influence.
28 The Action Group typically exercises a tight, centrally imposed discipline over its members. (See Richard L. Sklar, *Nigerian Political Parties* [Princeton, 1963].) That the party's apparent decision to field instead a candidate it believed to be stronger was obeyed, would therefore be in keeping with the comportment usually demanded by the party.
29 Interview with Malam Mudi, Argungu, August 24, 1959.

A limited survey of opposition candidates for election in the years 1956, 1959, and 1961 disclosed many whose backgrounds would suggest other cases of the kind of motivations explicitly acknowledged by a Malam Abdulmumuni or a Malam Mudi. An Action Group candidate for Sokoto Central was M. Haruna, a dismissed head of the Sokoto N.A. police, who was of the Sokoto Toronkawa, and a first cousin of the *Sardauna*. The A.G. candidate for the Kiru constituency in Kano emirate was another Sokoto Bataranke who had lost his N.A. post. That same party's candidate for the Bauchi Central seat was M. Muhammadu Balarbe, son of Yakubu Ill, the late Emir of Bauchi, and formerly district head of Jama'a (dismissed in 1956 for embezzlement). The NEPU candidate in the same constituency, M. Muhammadu Gidado, had been dismissed from his post as Supervisor of the N.A. Works Department one year before. In 1961 the NEPU candidate for the consituency of Minjibir, in Kano, was the ex-*Turaki*. In Wudil, also a Kano constituency, a member of the dispossessed hereditary *sarauta* family (Jobawa) sought the NEPU nomination (he was turned down, allegedly because NEPU declined to meet his terms—liquidation of his personal debts); he succeeded in becoming the NPC candidate, reportedly thanks to the special efforts of the Emir, whom the man told he would otherwise stand as a NEPU candidate. In 1961 one of the seats in Dawakin Tofa district of Kano was contested unsuccessfully by a son of the former district head under the A.G. banner. An exhaustive survey would doubtless have uncovered many more examples, but these should indicate the pattern.

THE CANDIDACY of M. Abubakar Zukogi, who were encountered earlier, exemplifies the third general category—those whose participation in modern electoral competition represented in part, at least, an outlet for the expression of grievances which stem from peculiar, historically contingent features of the structure of a traditional emirate. In 1959, 1961, and 1964 Abubakar Zukogi was a NEPU candidate in Bida.

It was intimated above that Bida emirate traditionally chooses its emir, or *Etsu*, as that office is called in the indigenous Nupe language, from one of the three branches of its ruling dynasty in a system of strict rotation. The three royal lineages are each derived from one of three sons of Malam Dendo, the Fulani devout who, with recognition from the Emir of Gwandu (overseer of the eastern half of the Fulani Empire), established his authority by conquest over the ancient kingdom of Nupe.[30] The three sons were Usuman Zaki, Masaba (the first two Fulani Emirs of Bida), and Mamudu Majigi, whose son, Umoru Majigi, was the third Fulani *Etsu Nupe*. Thus the royal houses of Bida are called after the first three Fulani emirs; and their genealogy reflects the once unbroken cycle of three-way rotation.

Notwithstanding this formal tripartite structure, there is a tendency for the Masaba house to be aligned politically against the other two, a condition deriving from further circumstances of ancestry and history. Unlike Usuman Zaki and Umoru Majigi, whose mothers were Fulani, Masaba was Malam Dendo's son by a Nupe wife. When, on succeeding his father, Usuman Zaki failed to make Masaba the heir apparent to the throne, Masaba became resentful and, emphasizing his Nupe maternity, effectively plotted with the vanquished Nupe rulers against Usuman Zaki,[31] who received the support of Umoru Majigi.[32] This enmity was later compounded by machinations by the British Royal Niger Company in its "pacification" of Nupe around 1895-1897. The reigning emir at that time, Abubakar, a son of Masaba, forcibly resisted European penetration, in retaliation for which the company made a fateful pact with Muhammadu, a son of Umoru Majigi. Muhammadu had not been made heir apparent by Abubakar (an echo from the past). Harboring a grudge, Muhammadu conspired to withhold troops under his command from the decisive battle between Abubakar's forces and the company's, in return for which the company subsequently deposed Abubakar and made Muhammadu Emir of Bida. Bad blood between Masaba's descendants and those of "the other side", as the split is commonly alluded to in presentday Bida,[33] has persisted, being periodically replenished by various other sources of antagonism, such as the familiar cycles of dismissals and appointments invariably attendant upon the succession of a new Emir.

M. Abubakar Zukogi is a member of the royal house of Masaba,

[30] The classic study of Nupe or Bida traditional culture is S. F. Nadel, *A Black Byzantium* (London, 1942).

[31] S J. Hogben, *The Muhammadan Emirates of Nigeria* (London, 1929), pp. 127ff.

[32] Nadel, *Black Byzantium*, pp. 80-81.

[33] The land immediately surrounding Bida Town is divided into three royal estates, each in the control of one of the ruling houses. Bida Town itself is divided into three sections, the Masaba faction occupying the western portion, that of Usuman Zaki the north-eastern part, and that of Umoru Majigi residing largely in the eastern half of the southern part. See *ibid.*, pp. 40-43, 89, 161.

his grandfather having been the Emir Abubakar. His father once held a senior royal title customarily associated with the Masaba called *wacimbe*, and was a district head, a position he lost shortly after the succession in 1934 of M. Ndayako (of the Umoru Majigi house), the late Emir. Zukogi is one of the most articulate exponents of the NEPU ideology, and his name has been closely associated with other radical political groups.[34] Properly regarded as a regional leader and as a radical ideologue by conviction, his role as a modern politician in Bida was inextricably bound up in the fabric of Bida traditional politics. There, in 1959, he was also identified as a foe of the incumbent Emir in particular, and more generally as a *soi-disant* spokesman for the grievances of the Masaba house vis-à-vis "the other side." Allegedly, he once vowed to bring about the dethronement of the Emir; indeed, upon his release from prison in 1958 (where he served a four-year sentence),[35] some of his political followers presented him with a white horse, a symbolic act bound, under the circumstances, to carry highly provocative traditional connotations.[36] It is significant that Zukogi in 1959 tried to make an important election issue of the fact that the Emir had recently appointed one of his own kinsmen as *Shaba* (corresponding to the Hausa title of *Ciroma*, the heir apparent). Zukogi's contention was that the Emir thereby intended to violate the established order of rotation and to entrench his own line.[37] Unfortunately for Zukogi and the Bida NEPU, the susceptibility to antipathy of the pro-Masaba elements had been counteracted considerably by the fact that until 1963 the local NPC was led by a prominent member of the Masaba house, M. Usuman Sarki, *Sardauna* of Bida and Federal Minister of Information.[38] Returned to Lagos (and to the government bench) in 1959 from the constituency of Bida West (while Zukogi was losing out to his NPC opponent in Bida East), M. Usuman Sarki

[34] I.e. NEPA, the Zikist Movement, the Middle Belt Peoples' Party.

[35] Arraigned in the court of the Alkalin Bida on a charge of possession of stolen goods, he became embroiled in a scuffle involving other NEPU followers and the authorities. He was subsequently convicted on multiple counts of contempt of court, assault of an Alkali and of a police officer in the execution of his duties, and incitement to riot. The case was tried according to Islamic law.

[36] The horse (and especially a white horse) is a traditional symbol of rule in Bida, as in other emirates. See Nadel, *Black Byzantium*, pp. 61, 128, 130, 143, 202.

[37] In 1963 the order of rotation was indeed violated, but not in the manner envisioned by Zukogi. Had the traditional order of rotation been followed, a member of the Usman Zaki house would have succeeded Nkayako, of the Muhammadu Majigi house. In fact, the victorious candidate was Malam Usuman Sarki, former *Sardauna* of Bida and a Masaba.

[38] See Appendix A, No. 24.

made clear his loyalty to the incumbent emir, Ndayako, who toured his districts during the electoral campaign on the *Sardauna* of Bida's behalf. On Ndayako's death in 1963 Usuman Sarki became the first *Etsu Nupe* chosen out of rotation.

Table 35: Genealogy of the (Fulani) Emirs of Bida

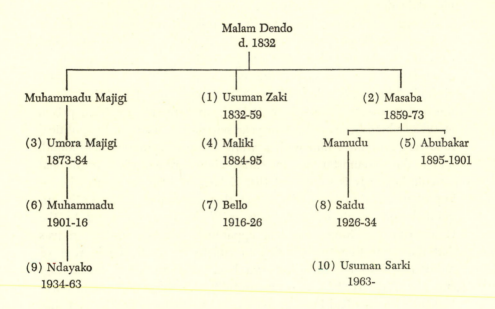

The role of Abubakar Zukogi in Bida was not the only example of this third category of interaction between modern and traditional rivalry, although his prominence in NEPU makes his case particularly striking. Aspects of modern politics in parts of old Adamawa, and possibly in southern Katsina emirates, would seem similarly to reflect certain structural tensions in those emirates.

In Adamawa a case in point was the role of one Malam Hamman Jalo in the United Nations plebiscite conducted in November 1959 to determine the future disposition of the Northern Cameroons Trust Territory, of which certain districts of Adamawa were a part (along with Dikwa emirate and a small enclave in Benue province). There were two alternatives posed in the plebiscite for the people of the Northern Cameroons: (1) to remain part of the Northern region (remaining part of the existing administrative units seemed to be implied) after Nigerian independence, or (2) to defer a decision to a later date. The result of the plebiscite (a clear majority in favor of deferring a decision) revealed widespread discontent in the districts concerned vis-à-vis the Adamawa Native Authority, particularly on the part of the non-Fulani, non-Muslim subject peoples.

One related source of discontent, however, involved an old dispute between a noble Fulani family, once hereditary rulers in one of the northern districts—Madagali—and the royal family of Adamawa, who were residents of Yola, the capital. The latter historically had legal authority over the emirate as a whole; but in actuality its control over outlying districts and their local hereditary rulers had always been weak; this weakness had continued to plague the Native Authority in recent years.[39] Madagali District, which was in the Cameroons Trust Territory, had long been a particularly sore spot. During the German occupation of the Cameroons, the hereditary District Head of Madagali was Hamman Yaji, whose tyrannical exploits are an Adamawa legend. After the transfer of the Cameroons to British authority, Hamman Yaji was deposed (1926) on various charges, including that of slave-raiding. From that time, the Emir, or Lamido, of Adamawa appointed the district heads of Madagali directly, and descendants of the Hamman Yaji were deliberately excluded from the competition.

In 1953 a district head of Madagali was deposed. The Lamido's new appointee was a son of the *Galadima* of Adamawa. The previous Lamido, however, apparently had predicted that "in their time, the people of Madagali would see the house of Hamman Yaji returned to power". Embittered at the appointment of the *Galadima's* son, the descendants of the Hamman Yaji and their followers staged a riot when the Lamido attempted to install his appointee. The revolt was unsuccessful; nevertheless, the new district head found it expedient to live away from the headquarters of his district for some time, where the Hamman Yaji (with the help, incidentally, of Yerima Bala, the local NEPU leader) continued to agitate for possession of the *sarauta*.

The 1959 UN plebiscite provided an opportunity for the Hamman Yaji to settle a score with Yola. A political "party", the Northern Kameroon Democratic Party, was organized in the Northern districts

[39] See A.H.M. Kirk-Greene, *Adamawa: Past and Present* (London, 1958), pp. 150-51.

specifically to persuade the people of that area to approve the second alternative, deferring a decision, thinking its adoption would be a repudiation of the Adamawa Native Authority. In fact, the result of the voting precipitated extensive reform measures by the government, including the unprecedented step of dismembering the traditional emirate. The president of the N.K.D.P., as an oracle of traditional politics might have presaged, was M. Hamman Jalo, headmaster of a junior primary school, son of Hamman Yaji, and in 1953 the disappointed rival candidate for the district headship of Madagali.

Certain districts of southern Katsina, like the northern ones of Adamawa, have traditionally been highly independent of the central regime. Before the British, the degree of independence of some titleholders (afterwards made district heads in southern Katsina) from the Emir of Katsina was probably unique in the Northern emirates. As in Adamawa, this historic relationship had left a legacy of political and administrative problems to the Katsina Native Authority. Attempts by the Katsina N.A. to impose stricter control over some of the hereditary rulers of its southern districts characteristically had caused dissension between the throne and the families who resisted integration. It is therefore tempting to speculate, in the absence of direct investigation (which was possible for the Adamawa plebiscite), that this situation had something to do with the extraordinary fact that in 1959 the Action Group candidates in three constituencies of southern Katsina—Malumfashi, Maska, and Marusa—Mashi were all members of the Danezawa (*Gidan Galadima*) clan of Fulani, a family that traditionally furnishes the district heads of Malumfashi and Maska. The A.G. candidates opposed the nominees of the divisional NPC which in Katsina, as elsewhere, was dominated by officials of the central Native Authority. It will also be recalled that M. Abdulmumuni, the successful "independent cum NEPU" candidate in 1956 for Malumfashi, was likewise a member of this family. If this interpretation is correct, as seems likely, by 1961 the NPC had learned a lesson: in five Katsina constituencies (Danya, dan Yusufu-Kaura, Kankara-Nogo, Marusa-Mashi, and Malumfashi) the NPC candidates were Danezawa, and all these candidates except one (M. Abdulmumuni) became newly elected members.

MY ANALYSIS in this chapter further demonstrates the major theme of this book—the great extent to which traditional values and responses permeated the modern representative institutions of Northern Nigeria. As I suggested at the beginning of the chapter, a bending of new institutions to the purposes of traditional ones was a logical consequence of the political dominance of the traditional ruling elite, which projected its patterns of behavior into the system of modern elections. Thus modern democratic elections became a vehicle for the pursuit of the interests, ambitions, and conflicts peculiar to that elite.

But the analysis also suggests that this playing out of old patterns of behavior in the context of a new institution was not a one-sided process. Rather, as a result of the interaction of institutions, the patterns of behavior characteristic of each were affected or modified. Thus institutional convergence had wider implications for the development of a modern democratic system and for the evolution of the traditional system. Some aspects of the impact of convergence on democratic development are perhaps more readily apparent than others. The adaptation of democratic elections to the interests and pursuits of an established ruling class militated against its usefulness as a means of posing fundamental questions about the basic purposes and structure of government. It certainly tended to minimize rational discussion of important contemporary issues, such as alternative development policies; and generally it perpetuated a recrudescent and parochial political outlook, as witness the impact of dynastic rivalry on election campaigns in Kazaure.

I suggested above that holding elective office was instrumental for participation in *neman sarautu* and that, conversely, a *sarauta* was an asset in electoral contests. The result was the creation of a relatively closed cycle of advantages for members of the traditional elite, which contributed to the tendency to confine the recruitment of modern political leadership to that restricted and unrepresentative social base.

Furthermore, modern elective office sometimes provided political shelter and compensation in wealth and prestige to those who lost their *sarauta* because of failure to meet the modern standards of administrative competence and integrity. This cushioned the impact on the privileged members of the ruling class of reform measures in recruitment and discipline.

The development of the NPC party along the lines of the modern

British prototype was also effected. Serious problems confronted the NPC as it worked for party discipline. In fact, in this regard, the party was caught in a dilemma: Its commitment to formulating and executing a coherent plan of economic and social development regionally and nationally required the ability to control the selection and conduct of its parliamentary rank and file and its government ministers in Kaduna and Lagos. This task implied centralized control over nominations or candidacies, and the imposition of discipline in cases of infringement at the constituency level.

On the other hand, the NPC branches in the emirates were largely made up of local traditional elites whose concept of political office was the notion that legitimately all such offices should be objects of competition between members or segments of these elites. Clearly the ideal modern party concept and the pure traditional concept of office clashed badly. Yet the national party leadership was itself largely composed of the members of local traditional elites; moreover, the leadership was committed to the preservation of the emirate system and thus to its key institutions. Consequently the party was unable consistently or wholeheartedly to prevent manipulation of modern elections for traditional purposes.

The dilemma caused the NPC intermittently to lean in opposite directions with respect to discipline: now enforcement, now laxity. As expected, the will to enforce grew in the face of effective opposition from the NEPU or the Action Group, but even then party discipline was not always actually observed locally, or imposed from above.[40] Thus prior to 1959, there was only one case of expulsion or

---

[40] There were a few cases in which the NEPU won seats in the emirates by split voting of NPC supporters between the official candidate and an "independent" NPC candidate. Probably the most celebrated of these was the NEPU victory in 1956 in Zaria Central where the combined number of votes for the official nominee and an "independent" who was also an NPC member was greater than the NEPU total. Similarly, in the constituency of Kankara Kogo in 1959, the NPC-Independent tally barely surpassed that of the NEPU candidates who won. This election was notable in another respect pertinent to this problem: The district heads of the two districts contained in this constituency (Kankara and Kogo) had both desired the official party nomination, but struck an agreement between themselves which provided that one would run as the nominee for the 1959 federal election and the other would await the next regional election. When both were passed over in favor of M. Hassan Rafindadi, a client of the Emir of Katsina and a national party leader, the two district heads are said on good authority to have retaliated either by surreptitiously supporting the NEPU candidate, or (in another version of the story) by withholding from the official candidate in the election the considerable support district heads were usually in a position to give. In the next federal election the constituency was redrawn; Kankara district was placed in one constituency and Kogo in another.

suspension of an NPC member for opposing the official candidate, and that case was not germane to the problem being discussed.[41] After 1959 the party threatened automatic expulsion and/or exclusion from membership of the parties in parliament for anyone who opposed its official candidate. In the case of the Emir of Gombe's four favorites who defied the edict, the party announced its intention of making good its threat, but in the end relented. There were a number of similar cases in the 1959 and 1961 elections. For the most part, the party's practice has been to welcome victorious NPC-Independents to its side of the regional and federal legislative houses.

While the dilemma helps account for the many instances of laxity, it also helps explain why there were not many more independent candidacies, or in other words, why traditional rivalries or conflict did not extend to the electoral domain more frequently or more seriously than was actually the case. For, being aware of the dangers to the party's role as the political instrument of economic modernization (to say nothing of the potential dangers to its capacity to compete with opposition parties), the party constantly strove to minimize traditional convolutions, or to keep them confined to the preelection stage of nominations.

Ironically, one of its favorite means of accomplishing this was to rely on the authority of the emir (plus, depending on the emir's position, that of his important councillors) to ensure a measure of equity in the allocation of electoral opportunities among local traditional interests. The irony lies in the fact that use of this device put the NPC in the business of helping to adjudicate traditional claims; it thereby became indirectly concerned with the politics of *sarauta*. Thus the dilemma posed by the convergence of institutions was never wholly escaped.

That an emir sometimes played this kind of pivotal role in nominations touches on another problem of democratic development. For the role of the emir inevitably influenced and was influenced by the dynamics of modern electoral competition. Generally speaking, an emir had two choices as to the role he played, neither one of which permitted him the political aloofness characteristic of the modern constitutional monarch (a proposition explored extensively in Chapter 6). He could adopt or be persuaded to acquire a position of rela-

---

[41] The person in question, Barrister Abdul Razaq (the legal counsel of the NPC) did not run in his emirate of origin—Ilorin—but in Zaria. It turned out that within a year the party reinstated him.

tive impartiality between the various conflicting interests in his emirate. The alternative was to remain identified in the context of electoral competition with the particular interests of his dynasty (e.g. the Emir of Kazaure) or those of his immediate family and clients (the Emir of Gombe). If he was actively partisan he was constantly engaging himself directly in political disputes within and between the political parties. But if the emir enjoyed a local reputation for impartiality, one of the parties—the NPC, in effect—appealed to him to use his prestige and authority to protect and stabilize its local organization, especially in matters involving conflicts over party nominations. In either case, the realities of institutional convergence (positive displacement of an old institution) involved him on one level or another in "politics", and precluded action free of difficulties.

At the same time, it must also be noted that, insofar as some sort of political opposition was to be regarded as a desirable element of democratic government, behavioral transference from the traditional institution to the modern one was not totally detrimental to democratic development. How far the end of rational deliberation on political policy was in this way served is highly questionable, as I have suggested. Nevertheless, the persistence of traditional habits contributed to the emergence of a degree, however small, of intraparty factionalism and effective interparty competition, which hindered the forging of the NPC into an instrument of a monolithic political structure. In this sense, the salutary aspect of weak discipline in the NPC was the availability of some source of support which was used to advantage by ideologically oriented opposition parties. While this source did not prove adequate in terms of basic goals, the efforts of the opposition parties to utilize it gave them some political leverage. Nor could the possibility be discounted that a more highly organized version of NEPU, making a more sustained effort to exploit or exacerbate dissension within the traditional ruling class, might have eventually found this source more fruitful—which in itself probably exerted some restraint on the NPC.

The advent of democratic elections also affected the traditional system, but more subtly than in the reverse case. The traditional antagonism between the *Gidan* Adamu and the *Gidan* Umaru in Kazaure was intensified as a result of the 1959 and 1961 elections. These elections provided the Umaru faction with an opportunity to challenge the incumbent regime, an opportunity the traditional system per se did not offer (i.e. short of extralegal means such as rebellion or sabotage). The initial success of the challenge, in turn, led the Adamu regime to take retaliatory measures whose effect was to produce in Kazaure an unprecedented imbalance of power in favor of the *Gidan* Adamu.

Further, modern electoral contests occasionally produced co-rivalries which the strict traditional rules of *neman sarautu* would have precluded, or which would at least have been anomalous from the standpoint of that institution. There were several instances of a candidate defeating an opponent with whom he would not ordinarily be eligible or able to compete (e.g. the 1956 regional election in a southern Katsina constituency where the district head of Ingawa was defeated by his village head). Such electoral triumphs of individuals of relatively inferior status and position over their "betters", in terms of the traditional hierarchical order, was naturally a source of some consternation to those with a vested interest in the maintenance of that order. Although the extent is not to be exaggerated, there is no doubt that the introduction of democratic elections imparted an added measure of flexibility and of personal mobility to the *sarauta* system. It is unlikely, for example, that individuals such as Ndagi Farouk of Bida and Maitama Sule of Kano[42] would have attained their respective *sarautu* had they not first won influence, money, and fame in the offices they reached via election. Furthermore, the desire of an emir to deprive a "disloyal" subordinate or enemy of the fruits of *sarauta*, formerly accomplished automatically by removing him from administrative office, was on occasion partially thwarted by the victim's later success at the polls.

There are other consequences in regard to both democracy and tradition which might be discussed here, doubtless including effects of which I am not aware. These observations should suffice to show, however, that the juxtaposition and interaction of a modern and a traditional institution had ramifications in each other's domain, and, what is perhaps more important, that these ramifications were anything but unambiguous.

THE AMBIGUOUS political consequences which seem to have followed the dynamic interrelationship of a traditional and a modern institution in Northern Nigeria prompts two related observations of theoretical import about the process of political change. Students of the phenomenon of change in human institutions have often specu-

---

[42] See Appendix A, Nos. 11 and 26.

lated about various conditions that may promote or inhibit a given culture's acceptance of a new pattern of behavior. One such condition, already discussed, is the ability of a people to recognize in a new institutional pattern certain aspects of their own preexisting culture. Some observers have given to this process by which new institutions are identified with or reinterpreted in terms of old ones the name "syncretism". Perhaps the most familiar application of the concept has been in analyses of change in religious behavior and institutions, usually to the effect that the adoption of a new faith was facilitated by the fact that certain aspects of the myths, rituals, legends, symbols, or key figures of that faith corresponded to those of old religious institutions or cults. The concept of syncretism seems to have given rise to a general proposition that the greater the similarity of the institution or behavioral trait being introduced to that of a preexisting institution or trait, the greater the likelihood that the new pattern will take hold in the society. George M. Foster argues: "The lesson of syncretism is important to the strategy of planned culture change: the probability of acceptance is increased to the extent that innovations are susceptible to reinterpretation in the conceptual framework of the recipient group".[43]

The findings in this chapter would seem to have some critical bearing on both the concept of syncretism and the general proposition it has stimulated. First, the concept of syncretism seems to be primarily directed to an interest in the fate of the institution being introduced, rather than to a concern with the destiny of the old institution through which the new institution is interpreted. This concept presupposes situations of innovation in which the new institution or pattern has displaced or is in process of displacing the old. But clearly not all situations of innovation are ones in which even gradual displacement is taking place. On the contrary, the introduction of democratic elections alongside the ubiquitous custom of *neman sarautu* in Northern Nigeria is one example of the possibility that in some situations an old institution may continue actively to operate co-extensively with a new institution with which is shares certain important features. In such situations, to ask questions about only what happens to the innovation may be to overlook the impact of that innovation on a comparable preexisting pattern that persists. An attempt to include this latter aspect of the phenomena was made in this chapter.

[43] *Traditional Cultures and the Impact of Technological Change* (New York, 1962), p. 28.

The desirability of keeping in mind the consequences of innovation, both in terms of the new institution being introduced, and in terms of the old institution to which it is being compared, suggests the usefulness of a concept broader than that of syncretism, one that is alert to both directions of possible effects. I am suggesting that the term institutional convergence more fully encompasses the range of possibilities inherent in the confrontation of two comparable yet alien social or political institutions. Accordingly, the concept of syncretism might more appropriately be regarded as a special case of convergence, or as only one aspect (the fate of the innovation) of a situation in which a protracted confrontation of institutions, requiring reinterpretation, occurs.

Concerning the general proposition with which syncretism has come to be associated, this chapter also points to the need for reformulation. On the basis of the analysis of the case of institutional convergence presented above, it is reasonable to assert, in one sense, that the susceptibility to reinterpretation of modern democratic elections in terms of *neman sarautu* facilitated the acceptance of the former institution by the Northern Nigerian society. That is, because democratic elections had in common with a traditional institution certain significant features, the society "made more sense" of that alien political institution than it might have otherwise. This argument might proceed to the effect that, precisely because the rules of democratic elections did not require the political leaders and people of Hausaland to depart drastically from a pattern of behavior already established regarding the traditional institutions, they were able more readily to accept the innovation—more so than might have been the case were traditional political recruitment based on some principle of a relatively fixed order of succession, e.g. primogeniture. Thus the *relative* comparability of the institution of *neman sarautu* and the notion of an open recruitment system of competition for political office could be identified as a crucial element in a syncretic process.

Yet the facts and conclusions adduced above pose certain difficulties for this proposition that are perhaps much more significant. We have seen how the traditional elite (with the tacit concurrence of the electorate) tended, in effect, to assimilate the competitive modern electoral process to the competition for traditional office and title, without necessarily adopting many of the fundamental objectives which elections are intended to serve in Western democratic societies—representative selection of leadership, political accountability, rational deliberation of issues. In fact, I have suggested that, from the perspective of the democratic development of the political system as a whole, this reinterpretation of elections in terms of *neman sarautu* had several significantly, but not exclusively, negative ramifications.

This combination of a ready identification and utilization of an institution and an apparent indifference to or neglect of its original purposes seems to invite a distinction between an adoption of form, on one hand, and function on the other. Many of the formal rules, procedures, and conventions associated with modern elections may have been accommodated in the emirates of Northern Nigeria within the traditional pattern of behavior, and vice-versa. But clearly, reception of the aims and purposes of the modern institution by the traditional society did not take place concomitantly. In this case it seems no exaggeration to say that, far from having facilitated a substitution of the political *functions* of a democratic election for traditional ones, the process of reinterpretation provided new means (via the *forms* of the new institution) for the gratification of traditional ends.

All this seems to cast doubt on the adequacy of the syncretic proposition. Doubtless there are many circumstances in which reinterpretation has positive implications for the capacity of a society to absorb new institutions, but it would appear that such is not invariably or categorically so.

I have suggested that a satisfactory reformulation of some such general proposition is required to take account of (1) a distinction between formal and functional aspects of innovation and (2) the necessity for stipulating specific conditions under which reinterpretation leads to formal or functional innovation (or rejection), respectively.

I further suggested that such a reformulation must confront three other difficulties or complications, namely (3) the necessity to make clear precisely in what sense two institutions are comparable; (4) the possibility that reinterpretation may have multiple or conflicting implications, that is, that reinterpretation may at once be conducive to the absorption of certain elements or properties of a new institution and useful for the rejection of others; or alternatively, that reinterpretation may lead to complete or partial absorption in one area of the political system and complete or partial rejection in another; (5) the need for some kind of objective index for identifying and measuring the degree of absorption of an innovation.

The nature of the theoretical inquiry involved in such concepts as syncretism and convergence, and the kind of propositions they suggest, could perhaps be restated concisely as the question of whether and in what way the reception of an innovation may be influenced by the presence in the recipient culture of correlatives of the innovation. Clearly this is a question of enormous scope and complexity. Adequate general propositions would have to await investigation and analysis of a wide variety of cases and conditions. Hopefully this analysis of dynamic interplay between the political institutions of democratic elections and *neman sarautu* will illuminate some of the complexities of such an inquiry, and warn that at this stage acceptance of any sweeping proposition about such results is unsound.

Having confessed the need for more data and for caution against theoretical oversimplification, I should nevertheless reiterate the one hypothesis made explicit earlier in this chapter—that a structure of social and political domination decisively influences the reception and reinterpretation of innovation, or, more generally, that the particular nature of a social and political structure is a crucial determinant of any society's experience of change.

CHAPTER 10

Conclusion

IN THE INTRODUCTION to this book the idea of a valid application to all contemporary "traditional" societies undergoing "modern" influences (I called them "confrontation societies") of conceptual tools or heuristic devices derived from the Western experience of "modernization" was tentatively challenged in general terms. The widespread attempts to apply a universal model based on those constructs, it was suggested, have led to conclusions about the nature and direction of such societies in general which in particular cases could turn out to be oversimplified or premature. Specifically, I suggested that conceiving of the process of change in confrontation societies in terms of an unavoidable choice between certain incompatible norms or principles of behavior has given rise to such questionable assertions as that confrontation societies are inevitably racked with strain, conflict, or instability, and that insofar as confrontation societies accept or absorb elements of modern Western societies, the effect must be the displacement of corresponding elements of the traditional society. I then considered some conceivable circumstances which might invalidate these assumptions. This in turn led me to advance, in place of the simple acceptance-displacement hypothesis concerning the outcome of confrontation, the hypothesis that the experience of confrontation might have one of a number of broad outcomes. These multiple possibilities, I said, indicate the desirability of close empirical investigation of different confrontation situations.

One of the several possible results of confrontation is partial acceptance of modernity with partial rejection or displacement of tradition. This tentative hypothesis, which I suggested would be borne out in the case of Northern Nigeria in relation to the traditional system of the emirates, is equivalent to the hypothesis that confrontation may result in the creation of a more or less stable mixture or combination of elements deriving from a "traditional society" on the one hand and from "modern" Western society on the other. I would now like to relate these tentative observations to various aspects of postwar political development in Northern Nigeria contained in the preceding chapters and draw firmer conclusions.

It may be helpful to begin by summarizing what the book shows did *not* occur in Northern Nigeria. Clearly a synthesis, or fusion, of the traditional and modern systems, in the sense of a full realization of all the fundamental objectives, practices, and values associated with each, did not result, notwithstanding the fact that the postulation of such a synthesis was part of the government's rationalization for the policy of preserving key traditional institutions, "as a framework for democratization and modernization of local government". Thus the chapters that dealt with the evolution and implementation of the government's program of local government reform pointed to many important instances in which maintaining the traditional "framework" meant having to reject certain modern and democratic desiderata. Examples include: the failure to adopt the procedure of handling the recruitment, promotion, and discipline of Native Authority personnel through an independent agency operating on the basis of a mandatory, comprehensive, and precise legal code (the proposed N.A. Staff Standards Boards); the failure to adopt a similar arrangement in regard to native court personnel, and, in the same domain, the failure to extend the principle of separation of executive and judicial powers to the institution of the emir's courts: the emirs' inability to behave impartially or abstain from action in connection with the affairs of political parties; the government's related refusal to prohibit active political partisanship on the part of N.A. staff; the government's dissolution of the radical-opposition-party-controlled Ilorin N.A. Council; the nonadmission of popularly elected majorities to the central councils of the large emirate Native Authorities; the restrictions imposed on the powers of subordinate councils; and the failure to rationalize the size of administrative units.

But neither did total rejection of modernity nor preservation of the pristine traditional system occur. Modern institutions were absorbed on the regional level—parliamentary representation, the British cabinet system, popular suffrage and political parties. At the local level, traditional institutions were definitely altered—the legal and, to a lesser extent, social composition of central councils changed (as did that of traditional councils). There was a limited application of the electoral principle to the central councils and more extensively to subordinate councils; the legal and political controls exercised over Native Authorities by the regional government were increased in number, scope and intensity. Serious legal and judicial reforms included the adoption of a new penal code, the elimination of the category of "offences against native law and custom", and the introduction of an integrated Nigerian appellate structure. Judicial personnel were excluded from Native Authority Councils, as well as from the Regional House of Assembly. In sum, the political policy-makers in Northern Nigeria neither clung to a strict pattern of traditional government nor accepted modern elements indiscriminately. Frequently the course of reform in local government was a selective process in which certain innovations were selected from a wide range of modern Western practices by the regional government and then adapted to suit traditional preconceptions (e.g. the General Purposes Committee and the cabinet system as used in local government, the Shari'a court of appeal, etc.).

If within various important contexts of action, total rejection and total acceptance of modernity and total displacement and total preservation of tradition are ruled out as accurate characterizations of what took place in postwar Northern Nigeria, as evidently they must be, we come by virtue of the process of elimination to the conclusion that a mixture or combination of elements of modernity and tradition came into being. But the matter is much more emphatic than that. In virtually every political institution and pattern of behavior examined in this book, we have seen complex manifestations of the dynamic interplay of these elements. The point on which further comment is in order here is the attachment of the adjective "stable" to this state of affairs. Another adjective which might be used is "viable". These adjectives are meant to suggest that the political development of Northern Nigeria since World War II cannot be regarded as a slow but straightforward movement from a traditional to a modern pattern as it exists in the West. Many features of the traditional political system of the emirates have been shown to have been extremely resilient and in a practical sense compatible with certain modern institutional innovations. Far from modern institutions having simply driven out traditional ones, elements of the institutions of each type or origin coalesced to form a workable system of power and authority, one neither purely traditional nor purely modern, yet that was conspicuous for its relative lack of strain and friction. From the foregoing discussion of various institutions and patterns it is possible to discern some of the conditions and factors that supported this result.

Two such factors and conditions were first mentioned at the very outset—the scope of the traditional system in relation to the modern political unit of Northern Nigeria and the federal structure of the government of Nigeria. Although the boundaries of the traditional system of the emirates were not coextensive with Northern Nigeria, they did make up the largest portion of its territory and the preponderant majority of its population. Hence the regional institutions of government were bound primarily to reflect the political climate prevailing in the land of the emirates, as by the same token did Nigeria as a whole. The relationship between persisting traditional emirate patterns and Nigerian federalism was thus a chicken-and-egg affair. On one hand, the location at the regional level of the constitutional powers that most vitally affected the destiny of local institutions promoted the insulation of Northern Nigeria from antagonistic social and political influence in the south. At the same time, regionalization of power produced a prodigious new concentration of wealth, opportunity and perquisites—access to and control of which persons traditionally enjoying disproportionate political influence and power in the emirates also had a disproportionate share. These cumulative and reciprocal advantages, in turn, were new means for the pursuit and protection of these persons' special interests and values. At the same time, the federal structure of Nigeria allowed political leaders to shape the political destiny of the emirates free of southern Nigerian influence. As important as these factors were, even they were at best necessary conditions of a situation with deeper sources.

The mitigating possibilities (which were tentatively suggested in the introduction) that might lead to an incomplete or equivocal reception of modernity into a confrontation society may be reiterated at this point: contingencies and circumstances might mitigate an irreconcilable clash of traditional and modern elements; some elements of tradition might be functional for the maintenance of certain modern institutions or patterns (and, conversely, some modern elements might be functional for the maintenance of some traditional institutions); a given society might behave inconsistently with regard to values indefinitely (or over long periods of time); those originally possessing political power might make "creative adjustments", i.e. take steps to realize certain aspects of modernity in a way that would also conserve important traditional patterns or interests. We can now see, in the case of Northern Nigeria, how each of these possibilities was in fact manifested in concrete instances.

A major example of a historical contingency mitigating a potential clash of elements was early educational policy under the British colonial power. This policy, we saw, worked to make compatible to a great extent in this generation (and for the foreseeable future) the norms of both achievement and ascription in leadership recruitment to the new regional governmental institutions (and to a lesser extent in local institutions as well). Katsina College, a prime fruit of this policy, facilitated cohesiveness among the physically dispersed, and in some instances also ethnically or historically diverse, ruling strata of the emirates. Furthermore, it was pointed out that far from the added emphasis on Western-type education having caused a redistribution of power and prestige to traditionally low status groups, Western education came to represent an additional attribute separating many of the traditional ruling class from most of the traditionally subject population, while at the same time reinforcing that class's special claim to a right to govern. In a broader sense, the entire British colonial presence was a mitigating contingency. For indirect rule provided a local model for a policy of pragmatic mediation of the conflicting values of "tradition" and "modernity"; indeed, British society itself pointed to the efficacy of such a policy for assuring the longevity of established rulers.

There is abundant evidence in this book of persistent inconsistency or ambivalence on the part of Northern political leaders toward many significant matters associated with modernity. It was observed that, on the one hand, the NPC government encouraged emirs and chiefs to be "above party politics". On the other hand, it assigned them to and sustained them in unmistakably political roles and functions. The NPC as a party utilized and cultivated the political influence of emirs, but decried exhortations to the chiefs' neutrality emanating from NEPU. In Ilorin the government denounced political "victimization" of N.A. staff at the hands of the ITP Council; yet it declined to exclude that staff from the active participation in local politics which engendered the council's distrust. It fostered the idea of democratic conduct of subordinate councils, but withheld from them even the elementary democratic privilege of selecting a chairman, along with other effective powers and resources. The Northern leaders in principle subscribed to the norm of an impersonal relationship with civil servants; yet they countenanced practices and attitudes set by custom.

Was Northern Nigeria in this period a secular or an Islamic polity? The modified Northern legal and judicial systems were one reflection of the Northern political leaders' profound ambivalance on this issue. In his proselytizing activities, the Sardauna especially seems to have forfeited all claims to a strictly secular definition of governmental legitimacy. Yet the same government party of which he was also head had as its slogan, "One North, One People", and disclaimed any desire to dominate non-Muslim minorities. It was observed that district heads (in fact, it might be said of high Native Authority officials in general) were expected to maintain a social and political role the financial requirements of which normally exceeded official emoluments—which encouraged the very abuses of office which the government was pledged to eradicate and was unevenly constrained to punish. There were no signs of any resolution of basic tension between Northern leaders' positive valuation of development and the private use to which they put public revenue. The tension was not soothed by the association of strictures of financial integrity with former British colonial overlords whose implicit claim to moral superiority was to those leaders a source of deep resentment, and sometimes disillusionment (especially as the British and themselves practiced selective reinforcement). But perhaps some of the most interesting phenomena encountered in this study were the various points at which modern and traditional institutions, and patterns were in a practical or functional sense, mutually reinforcing.

Thus the marked *internal* political stability of Northern Nigeria, which primarily stemmed from the persistence of an authoritarian relationship of traditional rulers to subjects in the emirates, was also both a selling point in the attraction of capital for economic development and a convenience for the involuntary introduction of various technological innovations into emirate society. Similarly, reforms in the direction of modern norms were sometimes facilitated by manipulation of a traditional role (e.g. the *Waziri* of Bornu in relation to Bornu emirate) or exploitation of traditional prestige (the *Sardauna* of Sokoto in relation to the emirates in general). Because Hausa society continued to accord the highest degree of respect and prestige to persons whose social position most closely approximated that occupied by members of their family in past generations, many Western-educated commoners who aspired to political leadership deduced that their own aspirations were apt to be more nearly and quickly fulfilled by achieving an accommodation and association with the established ruling class than through directly making a bid for recognition from the society at large.

Perhaps the clearest instances of the usefulness of traditional phenomena in terms of modern institutions were afforded by the activities of the Northern political parties. A principal function of any "modern" political party operating under a system of representative government on a foundation of mass suffrage is to mobilize the mass electorate for the exercise of choice at the ballot box. A cardinal aspect of this function is communication with the electorate: the formulation and articulation of issues and interests which will stimulate the attention, sympathy, and support of as many of that electorate as possible. Both principal Northern parties (NPC and NEPU) performed this function largely through manipulating traditional presuppositions, experience, expectations, and values. For the NPC such themes as a religious duty to obey and protect hereditary rulers, the virtue of unity in an Islamic community, the efficacy and benefits of traditional styles of political action (clientage, patronage, allegiance) proved extremely effective. NEPU was to some extent able to pierce the otherwise solid phalanx of NPC adherents through activating or exploiting the latent and manifest cleavages within traditional society, such as between *talakawa* and *sarakuna*, *Habe* and Fulani, the Gobirawa and Gimbanwa of Jega, the Ngizem-Karekere versus Bolewa cleavage in Fika, the *Yan Wazifa* Tijaniyya and Khadiriyya split, and in as many situations of dynastic rivalry as possible. NEPU tried to invoke what it considered to be authentic but dormant ideals of the Fulani *jihad*, while both NPC and NEPU made use of tradition-laden symbols (the figure of dan Fodio, the color green, the figure of Askia the Great, the star and crescent. In the case of Ilorin, we saw that ideologically radical parties found it prudent to communicate with the mass electorate in traditional terms, not only for the sake of initially mobilizing political power, but in order to retain or consolidate it as well.

Several instances may also be cited of the converse situation in which elements of modern institutions proved functional for the maintenance of traditional patterns. For example, the modern institution of party control of the economic and legal resources was a mechanism for rewarding politically loyal aristocrats. In pursuing economic development the NPC was often able at the same time to accord favorable entrepeneurial opportunities to local traditional rulers (highly remunerative memberships in regional and national boards and corporations). In a more general way we saw how Native Authorities were given an economically and politically advantageous role in the dispensation of modern services and in the legal regulation of economic activity which governmental control of modern services and development projects entailed. Most of these services and regulations originated in the regional government, but to the masses of peasants, frequently the sole source of these new blessings and burdens appeared (thanks to the division of local and regional functions) to be their local Native Authority, which served to sustain the attitudes of awe and respect if not subservience which peasants had customarily displayed in relation to their traditional rulers.

Similarly, in adopting certain trappings and practices of traditional rule, political leaders in modern institutions confirmed popular conceptions of what someone in authority "ought to be like", which in turn renewed the popular estimation of traditionally high status persons (in both local and regional institutions). Being elected to a legislature brought rewards that were available for *reinvestment* in the competition for traditional honors, which further excited the envy of traditional rivals, which redoubled the efforts of other such persons to win elected office, and so on, in a chain of responses that reinvigorated traditional political patterns.

The infusion of modern political standards into the administrative process also sometimes subserved traditional purposes. To wit, government-inspired investigations into Native Authorities were often skillfully manipulated (or, almost as important, were thought to be) at the local level so as to injure members of rival dynasties or lineage segments. Appointments emirs could not have made according to purely hereditary traditional rules (e.g. a hereditarily ineligible client to a restricted district headship), but which served to enhance the emir's personal control and influence, became possible on the grounds of raising the education level of local administrative personnel.

The response of persons in positions of power and authority to proposed changes which were potentially detrimental to their interests or objectives was often to take steps designed to offset or minimize the impact of the change rather than to reject or oppose the change as such. Some of the countermeasures indeed seem to fit the phrase "creative adjustment to change".[1] Instances of such adjustments fall into two categories: formal or legal, informal or extralegal.

A cardinal example of the first category was the electoral college and the "ten percent injection" procedures employed in connection

---

[1] The phrase "creative adjustment" is intentionally used here in preference to the more familiar "pragmatic adjustment" because the latter seems to suggest reactions of an essentially negative character—acquiescense or graduated retreat—whereas the former serves to emphasize the element of invention involved.

with the 1951 election to the Northern House of Assembly. These procedures, which were provided for by law, allowed nonelected traditional authorities in the North to control the outcome of the election, although the institution of election had been proposed and in principle accepted as a means of securing popular representation. It is worth observing that although these procedures were later revoked, they undoubtedly served to help induct prospective candidates into what later became the standard practice of seeking the sanction of the emir before offering themselves for election. Other examples included the constitutional powers of the House of Chiefs, the institution of the Council of Chiefs, the position of the district head in subordinate councils—all of these being legal arrangements designed to minimize the impact of representative institutions on the power of traditional rulers rather than to reject the institutions as such.

A primary example of an extralegal or informal "creative adjustment" was the *"majalisar dare"*, an inner clique of traditionally powerful councillors who made the important decisions about council business outside the forum of the expanded, partly elected, control council which had been produced by "democratic reforms". Another example was the failure to convene the regular annual conventions of the NPC or to elect party officers annually, as provided for in the party's constitution in the years after 1956.

In general, the increasing willingness of the traditional ruling classes to assume functions and skills which might have otherwise occasioned a shift of power to others constituted one of the more effective antedotes to the politically disruptive potentialities of "modernization". The delegation of new functions and powers to educated persons of the traditional slave or servant class, as in Kazaure was a shrewd variation on this capacity for flexible response. The "selective" recruitment or co-optation of wealthy merchant-traders and educated individuals into the ranks of political leadership who were traditionally excluded from or very lowly placed in the traditional hierarchy was similarly astute. In addition to this "vertical assimilation" of persons from traditionally lower social strata, there was an equally important degree of "horizontal integration" of elite members of traditionally diverse (and sometime historically antagonistic) ethnic groups. The union of Fulani and Kanuri traditional aristocracies represented a particularly vital example of this process, but the rapprochement between the Muslim aristocracies of the emirates and leaders of the ethno-religious minorities in the Middle Belt, although not much explored in this book, was perhaps the most remarkable of all.

These are some of the factors that promoted the condition of political continuity in Northern Nigeria under a parliamentary regime. The crux of all this is that significant elements of the traditional political system of the emirates proved to be compatible in practical terms with significant features of a modern state. To be sure, the resulting political system reflected normative ambiguity and ambivalence, but the system was no less viable and effective because of it. To say that the outcome of confrontation in Northern Nigeria may be characterized as the creation of a stable mixture—or perhaps more precisely, *a stable symbiosis* of modern and traditional elements—seems a fair characterization, certainly one much closer to the realities discussed here than to the image of an inherently unstable and progressively disintegrating society conjured up by the conceptualization of confrontation situations in terms of an inherent irreconcilability of modernity and tradition.

The materials and conclusion of this book give rise to a final reflection on the concept of modernization. In retrospect, to insist that in any given context significant features of a traditional society *must* be eliminated to the extent that it absorbs important elements of Western modern society, is an assertion which has no doubt derived much comfort and support from a tendency to assume, a priori, that normative consensus is somehow an imperative condition of any society. (Related to that assumption, in turn, are other equally supportive and questionable postulates, such as that normative consistency is necessary to psychological stability and social institutions are so interdependent or interlocked that any significant change in any of them perforce leads to total systemic transformation.)

The questionable inference involved here may be stated as follows: because a principle or norm mentally adduced from the existence of social institution X is logically incompatible with a norm similarly extrapolated from social institution Y, any Y society, as a consequence of adopting an X institution, must arrive at and act in accordance with consensus in favor of the X norm or principle. Indeed, this seems a classic instance of the fallacy of reification—mistaking a mentally coherent formulation for the substance of reality. Thus, except on a priori grounds, there is no necessary reason why a given society might not subsist while acknowledging conflicting norms of behavior, let alone find it impossible to make practical uses of institutional arrangements which happen to be mutually alien in origin. The experience of Northern Nigeria, in any case, hardly accords with these assumptions, and it may well be that other societies operate without benefit of normative consensus.[2]

Finally it should be stated that a term such as "stable symbiosis", which I have used generally to characterize experiences of change described and analyzed in this book, is also a conceptualization, if a rather crude one. As such, it is no less open to empirical scrutiny, disconfirmation, or refinement, and no less susceptible to the fallacy of reification in the context of empirical analysis than any other concept. To have great importance attached to this term, much less to have it taken as a general conceptual *substitute* for "modernization", has *not* been my intention here. But if the term and the analysis from which its use here stems helps draw attention to the shortcomings of picturing a universal, inexorable, and fatal retreat of traditional forces in the face of "the challenge of modernity", this study may have served a generally useful purpose.

[2] See M. G. Smith's statement on this point in the preface to a collection of his essays, *The Plural Society in the British West Indies* (Berkeley and Los Angeles: University of California Press, 1965), pp. vii-xviii; and Leo Kuper and M. G. Smith, *Pluralism in Africa* (Berkeley and Los Angeles: University of California Press, 1968).

Appendices

Appendixes

A Selected Biographical Directory of Northern Nigerian Political Leaders: 1946-1966

(Including all members of the Northern House of Assembly in 1956-1961, 1961-1965, from constituencies that lie within the Northern emirates)

KEY

b:	born	tt:	traditional title
eth:	ethnic background	occ:	occupation
trad. class:	traditional class	educ:	education
Sar:	Sarakuna	const:	constituency
(r)	royalty	relig:	religion
(n)	nobility	†	first elected in 1952
(c)	clientage	§	elected in 1956 and 1961
(v)	vassalage		
(m)	marriage	M	1956 member who became a minister in 1961
Tal:	Talakawa	PS	1956 member who became a parliamentary secretary
		PC	1956 member who became a provincial commissioner

Premier of the Northern Region, 1953-1966

1. Bello, A. Sir Ahmadu, b: Sokoto, 1909; eth: Fulani; trad. class:
§M§ Sar (r); tt: *Sardauna*; occ: N.A. councillor; educ: Middle VI (Katsina College); const: Sokoto Central; relig: Islam (Khad.); father's occ: district head; father's tt: *Sarkin* Rabah; career: teacher, Sokoto Middle School, District Head Rabah, N.A. councillor; remarks: contestant for succession to the throne of Sokoto in 1938, first cousin, reigning Sultan of Sokoto, matrilineal descendant ruling dynasty of Kano. Assassinated January 1966.

Prime Minister of Nigeria, 1957-1966

2. Balewa, A. Sir Abuaker Tafawa, b: Bauchi, 1912; eth: Gerawa; trad. class: Tal; tt: none; occ: N.A. education officer; educ: Middle VI (Katsina College); const: Bauchi South West; relig: Islam (Khad.); father's occ: servant of the district head of Lere; father's tt: *Shatima* or *Shamaki*; career: teacher, Bauchi Middle School, headmaster, N.A. councillor, education assistant, N.A. education officer; remarks: slave descendant, diploma in education, University of London. Assassinated January 1966.

Other Ministers of the Northern Region of Nigeria, 1956-1961

3. Abdullahi, M., b: Adamawa, 1924; eth: Fulani; trad. class: Sar (n); tt: *Dan* Buram; occ: district head; educ: Middle IV; const: Adamawa Southern Trust Territory; relig: Islam; father's occ: ?; father's tt: ?; career: N.A. agricultural assistant, N.A. supervisor of agriculture.

4. Ahmadu, A., b: Pategi, 1914; eth: Nupe; trad. class: Sar (n);
†§M   tt: *Galedima*; occ: N.A. councillor; educ: Middle IV; const: Lafaigi; relig: Islam; father's occ: traditional councillor; father's tt: Ndeji; career: N.A. chief scribe, N.A. schools manager, N.A. councillor.

5. Aliyu, A., b: Bida, 1906; eth: Nupe; trad. class: Tal; occ: N.A.
†§M   councillor; tt: *Makama*; educ: Middle VI (Katsina College); const: Bida-Agaie; relig: Islam; father's occ: Koranic *Malam*; career: teacher, then headmaster, Bida Middle School, N.A. councillor; remarks: see Chapter 7.

6. Baki, A. Usman Laden, b: Katsina, 1926; eth: Fulani; trad. class:
†§   Sar (r); tt: *Wazzirin Ayyuka*; occ: N.A. department head; educ:
PC   Middle VI (Kaduna College); const: Katsina Town; relig: Islam (Tij.); father's occ: district head; father's tt: *Sarkin* Kankiya; career: employee in a works department; remarks: grandson of the Emir of Katsina, Dikko, nephew of present Emir, Alhaji Usman Nagogo, married to daughter of Tafidan Katsina, formerly councillor for development and works, Katsina, N.A., now federal minister. Resigned post for parliamentary secretary in 1959 to become *Wazzirin Ayyuka*.

7. Bashar, M. Muhammadu, b: Daura, 1926; eth: *Habe*; trad. class:
†§M   Sar (r); tt: *Wombai*; occ: district head; educ: Middle VI (Kaduna College); const: Gwandu Central; relig: Islam; father's occ: district head; father's tt: *Bunturawa*; career: N.A. scribe, chief scribe, district head, Sandamu, district head, Baure; remarks: grandson of past Emir of Daura, brother of reigning Emir of Daura. Frequently mentioned as likely successor to the throne.

8. Bida, A. Dalhatu, b: Bida, 1921; eth: Nupe; trad. class: Sar (r);
†PS   tt: none; occ: school teacher; educ: Middle VI (Kaduna College); const: Gwandu Central; relig: Islam; father's occ: emir; father's tt: *Etsu Nupe*; career: teacher, Birnin Kebbi Middle School, headmaster; remarks: member of the royal dynasty of Bida (Masaba). Brother is Alhaji Usman Sarki (in 1959 a fed-

eral minister, now *Etsu Nupe*, Emir of Bida). Formerly married to a daughter of the Emir of Gwandu; also married into alternate royal dynasty of Bida.

9. Biu, A. Ibrahim, b: Bornu, 1922; eth: Kanuri; tt: Sar (r);
§M   occ: N.A. department head; educ: Middle IV; const; Biu; relig: Islam (Tij.); father's occ: emir's councillor; father's tt: *Chamallwa*; career: school teacher, N.A. works department technical assistant, N.A. supervisor of works, N.A. councillor in charge of works.

10. Dutse, M. Abdullahi Maikano, b: Kano, 1915; eth: *Habe*; trad.
§   class: Sar (v); tt: none; occ: N.A. department head; educ: Middle VI (Katsina College); const: Dutse; relig: Islam (Tij.); father's occ: district head; father's tt: *Sarkin* Dutse; career: district scribe, N.A. central office clerk, senior assistant chief clerk, hospital supervisor, N.A. chief clerk, N.A. forestry department; remarks: resigned ministerial post in 1960 to succeed his deceased father as *Sarkin* Dutse, District Head of Dutse District, Kano emirate.

11. Faruk, M. Ndagi, b: Bida, 1924; eth: Nupe; trad. class: Sar
§PC   (n); tt: *Tafidan* Bida; occ: N.A. councillor; educ: Middle IV; const: Bida Town; relig: Islam (Tij.); father's occ: native court judge; career: N.A. medical supervisor, N.A. councillor; remarks: married to the granddaughter of the late Emir of Bida, Ndayako.

12. Fatika, A. Ahmadu, b: Zaria, 1916; eth: Fulani; trad. class: Sar
§M   (n); tt: *Sarkin* Fada; occ: N.A. councillor; educ: Middle VI (Katsina College); const: Zaria West; relig: Islam; father's occ: district head; fathers' tt: *Sarkin* Fatika; career: teacher, N.A. junior primary school, teacher, middle school, school manager, councillor in charge of education, police and veterinary services, councillor in charge of education, local government and development.

13. Gasash, A. Ibrahim Musa, b: Kano, 1910; eth: Tripolitanian Arab; trad. class: Tal; occ: merchant-trader; educ: self-educated; const: Kano City West; relig: Islam (Tij.); father's occ: trader; career: import and retail trade; remarks: father first came to Northern Nigeria on a trans-Saharan caravan originating in Tripoli. Father was the slave servant of a Tripolitanian Arab merchant named Gasash, from whom the father took his name.

14. Gaya, M. Sule, b: Kano, 1925; eth: Fulani; trad. class: Sar
§M   (n); tt: none; occ: school teacher; educ: Secondary II (Kaduna
     College); const: Gaya; relig: Islam; father's occ: village head;
     father's tt: *Gabarme*; career: teacher, Gaya Junior Primary
     School, teacher, Kano Middle School, headmaster, Birnin Kudu
     Senior Primary School.

15. Habib, M. Abba, b: Dikwa, 1914; eth: Shuwu Arab; trad. class:
§†   Sar (n); tt: none; occ: N.A. councillor; educ: Middle VI (Kat-
     sina College); const: Dikwa North; relig: Islam; father's occ: dis-
     trict head; father's tt: ?; career: teacher, Bornu Middle School,
     teacher, Kaduna College, teacher, Zaria Middle School, chief
     scribe, Dikwa N.A.; remarks: member of the Ahmed Gonimi fam-
     ily of Bornu. Ahmed Gonimi was one of the four advisors to
     the first Shehu of Bornu. Malam Abba Habib is often spoken
     of as a leader of the "radical" wing of the NPC.

16. Hashim, A. Tijjani, b: Kano, 1931; eth: Fulani; trad. class; Sar
§PS (r); tt: none; occ: scribe (clerk), N.A. veterinary department;
     educ: Middle III; const: Kano South East; relig: Islam; father's
     occ: district head; father's tt: *Turakin* Kano; career: scribe
     (clerk), veterinary department, Kano N.A.; remarks: the late
     Emir of Kano, Bayero, was his father's brother.

17. Kabir, M. Muhammadu, b: Katagum, 1928; eth: Fulani; trad.
§†M class: Sar (r); tt: *Ciroma*; occ: district head; educ: Middle
     IV; const: Katagum North; relig: Islam; father's occ: emir; fa-
     ther's tt: *Sarkin* Katagum; career: central office scribe (clerk),
     N.A. central office, since 1952 district head of Sokwa.

18. Kaita, A. Isa, b: Katsina, 1912; eth: *Habe*; trad. class: Sar (v);
§†M tt: *Madawaki*; occ: N.A. councillor; educ: Middle VI (Katsina
     College); const: Katsina South; relig: Islam (Tij.); father's occ:
     N.A. councillor; father's tt: *Madawaki* or *Waziri*; career: teach-
     er, Katsina N.A., broadcasting officer, Accra, Ghana, personal
     assistant Emir of Katsina, N.A. chief scribe, N.A. development
     secretary, N.A. councillor.

19. Mungono, A. Mustapha, b: Bornu, 1919; eth: Kanuri; trad.
§M   class: Sar (c); tt: none; occ: chief scribe; educ: Middle VI;
     const: Bornu North East; relig: Islam; father's occ: village
     head; father's tt: ?; career: N.A. treasury accountant, N.A. as-
     sistant chief scribe, N.A. printer, N.A. chief scribe.

20. Usman, M. Shehu, b: Katsina, 1925; eth: Fulani; trad. class:
§M   Sar (n); tt: *Galadiman* Maska; occ: village head; educ: Middle

VI; const: Katsina South West; relig: Islam (Tij.); father's occ: district head; father's tt: *Sarkin* Maska; career: N.A. district scribe, N.A. village head.

Ministers of the Government of the Federation of Nigeria from the Northern Region, 1959-1964

21. Dipcharima, M. Zanna Bukar, b: Bornu, 1919; eth: Kanuri; trad. class: Sar (n); tt: *Zanna*; occ: district head; educ: Middle VI (Katsina College); const: Yerwa Town; relig: Islam; father's occ: village head; father's tt: *Lawan* Dipchari; career: teacher, Bornu Middle School, clerk, John Holt & Co., district head, and N.A. councillor; remarks: member of the NCNC press delegation to London in 1947.

22. Ibrahim, M. Waziri, b: Bornu, 1926; eth: Kanuri; trad. class: Tal; occ: district manager, United Africa Company; educ: Middle VI (Kaduna College); relig: Islam; father's occ: *Imam* of Damataru; father's tt: none; career: teacher, Bornu Middle School, clerk, United Africa Company, personnel manager, United Africa Company; remarks: M. Ibrahim comes from a family of learned *Malams*. He was the founder of the Damataru branch of NEPU in 1950, of which he was chairman from 1950 to 1951.

23. Olarewaju, Mr. M.A.O., b: Ilorin, 1916; eth: Yoruba; trad. class: Tal; occ: N.A. forest ranger; educ: Middle IV; const: Ilorin East; relig: Christianity (Protestant); father's occ: farmer and emir's representative; tt: none; career: N.A. forest guard, N.A. forest ranger.

24. Sarki, A. Usman, b: Bida, 1920; eth: Nupe; trad. class: Sar (r); tt: *Sardauna*; occ: N.A. department head; educ: Middle VI (Kaduna College); const: Bida West; relig: Islam (?); father's occ: Emir of Bida; father's tt: *Etsu Nupe* (Masaba dynasty); career: N.A. engineering assistant, supervisor of works department; remarks: became *Etsu Nupe*, the Emir of N.A. Bida, in 1962.

25. Shagari, M. Shehu, b: Sokoto, 1924; eth: Fulani; trad. class: Sar (n); tt: none; occ: senior visiting teacher; educ: Secondary III and Grade II Teacher Training (Kaduna College); const: Sokoto West; relig: Islam (Khad.); father's occ: village head; father's tt: *Sarkin* Shagari; career: teacher, Zaria Middle School, teacher, Sokoto Middle School, teacher, Argungu Senior Primary

School, senior visiting teacher, Sokoto; remarks: member of a prominent Fulani family of ruling family of Sokoto. The Yola-rabe Toronkawa antedate Shehu dan Fodio.

26. Sule, M. Maitama, b: Kano, 1927; eth: *Habe*; trad. class: slave; tt: *Dan Masani*; occ: senior visiting teacher; educ: Middle VI and Grade II Teacher Training (Kaduna College); const: Dawakin Tofa West; relig: Islam (Khad.); father's occ: slave-servant of the Madakin Yola, an emir's messenger; father's tt: none; career: teacher, Kano Middle School, teacher, Provincial School (Kano), N.A. information officer, senior visiting teacher; remarks: descendant of Kano *Cucunawa* (royal slaves of Kano).

27. Ribadu, M. Mohammadu, b: Adamawa, 1910; eth: Fulani; trad. class: Sar (n); tt: none; occ: district head and N.A. treasurer; educ: Middle IV; const: Adamawa Central; relig: Islam (?); father's tt: *Ardo* Ribadu; career: N.A. chief accountant, district head, N.A. treasurer; remarks: member of the Sukur'en family of Adamawa emirate, which is connected through marriage to the Ba'en family, the royal dynasty of Adamawa.

28. Wada, A. Inuwa, b: Kano, 1917; eth: Fulani; trad. class: Sar (n); tt: *Magajim Gari*; occ: Kano N.A. Electricity Undertaking clerk; educ: Middle VI (Katsina College); const: Sumaila; relig: Islam; father's occ: native court judge; father's tt: *alkalin* Kano; career; itinerant scout commissioner clerk, Electricity Undertaking, N.A. information officer, N.A. chief scribe; remarks: member of the prominent family of Kano called Genawa, a judicial lineage. A. Inuwa Wada is related to M. Aminu Kano and other prominent Kano personalities (M. Isa Wali, Dr. Abubaker Imam, etc.).

29. Yar'aduwa, M. Musa, b: Katsina, 1919; eth: *Habe*; trad. class: Tal; tt: *Tafida*; occ: N.A. development secretary; educ: Middle VI; const: Katsina Central; relig: Islam; father's occ: N.A. treasurer; father's tt: *Mutawalli*; career: Middle School teacher, N.A. liaison officer, assistant development secretary, development secretary; remarks: M. Musa Yar'adauwa's father was a retainer of M. Dikko, later Emir of Katsina.

NPC members of the Northern House of Assembly, 1956-1961 (government backbenchers)

30. Abdulkadiri, A., b: Katagum, 1907; eth: Fulani; trad. class: Sar (n); tt: *Sarkin* Giade; occ: district head; educ: Elementary 7;

const: Katagum West; relig: Islam; father's occ: ?; father's tt: ?; career: N.A. scribe, district head Giade and chairman, N.A. outer council.

31. Abdullahi, A. Maje, b: Kano, 1924; eth: Fulani; trad. class: Sar
†§ (r); tt: *Turaki*; occ: district head; educ: Middle IV; const: Kano
PS South West; relig: Islam (Tij.); father's occ: emir; father's tt: *Sarkin* Kano (M. Abdullahi Bayero); career: N.A. scribe, N.A. police corporal, N.A. development secretary, district head; remarks: Alhaji Maje Abdullahi was one of the founding members of NEPA, predecessor party of NEPU.

32. Abdulmumuni, M., b: Katsina, ?; eth: Fulani; trad. class: Sar
§† (n); tt: (ex-*Galadima*); occ: trader, United Africa Company employee; relig: Islam; father's occ: district head; father's tt: *Galadima*; career: village head, district head; remarks: M. Abdulmumuni's father, the *Galadima* Mulumfashi Adamu, was a supporter of the Emir of Katsina Nagogo's candidacy for the throne.

33. Abubukas, A. b: Sokoto, 1918; eth: Fulani; trad. class: Sar (n);
§† tt: *Alkalin Alkalai*; occ: N.A. councillor; educ: Elementary III (School of Arabic Studies, Kano); const: Sokoto Town; relig: Islam (Khad.); father's occ: chief judge of Sokoto; father's tt: *Alkalin Alkali*; career: *Mufti* (assessor) of native court, district *Alkali*, N.A. legal advisor; remarks: member of traditional judicial lineage in Sokoto.

34. Abubakar, A., b: Sokoto, 1906; eth: *Habe*; trad. class: Sar (v);
† tt: *Madawaki*; occ: N.A. councillor; educ. Middle VI (Katsina College); const: Sokoto North West; relig: Islam (Khad.); father's occ: *bara* (servant) of the Sultan of Sokoto; father's tt: none; career: N.A. Middle School teacher, scribe of Sokoto, visiting teacher, N.A. treasurer; remarks: Alhaji Abubakar, *Madawaki* Sokoto, is a descendant of a prominent royal Sokoto slave family. Along with Alhaji Abubakar, Tafawa Balewa, Mietama Sule and Alhaji Aliyu, Makamah Bida, reportedly he was originally sent to school in lieu of a royal or noble son.

35. Abuja, M. Hassan; b: Abuja, 1908; eth: *Habe*; trad. class: Sar
§† (r); tt: *Makama*; occ: N.A. councillor; educ: Middle VI (Katsina College); const: Abuja-Lapai; relig: Islam; father's occ: emir; father's tt: *Sarkin* Zazzau (of Abuja); career: teacher, Bida Middle School, N.A. chief scribe, N.A. development secretary, N.A. councillor in charge of education; remarks: co-author *A*

Chronicle of Abuie, former assistant lecturer, School of Oriental and African Studies, University of London.

36. Adamu, M., b: Bauchi, ?; eth: *Habe* (Gerawa); trad. class: Sar
§† (r); tt: *Sarkin* Duguri; occ: district head; educ: Elementary III; const: Bauchi Central; relig: Islam (Khad.); father's occ: district head; father's tt: *Sarkin* Duguri; career: government agricultural field overseer, N.A. district scribe, N.A. storekeeper and treasury scribe; remarks: member of (*Habe*) ruling dynasty of Bauchi emirate.

37. Ahmadu, M., b: Adamawa, 1908; eth: Fulani; trad. class: Sar
§ (n); tt: *Ardo* Malabu; occ: district head; educ: Elementary III; const: Adamawa North Central; relig: Islam; father's occ: ?; father's tt: ?; career: N.A. district scribe, trader, district head; remarks: member of the prominent Fulani family of Adamawa called Wolarabe.

38. Ahmed, M. Sumaila, b: Zaria, ?; eth: Fulani; trad. class: Sar
§PC (c); tt: *Sarkin* Tsapta; occ: N.A. sanitary inspector; educ: Middle IV; const: Zaria East; relig: Islam (Tij.); father's occ: village head; father's tt: *Sarkin* Karau; career: ?

39. Aliyu, M., b: Sokoto, 1916; eth: Fulani; trad. class: Sar (n);
§† tt: *Magajin Gari*; occ: N.A. councillor; educ: Middle IV; const:
PC Sokoto Town West; relig: Islam (Khad.); father's occ: N.A. councillor; father's tt: *Magajin Gari*; career: N.A. scribe, district head, N.A. councillor; remarks: in Sokoto the title of *Magajin Gari* is always awarded to the first descendant of the first Sokoto or the first *Magajin Gari* who was the advisor and supporter of Shehu Usman dan Fodio, founder of the Fulani empire; thus M. Aliyu is a direct descendant of the first *Magajin Gari* of Sokoto.

40. Alkali, M. Abba dan, b: Kano, 1924; eth: Fulani; trad. class: Sar (n); tt: none; occ: chief scribe, Kano Native Court; educ: Middle VI (School for Arabic Studies); const: Kano North; relig: Islam (Tij.); father's occ: chief judge of Kano emirate; father's tt: *Alkalin Alkalai*; career: court inspector, chief scribe, Native Court; remarks: member of the Emir of Kano's judicial council. Father married sister of the Emir (Bayero) of Kano.

41. Aminu, M. Mohammadu, b: Kano, 1907; eth: Fulani; trad. class:
§ Sar (r); tt: formerly *dan Iya*; occ: district head; educ: self-educated; const: Bichi; relig: Islam (Tij.); father's occ: emir;

father's tt: *Sarkin* Kano; career: district head Dawakin Kudu; remarks: father Alhaji Abdullahi Bayero, late Emir of Kano.

42. Anace, A. Abdu, b: Kontagora, 1918; eth: Fulani; trad. class: Sar (r); tt: *Magajin Gari*; occ: N.A. councillor; educ: Middle VI (Kaduna College); const: Kontagora-Wushishi; relig: Islam; father's occ: emir; father's tt: *Sarkin* Sudan (of Kontagora emirate); career: N.A. chief scribe, N.A. school manager, N.A. councillor in charge of local government.

§† PS

43. Bello, M. Muhammadu, b: Sokoto, ?; eth: Fulani; trad. class: Sar (r); tt: *Sarkin* Gandu; occ: N.A. department head; educ: ?; const: Sokoto Town East; relig: Islam (Khad.); father's occ: ?; father's tt: ?; remarks: younger brother of the reigning Sultan of Sokoto.

§

44. Bello, M. Muhammadu, b: Sokoto, 1932; eth: Fulani; trad. class: Sar (r); tt: *Marafan* Asara; occ: village head; educ: Elementary IV; const: Sokoto North; relig: Islam (Khad.); father's occ: district head; father's tt: *Sarkin* Gobir Gwadabawa; career: village head; remarks: member of the chamber of one of the rival royal lineages of Sokoto (the Atikawa).

45. Boyi, M. Muhammadu, b: Adamawa, 1915; eth: Gwoza (Fulani mother); trad. class: Tal; tt: *Galadima*; occ: district head; educ: illiterate; const: Dikwa South; relig: animist; father's occ: farmer; father's tt: none; career: N.A. messenger, district head; remarks: chief of a pagan enclave of Gwoza in Dikwa emirate.

46. Cigari, M. Shehu, b: Sokoto, 1931; eth: Fulani; trad. class: Sar (r); tt: none; occ: Sultan's representative; educ: privately educated; const: Sokoto South West; relig: Islam (Khad.); father's occ: emir; father's tt: *Sarkin* Musulmi (of Sokoto); remarks: lost seat in 1959 when he was sentenced to two years at hard labor on a charge of malicious assault of an Action Group field secretary.

§

47. Dankantoma, M. Baba, b: Sokoto, 1911; eth: *Habe*; trad. class: Tal; occ: producer buyer, trader, general merchant; educ: illiterate; const: Gusau Town; relig: Islam; father's occ: trader; father's tt: none.

48. Dasuki, M. Ibrahim, b: Sokoto, 1908; eth: Fulani; trad. class: Sar (r); tt: *Marafan* Gada; occ: district head; educ: Elementary VI; const: Sokoto North Central; relig: Islam (Khad.); father's occ: district head; father's tt: *Sarkin* Gobir; career: agri-

§

cultural *malam*, district head; remarks: member of the royal rival lineage of Sokoto emirate (Atikawa).

49. Daura, A. Jibir, b: Daura, 1909; eth: *Habe*; trad. class: Sar
† (r); tt: *Magatarkada*; occ: registrar, Kano Emir's Court; educ: Middle VI (Katsina College); const: Kano Central; relig: Islam (Tij.); father's occ: Arabic teacher, district scribe; career: teacher, Middle School, N.A. scribe, registrar, Emir's Court; remarks: member of the royal house of Daura emirate. An influential advocate of religious orthodoxy in legal matters in Kano emirate and in the Northern Region generally.

50. Demsa, M. Ibrahim; b: Adamawa, 1908; eth: Fulani; trad.
§ class: Sar (n); tt: *dan Iya*; occ: district head; educ: Middle VI (Katsina College); const: Adamawa Northern Trust Territory; relig: Islam (Tij.); father's occ: district head; father's tt: *Ardon* Demsa) career: teacher, N.A. department head; remarks: member of a prominent Fulani family of Adamawa called Wolarabe. Married to the mother of the *Lamido* of Adamawa.

51. Dingyadi, M. Sani, b: Kano, 1907; eth: *Habe*; trad. class: Tal;
† tt: *Makama*; occ: N.A. councillor; educ: Middle VI (Katsina College); const: Sokoto West; relig: Islam (Khad.); father's occ: blacksmith; father's tt: *Sarkin* Makera; career: former master, Katsina College; remarks: M. Sani Dingyadi is a member of a family whose male members traditionally are blacksmiths in Kano emirate. Blacksmith is a low-status occupation in Hausa society.

52. Diso, A. Mahamud, b: Kano, 1907; eth: Fulani; trad. class: Sar (r); tt: none; occ: N.A. chief surveyor; educ: Kano Survey School; const: Kano City South; relig: Islam (Tij.); father's occ: Koranic *Malam*; father's tt: none; remarks: Sulebawa royal dynasty member.

53. Dodo, A. Muhammadu, b: Katsina, 1917; eth: Fulani; trad. class:
† Sar (n); tt: *Alkalin* Karami; occ: Native Court judge; educ: Kano Law School; const: Katsina North East; relig: Islam (Tij.); father's occ: chief native court judge; father's tt: *Alkalin Alkalai*; career: native court scribe, chief registrar of native courts, inspector of native courts; remarks: married to a daughter of the district head of Kankiya of Katsina emirate. The district head was the son of M. Dikko, the late Emir of Katsina.

54. Dokaji, A. Abubakar, b: Kano, 1908; eth: Fulani; trad. class: Sar
† (n); tt: *Dokaji*; occ: district head; educ: Middle VI (Katsina
College); const: Kuru; relig: Islam (Khad.); father's occ:
N.A. councillor; father's tt: *Waziri*; career: N.A. school teacher, N.A. scribe, N.A. treasury scribe, district head; remarks:
member of the Kano noble family called Bornawa.

55. Fakkai, M. Muhammadu, b: Argungu, 1931; eth: Kabbawa
(*Habe*); trad. class: Sar (r); tt: *Sarkin* Gobir; occ: district
head; educ: Middle IV; const: Argungu; relig: Islam; father's tt:
Sarkin Argungu (dismissed 1959); career: district scribe, native
treasury scribe, district head.

56. Gyani, M. Maude Ahmadu Sidi, b: Zaria, 1921; eth: Jaba; trad.
§ class: Tal; tt: none; occ: farmer; educ: Middle VI (C.M.S. Mission School); const: Zaria South West; relig: Christianity; father's occ: village head; father's tt: *Sarkin* Gyani; career: native
court member.

57. Hurdi, M. Muhammadu, b: Hadejia, ?; eth: Fulani; trad. class:
§ Sar (r); tt: none; occ: N.A. department head; educ: Middle
II; const: Hadejia South West; relig: Islam; father's occ: district
head; father's tt: *Ciroma*; career: N.A. school teacher, N.A.
school's manager, councillor in charge of education.

58. Ibrahim, A., b: Gumel, 1913; eth: Kanuri; trad. class: Sar (n);
§† tt: *Waziri*; occ: N.A. councillor; educ: Middle II; const: Gumel;
relig: Islam (Tij.); father's occ: N.A. councillor; father's tt:
Wazirin Gumel; career: district scribe, prison scribe, agricultural Malam, head of N.A. agricultural department, N.A. councillor; remarks: member of the Gumel family which traditionally
furnishes an N.A. councillor.

59. Idirisu, M., b: Adamawa, 1910; eth: Fulani; trad. class: Sar (n);
† tt: *Tafida*; occ: N.A. councillor; educ: Middle VI (Katsina College); relig: Islam (Tij.); father's occ: trader; father's tt: none,
career: N.A. school teacher, district head, N.A. development secretary; remarks: member of a prominent Hausa family in Adamawa, whose ancestor assisted the first *Lamido* of Adamawa
in waging the *Jihad*.

60. Idrisu, M. Maina, b: Fika, 1917; eth: Bolewa; trad. class: Sar
§ (r); tt: *Maina*; occ: N.A. chief scribe; educ: Middle VI (Katsina College); const: Potiskum; relig: Islam; father's occ: emir;
father's tt: *Sarkin* Fika; career: adult education officer, N.A.

chief scribe; remarks: eldest son of reigning Emir of Fika, A. Muhammadu.

61. Imam, M. Baba Kura, b: Bornu, 1925; eth: Kanuri; trad. class: Sar (n); tt: none; occ: N.A. inspector of Native Courts; educ: Elementary IV; const: Bornu North; relig: Islam; father's occ: chief judge; father's tt: *Alkalin Alkalai*; career: Arabic teacher, district alkali, inspector of native courts; remarks: M. Baba Kura Imam is the younger brother of M. Ibrahim Imam, leader of the opposition in the Northern House of Assembly (see number 106).

62. Inuwa, A. Muhamadu, b: Kano, 1901; eth: Fulani; trad. class:
§† Sar (r); tt: *Galadima*; occ: district head; educ: School of Arabic Studies (Kano); const: Dawakin Kndu; relig: Islam (Tij.); father's occ: emir; father's tt: *Sarkin* Kano; career: District Head, Ungogo, District Head, Minjibir; remarks: became Emir of Kano in 1960, upon the resignation of A. Muhamadu Sanusi.

63. Ja'afar, M. Abdullahi, b: Bornu, 1922; eth: Kanuri; trad. class:
§ Sar (n); tt: none; occ: N.A. deputy sanitary inspector; educ: Middle II; const: Bornu North West; relig: Islam; father's occ: chief judge; father's tt: *Alkalin Alkalai*; career:?

64. Jafarta, M., b: Muri, 1920; eth: Fulani; trad. class: Tal; tt: none; occ: emir's representative; educ: Koranic School and adult education; const: Muri Southwest; relig: Islam; father's occ: tailor; father's tt: none; career: emir's representative.

65. Jatau, M. Gwani, b: ?; eth: Kagoma; trad. class: Tal; tt: none;
§PS occ: N.A. teacher; educ: Teacher Training School; const: Jama'a; relig: Christianity (Protestant); father's occ: village chief; father's tt: none.

66. Dantata, A. Ahmadu; b: Kano, 1916; eth: *Habe*; trad. class: Tal; tt: none; occ: trader, transport owner, merchant; educ: privately educated; const: Kano City East; relig: Islam (Tij.); father's occ: trader, merchant trader; father's tt: none; remarks: in 1959 the wealthiest of Kano merchants. Deceased 1960.

67. Kassim, A. Haruna, b: Kano, 1914; eth: *Habe*; trad. class: Tal;
§ tt: none; occ: merchant trader; educ: Elementary VI; const: Kano West; relig: Islam; father's occ: village head; father's tt: none; remarks: operates prosperous pilgrimage agency in Kano City; married into the prominent Fulani family of Kano called Yolawa (to the daughter of the *Madakin* Kano's brother).

68. Kwairanga, M. Muhammadu, b: Gombe, 1931; eth: Fulani; trad.
§ class: Sar (r); tt: *Ciroma*; occ: district head; educ: Elementary
IV; const: Gombe South; relig: Islam; father's occ: emir; father's
tt: *Sarkin* Gombe; career: N.A. messenger, district head; remarks: son of the reigning head of Gombe, A. Abubakar,
nephew of the *Yeriman* Gombe (see number 84).

69. Kurawa, M. Ahmadu Tijani, b: Kano, 1914; eth: Fulani; trad.
class: Tal; tt: none; occ: N.A. assistant land registrar; educ:
Elementary VI; const: Kano South East; relig: Islam; father's
occ: N.A. supervisor of prisons and *Bafada* (courtier); father's tt:
none; career: N.A. tax scribe, trader, English teacher, Kano assistant land officer.

70. Kyari, M. Maina Abba, b: Bedde, 1928; eth: Bede; trad. class:
Sar (r); tt: *Abba*; occ: N.A. medical dispenser; educ: Middle III; const: Bebbe; relig: Fulani; father's occ: emir; father's
tt: *Mai* Bedde (the Emir of Bedde); remarks: younger brother
of the reigning Emir of Bedde.

71. La'aro, A. Ibrahim, b: Ilorin, 1918; eth: Yoruba; trad. class: Tal;
tt: none; occ: owner, commercial transport firm; educ: Middle
VI (Kaduna College); const: Ilorin Town; relig: Islam; father's
occ: ?; father's tt: ?; career: assistant treasurer of Ilorin N.A.

72. Lame, M. Yakubu, b: Bauchi, 1922; eth: Fulani; trad. class: Sar
§PC (n); tt: *Magajin Gari*; occ: N.A. councillor; educ: Middle IV;
const: Bauchi West; relig: Islam (Tij.); father's occ: ?; father's
tt: ?; remarks: now *Wazirin* Bauchi.

73. Lamido, M. Mi'azu, b: Sokoto, 1926; eth: Fulani; trad. class: Sar
§M (r); tt: none; occ: secretary to N.A. council; educ: Middle IV;
const: Sokoto North East; relig: Islam (Khad.); father's occ:
emir; father's tt: *Sarkin* Musulmi (Sultan of Sokoto); career:
N.A. clerk, N.A. cotton supervisor, Sultan's private secretary;
remarks: eligible for the throne of Sokoto.

74. Lawal, A. Muhammadu, b: Katsina, 1898; eth: Fulani; trad.
§ class: Sar (r); tt: *Sarkin* Yandaka; occ: district head and N.A.
councillor; educ: Elementary VI (Kano Sons of Chief's
School); const: Katsina Central; relig: Islam; father's occ: district head; father's tt: *Yandaka*; career: village head, district
head; remarks: suspended as district head in 1957, member of
the Yerubawa Fulani family of Katsina, whose ancestor was one
of the three original flag holders under Shehu Usman dan Fodio.
See Chapter 4.

75. Limam, A. Usman, b: Katsina, 1901; eth: Fulani; trad. class: Sar
§† (r); tt: *Sarkin* Musawa; occ: district head; educ: Elementary
VI; const: Katsina East Central; relig: Islam (Tij.); father's occ:
emir; father's tt: *Sarkin* Katsina; career: N.A. medical department employee, district head; remarks: competed with A. Ma-
gogo for the Emirship of Katsina.

76. Maccido, M. Muhammadu; b: Sokoto, 1926; eth: Fulani; trad.
§† class: Sar (r); tt: *Sarkin* Kudu; occ: N.A. councillor; educ: Middle IV (diploma in public administration, Devon Technical College, England); const: Sokoto South Central; relig: Islam
(Khad.); father's occ: emir, father's tt: *Sarkin* Musulmi; career:
N.A. scribe, assistant to councillor (the Sardauna of Sokoto,
1951-1953), district head, councillor in charge of works, in
charge of natural resources; remarks: said to be a personal protégé of the *Sardauna*. The *Sarkin* Kudu and the *Sardauna* are
perhaps the main contenders in the line of succession in Sokoto.

77. Maihaja, M. Yanusa, b: Bornu, 1916; eth: Kanuri; trad. class:
§ Tal; tt: none; occ: trader; educ: illiterate; const: Bornu Town;
relig: Islam; father's occ: ?; father's tt: ?

78. Mairiga, M. Jibrin, b: Nassarawa, 1922; eth; *Habe*; trad. class:
Sar (v); tt: none; occ: N.A. councillor; educ: Middle II; const:
Nassarawa; relig: Islam; father's occ: N.A. chief scribe; father's
tt: *Sarkin Malam*; career: N.A. scribe, N.A. chief scribe, councillor for finance, works and local government; remarks: member of the Makama Dogo family of Katsina emirate, whose ancestor gave allegiance to the first Fulani Emir of Katsina.

79. Malam, Alhaji Muhammadu Dan, b: Katsina, 1914; eth: Fulani;
§† trad. class: Sar (r); tt: *Wambai*; occ: N.A. department head
and councillor; educ: Middle V (Katsina College); const: Katsina East; relig: Islam (Tij.); father's occ: village head; father's
tt: ?; career: N.A. sanitation inspector, N.A. health department
head, councillor for medical and health services.

80. Maiwada, Alhaji, b: Kano, 1918; eth: *Habe*; trad. class: Sar
† (c); tt: none; occ: trader; educ: privately educated; const:
Wudil; relig: Islam (Tij.); father's occ: Bafada (courtier); father's tt: none.

81. Muhammadu, A. Musa, b: Borgu, 1929; eth: uncertain; trad.
§PS class: Sar (r); tt: *Magajin Gari*; occ: N.A. councillor; const:
Borgu; relig: Islam; father's occ: emir; father's tt: *Sarkin* Borgu;
career: N.A. schoolteacher, N.A. veterinary assistant, acting na-

tive development secretary and treasurer, N.A. councillor; remarks: eldest son of the ruling Emir of Borgu. A. Musa Muhammadu formerly held the title of *dan Galadima*.

82. Mu'azu, A., b: Katsina, 1900; eth: Fulani; trad. class: Sar (c);
§ tt: *Sarkin* Ruma; occ: district head; educ: Elementary VI (Kano Sons of Chiefs School); const: Katsina North West; relig: Islam; father's occ: district head; father's tt: *dan Waire*; career: N.A. storekeeper, village head, district head; remarks: A. Mu'azau's father, *dan Waire*, was a famous Katsina warrior.

83. Muhammadu, A., b: Kazaure, 1918; eth: Beriberi (Kanuri);
§†
PC
trad. class: slave; tt: *Magajin Gari*; occ: N.A. councillor; educ: Middle V; const: Kazaure; relig: Islam (Khad.); father's occ: *Bafada* (courtier); father's tt: *Tarno*; career: Kano N.A. central office and treasury scribe, Kazaure N.A. supervisor of works, N.A. councillor; remarks: married to daughter of the reigning Emir of Kazaure, Adamu.

84. Muhammadu, M., b: Gombe, 1903; eth: Fulani; trad. class: Sar (r); tt: *Yeriman* Gombe; occ: district head; educ: Elementary II; const: Gombe North; relig: Islam (Khad.); father's occ: emir; father's tt: *Sarkin* Gombe; career: village scribe, N.A. treasury scribe, central office scribe, village head; remarks: brother of the reigning Emir of Gombe, Abubakar.

85. Muhammadu, M., b: Muri, 1904; eth: Fulani; trad. class: Sar
§ (r); tt: *Ubandoma*; occ: district head; educ: Elementary IV; const: Muri North East; relig: Islam (Tij.); father's occ: emir; father's tt: *Sarkin* Muri; career: district scribe, district head.

86. Mukkadam, A. Othman, b: Bornu, 1902; eth: Kanuri; trad.
§ class: Sar (n); tt: *Mukkadam*; occ: N.A. councillor (retired); educ: Elementary III; const: Bornu East; relig: Islam (Tij.); father's occ: chief judge; father's tt: *Imam* and *Alkalin Alkalai*; career: N.A. teacher, district head; remarks: M. Othman Mukkadam is the elder brother of M. Ibrahim Imam, leader of opposition in the Northern House of Assembly.

87. Malabu, M. Bello; b: Adamawa, 1913; eth: Fulani; trad. class:
† Tal; tt: *Madawaki*; occ: N.A. councillor; educ: Middle IV (Katsina College); const: Adamawa South Central; relig: Islam; father's occ: ?; father's tt: none; career: N.A. teacher, N.A. schoolmaster, asst. lecturer, School of Oriental and African Studies, London University, N.A. schools manager.

88. Musa, A., b: Sokoto, 1911; eth: *Habe*; trad. class: Sar (v); tt:
§ *Sarkin* Danko; occ: district head; educ: Elementary IV; const:
Sokoto South; relig: Islam (Khad.); father's occ: ?; father's tt:
?; career: Sokoto N.A. driver, Sultan's chauffeur; remarks: was
Sultan's chauffeur when appointed district head of Bukuyum.

89. Master, M. Abba, b: Bornu, 1924; eth: Kanuri; trad. class: Sar
§PS (r); tt: *Abba*; occ: N.A. central office clerk; educ: Middle IV;
const: Bornu West; relig: Islam; father's occ: emir; father's tt:
Shehu (of Bornu); career: ?; remarks: fourth son of the reigning *Shehu* of Bornu.

90. Nabegu, A., b: Kano, 1899; eth: *Habe*; trad. class: Tal; tt: none;
† occ: merchant trader; educ: literate in Hausa *Ajami*; const:
Kano South; relig: Islam (Tij.); father's occ: farmer; father's tt:
none; career: trader, appointed N.A. councillor in 1955 to represent Kano traders; remarks: married to a daughter of the
Galadimam Kano who, since 1960, is the Emir of Kano.

91. Nadada, A. Muhammadu Sada, b: Katsina, 1903; eth: Fulani;
§† trad. class: Sar (r); tt: *Sarkin* Kankiya; occ: district head; educ:
Middle VI (formerly teacher, Katsina College); const: Katsina
North; relig: Islam (Tij.); father's occ: emir; father's tt: *Sarkin*
Katsina; career: N.A. department head (with *Wazirin Ayyuka*),
district head (with title *Sarkin* Sulebawa).

92. Ringim, A. Abdurahaman Uba, b: Kano, 1919; eth: *Habe*; trad.
† class: Tal; tt: none; occ: trader, motor transport owner; educ:
Koranic School; relig: Islam (Tij.); father's occ: trader; father's
tt: none; remarks: associate of Ibrahim Nyas, Tijaniyya leader
from Kaolack in Senegal.

93. Sanusi, A. Ado, b: Kano, 1930; eth: Fulani; trad. class: Sar (r);
§† tt: *dan Iya*; occ: N.A. development inspector; educ: Middle VI
(Kaduna College); relig: Islam (Tij.); father's occ: emir; father's
tt: *Sarkin* Kano; career: N.A. council clerk; remarks: formerly
married to a ward of the *Sardauna* of Sokoto.

94. Shatambaya, M. Adamu, b: Yauri, 1917; eth: *Habe*; trad. class:
Sar (v); tt: none; occ: N.A. court scribe; educ: Elementary
VI; const: Yauri and Gwandu South; relig: Islam (Khad.);
father's occ: village head; father's tt: none; career: ?.

95. Shehu, M., b: Gwandu, 1917; eth: Fulani; trad. class: Sar (r); tt:
Marafan Bunza; occ: district head; educ: Middle IV; const:
Gwandu North; relig: Islam (Tij.); father's occ: emir; father's

tt: *Sarkin* Gwandu; remarks: younger brother of reigning Emir of Gwandu. Title is now *Sarkin* Gabas (the district head of Gwandu).

96. Shettima, A. Yakubu, b: Kano, ?; eth: *Habe*; trad. class: slave; tt: none; occ: trader, contractor, *Bafada* (courtier); educ: illiterate; const: Dawakin Tofa; relig: Islam (Tij.); father's occ: *Bafada* (courtier); father's tt: none; remarks: *Bafada* (courtier to the Emir of Kano).

97. Shuwa, M. Abba Kyari, b: Bornu, 1904; eth: Kanuri; trad.
§† class: Sar (r); tt: ex-*Galadima*; occ: trader (ex-district head); educ: Elementary III; const: Bornu South; relig: Islam; father's occ: emir; father's tt: *Shehu* (of Bornu); career: village head, district head, Mungono, district head, Nguru, district head, Marghi; remarks: cousin of the reigning *Shehu* of Bornu.

98. Tureta, M. Muhammadu Maigwadabawa, b: Sokoto, 1914; eth:
§† *Habe*; trad. class: Sar (v); tt: *Truaki*; occ: N.A. councillor; educ: Middle VI (Katsina College); relig: Islam (Khad.); father's occ: district head; father's tt: *Sarkin* Burmi (of Tureta); career: village head, N.A. chief scribe, N.A. councillor.

99. Umaru, A. Babura, b: Kano, 1915; eth: Fulani; trad. class: Sar
§M (n); tt: *Sarkin* Fulani Ja'idanawa; occ: N.A. councillor; educ: Middle VI (Katsina College); const: Dambatta; relig: Islam (Tij.); father's occ: ?; father's tt: ?; career: government agricultural assistant, district head; remarks: member of the prominent Fulani family of Kano called Danbazawa. Married to a daughter of the late Emir of Kano, Bayero.

100. Usman, M., b: Sokoto, 1927; eth: Fulani; trad. class: Sar (r);
§ tt: *Sarkin* Baura; occ: district head; educ: Middle IV; const: Sokoto West Central; relig: Islam (Khad.); father's occ: ?; father's tt: ?; career: village head, district head; remarks: younger brother of the reigning Sultan of Sokoto. Title is now *Sarkin* Gabas (district head of Talata Mafara).

101. Usman, M. Shehu, b: Lafia, 1921; eth: *Habe*; trad. class:
§ Tal; tt: *Sarkin* Daji; occ: N.A. chief forest guide; educ: Elementary VI; const: Lafia Town; relig: Islam (Tij.); father's occ: farmer; father's tt: none.

102. Yola, M. Umaru (Dan Madaki), b: Kano, 1914; eth: Fulani;
§† trad. class: Sar (n); tt: none; occ: N.A. chief adult education organizer; educ: Elementary VI; const: Kano East Central; relig: Islam (Tij.); father's occ: N.A. councillor; father's tt:

Madakin Kano; career: N.A. teacher, N.A. chief adult education officer; remarks: member Kano Fulani family called Yolawa. Brother of present *Madakin* Kano, speaker of Northern House of Assembly.

103. Yusufu, A., b: Hadejia, 1902; eth: *Habe*; trad. class: Sar (v);
§† tt: *Galadima*; occ: N.A. councillor; educ: Elementary VI; const: Hadejia North East; relig: Islam (Tij.); father's occ: N.A. councillor; father's tt: *Galadima*; career: teacher (N.A.), N.A. department head, district head; remarks: formerly held title *Sarkin* Bai.

Opposition Party Members of the Northern House of Assembly

104. Basharu, M., b: Bornu, 1915; eth: Kanuri; trad. class: Sar (c); tt: none; occ: trader and motor transport owner; educ: adult education; const: Yerwa Town North; relig: Islam; father's occ: ward head; father's tt: *Mai* Angwa; career: N.A. auto driver (dismissed in 1954 for taking part in a strike against the Bornu Native Authority); remarks: defeated Shettima Kashim, former regional government minister and federal government minister (now governor of Northern Region) in the 1956 election. Member Bornu Youth Movement.

105. Ekunrin, Mr. J. G., b: Ilorin, 1919; eth: Igbomina Yoruba; trad. class: Tal; tt: none; occ: Action Group organizing secretary; educ: Elementary VI (plus three years S.I.M. Seminary School); const: Ilorin South; relig: Ekunrin is an ordained Protestant minister; remarks: member Tgbomina *Talaka Pasapo* and ITP Grand Alliance (see Chapter 3).

106. Imam, M. Ibrahim, b: Bornu, 1916; eth: Kanuri; trad. class: Sar
† (n); tt: none; occ: trader, contractor; educ: Middle VI (Katsina College); const: Yerwa Town South; relig: Islam; father's occ: chief judge; father's tt: *Alkalin Alkali*; career: N.A. engineering assistant, N.A. supervisor of works department, N.A. councillor; remarks: Sefawa family, formerly ruling dynasty of Bornu.

107. Keffi, M. Bala, b: Keffi, 1919; eth: *Habe*; trad. class: Tal; tt: none; occ: trader, contractor; educ: Elementary IV; const: Kaduna; relig: Islam (Tij.); father's occ: ?; father's tt: ?; career: member Nigerian police.

108. Mahiru, M. Shehu, b: Zaria, 1922; eth: *Habe*; trad. class: Tal; tt: none; occ: bicycle mechanic; educ: adult education; const:

Zaria Urban; relig: Islam (Tij.); father's occ: servant of late Emir of Zaria; father's tt: none; career: ?

109. Mahmud, Ibrahim, b: Misau, 1917; eth: Fulani; trad. class: Sar (n); tt: none; occ: contractor; educ: Middle VI (Katsina College); const: Misau; relig: Islam; father's occ: district judge; father's tt: *Alkali*; career: N.A. technical assistant, works department; remarks: dismissed from N.A. post in 1954 for financial irregularities. M. Ibrahim Mahmud contested the 1956 elections as an independent candidate; thereafter declared for NEPU.

110. Maito, A. Sulaimanu, b: Ilorin, 1901; eth: Yoruba; trad. class: Tal; tt: none; occ: cattle trader; educ: illiterate; const: Ilorin North; relig: Islam (Tij.); father's occ: ?; father's tt: ?

111. Olawoyin, Mr. J. S., b: Ilorin, 1925; eth: Ibolo Yoruba; trad. class: Tal; tt: none; occ: Action Group organizing secretary; educ: Secondary VI (Offa Grammar School); const: Offa Town; relig: Christianity; father's occ: minister and founder of the Iyera Okin African Church, carpenter; father's tt: none; career: Nigeria Railway employee, trader, British Cotton Grower's Association weighing clerk, assistant sales clerk London and Kano Company, Action Group organizing secretary. Was publicity secretary of the Middle Belt People's Party in 1953. Was first associated with Chief Abafami Awolowo, leader of the Action Group during 1953 Constitutional Conference in London.

112. Soba, M. Usman Ango, b: Zaria, 1919; eth: Fulani; trad. class: Sar (r); tt: none; occ: farmer; educ: Middle IV; const: Zaria North; relig: Islam (Tij.); father's occ: district head; father's tt: ?; career: clerk, emir's office, emir's gardener; remarks: by birth member of Bornawa royal dynasty of Zaria.

113. Tela, M. Haruna, b: Sokoto, 1914; eth: *Habe*; trad. class: Tal; occ: Koranic Malam, tailor, small trader; educ: adult education; const: Kaura Namoda; relig: Islam (Tij.); father's occ: ?; father's tt: ?; remarks: associated with the *dan Wazifa* wing of Tijannia brotherhood in eastern Sokoto.

Ministers without Portfolio, 1961-1965

114. Aliyu, A., b: 1908; eth: Fulani; trad. class: Sar (c); tt: *Turakin*
† Zazzau; occ: politician; const: Zaria Central; career: teacher, Zaria Middle School, E.T.C. Katsina, Kano Middle School, sen-

ior accountant Zaria N.A. treasury, clerk, in charge of Zaria N.A. central offices, Zaria N.A. supervisor of works and P.W.D., attended Ibadan conference on the review of the Richardson Constitution, 1950, elected to Northern House of Assembly, 1954, appointed minister of trade and industry, retired from Zaria N.A., appointed chairman N.R.D.C., resigned from N.R.D.C. following election to Northern House of Assembly, 1961.

115. Karim, M. Umaru Abba, b: 1930; tt: *Walin* Muri; occ: politician; const: Muri South West; career: treasury accountant, Muri N.A. secretary Muri N.A. council, development secretary, Muri N.A., elected to Nigeria House of Representatives, 1954 and 1959, appointed parliamentary secretary to Federal Minister of Mines and Power.

Parliamentary Secretaries, 1961-1965

116. Ahmed, A. Hassan, b: 1933; tt: none; occ: teacher; const: Nassarawa; career: teacher.

117. Hong, A. Haliru Zarma, b: 1936; eth: Kilba; trad. class: Sar (v); tt: none; occ: headmaster and teacher; const: Adamawa North West; career: teacher, Adamawa N.A. and Micika Senior Primary School, headmaster Mubi Senior Primary School and Girei Senior Primary School.

118. Muhammadu, M., b: 1916; tt: *Wakalin Ayyuka* Gusau; occ: N.A. councillor; career: Sokoto N.A. councillor, parliamentary secretary, Ministry of Justice.

119. Sulaiman, A. Muhammadu, b: 1933; tt: none; occ: headmaster; const: Keffi; career: teacher, Keffi Junior Primary School, Abuja Secondary School, Laminga Senior Primary School, headmaster, Keffi Senior Primary School.

Provincial Commissioners, 1961-1965

120. Bele, M. Dauda Jamtari, eth: Kanuri; trad. class: Sar; tt: none; occ: ?; const: Mubi; career: ?

121. Benisheik, M. Zanna Umara, b: 1918; eth: Kanuri; trad. class: Sar (n); tt: *Zanna*; occ: N.A. employee; const: Fume Gujba; career: N.A. technical assistant, Bornu, prison scribe, court scribe, supervisor of wells, then of works, town councillor, Bornu, provincial councillor, Bornu, in Assembly, parliamentary secretary, Premier's office.

122. Okin, A. Sanni Olarewaju Brairmoh, b: 1910; eth: Yoruba; tt: none; occ: N.A. employee; const: Ilorin Central; career; teacher, Lagos, and Ilorin, transferred to Ilorin N.A. central office, court registrar, treasurer, provincial supervisor of accounts and stores, and local government secretary, Ilorin N.A., member Ilorin provincial council, parliamentary secretary, Ministry of Agriculture.

123. Salihu, A. Muhammadu Gonto, trad. class: Sar (r); tt: *Turakin* Wase; occ: ?; const: Lowland East; father's occ: Emir of Wase; career: ?

Newly elected NPC members of Northern House of Assembly, 1961-
1965, government back-benchers

124. Abdullahi, A. Sarkin Yola, b: 1934; eth: Fulani; trad. class: Sar (n); tt: *Sarkin* Yola; occ: clerk, Kano city council, and N.A. councillor; const: Bici West; father's tt: *Sarkin* Shanu of Kano; career: water revenue clerk, Kano N.A., clerk, Kano city council.

125. Abdurrahman, A. Sarkin Gobir, eth: Fulani; trad. class: Sar (r); tt: *Sarkin* Gobir; occ: district head; const: Gwadabawa North; career: ?

126. Abubakar, A., b: 1915; eth: Kebbawa; trad. class: Sar (c); tt: *Magajin Gari* (Argungu); occ: N.A. councillor and department supervisor; const: Argungu East; career: dispensary attendant, Argungu N.A., supervisor of medical services, with title *Wakalin Magani*, Argungu N.A. councillor of works, medical services and health, with title *Magajin Gari*.

127. Addiya, M. Sarkin Gobir, b: 1911; tt: none; occ: trader; const: Binji-Tangaza; career: trader.

128. Afolayan, Olarewaju Mofoluwasho, b: 1931; eth: Yoruba; trad. class: Tal; tt: none; occ: politician, administrative secretary; const: Ilorin South; career: teacher, civil servant, administrative secretary, NPC, Ilorin South, active Baptist church worker.

129. Ahmadu, M. Sarkin Pindiga, tt: *Sarkin* Pindiga; occ: village head; const: Ako; career: ?

130. Alam, M. Muhammadu, b: 1930; eth: Yungur; trad. class: Sar (v); tt: *Iyan* Yungar; occ: district head, N.A. councillor, farmer; const: Adamawa West; career: village scribe, district scribe, Yungur, district head, Yungur N.A. councillor, Adamawa.

131. Albishir, M. Muhammadu (Rimi), b: 1920; eth: Fulani; trad. class: Sar (r); tt: *Fardami*; occ: village head; const: dan Yusufa-Kaura; father's occ: village head; father's tt: *Fardami*; career: veterinary assistant, village scribe, village head, *Fardami*, in Kaura district.

132. Alkali, M. Muhammadu Nura, b: 1932; eth: Fulani; trad. class: Jud; tt: none; occ: district scribe; const: Tudun Wada (Kano); father's tt: *Alkalin* Riruwe Kano; career: forest guard, acting forester, Kano N.A., district scribe, Kano N.A.

133. Andrew, Sidi, b: 1932; tt: none; occ: teacher; const: Zangon Katab; career: teacher, Roman Catholic mission.

134. Bajini, M. Muhammadu, b: 1929; eth: Fulani; trad. class: Sar (n); tt: none; occ: N.A. employee and member Sokoto Town health committee; const: Dange Shuni; father's tt: *Galadiman* Gari; career; health inspector Sokoto N.A., head of vaccination team in 1955, worked in various rural districts, secretary, Sokoto Town Council Health Committee, clerk and storekeeper, Sokoto N.A. health department, provincial president, NPC Youth Association, and member, NPC provincial executive committee.

135. Balewa, M. Adamu Tafawa, b: 1925; eth: Fulani; trad. class: Sar (n); tt: *Ajiyan* Bauchi; occ: district head; const: Bauchi South West; career: government 1st class clerk, district head.

136. Batulbe, M. Bukar, b: ?; eth: Kanuri; trad. class: Jad; occ: trader; const: Yerwa; career: ?

137. Bayero, A. Salihi Turaki, b: ?; eth: Fulani; trad. class: Sar (r); tt: *Turaki* Bayero; occ: secretary N.A. council; const: Bici East; career: clerk, Kano chief alkali's court, assistant clerk, then secretary Kano N.A. council.

138. Bayero, M. Yusufu, b: 1932; eth: Fulani; trad. class: Sar (r); tt: none; occ: senior scribe; const: Sumaila; father's occ: Emir of Kano; career: Kano N.A. employee, Health Office, printing press, scribe North Ward office, Kano City senior scribe West Ward; remarks: brother is Emir of Kano, A. Sar Muhammadu Sanusi.

139. Dantata, A. Aminu, b: 1931; eth: Hausa; trad. class: Tal; tt: none; occ: director, Alhassan Dantata and Sons firm; const: Kura; father's occ: trader ?; career: produce buyer, Sokoto province manager, assistant director then director Alhassan, Dantata and Sons.

140. Darazo, M. Sule, b: 1917; eth: Hausa; trad. class: Sar (n); tt: none; occ: teacher; const: Bauchi North East; father's tt: *Banayan* Darazo; career: teacher.

141. Diso, A. Muhammadu, b: 1900; tt: ex-*Falaki* of Kano (deposed); occ: N.A. employee; const: Gezawa; career: government civil service, transferred to Kano N.A.

142. Gande, A. Garba Dikkon, b: 1920; eth: Fulani; trad. class: Sar (n); tt: *Sarkin* Gande; occ: N.A. employee; const: Sokoto West Central; father's tt: *Sarkin* Gande; career: trader, now Gande village head, member Sokoto Provincial Council, assistant chairman Silame District Council, director, Sokoto Trading Co., member executive committee, assistant treasurer, and legal advisor, NPC, Sokoto branch.

143. Gashua, Malam, A., b: 1924; eth: Fulani; trad. class: Sar (r); tt: none; occ: adult education senior organizer; const: Bedde division, Gashua; father's tt: *dan* Nyileci; career: adult education senior organizer.

144. Gaya, M. Muhammadu Kabir, b: 1932; eth: Fulani; trad. class: Sar (r); tt: none; occ: district scribe; const: Gaya North; father's occ: district head Gaya; father's tt: ?; career: district scribe Gaya.

145. Gusau, A. Hashimu, b: 1925; eth: Hausa; trad. class: Tal; tt: none; occ: trader; const: Chafe-Gusau; career: trader, Kano and Gusau, president, Gusau branch of "A.N.M.U."

146. Gwarzo, M. Ado Salihu Shehu, b: 1933; eth: Fulani; trad. class: Jud; tt: none; occ: elementary school crafts teacher; const: Gwarzo West; father's occ: Native Court judge; father's tt: *Alkalin* Gwarzo; career: elementary school crafts teacher.

147. Hadejia, M. Abdulkadir Maigari, b: 1919; trad. class: Sar (n); tt: none; occ: teacher; const: Hadejia East; career: teacher, Hadejia Junior Primary School, headmaster Hadejia Central Junior Primary School, acting manager, Hadejia N.A. schools.

148. Haruna, A., b: 1898; eth: Fulani; trad. class: Sar (r); tt: *Sarkin* Kebbin Jega; occ: district head, N.A. councillor; const: Gwandu East, career: veterinary assistant, village head, district head, Jega, member Gwandu N.A. council.

149. Idiaro, M. Hannafi, b: 1907; eth: Fulani; trad. class: Sar (c); tt: none; occ: teacher; const: Ilorin North; career: teacher, visiting teacher, bursar Provincial Secondary School.

150. Idirisa, A. Makaman Katsina, b: 1905; eth: Fulani; trad. class: Sar (r); tt: *Makaman* Katsina; occ: district head; const: Danja; father's tt: *Iya*; career: district head Bakori.

151. Isa, M. Labo Na, b: 1920; tt: none; occ: trader; const: Yauri; career: general trader, petrol agent of the United Africo Company, Ltd., Yelwa.

152. Ja'afar, A. Abba (Abdullahi Abubaker), b: 1922; eth: Fulani; trad. class: Sar (n); tt: none; occ: N.A. sanitary inspector; const: Dawakin Tofa West; career: N.A. sanitary inspector.

153. Kafarati, M. Abdu Yeriman, b: 1925; eth: Bolawa; trad. class: Sar (n); tt: *Yeriman* Kafarati; occ: N.A. employee; const: Duka Kwani; father's tt: *Sarkin* Kafarati; career: former clerk, Gombe Transport and Traders Co., Ltd., former supervisor N.A. medical department, Gombe.

154. Kanam, M. Muhammadu Ciroman, b: 1926; trad. class: Sar (r); tt: *Ciroman* Kanam; occ: district head; const: Kanam; career: district scribe, forest guard, district head Kantana.

155. Kauran, A. Ya'u, b: 1926; tt: none; occ: trader; const: Kaura-Namoda; career: trader, member district heads' council.

156. Kura, A. Ladan, b: 1920; tt: none; occ: government and N.A. general contractor; const: Bauchi Central; career: government and Bauchi N.A. general contractor.

157. Lere, M. Ya'u, b: 1924; tt: none; occ: N.A. department head; const: Kauru-Lere; father's tt: *Sarkin* Lere; career: senior sanitary inspector, Zaria N.A., member NPC Zaria branch executive committee, health department head (*Wakilin Tsapta*).

158. Mahdu, M. Muhammadu, b: 1924; tt: none; occ: N.A. administrative secretary; const: Katagum West; career: administrative secretary, Katagum N.A.

159. Mai'aduwa, A. Ahmadu, b: 1932; eth: Hausa; trad. class: Sar ?; tt: *Galadima*; occ: village head; const: Daura West; father's tt: *Galadima*; career: village head scribe, village head, Danyashe, member Katsina provincial council, provincial education committee, Daura outer council, and Mai'aduwa district head council, president Danyashe village council, awarded NPC medal by Premier for loyal service.

160. Makama, M. Maikano Wudil, b: 1911; eth: Fulani; trad. class: Sar (n); tt: none; occ: trader and farmer; father's occ: district head Wudil; father's tt: ?; career: successful trader and farmer.

161. Marama, M. Madu, b: ?; tt: none; occ: N.A. employee; const: Biu South; career: ?

162. Marusa, A. Ibrahim, b: 1890; eth: Fulani; trad. class: Sar (r); tt: *Marusa*; occ: district head, farmer; const: Marusa-Mashi; father's tt: *Marusa*; career: Arabic teacher, district head Dutsi.

163. Masu, Zanna Mu'azu, b: ?; tt: *Zanna*; occ: ?; const: Dikwa Central; career: not given.

164. Mohammed, M. Alhassan, b: 1935; eth: Hausa; trad. class: Sar (r); tt: *Tafidan* Gumel; occ: district head; const: Gumel East; father's occ: emir; father's tt: *Sarkin* Gumel; career: Gumel N.A. clerk, district head Gagarawa.

165. Muhammadu, M. Dakin Gari, b: 1929; trad. class: Sar; tt: *Sarkin* Kudin Dakin Gari; occ: district head; const: Gwandu South; career: dispensary attendant, Gwandu N.A. village head, district head Dakin Gari.

166. Muhtar, A., b: 1916; eth: Fulani; trad. class: Sar (r); tt: *Sarkin* Pawa Kankara; occ: district head; const: Kankara-Nogo; father's tt: *Sarkin* Gwari; career: village head, Jargaba and Dauja, district head Kankara.

167. Musa, A. Kamba, b: 1904; eth: Kebbawa; trad. class: Sar (n); tt: *Sarkin* Shiko Kamba; occ: district head; const: Argungu West; father's tt: *Sarkin* Shiko; career: teacher, district head Dendi.

168. Mustafa, M. Yerima, b: 1901; trad. class: Sar (r); tt: *Yerima*; occ: district head; const: Geidam; career: sanitary inspector, Bornu N.A., Shehu's personal health and medical attendant, district head Fune, promoted to Maidugure and then to Geidam, Bornu N.A. councillor; remarks: member Ycrima family.

169. Nabegu, A. Baba, b: 1926; eth: Hausa; trad. class: Tal; occ: successful merchant-trader; const: Rano; career: trader and merchant.

170. Ojo, M. Moses Ade, b: 1926; tt: none; occ: general contractor and photographer; const: Ilorin East; career: general contractor, photographer, Ilorin and Kabba provinces.

171. Rabiu, A., b: 1920; tt: none; occ: hospital chief nurse; const: Babura Garki; career: nurse in charge of Kano City hospital medical ward, then of out-patient department, promoted to chief nurse, president Kano NPC branch.

172. Ringim, A. Uba Ibrahim, b: 1921; eth: Hausa; trad. class: Tal ?; tt: none; occ: trader; const: Sumaila; career: trader.

173. Rufa'i, M. Ahmadu Danyama, b: 1919; eth: Fulani; trad. class: Sar (n); tt: none; occ: politician; const: Misau; father's tt: *Turakin* Misau; career: agricultural assistant, transporter, produce buyer, onetime U.A.C. employee, hides, and skin officer Ministry of Animal Health and Forestry, loans officer N.R.D.C.

174. Sambo, M. Muhammadu, b: 1924; tt: *Wakilin Zinna*; occ: assistant district head; const: Muri East; career: N.A. timekeeper,

assistant district scribe, district scribe, department head (*Waki-lin Zinna*).

175. Tangaza, M. Abdu, b: 1916; eth: Fulani; trad. class: Sar (r); tt: none; occ: secretary to N.A. councillor; const: Gandi-Goronyo; father's occ: district head Tangaza; father's tt: *Marafa;* career: scribe, N.A. central office, N.A. treasury accountant, office typist, senior scribe, officer chief recorder, secretary to N.A. councillor.

176. Tudu, A. Aliyu Isa, b: 1906; trad. class: Sar; tt: none; occ: district head; const: Isa; career: district head Isa.

177. Umar, M. Abdu, trad. class: Sar (n); tt: *Ciroman* Shira; occ: N.A. employee; const: Katagum South; career:?

178. Umaru, M. Bashari, b: 1931; tt: none; occ: N.A. pharmacist; const: Birnin Kudu; career: government pharmacist, Kano N.A. pharmacist.

179. Usman, A. Ibrahim Makarfi, b: 1912; tt: none; occ: groundnut buying agent and contractor; const: Ikara-Makarfi; career: groundnut buying agent and contractor.

180. Usman, A. Sarkin Gabas, b: 1917; trad. class: Sar (r); tt: *Sarkin* Gabas Gwandu; occ: district head; const: Gwandu North; career: Birnin Kebbi prison scribe, Kalgo district scribe, district head Bun then Gwandu (with title *Sarkin* Gabas); remarks: younger brother of Emir of Gwandu, Alhaji Haruna.

181. Usmar, M. Sule, b: 1933; eth: Fulani; trad. class: Sar (r); tt: *Sarkin* Sulebawa; occ: N.A. employee and district head; const: Ingawa; father's occ: Emir of Katsina; career: Katsina N.A. employee of forestry then agriculture department.

182. Wushishi, A. Usman, b: ?; eth: Hausa; trad. class: Tal; tt: none; occ: N.A. employee; const: Kontagora South East; father's occ: Koranic *malam*; career: government veterinary assistant, Kontagora N.A. employee.

183. Yakubu, A. Faruku, b: 1931; trad. class: Tal; tt: none; occ: general contractor; const: Kiru; career: general contractor.

184. Yari, A. Tijjani, b: ?; tt: *Sarkin* Dawaki; occ: N.A. employee; const: Karaye; father's occ: district head Gwarzo; career: ?

185. Yola, M. Mukhtar, b: 1934; eth: Fulani; trad. class: Sar (n); tt: none; occ: N.A. treasury accountant; const: Dawakin Tofa East; career: N.A. treasury accountant, Kano.

186. Yola, M. Mustafa Baba, b: 1928; trad. class: Sar (r); tt: none;

occ: N.A. councillor; const: Adamawa Central; career: veterinary assistant, Lamido's private secretary.

187. Zango, A. Mudi, b: 1911; trad. class: Sar (?); tt: *Mai'unguwa*; occ: village head; const: Kunbotso; career; village head.

188. Zubairu, M. Kaigama, b: 1923; trad. class: Sar (s); tt: none; occ: district head; const: Kaga-Marghi; career: district head; remarks: member of Kaigama family, a royal slave family.

APPENDIX B

The Native Authorities (Customary Presents) Orders Publication Notice, 1955

FIRST SCHEDULE
Prohibited Customary Presents

All gifts and presents of all kinds passing to and from or between—

A. chiefs and their people;
B. district heads and their people;
C. village heads and their people;
D. chiefs, district heads and village heads and any of them;
E. native authority officials and members of the public;
F. officials of native authorities (other than subordinate native authorities) and subordinate native authority officials;
G. superiors and inferiors as defined in this order.

EXCEPTING those gifts and presents specifically permitted by this order, but

INCLUDING (without prejudice to the generality of the foregoing) the following by way of examples—

Examples

1. All gifts made by any person in connection with appointments or promotions to native authority posts or traditional *Sarauta* titles including (without prejudice to the generality of the foregoing) the following gifts—

(a) gifts to a chief or other superior in order to obtain a post;
(b) services rendered to a chief or other superior either before or after being appointed to a post;
(c) gifts or money distributed to the public by a candidate for a post in order to increase the prestige of the candidate or to obtain votes, support or other favour or advantage in obtaining the post in question;
(d) gifts made by any person to the person appointed to the post after such appointment;

Provided always that nothing herein contained shall be deemed to prohibit the giving of traditional *Kayan Sarauta* if the same is paid for out of the funds of the native authority concerned.

2. All gifts and payments made by any person in order to secure some favour which the giver would not otherwise be entitled to expect and all gifts or payments made in gratitude for some favour unlawfully shown or given to any person in the past including (without prejudice to the generality of the foregoing) gifts, whether rendered in goods, services or money with the object of—

(a) obtaining preferential treatment over another person;

(b) avoiding the attentions of officials performing their normal duties;

(c) concealing wrong-doing or negligence; or

(d) mitigating a punishment.

3. All gifts made by an inferior to a superior in the knowledge that under local custom the superior would be obliged to give some larger present in return and with the intention that the superior should thus be induced to give such larger present;

Provided that nothing in this paragraph contained shall be deemed to prohibit the exchange of small symbolic gifts of kolanuts.

4. All gifts made by any person to a chief, district head, or village head or by a chief, district head or village head to any person (including one another) on any of the following occasions—

(a) the religious festivals of the Greater Bairam, the Lesser Dairam and the Prophet's Birthday and any Salla time;

(b) on the arrival of the chief, district head or village head at any place during a tour or on a visit:

Provided that nothing herein contained shall be deemed to prohibit the supply of an adequate quantity of food for the chief, district head or village head and for a reasonable number of his retainers by way of subsistence during his stay; and

Provided also that such supply is confined to such amount of food as can reasonably be consumed by the persons for whom it is provided while they are staying in the place in question and is not excessive in amount and does not include whole animals or large quantities of food to be carried away;

(c) on the departure of a chief, district head or village head from a place on tour;

(d) on the departure of a chief, district head or village head from their respective headquarters on journeys undertaken for a particular purpose;

499

(e) on the return of a chief, district head or village head to their respective headquarters from journeys undertaken for a particular purpose;

(f) to a chief, district head or village head on being summoned by any of them for official reasons such as for council meetings or in order to receive instructions or for reprimand:

Provided that nothing herein contained shall be deemed to prohibit the supply of an adequate quantity of food to a village or district head by his superior when each village or district head visits the headquarters of his superior;

(g) on the arrival of visitors in any place, by way of contribution to the entertainment of such visitors;

(h) on any other special occasion such as the accession of a person to a title, the birth or marriage of a relation of a chief or district head or village head, or at the harvest:

Provided always that nothing herein contained shall be deemed to prohibit unsolicited gifts to a chief or district head or village head from members of their respective families on the celebration of family occasions.

5. All gifts or payments made by any person to a district head or village head in consideration of the performance by such district head or village head of any duties which he is bound by custom to perform without payment, including (without prejudice to the generality of the foregoing) the following—

(a) the witnessing of transactions involving the transfer or dealing with land or other property;

(b) the summoning of recalcitrant or runaway wives:

Provided that nothing herein contained shall be deemed to prohibit the payment of a reasonable honorarium only to the messenger who discovers or brings back to her husband the wife at the direction of the district or village head.

6. All gifts made to a chief or district or village head or other superior by any person or group of persons out of the proceeds of their hunting or fishing, or by way of a proportion of the communal forest produce or the harvest collected by any such person or persons.

7. All gifts of payments of any kind (other than payments authorised by law) made to any person connected in any way with a native court whether alkali, court member, mufti, scribe, assessor, messenger or any other official whatsoever by any person connected

with any case which has been, is or will be before the court, whether such person is a party to the case or a witness or is otherwise interested therein.

8. All gifts and payments made by any person to a messenger or other go-between who is sent to such person as a representative of a chief or district head including (without prejudice to the generality of the foregoing) the following—

(a) gifts and payments made by a person to such messenger or go-between on his bringing a message or instructions to such persons;

(b) all gifts and payments made to a messenger or go-between with the object to conciliating him or any other person in the hope that he or such other person shall influence the chief or district head in favour of the giver of the present.

9. All gifts and payments made to a native authority official in connection with the carrying out of his official duties whether the gifts or payments or any part thereof are intended for such official or for any of his superiors:

Provided that nothing herein contained shall be deemed to prohibit the provision of food and lodging for a native authority official by persons of adequate means while such native authority official is on tour in an official capacity if such food and lodging is limited to what is adequate for not more than three days at any one place and if the amount of the food is limited in manner prescribed in the second proviso to sub-paragraph (b) of paragraph 4 of this Schedule.

10. Gifts or payments in cash or in kind to village heads by their villagers for or on any special occasion; and collections in cash or in kind made by village heads from their villagers on such occasions.

11. All presents made by nomad Fulani to a village head on the arrival of the Fulani in the area of the village head:

Provided that nothing herein contained shall be deemed to prohibit the giving by such Fulani of a small amount of milk and butter only to the village head sufficient for the needs of himself and his family during the period of the stay of the Fulani concerned.

SECOND SCHEDULE

Permissible Customary Presents

1. Unsolicited gifts to chiefs and district or village heads on the celebration of family occasions such as the marriage of the chief or

district or village head or of a child of a chief, district head or village head, from members of their respective families:

Provided that nothing herein contained shall be deemed to authorise the giving or acceptance generally of gifts to a superior from all his subordinates on such occasions.

2. Small personal presents from chiefs or district or village heads:

(a) at festivals and family occasions;

(b) to important visitors;

(c) by way of religious alms.

3. The supply by persons of adequate means to native authority officials on tour in an official capacity of adequate food or lodging or both for not more than three days at any one place:

Provided that such supply of food is confined to such amount of food as can reasonably be consumed by the persons for whom it is provided while they are staying in the place in question and is not excessive in amount and does not include whole animals or large quantities of food to be carried away.

4. Small presents by native authority officials on tour to the families and servants of any person who has lawfully supplied them with food and lodging.

5. Presents to a person selected for an important native authority appointment or a traditional title of gowns or cloaks or other traditional presents:

Provided that the cost of such presents shall be defrayed from native authority funds.

6. Presents by way of reasonable assistance to village or district heads who have suffered some serious mishap, e.g., loss of house by fire.

Questions For Administrative Officers on Certain Aspects of the Development of Native Authorities, 1946-1959

I. GENERAL DEVELOPMENT OF THE N.A.

(1) Organisation of the N.A. (inner council) before 1950.

(2) What have been the principal reorganisation(s) of the N.A. since 1950?

(3) Emir-in-council: have there been any instances of disagreement between the emir and his council since the N.A. Law, 1954, was passed? How were they resolved? Can you cite any instances of the effect of the 1954 Law (increased powers of councillors) on a decision(s) of the N.A.?

(4) Do heads of departments hold *traditional* titles (i.e., not including 'Wakilin Ayyuka,' etc.)? Did they in the past? Is there a policy on this matter?

(5) Committees of the council: to what extent is the business of the N.A. conducted by committees?

(6) Services: have particular services been emphasized by
    (a) the N.A.?
    (b) Administration?
Has there been any change of emphasis over the past ten years or so?
Have services been evenly distributed between urban and rural areas? Within urban areas? Between districts?

II. RELATIONSHIP BETWEEN ADMINISTRATION AND NATIVE ADMINISTRATIONS

(7) Has there been any change in the relationship between Administration and the Native Administrations—
    (a) from the point of view of the officer—practical or psychological, if not legal?
    (b) with regard to the willingness of the N.A. to accept advice? Instances?
—i.e., either since 1954, or since self-government became imminent?

(8) What are the principal means of supervision and control by the provincial/divisional administration over the activities of the Native Administrations?

Have these changed or not during the last ten years?

III. STAFF

(9) To what extent do you think the principles and practice of employment, promotion, and discipline on merit are in operation in the Native Authority Service?

    (a) at the level of district head, N.A. councillor, and head of department?

    (b) at the level of employees in departments (agricultural, veterinary, health *malams*, etc.) and clerical staff?

(10) What has been the effect, if any, of setting up an establishment committee?

(11) Has the possibility of setting up a staff standards board or similar body, or increasing the powers of the establishment committee, been discussed with the N.A.? What is the position?

(12) Have there been any instances of the minister for local government exercising his power to disapprove any appointment over 360 pounds per annum? Has the question ever arisen?

(13) To what extent have qualifications for posts as in (9)(a) and/or (9)(b) risen in the past ten years?

IV. HUDSON COMMISSION

(14) What was the position taken by the N.A. toward the Hudson Commission recommendations?

What specific recommendations were

    (a) acceptable,

    (b) controversial,

    (c) rejected?

(15) Do you see any reason why the substance of the proposals were rejected by the Native Administrations as a whole from the point of view of your N.A.?

V. FINANCE

(16) How much money is handled per annum by the N.A. or provincial body in respect of

    (a) loans,

    (b) contracts?

(17) In your opinion, does self-government mean more or less autonomy in practice and/or principle for the N.A. (from the regional government)? Any signs for the future?

Can you cite any instances of the regional government clamping down on an act or activity of the N.A. since 1957?

VI. SUBORDINATE COUNCILS: OUTER COUNCILS

(18) Are there any instances of the N.A. having adopted recommendations by the outer council? instances?

(19) Is the outer council an effective source of constructive criticism of the activities of the N.A. (services or administration)? Instances?

(20) What sort of person, in terms of traditional status, education, or occupation, is most articulate in the outer council?

VII. DISTRICT COUNCILS

(21) As in (18), (19), and (20) above.

(22) Is there any political party activity in any districts of the N.A.?

(23) What is the financial position of district councils:
   - (a) formal: D.C.F. or D.F.R.? If the latter, has any use been made of rating powers? For what services? What was the incidence?
   - (b) sources of revenue?
   - (c) amount of revenue? (Please note any increases or decreases.)
   - (d) amount of expenditure? (Reserves?)

(24) What are the services for which district councils have been made responsible?

(25) In your opinion, could more services be handled satisfactorily by district councils if delegation were made by the N.A.?

(26) What are the principal means of control by the N.A. over the activities of district councils? Are councils either under-controlled or over-controlled, in your opinion?

(27) How many districts of the N.A. have gazetted councils? Are there any immediate plans for more?

(28) What plans or recommendations have been presented to the N.A. with regard to future (immediate or distant) development of district councils in respect of:
   - (a) composition of the councils,
   - (b) powers of the councils,

(c) responsibilities of the councils,

(d) finance of the councils.

(29) From your experience, what should be the future relationship between the district head and the district council—i.e., should the chairman of the council continue to be appointed by the N.A. or should he become an elected official? Should his powers increase, decrease, or remain the same? Has this question ever been discussed with the N.A.? What was the position?

VIII. Town Councils

(30) As in (18), (19), (20), (23), (24), (25), (26), (27), (28), (29) above.

(31) Political parties in town councils:

(a) Have there been any issues of contention between majority and minority parties in the town council(s)? Please cite as many instances as you can.

(b) Have there been any issues of contention between the N.A., on the one hand, and both majority and minority parties, on the other? Please cite as many instances as you can.

(32) Does the town council(s) control appointments? What are their legal powers? How is hiring done in practice?

(33) How many of the staff controlled by the council are employed directly, and how many on seconding from the N.A.?

(34) Committees of the town council:

Are committees given a reasonably free hand, or are there problems of too much scrutiny of committee work by the full council?

Is most of the work of the council done in committee or in plenary session?

Is there party representation on committees (i.e., majority-minority)?

(35) In your opinion, does the public distinguish between projects carried out by the N.A. and those by the town council? Have there been any instances of representations made to the council concerning administration of a service by the council?

(36) What services have been most successfully handled by the town council? To what would you attribute such success?

(37) Are traditional and nominated members politically independent in practice, or do they tend to support the party in power? Or the N.A.?

(38) Is the town council, or should it be in future, associated with the work of assessment of *attajirai* within the town?

(39) What functions or responsibilities have been added to the council as a result of demand on its part?

(40) Please remark on:

    (a) standards of debate in the council,

    (b) general interest of the public in the council's activities.

(41) What major problems come to mind as having presented difficulties in the past or as likely to do so in future in the development of the town council?

Selected Bibliography

I. Books: general

Abraham, R. C. *The Tiv People*. London: Crown Agents, 1940.

Africanus, Leo. *History and Description of Africa*. 3 vols. Translated by Pory. London: printed for the Hakluyt Society, 1896. Annotated and translated French edition, *Description de l'Afrique*. 2 vols. Paris: Epaulard, 1956.

Ahmadu, Bello, the Sardauna of Sokoto. *My Life*. Cambridge: Cambridge University Press, 1962.

Ajayi, J. F. Ade, and R. S. Smith. *Yoruba Warfare in the Nineteenth Century*. Cambridge: Cambridge University Press, 1964.

Akinyede, G.B.A. *The Political and Constitutional Problems of Nigeria*. Lagos: Nigerian Printing and Publishing Co., 1957.

Akpan, Ntieyong U. *Epitaph to Indirect Rule*. London: Cassell and Co., 1956.

Aluko, S. A. *The Problems of Self-Government for Nigeria, A Critical Analysis*. Devon: Stockwell, 1955.

Ames, C. G. *Gazatteer of the Plateau Province, Nigeria*. Jos: Niger Press for Native Administration, 1934.

Anderson, J.N.D. *Islamic Law in Africa*. Colonial Research Publication No. 16. London: H. M. Stationery Office, 1954.

Anyiam, Frederick Uzoma. *Men and Matters in Nigerian Politics, 1934-1958*. Yaba: Okwesa, 1959.

Apter, David E. *The Gold Coast in Transition*. Princeton: Princeton University Press, 1955.

Arnett, Edward J. *Gazatteer of Sokoto Province*. London: Waterlow, 1920.

———. *Gazatteer of Zaria Province*. London: Waterlow, 1920.

———. *The Rise of the Sokoto Fulani, Being a Paraphrase and in Some Parts a Translation of the Infaku'l Maisuri of Sultan Mohammed Bello*. Kano: Emirate Printing Department, 1922.

Awa, Eme O. *Federal Government in Nigeria*. Berkeley: University of California Press, 1964.

Awolowo, Obafemi. *Awo: The Autobiography of Chief Obafemi Awolowo*. Cambridge: Cambridge University Press, 1960.

———. *Forward to a New Nigeria*. Speeches at the Nigerian Constitutional Conference and other occasions. London: n.p., 1957.

————. *I Am On My Way.* Speeches on Nigerian Unity. Ibadan: Action Group Bureau of Information, 1957.

————. *The Path to Nigerian Freedom.* London: Faber, 1947.

————. *Thoughts on the Nigerian Constitution,* Ibadan: Oxford University Press, 1966.

Azikiwe, Nnamdi. *The Development of Political Parties in Nigeria.* London: The Office of the Commissioner in the United Kingdom for the Eastern Region of Nigeria, 1957.

————. *Economic Reconstruction of Nigeria.* Lagos: n.p., 1942.

————. *Land Tenure in Northern Nigeria.* Lagos: n.p., 1942.

————. *Political Blueprint of Nigeria.* Lagos: African Book Co., 1943.

————. *Renascent Africa.* Accra: privately printed, 1937.

————. *Zik: A Selection from the Speeches of Nnamdi Azikiwe,* ed. Philip Harris. Cambridge: Cambridge University Press, 1961.

Balogun, Kolawole. *My Country Nigeria.* Yaba: printed by Sankey Printing Works, 1955.

Baxter, R. W. *Our North: The Story of Northern Nigiera in Its Self-Government Year,* 1959. Kaduna: Ministry of Information, 1959.

Benton, P. A. *A Bornu Almanack.* London: n.p., 1914.

————. *The Sultanate of Bornu.* London: H. Milford, 1913. Translation of a monograph by Dr. A. Schultze.

Bittinger, D. W. *Educational Experiment in the Sudan* (Elgin, Ill., 1941).

Blitz, L. Franklin. *The Politics and Administration of the Nigerian Government.* London: Sweet and Maxwell; Lagos: African Universities Press, 1965.

Bohannan, Laura and Paul. *The Tiv of Central Nigeria.* London: International African Institute, 1953.

Bohannan, Paul. *Justice and Judgment among the Tiv.* London: Oxford University Press, 1957.

————. *Tiv Farm and Settlement.* Colonial Research Studies No. 15. London: Great Britain Colonial Office, 1954.

Bovill, E. W. *Caravans of the Old Sahara.* London: Oxford University Press, 1933.

————. *The Golden Trade of the Moors.* London: Oxford University Press, 1958.

Bowen, Elenore Smith. *Return to Laughter.* London: Gollancz, 1954.

Brett, Lionel, ed. *Constitutional Problems of Federalism in Nigeria.* Lagos: Times Press, 1961.

Bretton, Henry L. *Power and Stability in Nigeria: The Politics of Decolonization.* New York: Frederick A. Praeger, 1962.

Buchanan, Keith M., and J. C. Pugh. *Land and People in Nigeria: The Human Geography of Nigeria and Its Environmental Background.* London: University of London Press, 1955.

Buell, Raymond Leslie. *The Native Problem in Africa.* 2 vols. New York: Macmillan, 1928.

Burdon, John A. *Historical Notes on Certain Emirates and Tribes* [in Northern Nigeria]. London: Waterlow, 1909.

Burke, Fred. G. *Local Government and Politics in Uganda.* Syracuse: Syracuse University Press, 1964.

Burns, Sir Alan C. *History of Nigeria.* London: Allen and Unwin, 1956. First edition 1929.

Busia, K. A. *The Position of the Chief in the Modern Political System of Ashanti.* London: Oxford University Press, 1961.

Cameron, Sir Donald. *Principles of Native Administration and their Application.* Lagos: Government Printer, 1934.

Campbell, M. J. *Law and Practice of Local Government in Northern Nigeria.* Lagos: African Universities Press; London: Sweet & Maxwell, 1963.

————. *Principles of Local Government in Northern Nigeria.* London: Oxford University Press, 1963.

Carney, David E. *Government and Economy in British West Africa.* New York: Bookman's, 1961.

Cary, Joyce. *The African Witch.* London: Gollancz, 1936.

————. *An American Visitor.* London: Joseph, 1949.

————. *Ayissa Saved.* London: Joseph, 1949. (First American edition, New York: Harper & Row, 1962).

————. *Mr. Johnson.* London: Joseph, 1947.

Clapperton, H. *Journal of a Second Expedition into the Interior of Africa from the Bight of Benin to Soccatoo.* London: Murray, 1829.

Cole, Taylor, and Robert O. Tilman, eds. *The Nigerian Political Scene.* Durham: Duke University Press, 1962.

Coleman, James S. *Nigeria: Background to Nationalism.* Berkeley: University of California Press, 1958.

Cook, A. N. *British Enterprise in Nigeria.* Philadelphia: University of Pennsylvania Press, 1943.

Cowan, L. Gray. *Local Government in West Africa.* New York: Columbia University Press, 1958.

Crocker, W. R. *Nigeria—A Critique of British Colonial Administration.* London: Allen and Unwin, 1936.

Crowder, Michael. *A Short History of Nigeria.* New York: Frederick A. Praeger, 1962.

———. *The Story of Nigeria.* London: Faber and Faber, 1962.

Davies, Chief H. O. *Nigeria: Prospects for Democracy.* London: Weidenfield and Nicholson, 1961.

Davies, J. G. *The Biu Book: A Collation and Reference Book on Biu Division.* Zaria: Northern Regional Literature Agency, 1954-1956.

Denham and Clapperton. *Narrative of Travels in Northern and Central Africa.* 2 vols. London: Murray, 1826.

Dike, K. Onwuka, ed. *Eminent Nigerians of the Nineteenth Century.* Cambridge: Cambridge University Press, 1960.

Dupigny, Elliott G.M. *Gazatteer of Nupe Province.* London: Waterlow, 1920.

East, Rupert M., tr. *Akiga's Story: The Tiv Tribe as Seen by One of its Members.* London: Oxford University Press, for the International Institute of African Languages and Cultures, 1939.

———. *Stories of Old Adamawa.* Zaria: NORLA, 1935.

Edgar, F. *Hausa Folktales and Miscellany.* tr. Neil Skinner, n.p., 1965.

Egbe Omo Oduduwa. *Proposals for 1950 Constitutional Reforms.* Lagos: n.d.

Elias, T. Olawale. *Groundwork of Nigerian Law.* London: Routledge & Kegan Paul, 1954.

———. *Nigerian Land Law and Custom.* 3rd ed. rev. London: Routledge & Kegan Paul, 1962.

———. *The Nigerian Legal System.* 2nd ed. rev. London: Routledge & Kegan Paul, 1963.

Elphinstone, K. V. *Gazatteer of Ilorin Province.* London: Waterlow, 1921.

English, M. C. *An Outline of Nigerian History.* London: Longmans, Green and Company, 1959.

Epelle, Sam. *The Promise of Nigeria.* London: Pan Books Ltd., 1960.

Ezera, Kalu. *Constitutional Developments in Nigeria.* Cambridge: Cambridge University Press, 1960.

Finer, Herman. *English Local Government.* London: Methuen and Co., Ltd., 1933.

Flint, J. E. *Sir George Goldie and the Making of Nigeria.* London: Oxford University Press, 1960.

Forde, C. Daryll and others. *Peoples of the Niger-Benue Confluence.* Ethnographical Survey, West Africa, No. 10. London: International African Institute, 1955.

Fortes, M., and E. E. Evans-Pritchard, eds. *African Political Systems.* London: Oxford University Press, 1940.

Fremantle, John M. ed. *Gazatteer of Muri Province.* London: Waterlow, 1922.

Frodin, Reuben. "A Note on Nigeria." A publication of the American Universities Field Staff. West African Series, Vol. IV, No. 6, 1961.

Gall, F. B. *Gazatteer of Bauchi Province.* London: Waterlow, 1920.

Gervis, Pearce. *Of Emirs and Pagans.* London: Cassell, 1963.

Gouilly, Alphonse. *L'Islam dans l'Afrique Occidentale Française.* Paris: Editions Larose, 1952.

Gowers, Sir William F. *Gazatteer of Kano Province.* London: Waterlow, 1921.

Greenberg, Joseph H. *The Influence of Islam on a Sudanese Religion* [in Hausa country]. American Ethnological Society, Monograph No. 10. New York: J. J. Augustin, 1946.

Guillaume, Alfred. *Islam.* London: Penguin Books, 1956.

Gunn, Harold D. *Pagan Peoples of the Central Area of Northern Nigeria.* Ethnographical Survey, West Africa, No. 12. London: International African Institute, 1956.

————. *Peoples of the Plateau Area of Northern Nigeria.* Ethnographical Survey, West Africa, No. 7. London: International African Institute, 1953.

Gunn, Harold D., and F. P. Conant. *Peoples of the Middle Niger Region, Northern Nigeria.* London: International African Institute, 1960.

Hailey, Lord. *An African Survey.* London: Oxford University Press, 1937.

————. *An African Survey Revised 1956.* London: Oxford University Press, 1957.

————. *Native Administration in the British African Territories: Part III. West Africa: Nigeria, Gold Coast, Sierra Leone, Gambia.* London: H. M. Stationery Office, 1951.

————. *Native Administration and Political Development in British Tropical Africa.* London: Colonial Office, 1940.

Hazelwood, Arthur. *The Finances of Nigerian Federation.* Oxford

University Institute of Colonial Studies, Reprint Series No. 14. London: Oxford University Press, 1955.

Herman-Hodge, H. B. *Gazatteer of Ilorin Province*. London: Allen and Unwin, 1929.

Hicks, U. K. *Development from Below*. Oxford: Clarendon Press, 1961.

Hinden, Rita, ed. *Local Government and the Colonies—1947*. Report to the Fabian Colonial Bureau. London: Allen and Unwin, 1941.

Hiskett, M., tr. *Tazyin al Waraqat*, by Abdullahi. Ibadan: Ibadan University Press, 1963.

Hodgkin, Thomas. *African Political Parties*. Harmondsworth: Penguin Books, 1961.

———. *Nationalism in Colonial Africa*. London: Frederick Muller, 1956.

———. *Nigerian Perspectives, An Historical Anthology*. London: Oxford University Press, 1960.

Hogben, S. J. *The Muhammadan Emirates of Nigeria*. London: Humphrey Milford, 1929.

Hogben, S. J., and A.H.M. Kirk-Greene. *The Emirates of Northern Nigeria*. London: Oxford University Press, 1966.

Hopen, C. Edward. *The Pastoral Fulbe Family in Gwandu*. London: Oxford University Press, 1958.

Howard, C., ed. *West African Explorers*. London: Oxford University Press, 1961.

Ikejiani, Okachukwu, ed. *Nigerian Education*. Ikeja: Longmans of Nigeria, 1964.

Ikeotuonye, U.C. *Zik of New Africa*. London: P. R. Macmillan, 1961.

Imrie, J., and D. G. Lee. *Report of the West African Survey Mission on the Training of Cvil Servants in Nigeria*. Lagos: Government Printer, 1954.

Keay, E. A., and S. S. Richardson. *The Native and Customary Courts of Nigeria*. London: Sweet & Maxwell; Lagos: African Universities Press, 1966.

Kirk-Greene, A.H.M. *Adamawa: Past and Present*. London: Oxford University Press, 1958.

———. *Barth's Travels in Nigeria: Extracts from the Journal of Heinrich Barth's Travels in Nigeria, 1850-1855*. London: Oxford University Press, 1962.

———. *Maiduguri and the Capitals of Bornu*. Zaria: Gaskiya Corp., 1958.

————, ed. *The Principles of Native Administration in Nigeria, Selected Documents, 1900-1947*. London: Oxford University Press, 1965.

Levy, Reuben. *The Social Structure of Islam*. London: Cambridge University Press, 1957.

Lugard, Flora, L. S. *A Tropical Dependency*. London: J. Nisbet & Co., 1905.

Lugard, Sir Frederick. *The Dual Mandate in British Tropical Africa*. 4th ed. London: William Blackwood, 1929.

Maghili, Al (c. 1450-1504). *The Obligations of Princes*. tr. T. H. Baldwin. Beirut: n.p., 1932.

Maiden, R. L. *Historical Sketches*. Zaria: NORLA, 1955.

Meek, Charles K. *The Northern Tribes of Nigeria: An Ethnographical Account of the Northern Provinces of Nigeria, together with a Report on the 1921 Decennial Census*. 2 vols. London: Oxford University Press, H. Milford, 1925.

————. *Tribal Studies in Nigeria*. 2 vols. London: Kegan Paul, 1931.

Mellanby, Kenneth. *The Birth of Nigeria's University*. London: Methuen, 1958.

Middleton, John and David Tait. *Tribes without Rulers*. London: Routledge & Kegan Paul, 1958.

Miller, Walter R. S. *Have We Failed in Nigeria?* London: United Society for Christian Literature, 1947.

————. *Reflections of a Pioneer*. London: Church Missionary Society, 1936.

————. *Success in Nigeria? Assets and Possibilities*. London and Redhill: United Society for Christian Literature, Lutterworth Press, 1948.

————. *Walter Miller: An Autobiography, 1872-1952*. Zaria: Gaskiya Corp., 1952.

————. *Yesterday, Today, and Tomorrow in Northern Nigeria*. London: Student Christian Movement Press, 1938.

Morel, Edmund E. *Nigeria: Its People and Problems*. London: Smith Elder, 1911.

Muffett, D. J. *Concerning Brave Captains*. London: Deutsch, 1964.

Nadel, Siegfried F. *A Black Byzantium: The Kingdom of Nupe in Nigeria*. London: Oxford University Press for the International African Institute, 1942.

————. *Nupe Religion*. London: Routledge & Kegan Paul, 1954.

Na'Ibi, Malam Shuaibu and Alhaji Hassan. *The Gwari Tribe in Abuja Emirate*. Lagos: *Nigeria Magazine* special publication.

Nduka, Otonti. *Western Education and the Nigerian Cultural Background*. Ibadan: Oxford University Press, 1964.

Nigeria 1965, Crisis and Criticism. Selections from Nigerian Opinion. Ibadan: Ibadan University Press, 1966.

Niven, Cecil R. *How Nigeria is Governed*. London: Longmans, Green and Company, 1950.

————. *A Short History of Nigeria*. London: Longmans, Green and Company, 1948.

Northern Elements Progressive Union. *Sawaba Creed: Why I Join the Sawaba Crusade*. n.p.n.d.

————. *Sawaba Declaration of Principles*. Kano: n.p., 1950.

Northern Peoples' Congress. *Constitution and Rules*. Zaria: Gaskiya Corp., n.d.

————. Central Headquarters Secretariat, Kaduna. *Half-Yearly Parliamentary Reports*.

Nwabueze, B. O. *Constitutional Law of the Nigerian Republic*. London: Butterworths, 1964.

————. *The Machinery of Justice in Nigeria*. London: Butterworths, 1963.

Odumosu, Oluwole Idowu. *The Nigerian Constitution, History and Development*. London: Sweet & Maxwell, 1963.

Ojo, Chief Samuel. *Short History of Ilorin*. Shaki: n.p., 1957.

Okigbo, Pius N. *Nigerian National Accounts 1950-1957*. Enugu: Government Printer, 1962.

————. *Nigerian Public Finance*. Evanston: Northwestern University Press, 1965.

Orr, Charles William James. *The Making of Northern Nigeria*. London: Macmillan & Co., Ltd., 1911.

Palmer, Sir Herbert R. *The Bornu Sahara and Sudan*. London: Murray, 1936.

————. *The Occupation of Hausaland in 1900-1904*. Lagos: 1927.

————. *Sudanese Memoirs, Being Mainly Translations from a Number of Arabic Manuscripts Relating to the Central and Western Sudan*. 3 vols. Lagos: Government Printer, 1928.

Park, Andrew. *Sources of Nigerian Law*. London: Sweet & Maxwell, 1964.

Perham, Margery F. *Lugard Vol. I: The Years of Adventure, 1858-1898*. London: Collins, 1956.

————. *Lugard Vol. II: The Years of Authority, 1898-1945.* London: Collins, 1960.

————. *Native Administration in Nigeria* London: Oxford University Press, 1937.

————. ed. *The Economics of a Tropical Dependency.* 2 vols. London: Faber, 1946-1948.

Phillips, Claude S. *The Development of Nigerian Foreign Policy.* Evanston: Northwestern University Press, 1964.

Phillipson, Sir Sydney, and S. O. Adebo. *The Nigerianisation of the Civil Service: A Review of Policy and Machinery.* Lagos: Government Printer, 1954.

Post, Kenneth W.J. *The New States of West Africa.* Harmondsworth: Penguin Books, 1964.

————. *The Nigerian Federal Election of 1959.* London: Oxford University Press, 1963.

Prest, A. R., and I. G. Stewart. *The National Income of Nigeria, 1950-1951.* London: H.M. Stationery Office, 1953.

Richardson, Samuel, and T. H. Williams. *The Criminal Procedure Code of Northern Nigeria.* London: Sweet & Maxwell, 1963.

Robinson, Charles H. *Hausaland, or Fifteen Hundred Miles Through the Central Sudan.* London: Sampson, Low, 1896.

Rothchild, Donald. *Toward Unity in Africa: A Study of Federalism in British Africa.* Washington, D.C.: Public Affairs Press, 1960.

Royal Institute of International Affairs. *Nigeria: The Political and Economic Background.* London: Oxford University Press, 1960.

St. Croix, F. *The Fulani of Northern Nigeria.* Lagos: Government Printer, 1945.

Scarritt, James R. *Political Change in a Traditional African Clan: A Structural-Functional Analysis of the Nsit of Nigeria.* Social Science Foundation and Graduate School of International Studies. Denver: University of Denver, 1965.

Schatz, Sayre P. *Development Bank Lending in Nigeria: The Federal Loans Board.* Ibadan: Oxford University Press, 1964.

Schultze, A. *Sultanate of Bornu.* Tr. from the German with additional appendices by P.A. Benton. London: Oxford University Press, 1913.

Schwarz, Frederick A.O., Jr. *Nigeria, The Tribes, The Nation, or The Race—The Politics of Independence.* Cambridge: M.I.T. Press, 1965.

Sklar, Richard L. *Nigerian Political Parties.* Princeton: Princeton University Press, 1963.

517

Smith, Mary F. *Baba of Jaro, A Woman of the Muslim Hausa.* London: Faber, 1954.

Smith, M. G. *Government in Zazzau.* Oxford: Oxford University Press, 1960.

Smythe, Hugh H. and Mabel M. *The New Nigerian Elite.* Stanford: Stanford University Press, 1960.

Sokolski, Alan. *The Establishment of Manufacturing in Nigeria.* New York: Frederick A. Praeger, 1965.

Stapleton, G. Brian. *The Wealth of Nigeria.* London: Oxford University Press, 1958.

Stenning, Derrick J. *Field Study of Nomadic Fulani in Northern Nigeria: Interim Report.* London: International African Institute, 1953.

————. *Savannah Nomads.* London: Oxford University Press for International African Institute, 1959.

Temple, Charles L., ed. *Notes on the Tribes, Provinces, Emirates and States of the Northern Provinces of Nigeria, compiled from Official Reports of O. Temple.* Lagos: C.M.S. Bookshop, 1919.

Trimingham, J. Spencer. *History of Islam in West Africa.* London: Oxford University Press, 1962.

————. *Islam in West Africa.* Oxford: Clarendon Press, 1959.

Urvoy, Yves. *Histoire de l'Empire du Bornu.* Paris: Larose, 1949.

Warren, J. H. *The English Local Government System.* London: Allen and Unwin, Ltd., 1949.

Weiler, Hans, ed. *Education and Politics in Nigeria.* Published in German and English. Freiburg im Breisgau: Verlag Rombach, 1964.

Wheare, Joan. *The Nigerian Legislative Council.* London: Faber and Faber, Ltd. 1950.

Whitting, C.E.J., tr. *History of Sokoto by Hajji Sa'id.* Kano: Ife-Olu Printing Works, 1949.

Wilson, C. H. *Essays on Local Government.* Oxford: B. Blackwell, 1948.

Wraith, Ronald E. *Local Government.* rev. ed. London: Penguin Books, 1956.

————. *Local Government in West Africa.* London: Allen and Unwin, Ltd. 1964.

Yesufu, T. M. *An Introduction to Industrial Relations in Nigeria.* London: Oxford University Press, 1962.

II. ARTICLES: GENERAL

Abernethy, David B. *"Nigeria Creates a New Region"*, *African Report*, Vol. IX, No. 3 (March 1954).

Adebayo, Durosinlorun. "Daura, The Cradle of the Hausa Race", *Nigerian Citizen* (February 1962).

Adebo, S. O. "The Civil Service in an Independent Nigeria", *The New Nigerian: Journal of the Nigeria Society*, Vol. 1, No. 1 (August 1961).

"Administration of Urban Areas in the Northern Region of Nigeria", *Journal of African Administration*, Vol. VI (February 1954).

Allot, A. N. "Legal Problems in Northern Nigeria", *West Africa* (March 9, 1957).

————. "The Moslem Court of Appeal", *West Africa* (August 10, 1957).

Anderson, J.N.D. "Conflict of Laws in Northern Nigeria", *Journal of African Law*, Vol. I (Summer 1957).

————. "Conflict of Law in Northern Nigeria: A New Start", *International and Comparative Law Quarterly*, Vol. VIII (1959).

————. "Islam Law in Africa: Problems of Today and Tomorrow", in Anderson, ed., *Changing Law in Developing Countries*. London: Allen and Unwin, 1963.

————. "A Major Advance", *Modern Law Review*, Vol. 24, No. 5 (September 1961).

————. "The Relationship between Islamic and Customary Law in Africa", *Journal of African Administration*, Vol. XII, No. 4 (1960).

Anglin, Douglas G. "Brinkmanship in Nigeria", *International Journal*, Vol. XX, No. 2 (Spring 1965).

————. "Nigeria: Political Non-alignment and Economic Alignment", *Journal of Modern African Studies*, Vol. II, No. 2 (July 1964).

Arikpo, Okoi. "Is There a Nigerian Nation?" *West Africa Review*, Vol. 31 (February 1960).

Armstrong, Robert G. "The Idoma-Speaking Peoples", in C. D. Forde et al. *Peoples of the Niger-Benue Confluence*. London: International African Institute, 1955.

————. "The Igala", in C. D. Forde et al. *Peoples of the Niger-Benue Confluence*. London: International African Institute, 1955.

Arnett, E. J., tr. "A Hausa Chronicle" (Daura Makas Sariki), *Journal of the Royal African Society*, Vol. 9, No. 34 (January 1910).

Awa, Eme O. "The Federal Elections in Nigeria, 1959", *Ibadan*, No. 8 (March 1960).

———. "Local Government Problems in Nigeria", in H. Passin and K.A.B. Jones-Quartey, eds., *Africa: The Dynamics of Change.* Ibadan: Ibadan University Press, 1963.

———. "Roads to Socialism in Nigeria", in *Conference Proceedings of the Nigerian Institute of Social and Economic Research*, March 1962. Ibadan: N.I.S.E.R., 1963.

Azikiwe, Nnamdi. "Essentials for Nigerian Survival", *Foreign Affairs,* Vol. XLIII, No. 3 (April 1965).

———. *"Nigeria in World Politics"*, *Presence Africaine*, Vols. IV, V, Nos. 32, 33 (1960).

———. "Nigerian Political Institutions", *Journal of Negro History*, Vol. XIV (July 1929).

Baker, T. M. "Political Control among the Birom", *West African Institute of Social and Economic Research, Annual Conference, 1956.*

Balewa, Sir Abubakar Tafawa. "Nigeria Looks Ahead", *Foreign Affairs*, Vol. XLI, No. 1 (October 1962).

Bivar, A.D.H. "Arabic Documents of Northern Nigeria", *Bulletin of the School of Oriental and African Studies*, Vol. XXII, No. 2 (1959).

———. *"Wathiqat ahl al Sudan"*, *Journal of African History*, Vol. 2 (February 1961).

Bivar, A.D.H., and M. Hiskett. "The Arabic Literature of Nigeria to 1804: A provisional account", *Bulletin of the School of Oriental and African Studies*, Vol. XXV, No. 1 (1962).

Bohannan, Paul. "Extra-Processual Events in Tiv Political Institutions", *American Anthropologist*, Vol. 60, No. 1 (February 1958).

———. "The Impact of Money on an African Subsistence Economy", *Journal of Economic History*, Vol. XIX, No. 4 (1959).

———. "The Migration and Expansion of the Tiv", *Africa*, Vol. 24, No. 1 (January 1954).

———. "Some Principles of Exchange and Investment among the Tiv", *American Anthropologist*, Vol. 57, No. 1 (1955).

———. "A Tiv Political and Religious Idea", *South-West Journal of Anthropology*, Vol. 2, No. 2 (Summer 1955).

"The Bolewa of Fika", *Nigeria*, No. 51 (1956).

Bourdillon, Bernard. "Nigeria's New Constitution", *United Empire*, Vol. 37 (March-April 1946).

Bovill, E. W. "Jega Market", *African Affairs*, Vol. XXIII, Nos. 91 and 92 (1924).

————. "Muhammad El Maghili", *African Affairs*, Vol. XXXIV, No. 134 (1935).

Brett, Lionel. "Digest of Decisions on the Nigerian Constitution", *Journal of African Law*, Vol. VIII, No. 3 (Autumn 1964).

Buchanan, Keith. "The Northern Region of Nigeria: The Geographical Background of its Political Duality", *The Geographical Review*, Vol. XLIII, No. 4 (October 1953).

Bull, Mary. "Indirect Rule in Northern Nigeria, 1906-1911", in Kenneth Robinson and Frederick Madden, *Essays in Imperial Government*. Oxford: Basil Blackwell, 1963.

Bunting, Reginald. "Nigeria", in Helen Kitchen, ed., *The Educated African*. New York: Frederick A. Praeger, 1962.

Burdon, John A. "The Fulani Emirates of Northern Nigeria", *Geographical Journal*, Vol. 24 (1904).

Clifford, Miles. "A Nigerian Chiefdom. Some Notes on the Igala Tribes in Nigeria and their 'Divine King'", *Journal of the Royal Anthropological Institute*, Vol. 66 (1936).

Cohen, Ronald. "The Analysis of Conflict in Hierarchical Systems: An Example from Kanuri Political Organization", *Anthropologica* N.S., Vol. IV, No. 1 (1962).

————. "The Bornu King Lists", *Papers in African History*, Boston, 1964.

Coker, Increase. "The Nigerian Press, 1929-1959", in Ayo Ogunsheye, ed., *Report on the Press in West Africa*. Ibadan: mimeo., 1961.

Cole, C. W. "Village and District Councils in the Northern Region of Nigeria", *Journal of African Administration*, Vol. III (April 1951).

Cole, Taylor. "Bureaucracy in Transition: Independent Nigeria", *Public Administration*, Vol. 38 (Winter 1960).

————. "The Independence Constitution of Federal Nigeria", *The South Atlantic Quarterly*, Vol. LX, No. 1 (1961). *Duke University Commonwealth—Studies Reprint Series*, No. 6.

Coleman, James S. "The Emergence of African Political Parties", in C. Grove Haines, ed., *Africa Today*. Baltimore: The Johns Hopkins Press, 1955.

————. "The Foreign Policy of Nigeria", in Joseph E. Black and Kenneth W. Thompson, eds., *Foreign Policies in a World of Change*. New York: Harper & Row, 1963.

Cotter, William R. "Taxation and Federalism in Nigeria", *British Tax Review* (March-April 1964).

Coulson, N. J. "The State and the Individual in Islamic Law", *The International and Comparative Law Quarterly*, Vol. 6, Part 1 (January 1957).

Cowan, L. Gray. "Local Politics and Democracy in Nigeria", in G. M. Carter and W. O. Brown, eds., *Transition in Africa: Studies in Political Adaptation*. Boston: Boston University Press, 1958.

"Criminal Law Reform in Northern Nigeria", a symposium, *Modern Law Review*, Vol. 24, No. 5 (September 1961).

Crowder, Michael. "Islam in Northern Nigeria", *Geographical Magazine*, Vol. 31, No. 6 (October 1958).

———. "Islam on the Upper Niger", *Geographical Magazine*, Vol. 31, No. 5 (September 1958).

———. "Political Tensions in Northern Nigeria", *West Africa* (January 11, 1958).

Currie, Sir James, K.B.E. "Indirect Rule and Education in Africa", *United Empire*, Vol. 23, No. 11 (November 1932).

Daniel F. deF. "The Regalia of Katsina, Northern Provinces of Nigeria", *Journal of the African Society*, Vol. 31, No. 122 (January 1932).

———. "Shehu Dan Fodio", *Journal of the African Society*, Vol. 25, No. 99 (April 1926).

Daniels, W. C. "The Federation of Nigeria", in A. N. Allott, ed., *Judicial and Legal Systems in Africa*. London: Butterworths, 1962.

"Daura", in *Nigeria*, No. 50 (1956).

Davies, H. O. "The New African Profile", *Foreign Affairs*, Vol. XL, No. 2 (January 1962).

Dent, M. J. "Elections in Northern Nigeria", *Journal of Local Administration Overseas*, Vol. I, No. 4 (October 1962).

Diamond, S. "The Weight of the North", *Africa Today*, Vol. 10, No. 1 (1963).

Dry, D.P.L. "The Hausa Attitude Toward Authority", *West African Institute of Social and Economic Research, Annual Conference 1952*.

Dudley, B. J. "The Nomination of Parliamentary Candidates in Northern Nigeria: An Analysis of Political Change", *Journal of Commonwealth Political Studies*, Vol. II, No. 1 (November 1963).

Elias, T. O. "The New Constitution of Nigeria and the Protection of Human Rights and Fundamental Freedoms", *Journal of the International Commission of Jurists*, Vol. II (1959-60).

522

"The Emir [of Abuja] Pushes His People", *West Africa*, No. 1,751 (September 1950).

Epsie, Ian. "Decade of Decision", *Ibadan*, No. 11 (February 1961).

Fabunni, L. A. "Egypt and Africa", *West Africa* (December 28, 1957).

Fagg, Bernard. "The Nok Culture", *West African Review*, Vol. 27 (December 1956).

———. "The Nok Culture in Prehistory", *Journal of the Nigerian Historical Society* (December 1959).

Farrington, J. L. "Northern Nigeria: An Awakening Giant", *African Affairs*, Vol. 62 (1963).

Fisher, Humphrey J. "The Ahmadiyya Movement in Nigeria", in Kenneth Kirkwood, ed., *African Affairs*. Carbondale: Southern Illinois University Press, 1961.

Forde, C. Daryll. "Government in Umor: A Study of Social Change and Problems of Indirect Rule in a Nigerian Village Community", *Africa*, Vol. 12 (1939).

———. "The Nupe", in C. D. Forde et al. *Peoples of the Niger-Benue Confluence*. London: International African Institute, 1955.

Foster, Joan. "Women's Teacher Training in Northern Nigeria", *Overseas Education*, Vol. 31, No. 4 (1960).

Fremantle, John M. "A History of the Region Comprising the Katagum Division of Kano Province", *Journal of the African Society*, Vol. 10, No. 39 (April 1911), No. 40 (July 1911), Vol. 11, No. 41 (October 1911), No. 42 (January 1912).

"From Maiduguri to Lake Chad", *Nigeria*, No. 79 (1963).

Greenberg, Joseph H. "Islam and Clan Organization among the Hausa", *Southwest Journal of Anthropology*, Vol. 3, No. 3 (Autumn, 1947).

———. "Some Aspects of Negro-Mohammedan Culture-Contact among the Hausa", *American Anthropologist*, Vol. 43, No. 1 (1941).

Grove, David L. "The 'Sentinels' of Liberty? The Nigerian Judiciary and Fundamental Rights", *Journal of African Law*, Vol. 7 (1963).

Hallett, R. "El Kanemi of Bornu", in K. O. Dike, ed. *Eminent Nigerians*. Cambridge: Cambridge University Press, 1960.

———. "Umaru and Ibrahim Ngwamatse", in K. O. Dike, ed., *Eminent Nigerians*. Cambridge: Cambridge University Press, 1960.

Harris, Richard. "Nigeria: Crisis and Compromise", *African Report*, Vol. 10, No. 3 (March 1965).

Helleinner, Gerald K. "Nigeria and the African Common Market", *The Nigerian Journal of Economic and Social Studies*, Vol. 4, No. 3 (November 1962).

Hiskett, M. "*Kitab-al-Farq*: A work on the Habe kingdoms attributed to 'Uthman dan Fodio' ", *Bulletin of the School of Oriental and African Studies*, Vol. 23, Part 3 (1960).

——. "Material Relating to the State of Learning Among the Fulani Before Their Jihad", *Bulletin of the School of Oriental and African Studies*, Vol. 19 (1957).

Hodgkin, Thomas. "Background to Nigerian Nationalism", *West Africa* (August 4-October 20, 1951).

——. "Disraeli on Northern Nigeria", *West Africa* (May 9, 1953).

——. "Islam, History, and Politics", *Journal of Modern African Studies*, Vol. 1, No. 1 (March 1963).

——. "Muslims South of the Sahara", *Current History*, Vol. 32, No. 190 (June 1957).

——. "Political Parties in British and French West Africa", *Information Digest, Africa Bureau*, No. 10 (August 1953).

——. "Uthman Dan Fodio", in *Nigeria 1960*, the Special Independence Issue of *Nigeria*. Lagos: Federal Ministry of Information Printing Division, 1960.

Holland, D. C. "Human Rights in Nigeria", *Current Legal Problems*, Vol. 15 (1962).

Howell, D. R. "The Status of Teachers in Nigeria", *Overseas Education*, Vol. 30, No. 3 (1958).

"Ilorin", in *Nigeria*, No. 49 (1956).

"In the Footsteps of the Shehu", in *Nigeria*, No. 78 (1963).

Jack, Homer A. "Mallam Aminu Kano—A Profile", *Africa Today*, Vol. 6 (September 1959).

Jeffries, W. F. "The Literacy Campaign in Northern Nigeria", *Fundamental and Adult Education*, Vol. 10 (1958).

Jelf, H. G. "The Northerner Goes to the Polls", *Corona*, Vol. 5, Nos. 5, 6, 7 (May-July 1953).

"Jibiya: A Border Market", in *Nigeria*, No. 60 (1959).

Kaplan, Philip J. "Fundamental Rights in the Federation of Nigeria", *Syracuse Law Review*, Vol. 13 (1962).

"Katsina", in *Nigeria*, No. 51 (1956).

Kingsley, J. Donald, "Bureaucracy and Political Development with Particular Reference to Nigeria", in Joseph La Palombara, ed., *Bureaucracy and Political Development*. Princeton: Princeton University Press, 1963.

524

Kirk-Greene, A.H.M. "The Battles of Bida", *West African Review*, Vol. 27 (January 1956).

———. "Bureaucratic Cadres in a Traditional Milieu", in James S. Coleman, ed., *Education and Political Development*. Princeton: Princeton University Press, 1965.

———. "A Redefinition of Provincial Administration: The Northern Nigerian Approach", *Journal of Local Administration Overseas*, Vol. 4 (January 1965).

———. "The Residencies of Northern Nigeria", *West African Review*, Vol. 33 (1962).

———. "Tax and Travel among the Hill-tribes of Northern Adamawa", *Africa*, Vol. 26, No. 4 (October 1956).

———. "A Training Course for Northern Nigerian Administrative Officers", *Journal of African Administration*, Vol. 2 (1959).

"Legal and Judicial Reform in the Northern Region", *West Africa* (September 24, 1960).

Lloyd, Peter C. "The Changing Role of the Yoruba Traditional Rulers", *Proceedings of the Third Annual Conference of the West African Institute of Social and Economic Research*. Ibadan: University College, 1956.

———. "Lugard and Indirect Rule", *Ibadan*, No. 10 (November 1960).

———. "Some Comments on the Election in Nigeria", *Journal of African Administration*, Vol. 4 (July 1952).

———. "The Traditional Political System of the Yoruba", *Southwestern Journal of Anthropology*, Vol. 10 (Winter 1954).

MacInnes, Colin. "Welcome, Beauty Walk", *Encounter*, Vol. 15 (October 1960).

Mackintosh, John P. "Electoral Trends and the Tendency to a One-Party System", *The Service*, Vol. 2, Nos. 81-83 (April 7-21, 1962).

———. "Federalism in Nigeria", *Political Studies*, Vol. 10, No. 3 (October 1962).

———. "Nigeria's External Relations", *Journal of Commonwealth Political Studies*, Vol. 2, No. 3 (November 1964).

———. "The Nigerian Federal Parliament", *Public Law* (Autumn 1963).

Mahood, M. M. "Joyce Cary in Borgu", *Ibadan* (June 1960).

Mair, Lucy P. "Representative Local Government as a Problem in Social Change", *Journal of African Administration*, Vol. 8, No. 1 (January 1958).

————. "Some Social Implications of Economic Change in Nigeria", *Nigerian Journal of Economic and Social Studies*, Vol. 1 (1959).

Marty, Paul L. "L'Islam et les Tribus dans la Colonie du Niger", (ex-Zinger), *Revue des Etudes Islamiques*, Vol. 4 (1930).

McStallworth, P. "Nigerianization at Dawn: The Federal Civil Service", *Journal of Negro History*, Vol. 46 (1961).

Mercier, Paul. "Historie et legende: la tataille d'Illorin", *Institut français d'Afrique noire*, Vol. 47 (Juillet 1950).

Miner, H. "Culture Change under Pressure: A Hausa Case", *Human Organization*, Vol. 19 (1960).

Mott, William P. "Nigeria's Experience in Internal Financing of Development Plans", in Warren H. Hausman, ed., *Managing Economic Development in Africa*. Cambridge: M.I.T. Press, 1963.

Nadel, Siegfried F. "The Kede: A Riverain State in Northern Nigeria", in M. Fortes et al., *African Political Systems*. London: Oxford University Press, 1940.

"Native Courts and Native Customary Law in Africa: Judicial Advisors' Conference", Supplement to *Journal of African Administration*, Vol. 5 (October 1953).

Nicholas, W. B. "Progress of a District Council in Northern Nigeria", *Journal of African Administration*, Vol. 5 (January 1953).

Niven, C. R. "Elections in Northern Nigeria", *Corona*, Vol. 4 (May 1952).

————. "Nigerian Pilgrimage to Mecca", *Corona*, Vol. 2 (November 1950).

"The Nupe of Pategi", in *Nigeria*, No. 50 (1956).

Obayan, E. O. "The Machinery of Planning in the Federation of Nigeria", *Nigerian Journal of Economic and Social Studies*, Vol. 4, No. 3 (November 1964).

Odumosu, Olu. "The Northern Nigerian Codes", *Modern Law Review*, Vol. 24, No. 5 (September 1961).

Ogunsheye, Ayo. "Nigeria", in James S. Coleman, ed., *Education and Political Development*. Princeton: Princeton University Press, 1965.

Ogunsheye, Ayo. "Nigeria's Political Prospects", *Ibadan*, No. 11 (February 1961).

————. "Societe traditionelle et democratie", *Presence Africaine*, Vol. 23 (December 1958-January 1959).

Oloko, Tunde. "Religion and Politics in Nigeria", *West Africa* (February 2, 9, 1957).

Onitri, H.M.A. "Nigeria's International Economic Relations: A Survey", *Nigerian Journal of Economic and Social Studies*, Vol. 3, No. 1 (November 1961).

Palmer, Herbert R. "An Early Fulani Conception of Islam", *Journal of the African Society*, Vols. 13 (1913-14) and 14 (1914-15).

————. "History of Katsina", *Journal of the African Society*, Vol. 26, No. 103 (1927).

————, tr. "The Kano Chronicle", *Journal of the Royal Anthropological Institute*, Vol. 38 (1908).

————. "A Muslim Divine of the Sudan in the Fifteenth Century", *Africa*, Vol. 3, No. 2 (April 1930).

"The Pategi Regatta", *Nigeria*. No. 52 (1956).

Perham, Margery. "Some Problems of Indirect Rule in Africa", *Journal of the Royal African Society*.

Perry, Ruth. "New Sources for Research in Nigerian History", *Africa*, Vol. 25, No. 4 (October 1955).

Phillips, Claude S. "Nigeria and Pan-Africanism", *Ibadan*, No. 10 (October 1962).

Post, Kenneth W. J. "The Federal Election: An Outside View", *Ibadan*, No. 8 (March 1960).

————. "Forming a Government in Nigeria", *Nigerian Journal of Economic and Social Studies*, Vol. 2, No. 1 (June 1960).

————. "Nigeria Two Years after Independence", *World Today*, Vol. 18, No. 11 (November 1962) and No. 12 (December 1962).

————. "Nigerian Election Afterthoughts", *West Africa* (July 23, 1960).

"Preserving Nigeria's Heritage: New Nigerian Museum of Antiquities at Lagos", *West African Review*, Vol. 28, No. 355 (April 1957).

Pribytkovsky, L., and L. Fridman. "The Choice Before Nigeria", *International Affairs* (Moscow), Vol. 9, No. 2 (1963).

Price, Justin H. "Islam in West Africa", *Times Colonial Review*, Vol. 9 (September 1956).

————. "Retrograde Legislation in Northern Nigeria?" *Modern Law Review*, Vol. 24, No. 5 (September 1961).

"A Review of the State of Development of the Native Authority System in the Northern Region of Nigeria on the First of January, 1955", *Journal of African Administration*, Vol. 7 (April 1955).

Richardson, S. S. "Training for Penal Reform in Northern Nigeria", *Journal of African Administration*, Vol. 13, No. 1 (1961).

Robinson, R. E. "Why 'Indirect Rule' Has Been Replaced by 'Local Government' in the Nomenclature of British Native Administration", *Journal of African Administration*, Vol. 2 (April 1950).

Rogers, A. A. "A Study of Race Attitudes in Nigeria", *Rhodes-Livingstone Journal*, No. 26 (December 1959).

Rothchild, Donald, "Safeguarding Nigeria's Minorities", *Duquesne Review*, Vol. 8, No. 2 (Spring 1963).

Salihu, Bajoga. "The History of Bornu", *Nigerian Citizen* (April 1963).

"Sallah at Ilorin", in *Nigeria*, No. 70 (1961).

Schachter, Ruth. "Single Party Systems in West Africa", *American Political Science Review*, Vol. 55, No. 3 (June 1961).

Schatz, Sayre P. "The Influence of Planning on Development: the Nigerian Experience", *Social Research*, Vol. 27 (Winter 1960).

———. "Nigeria's First National Development Plan (1962-1968), An Appraisal", *Nigerian Journal of Economic and Social Studies*, Vol. 5, No. 2 (July 1963).

Shehu, Zanna Ibrahim. "Meet Alhaji Abubakar Imam, One of the Architects of the Richards Constitution", *Nigerian Citizen* (June 27 and July 1, 1959).

Sklar, Richard L. "Contradictions in the Nigerian Political System", *Journal of Modern African Studies*, Vol. 3, No. 2 (1965).

Sklar, Richard L., and C. S. Whitaker, Jr. "The Federal Republic of Nigeria", in Gwendolen M. Carter, ed., *National Unity and Regionalism in Eight African States*. Ithaca: Cornell University Press, 1966.

———. "Nigeria", in J. S. Coleman and C. G. Rosberg, eds., *Political Parties and National Integration in Tropical Africa*. Berkeley: University of California Press, 1964.

Smith, H.F.C. "The Dynastic Chronology of Fulani Zaria", *Journal of Nigerian Historical Society* (December 1961).

———. "A Fragment of 18th-Century Katsina", *Bulletin of the Nigerian Historical Society*, Vol. 5, No. 4.

———. "A Further Adventure in the Chronology of Katsina", *Bulletin of the Nigerian Historical Society*, Vol. 6, No. 1.

———. "Muhammadu Bello, Amir Al-Mu'minin", *Ibadan*, No. 8 (June 1960).

———. "A Neglected Theme of West African History: The Islamic Revolutions of the Nineteenth Century", *Journal of the Historical Society of Nigeria*, Vol. 2, No. 2 (December 1961).

Smith, H.F.C. "Usmanu dan Fodio", in K. O. Dike, ed., *Eminent Nigerians*. Cambridge: Cambridge University Press, 1960.

Smith, M. G. "The Hausa System of Social Status", *Africa*, Vol. 29, No. 3 (July 1959).

————. "The Beginnings of Hausa Society: A.D. 1000-1500", in J. Vansina et al., eds., *The Historian in Tropical Africa*. London: Oxford University Press, published for the International African Institute, 1964.

————. "Historical and Cultural Conditions of Corruption among the Hausa", *Comparative Studies in Society and History*, Vol. 6, No. 2 (January 1964).

————. "Kagoro Political Development", *Human Organization*, Vol. 19, No. 3 (Fall 1960).

————. "Kebbi and Hausa Stratification", *British Journal of Sociology*, Vol. 12, No. 1 (March 1961).

————. "Secondary Marriage in Northern Nigeria," *Africa*, Vol. 23, No. 4 (1953).

————. "Slavery and Emancipation in Two Societies (Jamaica and Zaria)", *Social and Economic Studies*, Vol. 3, No. 4 (1954).

————. "The Social Functions and Meaning of Hausa Praise-Singing", *Africa*, Vol. 27, No. 1 (January 1957).

Smythe, H. H. "Human Relations in Nigeria: The Young Elite", *Journal of Human Relations*, Vol. 6, No. 2 (1958).

————. "Nigeria's Marginal Men", *Phylon*, Vol. 19 (1958).

————. "Problem of National Leadership in Nigeria", *Social Research*, Vol. 25 (1958).

————. "Social Stratification in Nigeria", *Social Forces*, Vol. 37 (1958-59).

"Some Problems of Girls' Education in Northern Nigeria", an interview with Miss F. I. Congleton, *Overseas Education*, Vol. 30 (July 1958).

Song, Malam Muhammadu. "Nigerian Local Government in Transition", *Journal of African Administration*, Vol. 12, No. 2 (1960).

Stenning, D. J. "Transhumance, Migratory Drift, and Migration: Patterns of Pastoral Fulani Nomadism", *Journal of the Royal Anthropological Institute*, Vol. 87, Part I (1957).

Stewart, Ian G. "Nigeria's Economic Prospects", *The Three Banks Review*, No. 49 (March 1961).

"Strong Man of the North", *West Africa* (January 3, 1953).

"A Survey of the Development of Local Government in African Territories since 1947", *Journal of African Administration*, Vol. 4 (January and October 1952).

"Symposium on the New Nigerian Development Plan", *Nigerian Journal of Economic and Social Studies*, Vol. 4, No. 2 (July 1962).

Temple, Charles L. "Northern Nigeria", *Geographical Journal*, Vol. 40 (1912).

"Translation of Arabic Letter from Sultan of Sokoto to Colonel T.L.N. Morland", in H. F. Backwell, ed. tr., *The Occupation of Hausaland*. Lagos: Government Printer, 1927.

Tremearne, Arthur J. N. "Notes on the Origin of the Hausas", *Journal of the Royal Society of Arts*, No. 58 (1910).

————. "Notes on Some Nigerian Tribal Marks", *Journal of the Royal Anthropological Institute*, Vol. 41 (1911).

"Tribal Rivalries within Islam", *The Times of London*, June 4, 1958.

Tugiyele, E. A. "Local Government in Nigeria: Some Suggestions for Solving Some Problems of Structure and Finance", *Journal of Local Administration Overseas*, Vol. 1 (October 1962).

"Ubiquitous Hausa Traders", *Times British Colonies Review, The Times*, No. 24 (1956).

United Kingdom, Colonial Office, African Studies Branch. "A Survey of the Development of Local Government in the African Territories since 1947", *Journal of African Administration*, Vol. 4, No. 4 (October 1952).

Varma, S. N. "National Unity and Political Stability in Nigeria", *International Studies*, Vol. 4 (1963).

Wachuku, J. "Nigeria's Foreign Policy", *University of Toronto Quarterly*, Vol. 31 (1961).

Wallace, J. G. "The Tiv System of Election", *Journal of African Administration*, Vol. 10 (April 1958).

Westermann, Diedrich H. "Some Notes on the Hausa People and their Language", in G. P. Barbery, *A Hausa-English Dictionary and English-Hausa Vocabulary*. London: Oxford University Press, H. Milford, 1934.

Whitaker, C. S., Jr. "Three Perspectives on Hierarchy: Political Thought and Leadership in Northern Nigeria", *Journal of Commonwealth Political Studies*, Vol. 3, No. 1 (March 1965).

Whitting, C.E.J. "Extracts from an Arabic History of Sokoto (by Hajji Sa'id)", *African Affairs*, Vol. 47, No. 188 (July 1948).

————. "The Unprinted Indigenous Arabic Literature of Northern Nigeria", *Journal of the Royal Asiatic Society*.

Wraith, R. E. "Local Government Democracy: 1. Intention and Achievement. 2. Councils without Clothes", *West Africa* (September 3, 10, 1955).

Yeld, E. R. "Islam and Social Stratification in Northern Nigeria", *British Journal of Sociology*, Vol. 11, No. 2 (June 1960).

Yesufu, T. M. "Nigerian Manpower Problems: A Preliminary Assessment", *Nigerian Journal of Economic and Social Studies*, Vol. 4, No. 3 (November 1962).

III. OFFICIAL PUBLICATIONS, NORTHERN NIGERIA REGIONAL GOVERNMENT

Ahmadu, Sardauna. *Local Government Development in the Northern Region*. Zaria, 1953.

Annual Report of the Northern Region Co-operative Department 1957-1958. Kaduna, 1959.

Cole, C. W. *Duties of the Administrative Officer in Northern Nigeria*. Kaduna, 1952.

————. *Report on Land Tenure in the Niger Province of Nigeria*. Kaduna, 1949.

————. *Report on Land Tenure in the Varia Province of Nigeria*. Kaduna, 1949.

Committee on the Future Administration of Urban Areas. *Report*. Kaduna, 1953.

Committee on Higher Moslem Education. *Report*. Kaduna, 1953.

Committee to Investigate the Movement of Locally Grown Foodstuffs. *Movement of Local Foodstuffs*. Kaduna, 1958.

Davies, J. G. *The Eiu Book: A Collation and Reference Book on Biu Division*. Zaria, 1954-1956.

Grove, A. T. *Land and Population in Katsina Province*. Kaduna, 1957.

Heath, Frank, tr. *A Chronicle of Abuja*. Tr. and arranged from the Hausa of Malam Hassan, Sarkin Ruwa, Abuja, and Malam Shuaibu, Mukaddamin Makarantar, Bida. Ibadan, for Abuja Native Administration, 1952.

Hudson, R. S. *Commission Appointed to Advise the Government on Devolution of Powers to Provinces. Provincial Authorities. Report by the Commissioner*. Kaduna, 1957.

Kingsley, J. Donald and Sir Arthur Rucker. *Staffing and Development of the Public Service of Northern Nigeria*. Kaduna, 1961.

Kirk-Greene, A.H.M. *How Northern Nigeria Trained its Administrative Officers*. Kaduna, 1960.

Maddocks, K. P., and D. A. Pott. *Report on Local Government in the Northern Provinces of Nigeria*. Kaduna, 1951.

Northern Nigeria's Day of History: Speeches Made by H. E. The Governor, Sir Gawain W. Bell and the Hon. Premier Alhaji Sir Ahmadu Bello, on Sunday, 15th March, 1959. Kaduna, 1959.

Northern Provinces Advisory Council. Record of proceedings at full meetings with emirs and chiefs. Kaduna.

Northern Region of Nigeria. *Annual Report of the Ministry of Works, 1958–59*. Kaduna, 1959.

———. *Annual Reports of the Northern Region Development Corporation, 1956-59*.

———. Audit Department. *Report of the Director of Audit on the Accounts of the Government of the Northern Region of Nigeria*. Kaduna, annual.

———. Civil Secretary. *Implementation Report of the Government of the Northern Region on the Report of the Commission on Public Services in the Federation of Nigeria, 1954-55*. Kaduna, 1955.

———. *Colonial Reports*, 1901, 1903, 1907-1908. London.

———. Co-operative Department. *Report on the Progress of Co-operation in the Northern Region of Nigeria*. Kaduna, annual from 1951-52.

———. Development Board. *Report*. Kaduna, annual from 1949-50.

———. Education Department. Adult Education Branch. *Adult Literacy Campaign, Northern Region, Handbook for 1952*. Zaria, 1952.

———. Education Department. *Educational Problems and Progress in 1952 in the Northern Region of Nigeria*. Kaduna, 1953.

———. Education Department. *Religious and Moral Instruction in the Training Centres and Schools of the Northern Region*. Kaduna, 1954.

———. Education Department. *Report*. Kaduna, annual from 1950-51.

———. *Educational Development*. Kaduna, 1961.

———. Ilorin Native Authority Central Office. "Constitution of Ilorin Native Authority Council." Typewritten.

———. Information Services. *Festival of Kano, 1959*. London, 1959.

———. Information Services. *The Institute of Administration—Zaria. Origin, Organization, Achievement, Potential*. Kaduna, 1958.

———. *Kano Native Authority Rules and Orders*. 1949.

———. *Law Reports of the Northern Region of the Federation of Nigeria*. 1956, 1957, 1958, 1959.

———. Legislature. *House of Assembly Debates*. 1952-1960.

532

————. Legislature. *House of Chiefs Debates.* 1952-1960.

————. Marketing Board. *The Regional Marketing Board: Bringing Prosperity to the North.* Kaduna, n.d.

————. Marketing Board. *Report.* Kano, annual.

————. Ministry of Education. *Citizens of the North.* Part II. Kaduna, n.d.

————. Ministry of Finance. "Northern Region Works Registration Board. Register of Northern Region Contractors, N. F. 2130B." (mimeo.)

————. Ministry for Local Government. *Magilisarku.* No. 5, 1958.

————. Ministry for Local Government and Community Development. *Local Government in the Northern Region.* Kaduna, 1953.

————. *Native Administration Estimates, Zaria Province.* 1949-50, 1950-51.

————. *Native Authority Law of 1954.* Kaduna, 1954.

————. *Native Authority Law of 1963, Revised Edition.* Kaduna, 1965.

————. *The Northern House of Assembly (Elected Members) Electoral Regulations, 1956.* N.R.L.N. 249 of 1956.

————. *Northern Region Native Authority.* Kaduna, 1954.

————. *Northern Region of Nigeria Provincial Annual Reports.* 1951-63. Kaduna.

————. *Northern Regional Legislature Who's Who, 1957.* Kaduna, 1957.

————. *Notes on District Council Funds.* Kaduna, 1955.

————. *Policy for Development, 1955-56.* Kaduna, 1955.

————. *Preliminary Statement of the Government of the Northern Region of Nigeria on the Report of the Commissioner Appointed to Advise the Government on the Devolution of Powers to the Provinces.* 1957.

————. Production Development Board. *Report.* Kaduna, annual from 1949-50.

————. *Progress Report on the Development Finance Programme of the Northern Region 1955-60, up to 31st March, 1959.* Kaduna, 1959.

————. *Proposal for Self-Government of the Northern Region of Nigeria.* Kaduna, 1958.

————. Public Relations Office. "Training for Local Government in Northern Nigeria", *Journal of African Administration,* Vol. 5 (April 1954).

————. Public Service Commission. *Report.* Kaduna, annual.

————. *Recent Trends and Possible Future Developments in the Field of Local Government in the Northern Region of Nigeria.* Published by Authority. Kaduna, 1952.

————. *Referendum on the Constitution to Provincial Conferences and Subsidiary Meetings.* 1953.

————. Regional Council. *House of Assembly Debates.* 1947-51.

————. Regional Council. *House of Chiefs Debates.* 1947-51.

————. Registrar of Co-operative Societies, *Report on the Progress of Co-operation.* Kaduna, annual from 1951-52.

————. *Report of the Committee on the Future Administration of Urban Areas.* Kaduna, 1953.

————. *Report on the Exchange of Customary Presents.* Kaduna, 1954.

————. *Report on the Kano Disturbances, 16th, 17th, 18th and 19th May 1953.* Kaduna, 1953.

————. Secretariat. *Duties of a District Head to His District and Its People.* Zaria, 1952.

————. Secretariat. *Financial Memoranda for Use in Native Treasuries.* Kaduna, 1951.

————. Secretariat. *Memorandum: Delegation of Financial Responsibility by Native Authorities to District Councils; Allocation of Funds and Budgetary Procedure.* Zaria, 1951.

————. *Social and Economic Progress in the Northern Region of Nigeria.* Zaria, 1957.

————. *Staff List.* Kaduna, irregular from 1955.

————. *Statement of Government Activities in the Northern Region Presented by the Governor to the Budget Meeting of the Northern Regional Legislature in 1957.* Kaduna, 1957.

————. *Statement by the Government . . . on the Reorganization of the Legal and Judicial Systems of the Northern Region.* December 1958.

————. "Statement of the Government of the Northern Region on the Report of the Committee of Inquiry appointed to Investigate Allegations about Ilorin N.A." Kaduna, 1958.

————. *Statement by the Premier on the Region's Need for Overseas Capital.* Kaduna, 1956.

————. *Statement of Policy on the Development Finance Program, 1955-60.*

————. Treasury. *Native Administration Estimates.* Kaduna, annually 1947-1959.

Pott, D.A. *Progress Report on Local Government in the Northern Region of Nigeria*. Kaduna, 1953.

Prothero, R. M. *Migrant Labour from Sokoto Province, Northern Nigeria*. Kaduna, 1958.

Report of the Resident: Sokoto Provincial Conference on Review of the Constitution, August 3-4, 1949.

Rowling, Cecil W. *Report on Land Tenure, Kano Province*. Kaduna, 1949.

————. *Report on Land Tenure, Plateau Province*. Kaduna, 1949.

Second Annual Report of the Northern Region Development Corporation. Kaduna, 1956.

Sharwood-Smith, Sir Bryan. Address to the Budget Meeting of the Northern Regional Legislature. Kaduna, 1953.

————. Address to the Northern House of Assembly, March 2, 1955. Kaduna.

————. Address to the Northern House of Assembly, December 12, 1956. Kaduna.

————. Address to the Northern House of Assembly, February 20, 1957. Kaduna.

————. Address to the Northern House of Chiefs, February 8, 1954. Kaduna.

————. Address to the Northern House of Chiefs, February 27, 1954. Kaduna.

————. Address to the Northern House of Chiefs, December 17, 1956. Kaduna.

————. *Sokoto Survey*. Zaria, 1948.

————. Statement of Government Activities in the Northern Region to the Budget Meeting of the Northern Regional Legislature. Kaduna, annual, 1954-59.

Statement by the Government of Northern Region of Nigeria on Additional Adjustments to the Legal and Judicial Systems of Northern Nigeria. Kaduna, 1962.

White Paper on Judicial and Legal Reform in Northern Nigeria. Kaduna, 1958.

White, Stanhope. *Report of the Department of Commerce and Industries; Its Role in the Northern Region and Suggested Projects for Operation Therein by the Department*. Kaduna, 1951.

Williams, D. H. *A Short Survey of Education in Northern Nigeria*. Kaduna, 1959.

Yakin Jahilci Committee [on Education]. *Report*. Kaduna, 1953.

IV. Official Publications,
British and Nigerian Governments

Administrative and Financial Procedure under the New Constitution: Financial Relations between the Government of Nigeria and the Native Administrations. Lagos, 1947.

Advisory Committee on Education in the Colonies. *Education for Citizenship in Africa.* London, 1948.

Annual Abstract of Statistics. Lagos.

Archer, J. N. *Educational Development in Nigeria: 1961–70.* Lagos, 1961.

Arikpo, Okoi. "Who Are the Nigerians." Lagos, 1957.

Ashby, Sir Eric et al. *Investment in Education. The Report of the Commission on Post-School Certificate and Higher Education in Nigeria.* Lagos, 1960.

Blackwell, H. F., ed. *The Occupation of Hausaland 1900-04, Being a Translation of Arabic Letters Found in a House of the Wazir of Sokoto, Bohari, in 1903.* Lagos, 1927.

Bourdillon Bernard. *A Further Memorandum on the Future Political Development of Nigeria.* Lagos, 1942.

————. *Memorandum on the Future Political Development of Nigeria.* Lagos, 1939.

Brooke, Mr. Justice. *Report of the Native Courts (Northern Provinces) Commission of Enquiry.* House of Representatives Sessional Paper No. 1 of 1952. Lagos, 1952.

Clifford, Sir Hugh (governor, 1919-1925). *Address to the Nigerian Council* [last meeting], February 26, 1923.

Dawn of Africa: Nigeria and African Unity. Apapa, n.d.

de St. Croix, F.W. *The Fulani of Northern Nigeria.* Lagos, 1944.

Department of Education Statistics, 1960. Lagos, 1960.

Development of Local Government in the Colonies. London, 1956.

Federal Electoral Commission. *Report on the Nigeria Federal Elections, December, 1959.* Lagos, 1960.

Federation of Nigeria Official Gazette. Lagos.

Gana, Abba M. *Our Land and People, Part 2—The North.* Crownbird Series No. 32. Lagos.

General Report and Survey on the Nigeria Police Force for the Year 1958. Lagos, 1959.

Guide to the Parliament of the Federation. Lagos, n.d.

The Integration of Departments with Ministries. Lagos, 1959.

International Bank for Reconstruction and Development. *The Economic Development of Nigeria; Report of a Mission Organized by the International Bank for Reconstruction and Development at the Request of the Governments of Nigeria and the United Kingdom.* Lagos, 1954. Baltimore: The Johns Hopkins Press, 1955.

Lugard, Sir Frederick J. D. [Governor-General of Nigeria, 1914-1919]. *Nigeria. Report on the Amalgamation of Northern and Southern Nigeria, and Administration, 1912-1919.* London, 1920.

————. *Northern Nigeria. Memorandum on the Taxation of Natives in Northern Nigeria.* London, 1907.

————. *Political Memoranda.* Lagos, 1910 and 1918. London, 1919.

————. *Revision of Instructions to Political Officers on Subjects Chiefly Political and Administrative 1913-1918.* London, 1919.

Mbanefo Commission. *Review of Salaries and Wages.* Lagos, 1959.

Nigeria. *Annual Report of the Northern Province.* 1900-1957. Lagos.

————. *Apportionment of Duties Between the Government of Nigeria and the Native Administrations.* Lagos, 1947.

Federal Republic of Nigeria. *The Constitution of the Federal Republic of Nigeria.* Lagos, 1963. This contains the Constitution of the Federation and the Constitutions of Northern, Eastern, and Western Nigeria. The Constitution of Midwestern Nigeria is published in the *Supplement* to the *Official Gazette Extraordinary*, No. 99, Vol. 50, December 16, 1963—Part C.

The Nigeria (Constitution) Order-in-Council, 1954-58. Supplement to *Official Gazette*, No. 4, Vol. 46, January 15, 1959.

The Nigeria (Constitution) Order-in-Council, 1960. S.I. No. 1,652. Published in the *Supplement* to the *Official Gazette Extraordinary*, No. 62, Vol. 47, September 30, 1960—Part B. This contains the Constitution of the Federation of Nigeria and the Constitutions of the Northern, Western, and Eastern Regions.

Nigeria Constitutional Discussions Held in London, May 1960. London, 1960. Cmnd. 1063.

Nigeria. *The Debates on Self-Government in the Federal House of Representatives on the Twenty-Sixth March, 1957, as Recorded in the Official Report.* Lagos. n.d.

————. "Decision of His Excellency the Governor on the Claim for a Revision of the Inter-Regional Boundary between the Northern and Western Regions," *Nigeria Gazette Extraordinary*, Vol. XXXIX (September 3, 1952).

Government of the Federation of Nigeria. Department of Commerce and Industries. *Handbook of Commerce and Industry in Nigeria.* Lagos, 1957.

———. "Dispatches from the Secretary of State for the Colonies, Dated 15th July, 1950, 10th April, 1951, and 30th June, 1951 and from the Governor of Nigeria Dated 15th May, 1951 on the Proposals for Constitutional Reform in Nigeria", *Nigeria Gazette Extraordinary*, Vol. 38 (July 1951).

Federation of Nigeria. *The Economic Program of Development of the Federation of Nigeria, 1955-60.* Sessional Paper No. 2 of 1956.

Government of Nigeria. *Estimates of the Government of the Federation of Nigeria for 1961-62.* Lagos.

Government of the Federation of Nigeria. Federal Information Service. *Who's Who of the Federal House of Representatives.* Lagos, 1958.

Federation of Nigeria. *Final Report of the Parliamentary Committee on the Nigerianisation of the Federal Public Service.* Lagos, 1959.

———. *Fundamental Human Rights and Rights of Appeal.* Federal Gazette No. 46 of October 27, 1959. Legal Notice 228 of 1959.

Government of Nigeria. *House of Representatives Debates, 1952-1954.*

Government of Nigeria. *Legislative Council of Nigeria Debates, 1924-1951.*

Federation of Nigeria. *Matters Arising from Final Report of the Parliamentary Committee on the Nigerianisation of the Federal Public Service. Statement of Policy by the Government of the Federation.* Sessional Paper No. 2 of 1960. Lagos, 1960.

Government of Nigeria. Ministry of Information. *100 Facts about Nigeria.* Lagos, N.D.

Federation of Nigeria. *National Development Plan, 1962-1968.* Lagos, 1962.

Government of the Federation of Nigeria. National Economic Council. *Economic Survey of Nigeria, 1959.* Lagos, 1959.

———. *The Nigeria Handbook.* London, 1953.

———. *Population Census of the Northern Region of Nigeria, 1952.* Lagos: Census Superintendent, Bulletins 1-13, 1952-1953.

Government of Nigeria. *Proceedings of the General Conference on Review of the Constitution, January, 1950.* Lagos, 1950.

Government of Nigeria. *Progress Report on the Economic Programme, 1955–60.* 1st-3rd Reports. Lagos, 1957-1960.

Federation of Nigeria. *Proposals for the Constitution of the Federal Republic of Nigeria.* Sessional Paper No. 3, 1963. Lagos, 1963.

Government of the Federation of Nigeria. *Report by the Ad-Hoc Meeting of the Nigeria Constitutional Conference Held in Lagos in February 1958.* Lagos, 1958.

Federation of Nigeria. *Report of the Commission on the Public Services of the Governments in the Federation of Nigeria, 1954-55.* Lagos, 1955.

Government of the Federation of Nigeria. *Report of the Constituency Delimitation Commission, 1958.* Lagos, 1958.

Nigeria: Report of the Fiscal Commission. London, 1958.

Government of the Federation of Nigeria. *Report of the Resumed Nigeria Constitutional Conference Held in London in September and October, 1958.* Lagos, 1958.

Federation of Nigeria. *The Role of the Federal Government in Promoting Industrial Development in Nigeria.* Sessional Paper No. 3 of 1958.

Federation of Nigeria. *Views of the Government of the Federation on the Interim Report of the Committee on Nigerianisation.* Sessional Paper No. 7 of 1958. Lagos, 1958.

Nigeria Trade Journal. Lagos, 1953 forward.

Nigeria 1960. The special Independence Issue of *Nigeria.* Lagos, October 1960.

Niven, C. R. *Our Emirates.* Crownbird Series No. 36. Lagos.

Palmer, Herbert R. *Gazeteer of Bornu Province.* Lagos, 1929.

———, tr. *History of the First Twelve Years of the Reign of Mai Idris Alooma of Bornu (1571-1583) by His Imam, Ahmed ibn Fartua.* Lagos, 1926.

Political and Constitutional Future of Nigeria. Sessional Paper No. 4 of 1945. Lagos, 1945.

Quarterly Abstract. Lagos.

Report on Electoral Reform in the Northern Region. Lagos, 1953.

Report on Employment and Earnings Enquiry. Lagos, 1958.

Report of the Federal Advisory Committee on Technical Education and Industrial Training. Lagos, 1959.

Review of the Constitution, Regional Recommendations. Lagos, 1949.

Sharwood-Smith, B. E. *Kano Survey.* Lagos, 1950.

Smith, M. G. *The Economy of Hausa Communities of Zaria*. A Report to the Colonial Social Science Research Council. London, 1955.

Triennial Survey of the Work of the Federal Department of Education for the Years 1955 to 1957. Lagos, 1959.

United Kingdom. Colonial Office. *Commission Appointed to Enquire into the Fears of Minorities and the Means of Allaying Them. Report*. Cmnd. 505. London, 1958.

————. *Nigeria, 1953*. London, 1955.

————. *Nigeria, 1955*. London, 1958.

————. *Report by the Conference on the Nigerian Constitution Held in London in July and August, 1953*. Cmnd. 8,934. London, 1953.

————. *Report of the Fiscal Commission for Nigeria*. Cmd. 481. London, 1958.

————. *Report of the Fiscal Commissioner on the Financial Effects of the Proposed New Constitutional Arrangements*. Cmnd. 9,026. London, 1953.

United Kingdom. Colonial Office. *Report by the Nigerian Constitutional Conference Held in London in May and June 1957*. Cmnd. 207. London, 1957.

————. *Report by the Resumed Conference on the Nigerian Constitution Held in Lagos in January and February, 1954*. Cmnd. 9050. London, 1954.

White Paper on the Reorganisation of the Ministries. Ibadan, Sessional Paper No. 2 of 1959.

V. Unpublished Documents

Awa, E. O. "Local Government Problems in a Developing Community (Nigeria)". Paper delivered at an International Conference on Representative Government and National Progress, Ibadan, March 1959. Mimeo.

Awolowo, Obafemi. Presidential Address at the Conference of the Action Group held in Jos, 9 September 1958. Mimeo.

————. Presidential Address at the Emergency Congress of the Action Group held at Kano on 12 December 1958. Mimeo.

Azikiwe, Nnamdi. "The Evolution of Federal Government in Nigeria". An address at a public meeting arranged by the Nigerian Union of Students, London, October 14, 1955.

Bamalli, M. Nuhu. "The Northern Peoples' Congress". 1959. Mimeo.

Bohannan, Laura. "*A Comparative Study of Social Differentiation*". Doctor of Philosophy thesis, Oxford University, 1951.

Bohannan, Paul. "Some Economic and Political Aspects of Land Tenure and Settlement Patterns among the Tiv of Central Nigeria". Ph.d. thesis, Oxford University, 1951.

Bohannan, Paul and Laura. *Three Source Notebooks in Tiv Ethnography.* Unpub. manuscript. Human Relations Area Files. 1959.

Bornu Youth Movement. Secretariat Records. Maiduguri.

Daniel, F. de F. *A History of Katsina.* c. 1937, private circulation.

Davies, J. G. "Provincial Annual Reports for 1957", unpublished. Provincial Files, Ilorin.

Dees, G.R.I. "Papers on Native Authority Finance". No. 3, 1959. Mimeo.

————. "A Survey of Native Authority Finance in the Northern Region". No. 2. 1959. Mimeo.

Ellison, R. E., and Kaka Malam. "Notes for a History of Bornu". 1934, unpub. manuscript.

Harria, P. G. "Sokoto Provincial Gazetteer". 1938, unpub. manuscript.

Ilorin Native Authority Office. Minutes of the Ilorin Native Authority Council, May 8, 1957 to August 1958 inclusive. Mimeo.

Imam, Abudakar. "The Problems of Northern Nigeria as the Natives See It. An Account of an Interview with Lord Lugard". Typewritten.

Kano, Malam Aminu. Address by the NEPU Delegation to the All-African Peoples' Conference, Accra, December 1958. Mimeo.

————. Presidential Address to the Fifth Annual Conference of the Northern Elements Progressive Union. 1955.

————. Presidential Address to the Seventh Annual Conference of the Northern Elements Progressive Union. Ibadan, 26 September 1957.

————. Statement on the Founding of the Northern Elements Progressive Union. Typewritten.

Kotoye, N.A.B. "Further Suggestions about Judicial Reform in the North". Prepared for the Action Group Delegation to the Resumed Constitutional Conference of 1958. Typewritten.

————. "Spotlight on Justice in the North". Prepared for the Action Group Delegation to the Resumed Constitutional Conference of 1958. Typewritten.

Low, V. et al. "Notes for a Preliminary History of Bauchi Province". 1960. Unpub. typescript.

Maikwaru, Abba M. "The Song: We Recognise Those Who Have Wronged Us". Undated private printing in Hausa.

Masterton-Smith. *Abuja, the Heart of Nigeria.* Ex. M.P. 36002.

NCNC Constitution of Kaduna Capital Territory (NEPU/NCNC) Supreme Council, October 1958. Mimeo.

National Muslim League. (*Egbe Muslumi Parapo*). Constitution, Rules and Regulations. Abeokuta, 1957.

———. Memorandum on the Fears of the Muslim Minorities in the Regions. December 1957. Mimeo.

Northern Elements Progressive Union. *Jam'iyyar Neman Sawaba, Manufa, Sharudda da Ka'idodi.* Kano, n.d. (Constitution and Rules.)

———. National Headquarters Secretariat Files, Kano. Auditors Report to the Seventh Annual Conference, September 20, 1957. Mimeo.

———. Delegation to the United Kingdom, 19 December 1955. Memorandum. Mimeo.

———. Election Manifestos.

Northern Elements Progressive Union. National Headquarters Secretariat Files, Kano. Memorandum on Civil Liberties, presented to Rt. Hon. A. T. Lennox-Boyd, Secretary of State for the Colonies, at Kano, Nigeria, 30 January 1957.

———. Memorandum of the Northern Elements Progressive Union to the Secretary of State for the Colonies, July 1952. Mimeo.

———. Names of NEPU Members who were convicted and sentenced by the Native Courts in Kano Province, 1954-1957. Typewritten.

———. Officers of the NEPU, September 1957-September 1958. Mimeo.

———. "Northern Elements Progressive Union Views on the Nigerian Constitution." 1956. Typescript.

Northern Peoples' Congress. Central Headquarters Secretariat, Kaduna. Communications with branches.

———. Election Manifestos.

———. Memorandum on the Foundation of the Northern Peoples' Congress. Typewritten.

———. Proposals for party organization.

———. Records of members, branches, and affiliated organizations.

———. Central Headquarters Secretariat, Kaduna. Records of the proceedings of conferences and minutes of meetings. Mainly in Hausa.

———. "Declaration of *Jam'iyyar Mutanen Arewa* (Northern Peoples' Congress), 1st October, 1951".

———. *Minutes*, NPC Emergency Convention, November 21, 1953. Mimeo. in Hausa.

Northern Peoples' Congress. *Minutes,* NPC Executive Committee, January 3, 1954. No. F. 7. Mimeo. document in possession of author.

―――. Secretariat. "Sake Tsarin Jam'iyyan Mutanen Arewa". Kaduna, December 13, 1953. Mimeo.

Perry, Ruth. A *Preliminary Bibliography of the Literature of Nationalism in Nigeria.* London: International African Institute, n.d. Mimeo.

Report of the Committee of the Zaria Native Authority on the Reorganization of the Native Authority Council and of the Native Authority's Central Administrative Structure. Mimeo.

Reynolds, C.J.L., Senior Resident. *Provincial Annual Report on Ilorin.* 1958.

Sarkesian, Sam C. "Nigerian Political Profile: The Emerging Political Interest Groups". Unpub. thesis, Department of Government, Columbia University, 1962.

"Schools for the Sons of Chiefs". File 2856 (Bornu) 1937048, Item #244, Archives, Kaduna.

United Middle Belt Congress. Constitution and By-Laws. Ilorin, 1955. All mimeo.

―――. Draft Constitution, 1957.

―――. Memorandum on Constitutional Reform, 1957.

―――. Memorandum on the Creation of a Separate Middle Belt Region, 1956.

―――. Minutes of the Conference at Kafanchan 26 August 1956.

―――. Minutes of a Meeting between the Action Group and the UMBC, April 19, 1957.

―――. Report of the Convention Held in Lafia, January 15-17, 1957.

―――. United Muslim Party. Letter to the Prime Minister of the Federation from M.R.B. Ottun, July 17, 1958.

―――. United Muslim Party. Memorandum on the Creation of a Lagos Region submitted to the Resumed Constitutional Conference, September 1958.

―――. Representations on the Nigerian Constitutional Conference, May 23, 1957.

―――. Warri Peoples' Party. Memorandum to the Minorities Commission on behalf of the Warri and Western Ijaw Peoples, 1957.

Vischer, Hans. Quarterly Report: Education Department (Quarter ending June 30th, 1910), submitted to H. E. the Governor at Zaria, July 1910, by Hans Vischer. Archives, Kaduna, #3666. 1910.

Warri National Union Newsletter, Anniversary Issue, No. 12 (September 1955).

Wilcox, Dave. *The Roots of Nigerian Foreign Policy.* Ibadan: Institute of African Studies, University of Ife, Ibadan Branch, 1963.

VI. JOURNALS AND NEWSPAPERS

Black Orpheus: A Journal of African and Afro-American Literature. Three issues per year, Ibadan University.

Daily Comet. Comet Press Ltd., Kano (Zik Group).

Daily Express. Lagos.

Daily Service. Amalgamated Press, Lagos.

Daily Times. Nigerian Printing and Publishing Company. Lagos.

Gaskiya Ta Fi Kwabo. Twice weekly (Hausa), Gaskiya Corp. Zaria.

Gaskiya Ta Fi Kwabo. Weekly, Eastern Nigeria Information Service, Enugu.

Ibadan. Three issues per year, Ibadan University.

Journal of the Historical Society of Nigeria. Irregular, Ibadan University. The Society's *Bulletin* lists current historical publications relating to Nigeria.

Journal of the Nigerian Society of Economic and Social Studies. Three issues annually.

Kano Daily Mail. Kano.

Morning Post. Lagos.

New Nigerian. Kaduna.

News from Nigeria. Biweekly processed newssheet. Federal Information Service, Lagos, 1955—

Nigeria (or *Nigeria Magazine*). Quarterly, Federal Government Printer, Lagos. Mostly art, archeology, and style of life throughout the country.

Nigeria Year Book. 1957-1959. Nigerian Printing and Publishing Company, Lagos.

Nigeria Year Books. 1958-1961. Times Press, Apapa.

The Nigerian. London.

Nigerian Citizen. Twice weekly. Gaskiya Corp., Zaria.

Nigerian Field. 1931-1960. Nigerian Field Society, Stroud, Glos.

Nigerian Opinion. Ibadan.

Nigerian Publications. Annually, Ibadan University Press, Ibadan.

Nigerian Tribune. Amalgamated Press, Nigerian Ltd., Ibadan.

Northern Region of Nigeria. *Majilasaku: Local Government Journal* July 1956—

Northern Regional Daily Press Service, Kaduna.

Proceedings of the Nigerian Institute of Social and Economic Research. Annually, Ibadan.

West African Pilot. West African Pilot Ltd., Lagos (Zik Group).

Sunday Times. Weekly. Nigerian Printing and Publishing Company, Lagos.

Who's Who in Nigeria. Nigerian Printing and Publishing Company, Lagos, 1956.

VII. Bibliographies

African Studies Bulletin. Three times a year. Stanford University.

Africana Newsletter. Semi-annually, Stanford University.

Coleman, James S. *Nigeria: Background to Nationalism.* Berkeley: University of California Press, 1958, pp. 481-96.

―――. "A Survey of Selected Literature on the Government and Politics of British West Africa", *American Political Science Review.* Vol. 49 (December 1955).

Conover, Helen F. *African Libraries, Book Production and Archives.* Reference Department, Library of Congress, Washington, D.C., 1962.

―――. *Nigerian Official Publications, 1869–1959: A Guide.* Reference Department, Library of Congress, Washington, D.C., 1959.

Harris, John. *Books about Nigeria: A Select Reading List.* Ibadan: Ibadan University Press, 1959.

Hazlewood, Arthur. *The Economics of "Underdeveloped" Areas: An Annotated Reading List of Books, Articles, and Official Publications.* Second ed. London: Oxford University Press, 1959.

Hewitt, Arthur R. *Guide to Resources for Commonwealth Studies in London, Cambridge, with Bibliographical and Other Information.* London: Published for the Institute of Commonwealth Studies by the Athlone Press, University of London, 1957.

Holdsworth, Mary. *Soviet African Studies 1918-1959: An Annotated Bibliography.* Oxford: Oxford University Press, Distributed for the Royal Institute of International Affairs, 1961.

Kensdale, W.E.N. *Field Notes on the Arabic Literature of the Western Sudan.* [With lists of the writings of Shehu Usuman dan Fodio.] Journal of the Royal Asiatic Society, October 1955.

Nigerian Publications. University Library, Ibadan University. Annually.

545

O'Connel, James. "A Survey of Selected Social Science Research on Nigeria since the End of 1957", Appendix to Robert O. Tilman and Taylor Cole, *The Nigerian Political Scene*, Durham: Duke University Press, 1962.

Perry, Ruth. *A Preliminary Bibliography of the Literature of Nationalism in Nigeria*. Transcript.

United Kingdom. Colonial Office. *Government Publications. Sectional List No. 34*. Revised to 30 November 1958. London: H.M. Stationery Office, 1958.

Index

Abdu, Magaji, 428
Abdulaz, Hassam, 330
Abdullah, Raje, 358
Abdullahi, brother of dan Fodio, 23-24, 295, 350, 394; writings, 24
Abdullahi, Yarimi, 428
Abdulmumuni, ex-*Galadima* of Katsina, 441-43, 448, 477
Abdusalame, Emir of Ilorin, 123
Abokin talakawa (friend of the commoners), 49
Abubakar, Emir of Bida, 444, 445
Abubakar, Sir, *see* Sokoto, Sultan of
Abuja, Emir of, 291, 360
Abuja emirate, 20; *habe* dynasty, 20; subordinate councils, 242
Abuja, Hassan, 345-46, 477-78
Action Group (AG), 30, 130-31, 156, 172, 377, 443, 448, 450; alliance with ITP, 137-45; drive for support, 141; in Kazaure elections, 429
Adalci (righteousness), 291, 397
Adamawa emirate, 201, 215, 377, 397; plural emirate, 203; UN plebiscites, 205-208, 446-48; council, 201; subordinate councils, 240, 241, 243; forced resignation of Lamido (1953), 272, 274; succession crisis, 289-91; structural tensions, 446-48
Adamawa, *Galadina* of, 447
Adamawa, Lamido of, 272, 274, 389, 447
Adamawa, Waziri of, 289-90
Adamawa province, 16
Adamu, Emir of Kazaure, 283-85, 428, 429, 434, 452; and Muhammadu, 284
Afon, District Head of: dismissal and reinstatement, 149, 162-63
Afonja, governor of Ilorin, 122-24, 134
AG, *see* Action Group
Agaie emirate, 209; subordinate councils, 242
Aguiyi-Ironsi, Maj. Gen., 353
Ahmadu Bello University, 247
Ahmadu, Lamido of Adamawa, 290; forced resignation (1953), 274; NEPU candidates (1959), 373
Ahmed of Zaria, 346
Ajami script, 17, 23, 327
Ajikobi, Balogun, 123, 133, 168, 171
Alanamu, *Balogun* of Ilorin, 123, 127
Alheri Youth Association, 386

Alimi, Fulani leader in Ilorin, 122-23
Aliu, *Tarakin Zazzau*, Chairman of Marketing Board, 388
Aliyu, Makaman Bida, 472; of Finance, 336-37, 339; acting premier, 337
Aliyu, *Sarkim* Kudu, 437
Alkali (Muslim judges), 25, 105, 119, 228, 229, 315, 316, 329, 330; *alkalin alkali* (chief judges), 222, 333; courts, 222
Al-Kanemi (Shehu Laminu), 328
Alkyabba (cloak signifying authority), 350
Almond, Gabriel, 80
Amalgamation of emirates, 209-10
Aminu, ex-*Dan Iya* of Kano, 441, 478-79
Apter, David, 76
Arabic language, 24, 327
Arago people, 204, 384
Are (governor), 122
Are Magajin, *Balogun*, 134, 165
Argunga emirate, 19, 24, 234, 397, 442; alleged nepotism of Emir and his resignation (1960), 272, 274-77, 303, subordinate councils, 243
Aroja (payment by market people to officials), 143; suppression of, 150
Arziki (good fortune), 332
Askia, Muhammed, 393, 464
Askianist (Aminiyya) movement, 393-94, 413
Atikawa, Toronkawa lineage, 347, 419
Atiku Abubakar, Sultan of Sokoto, 347, 419
Attajirai (merchant traders), 248, 315; and government contracts, 334; distribution of largesse, 333; in Northern House of Assembly, 331-36; NPC candidates and executive members, 333-34, 371
Azikiwe, Dr. Nhamdu ("Zik"), 258, 385

Babakekeres (middlemen in law courts and fief-holders), 127-28, 140, 143, 150
Bacucune (royal slave-descendant), 337, 338
Bakwai (seven "true" Hausa states), 20; *banza bakwai* (bastard seven), 20, 23
Bala, Yerima, 447

547

BOOKS WRITTEN
UNDER THE AUSPICES OF THE
CENTER OF INTERNATIONAL STUDIES
PRINCETON UNIVERSITY

Gabriel A. Almond, *The Appeals of Communism* (Princeton University Press 1954)

William W. Kaufmann, ed., *Military Policy and National Security* (Princeton University Press 1956)

Klaus Knorr, *The War Potential of Nations* (Princeton University Press 1956)

Lucian W. Pye, *Guerrilla Communism in Malaya* (Princeton University Press 1956)

Charles De Visscher, *Theory and Reality in Public International Law*, trans. by P. E. Corbett (Princeton University Press 1957; rev. ed. 1968)

Bernard C. Cohen, *The Political Process and Foreign Policy: The Making of the Japanese Peace Settlement* (Princeton University Press 1959)

Myron Weiner, *Party Politics in India: The Development of a Multi-Party System* (Princeton University Press 1957)

Percy E. Corbett, *Law in Diplomacy* (Princeton University Press 1959)

Rolf Sannwald and Jacques Stohler, *Economic Integration: Theoretical Assumptions and Consequences of European Unification*, trans. by Herman Karreman (Princeton University Press 1959)

Klaus Knorr, ed., *NATO and American Security* (Princeton University Press 1959)

Gabriel A. Almond and James S. Coleman, eds., *The Politics of the Developing Areas* (Princeton University Press 1960)

Herman Kahn, *On Thermonuclear War* (Princeton University Press 1960)

Sidney Verba, *Small Groups and Political Behavior: A Study of Leadership* (Princeton University Press 1961)

Robert J. C. Butow, *Tojo and the Coming of the War* (Princeton University Press 1961)

Glenn H. Snyder, *Deterrence and Defense: Toward a Theory of National Security* (Princeton University Press 1961)

Klaus Knorr and Sidney Verba, eds., *The International System: Theoretical Essays* (Princeton University Press 1961)

Peter Paret and John W. Shy, *Guerrillas in the 1960's* (Praeger 1962)

George Modelski, *A Theory of Foreign Policy* (Praeger 1962)

Klaus Knorr and Thornton Read, eds., *Limited Strategic War* (Praeger 1963)

Frederick S. Dunn, *Peace-Making and the Settlement with Japan* (Princeton University Press 1963)

Arthur L. Burns and Nina Heathcote, *Peace-Keeping by United Nations Forces* (Praeger 1963)

Richard A. Falk, *Law, Morality, and War in the Contemporary World* (Praeger 1963)

James N. Rosenau, *National Leadership and Foreign Policy: A Case Study in the Mobilization of Public Support* (Princeton University Press 1963)

Gabriel A. Almond and Sidney Verba, *The Civic Culture: Political Attitudes and Democracy in Five Nations* (Princeton University Press 1963)

Bernard C. Cohen, *The Press and Foreign Policy* (Princeton University Press 1963)

Richard L. Sklar, *Nigerian Political Parties: Power in an Emergent African Nation* (Princeton University Press 1963)

Peter Paret, *French Revolutionary Warfare from Indochina to Algeria: The Analysis of a Political and Military Doctrine* (Praeger 1964)

Harry Eckstein, ed., *Internal War: Problems and Approaches* (Free Press 1964)

Cyril E. Black and Thomas P. Thornton, eds., *Communism and Revolution: The Strategic Uses of Political Violence* (Princeton University Press 1964)

Miriam Camps, *Britain and the European Community 1955-1963* (Princeton University Press 1964)

Thomas P. Thornton, ed., *The Third World in Soviet Perspective: Studies by Soviet Writers on the Developing Areas* (Princeton University Press 1964)

James N. Rosenau, ed., *International Aspects of Civil Strife* (Princeton University Press 1964)

Sidney I. Ploss, *Conflict and Decision-Making in Soviet Russia: A Case Study of Agricultural Policy, 1953-1963* (Princeton University Press 1965)

Richard A. Falk and Richard J. Barnet, eds., *Security in Disarmament* (Princeton University Press 1965)

Karl von Vorys, *Political Development in Pakistan* (Princeton University Press 1965)

Harold and Margaret Sprout, *The Ecological Perspective on Human Affairs, With Special Reference to International Politics* (Princeton University Press 1965)

Klaus Knorr, *On the Uses of Military Power in the Nuclear Age* (Princeton University Press 1966)

Harry Eckstein, *Division and Cohesion in Democracy: A Study of Norway* (Princeton University Press 1966)

Cyril E. Black, *The Dynamics of Modernization: A Study in Comparative History* (Harper and Row 1966)

Peter Kunstadter, ed., *Southeast Asian Tribes, Minorities, and Nations* (Princeton University Press 1967)

E. Victor Wolfenstein, *The Revolutionary Personality: Lenin, Trotsky, Gandhi* (Princeton University Press 1967)

Leon Gordenker, *The UN Secretary-General and the Maintenance of Peace* (Columbia University Press 1967)

Oran R. Young, *The Intermediaries: Third Parties in International Crises* (Princeton University Press 1967)

James N. Rosenau, ed., *Domestic Sources of Foreign Policy* (Free Press 1967)

Richard F. Hamilton, *Affluence and the French Worker in the Fourth Republic* (Princeton University Press 1967)

Linda B. Miller, *World Order and Local Disorder: The United Nations and Internal Conflicts* (Princeton University Press 1967)

Henry Bienen, *Tanzania: Party Transformation and Economic Development* (Princeton University Press 1967)

Wolfram F. Hanrieder, *West German Foreign Policy, 1949-1963: International Pressures and Domestic Response* (Stanford University Press 1967)

Richard H. Ullman, *Britain and the Russian Civil War: November 1918-February 1920* (Princeton University Press 1968)

Robert Gilpin, *France in the Age of the Scientific State* (Princeton University Press 1968)

William B. Bader, *The United States and the Spread of Nuclear Weapons* (Pegasus 1968)

Richard A. Falk, *Legal Order in a Violent World* (Princeton University Press 1968)

Cyril E. Black, Richard A. Falk, Klaus Knorr, and Oran R. Young, *Neutralization and World Politics* (Princeton University Press 1968)

Oran R. Young, *The Politics of Force: Bargaining During International Crises* (Princeton University Press 1969)

Klaus Knorr and James N. Rosenau, eds., *Contending Approaches to International Politics* (Princeton University Press 1969)

James N. Rosenau, ed., *Linkage Politics: Essays on the Convergence of National and International Systems* (Free Press 1969)

John T. McAlister, Jr., *Viet Nam: The Origins of Revolution* (Knopf 1969)

Jean Edward Smith, *Germany Beyond the Wall: People, Politics and Prosperity* (Little, Brown 1969)

James Barros, *Betrayal from Within: Joseph Avenol Secretary-General of the League of Nations, 1933-1940* (Yale University Press 1969)

Charles Hermann, *Crises in Foreign Policy: A Simulation Analysis* (Bobbs-Merrill 1969)

Robert C. Tucker, *The Marxian Revolutionary Idea: Essays on Marxist Thought and Its Impact on Radical Movements* (W. W. Norton 1969)

Harvey Waterman, *Political Change in Contemporary France: The Politics of an Industrial Democracy* (Charles E. Merrill 1969)

C. S. Whitaker, Jr., *The Politics of Tradition: Continuity and Change in Northern Nigeria, 1946-1966* (Princeton University Press 1969)